Sullivan's Hollow

Neace, Red Jack, and Wild Bill Sullivan, c. 1875

Sullivan's Hollow

By Chester Sullivan

 University Press of Mississippi

For Peggy With Love

This investigation was supported by University of Kansas General
Research allocations No. 3762-x038 and No. 3179-x038.

Library of Congress Cataloging in Publication Data

Sullivan, Chester.
  Sullivan's Hollow.

  Bibliography: p.
  SUMMARY: Presents a history of Sullivan's Hollow,
Mississippi, a place purportedly synonymous with lawless-
ness.
  1.   Sullivan's Hollow, Miss.–History. 2.   Sullivan's
Hollow, Miss.–Genealogy. [1. Sullivan's Hollow, Miss.–
History] I. Title.
F349.S93S94   976.2'582   78-11484
ISBN 0-87805-080-9

Preface

Once when I was on a trip to Jackson as a child a man asked me my name. I told him, and he said, "I hope you aren't one of those Sullivans from *Sullivan's Hollow!*" Perplexed by his reaction, I remember saying, "Well yes, I am." It was nothing special to me then, because then I thought the world was like Sullivan's Hollow. But my memory of that encounter stayed with me, and as I learned other places I began to understand the ways in which the Hollow is indeed special. It was years later when I read in *A Guide to the Magnolia State*, "The Hollow. . . Every Mississippian knows of it and uses its name as a synonym for lawlessness." When I read that I remembered the man in Jackson, and I felt a strong impulse to go back and retrieve what I could of the old-time myth. The search was a pleasant one, and these pages contain most of what I found. It is fragmentary, and because of the nature of the material there is little first-hand documentation. Taken on the whole, however, I believe that it is a fair representation of the people and the place.

For their courtesy and hospitality I gratefully thank everyone who agreed to tell once again what they'd seen or heard, even those who thought that a book "on the dark side" should not be written. I am grateful to Patti Carr Black of the Mississippi Department of Archives and History, who

v

showed the way, and I am especially indebted to Grover
Bishop, who in 1938, under the auspices of the Works Pro-
gress Administration, conducted numerous interviews with
Sullivans and with people who knew the Sullivans. Valuable
information was also preserved by Ann Hammons, C. Sessions
Fant, Harry Henderson, Sam Shaw, and Minnie Davis.

Contents

Sullivan's Hollow

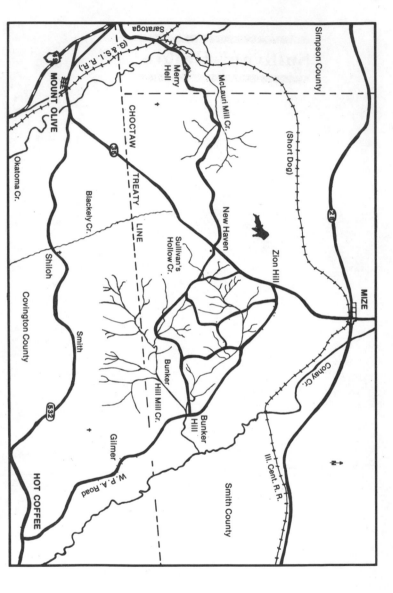

Sullivan's Hollow, Smith County, Mississippi

1 The Piney Woods

Hills, trees, and water characterize the piney woods, where for every hill there is a hollow with its spring of water and where every hollow descends into yet another hollow until finally, through the addition of spring to spring a branch develops, perhaps intermittent at first but then as it flows on down it becomes wider and deeper until finally it runs year round. It is a creek. That creek flows until it joins another creek, making it impossible to distinguish the water of one creek from the water of another. No matter. There is always the high ground to your left, to your right, behind you—and you are surrounded by lush trees bound together by vines and shrubs. Follow the water as it turns one way and another until you come to the deep swamp; there the creek becomes a river, like the Cohay.

Until 1900 the piney woods were covered by forests of long-leaved yellow pines mixed with hardwoods, beeches, bays, and gums in the creek and river bottoms. Piney woods soil is sandy and clayey, and except for the swamps it is well drained by numerous fresh creeks. At the turn of the century the land was swept clean by skidder logging operations, which caused sand and gravel to wash into the smaller creeks, leaving them golden bottomed, shallow, bright, and clear, but (as in the case of Bunker Hill Mill Creek) ruined for older

3

inhabitants, who remember them as being "dark and deep and over your head and full of trout."[1] After the timber was cleared, years of row-crop farming on the hillsides continued the silting process.

The longleaf pines were native to the piney woods area of southern Mississippi. By all accounts, they were enormous and spectacular. When standing they were surprisingly fire resistant, living on when the Indians burned the brush under them for the purposes of their own agriculture. White settlers continued that practice, which resulted in a parklike effect with the magnificent pines well spaced, the underbrush killed back, and the floor of the forest covered with either fresh grass or a clean layer of brown pine needles. The serenity and beauty overpowered early travelers to the piney woods: "Much of it is covered exclusively with the long leaf pine; not broken, but rolling like the waves in the middle of the great ocean. The grass grows three feet high and hill and valley are studded all over with flowers of every hue."[2] An observer who saw the forest floor burning wrote, "It was an exceedingly pretty sight. A bright flaming ring, about a foot in height, and three or four hundred yards in diameter, kept spreading itself in all directions, meeting and enclosing trees, burning up shrubs with great avidity."[3]

Those trees were known as long-straw pines, and their wood was known as fat pine, heart pine, lightwood, kindling, or lightard. A knot of it was especially prized for keeping a night-fishing fire going. In my youth, our schoolboy threats at Frog Pond usually carried the potential of someone getting hit over the head with a lightard knot. The fat-pine wood burned infinitely better than the wood of other pines because it was saturated with pitch, or rosin, as it was called in the piney woods. Because of the rosin, lightard was extremely rot resistant, and wood lice (termites) couldn't eat it.

4

Today it is easier for us to imagine what the longleaf forests were like than to imagine how they could have been so thoroughly destroyed in only eleven years. The lumbering boom in Mississippi lasted from 1904 to 1915. Fortunes were made quickly, and greed led to the destruction of the longleaf pine forests. White pine in the North was getting scarce; Mississippi was two thousand miles closer to the northern, eastern, and international markets than were the forests of the Pacific Coast; technological advances rapidly increased mill capacities; Mississippi's mild climate allowed year-round operation; and of course the lumber companies were interested in making money—as much as they could, as fast as they could.

In 1890 there were 338 sawmills in Mississippi. In 1899 there were 608, and in 1909 there were 1,761. In 1899 the Gulf & Ship Island Railroad was 65 miles long, from the Gulf of Mexico up to Hattiesburg, and 18 sawmills sat along it. Three years later there were 60, and in 1909, 800 million board feet of yellow-pine lumber were shipped on the Gulf & Ship Island.[4] All that remains of the pine forest's splendor and magnificence is summarized by an advertisement that sometimes appears in the local papers, placed there by a company that manufactures dynamite:

Wanted to buy—Stumps
Hercules Incorporated will buy, uproot and remove your original growth pine stumps and top wood, commonly called lighterwood. Call collect.

Sullivan's Hollow in the piney woods lies between the Okatoma and the Cohay creek systems. *Okatoma* in Choctaw means "shining water." Both the Okatoma and the Cohay flow southeasterly into the Leaf River, which was called *Hastabucha* ("leafy") by the Choctaws.

5

The Hollow was settled by Thomas Sullivan, who was born in 1785. In 1807 he came to Mississippi from Bishopville, in up-country South Carolina, bringing his wife Elizabeth, four or five of their children, and his brother John. They came west in wagons drawn by horses and oxen on the Natchez to Fort Stephens Wagon Road, which passed within five miles of Old Jaynesville. Sometimes people moving into the Southwest would settle temporarily and make a crop along the way. The Sullivan family followed that practice by spending a year in Alabama. John did not stay long in Mississippi before returning to South Carolina. Originally settling in southeastern Simpson County on the upper reaches of Bowie Creek near what became Old Jaynesville, the Sullivans later moved twelve miles east into what would become Smith County, where they built the log house still inhabited by their descendants.

After the War of 1812 large numbers of people moved into the piney woods traveling the Three-Chopped Way, the Natchez to Fort Stephens Wagon Road, and the Jackson Military Road. Some of them, like the Sullivans, were not primarily farmers. Farmers passed through and went on to rich loess soils in the southwestern part of the state. The people who stopped off in the piney woods were stockmen and hunters, who were looking for a particular kind of unsettled country where they could have open range for their livestock and where they could hunt, fish, and build themselves a cabin. After they were settled they would enhance their lives with patch farming, stock pens, and small outbuildings. It is most important to note that above everything else they valued their independence and privacy. Those piney woods settlers were closely observed by a Natchez man in 1870:

Most of them were from the poorer districts of Georgia and the

6

Carolinas. True to the instincts of the people from whom they were descended, they sought as nearly as possible just such a country as that from which they came, and were really refugees from a growing civilization consequent upon a denser population and its necessities. They were not agriculturists in a proper sense of the term; true, they cultivated in some degree the soil, but it was not the prime pursuit of these people, nor was the location sought for this purpose. They desired an open, poor, pine country which forbade a numerous population. Here they reared immense herds of cattle which subsisted exclusively upon coarse grass and reeds which grew abundantly among the tall, long-leaved pine and along the small creeks and branches numerous in this section. Through these almost interminable pine forests the deer were abundant, and the canebrakes full of bears. They combined the pursuits of hunting and stock-minding, and derived support and revenue almost exclusively from these.[5]

2 The Hollow

Sullivan's Hollow lies south of Mize in a system of hills drained by Sullivan's Hollow Creek from its headwaters near Thomas Sullivan's house to where it joins Bunker Hill Mill Creek. Originally the Hollow was six miles long and three miles wide, running in a northerly crescent from west to east. But, as its reputation spread south and west and as the number of Sullivans dramatically increased, "Sullivan's Hollow" in time expanded until it encompassed the southwest corner of Smith County and parts of Covington and Simpson counties. By the turn of the century what was generally known as Sullivan's Hollow was the area bounded by Mize on the north, Hot Coffee[1] on the southeast, and Mount Olive and Saratoga on the southwest.

When Thomas settled, Smith County was still in the Choctaw Territory. His home was two miles north (on the Indian side) of the Mount Dexter treaty line of the 1805 first Choctaw session. The account handed down through generations has it that he and his sons built their house by cutting pine logs in the daytime and assembling them after dark, using large bonfires for light. After peeling the bark from the logs with a homemade peeler, they shaped them with a broadax. Then they cut V-shaped notches in both ends and fastened the logs together with wooden pegs. With a froe and maul they rived boards out of pine blocks to shingle the roof.

Their chimney was built of bricks, which they'd made by pressing clay mud into wooden molds. The molds were stacked beside a fire until the clay had dried hard. Originally the house had an earthen floor. The following account describes a piney woods cabin of the period:

> Often a crack by the fireplace was enlarged to give the mother a little more light on her sewing. The floor, if by good fortune it was of plank, was more costly than all the rest of the building. . . . Sawed lumber was costly and could be used only in building the family room. It was put down loosely and when well shrunken was driven up tight and nailed. The only planing it received was the frequent application of the scrub broom. A few people at a cost of much labor hewed out "puncheons" for floors; others built their cabins flat on the ground and there lived comfortably and contentedly with their families, waiting for better times.[2]

The Sullivans were typical settlers of the Southwest in that they worked hard days and lived by their skills and good husbandry. They caught fish from the creeks, hunted game in the woods, and gathered wild nuts, fruits, and vegetables. Food fish were catfish, trout, eel, and various kinds of perch. They ate bear, deer, rabbit, squirrel, opossum, and raccoon meat, and many kinds of birds were hunted or trapped, such as turkeys, quail, doves, pigeons, plovers, ducks, and geese. Edible plants included the grape, persimmon, chinquapin, hickory nut, blackberry, huckleberry, plum, pawpaw, pokeweed, sassafras, and wild onion, and there was wild honey. The rest of their food they raised themselves.

After clearing fertile patches of land, Thomas planted his corn with a stick. He raised sweet potatoes,[3] field peas, and a small amount of cotton, used to make the family's clothing. He took any excess cotton on a two-week trip to Mobile or Natchez, where he sold it, saving the money against the time when the Indian lands would officially be opened and sold to white settlers. He bought only coffee and salt. He and his family kept chickens, hogs, and sheep for wool, and "They had the woods full of cattle." It is likely that Thomas Sullivan obtained most of his cash money from the periodic sale of cattle.

When the weather turned cold in the fall Thomas would kill enough hogs to provide meat for the following year. After the hogs were dressed, a portion of the meat was salted down in barrels made from hollow logs, where it was left for three weeks. Then it was hung over a small hickory fire in a pine-log smokehouse, where it would slowly cure, dripping lard and salt onto the dirt floor. Hog meat, or "bacon," was a staple of their diet. It was eaten fresh in winter, cured in spring, and salted in summer. Fat bacon was used for seasoning vegetables, such as turnips, collards, cabbages, beans, and peas. If the Sullivans ran out of cooking salt before the time to go to market, they would dig up the earth of the smokehouse floor and boil it in water to extract the salt. They did not preserve beef.

Thomas Sullivan had two Negro slaves. It is said that he was good to them but "made them work mighty hard." He struck fire from flint, and his children "didn't know what a match was." Milk in gourds and butter in wooden piggins were kept cool by being lowered into pits dug into the ground or by being hung partway down the well, which wasn't dug until 1824. Until then, fresh water came from the creek.

Thomas Sullivan became known to his descendants as Pappy Tom. His first wife, Maud Elizabeth Arnold (1790–1846), was the mother of James, Margaret, Thomas (Hog Tom), Loderick, Stephen, Owen, Joseph, Dan, and Celia. The children of his second wife, Mary Polly Workman (1803–

1891), were Frederick, Thomas Jefferson, Caroline, Henderson (Hense), Eliza Jane, Mark, Wiley (Big Wiley), Mary Ann, Samuel, Cornelius (Conn), Loughton, Alexander, and Clarra. He fathered twenty-two children.

One version of the story is that Polly Workman and her mother came to live in the Hollow in a cabin Tom built for them down by the spring, which used to be in front of his house, and that while Elizabeth was still alive Polly began having his children. It was said that he set such high stock in Polly that she was the only person he would trust to carry the smokehouse key. Another version of the story has it that Polly was the daughter of a woman Tom knew in Natchez. On a trip there he found the woman critically ill, and she asked him to take Polly, then twelve or thirteen, back to the Hollow and provide for her, which he did. A third version holds that Tom and his brother Stephen immigrated to America bringing Polly with them as a maid. According to this one, Tom married her after Elizabeth died.

As time went by, Tom's children found husbands and wives for themselves and took parcels of land, as he had, by clearing it and living on it. They said that Pappy Tom took a great deal of pride in his frugal, self-reliant way of life and in being a patriarch, helping them to set up their own small farms.

There is no mention in the oral record of Tom Sullivan's having had trouble with the Indians. At that time, from 1795 until 1837, Choctaw lands were shrinking because of the overwhelming pressure being placed on them by white settlers, many of whom, like Tom Sullivan, were trespassers.

My uncle Stone Sullivan remembers his mother telling him about seeing Indians pass her house, single file, on their way to the Cohay bottoms, where they would camp and make

11

swamp-cane baskets, which they used as trade items. They would stay for a week or ten days. She said that they were a quiet, dispirited lot, who caused no trouble. She, Ophelia Sullivan, had Indian blood herself. She was a Burkhalter from Covington County, and I remember her taking me down on Sullivan's Hollow Creek when I was a child to cut button willow. She scraped off the sappy inner bark, cooked it down, and mixed it with honey to make cough syrup.

The Sullivans were well entrenched in the Hollow by the time of the final Choctaw cession, the Treaty of Dancing Rabbit Creek in 1830, after which the land was surveyed. On September 15, 1835, Pappy Tom paid $1.25 per acre for two hundred acres of the land on which he had been living for fifteen or twenty years. Tom's closest neighbors, Benjamin Keyes and William Keyes, also bought land at that time. Dr. James Carr moved into the Hollow about that time, becoming a neighbor, friend, and physician to Pappy Tom.

In 1855, Thomas Sullivan died in the house that he had built. It was said that before his death he complained of darkness in the daylight. He suffered greatly in dying and had fits and foaming at the mouth. The people waiting on him were "just about ready to drop from having to be around him the way that he was going on."

Tom's twenty-two children generally lived quiet lives, and most of them married and had large families averaging ten or eleven children. (Samuel had twenty-two.) They named their children after their own brothers and sisters, creating such a duplication of names that it soon became necessary to add distinguishing prefixes to given names. Those prefixes then were retained by family branches, such as the Hog Toms, the Wild Bills, the Red Jacks, the Big Buds, and so on.

The best story remembered about Thomas Sullivan concerns the time he refereed a fight. One day, Pappy Tom was in Old Westville, then the Simpson County seat, when Tilman Bishop and an Irishman got into an argument. People began to gather around them, and it was soon decided that the two men should fight it out bareknuckle. Pappy Tom was picked to be the referee. The two men fought for about an hour, and the fight was so fierce and bloody that when it ended Tom used his pocketknife to pick shreds of knuckle skin out of their teeth. A significant detail of this story is that one of the fighters was an "Irishman." Tom Sullivan and a goodly number of the other piney woods settlers termed themselves Scotch-Irish, a name adopted by many Americans after 1846 to distinguish themselves from the newer immigrants from southern Ireland.

3 The Scotch-Irish Settlers

The Scotch-Irish settlers of the American frontier were vigorous people who in 1776 comprised roughly one-tenth of the population. Formed by their history, they were tough and ideally suited to the hardships of immigration. Around 1600 they had moved from the lowlands of Scotland to Ulster, in northern Ireland. Between 1717 and 1775, because of adverse economic conditions in Ulster, many of them had come to American, where they were known simply as Irish. Severely religious, they were also described as poor, Presbyterian, pertinacious, dour, and clannish. They were known as a people with limited outlook and abiding prejudices. An English colonist, loyal to the crown, said of them, "They are the most God-provoking Democrats on this side of Hell."[1] Others, commenting on their fervent religiosity and their violent nature, have observed that the Scotch-Irish were so afraid of God that they didn't have time to be afraid of anything else.

After the potato famines of 1845-1846 brought large numbers of Catholic Irish to America, the Scotch-Irish adopted their double name to distinguish themselves from people whom they considered inferior. They assimilated quickly and became so thoroughly a part of the landscape that some historians have described their basic Scotch-Irish characteristics and attitudes as being typical of nineteenth-century America. Both of Andrew Jackson's parents were Scotch-Irish, and ten other presidents of the United States had Scotch-Irish ancestry.

When the Scotch-Irish arrived in America they naturally wanted land. Few of them had been landowners, and the raising of rents on long-standing Ulster leases was the very reason that most of them had left Ireland. Because the Eastern Seaboard was already taken, most of them passed through settled areas, going west and south to the Appalachian frontier.

It is likely that Tom Sullivan's parents came to America with the fourth wave of Scotch-Irish immigrants in 1754-1755 and that the pressures of an expanding population in South Carolina prompted Tom, when he was twenty-two years old, to journey deeper into the Southwest until he settled the hollow bearing his name. That name is also clearly Irish, which shows that mixing occurred in northern Ireland between Thomas Sullivan's ancestors, who would have been Irish and Scotch-Irish. The addition of Irish blood to the family stock resulted in typically "Irish" characteristics also being common to the Hollow Sullivans. At the risk of drawing a caricature we might identity some of those traits as an affinity for storytelling, dancing, music, jokes, whiskey, and sentimentality.

Because the land had to be cleared of trees before it could be farmed, logrollings became important social events. They were frequently accompanied by a quilting and followed by a frolic. Before a logrolling, it was customary for the host to go himself or to send a son to invite his neighbors. On the set day the logs, which the host had previously cut from the trees. would be piled for burning, split into fence rails,[2] or possibly moved to a house site. That was before sawmills and railroads made the enormous pine logs marketable. Men handled the logs; some women quilted, while others prepared food; the children played. At dinnertime one of the women blew a horn to call the men in to eat corn pone, greens, and coffee, all of which had been cooked at the fireplace. A large pot of turkey and dumplings had been simmered out in the yard, there being plenty of turkeys in the Hollow in those days. After dinner the people sat around for an hour to rest and talk. Then they went back to work until dusk, when they would clean up, eat supper, and get ready for the frolic.

In 1878 Sarah Harvey was a young girl living with one of Pappy Tom's grandsons, her uncle Wilkie Sullivan, about a mile north of the old Dr. Carr place in the Hollow. One of her chores was to carry water from a spring that lay a mile from the house. If she was gone longer than Wilkie thought necessary, he would beat her with a stick until he'd raised knots on her back. One winter day she was cooking dinner at the fireplace, where Wilkie sat with his bare feet stuck far up into the hearth. While she was tending to the cornbread her fire stick slipped, knocking some hot ashes onto his foot. The next thing she knew she was lying on the other side of the house. He had struck her with his fist so hard that she had hit the corner of the wall, knocking a hole in her head. Her blood covered the floor, she said, and she commented that she did not stay with him much longer after that. She left when she was thirteen.

Wilkie Sullivan gave a logrolling while Sarah was living in his house, his wife gave a quilting, and that night they had an old-time frolic. Sarah remembered that the only kind of music they had was from fiddle players, and they had some good ones back in the Hollow then. There were usually two fiddlers at a frolic, and the caller was referred to as the prompter. Two dances were popular, the breakdown reel and the "old-time" square dance. For these dances, about ten girls and ten boys would line up in rows facing each other. At Wilkie's frolic old man Frank Sullivan, Mark's son, was the prompter, but there was no one as good as old man Frank Russell, who lived north of the Hollow, had been born in 1849, and remembered all about "the war." He was the most sought-after prompter in the Hollow.

The style of dancing had changed considerably by 1938, when Grover Bishop observed, "In the Hollow now when they have a dance it is well advertised, but they don't have a logrolling nor a quilting. They come in their cars about nine o'clock and bring the young girls with them, also their liquor bottles. They have violins and guitars for music, and they hug up as close as they can get, with each other's arms around one another. After dancing for awhile they go out to the cars, boys and girls, and take a drink and stay out there about an hour and make love to one another. Before the dance is over about half of them are drunk, and sometimes there are two three fights."

In Sullivan's Hollow, dinner-on-the-ground meetings, revivals, and churchgoing have always been important events. A number of churches flourished in the Hollow, which by one count has twelve cemeteries. That many burying places for such a small area attests both to denominational preferences and to the internecine strife of the third generation.

In 1835 Zion Hill Baptist Church was organized. It was commonly known as Lick Skillet, and Jim Hitt was its first preacher. Preacher Gunn organized Sardis Baptist, around 1860. On one cold day, after church, Joseph Sullivan's wife gave Preacher Gunn a wool blanket to wrap up in on his way home. The next thing the congregation knew was that he had

17

left his wife and children and run off with another woman. He was never heard of after that. Then Calvary Presbyterian Church was organized. Frontier hardships impeded many of the formal aspects of Presbyterian worship, and, despite the fact that some Presbyterian ministers experimented with direct evangelism, many Scotch-Irish, because of isolation and for other reasons, became Baptists or Methodists.

Raw frontier humor was also a prevalent social institution. Many accounts of jokes and tricks played at others' expense have been interesting enough to be told and retold until today, even though the exact words, the manner in which the words were said, and much knowledge of the personalities involved have all been lost. Although we cannot reconstruct them exactly, it is easy to see the kernel of humor in many of those legendary jokes.

As an example of that tough humor, Pappy Tom's son Loderick had a saying that he applied to his wife, Lizzie. Loderick and Lizzie had thirteen children, and Lizzie lived to be eighty-four, but when she was in labor with her first child the midwife, because it was an extremely difficult birth, told her that if she ever got pregnant again it would surely kill her. Two years later Lizzie had her second child, and after that, with each new baby, Loderick would say, "Boys, you cannot kill them, and whoever said that you could just didn't know what he was talking about!" When he was an old man some young fellows went 'possum hunting on his place and through their carelessness managed to set the woods afire. An angry Loderick caught them and, addressing them as children, said, "The next time you boys get hungry I want you to stay off my land and *leave my 'possums alone*! I'll kill you a cow to eat, if you're that hard up!"

For many years the ratio of Sullivans to other people in

the Hollow was ten to one. The Sullivans were suspicious of strangers, making them reveal their business quickly, and if a stranger did not seem to have a good reason for being there they would turn him around and send him back the way he had come. That coolness toward outsiders shows that for a long time the people who lived in the Hollow held a clearly defined us them attitude relative to the outside world.

Peach-tree peddlers had a reputation for being dishonest, sometimes selling trees in the winter that leafed out in the spring to be something less than a peach. One such peddler encountered the infamous Wild Bill and Neace plowing in a field. They only had one mule, and they were each taking turns in the harness with the mule. The salesman made some comment on their situation, whereupon the brothers promptly hitched him to the plow and made him pull with the mule for an hour or two. Then, at dinnertime, they took him to the house and put him in the mule's stable, where they gave him corn and fodder, which they made him eat. One version of the story has it that they then took him to the house and set him down to a big, fine dinner. At any rate, he and other peddlers like him spread the word in all the hotel lobbies of the South that Sullivan's Hollow was "one hell of a mean place."

The hostile attitude that Hollow natives expressed toward outsiders was not restricted to raw humor, however. Around 1885 an Irishman came through looking for work, and Big Dan Sullivan, Pappy Tom's grandson, hired him. Big Dan mistrusted and disliked the Irishman, watching him closely all the while that he worked. When the job was finished Big Dan paid $150 to the Irishman who left, looking for more work. Dan followed him into the swamp, where he killed him and took back his $150. After putting the man's body into a hollow log, he buried him in the mud there in the swamp. Years later Lyers Clark moved into the Hollow and bought some land. While he was clearing some ground he dug up the log and the Irishman's bones. Dan was "talked to" about the killing but nothing could be proved against him.

The people of the Hollow have, from the beginning, been absorbed by an interest in law and politics. Sometimes, as in the case of Pappy's son Mark, interest in law and the impulse to joke were at loggerheads. The sheriff of Smith County once gave Mark a summons to appear in Raleigh the following Monday morning for jury duty. Mark, knowing what was on the docket for that week, did not want to serve, but he arose early Monday morning, long before sunup, and made his way to Raleigh on horseback. He was in court early, and when court time finally came the little old courthouse was jammed with people, who didn't care so much about the county's affairs as they did about the news. Watching trials was entertainment for them. When his turn came to be qualified for the jury, Mark said, "Judge, I have an excuse. When I left my home this morning I left my wife and daughter both in bed, and I don't know which one of them is going to die first, and I would like to get off jury duty." The judge replied, "Why Mr. Sullivan, why hadn't you done and told me about this. Shore you can get off, and I am very sorry to hear about this, and I hope that they get well, and I want you to let me hear how they are getting along."

So Mark got up and left the courthouse and went on about his business. That afternoon when court had adjourned for the day, the judge went down into the courtyard, where he happened to see Mark talking with a group of men. He walked over and said, "Why Mr. Sullivan, I thought you said your wife and daughter were in a dying condition—and here you are still up here?" "No, Judge," Mark replied, "You see, when I left home this morning it was a way before daylight, and my wife and daughter were still in the bed, and you must have misunderstood me, because you ought to know, Judge, that I do not know which one of them will die first. They were not sick, but they were in bed when I left." The judge didn't say a word. He turned around and went about his business, knowing that Mark Sullivan had put one over on him. Mark went on to serve as constable for a long time while his son Mac was justice of the peace. "It was woe unto him who was caught violating the law, then. Old Mark would catch him, and Mac would sentence him."

My uncle Stone told me this story:

You know the first job I ever had? I made fifty cents from it—a fifty-cent piece. They used to make fifty-cent pieces. And Paw and all of 'em—I was a little bitty boy, and they all went to Taylorsville. They used to buy flour in a barrel, and they'd run out of flour for a month or two before they'd go after it. You didn't go to town then when you ran out of flour, you just waited until you went to town and got you a barrel. And they'd order up this old thing of whiskey and stuff, I guess, and a wagon load of stuff to take to town, maybe something to sell. They all came back with this barrel of flour, and they came up, and they were all so drunk or something. They came up to the back porch. It was a big barrel of flour, so big they couldn't get it in the kitchen, so they left it out on the back porch, and they had to have *biscuits for supper!* They were going to live high that night! A big conversation came up about the barrel of flour—they'd have to watch it that night—well, I didn't know what I was awatching—until I found out later. See they went and knocked the head out of it and got enough flour to cook with—maybe the neighbors came in too, maybe everybody came to have biscuits—it was a rare thing—my daddy or grandpaw or somebody gave me a

21

four-bit piece to watch the flour barrel, and he told me, I can remember this, he said when the chickens come here to roost, now, your job is to keep their tails turned outside! You know, he looked at me closely, to see if I'd gotten the point, the chickens were going to come up there and roost, and they'd be pecking in the flour, and it would be all right to let them peck in it, but don't let 'em roost there with their tails inside!

4 Mize, the Capital of Sullivan's Hollow

The first post office, Clear Creek Post Office, opened in 1895 a few miles north of the main Hollow in Clear Creek. It was owned by a man named Hopkins, who later sold it to John Mize, the sheriff of Smith County. The mail was carried on horseback, and after a few years Mize's post office was moved across the creek to the south side, near where it is today. When the branch line of the railroad came through, a couple of small stores were started alongside the post office, forming the town. Pauly Ainsworth owned the first store, which opened for business in 1901.

By then Sullivans were scattered all over Smith County. Mize was their principal gathering place, and where they gathered they fought. It was said that, until the early 1920s, on Saturdays there was nobody on the streets of Mize except Sullivans. Everybody else would stay home, and on Sunday morning, as a result of a knifing or a shooting, there would be one or two fewer Sullivans in the Hollow.

And for a long time there were no Negroes living in or near Mize. For that reason, and because no Negroes were wanted there, Mize acquired the nickname No Nigger. Sam McCollum, a Negro who lived in Magee, remembered that one day he was going through the Hollow and passed a Sullivan standing out in his yard. Sam didn't tip his hat as he passed, and for that

23

the man stopped him, gave him a whipping, and hooked him up to a plow and made him pull it. Then he turned him loose with the warning that if he ever passed through that way again he'd better tip his hat.

Alf Sullivan, one of Pappy Tom's slaves, stayed on after the war and is buried on the place. Marshal Keyes is the present owner of the site, there being a large oak tree at the head of the grave. Except for Alf, the freed slaves went south of Hot Coffee to a ridge, the highest point in Covington County, where they settled a prosperous community that they named Hopewell. It follows that whites called Hopewell and the area surrounding it Nigger Ridge. Alf's son was Frank, and Frank's son is Otho Sullivan, who told me the following story about my great-grandfather Neace: "Old Man Neace. I used to stay with him when I was a little old boy, pretty good-sized boy, and nobody couldn't do nothing with him but me. And stayed drunk all the time. He'd get off and get drunk, lay down—I'd go get in his bed with him. He'd go off to sleep, quit cuttin' up, and I'd go in his pocket and get me all kinds of money. And after he got sober he'd get up and count his money and miss it! 'Otho, you been in my damn pocket! You got my damn money! But I'm gonna let you have it.' They couldn't *nobody* do nothing with him."

Steave Howell, born in 1840, was one of the early settlers of the Hollow. He lived close to Mize, and it was observed that, when the Sullivans and the Howells married, those unions produced offspring that were politely called "pretty rough." A Confederate veteran, Howell attended a reunion at Gettysburg in 1938. When asked about the Sullivans, he replied, "I do not know anything about them only that they are all mean as hell."

The second most important town in Sullivan's Hollow is

Mount Olive, some six miles south of the old Hollow on the Okatoma Creek. Mount Olive was settled in 1810 by two families from North Carolina and became a town in 1856, named after an old Presbyterian church in the community. At its beginning, Mount Olive was on the Ellisville and Monticello (Arkansas) Road. The inhabitants were, for a long time, afraid of the wild Sullivans. Even in Grover Bishop's day it was difficult to get anyone to say anything about them, as "the Sullivans still come to Mt. Olive, and there are lots more of them now than there were then."

In the notorious early days, the days of the third generation, Mize and Mount Olive were the unofficial boundaries of the Hollow. The Sullivan boys would frequently start a fight in one of the towns and ride off to the other town, where they'd stay until the trouble blew over.

The tree-covered hollows provided water and privacy for people to make whiskey, which was called "liquor." Once Mark Sullivan was summoned to appear before a grand jury in Raleigh, and he was asked if he knew anything about anybody making liquor in the Hollow. He answered, "Yes. They all make liquor down there." The jury then asked who was making it the most, and he replied, "Most everyone." The members of the jury were excited by that bit of information, until Mark added, "Some of them make it out of peas and some make it out of greens, but either way, everybody makes it, and they call it pot liquor, down in the Hollow."

Pappy Tom's son Hog Tom was one of the first Sullivans to live close to Mize. The prevalent explanation for his name is that he was always getting his hogs mixed up with those of his neighbors and that sometimes when it came to sorting them out he took good measure. It has also been recorded that Hog Tom once said he'd just as soon kill a lean hog as a

25

fat one, because the liver of a lean hog tasted fine and liver was the only part he cared for. But the overriding notion is that he was fond of stealing and that hogs were his favorite grab. Once Allen Byrd, Hog Tom's brother-in-law, noticed that some corn was missing from his crib. The knothole was high, but reachable if one stood on the wooden block that happened to be there. The next morning when he went out to the crib to feed his horses he found Hog Tom there, standing on the wooden block with his arm inside the crib— and it was wintertime and cold weather.

Byrd said nothing until he'd finished feeding his horses. Then he looked up, as if he'd just seen Tom for the first time, and remarked, "Why Tom! Let's go in to breakfast!" Tom said, "Breakfast hell! I've got my hand hung in this damned trap you had set here to catch rats with." Byrd said, "No, Tom. I did not put it there to catch rats with. I put it there to catch the one that has been stealing my corn." Tom replied sheepishly, "Well, Allen. I just needed enough to go to mill on." Of course everyone knew that Tom had a crib full of his own corn at home.

5 The Lawless Years

The fights and "rackets" and "trouble" in Sullivan's Hollow tended to follow a random pattern, but one could place the violent period from the close of the War Between the States to the Battle of the Ball Game in 1922, which was the last notorious conflict.

Six of Thomas Sullivan's sons were directly involved in the War Between the States. Samuel was wounded; Mark was tried and convicted of desertion, but he was given a graveside pardon by Captain George Buchanan of Covington County. Tom's grandson Stephen, serving in his father's place, was killed at Shiloh. Tom's grandson, John Wylie Sullivan (Little Wylie), was the captain of a company in which Jim Byrd and Will Stubbs served. They revealed that he once caught them stealing food and severely chastised them, but then he told them under his breath, "If you're going to take it anyway, then why don't you get enough *for all of us*!"

An examination of the lawless attitude prevalent in Sullivan's Hollow during the late nineteenth and early twentieth centuries must include the histories of the towns Montrose and Ellisville. Each town is approximately twenty-five miles from Mize. Montrose lies to the northeast, in Jasper County, and Ellisville is to the southeast, in Jones County.

On April 24, 1863, Colonel Benjamin Henry Grierson had

27

his Sixth and Seventh Illinois Cavalry regiments two miles west of Montrose. His horses were used up, so he decided to move slowly into Smith County, capture fresh horses and mules if he could, and then join General U. S. Grant south of Vicksburg. As Grierson's scouts led by Sgt. Surby moved from Montrose to Raleigh, "the pines grew closer together, the straight trunks bare of limbs to extraordinary heights."

Through the forest the road twisted aimlessly, some places so narrow that two horsemen could not ride abreast, the trail's sandy texture covered with a carpet of brown pine needles. The needles silenced the horses' hooves, and in the light filtered through the trees the column must have seemed a ghost company, the men's heads and shoulders moving rhythmically up and down without a beat to mark the measures. The only sounds were the occasional snortings of the horses, the infrequent commands, and the soughing of the pines. Here the farms were small, and houses were few along the way. Sometimes they passed log cabins with pine groves almost to the doors, the tree trunks scarified in V-shaped slashes, gummy resin oozing into wooden cups. Pine fumes drifted from stills boiling turpentine somewhere down in the forests. This was the Piney Woods country, poor white country, the people owning few slaves or none, loyal neither to the Confederacy nor the Union, wanting only to be left alone. By 1863 Confederate conscription laws had aroused many of the Piney Woods dwellers to covert disloyalty. Small bands of deserters were already operating as bushwackers against conscripting agents. . . . Along the road to Pineville Surby halted his scouts in front of a double log house. Five women of varying ages were sitting on the doorstep, but not a man was in sight. As Surby approached he could read fear in the women's faces. At first he believed they had been warned of disguised Yankees, but soon learned that they feared him as a Confederate conscriptor. The women lied in a chorus: "Our husbands are all in the army at Vicksburg." No, they had no milk, only water. "I suppose you are conscripting. Well, you'll find no men around here. You'd better conscript all the women too. We have no one left to care for us. We don't own any blacks." But Surby discovered later from a chance remark that at least two of their men were hiding out in the woods, and when he convinced the women that he and his scouts were Yankees instead of conscripting agents, they brought out not only milk but bread, butter, and pies. The oldest of the women, according to Surby, opened a chest and showed him a Union flag which she had hidden away. [1]

The Conscription Act, passed to ensure a supply of soldiers for the confederacy, contained a provision known as the twenty-Negro rule, whereby one white man was exempted from military service for every twenty slaves nominally under his control. It was abundantly clear to the poor whites in the piney woods that this would exclude, on the basis of personal wealth, great numbers of white Mississippians. That rule, along with another provision of the Conscription Act whereby men of wealth could hire substitutes, led the poor whites to describe the war as "the rich man's war and the poor man's fight."

Ellisville lies in Jones County, which joins Smith County on the south. The land of neither county was conducive to the cotton and slave economy that was a central factor in the War Between the States. Although Jones County's delegate to the secession convention was bound by the voters to vote against secession, he was intimidated at the convention in Jackson and voted for it. His betrayal so enraged the citizens of Jones County that they burned him in effigy. As the war progressed, Jones County became a favorite hunting ground for Confederate conscription agents.

Despite what has been written about that war by twentieth-century romanticizers, it would be incorrect to assume that Sullivans eagerly fought for separation from the Union— considering where they were and who they were. John K. Bettersworth, a student of this period of Mississippi's history, writes, "The Piney Woodsman of the 1860's found himself

29

living a primitive, even pastoral, sort of life. He raised livestock and food crops largely for his own subsistence. Sometimes he would carry his surplus of garden and dairy products
to sell in Mobile or even fell the trees on his land and float
them down the river. . . . But on the whole he lived econom-
ically very much to himself."[2]

It was widely rumored that the citizens of Jones County
seceded from the Confederacy and set up a republic of their
own with Newton Knight as president. As a matter of fact, in
October of 1863 Knight organized a company of six officers
and seventy-six privates, with a number of men from Smith
County joining. The company raided Confederate ammunition
trains for arms, and they raided government stores at Paulding
in Jasper County. Colonel Henry Maury was sent in March of
1864 to suppress Newton Knight; he failed. In May, Robert
Lowrey was sent to do the job: "Lowrey proceeded vigorous-
ly, shooting and hanging a number of the rebels, and tracking
with bloodhounds those who escaped into the swamps. The
present-day community of Crackers' Neck earned its name as
the site of hangings by the dreaded cavalry. When the people
retaliated by gorging the dogs with food containing red pep-
per, Lowrey shut the old men and boys of the countryside
in pens and threatened to hang them if they did not reveal
the whereabouts of the deserters."[3]

Sullivan's Hollow was the western point of a triangle that
included the Free State of Jones and the Pineville Road
where yankee soldiers found sympathetic women. Men from
Jones County established the precedent of hiding out in the
Leaf River swamps to avoid demands of outside authorities,
and that type of evasion would be later repeated by Wild Bill
and Neace. Another instance of resistance to authority occurred with the dynamiting of cattle-dipping vats in 1916.

After the war ended there were hard times in the Hollow. People had no money, and the few old clothes that they had were usually dirty. Children frequently wore a single item of clothing, the long-tailed shirt, the year around. Therefore, one of the first things to be done by men returning from the war was to cut blackjack or post oak to make lye soap. The wood was stacked and burned, and the ashes were put into a hopper. Water was slowly poured on the ashes, several times a day, just a little bit, until the ashes were properly wet. Then the water would begin to drip through. That lye water was put into a washpot and boiled, and grease or meat scraps were added to make it thicken. But meat was so scarce that, if a hog happened to die and if it had any fat on it, the people would dress it and render out some soap grease—if they found it before it had begun to stink.

Hogs were raised in pens in the woods. Then, when the acorns and beech mast began to fall, people took their hogs to the swamps and turned them loose. The owners would tend their hogs about a week, when they called them up and fed them corn to keep them tame. The smaller variety of hog, which fattened more easily, was called the guinea hog; the larger variety was known as rakestraw. This was because, before a cold spell, it would rake straw with a forefoot until it had a small pile, then it would carry the straw in its mouth to a place, eventually making a big bed. When people saw the hogs predicting cold weather that way, raking and toting straw, they knew it was time to get active themselves and cut a good supply of firewood.

During those hard times people sifted the bran from corn-meal and cooked it to make a coffee substitute, because few people could afford to buy real coffee.

Immediately following the war, in part as a result of the

wartime experience with its accompanying sense of loss and isolation, some of the third-generation Sullivans engaged in a series of violent crimes that set Sullivan's Hollow apart from the rest of the state and made it infamous.

In the Hollow, and throughout the frontier for that matter, murder was considered to be an ignoble, tragic, and pitiable act. Murder combined such quintessential elements—intrigue, high adventure, violence, and death—that stories of murders were told and retold until they sometimes assumed near-mythic proportions. Almost everyone abhorred killing, yet many people recognized killing as the one thing that a man could do to obtain immediate personal justice. Murder was, in that sense, separate from law. Although law was a force to be reckoned with, it had little to do with justice, and the process of law was regarded as a struggle in which justice might not, in the end, be obtained.

Far from being alien to the American temper, that attitude prevailed. It resounds in Elizabeth Jackson's last words to her son Andrew: "I have nothing to give you but a mother's advice. Never tell a lie, nor take what is not your own, nor sue anybody for slander or assault and battery. *Always settle them cases yourself!*"[4] Another version puts the matter even plainer, reverberating with Scotch-Irish toughness: "Avoid quarrels as long as you can without yielding to imposition. But sustain your manhood always. Never bring a suit at law for assault and battery or for defamation. The law affords no remedy for such outrages that can satisfy the feelings of a true man."[5]

Violence in Sullivan's Hollow resulted from revenge, practical jokes, disputes over property, trespass, sexual advances (often a man was alleged to have "said something" to another man's wife, and the wife then told her husband), defamation of character, drinking, boasting, and gambling. Against that background, the coming of age of two brothers served as a catalyst for the numerous tales of lawless Sullivans. Those brothers, Wild Bill and my great-grandfather Neace, gave substance to the charge that in the third generation the "Sullivans went mean." They were grandsons of Pappy Tom.

Hard evidence is scant, but a case can be made that the Sullivan brothers' violent acts were caused by socioeconomic factors and psychological dependency upon one another as a "symbiotic pair." The traditional explanation given for the third-generation meanness is that, because of their isolation, Sullivans had intermarried, thereby reducing their genetic pool to disadvantage. An old-time observer said, "Just so they were not brothers and sisters was all that mattered when it came to getting married. It was a long way to the county seat, where there was any law, and besides, none of them cared anything about the law, and the law didn't care anything about them. They were not bothered at that time about most anything that they did, short of murder, and even when they were called in to investigate a murder the law didn't fool around any more than they had to."

First-cousin marriages increase the chances of undesirable recessive traits being passed on, but genetics doesn't account for the violence of Wild Bill and Neace. Both men reformed in their middle age and became respected members of the community. By most accounts, Wild Bill and Neace were violent because fate led them to violence, because they found from experience that they would survive violent encounters, because they enjoyed it, and because after they'd gained a reputation for being "mean" it gratified their sense of humor to maintain that reputation. Their father Henderson married Leah Howell, whose children were Cornelius (Neace), Mary,

33

Ann, William (Wild Bill), Louisa (Aunt Puss), Henderson (Hence), Red Jack, Harriet, Wilson (Wils), and Martha (Matt). Someone who knew them said, "When the boys of that family were young they seemed to be much like the other boys, then and now, but the older they got the rougher they got."

Bill and Neace were the closest of the brothers, and it was observed that when you saw one of them you would soon see the other and that when one of them started a fight he couldn't win the other one "would jump in and help him out." Bill, born in 1851, was tall, weighing 175 pounds. He wore a moustache and a large black hat. Neace, born in 1845, was a magnificent physical specimen, tall and straight and gaunt and hard-bitten, with piercing black eyes and a flowing black beard, which reached almost to his waist. He wore his shirt front open the year around. Neace died in 1920, and Bill died in 1932.

Both men kept fine saddle horses, which they rode everywhere, and they were good riders who could get the most out of a horse. The meanness of the pair surfaced when they started "running" with Crave McLemore and Josh Craft. Then they "went from bad to worse." Fred Sullivan said that it was dangerous for anyone to walk the roads at night because he might be mistaken for one of their enemies and killed.

Bill never met anyone whom he was afraid of, and he was never known to have started a "racket," but if anyone started any trouble with him he took care of himself. On the other hand, Neace was habitually getting involved in disputes or starting fights. The usual pattern was that Neace would start the fight and Bill would finish it. Neace was quiet about what he did, but Bill didn't care who knew of his deeds. He didn't care who it was or where it was, but if it took violence to settle a disagreement that suited him fine; if the disagreement couldn't be settled with fists, then he always had his gun. He came to be known as Wild Bill Sullivan, the King of the Hollow.

As a rule the fights that involved Bill and Neace occurred .at churches or other public gathering places, except for the times when they would lie in wait for an enemy or perhaps slip up on the person whom they were intent upon beating up or killing. They had fights at the old Shiloh Baptist Church, at Old Bunker Hill, and at dances.

By the 1870s the Hollow had a number of people living in and around it, and the Sullivans were marrying into other families. Notable families were the Chains, the Dikes, and the Gibbonses. Wild Bill, Neace, Pete Gibbons, Jim Tew, Gabe Chain, and others "ran together and were all the time getting into some kind of trouble." They would fight one another as often as not, and some of their intraclan fights resulted in serious consequences.

In the summer of 1871 a big revival was held at Shiloh Baptist Church, five miles west of Gilmer, which was attended by almost everyone in the Hollow. The fight that occurred here was of more local importance that anything that had ever happened, and it came to be called the Battle of Shiloh. Here Bill and Neace earned the reputation of having plenty of nerve. Because of that reputation most people later left them alone, especially when they were on one of their sprees.

Here's how it all came about. The Gibbons boys and Wild Bill and Neace got into a quarrel about something one of the Gibbons boys had said about one of the Sullivan wives. Apparently Gabe Chain had been trying to get Neace's wife to live with him. He had been going to Neace's house at

35

times when he knew that she was there alone, and Neace had learned of it. At the revival, Neace asked Gabe about his actions, and their exchange prompted the fight. Bill and Neace mounted their horses and told their friends to get out of the way, that they were going to "run over the damned Dikes and Chains and kill them." Bill and Neace started toward Blakley Creek, which runs about three hundred yards south of the church, and asked the Chains and Dikes to come with them.

Jim Tew was standing outside the church, telling his wife about the boys' having trouble and going down to the creek to fight it out. While he was talking, they heard a gunshot. Jim, who was holding their baby, handed it to his wife and said, "I'll go down there and see what they have done." When he got to the creek he found Gabe Chain lying in the road. Neace was sitting on the ground near the edge of the creek.

The story goes that when the men got to the creek Neace and Gabe were going to fight it out with their hands but, when Neace began getting the better of Gabe, Gabe pulled his knife and cut Neace across the stomach so badly that his exposed intestines fell onto the sand. That was when Frank Gibbons, according to one version, drew his gun and shot Gabe. Another version held that Wild Bill had detached himself from the argument and circled around to hide and watch the fight. When he saw Gabe pull the knife and cut Neace, he took aim and shot. But it is more likely that Neace's brother-in-law Frank Gibbons shot Gabe Chain and Jim Dikes, who was also killed. After the fight Frank left the county and stayed gone four years. When he was finally heard of in Arkansas the sheriff went there and got him, and he was tried for the murders of Gabe and Jim. He was found guilty and sent to prison for life.

After he was cut, it was said, Neace picked up his own intestines, walked to the creek, washed the sand off them, put them back into his body, and rode to a house, where he was sewn up. Then, some said, he went out into the yard, climbed upon a stump, flapped his arms like a rooster's wings, and crowed. Gabe Chain lay in bed so long before he died that his back was almost rotten.

Bill and Neace were involved in many notorious events, but the most serious one, the thing that caused them the most trouble, was their killing of Bryant Craft in 1874. Some said that there was an affair between Bill and Bryant's sister, that Bill lay in wait and ambushed Bryant because he knew too much about it. According to the story told by Bill and Neace, this is what happened. They were caught plowing in a field by Bryant Craft and another Craft boy, who were riding horses and had guns. They pointed their guns at Bill and Neace and made them dance. A short time after that, Bill and Neace managed to catch one of the Crafts alone, plowing. They made him unhitch his horse and get into the harness. Then they said, "Get up!" He looked up, thinking they might shoot at him, but they just laughed and rode off.

Sometime after that, the four of them met on the Derby Road, a little north of Old Bunker Hill. Shooting ensued. They all hid in the corners of a split-rail fence bordering the road, and one of the Sullivans, when he'd run out of bullets, yelled to his brother, "If you've ever done it, do it now!" That was when his brother shot Bryant Craft. The other Craft boy fled.

The killing of Craft happened three years after the Battle of Shiloh, and as a result Bill and Neace took to the woods and hid out for two years. They would be seen or heard of at one place one day and then another place maybe twenty miles away the next day; they depended on their good horses and their knowledge of the land to keep ahead of Sheriff John Mize, who spent most of his time hunting them but never succeeded in arresting them. Once the brothers went to Texas, to get some rest. In a store there Bill picked up a newspaper and saw his own picture staring up from the front page. He showed it to Neace, they exchanged glances but no words, and they left Texas immediately, returning to where they felt safest, Cohay swamp. Henry Eubanks was one of those who carried them food and water. He would slip out of his house at night and take it to them.

People often remarked that Bill and Neace were "on the average just as good as anybody else, until they were drinking or someone wanted to start a fight with them, and then they were two of the meanest boys that ever lived in Sullivan's Hollow." According to the Honorable R. C. Russell, who was their close friend, the two men epitomized all that was good and bad in the Sullivans. They both were scrupulously honest in their business dealings, fiercely loyal to their friends, and courageous to the point of recklessness. Russell said, "There were no better people anywhere than Bill and Neace and the other Sullivans. But they *would* drink whiskey, and they *would* fight."

Bill and Neace took great delight in rough humor. Once when they came upon their uncle Loughton plowing, they shot at his feet and made him dance. Then they unhitched his mules, put the harness on him, and plowed him for awhile. Not long after that, they plowed the peach-tree salesman mentioned earlier. Then they caught another salesman, painted his white horse black, and argued hotly with him that it was their horse. Wild Bill once offered to put up a salesman for the night, explaining, "So's I can kill you."

A man named Stubbs recounted the time he was on his way to see his girl friend in the Hollow. He was riding a fast horse, which he had borrowed for the day to impress her, and he was carrying a fresh bouquet of wild flowers. As he rounded a bend he came upon a wagon standing dead in the middle of the road, and sitting in the wagon was Wild Bill. Stubbs stopped, and Bill offered him a drink from his jug. Stubbs told him that he was already late and couldn't stop. "All of a sudden he lay over and came up with his pistol leveled at me, saying, 'Have a drink with me or I'll start shooting, and I'll start by shooting that bunch of flowers out of your hand!'" Stubbs thrust the bouquet from him, reared up the horse, and got away. He said, "Wild Bill sent word the next day that he was sorry about it. He said if I'd just come to Mize he'd get down on his knees and beg my forgiveness in the street. I thought maybe he would, because he was a mighty fine fellow, but on second thought I decided not to risk it."

In their later years, Bill and Neace liked to tell about the day they were in the swamps hunting for something to eat and Bill decided that he would have some fun. It was late in the day in the fall of the year, so it was beginning to get pretty cool. Bill circled through the underbrush until he was ahead of Neace and came to a bridge across Cohay Creek. This bridge, about ten feet above the water, was a long one for those days, when almost every crossing had to be forded. Bill crossed the bridge, shook a bush and hollered. "All right, boys! Get him!" Of course Neace thought it was the sheriff or some of the Crafts, and he certainly didn't intend to get caught by either group, so he made a running jump over the bridge railing into the water. When he came splashing up, clawing for the bank, he heard laughter and saw Bill standing at the end of the bridge howling for all he was worth. Neace pulled his pistol; Bill, seeing how mad he was, sold out, as the old saying goes. He ran as fast as he could, crashing down through the middle of the woods. Neace shot at him six times but never came close to hitting him.

Neace then worked up a plan of revenge. One afternoon when they lay resting under a large tree Bill went to sleep. Neace prowled around until he came across a long blacksnake at the edge of an old field. He killed it with a stick, brought it back to the tree, and tied it to Bill's pants leg. Then he lay back and waited for Bill to wake up. Finally, when Bill roused himself, Neace said, "Come on, Bill. I've got an uneasy feeling. Let's go." He started off down the path with Bill following him. They'd only gone a few steps when Bill felt the snake pulling at his leg. He looked back and saw it, and then he yelled and took off running. Neace stepped out of the path and let him pass. He said that Bill ran a quarter of a mile before he got out of breath and stopped to find that it was a dead snake tied to his pants leg. He came back up the path cursing Neace for everything he could think of, with his pistol in the air, but he didn't get close to Neace for quite a while, not until he'd cooled off. There was something between Bill and Neace that none of the other brothers had, something that kept them from killing each other, because they certainly would kill anyone else they got mad at.

One day they were fishing in Cohay around some stumps that stood out in the water, when Bill saw a big catfish down in the hollow of a stump. He tried to reach it with his hand but couldn't, so he called Neace over to help him. His plan was for Neace to hold his feet while he went down headfirst into the stump and groped for the catfish. Then Neace would pull him and the fish both out. They set about it, but when

Bill got all the way down in the stump Neace let go of his feet and wouldn't pull him out. Bill's arms, head, shoulders, and chest were all under water, and he almost drowned before he could let go of the catfish and work himself out of the stump.

During the time of their hiding, Bill and Neace had numerous encounters with the law, but when they met one or two lawmen the officers wouldn't attempt to make an arrest because they knew that only an overwhelming superiority of numbers could bring the brothers in. Many times Sheriff Mize raised a posse when he knew Bill and Neace to be in a particular place, but he was never successful in sneaking up on them with a large enough group of deputies to capture them.

Once when he was after them the brothers got the jump on him, stuck his head under the corner of a rail fence, and lowered the fence, leaving him gibbeted for three hours before turning him loose. On another occasion Bill and Neace got the drop on a posse, locked them in a barn, and prepared to make their escape. While they were untying the posse's horses they winked and fell into a big argument about whether they ought to set the barn on fire before they left.

Frank Russell, a deputy under Sheriff Mize, once learned that Bill was hiding in a vacant house. He decided he would try to persuade him to surrender to be tried for the murder of Bryant Craft. Bill had always said he wouldn't surrender because he couldn't get a fair trial as long as John Mize was sheriff. Frank recounted that when he rode up to the house Bill saw that he was alone, came out, and invited him to come in and rest for awhile. Inside Bill said that he wished they would quit chasing him so much and let him alone, because all his hair was coming out from running through the woods. Frank said, "No, Bill. We are going to keep trying to

41

bring you and Neace in because the people expect it of us."
Bill replied, "Well, you never will because I am not going to
give you a chance to."

After Mize's term expired, a new sheriff was elected, and
then Bill and Neace got on their horses, went home and
gathered up some of their kinfolk, rode into Raleigh, and
surrendered. They were released to await trial. One night the
Smith County Courthouse burned, destroying the record of
their indictment. It was widely rumored that the fire had
been set in their behalf. The Crafts had moved away, no one
else wanted to press charges, so the whole thing was dropped.

In all, suspicious fires have destroyed three Smith County
courthouses. After the first one burned, business was resum-
ed in the old Floyd Hotel, which burned in 1892. A new
courthouse was built, but it burned in 1912. The present-
day courthouse was built in 1913. These rumors of arson en-
hanced Smith County's reputation for lawlessness.

Hog Tom and Hence were half brothers, sons of Pappy
Tom. Hog Tom had a son named William, whom he called
Billie to distinguish him from Hence's son, Wild Bill. Some
people who knew both men said that Billie was almost as
mean as Wild Bill. In fact, some said that Billie did a lot of
the meanness attributed to Wild Bill. Billie married Rufus
King's daughter Mary, who lived at the edge of Sullivan's
Hollow, but they were not a happy couple. Almost every
day, on the slightest excuse, Billie would beat Mary. He was
extremely jealous of her, and when he left the house he
swept the dirt around the door with a yard broom so that he
would see tracks if anybody came while he was gone. Of
course Mary was a good woman, but Billie was mean and
wanted an excuse to beat her. He would tell her that he was
going to town and then slip around and hide close to the

house and watch her all day. Periodically Mary would leave and go to stay with her father. Then she would go back and live with Billie—until he would whip her again—then she would leave. Some people came to believe that he ought to have beaten her for living with him at all. But Mary didn't live long. People said that she died from bad treatment. After her death Billie married his daughter-in-law's sister, who was a Prine. She very soon left him and stayed gone. She said that once was enough for her.

It was observed that the difference between Wild Bill and Billie was that Billie was sly and sneaking with his devilment, whereas Wild Bill didn't care who knew what he did. When Wild Bill got ready to do something he did it and thought about it afterward.

Neace had the appearance of any ordinary man then or now, "as Christian gentlemen go." He was fine as long as everything went his way, but if something went contrary to his likes he could be "as mean as the old Devil himself." One day George Norris went to see Neace, and after he got there he decided to have dinner and spend the day visiting. When Neace had company for dinner he made all his family wait to eat until he and his guest were finished, so he and George sat alone at opposite ends of the table. The two were the very best of friends, having been together in "lots of rough trouble." While they ate they talked about first one thing and then another. After awhile some subject came up which they did not agree on, and the more they talked the madder they got, until before they knew it they were fighting. They began by throwing the dishes at one another. When they'd broken all the dishes on the table, they grabbed their chairs and began fighting with them. Then, in a pause between swings, they looked at one another and asked, "What in the hell do we mean by this?" The fight was over, and they were as friendly as they had been before the fight had started. Neace had thrown a coffee cup at George and hit him on the head, cutting part of his ear off. George was living in the southern part of Sullivan's Hollow when he was interviewed by Grover Bishop. At that time he wouldn't tell everything he knew about the Sullivans because he had been with them in a lot of the trouble, despite the fact that some of it had happened forty or fifty years before.

A contemporary's description of Wild Bill runs like this:

> There is an old saying that the more you tell a lie the bigger you tell, it, and there is another saying that if you go out looking for trouble you will find it. Both sayings applied to Wild Bill. He was not a wild man, neither was he crazy. He was bad, and he would do anything to get a laugh, but he had as much sense as anybody in Sullivan's Hollow, and he lived in a violent time when almost everybody carried a pistol. When trouble started the man who was the quickest on the draw was the lucky one, and Wild Bill was about the fastest man with a pistol in the Hollow. When he was at home, as long as you acted right, he would treat you mighty fine—according to his fashion.

One evening late a stranger stopped by Bill's house and asked if he might be put up for the night. He said, "I want to stay the night, if I can. Mainly, I want to stay as far away as possible from Wild Bill Sullivan." Bill invited him in and told his wife to fix the man supper. After supper they sat around talking for a time. Then Bill put the stranger to bed, treating him with all courtesy and respect, but didn't tell the man who he was. The next morning when the stranger started to leave, Bill shook his hand and said, "I'm awful glad you stayed with me, and if you're ever through this way again, stop and say hello. My name is Wild Bill Sullivan!" Bill commented that if he had stuck a knife in the stranger the man would not have bled one drop.

Polly Sullivan, granddaughter of Pappy Tom, married Tilman Bishop. They lived a mile north of Magee, and their nearest neighbor was Irvin Jones, who lived three miles north of them. People living around Magee then had to go to Ellisville to trade, and to do that they had to pass through the Hollow. Once Tilman and Irvin and some other people took five ox wagons on a five-day trip to Ellisville. The first night they made camp about two miles short of Wild Bill's house. The next morning the wagons started while Tilman and Irvin, who were riding horses, put out the breakfast fire and stood around a few minutes to smoke their pipes.

Tilman and Irvin had not caught the wagons by the time they got to Wild Bill's house, where Bill was out in the barnyard feeding his stock. Bill liked to dance, and he liked to see other people have a good time, too. When Tilman and Irvin got close to Bill they spoke, and he answered, telling them to stop for awhile. When they got off their horses Bill caught each of them by the hand, said, "Let's dance!" and began to go around and around, pulling them with him and whooping it up for quite a few turns—until they began to get tired and uneasy. But they were afraid to say anything. Finally Tilman remembered who he was and said, "Say, Bill. I married Polly." Bill asked, "Polly who?" Tilman replied, "Polly Sullivan!" Then Bill said, "Why hadn't you done and told me about it? Come in and have some coffee before you go!" Irvin Jones later said that that was one time he was certainly glad Tilman had married a Sullivan.

After Wild Bill came out of hiding, he was in the hotel cafe in Raleigh. The proprietor asked him to pay an old debt that dated from before he went into hiding. Bill asked what he owed money for, and the proprietor said that he owed for his bed and board. Bill paid the amount that the man asked, but then went upstairs and came back down with a mattress across his shoulder. When the owner protested, Bill commented, "Well, you said that I owed for board and bed. I've already had my board, so now I'm getting my bed." Bill took the bed home and kept it.

One day when Mount Olive was small Wild Bill was there in the only cafe, and he was drunk. He was acting bad, cursing and trying to start a fight with anyone who would pay attention to him. The marshal went to see if he could get him to leave town or at least stop cursing and behave himself. When Bill saw the marshal coming, he put his hand inside his shirt as if to draw a pistol. Then the marshal began to talk to Wild Bill telling him that he ought to be ashamed of himself. People said that Bill must have had a good heart, because he stopped cursing and quieted down. That was the only time Wild Bill was ever known to back down once he had started something.

Loughton Sullivan's grandson told his son that during an Old Bunker Hill revival meeting Wild Bill, Neace, and two other men asked Loughton to go with them down to the spring for a drink of water, their intention being to get him down there and give him a whipping. Loughton was Bill and Neace's uncle, the one they had once plowed. When they got to the spring they jumped on him, but as the fight developed "it looked like he was going to whip all of them with his fists, so one of them backed up a piece, pulled a pistol, and shot and killed Loughton."

Wild Bill and his brother Wils were close neighbors, so close that their wives visited back and forth and their children played together. But the children fell out, and then their mothers fell out, so then the brothers fell out, too. One night in January, 1903, at a church social Bill and his son Jack stabbed Wils to death. When Wils' oldest son heard about it he got a shotgun and shot Bill's horse from under him, but Bill escaped through the brush. Bill and Jack were arrested and charged, and hard feelings grew against Bill. People who had protected him when he and Neace were hiding out were for hanging him now. Wild Bill and Jack were arrested, but their trial was repeatedly postponed. Jack managed to get a gun and he committed suicide in September, 1903. That was the same year in which his brother Bobby was killed by Adams in Mize. When Wild Bill was tried in the Raleigh Circuit Court in September, 1904, he was found guilty. He was held at Rankin County Farm Prison, and his appeal to the Mississippi State Supreme Court reversed the Circuit Court's decision. He was then released from the Farm Prison and not tried again.

Irvin Jones, who was born around 1860, related the following account of Henry Holmes and the Sullivans. When Holmes moved to the Hollow the Sullivans did not like him, and it was not long before he and some of them had a fight, which Holmes got the best of by using his pocketknife. He killed one of the Sullivans, and when the grand jury met he was indicted for manslaughter. Holmes heard about the indictment before the sheriff had a chance to arrest him, so he left the Hollow for Alabama, but en route he stopped to take a job at a sawmill some fifty miles from the Alabama line.

Jack Ashley, who lived in Simpson County, learned Holmes's whereabouts and told the sheriff. They made a secret deal whereby Ashley would hire Holmes to come to his place and work, tell Holmes that he would keep him hidden, and then help the sheriff capture him. They planned to split the reward offered for Holmes. Some people said that Henry Holmes was a good man who had acted in self-defense and that he hadn't run away because he feared the courts but because he was afraid some of the Sullivans might kill him before his trial. After Ashley and the sheriff made their arrangements, Ashley wrote Holmes, asking him to come and work, which he did. On the day that he arrived, Ashley told him to go down in a field close to the swamp to do some work. After Holmes left, Ashley sent for the sheriff, who gathered his deputies and hid beside the road that Holmes would have to travel when he started in from work that evening.

Holmes came up the road; as he came close to the hidden deputies he saw one of them and turned to escape. The sheriff yelled for him to halt, but Holmes began to run. Then one of the deputies shot him in the back. That night he died, but before he died he said that if he had known who they· were he would have stopped. He said he thought they were Sullivans. Sheriff Busby, when he heard that, prayed that Holmes would live. They said the sheriff never got over his deputy's killing Holmes.

Millie Canoy, born in 1845, knew the Sullivans of her day well, and she didn't like them at all. When she lived with Dr. Carr in the Hollow, she had an upstairs room. She said that he kept a human skeleton in the corner of her room and that some nights she couldn't sleep for being afraid of it. The doctor owned an old blind Negro while she was there, blinded by Joe Carr, the doctor's brother, who had beaten his eyes out with corncobs. According to Millie, Hog Tom was every bit as bad as Wild Bill, the only difference being that Hog Tom never killed anybody. After she married and moved to Simpson County, one day Norris and Hog Tom stopped by her house on their way to court at Old Westville. They asked her to cook them something to eat because they had left home before breakfast and were hungry. She cooked them a fine breakfast, and then they "went off and talked about her cooking." Moreover, when they started to leave they told her that they would pay for the breakfast when they came through on their way back home, but while she was in the kitchen they gave one of her children a nickel. She said, "If I had been a man I would have beat the Devil out of them. No, I don't like them, and they had better leave me and mine alone!" Millie said that her father, Joe Bishop, went to see Hog Tom one day; Hog Tom invited him to stay and eat, which he did. Hog Tom passed the meat around to Joe, who took out one piece. When he had finished that piece he asked for the meat to be passed again, and Hog Tom said, "Joe, you have eat enough." When Tom said that, Joe stopped eating, and he never went back there to eat again. Millie said that Hog Tom was mean to his wife and children and that he ought to have never been born.

Bunker Hill, named for the Battle of Bunker Hill in the Revolutionary War, was on the hillside just north of Sullivan's Hollow Creek, a half mile west of the Cohay bottoms. It was about two hundred yards below where Sullivan's Hollow Creek joins Bunker Hill Mill Creek, and at that point Rob Dean built a dam on the creek and flooded a large area to supply water power for his mill. Bunker Hill, established about 1861, consisted of three stores and Rob Dean's mill, and it was known as the place where much whiskey was sold and where the first Sullivan feud started in 1886. The early post office was abolished in 1890, but a flag stop by the name of Bunker Hill was retained on the Gulf & Ship Island Railroad several miles northeast of the settlement. That flag stop came to be known as New Bunker Hill. The mill pond was the scene of a notorious killing. George Sullivan, son of Neace, was out on it in a boat fishing when Sam Sullivan, thinking George was Rob Dean, shot and killed him. After that, Rob Dean understandably sold the mill and moved to Mobile, never to return.

The last great fight took place in 1922 and was known as the Battle of the Ball Game. The scene was a dirt basketball court near the high school in Mize, and the action grew out of a basketball game between Magee and Mize. Warren Ashley, a deputy sheriff, resented a remark made to his wife by a Magee player. They started a tussle, and when Judge Hughes saw Warren's pistol sticking out of his pocket he cried, "Get the pistol!" meaning for someone to disarm Warren. Warren, however, got it first, and with three men hanging on to his arm he began firing between his legs. With those shots other people, who had brought their own pistols for various reasons, began shooting, and in the end three people were killed. Four others were wounded, including Constable A. W. Lack. There were hearings but no trial resulted from the melee.

6 Aunt Puss and Fortune-telling Steave

Tall, prosperous, and independent, Aunt Puss (Louisa) lived from 1853 to 1934. Although she never married, she bore six children—Sarah Ann, Effie, Dick, Taylor, Chester, and Tootie—and it was said that none of them had the same father. People said that when springtime came Aunt Puss would go with her sheep stick to stand in the road and wait for a man to pass. When one did she would invite him to her house for dinner. She was a wealthy woman who owned land, had a lot of stock, especially sheep, and had fine crops. If the man was impressed and if he suited her, she would let him stay on her farm. Maybe she would get pregnant, and maybe he would get to feeling prosperous—plant a big crop for her and work it well—then in the fall when the crop was in she would take her sheep stick and run him off.

It is not surprising that Aunt Puss was a legend because she came from a unique family, being the sister of Neace, Wild Bill, and Red Jack. The son of one of her summer men came through the country a few years after his father had, and she took him in just like she'd taken in his father.

Once she was sitting on the porch talking with a friend, who had a son named Peter. Peter was about the same age as her son Dick, and the two boys were playing together in the yard. Aunt Puss, looking at the two boys, remarked, "I'll bet

51

you my Dick is bigger than your Peter!" I'm sure that's the first joke I ever heard.

One Sunday Aunt Puss invited the preacher to her house for dinner. She stayed home all morning to cook at her wood stove. In the middle of her cooking some of her boys ran in yelling, "Momma! The house is on fire!" She stormed outside, grabbed a ladder, and shinnied onto the board roof, thinking the fire would be there at the hot flue. But it was a trick; there was no fire. The boys pulled down her ladder and ran, leaving her trapped on the roof. When the preacher arrived dinner was ruined, and Aunt Puss was pretty mad, sitting on top of her house.

My uncle Stone, whose grandfather was Neace, remembers Aunt Puss well. He told me about the time he and a group of young boys were playing naked down in a ditch of runoff water following a heavy spring rain. They were splashing and laughing when they looked up to see Aunt Puss, tall and severe with her long stick, staring down at them. After an interminable silence, she asked, "You boys seed any sheep?" They cowered speechless, afraid to answer. After another long silence she said contemptuously, "I'll bet you wish they'd never been a sheep seed!"

When she was an old woman she would walk from her place to the house of one of her brothers, visit there with them and "drink whiskey with them like a man," and then walk home alone, carrying her big sheep stick. People who remember Aunt Puss speak of her with reverence and pride.

Steave Sullivan held all the records for being clever, lazy, and loving to eat. He talked in a slow drawl, and because he hated work he learned early in life how to get money without working for it. He was Pappy Tom's grandson, son of Hog Tom. Steave was married three times, and each wife left him for the same reason—he would not make her a living.

52

It was a fact that Steave could eat as much as two ordinary men. Of course he had a lot of kin in the Hollow—he was related to almost everybody in one way or another—and people said that at mealtime you could count on looking up and seeing Steave. Although most people didn't want to bother with him, they usually didn't say so because they didn't want to hurt his feelings.

One day Steave went to visit some people who were in no way related to him, arriving at dinnertime. It goes without saying that he was always on time to eat but could never be found when it came to work. On that day the family had killed hogs, and it's likely that Steave knew they'd killed hogs; he was pretty smart. Anyway, the lady of the house was cooking "the best part of the hog," the chitlins, and Steave was fond of chitlins. He often said that he'd never had his fill of them. When the family saw him coming they invited him in; there was no way around it. He came in and prepared for dinner; then they sat down at the table and ate what food was on it. Of course the lady of the house, who was "refined to a certain degree," was ashamed of the chitlins and had not put them on the table. Everybody back then ate them, but many people wouldn't admit it.

When dinner was over they returned to the living room, the fireplace room, and started to talk about one thing and another. After the woman had cleaned her kitchen, she came in and joined the conversation. After awhile they talked about having killed hogs that day. Before people had freezers, chitlins had to be eaten fresh, so it was natural that hog-killing time was chitlin-eating time. Soon the subject of chitlins came up, prompted by Steave. Then, in a friendly mood, the lady admitted that she had cooked some but had not put them on the table, to which Steave replied in his slow southern drawl, "Well—Lady—you ought not to have done that—if there is anything that I like better than chitlins—it is more chitlins—I could eat one as long as the Gulf and Ship Island Railroad—with a paunch [stomach] at every station!" At that the woman went back into her kitchen and brought out a big platter of boiled chitlins. Steave fell in on them and ate every one of them just as if he'd had no dinner at all.

He was called Fortune-telling Steave because telling fortunes was a handy dodge for him. At someone's house he would offer to tell their fortunes if they would make some coffee so he could use the cup they had drunk from to tell it. Of course he got a free cup of coffee. If he met someone on the road he would offer to tell their fortunes and then he would charge them for it. They could pay him whatever they wanted to; he would take anything that they offered.

Once he saw two Negro preachers on the road. How he could always tell that they were preachers was anybody's guess, but he could always tell a person's business. He had to be able to do that so he could proceed with his own business. When he got close to them he stopped them and began to talk about the Bible. He said that he was a very sick man, unable to work, and he almost had them crying. Then he got them to kneel with him and pray. He prayed for thirty minutes. Then he slacked off and told them that he needed some medicine and was penniless. The Negroes, who had a little over two dollars between them, gave him every cent of it and wished him Godspeed. He returned their blessing and went his way, but when he got to town he told how he had done the two Negroes. Every time he told about it he would get tickled and fall over laughing.

Steave was so lazy that people thought there might be something else wrong with him. One day somebody mentioned to him that he might have pellagra, and it almost scared him to death. They advised him to go to Hattiesburg and see Dr. Betha, who was a good doctor on that disease, so Steave "hit out" for Hattiesburg, walking, and when he got there the doctor told him that there was nothing the matter with him. Steave said, "Well—Doctor—they say—I have pellagra," The doctor said, "I don't think so, Steave." Steave asked, "Well—what is the matter with me? I don't seem able to work—Doctor?" The doctor replied, "Steave, if you are not able to work, why don't you get yourself a begging permit and carry it around with you and ask people to help you." Steave said, "Well—Doctor—don't you think if I did that it might hurt my reputation?"

Steave did get someone to write him a begging paper, which stated that he was unable to work and that Dr. Betha had diagnosed him as having pellagra. He carried the paper a long time, and some people would give him money when he showed it.

In 1920 Steave was at the house of Webster Bishop, who was pastor of a small country church. Steave decided to go to church with Webster to hear him preach and also to get a free meal. At church he met a spinster, Sopronie Ranner, who lived nearby. Steave called her Phronie, and they courted for about a month, until the day Steave came walking up to Preacher Bishop's house and said," Webb, I want you to go with me up to Phronie's house. We have decided to get married, and I want you to marry us for nothing, because you and me are kin." Webster got out his horse and buggy and took Steave back up to Phronie's house. He found when they arrived that Phronie and Steave were supposed to have been married the previous day, but for some reason Steave was a day late. Steave drawled, "Well—Phronie—I have come to get married—and I have brought the preacher." She said, "Steave, you were supposed to have come yesterday, and you didn't. Here I am not dressed to get married. And furthermore, my people don't want me to marry you. They say you won't make me a living. Will you or won't you?" Steave said, "Yes—Phronie—I will make you a good living if you will marry me." Phronie then turned to the preacher and asked him what he would do if he were in her place. Webster said, "Now, I did not come up here to try to get you all to marry. I came to marry you, if that is what you want." Phronie said, "Well, Steave, I am going to marry you, and if you don't make me a living I am going to quit you." Steave said, "All right." So they stood up and told the preacher to go ahead and marry them, which he did. Phronie was barefooted, and her dress was tucked up with a safety pin, but they got married just the same.

After the ceremony the three of them had a nice visit, during which Steave and Phronie told Webster Bishop a funny story. A few days before, when they'd talked about getting married, they discussed their plans for setting up house. Steave's furniture and bits of kitchenware were at some of his kinfolks' place, and Phronie's things were at a sister's. They were discussing whether they should get their furniture and kitchenware and put it together before they were married or wait until after they were married to do that. According to Phronie, she said, "Steave, let's put our things together first, and then get married, and we will already have that tended to." She said Steave looked around the room, blushed, and slowly said, "No—Phronie. Let's get married first—and then put our things together."

About three months later, Steave came walking up to Preacher Bishop's house and said, "Well—Webster—I have left

Phronie. You know what the Bible says. It is better to live on the housetop alone than in the house with a brawling woman."[1]

Thomas Sullivan's house

7 Merry Hell

Merry Hell is an area about five miles square, which lies in the southwestern part of Sullivan's Hollow—not the old Hollow, but what the Hollow had grown to encompass by the 1860s. Merry Hell is drained by McLaurin Mill Creek, named after an early settler who was one of the first to own Negro slaves. The creek was so heavily timbered that it was dangerous for anyone to go there, even during the daytime, but once two men decided to go fishing there. Late in the day they started home, but hadn't walked through the thick woods long before they realized that they were back where they'd been. By that time it was getting dark, so they had to stay where they were and wait until morning.

There was a brand of whiskey named Merry Hell, which was popular with the people of the Hollow, and it was known to have an "awful fine kick to it." While the men sat there in the dark with no fire and no food and not even a gun, just their rolled-up fishing lines, they were quite uncomfortable. They talked and wished for a bottle of Merry Hell to help them make the night. One of them said that he wished McLaurin Mill Creek was running with Merry Hell. After they made their way out of the woods the following day, they told about being lost and about how they'd wanted some

Merry Hell. That started people calling the creek Merry Hell Creek and that part of the Hollow Merry Hell.

But the name fit for other reasons. After the Sullivans moved into Merry Hell some rough people came too. It became "a mighty bad place in which to live," especially when the railroad passed near there, bringing and mixing in the kind of devil-may-care people who built the railroads. Many of the Sullivans were good musicians, and they would all gather at somebody's house about every weekend for a frolic, where there would usually be a barrel of whiskey sitting in the corner for anybody who wanted to sample it. After a night of dancing and frolicking some of the people would be drunk. They would have a merry time, so the name accommodated that, too. Merry Hell is quiet now, but people remember when "it used to be a mighty bad place to go in and start any trouble with the old Merry Hell clan."

At the entrance to Merry Hell, Grover Bishop visited Celia Sullivan West, who was born in 1850. She told him that a man named Clark was the first preacher she remembered in Sullivan's Hollow and that her grandfather Pappy Tom used to walk fifteen or twenty miles to hear his favorite, old Preacher West. Preacher West, an avid fox hunter, had made plans one Friday night to go hunting after he finished preaching his sermon. The sermon was on repentance, and he was doing some hard preaching and doing it pretty fast so he could get through. But his hunting partner, who hadn't come to church, decided that he would turn the dogs out and have a fox up and running by the time Preacher West finished. The dogs jumped a fox about two miles from the church and were running it as hard as they could right down a hollow toward the church. Everybody could hear them coming, and the closer they came the faster Preacher West preached. When the dogs came alongside the church, Preacher West couldn't stand it any longer. Stepping out of the pulpit he said, "Brethren and sisters, you all can repent right now—or don't repent and go to Hell! I am going to the dogs!"

Celia West smoked a pipe like many of the women in her day, who used tobacco in one form or another. She told about the time they were going to church on horses. The women rode sidesaddle, and the men rode straight saddle. The women wore long riding skirts, and the woman with the longest was "supposed to be the grandest." It began to rain, and a lady by the name of Rutling was smoking her pipe as they rode along. She put it in the pocket of her skirt, thinking its fire was out, but before long she began to smell something burning. By the time she got dismounted and got her skirt off, it was completely burned up. That put her in a very embarrassing position.

Celia said that times were "lots better back in those days." If her daddy told his children to do something, they knew to do it right, and they never would have thought of talking to their parents like children do today. She recalled going to a school at the old Smith place, where the teacher was a man named Thompson. A stranger was killed in Merry Hell, and his body was found in the creek with Thompson's belt around it. The teacher insisted that he had not killed him, but it looked so bad for him that he decided to get out of the country. When he left, all the children cried. They thought a lot of him and hated to see him leave under those circumstances. Celia said that when she heard Wild Bill and Neace coming up the road she would take her children and go to the woods until the two brothers were gone.

In Merry Hell a long lane leads to an old, settled place with barns on the left and on the right the home of Jeff Sullivan, son of Joseph Sullivan. Jeff was born there in 1861. He married Jane Harvey, and they had ten children. Jeff wore a big black hat, had a red moustache, talked with a coarse southern drawl, and was reputed to be the most courteous man imaginable. He lived all his life on the place that his father had homesteaded in 1836. His father before him had raised ten children there. Joseph Sullivan never in his life bought a pound of lard, he raised everything he ate, and he always had plenty to eat. The Sullivan house was built of pine logs, sealed with planks inside and outside. The walls are sixteen inches thick. There are three chimneys in the house, and one of them is built of homemade brick. Jeff used the same smokehouse that his father had used since 1863, and the garden had been in the same place since 1853. Jeff remembered that when he was a boy they cooked biscuits only on Sunday mornings, and remembered thinking that Sunday would never come.

Jeff and his brother "Orlando" Jack bought the first steam sawmill in Sullivan's Hollow. The mill cost them six hundred dollars, and for years its steam whistle was the timepiece of the Hollow. Then Jack caught his foot in the belt that ran from the engine to the saw, and the accident cost him his leg. After this Jeff lost his fondness for the sawmill. He sold his interest in it to Jack for a bale of cotton and thought he'd made a good bargain in getting rid of it. One day Jasper Wells and his young son went to inspect the mill with the intention of buying it. For bargaining leverage, Jasper pretended that he and his son knew everything there was to know about sawmills. Before they even got started with the serious dickering, Jasper's son spied the steam gauge, which looked a bit like a clock, and said, "Hey, Pa! Let's go! It's already six o'clock!"

A man named McMinnin was the first teacher in that part

of the Hollow. The schoolhouse was a small pine-log building with a dirt floor, and the benches were made of pine logs that had been split in half. They stood on wooden legs. Jeff said that it was a hard matter to learn much after walking six or seven miles to get there and then having to sit on those seats.

He remembered one year buying thirteen barrels of flour for his family at eighteen dollars a barrel, but he said that he didn't mind paying that much for flour because he had to pay eight dollars for a gallon of whiskey.

When he was a boy there were no religious sanctions on Sunday, and children were allowed to do whatever they pleased, such as hunting, fishing, or swimming. That was to change by the 1930s and 1940s, when most preachers forbade those activities on Sundays, as well as mixed bathing (boys and girls swimming together) on all days.

Jeff said that the first bale of cotton ginned in Merry Hell was grown by Joseph Sullivan, who sold it to Sam Johnson, owner of the Emporium Store in Jackson. Johnson bought the bale of cotton on credit, not having the money to pay for it, but when he died he was "worth thousands of dollars."

Molly Sullivan was the wife of Tommie, son of Big John, son of Hog Tom, son of Pappy Tom. Molly, who was a Tew, remembered Wild Bill and many of his fights and killings. Her husband worked the Hollow's first mail route, which started at Saratoga and went by a small post office at Steave Sullivan's home and from there to Bunker Hill and back. Tommie used a mule to carry the mail, and he was paid a dollar a day. He often allowed his son to accompany him; once when a Negro man who lived nearby wanted an organ that Tommie owned, Tommie traded him the organ for labor, letting him carry the mail three months to pay for it. Zeke Sullivan, living at Bunker Hill, was the first postmaster in that part of the Hollow.

Around the turn of the century Bud Hall lived near Merry Hell. He was the son of Dock Hall, who lived at the lower end of the Hollow. Bud married Mary Sullivan, daughter of Big John. Bud was a large, strong man, who weighed over two hundred pounds, and he was very mean. Tommie Sullivan [not Mary's brother] married Bud's sister Mary, and he didn't get along with Bud. Bud was always picking at Tommie or his folks, and he was much larger than Tommie. One day they got into a squabble about something and had a fight in which Bud whipped Tommie. Another time Bud went to Tommie's house when he wasn't at home and held Tommie's wife (his sister) and made his own wife whip her. When Tommie got home and found out about that he was exceedingly angry. The next day he went before the justice of the peace and had papers made out against Bud. While he was in town doing that, Bud came by his house, where he saw one of Tommie's sons in the front yard with a gun in his hand. Bud took the gun away from the boy and broke it over a wagon wheel.

The case against Bud was set for the following Saturday in Magee, and a crowd of people came into town in mule-drawn wagons. Tommie put his team behind R. L. Everett's Store, then went to the courthouse. The trial proceeded, Bud was found guilty, and was fined. After court he went walking all around town, fuming, telling everybody that he was going to cut Tommie's head off. People warned him to leave Tommie alone, that he had already been found guilty once, but he wouldn't listen. He went behind Everett's Store holding his knife in his hand, and when he got to within twenty feet of where Tommie and his family were eating their dinner, Tommie told him to stop and not come any farther. Bud said, "I am going to cut your damned head off!" Tommie told him a second time not to come any closer, but Bud

63

kept coming until he was within six feet of Tommie. Tommie, reaching into the wagon behind him, picked up a new twelve-gauge shotgun. He pointed it at Bud, pulled the trigger, and blew Bud's head off even with his ears. Tommie was arrested, tried, and found not guilty, but a few years later his own son killed him.

8 Saratoga, the Railroad Town

In 1900 Captain Joseph T. Jones, a pioneer oil man and railroad builder from Buffalo, New York, sent S. S. Bullis to Mississippi to study the financial condition of the Gulf & Ship Island Railroad, which had gone bankrupt in its attempt to build a road from Gulfport to Chicago. Bullis contracted with the receiver to finish building the road, and with that contract a period of tremendous activity began. Construction work was done by the Bradford Construction Company, which Jones organized, and the road was built at the cost of $15,000 to $20,000 per mile.

The line crossed a place southwest of Merry Hell, which came to be known as Saratoga but was shortened by the Hollow people to Togcy.

The railroad was to run up to Brandon, some ten miles east of Jackson, thence north to Chicago, but that plan was changed, and the line was routed straight into Jackson. Today Saratoga is visible only as railroad tracks, an old depot, and the brushy bottomlands of Okatoma Creek. It is about two miles northwest of Mount Olive, on land that was first settled by David Smith in 1820.

When the railroad had been completed as far north as Saratoga, it paused there and began spreading out, making Saratoga an operating base. Bullis named it after Saratoga

Springs, New York, and at its peak it had a population of approximately one thousand. Bullis planned to make Saratoga a banner town, "the finest on the Gulf and Ship Island." He built machine shops, hotels, and sawmills, but his dream town failed, he said, because "the Merry Hellions stole everything that I had except the depot, and they would have got it too if they'd thought they could have gotten away with it." After several boxcars were broken into and looted, the railroad found that it could not even leave its rolling stock on the sidings in Saratoga.

Bullis was responsible for buying right-of-way lands, much of which he paid for with railroad money but registered in his own name. He bought the David Smith place from David's son Evander, but he also bought some land that was not on the planned right-of-way. When Captain Jones discovered those irregularities he fired Bullis, but then he had to buy back a lot of Saratoga land, paying Bullis $150,000 for it. Soon after that, Jones sold the railroad to Illinois Central.

Saratoga began with a large sawmill, a planer mill, an iron factor, and a powerful steam-driven water pump, which was run by the infamous Brown Lee. Lee was five feet six inches tall and of medium build with heavy muscles. He weighed 150 pounds and had a dark yellow-red complexion with heavy overhanging eyebrows and deep-seated black eyes. Almost every time he was seen he had a fresh shave, and he tried to stay clean at all times. He kept his red moustache trimmed quite short. His hands were short, his shoulders were square, and he wore number nine shoes. He had a fine voice and was always smiling. His word was his bond. He would tell the truth regardless of whom it hurt. He lived to be seventy years old, he was devoted to his family, and he was quiet. But he had an extremely bad temper, and he would fight, as some

Hollow people said, at the drop of a hat. He was known as the Tush Hog of Saratoga.

Not only did Brown Lee run the water pump, but he also served as the local bully. Anybody who offered him the slightest offense got hit with a coal scoop or monkey wrench. It was said that a Negro once offended Brown when he was in one of his mad spells and Brown picked him up, threw him into the furnace, and burned him up. He especially liked to pick on strangers. Once Billie Gardner came into Brown's pump house to warm his hands because it was cold weather. He walked up to the boiler engine, pulled the door open, and began to warm. Brown walked over beside him and closed the door, but didn't say anything. Gardner opened the door again, and Brown closed it again, still without speaking. The third time Gardner opened the door Brown Lee caught him by the seat of the pants and kicked him out of the boiler room clear across the railroad tracks, then ran out to where he had fallen, jerked him up, and beat him unmercifully.

Later some men came to the boiler room and said, "Brown, do you know who that was you beat up?" Brown replied, "I don't know, and I don't give a damn." Then they told him that Gardner was a railroad civil engineer, and Brown said, "I don't care if it was the president of the United States, nobody if going to come in my pump house and open the door to my engine and let the steam waste, because I am working for the company, and they want me to save all the money I can!" But, when Brown had gotten through with his work, he went to Gardner and apologized. After that, Brown and Gardner were "the best of friends."

There were several unmarried men living at Fannie's Boarding House. Among them was Leon Patterson, who sold whiskey and was himself a bully. One day Brown Lee decided he would go to the boardinghouse and give Patterson a whipping. Waiting until night, he got two or three of his buddies to accompany him. During the afternoon, however, Patterson had learned of Brown's intention, so he got two or three friends of his own and was waiting. When Brown Lee arrived at the boardinghouse he called Patterson out and started cursing him. But Patterson jumped on him and almost killed him before the others could stop him. Brown never bothered Patterson again. With a few exceptions, however, Brown would take advantage of anybody, and the sneak attack was his favorite strategy. But it was frequently observed that Brown never bothered the Sullivans and they never bothered him.

Bud Hicks, who lived in Saratoga, was as mean as Brown Lee. One day Bud and Brown got into a fight about Bud's wife. Bud shot both Brown Lee and his own wife, but he didn't kill either of them.

About 1898 I. W. Walker settled two miles west of Saratoga, where he opened a store that later became a post office. Another man named Broadwell moved there and built a sawmill. For some unknown reason the place was named Coat, and it became a Sullivan hangout. Hub Hicks, father of Bud, was one of the first settlers in Coat, as was Hulon Smith, who was also justice of the peace. For several years Coat was a bad place to stop unless you were able to take care of yourself, and the people there made, sold, and drank plenty of whiskey. If there wasn't a poker game in progress they would be shooting craps or playing one of their endless jokes on someone. For about five years, it was said, a Saturday night didn't pass without someone's having a fistfight in Coat, Mississippi. One such fight in 1902 at I. W. Walker's Store featured Bud and Hub Hicks, Killy Thames, and Kazzie Tullos. A prank likely started the fight, but in truth nobody knew for sure what it was. After the fight was about ten minutes old, Kazzie ran into Walker's Store, grabbed a twelve-gauge shotgun, and fired it at the bunch of them. A few of the shot hit Bud in the chest but "did not hurt him very much." Kazzie's shotgun broke up the fight, though. A fight of that kind seldom resulted in legal action because it was almost impossible to get anyone to testify at a trial.

Mrs. Wash Tullos lived in Saratoga in the old days and ran a little store. One day some Merry Hellions came asking her to sell them whiskey. She told them to go away, that she didn't sell whiskey. They said that they'd been told that they could buy whiskey there on the hill, to which she replied, "Well, there is plenty of it around here, but *I* don't keep the stuff, and don't you come back here asking for it!" That, according to her account, was the end of it.

In its boom Saratoga had a small school and a church, of which Manuel Grayson was the first preacher. Fannie Sullivan Carter said that she often heard him say, "Don't do like I do but like I *say* do." Grayson's church, the Church of Saratoga, was organized in 1915. There were other churches around Saratoga much earlier than that, but they weren't attended by the people who lived in Saratoga. The church had many members, some of whom came to it from Zion Hill, some from Sardis, and some from other churches in the Hollow. Members included Sullivans, Halls, Gentrys, and Tulloses. According to Grayson, Brown Lee didn't belong to the church, but he gave more money than any regular member, and "if it hadn't been for Brown Lee, most of the time the money would have been short." According to Grayson, when he organized his church Brown told him, "If anybody tries to start anything or causes a disturbance, you just let me know and I will take care of him, because I have the authority to do it with," whereupon Brown pulled out a .45 Smith and Wesson. There was never any serious trouble as long as the church stayed there. After a few years it moved over to the highway, three miles north of Mount Olive.

One time the railroad workers called a strike, and the construction company hired "scalawags." When the strikers ganged them one night with guns, axes, and anything they could lay their hands on, the scalawags broke and ran, but not before the strikers had killed two of them and thrown them into the Okatoma, where they stayed.

And once Brown Lee got into a fistfight with Mac Simpson. They were both drunk, and they fought for forty minutes, until Simpson whipped Brown. Brown swore that he was going to kill Simpson, but he never did. Then one time a man named Cooper whipped Bud, Brown's son. Brown ambushed Cooper and cut him across the back, and it was not long before Cooper died of the wound. Brown was never threatened by the law for that murder, because almost everyone was afraid to accuse him of any wrongdoing whatsoever.

When Bud Joe Sullivan was found dead in an old field in 1905, some people said that Brown Lee had killed him. Brown watched over his corpse all day and that night, after making a stretcher, carried Bud Joe's body to Ike Pickering's house. Ike was away attending court at Raleigh. After Brown and some other men had put the body in the house, they stood the stretcher beside the gate and left it there. When Ike came home that night he saw the stretcher standing beside the gate, and he said he saw a man rise from the foot of it and go straight up into the sky. Ike soon moved away.

Superstition has always been strong in the Hollow. Willis Sullivan and his wife had one child named Marshal, who got sick and died. One night during his sickness, Mrs. Sullivan got up to see about him. The fire had gone out, and they had no matches or any other way to start a fire. She went to the fireplace and prayed, "Lord, give me some fire," and the fire blazed up. But while she was on her knees she heard someone say, "Death, death, death." And that was the night Marshal died. Sarah Harvey said that Mrs. Sullivan didn't know what she was talking about, that a cat was lying beside the fireplace and sneezed, and that that was what Mrs. Sullivan had heard and just thought someone had said "Death."

Big Bud Sullivan, Joe's son and Pappy Tom's grandson, had his homestead about a mile north of Saratoga. His children were Fannie, Maggie, Becky, Walter, Joe, Betty, John, Rosie, Shelby, Steave, Ruthie, Ross, Bertha, Housten, and Jimmie. His daughter Fannie, who was born in 1867, met Frank Lucas at school when she was nineteen and married him. They had ten children. After Frank died, one day Taylor Sullivan took her to Saratoga to sell vegetables. The place looked good to her, so she used the money her father had given her to open her boardinghouse, which she ran during Saratoga's boom years. When Walter Carter came through that part of the country on a cattle-buying trip, he stayed at Fannie's place. She said that she "got to liking him and up and married him." They had one child. Fannie's house was built by John Ruff McInnis in 1878 for two thousand dollars.

Fannie said that it took a whole cow and a barrel of peas for dinner at her boardinghouse, that she fed her boarders well, and that she didn't mind charging them for it. She recollected that everybody didn't work for the railroad, that some of them farmed and raised cattle and made money by selling their produce to the railroad workers. Others trapped or hunted for a living. They would ship out wild-animal hides

71

and get money to buy whatever they wanted, and many of them wanted whiskey. Some people sold bootleg whiskey, which "back in those days they called moonshine, Blind Tiger, Merry Hell, and lots of other names—it didn't make much difference, just so it had a kick to it and would make them drunk so they would feel good."

Fannie sold whiskey to the men who stayed in her boardinghouse. In 1906 and 1908 grand juries indicted her on six counts of the unlawful sale of intoxicating liquors. She was arrested, and A. B. and W. A. Sullivan, who lived in Merry Hell, went her bond for $250. On the day of her trial, however, the district attorney called her name three times, but she did not come forward. Then he called A. B. and W. A. Sullivan three times, but they did not appear. Brown Lee was scheduled to be a witness, and the sheriff called him three times but he was not there either. Judge Bullard was the circuit judge presiding over the Thirteenth District, which comprised Smith, Jasper, Covington, and Simpson counties. He instructed the district attorney to take forfeiture on the two Mr. Sullivans, issue the proper papers, and give them to the sheriff. Then he ordered the sheriff to bring the two men to court to show why they did not have Fannie Lucas there. The judge remarked that he was getting tired of the way the Sullivans were ignoring his court. The charges against Fannie were eventually nol-prossed, and A. B. and W. A. never paid the bond money. No one ever said that the sheriff was afraid to collect the forfeiture, but it was observed that an officer might be awful brave and bad and in spite of all that he might tend to stay out of Saratoga and Merry Hell.

Fannie's daughter Terrie grew up in the boardinghouse during the time that Al McClendan lived there. Fannie always called him Mr. Al, and he worked for the railroad. He was a fine, tall, handsome man who always dressed well.

Mr. Al's room was next to Terrie's, with a locked door connecting the two. He developed a fondness for Terrie, and at some time he and Terrie slipped off and were secretly married. Then Terrie took the key to the connecting door out of Fannie's purse and gave it to Al, who had a copy made. Then she put the key back in her mother's purse. For years, at least three and maybe as many as five, Terrie used her key to go into Al's room. They spent the nights together, and then early in the morning she would slip back into her room, lock the door, "get up," and go downstairs to make his morning biscuits. Al wouldn't eat biscuits made by anyone except Terrie. Maybe it was that he secretly, in his pride, wanted his wife to make his biscuits, or maybe it was that Terrie's biscuits were better than Fannie's. Then word came that the railroad was transferring Al, so the next morning he and Terrie came downstairs together; he was holding a piece of paper, which he showed to Fannie, saying, "Here—you can see our marriage license. We have been married so many years, and Terrie is going with me." When Fannie heard that she went to pieces. She raged, threw a fit, and cried all day. It wasn't that she was losing a daughter and a good cook. What upset her so much was that for all those years Terrie and Mr. Al had cheated her out of the rent on that extra room.

After it had been in operation awhile, the Gulf & Ship Island ran a special excursion train from Jackson to Gulfport, and all of the people in Saratoga made the trip to see the Gulf. On the way back, over half the men were drunk and "having a big time." Then Tim Thames of Mendenhall, Bud Hicks, and Brown Lee got into a fight, and Thames cut Brown's throat from ear to ear—"like to have cut his head off," people said. Dr. E. L. Walker of Magee held the main artery until they came to the next town, where they stopped for Dr. Walker to sew Brown's neck up with a piece of common cotton thread and a sewing needle. Of course Brown lived many years after that. It is no wonder that mothers would tell their children at night that, if they didn't get quiet and go to sleep, old man Brown Lee would get them.

In 1908, the year of the coming of the boll weevil, the state legislature created the Livestock Sanitation Board. In 1916 a statewide dipping law was passed to protect cattle against the Texas fever tick, and the government dug and equipped a number of dipping vats. But many people in south Mississippi and the Hollow didn't want to dip their cattle. Their cattle were not improved breeds, and the people saw no advantage to dipping. They saw it only as a nuisance. People began dynamiting the vats. As soon as the government would get a vat built, somebody would blow it up. Then a government supervisor went to Brown Lee and told him that he had a job for him—to guard a dipping vat. Brown asked, "What do you want me to do if somebody starts to blow it up?" The supervisor told him to take his gun with him, that he knew what to do without being told. When word went out that Brown Lee was guarding the vats, the dynamiting stopped.

When Brown Lee was an old man, just before he died, he was at a gristmill talking with Warren Bishop and Joe Roberts, who was about thirty. Joe made Brown mad about something, and Brown jumped on him and would have whipped him if Warren hadn't caught and held him until he cooled off. Brown Lee was born about 1850, and he died about 1920. He was married twice. His first wife bore two children. When she died he married Susie Dilmore. They had no children. When Brown died he left her some land and some money, enough to take care of her until she died, she sold the land and spent the money. Grover Bishop said, "She is living at one place today and at another tomorrow, and she don't have anything with which to make a living."

In 1901 a branch line was built on the railroad running north from Saratoga until it turned east to Mize and then curled down southeast to Laurel. It was quite busy until the early 1930s. A one-coach passenger shuttle, affectionately called the Short Dog, ran from Laurel up to Mendenhall, where it would lay over until seven o'clock the next morning. It would wait at Saratoga until the train from Jackson passed through so that passengers from Jackson could change trains to go to Laurel, but it was said that there weren't many passengers other than Hollow people, because Saratoga had such a bad reputation that most outsiders were afraid to stop. Outsiders usually found another means of transportation.

Once Bobby Sullivan was riding on the Short Dog and got into an argument with a man named Adams. When the train arrived in Mize, Bobby got off one side of the train and Adams got off the other side. The train pulled out, and they started shooting. Bobby was killed. A bystander said to Adams, "You've killed him. How do you think Mrs. Sullivan is going to feel when she's told?" Adams replied, "I reckon she's gonna feel just a lot like Mrs. Craft did after the Sullivans killed her boy."

9 Tent Pulls

Around 1913 the Holiness church came to the Hollow. Some people called it the Holiness church, and some called it the Holy Rollers' church. A Holiness preacher set up a big tent in Mount Olive, right beside the railroad tracks, and started having an old-time meeting. Wild Bill and Neace were still alive, in their sixties, and some of the younger Sullivans wanted to maintain the old Hollow tradition of being mean and raising hell. A lot of them went to church just for the devilment they could stir up.

The tent was near the depot, and every night a passenger train came through about nine o'clock, traveling north. On the fifth night of the meeting the big tent was filled with people from all over the Hollow; the preacher was feeling good, and so was everybody else. The preacher was intoxicated with the Holy Spirit, but a lot of the others were overjoyed with whiskey. The preacher was preaching on hell, and the people were shouting and having a good time, while outside the tent some boys from the old Hollow and a bunch of Merry Hellions mingled. When they got together there was bound to be a joke played on somebody.

That night, when the train stopped at the station, the boys were ready with a long rope which they tied from the tent to the train. As the train pulled out the tent started shaking and flapping, ropes snapped, and down it came, just as the congregation was in the act of sending up a long prayer. Some of the people thought that the lifting of the tent was the work of the Lord, some thought it was a punishment, and some thought it was a reward—but, regardless of what they thought, they screamed and cried and yelled. Some of them went one way and some went another, but they all scattered.

Another time a large traveling motion picture show set up its tent down at Old Bunker Hill, right in the heart of the Hollow. Some of the Hollow boys didn't have the price of admission, at least so they claimed, but they intended to see the show anyway. They went to the manager and told him that he ought to let them in, since they were Sullivans and he was set up right in the dead middle of Sullivan's Hollow. But he apparently hadn't heard about Sullivan's Hollow, because if he had he would have said, "Come on in, boys. The treat is on me." Instead he refused their request, and the boys turned around, acting like they were going back home. They waited until night fell and the show started, then they went to the back of the tent, one standing beside each of the ropes that held it up. They took out their knives, and when one of them gave the signal they cut the tent down on the cash customers. It almost frightened the people inside to death. They screamed and came running out from under the tent in every direction. Some of them didn't stop to ask any questions but just kept running until they got home. The manager left that night and was never seen in the Hollow again.

The myth of Sullivan's Hollow is indeed based on fact. The Hollow was an early southwestern settlement, and violence and lawlessness were characteristic of the whole American frontier. But the Hollow heritage proved difficult for some later Sullivans to live up to. Melvin Sullivan was from Merry

Hell and thought that he was bad, until old man D. T. Taylor got on him. In 1923 D. T. Taylor, who had the only store in Saratoga, did a little credit business with the people who lived around there. Mel ran up a bill and wouldn't pay it, although D. T. asked him to pay, and Mel said something that the old man didn't like. So D. T. reached under the counter and brought out a shotgun. Mel began to run, but it was too late then, for old man Taylor let go and shot him in the back. The shot didn't kill him, but it taught him that D. T. Taylor was pretty mean, too.

The brothers Ob and Wilkie Sullivan were sons of Pappy Tom's oldest son, James. Their mother was Patsy Rollins. After their father died their mother went to live with Ob, taking what few things she had, including three old chairs. Wilkie decided that he wanted those chairs, so he went to Ob's house to get them. When he arrived he stated his business, and Ob told him that he was not going to get them, so they tied up for a fight. Wilkie pulled his pistol, and Ob hit him beside the head, knocking him down, but no sooner was he down than he was up again, pulling a long knife out of his pocket. Ob took the knife away from Wilkie, made a pass at him with it, and ripped his belly open, cutting his entrails out. Red Mack Sullivan was a witness, as was Wilkie's wife Polly Harvey. They picked Wilkie up and carried him home. They fetched Dr. Watkins, who lived northwest of Merry Hell, and he sewed Wilkie up. Wilkie lived to be an old man, but he never went back to Ob's house for those three chairs.

Bee was the son of Little Wylie, who was the grandson of Pappy Tom. Bee married Ida Sullivan, who was the daughter of Jeff, Pappy Tom's son. Ab (Albert) Sullivan was Ida's brother, and like Bee the older he got the meaner he got. Bee and Ab were cousins, as well as being brothers-in-law.

Ab's second wife was Ollie Sullivan, Bee's sister, making him Bee's brother-in-law two ways. Minnie King, Ab's first wife, was killed accidentally while Ab was helping her clean house. In those days almost every house had a shotgun hanging on a homemade rack, which was usually made from two forked sticks and was nailed to the wall. Ab and Minnie were moving the bedsteads and mattresses out of the living room so she could scrub the floor. Ab picked up a pair of bedsprings and as he went through the doorway into the yard the springs snagged the shotgun that hung on the wall, pulling it off the rack. The gun fell to the floor, discharged, and killed Minnie, who was standing on the other side of the room.

The young men in the Hollow at that time had a clan, membership in which required that they take an oath to do what the majority of the other members told them to do, or else they would be killed. Ab, Bee, and Bud Joe, among many others, belonged to the clan. Rumor had it that Bee and Ab stole a horse, took it out of the Hollow, and sold it. When the new owner of the horse later questioned their honesty, they took him out and beat him. Bud Joe knew about their having stolen the horse and beaten the man, and they were afraid that he would tell on them, so they decided to silence him before he had a chance to speak of it. Finding him out in an old field hunting his horse, they slipped up close to him, and Bee shot him down. Then for fear that Ab would tell it, Bee gave the gun to him and made him shoot Bud Joe too. When Bud Joe was found, his horse bridle was hanging around his shoulder. Bee and Ab were arrested on suspicion and were tried but found not guilty. (It was mentioned earlier that Brown Lee brought Bud Joe's body in from the field.)

Soon after this, Bee pretended to be crazy and left the Hollow. He was not heard from for many years, and people decided that he must be dead. Then, about twenty years later, Bee wrote to his brother-in-law John King, saying that he was living in Kansas City, Kansas. So Bernard Sullivan (Bee's nephew), Bernard's wife, and one of Bee's daughters, who had been born after he left the Hollow, went up to Kansas to see him. They found him to be a rich man, but they couldn't tell how he had made his money. He was working as a streetcar driver. Bee soon returned to Sullivan's Hollow, but he only stayed a short while before he went back to Kansas, taking his daughter with him.

After Bee and his daughter had left the Hollow, Newt, one of Bee's sons, went to Kansas City, where they were living. He shot and killed his father and brought his sister back home with him. The story that Newt told was that he had found them living together like man and wife and that he had killed Bee in a rage, when he had seen the incestuous situation. Some people said that Newt knew "good and well" that Bee was not the blood father of his sister, that he just used the story as an excuse to kill Bee and get his money. Bee's body was brought to the Hollow and buried in the old Sullivan graveyard below Shiloh Church. Not long after Newt killed his father, he was found dead in the railroad yards at Laurel. His death remained a mystery.

A few years after Ab married Ollie, he was killed by John Beavers, who lived in the Hollow. It was generally agreed that Ab was a mean man and a bully who had his bluff in on most people. He'd always picked on John Beavers and run over him, until the day John forgot himself and shot him. John Beavers was tried for the killing and found not guilty. A few years later he killed another man and was tried in Raleigh and convicted. Sentenced to life in the state penitentiary, he was a model prisoner for seven years, until he escaped. Five years later he was found living a good life in Arkansas and was taken back to prison.

Postscript

People who write about Sullivan's Hollow usually feel obligated to include a disclaimer to the effect that the Sullivans (of their day) are fine, generous, law-abiding people, as good as can be found anywhere. Apologists have compiled lists of individual Sullivans who have achieved distinction, and they have pointed to the Hollow's churches, schools, businesses, and prosperous farms. That is all very well, but easy accolades fall pitifully short of making a meaningful statement about the Hollow people. The truth is harder to get at, lying deep in the people and in the land. Anyone seeking it would do well to begin with this simple observation: without the Sullivans' love of storytelling, their sense of place, their sense of humor, and their abiding conviction of their own worth, the myths of Sullivan's Hollow would long since have been suppressed and the place would have ceased to exist as it was and still is, a community of individuals.

Appendix A
A Trip Through the Piney Woods*

They owned a large stock of cattle and the three boys (as the good mother called her sons, who were tall enough for Prussian grenadiers), were then absent with a drove. Finding ourselves welcome we stripped our horse and led him to a small stable that stood near. We found a trough filled with potatoes and the rack with hay made of the dry vines. Our horse ate them with great relish. On this farm, as on most of the others in the same locality, a few acres are cow-penned and planted for bread; an acre or two for rice; but the main crop is the sweet potato. Some nations boast of their palm tree which supplies them with food, oil, light, fuel, shelter and clothing, but it will be seen that we have in the potato a staple article scarcely inferior to it. It will grow upon soils too thin to produce corn and with little culture. It may be converted into a valuable manure. For forage it is excellent. Hogs and cows thrive upon it exceedingly. An acre properly cultivated will yield from three to five hundred bushels. Its farinacious properties make it almost equal to bread and it supplies some of the most delicious dishes for the dessert.

Supper was somewhat tardy; but in an adjoining house, lit up by a brisk fire, we heard sundry "notes of preparation".

*J. F. H. Claiborne, "A Trip Through the Piney Woods," *Publications of the Mississippi Historical Society,* IX, pp. 533-535.

It was a rare chance that brought a guest to that lone dwelling and its kind inmates were intent on making us comfortable. Lulled by the cheerful signs and savory odors we cast ourselves into an arm-chair and dozed until at length a gentle touch and a musical voice summoned us to the table. The repast was abundant, excellent and scrupulously neat—but almost every dish was composed of potatoes dressed in many various ways. There were baked potatoes and fried potatoes— bacon and potatoes boiled together—a fine loin of beef was flanked round with potatoes nicely browned and swimming in gravy. A hash of wild turkey was garnished with potatoes mixed up in it. A roast fowl was stuffed with potatoes, beside us stood a plate of potato biscuit, as light as sponge; the coffee, which was strong and well flavored, was made of potatoes, and one of the girls drew from the corner cupboard a rich potato pie. In about an hour a charming blue-eyed girl brought us a tumbler of potato beer that sparkled like champagne and rather archly intimated that there were hot potatoes in the ashes if we felt like eating one. The beer was admirable, and we were told that good whiskey, molasses and vinegar were sometimes made of potatoes.

At length we turned in. The little chamber we were shown to was the perfection of neatness. The floor was sprinkled over with white sand. A small mirror stood on the wall, from which was suspended a sort of napkin tastily worked all over. Above was a rosary of bird eggs of every color, and over the window and pinned along the white curtains of the bed were wreaths of flowers, now dry indeed, but retaining their beautiful tints and making a very pretty ornament. An old oaken chest, highly polished and waxed, set in a corner, and over that a range of shelves stored with quilts, comforts, coverlids of many colors, the work of the industrious household. The pillows were bordered with fringed network and the sheets as white as the untrod snow; but the bed itself, though soft and pleasant, was made of potatoe vines. Either from over fatigue, our late and hearty supper, or from our imagination being somewhat excited, we rested badly, the nightmare brooded over us; we dreamed that we had turned into a big potato, and that some one was digging us up. Perspiring, struggling, we clinched the bed and finally leaped up gasping for breath. It was some time before the horrid idea would quit us. In the morning, owing to the drenching of the previous day, we were an invalid and threatened with fever and sore throat. The kind old lady insisted on our remaining in bed and she immediately bound a mashed roasted potato, just from the ashes, moistened with warm vinegar, to our neck and gave profusely a hot tea made of dried potato vines. These applications acted like charm, and with the addition of a few simples from the woods were all the remedial agents ever used by this happy family. They could scarcely form a conception of a physician such as we see him here, riding day and night, keeping half a dozen horses, following the pestilence to enrich science with its spoils, attending the poor from charity, accumulating fortunes from the infirmities of the human family, but not infrequently losing life in the effort. The mistress of the house had never known a fever, old as she was, her blooming daughters looked incredulous when we described the ravages of disease in other parts of the State, and certain it is that none of them had ever before seen one the worse from having ridden six hours in wet clothes. When we took leave of our kind friends it was in vain that we offered them compensation. They welcomed us to everything and we set off with our pockets filled with biscuits, jerked venison and potato chips, a sort of crystallized preserves steeped in syrup and then dried in the sun.

Appendix B

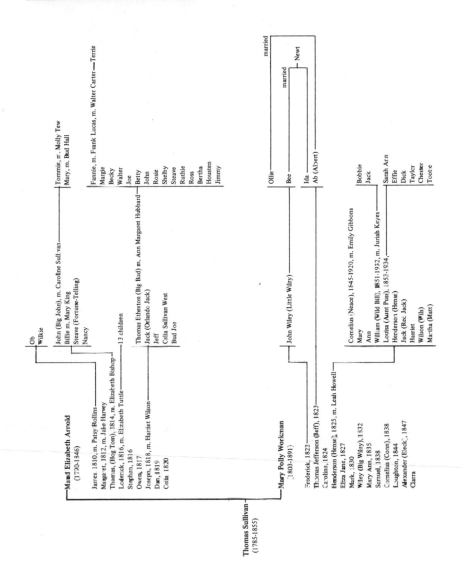

Notes

NOTES TO CHAPTER ONE

1. Until recent times, in this part of the country largemouth bass found in streams were called trout.

2. J. F. H. Claiborne, "A Trip Through the Piney Woods, " *Publications of the Mississippi Historical Society*, IX, 514.

3. Captain Basil Hall, *Travels in North America* (Edinburgh: Cadell and Co., 1829), III, 251.

4. Nollie W. Hickman, "Mississippi Forests," *A History of Mississippi* (Hattiesburg: University and College Press of Mississippi, 1973), II, 214-215.

5. William Sparks, 331.

NOTES TO CHAPTER TWO

1. Hot Coffee is famous throughout the state. Immediately following the Civil War, J. J. Davis of Shiloh opened a store on the Taylorsville-Williamsburg Road, which was a stretch of the old Jackson Military Road. He hung a coffeepot over his door and served delicious coffee made with fresh spring water and good beans from New Orleans, using molasses drippings to sweeten it. Customers could request either long or short sweetening, but Davis refused to serve cream, saying it ruined the taste. When he died in 1880, E. L. Craft from the Hollow took over the store, and for a while it went by the name of Davis' Store. Then one day a traveler found his coffee too hot, and as he strangled and sputtered he said, "Mister, this is *hot* coffee!" Craft liked the sound of it, so

he saw to it that there was a hot fire under the coffeepot, until the next drummer or traveler happened to ask him the name of the place. He was ready with his answer, "Mister, this is Hot Coffee!" Historically, Hot Coffee has been a crossroads of southern Mississippi. The exact point of intersection has not been located, but the east-west Natchez to Fort Stephens Wagon Road crossed the north-south Jackson Military Road either at or near Hot Coffee. Early accounts put Hot Coffee on the road to the following towns: Mobile, Alabama; Ellisville, Jackson, Martinville, Monticello, Taylorsville, and Williamsburg, Mississippi.

2. Mary J. Welsh, "Recollections of Pioneer Life in Mississippi," *Publications of the Mississippi Historical Society*, IV, 345-46.

3. In 1840 J. F. H. Claiborne took an extended trip through the piney woods and published a long essay entitled, "A Trip Through the Piney Woods." Part of that essay, in which Claiborne described the style of living he encountered in Covington County, is included herein as the appendix. It is both informative and amusing, especially on the subject of sweet potatoes.

NOTES TO CHAPTER THREE

1. Wayland F. Dunway, *The Scotch-Irish of Colonial Pennsylvania* (Chapel Hill: 1944), 130.

2. In the early days cattle ranged freely. Therefore, fields were fenced to keep cattle out of them, and the split rail was the type of fence used. "Old field" was a common term referring to a field that had been worn out and abandoned. "Newground" was the term applied to a field in its first year of cultivation.

NOTES TO CHAPTER FIVE

1. D. Alexander Brown, *Grierson's Raid* (Urbana: University of Illinois Press, 1945), 121, 122.

2. John K. Bettersworth, "The Home Front, 1861-1865," *A History of Mississippi* (Hattiesburg: University and College Press of Mississippi, 1973), I, 521.

3. *Ibid*, 524.

4. W. H. Sparks, *The Memories of Fifty Years* (Philadelphia: 1882), 147-48.

5. Augustus C. Buell, *History of Andrew Jackson* (New York: Scribner's Sons, 1904), 2 vols.; I, 56.

NOTES TO CHAPTER SIX

1. "It is better to dwell in a corner of the house top, than with a brawling woman in a wide house." Prov. XXI: 9.

Bibliography

BOOKS

Bettersworth, John K. "The Home Front, 1861-1865," in Richard A. McLemore, ed., *A History of Mississippi*, Vol. I. Hattiesburg: University and College Press of Mississippi, 1973.

Brown, D. Alexander. *Grierson's Raid*, Urbana: University of Illinois Press, 1954.

Buell, Augustus C. *History of Andrew Jackson*, Vol. I. New York: Scribner's Sons, 1904.

Davis, Minnie M. *True Confederates of Mississippi*, Hattiesburg: Geiger Printing Company, 1965.

Ford, Henry J. *The Scotch-Irish in America*, Princeton: Princeton University Press, 1915.

Hall, Capt. Basil. *Travels in North America*, Edinburgh: Cadell and Co., 1829, 3:251.

Hickman, Nollie W. "Mississippi Forests," in Richard A. McLemore, ed., *A History of Mississippi*, Vol. II. Hattiesburg: University and College Press of Mississippi, 1973.

Hilliard, Sam Bowers. *Hog Meat and Hoecake: Food Supply in the Old South, 1840-1860*, Carbondale: Southern Illinois University Press, 1972.

Holcomb, Gene, ed. *Mississippi: A Guide to the Magnolia State*, American Guide Series, New York: The Viking Press, 1938.

Knight, Thomas J. *Newton Knight*. Privately printed. Located in the Mississippi Department of Archives and History.

Lawson, James R., and Mrs. A. M. W. Mims. *History of Smith County*, privately printed in 1935, revised as the *Bicentennial Edition*, privately printed, 1977.

Leyburn, James G. *The Scotch-Irish: A Social History*, Chapel Hill: The University of North Carolina Press, 1962.

Montell, William L. *The Saga of Coe Ridge: A Study in Oral History*, Knoxville: The University of Tennessee Press, 1970.

Rogin, Michael Paul. *Fathers and Children: Andrew Jackson and the Subjugation of the American Indian*, New York: Random House, 1975.

Smith, William. *A Brief Review of the Conduct of Pennsylvania for the Year 1755*, cited in Wayland F. Dunaway, *The Scotch-Irish of Colonial Pennsylvania*, Chapel Hill: 1944.

Sparks, W. H. *The Memories of Fifty Years*, Philadelphia, 1882.

Wallace, David D. *The History of South Carolina*, New York: The American Historical Society, Inc., 1934.

Windsor, Jerry. *A History of Seminary, Mississippi*, privately printed, 1973.

Woodmason, Charles. *The Carolina Backcountry on the Eve of the Revolution*, ed. by Richard J. Hooker, Chapel Hill: University of North Carolina Press, 1953.

MANUSCRIPTS

Bishop, Grover. "History of Sullivan's Hollow," a manuscript totaling 98 typewritten pages, coded: 800-Sullivan's Hollow, Smith County, FC, received at the offices of the American Guide, individual reports dated: 1938, July 11, 18, Aug. 1, 8, 15, 22, 29, Sept. ?, 12, Oct. 3, 10, 17, 24, 31, Nov. 7, Dec. 3, 12. Manuscript located at Mississippi Department of Archives and History.

Connell, John T. "The Early History of the Gulf & Ship Island Railroad," a manuscript totaling 7 typewritten pages, coded: No. 414: FC. Manúscript located at Mississippi Department of Archives and History.

Fant, C. Sessions, "Sullivan's Hollow, Smith County," a manuscript totaling 7 typewritten pages, coded: 800-Sullivan's Hollow, Smith County, FEC. Undated. Manuscript located at Mississippi Department of Archives and History.

NEWSPAPERS

"Sullivan's Hollow Original Log Home Still Sullivans', " by Carl McIntire, Section G, p. 1, *Jackson Daily News*, Oct., 22, 1972.

"Sullivan Home 100 Years Old." *Daily Clarion-Ledger*, Dec. 31, 1937, p. 2.

MAGAZINES

Claiborne, J. F. H. "A Trip Through The Piney Woods," *Publication of the Mississippi Historical Society*, Vol. IX.

"The Sullivans of Sullivan's Hollow; Mississippi's Most Legendary Family," by Harry Henderson and Sam Shaw, *Collier's*, March 17, 1945.

Welsh, Mary J., "Recollections of Pioneer Life In Mississippi," *Publications of the Mississippi Historical Society*, IV, 345-46.

CALCULUS

A Short Course with Applications

CALCULUS

*A Short Course with Applications
to Business, Economics, and
the Social Sciences*

Gerald Freilich
QUEENS COLLEGE (CUNY)

Frederick P. Greenleaf
NEW YORK UNIVERSITY

W. H. FREEMAN AND COMPANY
San Francisco

Library of Congress Cataloging in Publication Data

Freilich, Gerald.
 Calculus: a short course with applications to
business, economics, and the social sciences.

 1. Calculus. I. Greenleaf, Frederick P., joint
author. II. Title.
QA303.F75   515   75–37569
ISBN 0–7167–0466–8

Printed in the United States of America

AMS 1970 subject classification: 00-01

2 3 4 5 6 7 8 9 10 KP 0 8 9 8 7 6 5 4 3 2

To Marion, Sandy, and David

To Sandra McKnight

Contents

Preface

This book gives an intuitive approach to the Calculus with emphasis on applications. It is written for the student whose mathematical background may include only a working knowledge of basic high-school algebra. With this audience in mind, we try to involve the reader constantly, and yet never overwhelm or distract him with technical details. We intentionally avoid most of the esoterica of the new math (set theory, abstract definitions, and ε-δ arguments). Instead we emphasize the fundamental ideas: functions and graphs, limits, derivatives, integrals, and functions of several variables. Examples and applied case studies are constantly presented to motivate the introduction of new ideas or show how they are used in practice.

Because of the diversity of student interests and course plans, this book is organized with flexibility of use in mind. There is a self-contained core (Chapters 1–3), followed by independent chapters which may be skipped or covered in any order desired. To meet the needs of students of diverse backgrounds, the first chapter includes a certain amount of optional review material. The core includes the following topics:

Chapter 1. Review of algebra; functions and their graphs; simple applications of the concept of function in economics, physics, and biology; equations of straight lines; solutions of inequalities.

Chapter 2. The concept of differentiation and some basic applications; tangent lines; the approximation principle; the "marginal" concept in economics; introduction to optimization problems.

Chapter 3. Standard differentiation techniques; second derivatives and their meaning; systematic study of optimization problems, with applications; curve sketching.

The remaining chapters include:

Chapter 4. Introduction to integration; an application to statistics via probability densities; integration techniques; improper integrals.

Chapter 5. Calculus of several variables (with emphasis on two variables); functions and their domains of definition; graphical presentations; level curves; partial derivatives and their meaning; optimization problems with and without boundary maxima; Lagrange multipliers; introduction to linear programming.

Chapter 6. Compound interest problems; exponentials and logarithms; growth and decay problems; elementary differential equations.

Chapter 1 includes a review of all necessary topics from high-school algebra. Students who are familiar with this material may skim, or even omit, many sections in this chapter. However, Sections 1.4–1.6 should always be covered. These are detailed case studies that introduce new terminology essential to later chapters. In Chapter 5 we have devoted special attention to a serious and realistic coverage of calculus of several variables, avoiding technical complexity while accurately conveying a feel for the subject.

The book includes more material than can be done in one semester. It seems unlikely that after the core material has been covered enough time will remain to do more than two of the later chapters. Some choice must be made, according to the aims of the course. We outline below several possible tracks for a one-semester course. The REGULAR tracks are appropriate for students requiring only moderate review of high school algebra. The ALTERNATE tracks provide more review for students with less background, or those who are returning to college after some time away from school. Parentheses indicate material to be covered lightly.

Economics, Business, and Accounting Students

REGULAR TRACK	ALTERNATE TRACK
Ch. 1: (1.1–1.3), 1.4–1.6, (1.8–1.10)	*Ch. 1*: 1.1–1.6, 1.8–1.10
Ch. 2: 2.1–2.6	*Ch. 2*: 2.1–2.6
Ch. 3: 3.1–3.5, 3.7	*Ch. 3*: 3.1–3.5, 3.7

Ch. 5: 5.1–5.2, 5.4–5.14   *Ch. 5*: 5.1–5.2, 5.4–5.7, (5.8), 5.9,
Ch. 6: 6.1, (6.2–6.3)   (5.10)
                                       Ch. 6: 6.1, (6.2–6.3)

In the tracks for business and management students we have deliberately emphasized the material on functions of several variables. Given the time limitations in a semester and the anticipated needs of these students, this seems to us the best choice. Of course, variations are possible: integration could be discussed by pruning the material in the above tracks. A more traditional program, outlined below, seems better suited for students in the biological and social sciences, or in the liberal arts.

Social Science, Biology, and Liberal Arts Students

REGULAR TRACK   ALTERNATE TRACK

Ch. 1: (1.1–1.3), 1.4–1.7, (1.8–1.10)   *Ch. 1*: 1.1 1.10
Ch. 2: 2.1–2.6   *Ch. 2*: 2.1–2.6
Ch. 3: 3.1–3.8   *Ch. 3*: 3.1–3.5, 3.7
Ch. 4: 4.1–4.7   *Ch. 4*: 4.1–4.7
Ch. 6: 6.1–6.4, (6.5)   *Ch. 6*: 6.1

It has been our experience that some students have a command of exponentials and logarithms, while others do not; in any case it is risky to presume familiarity with them. We mention exponentials and logarithms (and occasionally the trigonometric functions $\sin x$ and $\cos x$) throughout the book, but always in an inessential way. If a student has encountered these functions previously, their use in the text will enhance his feel for the material; if not, no harm will be done if he regards e^x, $\log x$, $\sin x$, and $\cos x$ as unfamiliar functions whose values are to be looked up in tables. The first half of Chapter 6 gives a self-contained explanation of the theory surrounding e^x and $\log x$.

Answers are given for almost every exercise. A solid dot (●) preceding an exercise indicates that a complete answer appears in the back of the book; a half-dot (◐) indicates that a partial answer is given. Starred (*) sections and exercises cover special topics, or require more mathematical skill than most parts of the book.

Tables for $\sqrt{x}$, e^x and e^{-x}, and $\log x$ are given at the end of the book. The method of interpolation, which can be used to extend the range of the tables, is explained with examples in Appendix 1.

We should like to express our appreciation to two of the editors at W. H. Freeman and Company: to George Fleming for many valuable discussions and continuing encouragement, and for persuading us to write the book in the first place; and to Peter Renz, who guided the book through the editorial process, read all its intermediate drafts, and helped hammer it into its present shape. Peter and George were instrumental in obtaining an extremely helpful set of reviews of the first draft; we should like to acknowledge our debt to those painstaking reviewers, particularly Frank Warner (University of Pennsylvania), Larry Goldstein (University of Maryland), Paul Knopp (University of Houston), and Richard Joss (California State University at Long Beach).

Finally, we thank the staff at W. H. Freeman and Company (particularly the editing and art departments) for their fine work.

Gerald Freilich
Frederick P. Greenleaf

August 1975

CHAPTER 1

Preliminary Concepts

1.1 The Concept of Number

As civilization and science developed so did the concept of number. This development has probably been paralleled in the life of the reader. The first numbers learned were the counting numbers: $1, 2, 3, \ldots$. Then the concept of number was enlarged to include all the integers, that is, positive and negative whole numbers and zero. After the arithmetic of the integers was learned, fractions were introduced as ratios of integers. Technically, these fractions are referred to as "rational numbers"; thus, a rational number is one that can be expressed as the ratio of two integers m/n, with the denominator n not zero. By the time elementary algebra was studied, we began to encounter problems that cannot be solved using only the rational numbers. For example, there is no rational number whose square is 2. To handle these and other situations irrational numbers, such as $\sqrt{2}$, were introduced. The set of all rational and irrational numbers together constitute the **real numbers.**

Every real number can be represented by a decimal expansion. Somewhere or other you have probably seen the first few terms of the decimal expansion of $\sqrt{2}$, given here to nine places:

$$\sqrt{2} = 1.414213562\ldots$$

In Exercise 11 we indicate how the successive entries in this expansion may be determined. For rational numbers such as

$$\frac{101}{33} = 3.06060606060\ldots$$

$$\frac{1}{4} = 0.2500000000\ldots$$

the expansion can be determined directly by long division. What do these decimals mean? The whole number to the left of the decimal point tells us the number of units to add on. The entries to the right of the decimal point tell us the number of $\frac{1}{10}$'s, $\frac{1}{100}$'s, $\frac{1}{1000}$'s, and so forth that should be combined to form the final number. Thus the decimal $3.060606\ldots$ stands for

$$3.060606\ldots = 3 + 0 \cdot \frac{1}{10} + 6 \cdot \frac{1}{100} + 0 \cdot \frac{1}{1000} + 6 \cdot \frac{1}{10,000} + \cdots$$

The operations of arithmetic—addition, multiplication, subtraction, and division—apply to the whole system of real numbers, with one important exception.

$$\textit{Division by zero is never permitted}! \tag{1}$$

The sum, product, and quotient of two real numbers can be determined by using their decimal expansions. You are probably used to such decimal calculations, so we shall not dwell on the details. When dealing with rational numbers written as fractions, you should recall the familiar laws of arithmetic:

$$\frac{a}{b} + \frac{c}{d} = \frac{ad + bc}{bd} \qquad\qquad \frac{\left(\dfrac{a}{b}\right)}{\left(\dfrac{c}{d}\right)} = \frac{a}{b} \cdot \frac{d}{c} = \frac{ad}{bc} \tag{2}$$

$$\frac{a}{b} \cdot \frac{c}{d} = \frac{ac}{bd}$$

We must often decide which is the larger of two numbers. Numbers given as fractions are not always easy to compare: is $73/63$ larger than $22/19$? Numbers written as decimals are much easier to compare. Going from left to right, we look for the first place where the expansions differ. The number with the larger entry in this position is the larger number. Compare π and its well-known rational approximation $22/7$:

$$\pi = 3.14159\ldots \quad \text{and} \quad \frac{22}{7} = 3.14285\ldots$$

These begin to differ in the third decimal place. Since 22/7 has a 2 there, while π has a 1, 22/7 is larger than π.

We use the following symbols to express the fact that a number x is larger than a number y:

$$x > y \quad \text{or} \quad y < x$$

For example, $22/7 > \pi$. Sometimes we know that x is either greater than y or equal to y, but we don't know which relation is true. In that case we use the symbols

$$x \geqslant y \quad \text{or} \quad y \leqslant x$$

Real numbers can be represented as points on a straight line. Starting with an unmarked line, choose one point and label it with the number 0 (this becomes the **origin**). Then choose a second point and label it with the number 1, as in Figure 1.1. These two points determine a "unit length" in the line and also specify a positive direction along the line, from 0 to 1 (to the right in Figure 1.1). By stepping off successive intervals of unit length to the right or left of the origin we can identify all positive or negative integers with points on the line. By dividing the unit interval, which extends from 0 to 1, into subintervals of equal length we can locate the point on the line corresponding to any rational number. For example, to locate 3/2 divide the unit interval in half and, moving to the right from the origin, step off three copies of this half interval. Arbitrary real numbers may be identified with points on the line by using decimal expansions. The position of $\sqrt{2} = 1.414\ldots$ is located as follows. The number 1 to the left of the decimal point means that $\sqrt{2}$ lies between the integers 1 and 2, $1 \leqslant \sqrt{2} \leqslant 2$. The digit 4 in the tenths' place gives the additional information that $\sqrt{2}$ lies between 1.4 and 1.5, so that $1.4 \leqslant \sqrt{2} \leqslant 1.5$. The digit 1 in the hundredths' place locates $\sqrt{2}$ with an accuracy of 0.01, namely $1.41 \leqslant \sqrt{2} \leqslant 1.42$. The point

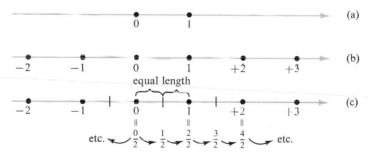

Figure 1.1
In (a) "0" indicates the origin in the number line, while "1" marks off a unit distance and determines a "positive direction" along the line, indicated by the arrowhead. In (b) the integers are marked in. In (c) we mark off fractions $\frac{1}{2}$, $\frac{3}{2}$, and so forth by dividing the unit interval in half and then stepping off copies of this half interval.

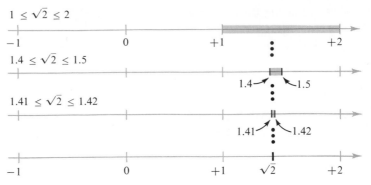

Figure 1.2
Locating $\sqrt{2} = 1.414\ldots$ within smaller and smaller intervals (shaded) in the number line. In the next step we would locate $\sqrt{2}$ with an accuracy of .001, namely $1.414 \leqslant \sqrt{2} \leqslant 1.415$.

corresponding to $\sqrt{2}$ is pinned down by taking more and more decimal entries into account. As we do this our uncertainty about its position in the number line becomes smaller and smaller, as shown in Figure 1.2. The exact location of $\sqrt{2}$ is determined by the full unending decimal $1.414\ldots$. This method applies just as well to decimal expansions of rational numbers. (Try your hand at locating $101/33 = 3.0606\ldots$ or $1/4 = 0.25000\ldots$.) Frequently, we shall only write out the first few terms of a decimal; these suffice to locate the number accurately enough for all practical purposes. Since real numbers may be identified with points on a line, the system of real numbers is often referred to as the **number line**. Real numbers will be regarded as points on a line or as decimal expansions, whichever is more convenient.

Geometrically, **inequalities** between real numbers describe the relative positions of two numbers a and b on the number line:

$$a < b \text{ means that } a \text{ lies strictly to the left of } b \tag{3}$$
$$(\text{or equivalently, } b \text{ lies strictly to the right of } a)$$

The symbol $a < b$ is read "*a is less than b*" or "*b is greater than a.*" For example,

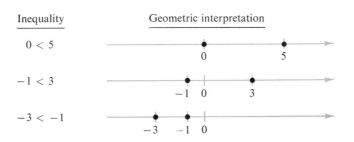

Do not be confused by the $(-)$ signs. Clearly, -3 lies to the left of -1, so that $-3 < -1$. As mentioned above, the symbol $a \leqslant b$ means that a either lies to the left of b or is equal to b. The symbol $a \leqslant b$ is read "*a is less than or equal to b.*"

The **positive** numbers are those to the right of the origin in the number line; the **negative** numbers are those to the left. In terms of inequalities

$$a \text{ is positive if } a > 0$$

$$a \text{ is negative if } a < 0 \tag{4}$$

The sign (positive or negative) of the product or quotient of two numbers is determined by the familiar **rule of signs**.

$$(+) \cdot (+) = (+) \qquad (+) \cdot (-) = (-) \qquad (-) \cdot (-) = (+)$$

$$(+)/(+) = (+) \qquad (+)/(-) = (-) \qquad (-)/(-) = (+)$$

We indicate that a number x satisfies a *pair* of inequalities, such as $a \leqslant x$ and $x < b$, by writing the inequalities together as a single symbol: $a \leqslant x < b$. This convention is handy for specifying sets in the number line, such as intervals. A **bounded interval** is defined by taking all x lying between two points $a < b$ in the number line. We get slightly different intervals depending on whether or not we include the **endpoints** a and b. Thus, bounded intervals are determined by pairs of inequalities such as $-\frac{1}{2} < x < \frac{3}{2}$, $-2 \leqslant x \leqslant 1$, and so forth. The intervals determined by these particular inequalities are shown in Figure 1.3.

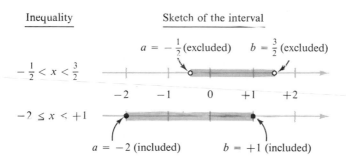

Figure 1.3
Some bounded intervals. The points in the interval are shaded. As for endpoints, an open dot indicates an excluded endpoint, while a solid dot indicates that the point is included as part of the interval.

Exercises

- 1. Express the following numbers as decimals. Plot these numbers as points on the number line.

    (*i*) $\frac{1}{3}$ (to three places)   (*iii*) $-\frac{11}{6}$ (to four places)

    (*ii*) $\frac{15}{7}$ (to eight places)   (*iv*) $\frac{15}{6}$ (to three places)

- 2. Which is the larger number, $x = 2.61414\ldots$ or $y = 2.613998\ldots$?

- 3. Which is the larger number: (*i*) $x = 17/19$ or $y = 6/7$? (*ii*) $x = 73/63$ or $y = 22/19$?

- 4. The sum of two decimals is obtained by lining up their decimal points and adding the entries in each decimal place. Using this idea, show that

    (*i*) $\sqrt{2} + \dfrac{1}{3} = 1.7475\ldots$ (*iii*) $\dfrac{2}{7} + \dfrac{\sqrt{5}}{3} = 1.0310\ldots$

    (*ii*) $\dfrac{1}{2} + \dfrac{1}{3} = 0.8333\ldots$ (*iv*) $\pi - \sqrt{2} = 1.7273\ldots$

    (Use $\pi = 3.14159\ldots, \sqrt{2} = 1.41421\ldots, \sqrt{5} = 2.23607\ldots$.)

- 5. Which of the decimals listed in Exercise 4 is the largest? The smallest? Locate each number as a point on the number line.

- 6. Using the ideas of Exercise 4, write out decimal expansions to three places for the following numbers:

    (*i*) $\dfrac{1}{7} - \dfrac{4}{3}$ (*iv*) $2\left(\sqrt{3} + \dfrac{1}{2}\right)$

    (*ii*) $\pi + \dfrac{1}{3}$ (*v*) $\pi - \sqrt{2} - \sqrt{5}$

    (*iii*) $\dfrac{4}{7} - \dfrac{\sqrt{5}}{3}$

- 7. Indicate whether true or false.

    (*i*) $1 < 3$ (*iv*) $-3 < -1$

    (*ii*) $1 \leqslant 3$ (*v*) $2 > 2$

    (*iii*) $-1 < -3$ (*vi*) $-2 \geqslant \frac{1}{2}$

- 8. Given any two real numbers a and b, exactly one of the following relations must hold:

    $$a < b, \quad a = b, \quad \text{or} \quad a > b$$

    For the following pairs, determine which relation is valid.

    (*i*) $a = 7/9, b = 8/10$ (*iv*) $a = \sqrt{2}, b = -1$

    (*ii*) $a = -14, b = -11$ (*v*) $a = \sqrt{2}, b = 2$

    (*iii*) $a = 99/100, b = 101/111$ (*vi*) $a = 4/3, b = 16/12$

- 9. Sketch the intervals in the number line determined by the following inequalities:

    (*i*) $0 < x < 1$ (*iii*) $-3 < x \leqslant -2$

(*ii*) $-1 \leqslant x < 3$ (*iv*) $-\sqrt{2} \leqslant x \leqslant \sqrt{2}$

●10. Sketch the points in the number line that satisfy the inequalities:

(*i*) $x > \frac{3}{2}$ (*iv*) $-5 \leqslant x \leqslant 2$

(*ii*) $x < \frac{3}{2}$ (*v*) $-4.50 < x < -1.75$

(*iii*) $x \geqslant \frac{3}{2}$ (*vi*) $-50 \leqslant x \leqslant 1000$

11. The square root $\sqrt{a}$ of a positive number a is the unique number x such that $x^2 = a$ and $x \geqslant 0$. We may locate $\sqrt{a}$ by trial and error. If we choose a number $x \geqslant 0$ and wish to see how close it is to $\sqrt{a}$, x is too small if $x^2 < a$ and is too large if $x^2 > a$. Using this principle we may locate $\sqrt{2}$ as follows.

(*i*) Since $1^2 = 1 < 2$ and $2^2 = 4 > 2$, $\sqrt{2}$ lies between 1 and 2.

(*ii*) Since $(1.4)^2 = 1.96 < 2$ and $(1.5)^2 = 2.25 > 2$, $\sqrt{2}$ lies between 1.4 and 1.5.

(*iii*) Since $(1.41)^2 = 1.98\ldots < 2$ and $(1.42)^2 = 2.01\ldots > 2$, $\sqrt{2}$ lies between 1.41 and 1.42.

Continuing in this way, we can locate $\sqrt{2}$ to any desired number of decimal places. The same procedure may be used to locate $\sqrt{a}$ for any positive number a. Use this method to check that the following decimal expansions are correct.

(*i*) $\sqrt{3} = 1.73\ldots$ (*iii*) $\sqrt{15} = 3.87\ldots$

(*ii*) $\sqrt{7} = 2.64\ldots$ (*iv*) $\sqrt{140} = 11.832\ldots$

1.2   Powers of a Real Number

In radiation experiments it is important to protect laboratory workers. If one inch of shielding permits only half the radiation to pass through, then two inches of shielding will pass only half the radiation that penetrates one inch of shielding, so that only $(\frac{1}{2})^2 = (\frac{1}{2}) \cdot (\frac{1}{2}) = \frac{1}{4}$ passes through two inches. Similarly, three inches will allow only $(\frac{1}{2})^3 = (\frac{1}{2}) \cdot (\frac{1}{2}) \cdot (\frac{1}{2}) = \frac{1}{8}$ through, half the amount penetrating two inches of shielding. In general, the fraction of radiation that penetrates n inches of shielding is $(\frac{1}{2})^n$. Suppose we write $(\frac{1}{2})^r$ for the fraction that penetrates r inches of shielding (r not necessarily an integer) How can we interpret this number? As an example, take $r = \frac{1}{3}$. Notice that three layers each $\frac{1}{3}$ inch thick afford the same protection as one layer one inch thick; therefore,

$$\left(\frac{1}{2}\right)^{1/3} \cdot \left(\frac{1}{2}\right)^{1/3} \cdot \left(\frac{1}{2}\right)^{1/3} = \frac{1}{2}$$

so that $(\frac{1}{2})^{1/3}$ must be the cube root of $\frac{1}{2}$, namely $0.793\ldots$. By similar reasoning we could interpret $(\frac{1}{2})^r$ for any r, and more generally, in this section we shall give meaning to the symbol a^r for any positive number a.

If n is a positive integer, the **nth power** of a real number a is obtained by multiplying a by itself n times

$$a^n = \underbrace{a \cdot \ldots \cdot a}_{n \text{ times}} \tag{5}$$

As examples, $1^5 = 1$, $2^4 = 16$, $(1/7)^2 = 1/49$. Obviously $a^1 = a$ for any a. In the expression a^n, the number a is called the **base** and n is called the **exponent**. Powers have two important algebraic properties, called **laws of exponents** .

$$a^m \cdot a^n = a^{m+n}$$

$$(a^m)^n = a^{mn} \tag{6}$$

These are easily deduced from the definition (5). For example

$$a^m \cdot a^n = \underbrace{(a \cdot \ldots \cdot a)}_{m \text{ times}} \cdot \underbrace{(a \cdot \ldots \cdot a)}_{n \text{ times}} = \underbrace{a \cdot \ldots \cdot a}_{m+n \text{ times}} = a^{m+n}$$

Similarly

$$(a^m)^n = \underbrace{(a^m) \cdot \ldots \cdot (a^m)}_{n \text{ times}} = \underbrace{(a \cdot \ldots \cdot a)}_{m \text{ times}} \cdot \underbrace{(a \cdot \ldots \cdot a)}_{m \text{ times}} \cdot \ldots \cdot \underbrace{(a \cdot \ldots \cdot a)}_{m \text{ times}}$$

Here there are n blocks, each containing m copies of a, so in all there are mn copies of a multiplied together. Thus $(a^m)^n = a^{mn}$.

If a is not zero, we define a^n for $n = 0, -1, -2, \ldots$ by taking

$$a^0 = 1$$

$$a^{-n} = \frac{1}{a^n} \quad \text{for } n = 1, 2, 3, \ldots \tag{7}$$

Thus, for example

$$5^0 = 1 \qquad 5^{-1} = \frac{1}{5} = 0.20 \qquad 5^{-2} = \frac{1}{25} = 0.04$$

and so on. If we define powers a^n in this way for all integers n, the laws of exponents given in (6) remain valid.

We can define **fractional powers** a^r for any fraction $r = p/q$ (p and q are integers, with $q \neq 0$), if we restrict our attention to positive numbers $a > 0$. Fractional powers of the form $a^{1/n}$ (n a positive integer) are interpreted as follows:

$$a^{1/n} = \text{the positive } n\text{th root of } a \tag{8}$$

This interpretation is not arbitrary; it is strongly suggested by our introductory remarks, where $r = 1/3$. Thus $a^{1/n}$ is the unique positive number whose nth power is a. For example, $a^{1/2} = \sqrt{a}$ (the square root), $a^{1/3} = \sqrt[3]{a}$ (the cube root), and so on. In particular,

$$2^{1/2} = \sqrt{2} = 1.414\ldots \qquad 8^{1/3} = \sqrt[3]{8} = 2 \qquad 25^{1/4} = \sqrt[4]{25} = \sqrt{5} = 2.236\ldots$$

Once we know how to interpret powers of the form $a^{1/n}$ we can interpret $a^{m/n}$ as follows:

$$a^{m/n} = (a^{1/n})^m = (a^m)^{1/n} \tag{9}$$

Thus there are two ways to calculate $a^{m/n}$:

> (i) Take a, form the positive nth root $a^{1/n}$, then take the mth power $(a^{1/n})^m = (a^{1/n}) \cdot \ldots \cdot (a^{1/n}) = a^{m/n}$.
>
> (ii) Take a, form the mth power a^m (also a positive number), then take the positive nth root $(a^m)^{1/n} = a^{m/n}$.

(10)

but both procedures yield the same value for $a^{m/n}$.

The exponent laws remain valid for fractional powers. As a result, it is no more difficult to manipulate fractional powers of a number than it is to manipulate integral powers a^n. Several laws of exponents that we have not yet mentioned are also valid. We give the full set of laws here.

The Laws of Exponents   Here $a, b, \ldots$ stand for positive real numbers and $r, s, \ldots$ for fractions.

$$
\begin{array}{ll}
(i)\ \ a^r \cdot a^s = a^{r+s} & (iv)\ \ a^{-r} = \dfrac{1}{a^r} \\[2mm]
(ii)\ \ (a^r)^s = a^{rs} & \\[2mm]
(iii)\ \ (ab)^r = a^r \cdot b^r & (v)\ \ \left(\dfrac{a}{b}\right)^r = \dfrac{a^r}{b^r}
\end{array}
\tag{11}
$$

Rather than prove these laws (time consuming, but not terribly difficult) we shall work out a few examples.

Example 1   Show that $4^{5/2} = 32$.

Solution   Although the procedures (10*i*) and (10*ii*) for evaluating $a^{m/n}$ always lead to the same answer, in this case it is easier to take the square root first, and then the 5th power. Compare the calculations:

$$4^{5/2} = (4^{1/2})^5 = 2^5 = 2 \cdot 2 \cdot 2 \cdot 2 \cdot 2 = 32$$

$$4^{5/2} = (4^5)^{1/2} = (1024)^{1/2} = \sqrt{1024} = 32$$

If we take the power first, we get the large number 1024, whose square root is not easy to recognize.

Example 2   Later, in Section 1.7, we shall examine population growth. The size of a certain population t years after the first census is given by the formula

$$N = 30{,}000{,}000 \cdot 2^{t/30}$$

In order to evaluate N we must calculate fractional powers of 2.

Initially, when $t = 0$, $N = 30{,}000{,}000 \cdot (2^0)$

After $t = 10$ years, $N = 30{,}000{,}000 \cdot (2^{1/3})$

After $t = 15$ years, $N = 30{,}000{,}000 \cdot (2^{1/2})$

After $t = 45$ years, $N = 30{,}000{,}000 \cdot (2^{3/2})$

Calculate the value of N after 15 years, after 45 years, and after 60 years.

Solution   Here $2^{1/2} = \sqrt{2} = 1.414$, so when $t = 15$ we get

$$N = 30{,}000{,}000 \cdot (1.414) = 42.42 \text{ million}$$

Similarly, $2^{3/2} = (2^{1/2})^3 = \sqrt{2} \cdot \sqrt{2} \cdot \sqrt{2} = 2\sqrt{2} = 2.828$, so that when $t = 45$

$$N = 30{,}000{,}000 \cdot (2.828) = 84.84 \text{ million}$$

Finally, $2^{60/30} = 2^2 = 4$, so that $N = 30{,}000{,}000(4) = 120$ million when $t = 60$.

Example 3   Evaluate $(\frac{1}{7})^{3/2}$ and $(\frac{1}{7})^{-3/2}$. Use the square-root tables (Appendix 2), where necessary.

Solution   We are free to use any of the laws of exponents (11). First apply (v), to get

$$\left(\frac{1}{7}\right)^{3/2} = \frac{1^{3/2}}{7^{3/2}}$$

From the definition (9) we get $1^{3/2} = (1^{1/2})^3 = 1^3 = 1$ and $7^{3/2} = (7^{1/2})^3 = (\sqrt{7})^3 = \sqrt{7} \cdot \sqrt{7} \cdot \sqrt{7} = 7\sqrt{7}$. Thus

$$\left(\frac{1}{7}\right)^{3/2} = \frac{1}{7^{3/2}} = \frac{1}{7\sqrt{7}} = 0.05399\ldots$$

There is no need to wrestle with similar calculations to determine $(\frac{1}{7})^{-3/2}$; just use $(11iv)$:

$$\left(\frac{1}{7}\right)^{-3/2} = \frac{1}{\left(\frac{1}{7}\right)^{3/2}} = \frac{1}{\left(\frac{1}{7\sqrt{7}}\right)} = 7\sqrt{7} = 18.5202\ldots$$

In practical calculations we often encounter very large or very small numbers, such as

$$x = 2{,}875{,}000{,}000 \quad \text{or} \quad y = 0.0000000437$$

These are not convenient to write down or calculate with; it is very easy to make a mistake in keeping track of the decimal place. For example, try calculating $x \cdot y$. Keeping track of the decimal place is made much easier by **scientific notation**. Most numbers can be written as a number of modest size times a suitable power of 10. Thus, after counting decimal places we may write x and y as

$$x = 2.875 \times 10^9 \quad \text{or} \quad 28.75 \times 10^8 \quad \text{or} \quad 0.2875 \times 10^{10}$$

$$y = 4.37 \times 10^{-8} \quad \text{or} \quad 43.7 \times 10^{-9} \quad \text{or} \quad 0.437 \times 10^{-7}$$

Now we can handle the powers of 10 separately in computations, which is a great convenience. For example

$$x \cdot y = (2.875 \times 10^9) \cdot (4.37 \times 10^{-8})$$

$$= (2.875 \times 4.37) \cdot (10^9 \times 10^{-8})$$

$$= 12.564 \times 10^1 = 125.64$$

Similarly

$$\frac{x}{y} = \frac{2.875 \times 10^9}{4.37 \times 10^{-8}} = \frac{2.875}{4.37} \times 10^9 \times 10^8 = 0.6579 \times 10^{17} = 6579 \times 10^{13}$$

(a number ending in 13 zeros).

Example 4   Calculate the value of the expression $P = -5{,}000{,}000 + 61q - 0.000122\, q^2$ when $q = 200{,}000$.

Solution   Rewrite all unwieldy numbers in scientific notation:

$$-5{,}000{,}000 = -5 \times 10^6 \qquad -0.000122 = -1.22 \times 10^{-4}$$

Now $q = 200{,}000 = 2 \times 10^5$, so that

$$q^2 = (2 \times 10^5) \cdot (2 \times 10^5) = 4 \times 10^5 \times 10^5 = 4 \times 10^{10}$$

Consequently

$$-0.000122 q^2 = (-1.22) \times 10^{-4} \times 4 \times 10^{10} = (-4.88) \times 10^6$$

$$61q = 61 \times (2 \times 10^5) = 122 \times 10^5 = 12.2 \times 10^6$$

$$-5{,}000{,}000 = -5 \times 10^6$$

Since each term involves the same power of 10, namely 10^6, it is easy to add them to get our answer.

$$P = (-5 \times 10^6) + (12.2 \times 10^6) + (-4.88 \times 10^6)$$

$$= (-5.0 + 12.2 - 4.88) \times 10^6$$

$$= +2.32 \times 10^6 = 2{,}320{,}000$$

NOTE: When a *sum* is formed, as in the last example, you must write all terms so they involve the same power of 10 before you add them. Only in products or quotients may different powers of 10 be combined, using the law $10^r \cdot 10^s = 10^{r+s}$.

Exercises

◖ 1. Make a list of the powers $a^4, a^1, a^0, a^{-1}, a^{-2}, a^{-3}$, and a^{-4} for each of the following numbers. Write each power as a decimal.

  (i) $a = 10$ (v) $a = -1$

  (ii) $a = 2$ (vi) $a = -2$

  (iii) $a = \frac{1}{3}$ (vii) $a = 0$

  (iv) $a = 1$ (viii) $a = \sqrt[3]{2} = 1.2599\ldots$

  NOTE: For $a = 0$ some of the powers are undefined. Which ones?

● 2. Find the value of

  (i) 8^0 (v) 8^{-2}

  (ii) $8^{1/3}$ (vi) $(8^2)^{1/3}$

  (iii) $8^{-1/3}$ (vii) $8^{-5/3}$

  (iv) $8^{4/3}$ (viii) $(\frac{1}{8})^{-1/3}$

  What is the relationship between $(8^2)^{1/3}$ and $(8^{1/3})^2$?

● 3. Evaluate the following fractional powers:

  (i) 4^0 (vi) 5^{-2}

  (ii) $1^{4/34}$ (vii) $32^{4/5}$

  (iii) $0^{4/35}$ (viii) $16^{-2.50}$

  (iv) 1^{-100} (ix) $(\frac{8}{27})^{5/3}$

  (v) 3^{-1} (x) $(0.01)^{3/2}$

  HINT: Write the exponent $2.50 = 5/2$. Write $0.01 = 1/100$.

● 4. Given the value $2^{1/3} = 1.2599\ldots$, what is the population N in Example 2 when $t = 10$ years? 20 years? 30 years? 40 years?

● 5. Evaluate the following fractional powers as decimals.

  (i) $8^{-5/6}$ (v) $4^{-1.25}$

  (ii) $27^{5/6}$ (vi) $1000^{3/2}$

  (iii) $125^{1/2}$ (vii) $(\frac{1}{500})^{1/2}$

  (iv) $125^{-1/2}$ (viii) $(\frac{2}{5})^{-3/2}$

  Use the square-root tables, Appendix 2, to look up any unfamiliar square roots you need.

● 6. The fraction of radiation transmitted by r inches of a certain type of shielding is $(\frac{1}{2})^r$. Write this number as a decimal, taking

  (i) $r = 1.00$ inch   (iii) $r = 1.50$ inches

  (ii) $r = 5.00$ inches   (iv) $r = 7.50$ inches

  Which of these thicknesses will stop all but 1% of the radiation? All but 0.1%? HINT: Write r as a fraction where necessary.

● 7. Use the exponent laws to evaluate the following expressions:

  (i) $(8 \cdot 27)^{1/3}$ (iii) $(256)^{-5/8}$

  (ii) $(8 \cdot 27)^{4/3} \cdot 6^{-3}$ (iv) $\left(\frac{4}{9}\right)^{5/2}$

(v) $2^{1/4}$

(vii) $\dfrac{9^{1/2}}{64^{1/3}}$

(vi) $\dfrac{1}{64^{-1/3}}$

(viii) $(0.0081)^{1/2} = \left(\dfrac{81}{10{,}000}\right)^{1/2}$

HINT: In (v), $2^{1/4} = (2^{1/2})^{1/2}$. Use the square-root tables.

8. Which number is larger?

    (i) 2^3 or 3^2

    (ii) 20^0 or 0^{20}

    (iii) 3^6 or 5^4

    (iv) $(\tfrac{1}{2})^9$ or $9^{1/2}$

    (v) $(0.20)^3$ or $(0.08)^2$

● 9. If a, b, and c are positive numbers, simplify the following expressions:

    (i) $\dfrac{a^{10}}{a^5}$

    (ii) $a^{-3} \cdot a^7$

    (iii) $\dfrac{(a^2 \cdot b^3 \cdot c)^4}{(a^3 \cdot b^{-1} \cdot c^2)^3}$

    (iv) $(a^3)^2$

    (v) $(a^2 \cdot b^{-3} \cdot c^{-1}) \cdot (a^4 \cdot b^3 \cdot c^7)$

    (vi) $\left(\dfrac{a^{1/3} b^{5/6}}{a^{4/3} b^{-1/6}}\right)^4$

10. Multiply out the following expressions:

    (i) $(a + b)^2$

    (ii) $(a + b)^3$

    (iii) $(a + b)^4$

    (iv) $(a + b)(a - b)$

    (v) $(a - b)^2$

●11. Write the following numbers in the form shown, where (. . .) indicates a suitable power of 10. For example, $0.00011 = 11 \times 10^{-5}$ and $1100 = 1.1 \times 10^3$.

    (i) $0.000098 = 98 \times (\dots)$

    (ii) $980{,}000 = 0.98 \times (\dots)$

    (iii) $10 = 1 \times (\dots)$

    (iv) $4421 = 4.421 \times (\dots)$

    (v) $9{,}842{,}000{,}000 = 9.842 \times (\dots)$

    (vi) $\dfrac{1}{100{,}000} = 1 \times (\dots)$

    (vii) $\dfrac{43}{10{,}000} = 4.3 \times (\dots)$

●12. Writing $x = 98{,}000{,}000$ as 9.8×10^7, calculate x^2 and express the answer in the form $(9.8)^2 \times (\dots) = 96.04 \times (\dots)$.

●13. Evaluate the following expressions involving powers of ten.

    (i) $\dfrac{3.172 \times 10^{13}}{6.231 \times 10^{23}}$

    (ii) $(15.1 \times 10^4) \cdot (0.23 \times 10^{-7})$

    (iii) $\dfrac{(3.1 \times 10^{13})^2}{4.9 \times 10^{23}}$

    (iv) $\sqrt{144 \times 10^6}$

●14. Evaluate the polynomial $P(x) = -800{,}000 + 500x - 0.02x^2$ for the following values of x:

    (i) $x = 1000$ (ii) $x = 5000$ (iii) $x = 12{,}000$

1.3 Functions and Their Graphs

In economics, business administration, biology, chemistry, and physics, one is frequently concerned with the dependence of a quantity upon other quantities. For example, a manufacturer might want to know how profit varies with the production level. In a typical biological problem one might study the dependence of the size of a bacterial population upon time, temperature, or the concentration of certain nutrients.

Mathematicians have abstracted from these problems the concept of function. The quantities to be measured and compared are called **variables**. To keep things simple we shall compare just two variables. A **function** is a rule or formula that gives the value of one variable if the value of the other variable is specified. For example, temperatures measured on the Celsius (centigrade) and Fahrenheit scales are connected by a simple formula

$$F = \frac{9}{5}C + 32 \tag{12}$$

If a newspaper reports that the temperature in Paris was 20° Celsius, it means that the Fahrenheit temperature was $(9/5)(20) + 32 = 36 + 32 = 68°F$ a pleasant day, rather than one on which you should worry about your antifreeze. Here the variables are F and C; the function is the rule (12) that gives the value of F when C is specified.

In a simple manufacturing problem the variables are the profit P (which might be measured in dollars per month) and the production level q (the number of units produced per month). A factory manager can set production at various levels. Once the production level has been set, the profit is determined. If the manager changes the number of units produced per month, then of course the monthly profits change too. The variables P and q play rather different roles here. The production level q may be set as the manager wishes, within reasonable limits. This is (unfortunately) not true of the profit variable. Asymmetry in the roles of the variables is typical of most functions. Usually, one variable may be varied freely, while the other is determined by the function. The "free" variable is called the **independent variable**, and the other the **dependent variable**. In (12) the independent variable is C, and F depends upon it. In a manufacturing problem the production level q is the independent variable, and the profit P is the dependent variable.

Example 5 Apples are priced at 49¢ per pound. Describe the relationship between cost and quantity bought.

Solution The natural independent variable x is the number of pounds bought. Then the dependent variable is the price paid, which we denote by y (measured in cents).

The function relating y to x is concisely expressed by the formula

$$y = 49x \qquad \text{for } x \geqslant 0$$

Notice that this relationship has meaning only for $x \geqslant 0$.

Often the set of values that the independent variable can take on is restricted. For example, in the manufacturing problem negative levels of production would not have meaning. The set of "allowable" or "feasible" values for the independent variable is called the **domain of definition** of the function. In Example 5 the domain of definition consists of all numbers $x \geqslant 0$.

Example 6   Upon what independent variable does the U.S. postage for a first-class letter depend? Specify the function involved.

Solution   The answer is supplied by the United States Postal Service. If you ask a postal clerk for the amount of postage required for a letter, he weighs it and then tells you the amount. The weight w (in ounces) is the independent variable. The dependent variable is the cost c (in cents) of the first-class postage. The independent variable w must be positive. Furthermore, suppose we concern ourselves with small letters only, say up to a maximum weight of 4 ounces. Then (in the year 1975) the function relating c to w is given by the rule

$$c = \begin{cases} 10 & \text{if } 0 < w \leqslant 1 \\ 20 & \text{if } 1 < w \leqslant 2 \\ 30 & \text{if } 2 < w \leqslant 3 \\ 40 & \text{if } 3 < w \leqslant 4 \end{cases}$$

which covers all possible choices of w for which $0 < w \leqslant 4$.

In Example 5 the function was expressed as an algebraic formula, while in Example 6 the rule for calculating the value of c was more complicated.

It is useful to have some standard notation for functions. We shall often let x stand for the independent and y for the dependent variable. If f is some function that relates x and y, the symbol

$$f(x) \qquad \text{(which is read "}f \text{ of } x\text{")}$$

stands for the value of the dependent variable when the independent variable is equal to x. This notation saves us a lot of verbiage. Thus if $y = 4$ when $x = -3$, we can indicate this by writing $4 = f(-3)$. If we are told that $1 = f(2)$, then y has the value 1 when x is set equal to 2. For example, if f is given by the algebraic rule $y = f(x) = x^2 - x + 1$, we have

$$7 = f(-2) \qquad 3 = f(-1) \qquad 1 = f(0) \qquad \tfrac{3}{4} = f(\tfrac{1}{2}) \qquad 1 = f(1) \qquad 3 = f(2)$$

as we can see by setting $x = -2, \ldots, x = +2$ in the formula and computing the corresponding values of y,

$$f(-2) = (-2)^2 - (-2) + 1 = 4 + 2 + 1 = 7$$

and so forth.

Although mathematicians often let x stand for the independent variable and y for the dependent variable, we shall occasionally use other more suggestive symbols for these variables, as in Example 6. After all, the names we give to the variables do not really matter. What matters is the way one variable depends on another. Thus the formulas

$$y = f(x) = x^2 - 1 \quad \text{and} \quad s = f(t) = t^2 - 1$$

describe the same function. In each case, the dependent variable is obtained by squaring the value of the independent variable and subtracting 1 from this square.

It may be an overstatement to say that "a picture is worth a thousand words," yet a picture of a function is very useful. This picture is called the **graph** of the function. In a plane, let us draw horizontal and vertical coordinate axes so that these perpendicular axes meet at the point corresponding to zero on each line (see Figure 1.4). The point where they meet is called the **origin**. In this **coordinate plane** we may label each point by a pair of numbers (a,b) called the **coordinates** of the point. These coordinates tell us how to find the point: the first number a tells us to move a units horizontally, starting from the origin. The second number b tells us then to move b units parallel to the vertical axis. If either a or b is negative, we must move parallel to the appropriate axis, but in the *negative* direction. For example, the origin O has coordinates $(0, 0)$. To locate the point Q with coordinates $(1, -2)$ as shown in Figure 1.4, we move 1 unit to the right along the horizontal axis, and then -2 units (2 units *down*) parallel to the vertical axis.

The **graph** of a function f is the set of points (x,y) in the plane such that $y = f(x)$. As an example, let us draw the graph of the function $y = 49x$ (for $x \geqslant 0$) discussed in Example 5. We do this by plotting enough points on the graph to suggest its shape, then drawing a smooth curve through these points. In Figure 1.5 we have listed several allowable values of x and have computed the corresponding values of $y = 49x$. Each entry in the table gives the coordinates $(x,y) = (x,49x)$ of a point on the graph. For example, $y = 98$ if $x = 2$, so $(2, 98)$ is on the graph. These graph

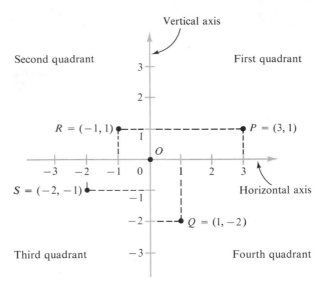

Figure 1.4
The point P in the coordinate plane has coordinates $(3, 1)$ since
we reach it by moving $+3$ units parallel to the horizontal axis
and $+1$ units parallel to the vertical axis. The origin O has
coordinates $(0, 0)$. Coordinates of other points Q, R, S are
indicated. The coordinate axes divide the plane into four pieces
called *quadrants*, which are labeled as shown.

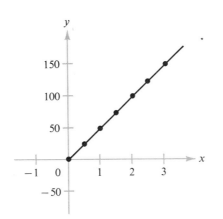

x	$y = 49x$
0	0
$\dfrac{1}{2}$	$\dfrac{49}{2} = 24.5$
1	49
$\dfrac{3}{2}$	$\dfrac{147}{2} = 73.5$
2	98
$\dfrac{5}{2}$	$\dfrac{245}{2} = 122.5$
3	147

Figure 1.5
The function $y = 49x$ of Example 5 is defined for $x \geqslant 0$. For selected values
of x the values of $y = 49x$ are tabulated at the right. The line indicates the
location of *all* points on the graph. For convenience we use different scales
of length on the two coordinate axes. The unit length on the vertical axis is
much smaller than the unit length on the horizontal axis. This strategy
allows us to sketch the graph in a reasonable amount of space.

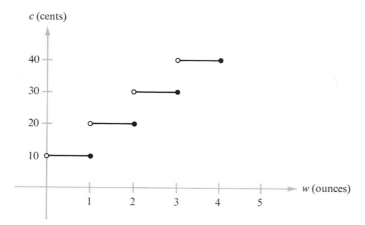

Figure 1.6
The graph of the postage function $c = c(w)$ in Example 6 is a "step
function." An open dot indicates that the point is *not* included in the
graph; solid dots *are* on the graph. Note the sudden breaks in the graph
at $w = 1$, $w = 2$, and $w = 3$. Compare this with the smoothness of the
graph in Figure 1.5. There is no algebraic formula for the postage
function, though there is a perfectly well-defined, logical rule for
calculating $c(w)$ when $0 < w \leqslant 4$.

points are indicated by solid dots in the figure. The complete graph is part of a straight
line emanating from the origin. Since the function is defined only for $x \geqslant 0$, there
are no graph points lying above negative values of x on the horizontal axis.

In sketching graphs we always associate the independent variable with the
horizontal axis (first coordinate) and the dependent variable with the vertical axis
(second coordinate), as in Figure 1.5.

Example 7   Draw the graph of the postage function in Example 6, relating $c = $ cost
to $w = $ weight.

Solution   Here the variables are labeled w and c instead of x and y. If w lies in the
range $0 < w \leqslant 1$ the related value of c is 10. Thus, as w moves from 0 to 1 along the
horizontal axis, the corresponding points (w,c) on the graph all have the same height
$c = 10$ above the horizontal axis; they lie on a horizontal line segment that is 10
units above the horizontal axis. If $1 < w \leqslant 2$ then $c = 20$, so the corresponding
points on the graph lie on a horizontal line segment 20 units above the w-axis. A
similar analysis of the remaining allowable values of w, $2 < w \leqslant 4$, shows that the
graph consists of four horizontal segments, as shown in Figure 1.6.

Example 8   Sketch the graph of the function $y = f(x) = x^2$.

Solution   First plot the graph points for a few values of x. The solid dots in Figure 1.7 correspond to the tabulated values of x and $y = x^2$. A few additional remarks will help us make an accurate sketch.

The square $y = x^2$ of any number x is positive, whether x is positive or negative. Thus the points on the graph all lie in the upper half of the coordinate plane. Also, $y = f(x)$ assumes the same value at $+x$ and $-x$, so that the points on the graph above $+x$ and $-x$ have the same height above the x-axis, namely $y = x^2 = (-x)^2$. This means that the graph is symmetric with respect to the y-axis, as shown in Figure 1.7. Finally, as x moves right along the x-axis taking on large positive values (or to the left, taking on large negative values), the dependent variable $y = x^2$ assumes large positive values. With these general observations in mind we can sketch the curve shown in Figure 1.7.

General observations about the behavior of $f(x)$ as x moves far to the left or right can be very useful in making an accurate sketch from a small number of plotted points. In the next example we shall use a simple fact about reciprocals:

$$\frac{1}{(\text{small positive})} = (\text{large positive})$$

$$\frac{1}{(\text{large positive})} = (\text{small positive})$$

(13)

For example 200,000 is quite a large number, while $1/200,000 = 0.000005$ is very small. For negative values the outcome, determined by the rule of signs $(+)/(-) = (-)$, is similar.

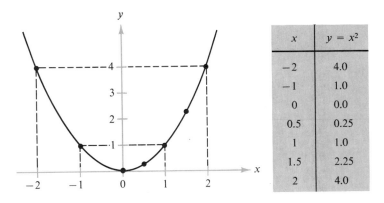

x	$y = x^2$
-2	4.0
-1	1.0
0	0.0
0.5	0.25
1	1.0
1.5	2.25
2	4.0

Figure 1.7
Graph of $y = x^2$. Points on the graph above $+x$ and $-x$ have the same height above the x-axis, namely $y = x^2$. This is shown for $x = \pm 1$ (which correspond to $y = 1$) and $x = \pm 2$ (which correspond to $y = 4$). Thus the graph is symmetric about the vertical axis.

Example 9   Sketch the graph of the function $y = 1/x$.

Solution   The function is not defined at $x = 0$; there is no point on the graph above $x = 0$. Generally, a graph has some sort of singular behavior wherever an algebraic formula for the function has denominator zero. It is a good idea to plot several points near such values of x (here $x = 0$). The general principle (13) can also be helpful. In Figure 1.8 we have tabulated some values of $y = 1/x$, taking several values of x near the troublesome point $x = 0$. We can save ourselves the trouble of calculating $f(x)$ for negative values of x by noticing that $f(-x) = (-1) \cdot f(x)$; the value at $-x$ is the negative of the value at x. Let us see what happens for small positive or small negative values of x.

$$x \text{ small positive}; \; y = \frac{1}{x} \quad \text{large positive (graph point high above } x\text{-axis)}$$

$$x \text{ small negative}; \; y = \frac{1}{x} \quad \text{large negative (graph point far below } x\text{-axis)}$$

This behavior is shown in the final sketch, Figure 1.8. What happens as x moves far to the right? The corresponding graph point approaches the x-axis, but is slightly

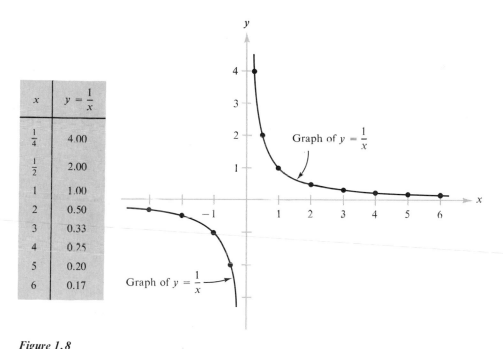

x	$y = \dfrac{1}{x}$
$\frac{1}{4}$	4.00
$\frac{1}{2}$	2.00
1	1.00
2	0.50
3	0.33
4	0.25
5	0.20
6	0.17

Figure 1.8
The graph of $y = 1/x$, defined for $x \neq 0$, consists of two separate curves. Values of $y = 1/x$ are tabulated for selected positive x; the value at $-x$ is (-1) times the values at $+x$, so there is no need to make a separate table for negative x.

above it because $y = 1/(\text{large positive}) = (\text{small positive})$. Likewise, as x moves far to the left, the graph approaches the x-axis from below, because $y = 1/(\text{large negative}) = (\text{small negative})$.

Exercises

- 1. For the function $y = f(x) = 3x - 2$, find the values $f(0)$, $f(-1)$, $f(1)$, and $f(8)$. For what value of x is $f(x) = 4$?

- 2. Find the values $f(-2)$, $f(0)$, $f(\frac{1}{2})$, $f(1)$, $f(5)$ for the functions determined by the following algebraic formulas:

  (i) $y = 4 - 13x$ (iii) $y = 4000 + 200x - 2.5x^3$

  (ii) $y = 5 - x + 2x^2$ (iv) $y = \sqrt{100 - 4x^2}$

  HINT: In (iv) use the square-root tables, Appendix 2.

- 3. Temperatures measured in degrees Fahrenheit are converted to temperatures on the Celsius scale by the formula

$$C = \frac{5}{9}(F - 32)$$

  obtained by solving equation (12) for C as a function of F. Convert the following commonly encountered Fahrenheit temperatures to their Celsius values.

  (i) $-5°$ (v) $90°$

  (ii) $0°$ (vi) $98.6°$ (body temperature)

  (iii) $32°$ (freezing)   (vii) $212°$ (boiling)

  (iv) $70°$ (room temperature)

- 4. The weight w (in pounds) of men with a certain body type varies with their height h (in feet) according to the formula

$$w = 0.9h^3$$

  (Can you think of a reason for the third power?) Two men with this build have heights 5'8" and 6'0". What are their weights? What is the ratio of their weights? The ratio of their heights?

- 5. A rectangular box has a square base, with each side of the base s inches long. If the height of the box is three times this base length, give a formula for the volume V of the box as a function of s. ANSWER: $V = 3s^3$.

- 6. Suppose the box in Exercise 5 is reinforced by applying fiberglass tape along each edge. How many edges are there? Give a formula for the length l of tape required as a function of s. ANSWER: 8 short edges, 4 long; $l = 20s$.

- 7. If the tape used in Exercise 6 costs \$2.80 per 100 feet, find the cost C of reinforcing 8000 such boxes as a function of s. NOTE: Be careful about converting from inches to feet! ANSWER: $C = (1120/3)s = (373.33)s$ dollars.

● 8. A large manufacturer of television sets has found that his yearly profit P depends on the number of sets q produced per year according to the formula

$$P = -5,000,000 + 61q - 0.000098q^2 \text{ dollars per year}$$

Calculate the profit if (i) $q = 0$, (ii) $q = 500,000$, (iii) $q = 125,000$, and (iv) $q = 311,000$ sets per year.

● 9. The area A of a circle depends on the radius r according to the formula $A = A(r) = \pi r^2$. Suppose A is the independent variable; find the corresponding radius $r = r(A)$ of a circle with given area A. Obtain $r(A)$ by solving $A = \pi r^2$ for r as a function of A. For what range of values of A does this formula make sense geometrically?

●10. Use graph paper to plot the following points in the coordinate plane.

(i) $(0, 0)$ (vi) $(3, -2)$

(ii) $(1, 0)$ (vii) $(-2, 3)$

(iii) $(0, 1)$ (viii) $(\frac{3}{2}, \frac{2}{3})$

(iv) $(-3, 0)$ (ix) $(2, 1 + \sqrt{2}) = (2, 2.414)$

(v) $(-1, -2)$

●11. A ball is dropped from the roof of a tall building. Let s (in feet) be the distance fallen t seconds after release. The following measurements were made:

t	0	0.25	0.5	1.0	1.5	1.75	2.0	2.25	2.5
s	0	1	4	16	36	49	64	81	100

Plot these points in the coordinate plane and sketch a reasonable approximation to the graph of $s - s(t)$. From the graph, estimate the value of s when $t = 1.25$ seconds. For which value of t is $s = 70$ feet?

●12. Sketch the graph of the function $y = f(x) = 1 - 3x$.

●13. Sketch the graph of the function $y = x^3$ by plotting points and drawing a smooth curve. Plot several points for x near zero to insure an accurate sketch.

●14. Sketch the graphs of the following functions:

(i) $y = f(x) = 3$ (a constant function)

(ii) $y = f(x) = x$

(iii) $y = f(x) = -2x + 3$

(iv) $y = f(x) = x^2 + 1$

(v) $y = f(x) = 2 - x - x^2$

(vi) $y = f(x) = \dfrac{2}{1 + x^2}$

(vii) $y = f(x) = 200x^2 - 400x + 500$

●15. By referring to the graph of $y = f(x) = x^2$ in Example 8, decide which values of x (if any) satisfy

(i) $f(x) = 4$ (ii) $f(x) = -1$

(*iii*) $f(x) \leqslant 4$ (*iv*) $f(x) > 1$

Sketch the solution sets for (*iii*) and (*iv*) as shaded regions on the number line. ANSWERS:
(*i*) $x = -2$ and $x = +2$; (*ii*) none; (*iii*) the interval $-2 \leqslant x \leqslant +2$; (*iv*) the two half lines
$x < -1$ and $x > +1$, taken together.

●16. Find the solution sets of the following inequalities by referring to the graph of $y = 1/x$ given
in Figure 1.8. Make diagrams showing each set as a shaded region on the number line.

(*i*) $\dfrac{1}{x} > 2$ (*ii*) $\dfrac{1}{x} < 1$

●17. In Figure 1.9 we show a graph of the U.S. Price Index for the years 1910–1974, plotted from
Government statistics. Here t = year number, and the index $I = I(t)$ tells you how many
dollars in the year t would buy the same amount of goods $1.00 could buy in the base year
1950. In effect, a 1950 dollar is worth $I(t)$ dollars in the year t. Obviously $I = \$1.00$ when $t =$

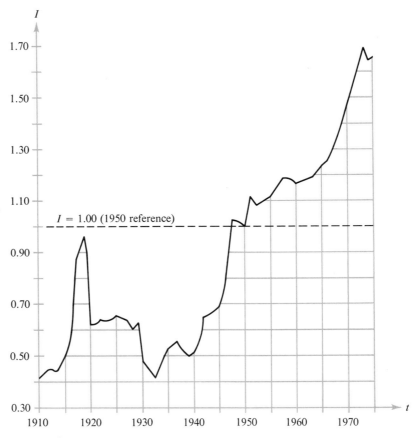

Figure 1.9
Graph of U.S. Wholesale Price Index (taking $I = 1.00$ in base year 1950). Source:
Bureau of Labor Statistics.

1950, which corresponds to the point (1950, 1.00) on the graph. Answer the following questions by inspecting this graph.

(*i*) What was the value of the price index in 1965? In 1930?

(*ii*) In which year(s) was the price index equal to 1.50? What does $I = 1.50$ tell about the value of the dollar in such years?

(*iii*) In which year(s) was the value of the dollar $\frac{3}{4}$ that of a 1950 dollar (that is, $I = 1 \div \frac{3}{4} = 1.33$)?

(*iv*) In which year(s) was the value of a dollar *twice* that of a 1950 dollar (that is, $I = \frac{1}{2} = 0.50$)?

(*v*) If a salary was $20,000 in 1974, what was its equivalent in the year 1938? In the year 1950?

●18. Calculate the values of the functions

    (*i*) $y = 2^x$ (*ii*) $y = 5 \cdot (2^x)$

for $x = -3, -2, -1.5, -1.0, -0.5, 0.0, +0.5, +1.0, +1.5, 2.0, 3.0$. Plot these values on graph paper and make a sketch of the graphs. Choose a vertical scale so that the graphs fit conveniently on the paper. HINT: Write exponents as fractions where necessary. Use $\sqrt{2} = 1.414$.

●19. Sketch the graph of the *square-root function* $y = \sqrt{x}$ using the square-root tables, Appendix 2, to plot points. Sketch at least the part of the graph for which $0 \leqslant x \leqslant 10$. Plot several points such that $0 \leqslant x \leqslant 1$, which is the hardest part of the graph to plot correctly. NOTE: $y = \sqrt{x}$ is defined only for $x \geqslant 0$, so the graph lies over the positive part of the x-axis.

20. Sketch the graph of $y = 1/x^2$. This function is not defined at $x = 0$. As in Example 9, special care should be taken for small positive and negative values of x. What happens as x gets small? Large positive? Large negative?

1.4   Motion of a Falling Body

We shall examine one of the earliest and most elementary problems in physics, the motion of a falling body. How does the position of a freely falling object vary with time under the influence of gravity?

We shall assume that the object is dense enough that air resistance is not an important factor.* The independent variable t is the time elapsed (in seconds), measured with a stopwatch, from the moment the object is released. The dependent variable is the position of the object, which can be described by measuring the distance s (in feet) that the object has fallen, as in Figure 1.10. Detailed physical experiments ever since the time of Galileo show that gravitational attraction at the Earth's surface causes *any* dense object to fall a distance $16t^2$ feet after an elapsed time of t seconds. This "free fall" does not depend in any way on the mass of the object: a cannon ball and

---

* On the airless surface of the moon *all* falling objects obey the same law, whether dense or not. This was demonstrated recently by an astronaut who dropped a feather and a hammer simultaneously. In the absence of air resistance, both struck the ground at the same time.

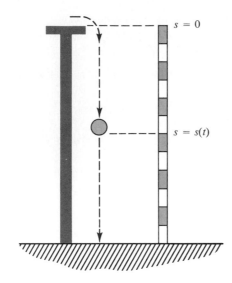

$s = 0$

$s = s(t)$

Figure 1.10
Position of a falling object, released from
rest, is described by the distance fallen
$s = s(t)$, measured in feet. The independent
variable is the elapsed time t, measured in
seconds. The distance s might be measured
with a reference yardstick, as shown.
Physical experiment and theory tell us that
the object's position is given by the formula
$s(t) = 16t^2$ from $t = 0$ until the object hits
the ground.

a ball bearing fall the same distance in a given amount of time. The relation between
s and t is given by the formula

$$s = s(t) = 16t^2 \qquad \text{for all } t \geq 0 \tag{14}$$

This function concisely represents the behavior of a falling object. It is a "mathematical
model" of the physical situation. With it we can predict the answers to many questions
without resorting to experimental work.

Example 10 Suppose we want to find the depth of an old-fashioned well by dropping
a stone and noting how long it takes to strike water. Determine the depth by using
equation (14), if the stone takes 2.5 seconds to hit bottom.

Solution If the stone falls for t seconds, it travels a distance of $s = 16t^2$ feet. Thus
the depth of the well is $16(2.5)^2 = 100$ feet.

So far we have described the motion of an object dropped from rest. What if we
give it a certain initial velocity at the moment of release? Think of throwing a baseball
into the air and watching it fall. For simplicity we shall only consider initial velocities
directed straight up (think of an overhead throw). Here it is natural to take the height
h (in feet) of the object above ground as the dependent variable; the elapsed time
t (in seconds) is still the independent variable. Note the difference between the variables s and h. Since s was the distance fallen, positive values of s correspond to downward distance; for the variable h, positive values correspond to upward distance. At
ground level, $h = 0$. Since we may not be at the ground level initially, we denote the

initial height of the object by h_0. Thus $h = h_0$ when $t = 0$. We denote the *initial velocity* of the object by v_0 (feet per second). In Figure 1.11 we have roughly indicated the path of the object. It starts moving up, but finally is pulled to the ground by gravity.

If there were no gravity, the initial velocity would cause the height to increase by v_0 feet every second, or by $v_0 t$ feet after t seconds. But during the same t seconds gravity does have an effect; it pulls the object down according to formula (14). The change in height due to gravity alone is therefore $-16t^2$ feet—a *negative* number, since gravity causes the height to *decrease*. Combining the independent effects of the initial velocity and gravity, we get an algebraic formula for the height after t seconds

$$h = h(t) = h_0 + v_0 t - 16t^2 \qquad \text{for } t \geqslant 0 \qquad\qquad (15)$$

Notice that $h = h_0$ when $t = 0$.

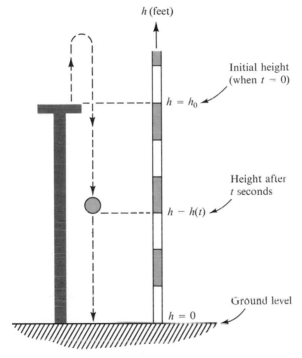

Figure 1.11
Position of a falling object as a function of time t may be described in terms of $h = h(t) =$ height above the ground (in feet). This might be measured with a measuring stick, as shown. Here $h_0 =$ initial height and v_0 is the initial velocity. Until the object hits the ground, it obeys the physical law $h(t) = h_0 + v_0 t - 16t^2$ for $t \geqslant 0$.

Example 11 From the top of a building 100 feet high, a boy throws a baseball directly up with a speed of 60 feet/second. (*i*) Express the height $h(t)$ as a function of elapsed time t. (*ii*) Determine when the ball hits the ground. (*iii*) How high does the baseball go?

Solution The initial height is $h_0 = 100$ and the initial velocity $v_0 = 60$ feet per second. Substituting these values into (15), we get

$$h(t) = 100 + 60t - 16t^2$$

Since h measures height above the ground, the ball strikes the ground when $h(t) = 0$. This leads to the quadratic equation

$$0 = h(t) = 100 + 60t - 16t^2$$

Factoring,* we get

$$0 = 4(25 + 15t - 4t^2) = 4 \cdot (5 + 4t) \cdot (5 - t)$$

The only way a product of numbers can equal zero is for one of the factors to be zero. Thus we must have either $5 + 4t = 0$ (and $t = -5/4$) or $5 - t = 0$ (and $t = 5$). We reject the negative value $t = -5/4$ because t must be positive in our problem; we conclude that the ball hits the ground 5 seconds after it was thrown.

To find how high the ball went, we might plot the graph of $h(t) = 100 + 60t - 16t^2$ (see Figure 1.12). By carefully measuring the coordinates of the highest point on the graph, we find that the maximum height is $h = 156.25$ feet, achieved when $t = 1.875$ seconds. (There are also algebraic methods for finding the maximum height, which we shall not discuss here.)

Exercises

●1. A stone is dropped into a well. Two seconds later it strikes bottom.

  (*i*) How deep is the well?

  (*ii*) How long after release was the stone halfway down?

●2. Repeat Exercise 1 if the stone hits bottom after 1.25 seconds.

●3. If a well is 36 feet deep, how long will a stone dropped into it take to reach bottom? How long will it take to fall the initial 20 feet? the final 20 feet?

---

* We shall review methods of factoring polynomials in Section 1.9.

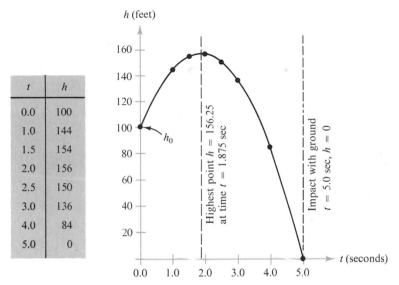

t	h
0.0	100
1.0	144
1.5	154
2.0	156
2.5	150
3.0	136
4.0	84
5.0	0

Figure 1.12

The height of a baseball thrown upward with velocity $v_0 = 60$ feet per second from an initial height of $h_0 = 100$ feet is given by the formula $h(t) = 100 + 60t - 16t^2$. Values of $h(t)$ for various t are tabulated at the left and plotted as solid dots on the graph. The ball strikes the ground ($h = 0$) at time $t = 5.0$ seconds. The highest point on the graph $h = 156.25$ is achieved when $t = 1.875$; thus $h = 156.25$ feet is the maximum height above ground reached by the ball.

●4. Suppose that a ball is thrown from the ground straight up into the air with initial velocity 100 feet per second. What is the formula expressing height $h(t)$ as a function of time t? How long will it take for the ball to fall back to the ground? Sketch the graph of $h(t)$, letting t range from $t = 0$ to $t = t_0$ (the impact time found above). In making your sketch plot (at least) the points corresponding to $t = 0, 1, 2, 2.75, 3, 3.25, 3.50, 4, 5, 6$. Using the graph, estimate the maximum height reached by the ball during its flight. NOTE: After reading Chapter 3, we shall be able to determine the maximum height by other means, without drawing the graph.

●5. A baseball is thrown straight up from the ground with an initial speed of 48 feet per second.

    (i) How high will it be 1 second later? two seconds later?

    (ii) When will the ball strike the ground?

    (iii) Draw a graph of the ball's height as a function of time and estimate the maximum height of the baseball.

●6. Suppose you throw a baseball straight up and catch it on its way down 4 seconds later.

    (i) How fast did you throw the ball?

    (ii) Draw a graph of the height of the ball as a function of time $h = h(t)$, and estimate the maximum height from the graph.

HINT: Substitute $h_0 = 0$ in equation (15) and use the fact that $h(4) = 0$ to solve for v_0.

1.5   Cost Functions

Two important functions in business administration and economics are the **cost function** and **demand function**. Suppose a firm produces a single product, such as refrigerators (the nature of the product does not really matter). If you are managing this firm you face many decisions. Clearly one of the major decisions is to set the rate of production. How can you do this? One way is to guess—if you guess correctly often enough you will be praised for your business acumen. If not, you may have plenty of time to ponder what went wrong. In that case you might realize that instead of, or perhaps in addition to, guessing you should have attempted to analyze the problem.

This suggests that you study the relationship between the rate of production and the **profit** P, which is just the difference between what comes in and what goes out. We call the last two variables the **revenue** R and the **cost** (or **operating cost**) C; thus

$$P = R - C \qquad (16)$$

Each of the variables P, R, and C depends upon the level of production, which is the independent variable. An analysis of P and R will be given in the next section. Here we shall consider the operating cost C.

In economic theory we fix a "short-run period of time": a week, a month, or some other convenient period. The **level of production**, indicated by q, is the number of units produced during this period. The plant can be run at different levels of production. At one extreme it can be left idle ($q = 0$ units); at the other extreme it can be run at full capacity. **Operating costs** are indicated by C, as above. Certain costs are independent of production level, and must be paid even if there is *no* production at all. These are the **fixed costs**, indicated by the symbol FC. They include such items as rent, interest paid to investors, amortization of the firm's equipment, and your salary during the short-run period. Other costs result from actual production, such as labor costs, costs of raw materials, and so on. These **variable costs** are indicated by VC. Clearly $C = FC + VC$.

Within certain limits the variable q is under direct control of an economic strategist. Once the level of production q is set, the operating costs C are determined by the price of raw materials and labor. Thus q is a natural independent variable and the cost C may be expressed as a function of q, giving us the **cost function** $C(q)$. In actual operations determination of the cost function would require detailed analysis of operating procedures, labor costs, costs of raw materials, and so on. Sometimes the total cost is given by a simple formula

$$C(q) = A + B \cdot q \qquad (A \text{ and } B \text{ fixed constants}) \qquad (17)$$

Here the constant A represents the fixed costs, the value of $C(q)$ when $q = 0$; the term $B \cdot q$ represents the variable costs. Formula (17) applies when the labor, raw material, and other variable costs are the same for each unit produced (namely B dollars per unit), so that the variable costs are proportional to q

$$VC = B \cdot q$$

Example 12 A retail gasoline station sells a single grade of fuel. The monthly costs of labor (salary of three regular employees) are $2520, and the monthly cost of insurance, property taxes, upkeep, and interest on invested capital amount to $1800. Suppose that you have a contract with a large supplier to provide gasoline at $0.30 per gallon, regardless of sales volume. Describe the total monthly costs of this operation.

Solution We assume that it takes three employees to man the station, whether the sales volume is high or low. We may therefore consider labor as part of the fixed cost in this problem. Labor and other regular monthly costs add up to the (monthly) fixed costs $FC = 2520 + 1800 = 4320$. We take q to be the number of gallons sold per month. Since the cost per gallon is just $B = \$0.30$, the variable cost is $VC(q) - 0.30q$ for any level of sales $q \geqslant 0$. Therefore the total cost is

$$C(q) = FC + VC = 4320 + 0.30q \qquad \text{for } q \geqslant 0$$

The graph of this function is shown in Figure 1.13. For example, if $q = 15{,}000$ gallons per month, the total cost would be $C(15{,}000) = 4320 + 0.3(15{,}000) = 4320 + 4500 = 8820$ dollars per month.

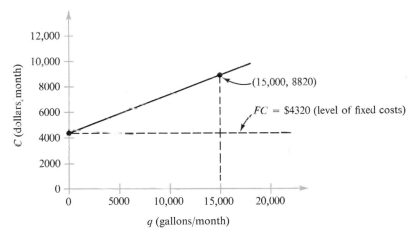

Figure 1.13
Total monthly costs for the gasoline station in Example 12. If $q = 0$ then $C(0) = FC + 0 = \$4320$ is just the fixed cost. The cost if $q = 15{,}000$ is indicated by the solid dot. The graph of $C(q) = 4320 + 0.30q$ is a straight line. The dashed horizontal line indicates the level of fixed costs $FC = \$4320$.

In the next example, the effects of a wholesale discount lead to a more complicated cost function.

Example 13   Suppose that the wholesale supplier in Example 12 offers a discount on the wholesale cost per gallon, according to the formula

$$(\text{wholesale cost per gallon}) = 0.30 - 0.000005q$$

if you order q gallons for the month.* What is the cost function in this case? Compare the cost without discount and the cost with discount if $q = 15{,}000$ gallons per month.

Solution   At sales level q gallons per month, the cost per gallon is $0.30 - 0.000005q$. Multiplying this by the number of gallons q we get the variable cost

$$VC = (\text{cost per gallon}) \cdot (\text{number of gallons}) = (0.30 - 0.000005q) \cdot q$$
$$= 0.30q - 0.000005q^2 \tag{18}$$

The fixed costs are \$4320, so the total costs per month are

$$C(q) = VC + FC = 4320 + 0.3q - 0.000005q^2 \tag{19}$$

This cost function is graphed in Figure 1.14 (solid curve). The dashed curve represents the cost function without the discount. If $q = 15{,}000$ the cost without the discount is \$8820 per month, as in Example 12. The cost with discount is obtained by substituting $q = 15{,}000$ into equation (19).

$$C(15{,}000) = 4320 + 0.3(15{,}000) - 0.000005(15{,}000)^2$$
$$= 7695 \text{ dollars}$$

In complex large-scale operations the variable costs are not proportional to q as in (17). As q increases from $q = 0$, the operation at first tends to become more efficient. Manpower is employed more effectively, and by investing capital in research more efficient products may be devised and labor-saving devices introduced. Such effects, referred to as **economies of size**, reduce the cost per unit. After q increases beyond a certain level we encounter **diseconomies of size**, which cause the cost per additional unit to rise. These effects might occur if some scarce raw materials are used, or if substantial overtime wages are paid. Figure 1.15 shows the graph of a typical cost function for a large range of q.

---

* At low volume you pay about \$0.30 per gallon. If you order 10,000 gallons you are charged only $0.30 - 0.000005q = 0.30{-}0.05 = \$0.25$ per gallon, making a total charge of $0.25 \times (10{,}000) = \$2500$ for the month.

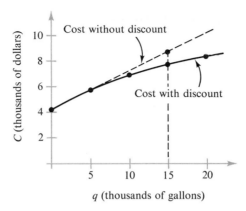

q	$C(q)$
0	4,320
5,000	5,695
10,000	6,820
15,000	7,695
20,000	8,320

Figure 1.14
Cost function for retail gasoline sales, including a discount on volume (an economy of size). The cost with discount is $C(q) = 4320 + 0.30q - 0.000005q^2$. Solid dots correspond to values in the table at left. The dashed line is the cost function without the discount (recall Example 12).

NOTE: Actually, in many situations the variable q can only take on integer values since the firm produces a whole number of units. To simplify the mathematics we adopt the fiction that q takes on all nonnegative real values. We "smooth" the data by plotting the points that correspond to integral values of q, then drawing a smooth curve through these points.

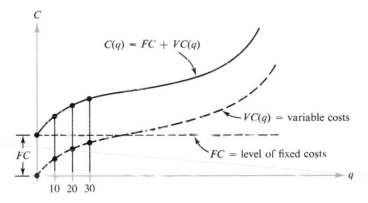

Figure 1.15
A realistic cost function. The dashed horizontal line represents the fixed costs; obviously $C(q) = FC$ when $q = 0$. The solid curve represents the total cost of producing q units; it is the graph of $C(q) = FC + VC$. As q begins to increase from zero, the costs $C(q)$ rise less and less steeply (the graph begins to flatten out) because economies of size predominate. For very large q costs once again begin to rise steeply, as diseconomies of size become overwhelming.

1.6   Demand and Profit Functions

The **demand function** and **profit function** are also important tools in economic analysis. To discuss them we must consider another economic variable, the **selling price** (or simply **price**) p. We could set p (dollars per unit) anywhere between 0 and $+\infty$, but an arbitrary choice will not guarantee optimum profit, or even any profit at all. To make a sensible choice we must test the market conditions to see how demand for the product varies with asking price.

   If a manufacturer produces a certain number of units per year and if the price per unit is set too low, the demand will be very great, leaving many unsatisfied customers willing to buy at this (low) price. He should raise the price in this case. On the other hand, if the price is too high, there will be too few customers and he should obviously lower his price to avoid accumulating unsold stock. Once the production level q is set, there is an equilibrium selling price $p(q)$ at which exactly q units will be sold, leaving no unsatisfied demand. We call the function $p(q)$ the **demand function*** since the price $p(q)$ directly reflects the market demand for the product.

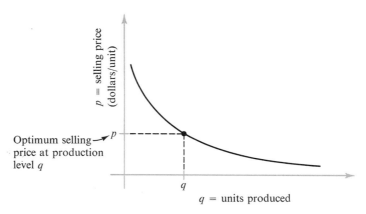

Figure 1.16
A typical demand function. The price is very large if the supply is small. Intuitively, the asking price $p(q)$ at which we will sell q units must decrease steadily as production increases. After all, is there any case in which increased supply leads to increased prices, all other factors being held constant? At high values of q the price must be kept very low to remain competitive and to sell this many units in a glutted market.

---

   * An alternative definition of the demand function occurs in economics texts, where the asking price p is taken as the independent variable. Then $q = q(p) = quantity\ sold\ at\ asking\ price\ p$ reflects the market demand for the product, and is regarded as the demand function. Actually, $q(p)$ is the "inverse" of our demand function $p(q)$. It is obtained by taking our function $p = p(q)$ and solving for q as a function of p (see Exercise 7 for an example). Given either one of these functions, the other can be determined. In the final analysis, either one can be taken as the demand function.

The equilibrium price $p(q)$ could be estimated by making market surveys or by extrapolating existing sales figures. This price is independent of the particular manufacturing methods used to produce the item. It reflects only the performance of the finished item on the sales market. In contrast, the cost function $C(q)$ gives the manufacturer's costs of producing q items, without reference to whether or not he can sell this many items, or sell them at an acceptable profit. Thus $p(q)$ and $C(q)$ measure independent but equally important relationships between a manufacturing business and the market in which it operates. With both functions in hand we can calculate many things of interest, such as the total revenue and total profit at various levels of production. We get the total revenue $R(q)$ at production level q by multiplying the number of units q times the selling price per unit $p(q)$. This gives us the **revenue function**

$$R(q) = q \cdot p(q) = \text{(number of units)} \cdot \text{(price per unit at production level } q) \quad (20)$$

Thus, by (16), the profit can be expressed as a function of q

$$P(q) = R(q) - C(q) = q \cdot p(q) - C(q) \qquad \text{for } q \geqslant 0 \tag{21}$$

once $C(q)$ and $p(q)$ have been determined. This is the **profit function**.

Example 14 A manufacturer of television sets can set his production anywhere between 0 and 1,000,000 units per year. Detailed analysis of plant operations leads to the following estimate of costs:

$$C(q) = 5,000,000 + 89.00q + 0.000012q^2 \qquad \text{for } 0 \leqslant q \leqslant 1,000,000$$

Fixed costs equal $5,000,000 yearly; the other terms (involving q) give the variable costs. At low production levels the cost per set is about $89.00, so that $VC = 89.00q$ (approximately). The extra term involving q^2 reflects diseconomies of size, which become substantial only for large q.

Market analyses yield an estimate for the equilibrium price (demand function) at various levels of production

$$p(q) = 150 - 0.000086q \qquad \text{for } 0 \leqslant q \leqslant 1,000,000$$

Determine the profit function and sketch its graph. Calculate the costs, revenue, and profit if $q = 500,000$ units per year. By examining the graph of the profit function $P(q)$, estimate the value of q yielding the highest profit, and the amount in dollars of this maximized profit.

Solution   Revenue is given by $R(q) = q \cdot p(q) = q \cdot (150 - 0.000086q) = 150q - 0.000086q^2$. The profit function is given by

$$P(q) = R(q) - C(q) = -5{,}000{,}000 + 61q - 0.000098q^2 \qquad (22)$$

for $0 \leqslant q \leqslant 1{,}000{,}000$. In particular, if $q = 500{,}000$ we get

$$C(500{,}000) = 5{,}000{,}000 + 89(500{,}000) + 0.000012(500{,}000)^2$$
$$= 52{,}500{,}000 \text{ dollars per year}$$

$$R(500{,}000) = 150(500{,}000) - 0.000086(500{,}000)^2$$
$$= 53{,}500{,}000 \text{ dollars per year}$$

$$P(500{,}000) = R - C = 1{,}000{,}000 \text{ dollars per year}$$

The graph of the profit function $P(q)$ is shown in Figure 1.17.

Note that $P(q)$ is negative (manufacturer operates at a loss) for some production levels. A visual estimate indicates that maximum profit is achieved at $q = 311{,}000$. Profits actually decline for higher values of q due to diseconomies of size. The maximum profit is $P = P(311{,}000) = 4.49$ million dollars per year. In the next chapters we shall see how to locate the point where profit is maximized without even drawing the graph of the profit function.

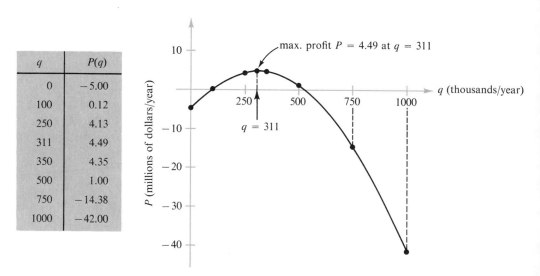

q	$P(q)$
0	-5.00
100	0.12
250	4.13
311	4.49
350	4.35
500	1.00
750	-14.38
1000	-42.00

Figure 1.17
Graph of the profit function $P = P(q)$ in Example 14. By a visual estimate of the coordinates of the highest point on the graph, we see that maximum profit occurs when $q = 311$ thousand per year. Then $P = \$4.49$ million per year.

Exercises

• 1. A manufacturer has fixed costs $FC = \$1500$ per week and variable costs $VC = 35q$ proportional to the level of production q. The demand function is given by $p(q) = 48 - 0.01q$. Determine

   (*i*) the cost function

   (*ii*) the revenue function

   (*iii*) the profit function

   as functions of q. Calculate the revenue and profit for $q = 100, 300, 800$, and 1000.

• 2. A manufacturer has fixed costs $FC = \$1000$ per month, and variable costs of $100 for each unit produced. If $q = $ number of units produced per month, find a formula for the monthly costs $C(q)$. Suppose that demand for his product is described by

$$p(q) = 300 - 2q \qquad \text{for } 0 \leqslant q \leqslant 40$$

Find the revenue function $R(q)$ and profit function $P(q)$. Sketch the graph of the profit function and estimate the maximum profit for $0 \leqslant q \leqslant 40$. What level of production yields maximum profit?

• 3. The cost function for a retail gasoline station selling q gallons of fuel per month is $C(q) = 4320 + 0.30q$, and the demand function is

$$p(q) = 0.80 - 0.00001q \text{ dollars per gallon for } 0 \leqslant q \leqslant 35{,}000$$

Determine the revenue function. Find the profit function and make a sketch of its graph. Estimate the value of q yielding the maximum profit. What is the maximum profit?

• 4. Repeat Exercise 3 using the following demand function and cost function:

$$p(q) = 0.80 - 0.00001q$$

$$C(q) = 4320 + 0.30q - 0.000005q^2$$

for $0 \leqslant q \leqslant 30{,}000$.

• 5. A group of studio apartments that rent for $200 per month yields a profit (over and above expenses) of $65 per month from each occupied apartment. However, each unoccupied apartment causes a net loss of $35 per month. There are 60 apartments in the complex.

   (*i*) Express the monthly profit P as a function of x, the number of occupied apartments. What is the feasible range of x in this problem?

   (*ii*) Express the monthly revenue R as a function of x.

   (*iii*) Find the break-even value of x, at which P becomes positive.

   (*iv*) Find the cost function $C(x)$ using the relation $P = R - C$.

   Sketch the graph of the profit function, showing the limited feasible range of the variable x.

• 6. In Example 14 the demand was described by giving the selling price p as a function of $q =$ number of units to be sold per year:

$$p(q) = 150 - 0.000086q \qquad \text{for } 0 \leqslant q \leqslant 1{,}000{,}000$$

Sketch the graph of this demand function. Choose scales of units on the q-axis (horizontal) and p-axis (vertical) so that your sketch fits nicely on a single piece of graph paper.

● 7. In Exercise 6, what is the range of values of p as q varies from 0 to 1,000,000? Take the demand function $p = p(q)$ and solve for q as a function of p, $q = q(p)$. For what range of prices is the latter formula valid?

● 8. Suppose that the selling price p (in dollars per unit) is taken as the independent variable in describing demand. Then the demand $q = $ *number of units sold per month at price p* is a function of the variable p. Suppose this demand function is given by

$$q = q(p) = 1500 + \frac{20,000}{p}$$

for prices in the range $1.00 \leqslant p \leqslant 10.00$. Answer the following questions:

(*i*) What is the demand (units per month) if we set $p = 1.00$, $p = 2.50$, $p = 5.00$, and $p = 10.00$?

(*ii*) If you wish to sell exactly 8000 units per month, what selling price p should you choose?

(*iii*) If your manufacturing plant has a maximum capacity of 15,000 units per month, what selling price should you choose in order to sell the entire output of the plant if it operates at full capacity?

● 9. Sketch the graph of the demand function $q = q(p)$ in Exercise 8. (This function is defined only for the feasible range of values $1 \leqslant p \leqslant 10$, so the graph lies over this interval in the p-axis.)

●10. In Example 14, suppose that the estimated cost and demand functions for the year are

$$C(q) = 5,000,000 + 89.00q + 0.000012q^2$$

$$p(q) = 150 - 0.00011q \qquad \text{for } 0 \leqslant q \leqslant 600,000 \text{ sets per year}$$

Show that the profit function $P = R - C$ is given by

$$P(q) = -5,000,000 + 61q - 0.000122q^2$$

Make a table of values $P(q)$ for $q = 0, 100, 200, 250, 300, 500,$ and 600 thousand sets per year. Plot the corresponding points on graph paper and sketch the graph of $P(q)$. Using the graph, estimate the value of q that yields the maximum possible profit. What is the corresponding value of P?

●11. A small-scale mercury smelter has fixed costs $FC = \$500$ per week and variable costs (mostly fuel, labor, and cost of raw ore) $VC = 2.7q$ proportional to the number q of pounds produced per week. Write out the cost function $C(q)$ for this smelter. Write out a formula for the *average cost per pound* produced

$$A(q) = \frac{C(q)}{q} = \frac{\text{(total cost)}}{\text{(total number of pounds produced)}}$$

Evaluate the total cost C and average cost per pound A for $q = 10, 50, 100, 200, 500,$ and 1000 pounds per week. Sketch the graph of $A(q)$. What happens to the average cost $A(q)$ as q gets very small? As q gets very large? If mercury sells for $3.70 per pound, at what production level does the smelter begin to break even?

*●12. Here is a more realistic wholesale discount arrangement than the one discussed in Example 13. Suppose a retail gasoline station operates under the following conditions:

(i) *Low volume* $(0 \leqslant q \leqslant 20{,}000)$ Three employees needed; fixed costs (including wages) are $4320. Price paid to supplier is $0.20 per gallon.

(ii) *High volume* $(q > 20{,}000)$ An additional employee must be hired to handle the work; monthly salary $1220. However, supplier offers a discount: all purchases beyond 20,000 gallons per month are made at $0.19 per gallon.

Describe the cost function for low- and high-volume operation. Sketch an accurate graph of the cost function $C(q)$. What happens to the graph when $q = 20{,}000$? Calculate the values of $C(q)$ when $q = 15{,}000$, $20{,}000$, and $25{,}000$ gallons per month. HINT: $C(q)$ will be given by *different* formulas on the intervals $0 \leqslant q \leqslant 20{,}000$ and $q > 20{,}000$.

*●13. Suppose that the gasoline station in Exercise 12 sells all of its fuel at $0.50 per gallon, regardless of sales volume. What is the formula for the revenue function $R(q)$? On graph paper plot the graphs of the cost function $C(q)$ (from Exercise 12) and the revenue function $R(q)$. Use this sketch to locate the *break-even point*, the sales volume at which $R(q)$ first exceeds $C(q)$.

1.7 Population Growth

In one more application of the function concept let us examine a growth problem from biology. However, the same mathematical methods apply to various kinds of growth phenomena, whether they arise in biology, economics, or elsewhere. Exponential functions make their appearance in all such problems.

Example 15 Country X has a population of 30,000,000, which is increasing at such a high rate that it will double in 30 years. Assuming that this rate of increase remains the same for the next 150 years, find a function that describes the population P as a function of time t for the next 150 years. What is the population when $t = 150$?

Solution The independent variable t is elapsed time (in years), with $t = 0$ the beginning time. The population $P = P(t)$ is the dependent variable. The fact that the population is presently 30,000,000 translates into the statement $P(0) = 30{,}000{,}000$. The fact that the population doubles in 30 years means that $P(30) = 2 \cdot (30{,}000{,}000) = 60{,}000{,}000$. If the rate of growth remains constant, doubling the population every thirty years, we must have $P(60) = 2 \cdot P(30) = 120{,}000{,}000$, $P(90) = 2 \cdot P(60) = 240{,}000{,}000$, and so on. In fact, the population will have doubled in thirty years starting from any time t, so that

$$P(t + 30) = 2 \cdot P(t)$$

In this way we obtain the values for P shown in Table 1.1.

t(years)	0	30	60	90	120	150
P(millions)	30	60	120	240	480	960

Table 1.1
Size of a population, initially 30 million, that doubles every 30 years.

How may we fit a function to these values? When we develop the calculus we shall be able to demonstrate an important fact about all growth phenomena: if the rate of growth remains constant, then the population $P(t)$ can always be expressed as an *exponential* function of t

$$P(t) = A \cdot 2^{kt} \qquad \text{for } t \geqslant 0 \tag{23}$$

where A and k are suitably chosen constants. How do we determine these constants? Since $2^0 = 2^{k \cdot 0} = 1$ when $t = 0$, it is clear that $A = P(0)$. In other words, A stands for the initial population, when $t = 0$; in our problem, $A = 30{,}000{,}000$. The other constant k is determined by noting that $60{,}000{,}000 = P(30) = A \cdot 2^{30k} = 30{,}000{,}000 \cdot 2^{30k}$, so that $2^{30k} = 2$. Now 2^x never has the same value for two different values of x; furthermore, $2^1 = 2$. Since $2^{30k} = 2$ and $2^1 = 2$, we must have $30k = 1$, or $k = 1/30$. Now we know the form of the growth function $P(t) = A \cdot 2^{kt}$

$$P(t) = 30{,}000{,}000 \cdot 2^{t/30} \qquad \text{for } t \geqslant 0 \tag{24}$$

This agrees with our remarks in the last paragraph: clearly formula (24) gives $P(0) = 30{,}000{,}000$ and $P(30) = 60{,}000{,}000$. If $t = 60$ we get

$$P(60) = 30{,}000{,}000 \cdot 2^{60/30} = 30{,}000{,}000 \cdot 2^2$$

$$= 30{,}000{,}000 \cdot 4 = 120{,}000{,}000$$

which is the correct value. To answer our original question, set $t = 150$ in (24). After 150 years the population will increase to quite a large value:

$$P(150) = 30{,}000{,}000 \cdot 2^{150/30} = 30{,}000{,}000 \cdot 32 = 960{,}000{,}000$$

The graph of the function $P(t)$ is shown in Figure 1.18.

It is unlikely that this rate of population growth could actually be maintained for a period of 150 years. Nevertheless, as long as the assumptions about the rate of growth prove correct (say for 50 years), formula (24) accurately describes the population as a function of time. Other examples of exponential population growth occur in con-

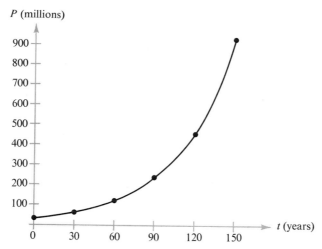

P (millions)

Figure 1.18
Graph of the function $P(t) = 30{,}000{,}000 \cdot 2^{t/30}$, which fits the
data in Table 1.1. The function has the form $A \cdot 2^{kt}$ where A and k
are constants; here the exponent kt varies, while the base 2 is
held fixed. Exponential functions make their appearance in all
kinds of growth problems. They will be discussed thoroughly in
Chapter 6.

trolled experiments with bacteria or one-celled animals. Another interesting example
of exponential growth is given in *The Natural Regulation of Animal Numbers,* by
D. Lack.* In 1937 two male and six female pheasants were released on an isolated
island where they had not been found previously, and where migration to or from the
island was geographically impossible. Under conditions that must be presumed conducive to the pheasants' tastes, their population grew from 8 in the spring of 1937 to
1325 in the spring of 1942. The actual pattern of growth is shown in Figure 1.19, and
is rather well fitted by an exponential function of the general form (23).

Exercises

●1. Calculate the values of the functions

  (i) $y = 2^x$ (ii) $y = 8 \cdot (2^x)$

  for $x = -3.0, -2.0, -1.5, -1.0, -0.5, 0.0, 0.5, 1.0, 1.5, 2.0,$ and 3.0. Plot these values on
  graph paper and make a sketch of the graph. Compare with Figure 1.18. HINT: Write exponents as fractions where necessary and use the square-root tables.

●2. Sketch the graph of $y = 2^{-x}$. This function has the form $y = A \cdot 2^{kx}$ with $A = 1$ and $k = -1$.
  It turns up in decay problems, as in Exercise 5 below.

---

* Lack, D. *The Natural Regulation of Animal Numbers,* Oxford University Press, New York, 1954.

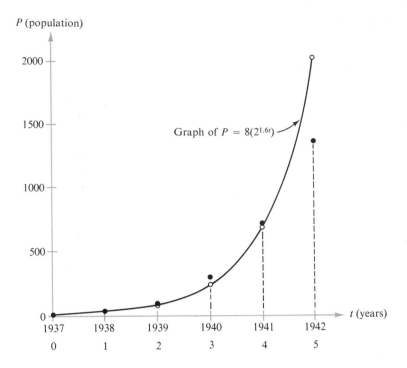

Year	1937	1938	1939	1940	1941	1942
t (years)	0	1	2	3	4	5
Population	8	30	81	282	705	1325
$8(2^{1.6t})$	8	24	73	222	676	2048

Figure 1.19
Tabulated values for the pheasant population in each year are plotted as solid dots. The population is approximately given by the exponential law $P = 8(2^{1.6t})$. The graph of $P = 8(2^{1.6t})$ is the solid curve; tabulated values of $8(2^{1.6t})$ are plotted as open dots. There are several reasons why the actual population begins to lag behind the predicted value $8(2^{1.6t})$. For example, the number of pheasants may be getting large enough to stress the limited environmental resources of the island. Once this happens, the assumptions leading to exponential growth are no longer valid.

●3. Suppose that a population of *E. coli* bacteria with an abundant supply of nutrients doubles in size every three hours. Then, as in all growth problems, we may expect the number $N(t)$ of bacteria after t hours to obey a law of the form $N(t) = A \cdot 2^{kt}$, where A and k are suitably chosen constants. Suppose we start with $N = 1000$ bacteria at time $t = 0$. Determine the constants A and k using the ideas of Example 15. Write out the function $N(t)$. Determine the number of bacteria after one day (24 hours) and two days. ANSWERS: $A = 1000$, $k = 1/3$, $N(t) = 1000(2^{t/3})$; $N(24) = 256{,}000$; $N(48) = 65.536$ million.

●4. The present population of a country is 50,000,000 and is increasing at such a rate that it will double in 50 years. Find a function of the form $P = A \cdot 2^{kt}$ describing the relation between the population P and the elapsed time t (in years), as in Example 15. Then sketch the graph of the function $P(t)$. From the graph, estimate when $P = 60{,}000{,}000$. When will the population reach 75,000,000?

●5. Radium undergoes radioactive decay at a steady rate: if we start with any amount Q, half of it will decay after 1600 years. This period of time T is called the *half-life* of radium. In decay problems, just as in growth problems, an exponential law holds. The amount $Q(t)$ left after t years is given by a function of the form $Q(t) = A \cdot 2^{kt}$, where A and k are suitably chosen constants. Evaluate the constants and write out $Q(t)$ explicitly, if the initial amount is 1 gram and t is measured in years. Then sketch the graph of $Q = Q(t)$; evaluate $Q(t)$ for whole multiples of the half-life, $t = nT$ for $n = 0, 1, 2, \dots$. How much radium will be lost after 800 years? What percentage of the initial amount remains after 800 years? HINT: Determine k by noticing what happens when $t = 1600$. ANSWERS: $A = 1$, $k = -1/1600$, $Q(t) = 1 \cdot 2^{-t/1600}$; if $t = 800$, $Q = 1 \cdot 2^{-1/2} - 1/\sqrt{2} = 0.707$ grams; 70.7% remains.

●6. When the growth of a population is limited by external factors, it starts to grow exponentially but eventually it levels off to some equilibrium level. Here is a formula that describes such a case: the number of bacteria in a culture medium deficient in nutrients is given in terms of the time t (in hours) by

$$N = \frac{1000 \cdot 2^t}{9 + 2^t} \qquad \text{for } t \geqslant 0$$

Use this formula to answer the following questions:

(i) How many bacteria are present initially, when $t = 0$?

(ii) Construct a table of values for $t = 0, 1, 2, 3, 4, 5, 6, 7$, and 8. Graph the function.

(iii) From the graph, estimate the values of t for which $N = 500$ and $N = 750$.

(iv) Do you think the population will ever reach $N = 1000$?

●7. In a tissue culture subjected to ionizing radiation, the number N of undamaged cells depends upon the exposure time t (in hours) according to the formula

$$N(t) = 10{,}000 \cdot 2^{-2t} \qquad \text{for } t \geqslant 0$$

Use this formula to

(i) Find the initial number of cells. HINT: At $t = 0$, no cells have been damaged.

(ii) Find the elapsed time t at which $N(t) = 5000$.

(iii) After how many hours are 3/4 of the cells damaged?

1.8 The Straight Line

The simplest curves in the plane are straight lines. In this section we shall review basic facts about the slope of a line and the equations that describe the line. If a line L is not vertical, its direction with respect to coordinate axes in the plane is described by a number called the **slope** of the line. Slope is measured by marking two points P_1 and P_2 on the line and computing the ratio

$$\text{slope}(L) = \frac{\text{change in } y\text{-coordinate}}{\text{change in } x\text{-coordinate}}$$

as we move from P_1 to P_2. For the reader's convenience, we outline here an orderly procedure for computing the slope.

Calculating the Slope of a Nonvertical Line L

STEP 1   Choose two points on L and write down their coordinates

$$P_1 = (x_1, y_1) \qquad P_2 = (x_2, y_2)$$

STEP 2   Compute the change in x as we move from P_1 to P_2

$$\Delta x = x_2 - x_1$$

STEP 3   Compute the corresponding change in y

$$\Delta y = y_2 - y_1$$

STEP 4   Compute the ratio of these changes

$$\text{slope}(L) = \frac{\Delta y}{\Delta x} = \frac{y_2 - y_1}{x_2 - x_1}$$

It is standard notation to use the symbol Δ to mean "change in" some quantity. Thus Δy means "the change in y" and Δx means "the change in x."

The slope of L does not depend on which pair of points we choose on L (see Figure 1.20), nor does it matter which point we label as P_1 and which as P_2 (see comments following Example 16). The slope is not defined for a vertical line: $x_1 = x_2$ and $\Delta x = 0$ for any two points on a vertical line, so that $\Delta y/\Delta x$ is undefined.

Example 16   Find the slope of line L if the points $P_1 = (1, -1)$ and $P_2 = (3, 0)$ lie on L. Find the slope of the line M passing through $(1, -3)$ and $(-2, 3)$.

Solution   (See Figure 1.21.) Here $(x_1, y_1) = (1, -1)$ and $(x_2, y_2) = (3, 0)$, so that $x_1 = 1$, $y_1 = -1$ and $x_2 = 3$, $y_2 = 0$. Therefore,

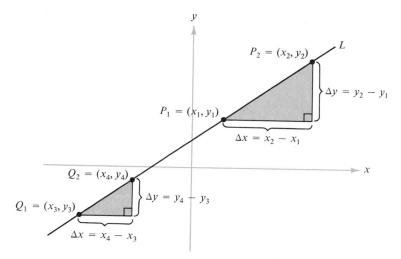

Figure 1.20
Given points $P_1 = (x_1, y_1)$ and $P_2 = (x_2, y_2)$ on a nonvertical line L, the slope
is $\Delta y/\Delta x = (y_2 - y_1)/(x_2 - x_1)$. Given any other pair of points $Q_1 = (x_3, y_3)$
and $Q_2 = (x_4, y_4)$ on L, the two triangles shown are similar, so that
$(y_2 - y_1)/(x_2 - x_1) = (y_4 - y_3)/(x_4 - x_3)$. Thus the slope does not depend
on the pair of points chosen.

$$\Delta y = y_2 - y_1 = 0 - (-1) = 0 + 1 = 1$$

$$\Delta x = x_2 - x_1 = 3 - 1 = 2$$

$$\text{slope}(L) = \frac{\Delta y}{\Delta x} - \frac{1}{2}$$

Similarly

$$\text{slope}(M) = \frac{3 - (-3)}{-2 - (1)} = \frac{6}{-3} = -2$$

What if we reverse the roles of initial and final points in Example 16, labeling $P_1 = (x_1, y_1) = (3, 0)$ and $P_2 = (x_2, y_2) - (1, \quad 1)$? In that case

$$\Delta y = y_2 - y_1 = -1 - 0 = -1$$

$$\Delta x = x_2 - x_1 = 1 - 3 = -2$$

$$\frac{\Delta y}{\Delta x} = \frac{-1}{-2} = \frac{1}{2}$$

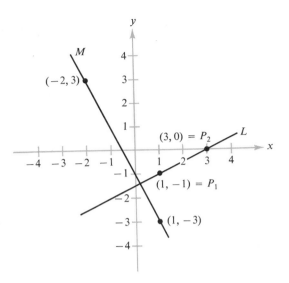

Figure 1.21
The line L contains $P_1 = (1, -1)$ and $P_2 = (3, 0)$. Its slope
is $1/2$. Observe that L rises as we move to the right, as is the
case for any line with positive slope. Line M has negative
slope -2, and falls as we move to the right.

The two minus signs attached to Δy and Δx cancel, giving exactly the same value for
slope(L) as before. Thus the labeling of points P_1 and P_2 is immaterial.

Many geometric statements may be translated into statements about the numerical value m of the slope. The slope of L is positive ($m > 0$) if the line rises as we move
to the right in the plane (see Figure 1.22). Similarly, m is negative if the line falls as
we move to the right. The slope is zero for horizontal lines. In general, the larger the
slope, the more steeply the line rises. Two non-vertical lines L_1 and L_2 with slopes
m_1 and m_2 are

(*i*) parallel if and only if $m_1 = m_2$.

(25)

(*ii*) perpendicular if and only if $m_2 = -1/m_1$ or, equivalently,
     if $m_1 \cdot m_2 = -1$.

Using (25*ii*) we see that the lines L and M in Example 16 are perpendicular. It is not
even necessary to sketch the lines to see this. Just compute and compare their slopes.

If we want to represent a straight line as the graph of some function, how do we
find an appropriate function? First notice that the slope of L is not enough to determine its position in the plane (any two parallel lines have the same slope); but if we
also know one point on the line, then its position is determined. Suppose L has
slope(L) = m and that L passes through some point $P = (a,b)$. If $Q = (x,y)$ is any

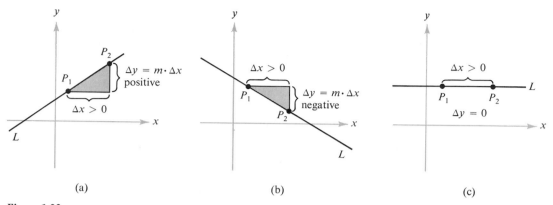

Figure 1.22

A rising line L has positive slope while a falling line has negative slope. In (a), (b) and (c), Δx is positive. In (a), Δy is positive and so is the slope m. In (b), Δy is negative and so is m. In (c), Δy and m are zero; since $\Delta y = m \cdot \Delta x = 0$, all points on L have the same y-coordinate and L must be horizontal.

point on L distinct from P, then by definition of slope

$$m = \frac{\Delta y}{\Delta x} = \frac{y - b}{x - a} \qquad\qquad (26)$$

This equation may be rewritten; multiplying both sides by $(x - a)$ we get

$$(y - b) = m \cdot (x - a) \qquad\qquad (27)$$

A point $Q = (x, y)$ in the plane lies on L if and only if its coordinates x, y satisfy equation (27). This identifies L as the solution set of (27), which is called the **point-slope** form of the equation for L.

Example 17 Find the equation of the line L that passes through $P = (-2, -1)$ with slope$(L) = 3$. Sketch the line.

Solution Since $P = (a,b) = (-2, -1)$ lies on L and the slope is $m = 3$, every other point $Q = (x,y)$ on L must satisfy the equation

$$3 = m = \frac{\Delta y}{\Delta x} = \frac{y - (-1)}{x - (-2)} = \frac{y + 1}{x + 2}$$

This is equivalent to (has the same solution set as) the equation

$$y + 1 = 3 \cdot (x + 2) = 3x + 6$$

or

$$y = 3x + 5 \qquad (28)$$

To determine the position of L in a sketch, we need the coordinates of one more point on the line besides $P = (-2, -1)$. We can get other points on L by setting fixed values of x in (28). If we let $x = -1$ we find that $y = +2$, so $Q = (-1, 2)$ lies on L, as shown in Figure 1.23.

Example 18   Find the equation of the line passing through the points $(-1, 1)$ and $(2, 3)$.

Solution   Since L contains $P_1 = (-1, 1)$ and $P_2 = (2, 3)$ its slope is

$$m = \frac{\Delta y}{\Delta x} = \frac{3 - 1}{2 - (-1)} = \frac{2}{3}$$

Since L also passes through $(-1, 1)$, a point-slope equation (27) for it is $(y - 1) = (2/3)(x - (-1)) = (2/3)(x + 1)$. This equation may be rewritten as

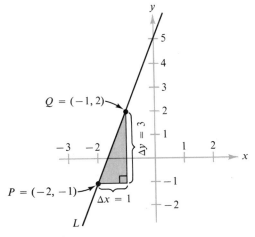

Figure 1.23
The line L has slope $m = +3$ and passes through $P = (-2, -1)$, indicated by a solid dot. Its equation is $y = 3x + 5$; that is, L is the solution set of this equation. The point $Q = (-1, 2)$ also lies on L, so we may draw L as the line through P and Q.

$$y = \frac{2}{3}(x - (-1)) + 1 = \frac{2}{3}(x + 1) + 1 = \frac{2}{3}x + \frac{5}{3}$$

Example 19   What is the slope of the line determined by the equation $y = 3x - 2$?

Solution   To find the slope it suffices to locate any two points that satisfy the equation $y = 3x - 2$. We can find such points by inserting specific values of x (or of y) into this equation. For example, if $x = 0$ then $y = 3 \cdot 0 - 2 = -2$, so that $P_1 = (0, -2)$ lies on the line. If we set $x = 1$, then $y = 3 \cdot 1 - 2 = 1$, so that $P_2 = (1, 1)$ also lies on L. Thus the slope is

$$\text{slope}(L) = \frac{\Delta y}{\Delta x} = \frac{1 - (-2)}{1 - 0} = \frac{1 + 2}{1} = 3$$

Suppose that at least one of the constants A and B is nonzero in the equation

$$Ax + By + C = 0 \qquad (A, B, \text{ and } C \text{ constants}) \tag{29}$$

In the plane, the solution set of such an equation is always a line, and furthermore every possible line is the solution set of an equation of this kind. For example, the equation $y = (2/3)x + (5/3)$ in Example 18 is equivalent to the equation $2x - 3y + 5 = 0$, which has this form ($A = 2$, $B = -3$, $C = 5$).

Example 20   What is the slope of the line L determined by the equation $3x + 4y - 5 = 0$? Where does the line cross the x-axis? The y-axis?

Solution   The point where L crosses the x-axis must have y-coordinate $y = 0$ (all points on the x-axis do). Substituting $y = 0$ into the equation for L, we get

$$3x + 4 \cdot 0 - 5 = 0, \qquad \text{so that } x = \tfrac{5}{3}$$

This is the x-coordinate of the crossover point; L crosses the x-axis at $P = (5/3, 0)$, as shown in Figure 1.24. Similarly, L crosses the y-axis where $x = 0$. Setting $x = 0$ in the equation for L we get

$$3 \cdot 0 + 4y - 5 = 0, \qquad \text{or } y = \tfrac{5}{4}$$

so L crosses the y-axis at $Q = (0, 5/4)$, as shown. Now that we know the coordinates of two points on L, we may compute the slope

$$\text{slope}(L) = \frac{\Delta y}{\Delta x} = \frac{\tfrac{5}{4} - 0}{0 - \tfrac{5}{3}} = -\frac{3}{4}$$

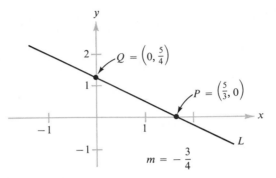

Figure 1.24
The solution set for $3x + 4y - 5 = 0$ is the line shown.
Its slope is $m = -3/4$. It meets the y-axis when $x = 0$;
substituting $x = 0$ into the equation for L, we get
$y = 5/4$. Therefore L meets the y-axis at $(0, 5/4)$.
Similarly, it meets the x-axis at $(5/3, 0)$ as shown.

We could find other points on L by fixing the value of x (or of y) and using the equation for L to solve for the value of the other coordinate.

Exercises

● 1 Compute the changes Δx and Δy in x and y as we move from $P_1 = (-2, 3)$ to $P_2 = (0, -1)$. Find the slope of the line joining these two points.

● 2. Find the slopes of the lines joining the following pairs of points.

    (i) $(1, -3)$ and $(-1, 3)$ *(iv)* $(-1, -1)$ and $(-4, 8)$

    (ii) $(4, 2)$ and $(6, 2)$ *(v)* $(-1, -4)$ and $(1, 2)$

    (iii) $(2, 2)$ and $(5, 3)$ *(vi)* $(1, 0)$ and $(7, 2)$

  3. In Exercise 2, which lines are parallel? Which lines are perpendicular?

● 4. Find the equation of the line L that passes through the points $P = (-1, 2)$ and $Q = (3, -1)$. What is the slope of L? Make a sketch of this line on graph paper.

● 5. Find the equation of the line that passes through $P = (2, -1)$ and has slope $m = 1/3$. Sketch the line.

● 6. Find the slope of the line whose equation is $2x + 3y = 6$; make a sketch of the line. Where does it cross the x-axis? Where does it cross the y-axis? Give both coordinates of the point where it meets the (horizontal) line whose equation is $y = 4$. ANSWERS: Crosses x-axis at $(3, 0)$; crosses y-axis at $(0, 2)$; slope $= -2/3$; crosses line at $(-3, 4)$.

  7. Find the coordinates of at least 6 *different* points on the line whose equation is

$$x + 2y = 200$$

by fixing various values of x or of y. Find both coordinates of the point where this line crosses the x-axis; likewise for the y-axis. Sketch the line. What is its slope? HINT: Try $x = 0, 10, \ldots,$ 50 and solve for the corresponding values of y.

• 8. Determine equations for the following lines in the coordinate plane.

     (*i*) The line through the points $(1, 2)$ and $(-1, 0)$

     (*ii*) The line through the points $(-4, 5)$ and $(1, -2)$

     (*iii*) The line through $(1, 4)$ that has slope $m = -1/2$

     (*iv*) The line through $(\pi, \sqrt{5} + 1)$ with slope $m = -5$

     (*v*) The line with slope $m = -1/3$ that crosses the y-axis at $y = +5$

     (*vi*) The line with slope $m = 2/7$ that crosses the x-axis at $x = 0$

◐ 9. Sketch the lines determined by the following equations. Find their slopes.

     (*i*) $4x + 3y = 0$ (*v*) $y - 2 = 0$

     (*ii*) $x + 2y - 3 = 0$ (*vi*) $-3x + 2y = 7$

     (*iii*) $x - y - 4 = 0$ (*vii*) $0.67x - 0.80y = 0.59$

     (*iv*) $y = 4x - \sqrt{5}$ (*viii*) $350x + 420y - 500 = 0$

•10. Based on past experience, a manufacturer knows that the demand function for his product is linear. At the production level $q = 1000$ he can command a price $p = 90$, while at $q = 1600$ the price must be reduced to $p = 80$. Find the equation of the demand function $p(q)$. What is the value of p when $q = 1450$? If the price is set at $p = 87$, find the corresponding level of production q.

◐11. Through market surveys, a bicycle store has estimated the potential demand q for the month of June at various selling prices p, as indicated in the following table.

p (\$)	80	85	90	95	100
q	860	770	680	590	500

Plot these points on graph paper, taking p as the horizontal axis. Do they lie along a straight line? If so, find the equation $q = q(p)$ of this line. For what range of values of p would you have reasonable confidence in the predictions of this "demand equation"?

•12. Let $y = f(x) = x^3 + x$. Find the coordinates of the points on the graph of f corresponding to $x = 1$ and $x = 2$. What is the slope of the line L through these points on the graph of f? What is its equation?

•13. If L is the line determined by the equation

$$Ax + By + C = 0 \qquad (A, B, \text{ and } C \text{ fixed constants}; B \text{ nonzero})$$

prove that

$$\text{slope}(L) = -\frac{A}{B}$$

HINT: Locate two points on L by taking $x = 0$ and $x = 1$ and solving for the corresponding values of y.

*14. On a single piece of graph paper, sketch the lines whose equations are

    (i) $3x - 4y = -1$ (iii) $3x - 4y = +1$

    (ii) $3x - 4y = 0$ (iv) $3x - 4y = +2$

by plotting the points where the lines cross the coordinate axes. What are their slopes? How are the lines related to each other geometrically? What can you say about the family of all lines L_c (c a real number) given by the equations

$$3x - 4y = c?$$

How does the position of L_c (the solution set of this equation) vary as the constant c increases?

1.9   Intersections of Graphs and Simultaneous Equations

The equilibrium price of a commodity in a competitive market is determined by the well-known condition: *supply equals demand*. More precisely, this equilibrium point is the intersection of the supply and demand curves for the given commodity. This is just one example of a practical problem with the following general mathematical form:

Problem   Given the graphs of two functions in the same coordinate plane, find the points where the graphs meet. These are called the **points of intersection** of the graphs.

Example 21   As prices rise, cattlemen are willing to put more beef on the market; when prices fall, they tend to cut back. Suppose this *supply relationship* for beef is given by the formula

$$p = \frac{1}{60}q + \frac{1}{2} \quad \text{for } 0 \leqslant q \leqslant 120 \tag{30}$$

Here p is the price (dollars per pound) at which producers are willing to supply q million pounds per week. On the other hand, consumer action produces opposite effects. Consumers buy less beef as the price increases, and more as the price decreases. Suppose that this *demand relationship* is described by

$$p = \frac{-1}{40}q + 3 \quad \text{for } 0 \leqslant q \leqslant 120 \tag{31}$$

This formula gives the price per pound p at which the public will buy q million pounds of beef per week. Find the point of intersection of the supply and demand curves. That is, find the level of production q at which the seller's price matches the price the consumer is willing to pay.

Solution   Both the supply function (30) and the demand function (31) are linear functions of q. Hence their graphs are straight lines, as shown in Figure 1.25. By examining the graphs we can see that $(q_0, p_0) = (60, 1.5)$ is their point of intersection. Economists refer to this as the **equilibrium point** and to $p_0 = 1.50$ dollars per pound as the equilibrium price. At the equilibrium price the quantity demanded by consumers, $q_0 = 60$ million pounds per week, equals the quantity that producers are willing to supply.

We can also find the equilibrium point by algebraic means. Observe that (q_0, p_0) lies on both the supply and demand curves. At the point of intersection the p values (height above the horizontal axis) are equal. Thus its coordinates must simultaneously satisfy the supply equation (30) and the demand equation (31)

$$p_0 = \frac{1}{60}q_0 + \frac{1}{2} \qquad p_0 = \frac{-1}{40}q_0 + 3$$

We may eliminate p_0 from these equations since

$$\frac{1}{60}q_0 + \frac{1}{2} = \frac{-1}{40}q_0 + 3 \; (= p_0)$$

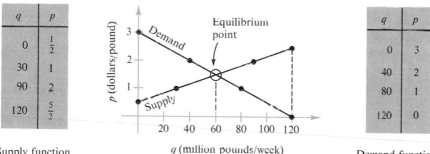

q	p
0	$\frac{1}{2}$
30	1
90	2
120	$\frac{5}{2}$

Supply function

q (million pounds/week)

q	p
0	3
40	2
80	1
120	0

Demand function

Figure 1.25
Both the supply function $p = (1/60)q + 1/2$ and the demand function $p = (-1/40)q + 3$ are linear, so their graphs are straight lines. If the price is $p = 1.00$, then producers are willing to produce only $q = 30$ million pounds per week, while consumers demand $q = 80$. This imbalance forces the price to rise. If the price is $p = 2.00$, consumer demand is $q - 40$, while producers are willing to supply $q = 90$, so the price falls. At the equilibrium point $(q_0, p_0) = (60, 1.50)$, where the graphs meet, the price $p_0 = 1.50$ corresponds to equal supply and demand, $q_0 = 60$, and the price is stable.

Solving this linear equation in one unknown for q_0 we get

$$\frac{1}{60}q_0 + \frac{1}{40}q_0 = 3 - \frac{1}{2}$$

or

$$\frac{5}{120}q_0 = \frac{5}{2}$$

which means that $q_0 = 60$. Once we know that $q_0 = 60$, we may find p_0 by substituting this value of q_0 into either the supply or the demand equation, to get

$$p_0 = \frac{1}{60}q_0 + \frac{1}{2} = \frac{1}{60}(60) + \frac{1}{2} = \frac{3}{2} = 1.50$$

In general, the *geometric* problem of locating the point(s) where the graphs of two functions $y = f(x)$ and $y = g(x)$ intersect reduces to an *algebraic* problem. We must find all values of x for which $y = f(x)$ and $y = g(x)$ are equal. This means precisely that the corresponding points on the graphs of f and g have the same height above the x-axis, so that the graphs intersect. But determining where $f(x) = g(x)$ is the same as locating all x for which

$$f(x) - g(x) = 0 \tag{32}$$

The solutions of such an equation are called its **roots** or **zeros**. If x is any root of equation (32), we may determine the value of y either from the function $y = f(x)$ or from $y = g(x)$ to obtain the coordinates (x,y) of a point where the graphs intersect. Ultimately our success with the algebraic approach depends upon our ability to find the roots, or zero values, of equation (32).

If the equation $f(x) - g(x) = 0$ is linear in x (as in Example 21 above) we can solve it by elementary algebra. We can also solve it if the equation is quadratic

$$Ax^2 + Bx + C = 0 \qquad \text{(where } A, B, \text{ and } C \text{ are constants, } A \neq 0\text{)} \tag{33}$$

by applying the **quadratic formula**. This formula from basic algebra states that such equations are satisfied by the following values of x:

$$x = \frac{-B + \sqrt{B^2 - 4AC}}{2A} \qquad x = \frac{-B - \sqrt{B^2 - 4AC}}{2A} \tag{34}$$

These two formulas differ only in the choice of a $(+)$ or $(-)$ sign in front of the radical, so they are often written together in a single expression

$$x = \frac{-B \pm \sqrt{B^2 - 4AC}}{2A}$$

The quadratic formula tells us explicitly how to find the roots of the quadratic equation from the given data, namely the coefficients A, B, and C. If the term $B^2 - 4AC$ under the radical is negative, the square root makes no sense (at least in the real number system). When this happens, the appropriate conclusion is that the equation $Ax^2 + Bx + C = 0$ *has no solutions* (in the real number system).

Example 22   Find the points of intersection of the graphs of $y = 3 - x - x^2$ and $y = x + 1$.

Solution   The graphs are plotted in Figure 1.26. We can either visually estimate coordinates of the intersection points using Figure 1.26, or locate them exactly by algebraic means. Eliminating y from the pair of equations yields

$$3 - x - x^2 = y = x + 1$$

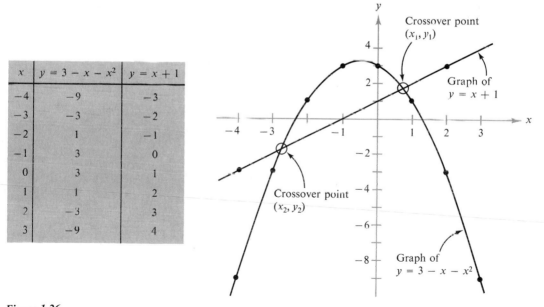

x	$y = 3 - x - x^2$	$y = x + 1$
-4	-9	-3
-3	-3	-2
-2	1	-1
-1	3	0
0	3	1
1	1	2
2	-3	3
3	-9	4

Figure 1.26
A table of values has been computed for each of the functions $y = 3 - x - x^2$ and $y = x + 1$. The corresponding points on the graphs are indicated by solid dots. The points of intersection of the graphs (represented by circles) may be estimated by inspecting the graphs: $(x_1, y_1) \approx (0.7, 1.7)$ and $(x_2, y_2) \approx (-2.7, -1.7)$. Using the algebraic approach we may calculate the exact intersection points: $(x_1, y_1) = (-1 + \sqrt{3}, +\sqrt{3})$ and $(x_2, y_2) = (-1 - \sqrt{3}, -\sqrt{3})$.

Transposing all terms to the right-hand side we obtain a quadratic equation

$$0 = x^2 + 2x - 2$$

with $A = 1$, $B = 2$, and $C = -2$. The solution set consists of two numbers given by the quadratic formula

$$x_1 = \frac{-B + \sqrt{B^2 - 4AC}}{2A} = \frac{-2 + \sqrt{2^2 - 4(1)(-2)}}{2}$$

$$= \frac{-2 + \sqrt{12}}{2} = -1 + \sqrt{3} = 0.732 \ldots$$

and

$$x_2 = \frac{-B - \sqrt{B^2 - 4AC}}{2A} = \frac{-2 - \sqrt{2^2 - 4(1)(-2)}}{2}$$

$$= \frac{-2 - \sqrt{12}}{2} = -1 - \sqrt{3} = -2.732 \ldots$$

For $x_1 = -1 + \sqrt{3}$ the corresponding value $y = y_1$ is

$$y_1 = x_1 + 1 = (-1 + \sqrt{3}) + 1 = \sqrt{3} = 1.732 \ldots$$

Similarly for $x_2 = -1 - \sqrt{3}$

$$y_2 = x_2 + 1 = (-1 - \sqrt{3}) + 1 = -\sqrt{3} = -1.732 \ldots$$

Therefore, the points of intersection are

$$(x_1, y_1) = (-1 + \sqrt{3}, \sqrt{3}) \quad \text{and} \quad (x_2, y_2) = (-1 - \sqrt{3}, -\sqrt{3})$$

We shall discuss the solution of zero-value problems no further, except to note that if a polynomial equation $h(x) = 0$ has degree 3 or higher, we should try to factor the polynomial. If we can guess one root of the equation $h(x) = 0$, then we can replace our original polynomial with one of lower degree. Hopefully, we can continue this process until we arrive at a quadratic equation, which we can always solve.

Example 23   Find the roots of the cubic (degree 3) equation $h(x) = x^3 - 8x - 3 = 0$.

Solution   Perhaps after some trial and error, we locate one of the roots $x_1 = +3$ by observing that $h(x_1) = h(3) = 3^3 - 8(3) - 3 = 0$. We do this by testing the values of $h(x)$ for various choices of x. Since $x = 3$ is a root, it follows that $(x - 3)$ may be factored out of $h(x)$; by long division we get

$$
\begin{array}{r}
x^2 + 3x + 1 \\
x - 3 \overline{)x^3 \qquad\quad - 8x - 3} \\
\underline{x^3 - 3x^2} \\
3x^2 - 8x \\
\underline{3x^2 - 9x} \\
x - 3 \\
\underline{x - 3} \\
0
\end{array}
$$

Thus $h(x) = x^3 - 8x - 3 = (x - 3)(x^2 + 3x + 1)$.* This product is zero if and only if one or the other of the factors $(x - 3)$, $(x^2 + 3x + 1)$ is zero. If $x - 3 = 0$ we get the root $x = 3$. If $x^2 + 3x + 1 = 0$, we get two more roots by applying the quadratic formula. The roots of the equation $x^2 + 3x + 1 = 0$ (with $A = 1, B = 3$, and $C = 1$) are

$$
x_2 = \frac{-3 - \sqrt{5}}{2} = -2.618\ldots \qquad x_3 = \frac{-3 + \sqrt{5}}{2} = -0.382\ldots
$$

We conclude that the solution set for $h(x) = 0$ consists of three numbers

$$
x_1 = 3, \qquad x_2 = \frac{-3 - \sqrt{5}}{2}, \qquad x_3 = \frac{-3 + \sqrt{5}}{2}
$$

Exercises

●1. Suppose the supply relationship for beef is

$$
p = \frac{1}{60} q + \frac{1}{2}
$$

and the demand relationship is

$$
p = \frac{200}{3q}
$$

where p is measured in dollars per pound and q in millions of pounds per week. Find the level of demand q and the price p when supply equals demand. (Solve the problem two ways: geometrically and algebraically.)

* If $x = p$ is a root of a polynomial equation $h(x) = 0$, then $(x - p)$ will always divide into $h(x)$ without remainder. This yields a factorization $h(x) = (x - p) \cdot k(x)$, where $k(x)$ is a polynomial of lower degree than $h(x)$. In our example, $p = 3$ and $k(x) = x^2 + 3x + 1$.

●2. Find both coordinates of the point of intersection for each of the following pairs of lines.

(*i*) $y = 4x + 10$ and $3x + y + 5 = 0$

(*ii*) $x - 3y + 1 = 0$ and $y = -x + 5$

(*iii*) $-x + 3y = 600$ and $2x + 2y = 500$

○3. Using the same set of coordinate axes, draw the graphs of the functions

$$y = 3x - 2 \quad \text{and} \quad y = 6 - 2x$$

Estimate the coordinates of the point of intersection by examining the sketch. Then calculate both coordinates of the point of intersection by using algebra.

●4. Carry out the steps in Exercise 3 using the functions

(*i*) $y = 2x + 6$ and $y = x^2 - 9$

(*ii*) $y = x^2 - x - 2$ and $y = 4 + 3x - x^2$

(*iii*) $y = 3x - 2$ and $y = x^3$

●5. Use the quadratic formula to find all roots of the following quadratic equations:

(*i*) $x^2 - 3x + 1 = 0$ (*v*) $8x^2 + 37 = 0$

(*ii*) $x^2 + x + 1 = 0$ (*vi*) $500,000 - 200x + .01x^2 = 0$

(*iii*) $x^2 + 4x - 8 = 0$ (*vii*) $500,000 - 20x + .01x^2 = 0$

(*iv*) $400x^2 - 1 = 0$

NOTE: If $B^2 - 4AC$ is negative, the term $\pm\sqrt{B^2 - 4AC}$ in the quadratic formula does not make sense (as a real number). In this event, the proper conclusion is that *there are no (real) roots* of the equation at hand.

●6. Suppose that the monthly costs of a manufacturing plant are given by

$$C(q) = 50,000 + 100q - 0.1q^2$$

where q = number of units produced per month. Suppose that all units are sold at a price of \$110, regardless of the production level. Calculate the revenue $R(q)$ as a function of q. Calculate the profit $P(q)$ as a function of q. What is the profit if you set q at 250 units per month? What is the break-even point (the value of q for which costs = revenue)?

●7. Find the zero values of the following polynomial equations. Use the quadratic formula wherever possible. Also use the principle that a product is zero if any one of the individual factors is zero.

(*i*) $x^4 - 1 = 0$ [HINT: $x^4 - 1 = (x^2 - 1)(x^2 + 1)$
                                        $= (x - 1)(x + 1)(x^2 + 1)$]

(*ii*) $x^2 + x - 2 = 0$

(*iii*) $x^2 - x + 1 = 0$

(*iv*) $x^3 - x^2 - x + 1 = 0$ [HINT: guess a root]

(*v*) $4x^2 - 2x - 7 = 0$

*●8. Prove that any quadratic polynomial $p(x) = Ax^2 + Bx + C$ may be factored as $p(x) = A \cdot (x - r_+) \cdot (x - r_-)$ where r_+ and r_- are the roots of the equation $Ax^2 + Bx + C = 0$

given by the quadratic formula. Factor the polynomials

(i) $x^2 + 4x - 21$ (ii) $x^2 - 2x - 2$

using this idea. HINT: Write out r_+ and r_- in terms of A, B, and C. Then multiply out $(x - r_+) \cdot (x - r_-)$. Could you have guessed the factorizations in (i) and (ii) without using this idea?

1.10 Inequalities

A publisher is preparing a book for which initial typesetting and editorial costs of $10,000 must be offset by revenue of $3.20 for each copy sold. If he sells x copies, his profit will be

$$P(x) = -10,000 + 3.20x$$

Obviously he is interested in knowing the values of x for which he makes a profit instead of a loss. Mathematically, he wants to determine when the inequality $P \geqslant 0$ is satisfied, that is

$$-10,000 + 3.20x \geqslant 0 \tag{35}$$

In this section we shall show how to solve problems involving inequalities.

Rules of Inequalities

(I) Inequalities are preserved when the same number is added to each side.

If $a < b$ and if c is any number, then $a + c < b + c$.   (36)

This is so whether the numbers are positive, negative, or of mixed type.

(ii) Inequalities are preserved when multiplied by a positive number. Let c be a positive number, $c > 0$. Then

If $a < b$ and if c is positive, then $ac < bc$.   (37)

As we shall see, positivity of c is essential here.

(iii) Inequalities are *not* preserved if we multiply both sides by -1, or by any other negative number. In fact, this *reverses* the original inequality.

If $a < b$ and if c is negative, then $ac > bc$.   (38)

For example, if $a = 1/2$ and $b = 3/5$ then $a < b$. But $(-1) \cdot a = -1/2$ is greater than $(-1) \cdot b = -3/5$, so that $-a > -b$ (see Figure 1.27).

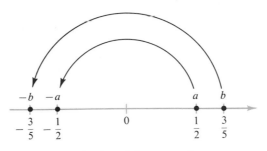

Figure 1.27
Effect on an inequality of
multiplication by -1.

Given an inequality involving an unknown x, say

$$3x - 7 > x + 2$$

the inequality holds for certain choices of x and fails for others. The set of real numbers x for which an inequality is true is called its **solution set**. The same term applies to the solutions of equations such as

$$3x - 7 = x + 2$$

From algebra you are familiar with the solution of equations. Inequalities, though they may be less familiar, are solved in much the same way. By applying the rules given above we can show that the inequality $3x - 7 > x + 2$ is equivalent to the simple inequality $x > 9/2$, in the sense that they have exactly the same solutions x.

Example 24   Describe the solution set for the inequality $3x - 7 > x + 2$.

Solution   The following inequalities are equivalent for the reasons indicated.

$$3x - 7 > x + 2 \qquad \text{Add } +7 \text{ to both sides (rule (36))}$$
$$3x > x + 9 \qquad \text{Add } -x \text{ to both sides (rule (36))}$$
$$2x > 9 \qquad \text{Multiply both sides by } \tfrac{1}{2} \text{ (rule (37))}$$
$$x > \tfrac{9}{2}$$

A number x satisfies $x > 9/2$ if and only if it lies strictly to the right of $9/2$ on the number line. The solution set is an "interval" extending to the right of $9/2$, the shaded portion of the line shown in Figure 1.28. The point $x = 9/2$ itself is *not* a solution. Had we started with the inequality $3x - 7 \geqslant x + 2$, which by the same reasoning

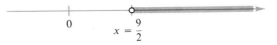

Figure 1.28
The shaded portion of the line is the solution set of
$x > 9/2$.

is equivalent to $x \geqslant 9/2$, the solution set would have been the shaded portion of the line together with the endpoint $x = 9/2$.

By similar methods we can find the solution of the publisher's problem (35). He makes a profit whenever

$$0 \leqslant -10,000 + 3.20x$$
$$10,000 \leqslant 3.20x \qquad \text{Add 10,000 to both sides}$$
$$3125 \leqslant x \qquad \text{Divide by 3.20}$$

The break-even point occurs when 3125 copies are sold.

   Later we shall want to decide which values of x make an algebraic expression positive (or negative). The next example illustrates a general procedure for doing this.

Example 25   Find all x such that $x^2 - x - 6 = (x + 2)(x - 3) < 0$. Sketch the solution set in the number line.

Solution   The expression has been written as a product of factors $(x + 2)$ and $(x - 3)$. It is easy to decide where in the number line each of the factors is positive or negative. For example

$$x + 2 > 0 \text{ when } x > -2 \quad (x \text{ to the right of } -2)$$

$$x + 2 < 0 \text{ when } x < 2 \quad (x \text{ to the left of } -2)$$

and similarly for the signs of $(x \quad 3)$. The signs for each factor are tabulated in Figure 1.29. The sign of their product $x^2 - x - 6$ is determined by the rule of signs. The solution set for the inequality $x^2 - x - 6 < 0$ is the shaded interval $-2 < x < 3$ shown in the last line of Figure 1.29. The endpoints -2 and $+3$, indicated by open dots, are not included in the solution set because the expression is equal to zero there. (They would have been included, had we considered the inequality $x^2 - x - 6 \leqslant 0$.)

Example 26   Find all x such that $x(x^2 - 1) > 0$ and sketch the solution set.

Solution   First factor the expression completely. Since $x^2 - 1 = (x - 1)(x + 1)$ we get

$$x(x^2 - 1) = x \cdot (x + 1) \cdot (x - 1) \qquad \text{for all } x$$

Next make a diagram showing the signs of each separate factor (see Figure 1.30):

$$x > 0 \text{ when } x \text{ lies to the right of the origin}$$

$$x + 1 > 0 \text{ when } x > -1 \quad (x \text{ to the right of } -1)$$

$$x - 1 > 0 \text{ when } x > +1 \quad (x \text{ to the right of } +1)$$

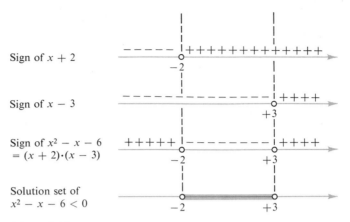

Figure 1.29
The first two lines show the signs of the factors $(x + 2)$ and $(x - 3)$
for x on various parts of the number line. The sign of their product
$x^2 - x - 6 = (x + 2)(x - 3)$ on various parts of the number line
is determined from the signs of the factors by the rule of signs.
The solution set for $x^2 - x - 6 < 0$ is the shaded interval shown
on the last line. The endpoints -2 and $+3$ are excluded because
$x^2 - x - 6$ is zero there.

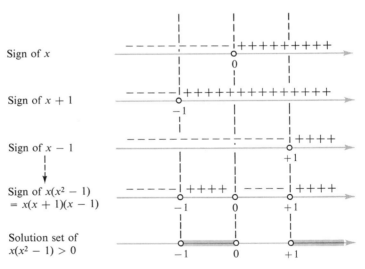

Figure 1.30
The first three lines show the signs of the factors x, $(x + 1)$, and $(x - 1)$,
whose product is $x(x^2 - 1)$. The solution set for $x(x^2 - 1) > 0$,
determined by the rule of signs, consists of the two shaded intervals
$-1 < x < 0$ and $+1 < x$ shown in the last line. The endpoints $-1, 0$,
and $+1$ are not in the solution set because the product is zero there.
What is the solution set for $x(x^2 - 1) < 0$?

Then use the rule of signs to determine the sign of their product $x(x^2 - 1)$ on various parts of the number line. The solution set for $x(x^2 - 1) > 0$ consists of the two shaded intervals shown in Figure 1.30.

Exercises

●1. Sketch the solution sets in the number line for the following inequalities:

(i) $x > -1$ (vi) $2 - x < 7$

(ii) $x < -1$ (vii) $2 - x < 2x + 11$

(iii) $x + 2 > 0$ (viii) $2 - x \geqslant 2x + 2$

(iv) $x + 2 < 0$ (ix) $-(\frac{7}{8})x + 1 \leqslant 2x + \frac{1}{2}$

(v) $x - 3 \geqslant 0$ (x) $2.0x - 500 \leqslant 100 + 1.5x$

●2. Suppose company A charges \$10 per day and 10¢ per mile to rent a certain type of automobile, while company H charges \$13 per day and 8¢ per mile. If you expect to drive x miles per day, for which values of x is it advantageous to rent from company A? From company H?

●3. Find the solution set for each of the inequalities below. Sketch each solution set in the number line, indicating which endpoints are part of the set.

(i) $(x + 1)(x + 4) > 0$ (v) $x^2 \leqslant 9$

(ii) $x(x - 5) < 0$ (vi) $x^2 + 4x + 4 \geqslant 0$

(iii) $x^2 - 2x - 15 \geqslant 0$ (vii) $x^2 + 3x \leqslant x^2 + 5x + 2$

(iv) $x^2 \leqslant 9x$ (viii) $2x^2 + 2x > x^2 + x + 6$

4. Sketch the solution sets for the inequalities

(i) $x^2 < 4$ (ii) $x^2 > 4$

HINT: $x^2 < 4$ holds if and only if $x^2 - 4 < 0$. Factor the polynomial and proceed as in Example 25.

●5. Determine where the polynomial $p(x) = x(x + 1)(x - 3)$ satisfies the inequality $p(x) \geqslant 0$. Where does $p(x) = 0$ hold? Sketch the solution set for the inequality $p(x) \geqslant 0$.

●6. Sketch the solution set for the inequality $x^3 > x$. HINT: Subtract x from both sides and use the methods of Example 26.

●7. Find the solution set for the inequality $(x + 1)(x + 2)(x - 3) > 0$.

●8. Find the solution set for the inequality

$$\frac{1}{x} < 4$$

by (i) first finding all positive solutions $x > 0$ (if any); (ii) then finding all negative solutions $x < 0$ (if any). Use rule (37) or (38) as appropriate in each case. NOTE: $x = 0$ is not a solution. The left side is not even defined if $x = 0$. HINT: See the graph of $y = 1/x$, Figure 1.8.

●9. The cost (in dollars) of constructing a certain type of condominium apartment building varies with the number of stories n according to the formula

$$C(n) = 2{,}000{,}000 + 200{,}000n + 2000n^2$$

The average cost per floor is therefore

$$A(n) = \frac{C(n)}{n} = \frac{2{,}000{,}000}{n} + 200{,}000 + 2000n$$

As n increases, $A(n)$ at first declines, but then begins to increase rapidly. If each full floor of apartments sells for $420,000, what range of heights n yields a profit for the builder?

CHAPTER 2

Derivatives and the Concept of Limit

2.1 An Example

We are now ready to introduce **differentiation**, the first of two fundamental operations used in the Calculus (the other being **integration**). We start with a physical problem whose mathematical description contains the seed ideas of differential Calculus.

In Section 1.4 we discussed the physical law governing the motion of falling bodies, such as a stone dropped into a well. The distance s that a stone falls in t seconds is given by the formula

$$s - 16t^2 \qquad (s \text{ measured in feet, } t \text{ measured in seconds}) \qquad (1)$$

We may ask what this law tells us about the speed (or velocity) of the stone at various moments during its fall. The surprising fact is that we can determine the speed from formula (1) without any physical measurements. To make things specific we shall determine the speed after one second has elapsed.

What do we know about speed? For one thing, there are two distinct types of speed—average and instantaneous. We are all familiar with the concept of **average**

speed. If we drive 165 miles in 3 hours, our average speed is

$$\frac{165 \text{ miles}}{3 \text{ hours}} = 55 \text{ miles per hour}$$

That is

$$\text{average speed} = \frac{\text{distance travelled}}{\text{time elapsed}} \qquad (2)$$

The concept of **instantaneous speed** (or speed at a given instant) is more subtle. In an "instant" no time elapses and consequently no distance is covered; if we substitute *time elapsed* $= 0$ and *distance travelled* $= 0$ into formula (2) we get the meaningless ratio $0/0$. To discuss instantaneous speed we need a new approach. Taking our cue from motion pictures, suppose we film the fall of a stone. By comparing successive frames, as in Figure 2.1, we may compute the average speed over the time interval

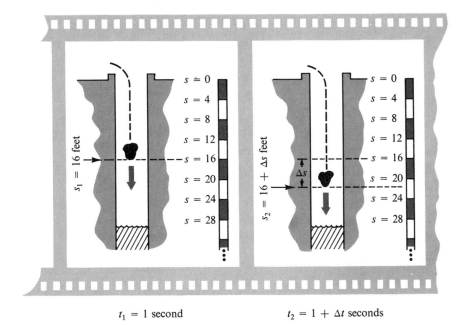

$t_1 = 1$ second $t_2 = 1 + \Delta t$ seconds

Figure 2.1
Here are two successive frames of a motion picture of a falling stone, the first frame taken at time $t_1 = 1$ second and the next at time $t_2 = 1 + \Delta t$ seconds (Δt is the time interval between frames). At time t_1 the stone has fallen $s_1 = 16$ feet. At the later time $t_2 = 1 + \Delta t$, the stone has fallen $s_2 = 16 + \Delta s = 16(1 + \Delta t)^2$ feet. The average speed over this time interval is just $\Delta s/\Delta t$. This average speed approximates the instantaneous speed at time $t = 1$ if the interval Δt is very small.

between frames. If we film more frames per second, we get a better approximation to continuous motion (compare the realism of modern films with those produced 60 years ago). The corresponding average speeds, computed for smaller time intervals, give a better approximation to the instantaneous speed. Here then is the key observation:

> If we fix a time t and consider average speeds for small time intervals beginning at t, then the average speeds tend toward a "limit value" as the time intervals get smaller and smaller. We take this limit value to be the instantaneous speed at time t.

Let us use this idea to find the instantaneous speed of a falling stone at time $t = 1$ second. Since the instantaneous speed is computed by means of average speeds, let us start with a sample calculation of average speed over the interval from $t_1 = 1.0$ to $t_2 = 1.5$. At time $t_1 = 1$ the stone has fallen $s_1 = 16(1)^2 = 16$ feet; at time $t_2 = 1.5$ it has fallen $s_2 = 16(1.5)^2 = 36$ feet. Between these times the stone falls a distance

$$\Delta s = s_2 - s_1 = 36 - 16 = 20 \text{ feet}$$

in an elapsed time of

$$\Delta t = t_2 - t_1 = 1.5 - 1.0 = 0.5 \text{ seconds}$$

Therefore the average speed is

$$\frac{\Delta s}{\Delta t} = \frac{20}{0.5} = 40 \text{ feet per second}$$

Similar computations, taking $t_1 = 1$ and $t_2 = 1 + \Delta t$, yield the average speed for an interval of length Δt seconds. Table 2.1 lists the value of $\Delta s / \Delta t$ for various choices of Δt.

NOTE: If x is a variable, we use the symbol Δx to indicate a change in this variable (difference between two nearby values). Here Δx is a single symbol, which stands for "the change in x." It is quite distinct from the symbol x, which stands for the variable itself. The symbol Δx is read as "delta x."

As shown in Table 2.1, the average speed seems to approach 32 feet per second as the elapsed time Δt decreases toward zero. We could calculate more entries by taking smaller increments, such as $\Delta t = 0.00001$, so that $t_2 = 1 + \Delta t = 1.00001$, but these computations become tedious. There is an easy way to circumvent all this numerical calculation. Using algebra we calculate the average speed over an arbitrary

Final time $t_2 = 1 + \Delta t$	Δt	Final distance s_2	$\Delta s = s_2 - s_1$	Average speed $\dfrac{\Delta s}{\Delta t} = \dfrac{s_2 - s_1}{t_2 - t_1}$
1.5	0.5	36.0	20.0	40.0
1.1	0.1	19.36	3.36	33.6
1.01	0.01	16.3216	0.3216	32.16
1.001	0.001	16.032016	0.032016	32.016
1.000				**32.000**
0.999	−0.001	15.968016	−0.031984	31.984
0.99	−0.01	15.6816	−0.3184	31.84
0.9	−0.1	12.96	−3.04	30.4
0.5	−0.5	4.0	−12.0	24.0

Table 2.1
The average speed $\Delta s/\Delta t$ of a falling stone in the time interval between initial time $t_1 = 1$ and various final times $t_2 = 1 + \Delta t$. During this interval the stone falls $\Delta s = s_2 - s_1 = s_2 - 16$ feet. The average speed is $\Delta s/\Delta t$ feet per second. Notice that the average speeds approach 32.00 whether Δt approaches zero through positive or negative values.

time interval, from $t_1 = 1$ to $t_2 = 1 + \Delta t$. The elapsed time is $t_2 - t_1 = \Delta t$. The initial value of s is $s_1 = 16(1)^2$ and the final value is $s_2 = 16(1 + \Delta t)^2$, obtained by substituting $t = 1 + \Delta t$ into formula (1). The stone falls a net distance

$$\Delta s = s_2 - s_1 = 16(1 + \Delta t)^2 - 16$$

$$= 16(1 + 2(\Delta t) + (\Delta t)^2) - 16$$

$$= 16 + 32(\Delta t) + 16(\Delta t)^2 - 16$$

$$= 32(\Delta t) + 16(\Delta t)^2$$

during this time interval, and the average speed is

$$\frac{\Delta s}{\Delta t} = \frac{32(\Delta t) + 16(\Delta t)^2}{\Delta t}$$

Now we may cancel Δt in the numerator and denominator since $\Delta t \neq 0$, to obtain a much simpler formula

$$\frac{\Delta s}{\Delta t} = 32 + 16 \, \Delta t \text{ feet per second} \tag{3}$$

Notice how easily (3) gives the entries in the last column of Table 2.1 once we are given the value of Δt from column 2.

The average speed cannot be defined if $\Delta t = 0$. To find the limit value of the average speeds we must therefore focus our attention on values of Δt that are close to, but not equal to, zero. Formula (3) shows quite clearly that the average speed $\Delta s/\Delta t$ approaches 32 feet per second as the elapsed time Δt approaches zero, because the constant term 32 stays fixed while the term $16\,\Delta t$ gets very small. Thus we are led to assign the value 32 feet per second as the instantaneous speed of the stone when $t = 1$.

instantaneous speed at time $t = 1$

$=$ limit value of $\Delta s/\Delta t$ as Δt approaches zero

$=$ 32 feet per second

We have determined the instantaneous speed by direct mathematical reasoning, given the formula (1), which describes position as a function of time.

By repeating these calculations (details left as Exercise 1) we could find the instantaneous speed 0.5 seconds after the stone is released. Taking $t_1 = 0.5$ and $t_2 = 0.5 + \Delta t$, the change in time is $t_2 - t_1 = \Delta t$, while the change in s is

$$\Delta s = s_2 - s_1 = 16(0.5 + \Delta t)^2 - 16(0.5)^2 = 16\,\Delta t + 16(\Delta t)^2$$

If $\Delta t \neq 0$ the average speed over this time interval is

$$\frac{\Delta s}{\Delta t} = \frac{16\,\Delta t + 16(\Delta t)^2}{\Delta t} = 16 + 16\,\Delta t$$

As Δt gets very small the second term $16\,\Delta t$ also gets very small, while the first term 16 stays fixed. Consequently

instantaneous speed when $t = 0.5$

$=$ limit value of $\Delta s/\Delta t$ as Δt approaches zero

$=$ 16 feet per second

The same kind of reasoning allows us to find the instantaneous speed at *any* time t. Taking averages for initial time $t_1 = t$ and final time $t_2 = t + \Delta t$ ($\Delta t \neq 0$), we get

$$\frac{\Delta s}{\Delta t} = \frac{16(t + \Delta t)^2 - 16t^2}{\Delta t} = \frac{16t^2 + 32t(\Delta t) + 16(\Delta t)^2 - 16t^2}{\Delta t}$$

$$= 32t + 16\,\Delta t$$

Now t is fixed and Δt approaches zero.* The second term gets very small so that the average speed approaches the value $32t$.

$$\text{instantaneous speed at time } t$$

$$= \text{limit value of } \Delta s/\Delta t \text{ as } \Delta t \text{ approaches zero} \tag{4}$$

$$= 32t \text{ feet per second}$$

for any value of t. For the particular values $t = 1$ or $t = 0.5$, we get the answers presented above.

Exercises

●1. Using the formula $s = 16t^2$ for the falling stone, write out formulas giving

  (*i*) The distance fallen s_1 at time $t_1 = 1/2$

  (*ii*) The distance fallen s_2 at time $t_2 = 1/2 + \Delta t$

  (*iii*) The average speed between times $t_1 = 1/2$ and $t_2 = 1/2 + \Delta t$

  in terms of Δt. Then find the instantaneous speed after $1/2$ second.

●2. Repeat Exercise 1 to find the instantaneous speed after 1.25 seconds.

●3. Use formula (4) to calculate the instantaneous speed of a falling object after the following elapsed times: (*i*) 0.1 second, (*ii*) 1 second, (*iii*) 2 seconds, (*iv*) 10 seconds. Convert your answers to *miles per hour* to get a better intuitive feel for the speeds involved. HINT: One mile $= 5280$ feet.

●4. A stone is dropped down a well 36 feet deep. How many seconds will the stone fall before striking bottom? What is its (instantaneous) speed when it hits bottom?

●5. How long does it take an object to fall (*i*) 1 foot, (*ii*) 10 feet, (*iii*) 100 feet, (*iv*) 1000 feet? HINT: Use the formula $s = 16t^2$. You are given s and must find t.

●6. If a 150-pound object falls from the top of a 10-story building, what will be its speed at impact *expressed in miles per hour*? What happens on a 20-story building? What if the weight of the object is doubled? Take one story to be 10 feet. HINT: One mile $= 5280$ feet, one hour $= 3600$ seconds. Formula (4) gives the speed in feet per second.

●7. In the February 26, 1974 issue of the *New York Times* there appeared a picture with the following caption:

  Dar Robinson made a swan dive off the roof of a seven-story building ... yesterday and, falling 80 feet a second, made a graceful landing into a 20-by-25-foot air cushion. Mr. Robinson, a 26-year-old stunt man from Los Angeles, was demonstrating the use of a new inflatable air bag that, its manufacturer says, could save hundreds of lives in fire and

---

* Again, notice the distinction between t and Δt; Δt is the change in t from its initial value, while t is the initial value itself.

emergency rescue operations. . . . He made one full flip during his one-and-a-half-second descent and landed on his back on a little red square that marks the top of the white air cushion. He disappeared for a moment into the nine-foot-tall cushion as it absorbed the force of his fall. . . .

(*i*) Assume that each story on the building is 10 feet high, and that Robinson fell from rest (that is, he had zero initial velocity). How long did he *actually* descend until landing on the top of the air cushion? With what velocity did he strike the cushion?

(*ii*) Redo (*i*), but assume that each story is 12 feet tall.

(*iii*) If you were the copy editor of the *Times*, what advice would you give to the reporter?

ANSWERS: (*i*) $t = 1.95$ sec, $v = 62.5$ ft/sec; (*ii*) $t = 2.17$ sec, $v = 69.3$ ft/sec; (*iii*) Read this book.

2.2   Average Rate of Change for Arbitrary Functions

In Section 2.1 we determined instantaneous speed by calculating the limit value of average speeds $\Delta s/\Delta t$ as Δt gets smaller and smaller. In this section we shall generalize this process, to calculate the rate of change of an arbitrary function $y = f(x)$. If the value of x is changed from an initial value x_1 to a new value x_2, the change in x is

$$\Delta x = x_2 - x_1$$

There is a corresponding change in the dependent variable y, namely

$$\Delta y = y_2 - y_1 = f(x_2) - f(x_1)$$

If $x_1 \neq x_2$ we define the **average rate of change** of y as x changes from $x = x_1$ to $x = x_2$ by the formula

$$\text{average rate of change} = \frac{\Delta y}{\Delta x} = \frac{y_2 - y_1}{x_2 - x_1} = \frac{f(x_2) - f(x_1)}{x_2 - x_1} \tag{5}$$

Sometimes the changes Δx and Δy are called the **increments** in x and y. We shall use this term frequently.

Example 1   Let $y = f(x) = x^3$. Taking $x_1 = 1$ and $x_2 = 3$, find the increments Δx and Δy, and the average rate of change $\Delta y/\Delta x$.

Solution   In going from $x_1 = 1$ to $x_2 = 3$ we find that

$$\Delta x = x_2 - x_1 = 3 - 1 = 2$$

The corresponding values of y are

$$y_2 = f(x_2) = f(3) = 3^3 = 27$$

$$y_1 = f(x_1) = f(1) = 1^3 = 1$$

Hence

$$\Delta y = y_2 - y_1 = 27 - 1 = 26$$

and the average rate of change is

$$\frac{\Delta y}{\Delta x} = \frac{26}{2} = 13$$

In specific applications the variables and the averages $\Delta y/\Delta x$ take on specific meanings.

Example 2 Suppose that the profit P of a manufacturer is related to the level of production q by the formula

$$P = 50q - 0.04q^2 - 10{,}000$$

Find the increment ΔP corresponding to a change in production level from $q_1 = 500$ to $q_2 = 600$ units. Find the average rate of change. What does it mean?

Solution At production level $q_1 = 500$ the profit is

$$P_1 = 50q_1 - 0.04q_1{}^2 - 10{,}000$$

$$= 50(500) - 0.04(500)^2 - 10{,}000$$

$$= 25{,}000 - 10{,}000 - 10{,}000 = 5000$$

If $q_2 = 600$, the profit is

$$P_2 = 50q_2 - 0.04q_2{}^2 - 10{,}000$$

$$= 50(600) - 0.04(600)^2 - 10{,}000$$

$$= 30{,}000 - 14{,}400 - 10{,}000 = 5600$$

Hence the increment in profit is

$$\Delta P = P_2 - P_1 = 5600 - 5000 = 600 \text{ dollars}$$

That is, the plant increases its profit by $\Delta P = \$600$ if the production level is increased by $\Delta q = 100$ units from 500 to 600. In general, $\Delta P > 0$ means that the production level q_2 is more profitable than the initial production level q_1, and $\Delta P < 0$ means that the production level q_2 is less profitable. The average $\Delta P/\Delta q = 600/100 = \$6$ per unit represents the average increase in profit for each of the 100 additional units produced when q is increased from 500 to 600.

The next example gives a geometric interpretation of the average rate of change.

Example 3   Given the function $y = f(x) = 2 + x + x^2$, find the average rate of change in y as x increases from $x_1 = 0$ to $x_2 = 1$.

Solution   Notice that $\Delta x = x_2 - x_1 = 1 - 0 = 1$; x moves one unit to the right on the horizontal axis in Figure 2.2. Thus

$$y_2 = 2 + 1 + 1^2 = 4 \quad \text{and} \quad y_1 = 2 + 0 + 0^2 = 2$$

so that

$$\Delta y = y_2 - y_1 = 4 - 2 - 2$$

The average rate of change in y with respect to x is therefore

$$\frac{\Delta y}{\Delta x} = \frac{2}{1} = 2$$

If $P_1 = (x_1, y_1) = (0, 2)$ and $P_2 = (x_2, y_2) = (1, 4)$ are the points on the graph of f over $x - 0$ and $x = 1$ on the horizontal axis, the average $\Delta y/\Delta x$ is just the slope of the straight line L passing through these points (see Figure 2.2).

This is true for any function $y = f(x)$. The average $\Delta y/\Delta x$ is always the slope of the line joining the corresponding pair of points on the graph of f.

Exercises

●1. Calculate the change Δy in the function $y = x^2 - x + 1$ as x changes from
   (*i*) $x_1 = 0$ to $x_2 = 1$
   (*ii*) $x_1 = 1$ to $x_2 = 2$
   (*iii*) $x_1 = 1$ to $x_2 = -1$
   (*iv*) $x_1 = 2$ to $x_2 = 2 + \Delta x$

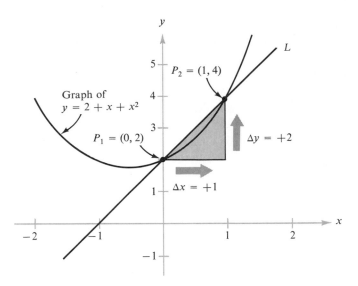

Figure 2.2
The graph of $y = 2 + x + x^2$ is a parabola. Points $P_1 = (0, 2)$ and
$P_2 = (1, 4)$ lie on it. As x moves from $x_1 = 0$ to $x_2 = 1$, there is an
increment $\Delta x = +1$ as shown, while $\Delta y = +2$. The average rate of
change is $\Delta y/\Delta x = +2/+1 = 2$. This average is precisely the slope
of the straight line L joining P_1 and P_2. In general, such a line is called
a *secant line*.

●2. In Exercise 1, calculate the average rates of change $\Delta y/\Delta x$.

●3. Let $y = f(x) = 1/x$. Taking the initial point $x_1 = 2$ and final point $x_2 = 2 + \Delta x$, find the
increment Δy if

    (*i*) $\Delta x = 1$ (*iii*) $\Delta x = -1$

    (*ii*) $\Delta x = 0.5$ (*iv*) $\Delta x = -0.5$

●4. Let $s = 4 - 3t$. Find the average rate of change of s with respect to t between $t_1 = 1$ and
$t_2 = 3$. What is the average rate of change between *arbitrary* t_1 and t_2? Answer: $\Delta s/\Delta t =
-3$ for any choice of t_1 and t_2.

◑5. Given $y = f(x) = x^2$, find the average rate of change of y with respect to x between

    (*i*) $x_1 = 1$ and $x_2 = 3$ (*ii*) $x_1 = 0$ and $x_2 = 2$

Draw the graph of the function and interpret these averages geometrically.

●6. If the cost per week of manufacturing an inexpensive transistorized audio amplifier is given by

$$C(q) = 50{,}000 + 100q - 0.1q^2$$

where q is the number of units produced per week, find the cost of producing (*i*) 500 units
per week and (*ii*) 600 units per week. What is the average rate of change of C with respect to
q, $\Delta C/\Delta q$, if the production level is increased from $q_1 = 500$ to $q_2 = 600$ units per week?

7. Suppose a ball thrown straight up in the air has height $h(t) = 64t - 16t^2$ after t seconds. The

average velocity over any time interval is just $\Delta h/\Delta t$. This velocity can be positive or negative: positive velocities correspond to a net increase in height h, negative velocities to a net decrease. Calculate the average velocity over the following time intervals:

(i) $t_1 = 0$ to $t_2 = 2.0$ (iii) $t_1 = 2.0$ to $t_2 = 3.0$

(ii) $t_1 = 0$ to $t_2 = 3.0$ (iv) $t_1 = 0$ to $t_2 = 4.0$

What is the physical interpretation of the zero average velocity in (iv)?

*●8. Consider $y = f(x) = x^3 + x$ and a fixed base point $x_1 = x$. For nearby values $x_2 = x + \Delta x$, write out formulas for

$$(i)\ \ y_2 = f(x_2) \qquad (ii)\ \ \Delta y = y_2 - y_1 \qquad (iii)\ \ \Delta y/\Delta x$$

Does $\Delta y/\Delta x$ approach a limiting value as Δx gets small? ANSWER: Limit value is $3x^2 + 1$ for any x.

2.3   The Derivative of a Function

Instantaneous speed has been defined as the limit value of the average speed $\Delta s/\Delta t$ as the elapsed time Δt approached zero. Likewise we may define the **instantaneous rate of change** of a function $y = f(x)$ to be the limit value of the averages $\Delta y/\Delta x$ as Δx approaches zero. The method we shall use is patterned after that in Section 2.1.

The "Delta Process" for Calculating Instantaneous Rate of Change   Fix a base point $x_1 = x$ and consider the values of f at nearby points $x_2 = x + \Delta x$ for small increments $\Delta x \neq 0$. Then compute as follows:

STEP 1   The value of f at the base point, namely $y_1 = f(x)$

STEP 2   The value of f at the nearby point, namely $y_2 = f(x + \Delta x)$

STEP 3   The corresponding change in y, $\Delta y = y_2 - y_1 = f(x + \Delta x) - f(x)$

STEP 4   The average rate of change over the interval from $x_1 = x$ to $x_2 = x + \Delta x$

$$\frac{\Delta y}{\Delta x} = \frac{y_2 - y_1}{x_2 - x_1} = \frac{f(x + \Delta x) - f(x)}{\Delta x}$$

STEP 5   The limit value of these averages as Δx approaches zero. If this limit exists we call it the **instantaneous rate of change of y with respect to x** at the point $x = x_1$.

The limit value of the averages $\Delta y/\Delta x$ is denoted by the following symbol

$$\lim_{\Delta x \to 0} \left\{ \frac{\Delta y}{\Delta x} \right\} \tag{6}$$

which is read as "*the limit of $\Delta y/\Delta x$ as Δx approaches zero.*" As an example of its use in practice, recall Section 2.1 where we considered $s = 16t^2$ near the base point $t = 1$. The averages were $\Delta s/\Delta t = 32 + 16(\Delta t)$, and they approached the limit value 32 as Δt approached zero. This we indicate by writing

$$\lim_{\Delta t \to 0} \left\{ \frac{\Delta s}{\Delta t} \right\} = 32 \quad \text{or} \quad \lim_{\Delta t \to 0} \{32 + 16(\Delta t)\} = 32$$

Here is a detailed example of the use of the delta process.

Example 4   Calculate the instantaneous rate of change of the function $y = f(x) = x^3$ at the base point $x = 1$. Then calculate the instantaneous rate of change at an arbitrary base point x.

Solution   STEPS 1 AND 2   Taking base point $x_1 = 1$ and nearby point $x_2 = 1 + \Delta x$ (with $\Delta x \neq 0$) we get

$$y_2 = (1 + \Delta x)^3 = 1 + 3(\Delta x) + 3(\Delta x)^2 + (\Delta x)^3$$

$$y_1 = 1^3 = 1$$

STEP 3   We get Δy by taking the difference $y_2 - y_1$

$$\Delta y = 3(\Delta x) + 3(\Delta x)^2 + (\Delta x)^3$$

STEP 4   Dividing by Δx we obtain the average rate of change

$$\frac{\Delta y}{\Delta x} = \frac{3(\Delta x) + 3(\Delta x)^2 + (\Delta x)^3}{\Delta x} = 3 + 3(\Delta x) + (\Delta x)^2$$

STEP 5   Obviously the first term, 3, stays fixed while the last two terms, involving Δx and $(\Delta x)^2$, get very small as Δx tends toward zero. Thus

$$\lim_{\Delta x \to 0} \left\{ \frac{\Delta y}{\Delta x} \right\} = \lim_{\Delta x \to 0} \{3 + 3(\Delta x) + (\Delta x)^2\}$$

exists and is equal to 3. This is the instantaneous rate of change at the base point $x = 1$.

For an arbitrary base point $x_1 = x$ we let $x_2 = x + \Delta x$. It follows that

$$y_2 = (x_2)^3 = (x + \Delta x)^3 = x^3 + 3x^2(\Delta x) + 3x(\Delta x)^2 + (\Delta x)^3$$

$$y_1 = (x_1)^3 = x^3$$

Hence

$$\Delta y = y_2 - y_1 = x^3 + 3x^2(\Delta x) + 3x(\Delta x)^2 + (\Delta x)^3 - x^3$$

$$= 3x^2(\Delta x) + 3x(\Delta x)^2 + (\Delta x)^3$$

The average rate of change is

$$\frac{\Delta y}{\Delta x} = \frac{3x^2(\Delta x) + 3x(\Delta x)^2 + (\Delta x)^3}{\Delta x} = 3x^2 + 3x(\Delta x) + (\Delta x)^2$$

for all small increments $\Delta x \neq 0$. Now let Δx get smaller and smaller. The base point $x = x_1$ does not vary, so the first term $3x^2$ stays fixed. The last two terms obviously get smaller and smaller as Δx approaches zero, so that

instantaneous rate of change of $y = x^3$ at any base point x

$$= \lim_{\Delta x \to 0} \left\{ \frac{\Delta y}{\Delta x} \right\} = 3x^2$$

If $x = 1$, the instantaneous rate of change is $3(1)^2 = 3$, as we found above. At another base point, say $x = 2$, we get a different rate of change, namely $3(2)^2 = 12$.

The instantaneous rate of change of a function $y = f(x)$ is called the **derivative** of f with respect to x.

Definition Given a function $y = f(x)$ and a point x in its domain of definition, we define the **derivative** $f'(x)$ of f at the base point x to be

$$f'(x) = \lim_{\Delta x \to 0} \left\{ \frac{f(x + \Delta x) - f(x)}{\Delta x} \right\} = \lim_{\Delta x \to 0} \left\{ \frac{\Delta y}{\Delta x} \right\} \tag{7}$$

provided this limit exists. In that case we say that f is **differentiable at** x.

If we apply the delta process to a function $f(x)$ we obtain its derivative $f'(x)$, which is a new function of the variable x. Various symbols are used for the derivative. In this book we shall use

$$f' \qquad y' \qquad \frac{df}{dx} \qquad \frac{dy}{dx} \qquad \frac{d}{dx}\{f(x)\} \tag{8}$$

interchangeably. It must be emphasized that both df/dx and dy/dx are single symbols, just as Δy is a single symbol. That is, the derivative dy/dx is not the ratio of two quantities dy and dx, even though it is the limit of ratios $\Delta y/\Delta x$. We could have tried to use just one of the symbols (8) throughout the book, but certain formulas are more suggestive if we use the appropriate notation. In some books you may find still other symbols for the derivative of a function $y = f(x)$, such as

$$Dy \qquad Df \qquad \dot{y} \qquad \dot{f}$$

They all stand for the same thing—the derivative function defined above.

Example 5   Let $y = f(x)$ be the constant function $y = 1$ for all x. Compute its derivative

$$\frac{dy}{dx} = \frac{d}{dx}\{1\}$$

Solution   For any point x and nearby point $x + \Delta x$, we find that

$$y = 1 \text{ at } x \quad \text{and} \quad y = 1 \text{ at } x + \Delta x$$

so that the increment in y is $\Delta y = 0$. Since $\Delta y/\Delta x = 0$ for *all* increments $\Delta x \neq 0$, the limit value of these averages is also zero:

$$\frac{dy}{dx} = \lim_{\Delta x \to 0}\left\{\frac{\Delta y}{\Delta x}\right\} = 0 \tag{9}$$

In other words, if y never changes as x varies, the instantaneous rate of change of y with respect to x is zero. The conclusion (9) holds for every base point x. Expressing the derivative as a function of x, we have $f'(x) = 0$ (a constant function) for all x.

The same conclusion applies to any constant function $f(x)$: its derivative is zero everywhere.

By similar reasoning we could compute the derivatives of $y = x$ and $y = x^2$ (see Exercises 1 and 2).

$$\frac{d}{dx}\{x\} = 1 \qquad \text{everywhere (constant function)}$$

$$\frac{d}{dx}\{x^2\} = 2x \tag{10}$$

We have already calculated the derivative of $y = f(x) = x^3$ in Example 4. There, referring to it as the instantaneous rate of change of $y = x^3$ with respect to x, we found that

$$f'(x) = \frac{d}{dx}\{x^3\} = \lim_{\Delta x \to 0} \left\{\frac{\Delta y}{\Delta x}\right\} = 3x^2$$

for any base point x. In particular, if we want the value of f' at $x = 2$ we just substitute $x = 2$ into this formula, $f'(2) = 3(2)^2 = 12$. Here are two more examples of the use of the delta process.

Example 6   In Example 2, the profit P was related to the level of production q by the formula $P = 50q - 0.04q^2 - 10,000$. Find the instantaneous rate of change of P with respect to q at production level $q = 600$. Give an economic interpretation of this rate of change.

Solution   Taking $q_1 = 600$ and nearby point $q_2 = 600 + \Delta q$, we get

$$P_2 = P(600 + \Delta q) = 50(600 + \Delta q) - 0.04(600 + \Delta q)^2 - 10,000$$

$$= 5600 + 2(\Delta q) - 0.04(\Delta q)^2$$

$$P_1 = P(600) = 50(600) - 0.04(600)^2 - 10,000 = 5600$$

so that

$$\Delta P = P_2 - P_1 = 2(\Delta q) - 0.04(\Delta q)^2$$

$$\frac{\Delta P}{\Delta q} = 2 - 0.04(\Delta q) \qquad \text{for all } \Delta q \neq 0$$

Clearly, this average tends toward the limit value 2 as Δq approaches zero:

$$\text{instantaneous rate of change} = \lim_{\Delta q \to 0} \frac{\Delta P}{\Delta q} = \lim_{\Delta q \to 0} \{2 - 0.04(\Delta q)\} = 2$$

That is, for small increments Δq away from the base level $q = 600$ we have

$$\frac{\Delta P}{\Delta q} \approx 2 \quad \text{or} \quad \Delta P \approx 2(\Delta q)$$

where ($\approx$) stands for "approximately equal to." This leads to a natural interpretation of the rate of change: if we increase production by *one unit* ($\Delta q = 1$) starting from the base level $q = 600$, we find that the profit increases by $\Delta P \approx 2(\Delta q) = \$2.00$. The instantaneous rate of change tells us (approximately) the profitability of producing additional units starting from production level $q = 600$; P increases by about \$2.00 for each additional unit produced, as long as Δq does not get too large.

The next example is a little more complicated, and introduces some new ideas for dealing with limits.

Example 7   If $y = \dfrac{1}{x^2}$, find the derivative $\dfrac{dy}{dx} = \dfrac{d}{dx}\left\{\dfrac{1}{x^2}\right\}$.

Solution   The function is undefined at $x = 0$. Derivatives can be defined only at points where f is defined, so there is no derivative at $x = 0$. For base points $x \neq 0$ we are interested in the behavior of $\Delta y/\Delta x$ for small increments $\Delta x \neq 0$. Then

$$y = \frac{1}{(x + \Delta x)^2} \quad \text{at } x + \Delta x \qquad y = \frac{1}{x^2} \quad \text{at } x$$

so that

$$\Delta y = \frac{1}{(x + \Delta x)^2} - \frac{1}{x^2}$$

$$\frac{\Delta y}{\Delta x} = \frac{\dfrac{1}{(x + \Delta x)^2} - \dfrac{1}{x^2}}{\Delta x} \qquad \text{for all small } \Delta x \neq 0$$

The limit value of $\Delta y/\Delta x$ is not at all apparent from this formula. But if we simplify the expression algebraically, some of the Δx cancel and it is easier to see what happens as Δx gets small.

$$\frac{\Delta y}{\Delta x} = \frac{\dfrac{1}{(x + \Delta x)^2} - \dfrac{1}{x^2}}{\Delta x} = \frac{x^2 - (x + \Delta x)^2}{x^2(x + \Delta x)^2(\Delta x)}$$

$$= \frac{x^2 - x^2 - 2x(\Delta x) - (\Delta x)^2}{x^2(x + \Delta x)^2(\Delta x)}$$

$$= \frac{(-2x - \Delta x)(\Delta x)}{x^2(x + \Delta x)^2(\Delta x)}$$

$$= \frac{-2x - \Delta x}{x^2(x^2 + 2x(\Delta x) + (\Delta x)^2)}$$

$$= \frac{-2x - \Delta x}{x^4 + 2x^3(\Delta x) + x^2(\Delta x)^2}$$

Now the numerator and denominator have well defined limit values as Δx gets small. All terms involving Δx get small while the remaining terms stay fixed:

$$\lim_{\Delta x \to 0} \{-2x - \Delta x\} = -2x$$

$$\lim_{\Delta x \to 0} \{x^4 + 2x^3(\Delta x) + x^2(\Delta x)^2\} = x^4$$

Clearly, if the numerator gets close to $-2x$ and the denominator gets close to x^4, then the quotient gets close to $-2x/x^4$. Therefore

$$f'(x) = \lim_{\Delta x \to 0} \left\{ \frac{\Delta y}{\Delta x} \right\} = \frac{-2x}{x^4} = \frac{-2}{x^3}$$

This analysis applies to every point $x \neq 0$, so that

$$\frac{d}{dx} \left\{ \frac{1}{x^2} \right\} = \frac{-2}{x^3}$$

Using the delta process to calculate derivatives can be very time-consuming, although sometimes there is no way to avoid it. In Chapter 3 we shall develop rules for calculating derivatives without using the delta process. For the moment, however, we shall set aside the problem of how to compute derivatives and get on to the important business of explaining what the derivative means and how it can be used. For this reason we shall borrow a simple differentiation rule from Chapter 3, and use it without proof in the rest of this chapter.

Many functions we encounter are **polynomials**, simple combinations of the powers $x^0 = 1$, $x^1 = x$, x^2, x^3, ... of the form

$$y = f(x) = a_0 + a_1 x + a_2 x^2 + \cdots + a_n x^n \tag{11}$$

where $a_0, a_1, a_2, \ldots, a_n$ are constants. For example, the profit function $P - -10{,}000 + 50q - 0.04q^2$ in Example 6 is a polynomial in the variable q (with $a_0 = -10{,}000$, $a_1 - 50$, $a_2 = -0.04$), and so are such functions as

$$y = x^3 + 3x - 7$$

$$y = -6x^4 + 20x^3 - x + 5$$

$$y = 3 - x \tag{12}$$

$$y = -14 \quad \text{(constant function, } a_0 = -14\text{)}$$

The derivatives of simple powers $y = x^n$ are easy to compute. From examples above, or the exercises below, it is evident that

$$\frac{d}{dx}\{1\} = 0 \qquad \frac{d}{dx}\{x\} = 1 \qquad \frac{d}{dx}\{x^2\} = 2x$$

$$\frac{d}{dx}\{x^3\} = 3x^2 \qquad \frac{d}{dx}\{x^4\} = 4x^3$$

In Section 3.1 we shall use the delta process to show that the simple pattern emerging here is valid for all powers $y = x^n$:

$$\frac{d}{dx}\{x^n\} = nx^{n-1} \qquad \text{for } n = 0, 1, 2, 3, \ldots \tag{13}$$

In Section 3.2 we shall show, further, that the derivative of any polynomial $y = a_0 + a_1x + a_2x^2 + \cdots + a_nx^n$ is readily calculated once we know how to differentiate simple powers:

$$\frac{dy}{dx} = a_0\frac{d}{dx}\{1\} + a_1\frac{d}{dx}\{x\} + a_2\frac{d}{dx}\{x^2\} + \cdots + a_n\frac{d}{dx}\{x^n\}$$

$$= 0 + a_1 + 2a_2x + 3a_3x^2 + \cdots + na_nx^{n-1} \tag{14}$$

For example, the derivatives of the functions (12) are

$$\frac{d}{dx}\{x^3 + 3x - 7\} = \frac{d}{dx}\{x^3\} + 3\frac{d}{dx}\{x\} - 7\frac{d}{dx}\{1\}$$

$$= 3x^2 + 3(1) - 7(0) = 3x^2 + 3$$

$$\frac{d}{dx}\{-6x^4 + 20x^3 - x + 5\} = -6\frac{d}{dx}\{x^4\} + 20\frac{d}{dx}\{x^3\} - \frac{d}{dx}\{x\} + 5\frac{d}{dx}\{1\}$$

$$= -6(4x^3) + 20(3x^2) - 1(1) + 5(0) = -24x^3 + 60x^2 - 1$$

$$\frac{d}{dx}\{3 - x\} = 3\frac{d}{dx}\{1\} - \frac{d}{dx}\{x\} = 3(0) - 1(1) = -1 \quad \text{(constant function)}$$

$$\frac{d}{dx}\{-14\} = -14\frac{d}{dx}\{1\} = -14(0) = 0 \quad \text{(constant function)}$$

Labeling the variable q instead of x, we may compute the derivative of the profit function mentioned above:

$$\frac{dP}{dq} = -10,000 \frac{d}{dq}\{1\} + 50 \frac{d}{dq}\{q\} - 0.04 \frac{d}{dq}\{q^2\}$$

$$= -10,000(0) + 50(1) - 0.04(2q) = 50 - 0.08q$$

Exercises

● 1. Calculate the derivative of $y = f(x) = x$ by using the delta process. ANSWER: $f'(x) = 1$ for all x (constant function).

● 2. Use the delta process to show that

  (i) $\dfrac{d}{dx}\{x^2\} = 2x$ (iii) $\dfrac{d}{dx}\{x^4\} = 4x^3$

  (ii) $\dfrac{d}{dx}\{3 - 4x\} = -4$ (constant)   (iv) $\dfrac{d}{dx}\left\{\dfrac{1}{x}\right\} = -\dfrac{1}{x^2}$ $(x \neq 0)$

  for any base point x.

● 3. Use the delta process to calculate the derivative

$$f'(x) = \lim_{\Delta x \to 0} \frac{\Delta y}{\Delta x}$$

  for the function $y = f(x) = 4 - x^2$. What is the value of f' when $x = 2$? For which value of x is $f'(x) = 1$? $f'(x) = 0$?

● 4. Calculate dy/dx by using the delta process if

  (i) $y = 2 - 3x$ (ii) $y = x^2 - x - 1$ (iii) $y = x - x^3$

● 5. Calculate the derivatives in Exercise 4 using the formula (14) for differentiating polynomials.

● 6. Use the differentiation rules (13) and (14) to find the following derivatives:

  (i) $f'(x)$ if $f(x) = x^7$ (v) $P'(q)$ if $P(q) = -10 + 3q$
  (ii) $f'(1)$ if $f(x) = x^7$ (vi) $f'(x)$ if $f(x) = 1 - x^4$
  (iii) $f'(-2)$ if $f(x) = x^2 + 2x + 3$ (vii) $f'(r)$ if $f(r) = 1 - r^4$
  (iv) $f'(x)$ if $f(x) = x^4 - x^2 + 2x$ (viii) $f'(x)$ if $f(x) = (1 + x)(1 + x^2)$

● 7. If a ball thrown straight up in the air has height $h(t) = 64t - 16t^2$ after t seconds, its instantaneous velocity at time t is just the rate of change dh/dt. Calculate velocity as a function of time (i) using the delta process; (ii) using formula (14).

● 8. On the surface of the moon the position of a falling body is given by the following equation:

$$s(t) = 2.33t^2 \qquad (s \text{ in feet, } t \text{ in seconds})$$

Calculate the instantaneous speed $ds/dt = s'(t)$ after t seconds, using the delta process. ANSWER: $ds/dt = 4.66t$ ft/sec.

● 9. Using the result of Exercise 8, determine the impact speed of an object dropped from the top of a 5-story building on the moon. Convert your answer from feet per second to miles per hour. Do you think you would survive a leap from a height of 5 stories on the moon? (One story = 11 feet) HINT: First calculate impact time from $s = 2.33t^2$. ANSWER: Impact time $t = 4.86$ sec; impact speed = 22.6 ft/sec = 15.4 mph; probably survive.

●10. Using the cost function $C(q) = 50{,}000 + 100q - 0.1q^2$, calculate

(i) ΔC (ii) the average rate of change $\Delta C/\Delta q$

for an arbitrary increment Δq from the base production level $q = 250$ units per week. What is the limit value of the average $\Delta C/\Delta q$ as you take smaller and smaller increments Δq? (This is the instantaneous rate of change of C with respect to q when $q = 250$.) ANSWER: Rate of change is 50 dollars/unit when $q = 250$.

*●11. The area A of a circle with radius r is $A(r) = \pi r^2$. Use formula (14) to show that $dA/dr = 2\pi r$. Draw two circles with the same center, one with radius r and the other with radius $r + \Delta r$. Then interpret ΔA as the area between these two circles. If Δr is small, is there a relation between $\Delta A/\Delta r$ and the circumference $2\pi r$ of the circle of radius r? Can you now give a geometric argument why dA/dr turns out to be the length of the circumference of the circle?

●12. Use the delta process to show that a *linear function* $y = Ax + B$ (A, B constants) has derivative

$$\frac{d}{dx}\{Ax + B\} = A \quad \text{(constant function)} \qquad \text{for all } x$$

2.4   Derivatives and Tangent Lines to Curves

If $y = f(x)$ is differentiable at a point $x = p$, there is an interesting and useful geometric interpretation of the derivative $f'(p)$ in terms of the graph of f. Through the point on the graph over $x = p$ there is a unique straight line L that passes through this point and is "tangent" to the curve. The slope of this tangent line turns out to be equal to the derivative $f'(p)$.

You have probably encountered the term "tangent line" in connection with circles. This concept may also apply to a curve that is the graph of some function $y = f(x)$. Given a point P on the graph we seek a straight line L through P that satisfies our intuitive notion of what a tangent line should be. If P and Q are points on a circle, as in Figure 2.3, we may join them by a straight line L_{PQ}, called the **secant line** through P and Q. If Q is allowed to move toward P, then L_{PQ} approaches L, the usual tangent line through P.

For general curves, such as the one in Figure 2.4, we may take nearby points Q on the graph, let Q approach P, and ask whether the line L_{PQ} joining P to Q approaches a limiting position. If it does, we take the line L in the limiting position to be the tangent line through P; if it does not, then there is no tangent line through P. One technical

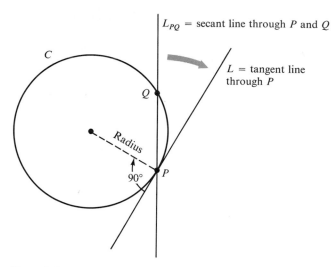

Figure 2.3
The tangent line to a point P on a circle is the limit of the secant lines L_{PQ} as Q approaches P.

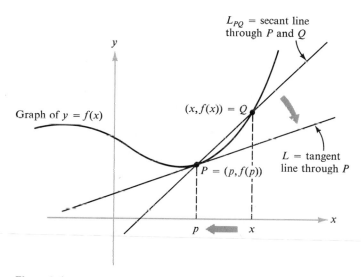

Figure 2.4
The tangent line L through a point P on the graph of $y = f(x)$. As Q moves along the graph toward P, the line L_{PQ} through P and Q approaches a limiting position. The limiting line L is called the *tangent line* to the graph at P. The lines through P and nearby points Q are called *secant lines* through P. In the figure, $P = (p, f(p))$ and $Q = (x, f(x))$, with $x \neq p$.

detail remains. We must make precise the notion "approaches a limiting position." Each of the lines passes through P, and so is completely determined by its slope. We say that the line L_{PQ} approaches a limit line L if slope(L_{PQ}) approaches slope(L) as Q approaches P.

Thus, for a function $y = f(x)$ and a point P on its graph corresponding to some base point $x = p$ on the horizontal axis, the **tangent line** L through P is defined to be the line through P whose slope is given by

$$\text{slope}(L) = \lim_{x \to p} \text{slope}(L_{PQ}) \tag{15}$$

Here the nearby point on the graph has the form $Q = (x, f(x))$ for x close to the base value p, as in Figure 2.4. To see how slope (L) is related to the derivative of f, we write $x = p + \Delta x \, (\Delta x \neq 0)$. Since L passes through P and Q, we find that

$$\text{slope}(L_{PQ}) = \frac{\Delta y}{\Delta x} = \frac{f(x) - f(p)}{x - p} = \frac{f(p + \Delta x) - f(p)}{\Delta x}$$

Since $\Delta x = x - p$ approaches zero as x gets close to p. we see that

$$\text{slope}(L) = \lim_{x \to p} \text{slope}(L_{PQ}) = \lim_{\Delta x \to 0} \frac{f(p + \Delta x) - f(p)}{\Delta x} = f'(p)$$

is the derivative of f evaluated at p. This may be summarized as follows:

Derivative as Slope of the Tangent Line   There is a well-defined tangent line to the graph of $y = f(x)$ at the point P on the graph above $x = p$ if f is differentiable at p. The slope of the tangent line through P is equal to the derivative $f'(p)$.

Example 8   If $y = f(x) = x + x^2$, find the slope of the tangent line through $P = (1, 2)$ on the graph. Find the equation of this tangent line.

Solution   The point P lies above $x = 1$ on the x-axis. By the above, the slope of the tangent line through P is equal to $f'(1)$. We use the differentiation rule for polynomials (14) to compute

$$f'(x) = \frac{d}{dx}\{x + x^2\} = \frac{d}{dx}\{x\} + \frac{d}{dx}\{x^2\} = 1 + 2x$$

If $x = 1$ we get $f'(1) = 1 + 2(1) = 3$. This is the slope of the tangent line through $P = (1, 2)$. Figure 2.5 shows this tangent line L; it also shows a typical secant line L_{PQ} passing through P and a nearby point Q on the graph, indicating how L_{PQ}

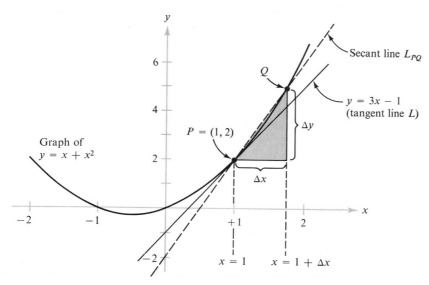

Figure 2.5
The tangent line through $P = (1, 2)$ on the graph of $y - f(x) = x + x^2$ has slope
$f'(1) = 3$. If Q corresponds to $x = 1 + \Delta x$, so that $Q = (1 + \Delta x, f(1 + \Delta x))$, the slope
of the secant line L_{PQ} is $\Delta y/\Delta x = 3 + \Delta x$. As Q approaches P, Δx must approach zero
and slope $(L_{PQ}) = 3 + \Delta x$ approaches the value $f'(1) = 3$. (See Exercise 2 for
calculation: slope $(L_{PQ}) = 3 + \Delta x$.)

approaches L. The equation of the tangent line is determined by its slope and the
coordinates of P:

$$3 - \text{slope} - \frac{\Delta y}{\Delta x} = \frac{y - 2}{x - 1} \qquad \text{for any point } (x, y) \text{ on } L$$

This may be rewritten in the form $3(x - 1) = y - 2$ or $y = 3x - 1$.

Example 9   Find the slope of the tangent line to the graph of $y = x^3$ at the point
$P = (2, 8)$.

Solution   Here $f(x) = x^3$. The required slope is $f'(2)$. Using formula (13), we have
$f'(x) = 3x^2$ for any x, so that $f'(2) = 12$ is the slope of the tangent line.

Exercises

1. Let P and Q be the points on the graph of $y = x + x^2$ corresponding to $x = 1$ and $x = 1 +$
   Δx $(\Delta x \neq 0)$. On a single piece of graph paper sketch the graph of $y = x + x^2$ and plot the

points Q for $\Delta x = +1.0$, $\Delta x = +0.5$, and $\Delta x = +0.2$. Then sketch

  (*i*) the corresponding secant lines L_{PQ}

  (*ii*) the tangent line L through $P = (1, 2)$

Do the secant lines L_{PQ} really approach L? Calculate the slopes slope(L_{PQ}) and compare with slope(L) = 3.0. HINT: Refer to Example 8.

●2. If $y = x + x^2$. find the coordinates of the points P and Q on the graph above $x = 1$ and $x = 1 + \Delta x$ (in terms of Δx). Show that the slope of the secant line is slope(L_{PQ}) = $3 + \Delta x$. What does this tell you about the slope of the tangent line through P?

●3. Calculate the slope of the tangent line through the given point on the graph for the following functions:

  (*i*) $f(x) = 1 - x^2$ at $P = (-2, -3)$

  (*ii*) $f(x) = 1 - x^2$ at $P = (0, 1)$

  (*iii*) $f(x) = x^4 - x + 1$ at $P = (1, 1)$

HINT: Use the differentiation formulas (13) and (14).

●4. If $y = f(x) = x^2$, find the slope of the tangent line through $P = (1, 1)$ on the graph. Find the equation of the tangent line through $P = (1, 1)$. On the same piece of graph paper draw the graph of $y = x^2$ and the tangent line through P.

●5. Calculate the derivative of $y = x^2 - 12x$. Then find all points on the graph for which the tangent line is *horizontal* (slope is zero).

●6. If $y = x^3$, determine the equation of the tangent line through each of the following points on the graph.

  (*i*) $(-1, -1)$ (*ii*) $(0, 0)$ (*iii*) $(2, 8)$

What is the slope in each case?

●7. The derivative of $y = 1/x^2$ is $dy/dx = -2/x^3$ (Example 7). Calculate the equation of the tangent line to the curve $y = 1/x^2$ through the point $(1, 1)$. What is its slope?

2.5   The Approximation Principle

Suppose we know the value of a function f at some base point p and want to compute its values $f(x)$ at points x close to p. If the formula for f is at all complicated this can be tedious. For example, if $f(x) = \sqrt{x}$ we know the value at $p = 100$, but calculating $f(x)$ for a nearby point such as $x = 103$ will take some time unless we can resort to tables or other devices. However, if f is differentiable at p there is a very simple approximation formula for values at nearby points. In fact, for $x \neq p$ the averages

$$\frac{\Delta f}{\Delta x} = \frac{f(x) - f(p)}{x - p}$$

approach the limit value $f'(p)$ as x gets close to p, by definition of the derivative. This means that

$$\frac{\Delta f}{\Delta x} \approx f'(p) \qquad \text{for all } x \text{ near } p$$

where "$\approx$" stands for "approximately equal to." We may rewrite this as

$$\Delta f \approx f'(p) \cdot \Delta x \qquad \text{for all } x \text{ near } p \tag{16}$$

In other words, the change $\Delta f = f(x) - f(p)$ corresponding to an increment $\Delta x = x - p$ away from p is roughly proportional to Δx. To put it another way, $\Delta f = f'(p) \cdot \Delta x$ plus an "error term" that gets very small compared to the "principal term" $f'(p) \cdot \Delta x$ as x approaches p.

Here is an example of the use of formula (16).

Example 10   Estimate $\sqrt{103}$ by using the approximation formula (16).

Solution   We are dealing with $f(x) = \sqrt{x}$; in Chapter 3 we shall show that

$$\frac{df}{dx} = \frac{1}{2\sqrt{x}}$$

We know the value of f at the point $p = 100$, namely $f(100) - 10$; we seek the value at the nearby point $x = 100 + \Delta x = 103$. To find $f(103)$ it suffices to find $\Delta f = f(103) - f(100)$ since $f(103) = f(100) + \Delta f = 10 + \Delta f$. Since $\Delta x = +3$, formula (16) tell us that

$$\Delta f \approx f'(100) \cdot \Delta x = \frac{1}{2\sqrt{100}} \cdot \Delta x = \frac{1}{20} \cdot 3 = 0.15000$$

Thus $f(103) = 10 + \Delta f \approx 10.15000$. The exact value is $f(103) = 10.14889 \ldots$.

More generally, we can estimate $\sqrt{100 + \Delta x}$ for any small increment Δx. Taking $f(x) = \sqrt{x}$ (with derivative $f'(x) = 1/2\sqrt{x}$) and base point $p = 100$ in formula (16), we get the approximate value of f at any nearby point $p + \Delta x - 100 + \Delta x$:

$$f(100 + \Delta x) = f(100) + \Delta f \approx f(100) + f'(100) \cdot \Delta x$$

$$= \sqrt{100} + \left(\frac{1}{2\sqrt{100}}\right) \cdot \Delta x = 10 + \frac{\Delta x}{20}$$

so that

$$\sqrt{100 + \Delta x} \approx 10 + \frac{\Delta x}{20} \qquad \text{for all small increments } \Delta x.$$

For example, if $\Delta x = -0.5$ we get $\sqrt{99.5} \approx 10 - (0.5/20) = 9.975$; the actual value of this square root is $\sqrt{99.5} = 9.97497 \ldots$.

For most practical purposes we may work with the approximate values $\Delta f \approx f'(p) \cdot \Delta x$ instead of the exact values, as long as the nearby point is fairly close to p. We summarize these observations as follows:

The Approximation Principle   If $y = f(x)$ is differentiable at $x = p$ and if we set $\Delta f = f(x) - f(p)$, then

$$\Delta f \approx f'(p) \cdot \Delta x$$

for all small increments Δx away from the base point p. Adding $f(p)$ to both sides, we get a similar formula for the value of $f(x)$:

$$f(x) \approx f(p) + f'(p) \cdot \Delta x = f(p) + f'(p) \cdot (x - p)$$

for all x near p.

Example 11   The volume of a sphere of radius r is given by the function $V(r) = (4/3)\pi r^3$. If the radius of the Earth is 3950 miles and the effective depth of the atmosphere is 20 miles, estimate the volume of the atmosphere in cubic miles.

Solution   The atmospheric volume is the difference in volume between spheres of radius $3970 = 3950 + 20$ (Earth + atmosphere) and 3950 (Earth alone). To apply the approximation principle, take $p = 3950$ and increment $\Delta r = 20$; the volume of the atmosphere is

$$\Delta V = V(p + \Delta r) - V(p) = V(3970) - V(3950)$$

The elementary differentiation formula (14) gives the derivative

$$\frac{dV}{dr} = \frac{4}{3}\pi \frac{d}{dr}\{r^3\} = \frac{4}{3}\pi(3r^2) = 4\pi r^2$$

Clearly $V'(p) = V'(3950) = 4\pi(3950)^2 = 1.96 \times 10^8$. By   the   approximation principle

$$\Delta V \approx V'(3950) \cdot \Delta r = (1.96 \times 10^8) \cdot 20 = 3.92 \times 10^9 \text{ cubic miles}$$

We leave calculation of the more exact value

$$\Delta V = \frac{4}{3}\pi(3970)^3 - \frac{4}{3}\pi(3950)^3 = 3.941 \times 10^9 \text{ cubic miles}$$

as Exercise 5.

The approximation principle has a geometric interpretation. Of all straight lines in the plane, the tangent line through a point P on the graph of a differentiable function $y = f(x)$ best approximates the graph of f near P (see Figure 2.6). To see

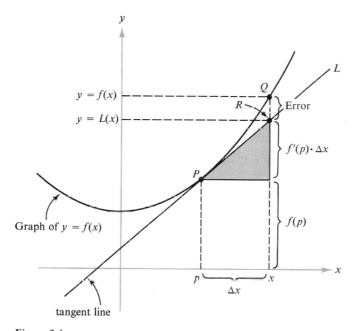

Figure 2.6
The line $y = L(x) = f(p) + f'(p)(x - p)$ is the tangent line to the graph of $y = f(x)$ at the point P. The tangent line best approximates the graph when x is near p. The actual error in approximating $f(x)$ by $L(x)$ is the length of the segment RQ shown above. As Δx approaches 0 this error gets to be very small, even in comparison to the small increment $\Delta x = x - p$. Thus $f(p + \Delta x) = f(p) + f'(p) \cdot \Delta x + \text{error} \approx f(p) + f'(p) \cdot \Delta x$ for small increments.

why, consider a base point $x = p$. The equation of the tangent line L through the corresponding point $P = (p, f(p))$ on the graph is given by

$$f'(p) = \text{slope}(L) = \frac{\Delta y}{\Delta x} = \frac{y - f(p)}{x - p}$$

or $y - f(p) = f'(p) \cdot (x - p)$. Thus the tangent line is the graph of the linear function

$$y = L(x) = f(p) + f'(p) \cdot (x - p)$$

Now compare the equation $y = L(x)$ of the tangent line with the formula in our statement of the approximation principle. The actual value $f(x)$ is closely approximated by $L(x)$:

$$f(x) = L(x) + \text{error}$$

with an error that gets very small as x gets close to p. The geometric significance of this error is illustrated in Figure 2.6.

Exercises

● 1. Given the functions $y = f(x)$ and base points p listed below, write out the approximation formula $\Delta y \approx f'(p) \, \Delta x$. Estimate Δy for $\Delta x = 0.1$ and $\Delta x = -0.1$ in each case.

   (i) $y = 1 - x^2$, $p = 1$

   (ii) $y = 1 + x^2$, $p = 3$

   (iii) $y = x^3 - x + 1$, $p = -1$

   ANSWERS: (i) $\Delta y \approx -2 \, \Delta x$, $\Delta y \approx -0.2$ if $\Delta x = +0.1$, $\Delta y \approx +0.2$ if $\Delta x = -0.1$;   (ii) $\Delta y \approx 6 \, \Delta x$, $\Delta y \approx +0.6$, $\Delta y \approx -0.6$;   (iii) $\Delta y \approx 2 \, \Delta x$, $\Delta y \approx +0.2$, $\Delta y \approx -0.2$.

● 2. Imitate Example 10 to compute $\sqrt{48}$ and $\sqrt{53}$ approximately. Use the fact that $dy/dx = 1/2\sqrt{x}$ if $y = \sqrt{x}$. Compare with the exact values in the square-root tables.

● 3. Use the approximation principle to estimate $\sqrt{49 + \Delta x}$ in terms of Δx for small increments Δx (refer to Exercise 2).

● 4. The value of $y = f(x) = 1/x^2$ is easily calculated for $x = 1.0$. Estimate the value of $f(x)$ at $x = 1.01795$ by using the approximation principle. Then compute the exact value for $f(1.01795)$. Is there much difference in the answers? (In the amount of work required?) HINT: $f'(x) = -2/x^3$ (Example 7); write $x = 1 + \Delta x$.

● 5. In Example 11 we gave an exact formula for the volume of the Earth's atmosphere

$$\Delta V = \frac{4\pi}{3}(3970)^3 - \frac{4\pi}{3}(3950)^3$$

and an approximate formula

$$\Delta V \approx 4\pi(3950)^2 \cdot \Delta r = 4\pi(3950)^2 \cdot (20)$$

Carry out these calculations. Which is easier?

● 6. Most weather phenomena are confined to the lowest 10 miles of the Earth's atmosphere. Estimate the volume of this part of the atmosphere in cubic miles.

● 7. The volume of the polar ice caps has been estimated at 8.3×10^6 cubic miles. If the Earth were a perfect sphere of radius 3950 miles and if the ice caps melted completely, to what depth (in feet) would the melt water cover the Earth? NOTE: This gives a rough estimate of how high the sea level would rise if all polar ice melted. HINT: One mile = 5280 feet.

● 8. At production level q units per week the profit of a certain manufacturer is $P = P(q) = -10{,}000 + 40q - 0.02q^2$. Use the approximation principle to estimate the change ΔP in profit if production is increased from $q = 500$ to $q = 520$. Compare this approximation with the exact change $\Delta P = P(520) - P(500)$.

● 9. A surveyor wants to find the area of a square plot of land. His measurements show that the length of a side is 100 feet, with a possible measurement error of ± 0.20 feet. Use the formula $A = s^2$ to find the uncertainty in the estimated area of 10,000 square feet.

●10. Blood flows very slowly along the walls of a blood vessel, and flows most rapidly along the center of the vessel. According to Poiseuille's law governing blood flow, the velocity v along the center is determined by the radius r of the vessel

$$v = k \cdot r^2 \text{ centimeters per second}$$

where k is a constant related to blood pressure and viscosity. Suppose $k - 2 \times 10^4$ and r is measured under a microscope to be 0.01 centimeters, with a possible measurement error of ± 0.001 centimeters. Find the estimated value of v and the corresponding error Δv.

*●11. The area of a square of side length s is $A(s) = s^2$. If the side length is increased by a small amount Δs from a base value s, write out formulas giving (in terms of Δs)

    (i) the exact change $\Delta A - A(s + \Delta s) - A(s)$

    (ii) the approximate value for ΔA given by the approximation principle

    (iii) the error $E = (\Delta A)_{\text{exact}} - (\Delta A)_{\text{approximate}}$

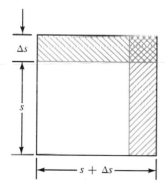

Figure 2.7
Squares with sides of length s and $s + \Delta s$. The increment in area, ΔA, is the entire shaded region.

In Figure 2.7 we show squares of side length s and $s + \Delta s$. The increment ΔA (shaded) is divided into two rectangular parts and a small square. Identify the terms in formulas (i)–(iii) with the areas of these regions.

2.6   Optimization and the "Marginal" Concept in Economics

The notion of derivative applies to any function, whether it describes the position of a moving object, the graph of a curve, or the profit from a manufacturing operation expressed as a function of production level. This general concept allows us to unify the analysis of many seemingly unrelated phenomena. Already we have used it to discuss the instantaneous speed of a falling object and the tangent line to a curve in the plane. In this section we shall take up a fruitful case study from economics and examine its implications.

Illustration   A manufacturer can run his plant at any level of production between $q = 0$ and $q = 2000$ units per week. Suppose that he has determined that his weekly profit is described by the function

$$P(q) = -1000 + 20q - 0.01q^2 \text{ dollars per week}$$

for $0 \leqslant q \leqslant 2000$. If he chooses a production level at random, say $q = 100$ or $q = 1500$ units per week, he might not be operating at maximum profit. The derivative dP/dq of the profit function can be used to determine the optimum level of production.

Discussion   We determine the derivative dP/dq using the differentiation rule for polynomials (14):

$$\frac{dP}{dq} = \frac{d}{dq}\{-1000 + 20q - 0.01q^2\}$$

$$= -1000\frac{d}{dq}\{1\} + 20\frac{d}{dq}\{q\} - 0.01\frac{d}{dq}\{q^2\} \qquad (17)$$

$$= -1000(0) + 20(1) - 0.01(2q)$$

$$= 20 - 0.02q$$

Economists give the derivative $dP/dq = P'(q)$ a special name, referring to it as the **marginal profit** at the production level under discussion. A mathematician would call it the derivative of the profit function. For small increments Δq in the production level away from base level q we have $\Delta P \approx P'(q) \cdot \Delta q$; an economist would put it this way:

$$\Delta P \approx (\text{marginal profit at level } q) \cdot \Delta q \qquad (18)$$

Similarly, if $C(q)$ is the cost function, its derivative at a certain production level is referred to as the **marginal cost** at that production level. In other words, by force of tradition economists tend to use the word "marginal" wherever a mathematician or physicist would use the phrase "derivative of." Marginal cost, marginal profit, and so forth are crucial concepts in formulating economic strategy. These concepts (hence also the notion of *derivative* on which they are based) pervade all modern discussions of economics. Furthermore, they provide the key to finding the optimum level of production.

Suppose the production level is set at $q = 100$, where $dP/dq = P'(100) = 20 - 2 = 18$. Is it more profitable to change the production level slightly? By the approximation principle, if we make a small change in production level to either side of the base level $q = 100$ (Δq positive or negative) we get

$$\Delta P \approx 18 \, \Delta q$$

by setting (marginal profit) $= P'(100) = 18$ in (18). Obviously a rational strategist will choose to increase profits if this is possible; that is, to make $\Delta P > 0$. But

$$\Delta P \text{ is positive (profit increases) if } \Delta q > 0 \, (q \text{ increased})$$

$$\Delta P \text{ is negative (profit decreases) if } \Delta q < 0 \, (q \text{ decreased})$$

Thus, *at the particular production level $q = 100$*, we can increase profits by increasing production somewhat.

Suppose we operate at a high level of production, say $q = 1500$ units per week. Should we maintain this level, increase it, or decrease it? Again, formula (18) and the sign of the marginal profit $P'(1500)$ at this production level tell us what to do. From (17) we see that $P'(1500) = 20 - 30 = -10$ dollars per unit. Since the marginal profit is now *negative*, the formula

$$\Delta P \approx P'(1500) \cdot \Delta q = -10 \cdot \Delta q$$

tells us that we should *decrease* production to increase profit. If $q = 1500$ the production level is so high that there are substantial diseconomies of size, and it pays to cut back production.

Ultimately we want to pick a production level that *maximizes* profits, so that P is as large as it can get for $0 \leqslant q \leqslant 2000$. If we randomly pick a production level, the preceding remarks tell us which way to move in order to increase our profit. They also tell us something else of great significance: if $P'(q) \neq 0$ there is *some* direction we can move q to achieve an even higher profit. By default:

> The only production levels at which P can possibly be a maximum are those for which $dP/dq = 0$.

There are not many values of q in the range $0 \leqslant q \leqslant 2000$ for which $P'(q) = 0$. In fact

$$0 = P'(q) = 20 - 0.02q$$

only if $q = 1000$. This is the "maximizing" choice of q, as can be seen from the graph of the profit function in Figure 2.8. However, notice that we were able to locate this point without ever taking the trouble to sketch the graph, which can be quite tedious.

In brief, we should calculate the marginal profit function $dP/dq = P'(q)$, then examine the points where $P'(q) = 0$. Maximum profit can occur only at these points.

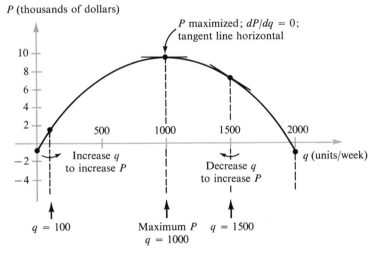

Figure 2.8

Graph of the profit function $P = -1000 + 20q - 0.01q^2$. At $q = 100$, marginal profit is positive ($dP/dq > 0$); thus P increases if q is *increased*. If $q = 1500$, then $dP/dq < 0$, so P increases if q is *decreased*. Profit reaches a maximum at $q = 1000$. Then $dP/dq = 0$ (horizontal tangent line). By solving the equation $dP/dq = 0$ we may find this point by using algebra. This is an improvement over the earlier method of carefully plotting the graph and locating the maximum by eye.

The preceding economic case study will be re-examined in the next chapter, where we shall fully discuss maximizing or minimizing an arbitrary function $y = f(x)$. For the moment, we point out that the previous discussion could be applied verbatim to *any* differentiable function $y = f(x)$. Let us fix a base point p at which the derivative is nonzero. Exactly as in our discussion of profit functions, if $f'(p) \neq 0$ the sign of f' tells us which way to move in order to increase or decrease the value of f, as shown in Figure 2.9. This is so because the basic formula $\Delta f \approx f'(p) \cdot \Delta x$ is valid. If we wish to maximize (or minimize) f, our attention is directed to the points where $df/dx = 0$. Otherwise, if $df/dx \neq 0$ we may move away from p so as to increase the value of $y = f(x)$ (moving in the opposite direction will decrease $y = f(x)$). This establishes a basic result:

The Optimization Principle   Let $y = f(x)$ be differentiable on an interval $a < x < b$. The points (if any) where $f'(x) = 0$ are the only ones at which f can achieve a maximum or a minimum value.

We were not interested in minimum values when we studied profit functions, but there are many applications in which the minimum values are what we seek.

This discussion also shows that whenever the derivative df/dx is nonzero its sign determines whether $y = f(x)$ is increasing or decreasing as x moves to the right in the number line (see Figure 2.9).

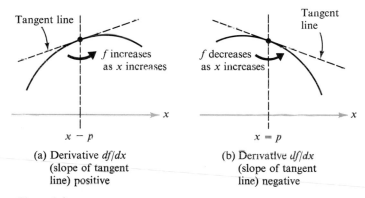

(a) Derivative df/dx (slope of tangent line) positive

(b) Derivative df/dx (slope of tangent line) negative

Figure 2.9
If $y = f(x)$ is differentiable at the point $x = p$ and df/dx is nonzero there, then the graph has the general shape (a) if $f'(p) > 0$, and the shape (b) if $f'(p) < 0$. In either case, the graph is very closely approximated by the tangent line. This line has slope $f'(p)$ and slopes upward if $f'(p) > 0$, downward if $f'(p) < 0$. Thus $f(x)$ increases as x moves past p from left to right if $f'(p) > 0$, and decreases if $f'(p) < 0$. The tangent line is horizontal when $f'(p) = 0$.

Significance of the Sign of df/dx   If $y = f(x)$ is differentiable on an interval $a < x < b$, then

(i) $y = f(x)$ is increasing throughout the interval if $\dfrac{dy}{dx} > 0$

(ii) $y = f(x)$ is decreasing throughout the interval if $\dfrac{dy}{dx} < 0$

Exercises

●1. If the cost function $C(q)$ for a manufacturing operation is known, the marginal cost $C'(q) = dC/dq$ at production level q is useful because it tells us (approximately) the cost of producing one additional unit starting from the given production level. Here we define

$$\text{Cost of producing } one \text{ more unit} = \Delta C = C(q + 1) - C(q)$$

taking $\Delta q = 1$. Use the approximation formula to explain why $dC/dq \approx \Delta C$. NOTE: The same ideas can be applied to other economic variables to define profit (revenue, demand, and so forth) per additional unit, and to relate it to the marginal profit dP/dq (marginal revenue dR/dq, marginal demand dp/dq, and so forth).

●2. The profit function in Example 14, Section 1.6, was

$$P(q) = -5,000,000 + 61q - 0.000098q^2 \qquad \text{for } 0 \leqslant q \leqslant 1,000,000$$

Where is the marginal profit $P'(q) = 61 - 0.000196q$ equal to zero? Make a sketch of the number line showing where P is increasing $(dP/dq > 0)$ and where it is decreasing $(dP/dq < 0)$ within the interval $0 \leqslant q \leqslant 1,000,000$. Use this information to determine the q for which P has the largest possible value. Which would you rather do: locate the maximum value of P by sketching the graph of $P = P(q)$, as in Example 14, Section 1.6, or by studying the marginal profit function dP/dq? ANSWERS: $dP/dq = 0$ at $q = 311,225$; increasing for $0 \leqslant q < 311,225$; decreasing for $311,225 < q \leqslant 1,000,000$; maximum at $311,225$.

●3. Calculate the derivative of $y = f(x) = x^3 - 3x$. Is f increasing or decreasing at $x = -2$? at $x = 0$? at $x = 0.5$? at $x = 3$?

●4. Find the derivative of $y = f(x) = x - 3x^2 + 1$. For which x is $y = f(x)$ increasing? decreasing?

●5. Calculate the derivative of $y = f(x) = x^3 - 3x$. For which x is $f(x)$ increasing? decreasing? HINT: Recall the methods introduced in Section 1.10 for determining the sign of a polynomial.

●6. Calculate derivatives and determine where each of the following functions is increasing or decreasing. In each case make a sketch of the number line showing the regions where the function increases or decreases.

(i) $y = f(x) = 40 - 13x$ (iv) $y = f(x) = 1 + 3x + 3x^2 + x^3$

(ii) $y = f(x) = 1 + x + x^2$ (v) $y = f(r) = 1 + r^3$

(iii) $y = f(x) = 2x^3 - 3x^2 - 12x + 1$ (vi) $P(q) = -10,000 + 153q - 0.003q^2$

●7. For the profit function $P(q) = 5q - 0.004q^2 - 1000$ calculate the marginal profit dP/dq. For which production levels in the feasible range $0 \leqslant q \leqslant 1000$ is the profit increasing with q? decreasing? Find the maximum feasible profit and the corresponding production level q. ANSWERS: Increasing for $0 \leqslant q < 625$; decreasing for $625 < q \leqslant 1000$; maximum $P =$ \$562.50 at $q = 625$; $dP/dq = 5 - 0.008q$.

*2.7   Limits and Continuity

The concept of limit turns up in many problems besides the calculation of derivatives. Here we give a general definition. Let $y = f(x)$ be an arbitrary function. If we fix a base point p we consider how the values of $f(x)$ behave as x gets close to p.

Definition   We say that the function f has a **limit** L at $x = p$, indicated by the notation

$$\lim_{x \to p} f(x) = L \tag{19}$$

if the values $y = f(x)$ get very close to L as x approaches p, keeping $x \neq p$.

The notion of limit is fundamental; all of the Calculus is built upon it and the techniques of algebra. We have already used this notion in defining derivatives, but it has many other uses as well.

You will note that x is excluded from taking the value p in the definition of limit (19). We don't even assume that f is defined at p; (19) is a statement about what $f(x)$ is doing for x *near* p, rather than *at* p itself. To see why this is natural, recall the formula for instantaneous speed of a falling object mentioned in Section 2.1:

$$\text{instantaneous speed} = \lim_{\Delta t \to 0} \left\{ \frac{\Delta s}{\Delta t} \right\} = \lim_{\Delta t \to 0} \{32 + 16(\Delta t)\} = 32$$

Here

Δt plays the role of the variable x in (19)

$\Delta s/\Delta t = 32 + 16(\Delta t)$ plays the role of $f(x)$ in (19)

0 plays the role of the point p in (19)

and the value of the limit L is 32. The average speed $\Delta s/\Delta t$ cannot be defined for $\Delta t = 0$; in this case the variable Δt can approach zero but not take on the value zero. This possibility is reflected in our general definition of limit, in which the variable x approaches p but does not take on the value p.

Example 12 Evaluate the limit $\lim\limits_{x \to 5} (3x - 4)$.

Solution Here $p = 5$ and we must examine the behavior of $f(x) = 3x - 4$ as x approaches 5. As x gets close to 5, the expression $3x$ gets close to 15, so that $3x - 4$ approaches $15 - 4 = 11$. Therefore

$$\lim_{x \to 5} (3x - 4) = 11$$

We can evaluate limits in an organized way by applying certain basic rules. Suppose $f(x)$ and $g(x)$ are two functions defined near p, and that

$$\lim_{x \to p} f(x) = L \quad \text{and} \quad \lim_{x \to p} g(x) = K$$

What can we say about the behavior of the **sum function** $f(x) + g(x)$ as x approaches p? Since $f(x)$ will be close to L and $g(x)$ will be close to K for all x close to p, it is clear that $f(x) + g(x)$ will be close to the value $L + K$. Expressed in symbols

$$\lim_{x \to p} \{f(x) + g(x)\} = L + K$$

There are similar rules for dealing with the **product** $f(x) \cdot g(x)$ and **quotient** $f(x)/g(x)$ of two functions $f(x)$ and $g(x)$, except that in the case of quotients we must avoid division by zero.

Properties of Limits Suppose that $\lim\limits_{x \to p} f(x) = L$ and $\lim\limits_{x \to p} g(x) = K$. Then

$$(i) \quad \lim_{x \to p} \{f(x) + g(x)\} = L + K = \left(\lim_{x \to p} f(x) \right) + \left(\lim_{x \to p} g(x) \right)$$

$$(ii) \quad \lim_{x \to p} \{f(x) \cdot g(x)\} = L \cdot K = \left(\lim_{x \to p} f(x) \right) \cdot \left(\lim_{x \to p} g(x) \right) \qquad (20)$$

$$(iii) \quad \lim_{x \to p} \left\{ \frac{f(x)}{g(x)} \right\} = \frac{L}{K} = \frac{\left(\lim\limits_{x \to p} f(x) \right)}{\left(\lim\limits_{x \to p} g(x) \right)} \quad \text{provided } K \neq 0$$

Example 13 Evaluate the limit $\lim\limits_{x \to 1} f(x)$ if $f(x) = x^3 + 6x^2 + x - 7$. How is the limit related to the value of f at the base point $p = 1$?

Solution It is clear that

$$\lim_{x \to 1} x = 1$$

All this says is that if x is close to 1 then x is close to 1. Using (20ii) repeatedly, we find that

$$\lim_{x \to 1} x^2 = \lim_{x \to 1} \{x \cdot x\} = \left(\lim_{x \to 1} x \right) \cdot \left(\lim_{x \to 1} x \right) = 1 \cdot 1 = 1$$

$$\lim_{x \to 1} x^3 = \lim_{x \to 1} \{x \cdot x^2\} = \left(\lim_{x \to 1} x \right) \cdot \left(\lim_{x \to 1} x^2 \right) = 1 \cdot 1 = 1$$

Thus

$$\lim_{x \to 1} \{x^3 + 6x^2 + x - 7\} = \left(\lim_{x \to 1} x^3 \right) + \left(\lim_{x \to 1} 6x^2 \right) + \left(\lim_{x \to 1} x \right) + \left(\lim_{x \to 1} -7 \right)$$

$$= \lim_{x \to 1} x^3 + \left(\lim_{x \to 1} 6 \right) \cdot \left(\lim_{x \to 1} x^2 \right) + \lim_{x \to 1} x + \lim_{x \to 1} -7$$

$$= 1 + 6 \cdot 1 + 1 - 7$$

$$= 1$$

We have used the obvious fact that the limit of any constant function $g(x) = k$ at any point p is just that constant k

$$\lim_{x \to p} g(x) = \lim_{x \to p} k = k$$

Notice that the value of f at p is $f(p) = f(1) = 1^3 + 6(1)^2 + 1 - 7 = 1$, so that

$$\lim_{x \to 1} g(x) = f(1)$$

By similar reasoning we can show that

$$\lim_{x \to p} f(x) = f(p)$$

for any polynomial $f(x)$ and any point p. Functions $y = f(x)$ with the property

$$\lim_{x \to p} f(x) = f(p) \qquad \text{for every } p \text{ in the domain of definition of } f \qquad (21)$$

are given a special name: **continuous functions**. Continuity does not play much of a role in differentiation, but we shall touch upon it in connection with integration (Chapter 4). Intuitively, a continuous function is one whose graph may be traced out without ever lifting the pencil from the paper. The simplest way a function can fail to be continuous is for its value to take an abrupt "jump" at some point p in its domain of definition (see Figure 2.10). Such a point is called a *jump discontinuity* for the function. The function is not continuous because $\lim_{x \to p} f(x)$ fails to exist at p. The "postage function" of Example 6, Section 1.3, has jump discontinuities at $w = 1$, $w = 2$, $w = 3$, and $w = 4$, as you can see from its graph (Figure 1.6); it is continuous for all other values of w.

Continuity also fails at p if $\lim_{x \to p} f(x)$ exists but disagrees with the value $f(p)$ of f at p, as in Figure 2.11(e). Or continuity may fail because the values $f(x)$ "blow up," becoming very large positive or negative as x approaches p, rather than tending toward a finite limiting value. An example of this is shown in Figure 2.11(b). In the other parts of Figure 2.11 we show the graphs of several other functions that are defined at and near a point $x = p$; the captions indicate which are continuous at p and which are not.

All polynomials are continuous. In fact, most functions given by algebraic formulas are continuous wherever they are defined (denominators nonzero). We give an illustration in the next example.

Example 14   For which points p is the function $f(x) = \dfrac{x^2 + 4}{x^2 + 2x}$ continuous?

Solution   First notice that f is not defined if the denominator $x^2 + 2x$ is equal to zero. But the roots of the quadratic equation $x^2 + 2x = 0$ are $x = 0$ and $x = -2$. Since f is undefined at 0 and at -2, we exclude these points in discussing continuity of f. For all other points p, $f(p)$ is defined. Consider the limit behavior of the

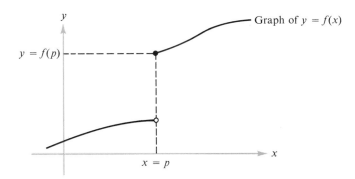

Figure 2.10
The solid curves together form the graph of the function $y = f(x)$ with a jump discontinuity at $x = p$. The open dot indicates a point *not* on the graph. The function is defined at p, but because of the jump the limit $\lim_{x \to p} \{f(x)\}$ does not exist.

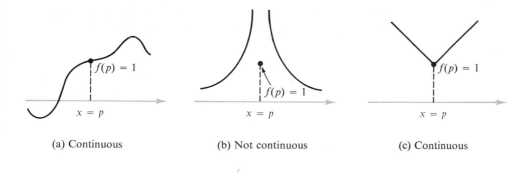

(a) Continuous   (b) Not continuous   (c) Continuous

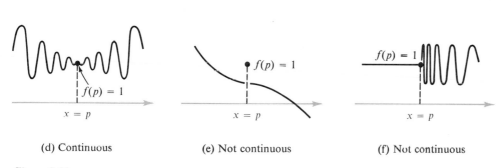

(d) Continuous   (e) Not continuous   (f) Not continuous

Figure 2.11

Graphs of functions defined near $x = p$. You should consider each figure with property (21) in mind to see why continuity fails or is valid. For example, in (b) and (f) the limit $\lim\limits_{x \to p} \{f(x)\}$ does not exist. In (e) the limit exists but does not coincide with the value of f at p: $f(p) = 1$ while $\lim\limits_{x \to p} \{f(x)\} = 1/2$.

numerator and denominator in f at such a point. We get

$$\lim_{x \to p} \{x^2 + 4\} = p^2 + 4 \quad \text{and} \quad \lim_{x \to p} \{x^2 + 2x\} = p^2 + 2p$$

Since the limit of the denominator is nonzero, we may apply (20*iii*) to get

$$\lim_{x \to p} f(x) = \lim_{x \to p} \left\{ \frac{x^2 + 4}{x^2 + 2x} \right\}$$

$$= \frac{\left(\lim\limits_{x \to p} x^2 + 4 \right)}{\left(\lim\limits_{x \to p} x^2 + 2x \right)} = \frac{p^2 + 4}{p^2 + 2p} = f(p)$$

so that f is continuous at p. Thus f is continuous at all points in its domain of definition.

There is a connection between continuity and differentiability: *if f is differentiable at p it must be continuous at p*. According to the approximation principle, for a differentiable function $f(x)$ we may write

$$f(x) = f(p) + f'(p) \cdot (x - p) + \text{error term}$$

for all x near p. We know that the error term gets very small as x approaches p. But the term $f'(p) \cdot (x - p)$ also gets small because $x - p$ approaches zero. In the limit only the constant term $f(p)$ persists, so that

$$\lim_{x \to p} f(x) = f(p) + 0 + 0 = f(p)$$

as required for continuity at p. We shall soon be able to differentiate many functions with ease. This guarantees that such functions are automatically continuous.

Exercises

●1. Evaluate

(i) $\lim_{x \to 0} 1$

(ii) $\lim_{x \to 1} 0$

(iii) $\lim_{x \to 0} x$

(iv) $\lim_{x \to 1} x$

(v) $\lim_{x \to -2} x$

(vi) $\lim_{x \to -2} (x^2 + 1)$

(vii) $\lim_{x \to -2} (x^2 + 3x)$

(viii) $\lim_{x \to \sqrt{2}} (x^3 - x^2 - 2x + 6)$

Here 1 and 0 stand for the constant functions $f(x) = 1$ and $f(x) = 0$. ANSWERS: (i) 1;   (ii) 0;   (iii) 0;   (iv) 1;   (v) -2;   (vi) 5;   (vii) -2;   (viii) 4.

●2. Evaluate

(i) $\lim_{x \to -3} (x^2 - 7)(x^2 + x + 1)$

(ii) $\lim_{x \to 7} (x - 7)(x^9 + x^5 - x)$

(iii) $\lim_{t \to 0} \dfrac{3t^2 - 2t + 4}{t^2 + t - 1}$

(iv) $\lim_{h \to 0} \dfrac{h^2 - h}{h}$

(v) $\lim_{t \to -1} \dfrac{t^2 - t - 2}{t + 1}$

(vi) $\lim_{x \to 0} \dfrac{x^3}{x^2}$

(vii) $\lim_{\Delta t \to 0} \dfrac{(\Delta t)^2 + 4(\Delta t)^3}{13 + (1 - \Delta t)^2}$

(viii) $\lim_{x \to 2} \dfrac{x^2 - 4x + 4}{x^2 - 4}$

HINT: In some cases simplify algebraically before applying the limit rules.

●3. For which points is the function $f(x) = 1/x$ continuous? For which points is the function $f(x) = 1/(1 - x^2)$ continuous? HINT: First exclude the points where the functions are undefined.

●4. Graph the following functions and determine which are continuous at the point 2.

(i) $\begin{cases} f(x) = 3 - x & \text{if } x < 2 \\ f(x) = x - 2 & \text{if } x \geqslant 2 \end{cases}$

(ii) $\begin{cases} f(x) = 3 - x & \text{if } x < 2 \\ f(x) = 2 & \text{if } x \geqslant 2 \end{cases}$

(iii) $\begin{cases} f(x) = x^2 - 2 & \text{if } x \leqslant 2 \\ f(x) = 1 + (x^2/4) & \text{if } x > 2 \end{cases}$

●5. The function $f(x) = (x - x^3)/(x - 1)$ is well-defined for all $x \neq 1$. How can we assign the value $f(1)$ at $x = 1$ so that f is continuous at $x = 1$? HINT: Evaluate $\lim\limits_{x \to 1} \{(x - x^3)/(x - 1)\}$ by simplifying the expression $(x - x^3)/(x - 1)$ algebraically.

●6. Let the function $y = f(x)$ be differentiable at the point p. The function $g(x)$ is defined by

$$g(x) = \frac{f(x) - f(p)}{x - p} \qquad \text{for } x \neq p$$

and

$$g(p) = a$$

How should we choose the value a so that g is continuous at p? HINT: What is $\lim\limits_{x \to p} g(x)$?

CHAPTER 3

Applications of Differentiation

3.1 Derivatives of Elementary Functions

We have previously computed the following derivatives:

Function $y = x^n$	Derivative
$f(x) = x^0 = 1$	$f'(x) = 0$ everywhere
$f(x) = x^1 = x$	$f'(x) = 1$ everywhere
$f(x) = x^2$	$f'(x) = 2x$
$f(x) = x^3$	$f'(x) = 3x^2$

A regular pattern seems to be emerging. If $y = x^4$ we might guess that $f'(x) = 4x^3$. More generally, if $f(x) = x^n$ it is reasonable to conjecture that $f'(x) = nx^{n-1}$ since this formula yields the correct result for $n = 0, 1, 2, 3$. This is correct: if n is any positive integer and if $f(x) = x^n$, then $f'(x) = nx^{n-1}$. In other words

$$\frac{d}{dx}\{x^n\} = nx^{n-1} \qquad \text{for } n = 0, 1, 2, \dots \tag{1}$$

To see this, consider a value of x and an arbitrary increment $\Delta x \neq 0$. The corresponding increment in y is

$$\Delta y = f(x + \Delta x) - f(x) = (x + \Delta x)^n - x^n$$

We expand $(x + \Delta x)^n$ by multiplying it out, concentrating our attention on the first two terms in the expansion.

$$(x + \Delta x)^1 = x + \Delta x$$

$$(x + \Delta x)^2 = x^2 + 2x(\Delta x) + (\Delta x)^2$$

$$(x + \Delta x)^3 = x^3 + 3x^2(\Delta x) + 3x(\Delta x)^2 + (\Delta x)^3$$

$$\vdots$$

$$(x + \Delta x)^n = x^n + nx^{n-1}(\Delta x) + \frac{n(n-1)}{2} x^{n-2}(\Delta x)^2 + \cdots + (\Delta x)^n$$

We have not written out the terms indicated by $(\cdots)$. All we need to know about them is that they all have $(\Delta x)^2$ as a common factor. Thus

$$\Delta y = (x + \Delta x)^n - x^n$$

$$= nx^{n-1}(\Delta x) + \frac{n(n-1)}{2} x^{n-2}(\Delta x)^2 + \cdots + (\Delta x)^n$$

so that the average rate of change $\Delta y / \Delta x$ is

$$\frac{\Delta y}{\Delta x} = \frac{nx^{n-1}(\Delta x) + \cdots + (\Delta x)^n}{\Delta x}$$

$$= nx^{n-1} + \frac{n(n-1)}{2} x^{n-2}(\Delta x) + \cdots + (\Delta x)^{n-1}$$

The omitted terms $(\cdots)$ each have a factor Δx, and so approach zero as Δx gets small. The first term nx^{n-1} *does not* have Δx as a factor and remains fixed, so that $\Delta y / \Delta x$ approaches nx^{n-1} as Δx gets small. Thus

$$f'(x) = \lim_{\Delta x \to 0} \frac{\Delta y}{\Delta x} = nx^{n-1}$$

as stated in (1).

Example 1 Find the derivative dy/dx if $y = f(x) = x^{20}$. What is the value of $f'(1)$?

Solution Apply (1) to the function $y = x^{20}$, taking $n = 20$. We get

$$\frac{dy}{dx} = f'(x) = nx^{n-1} = 20x^{19}$$

At $x = 1$ the derivative is equal to $f'(1) = 20(1^{19}) = 20$.

In Section 2.3 we used the delta process to find the derivative of $y = 1/x^2$, $dy/dx = -2/x^3$ for $x \neq 0$. It is more suggestive to write this function and its derivative as powers of x:

$$y = x^{-2} \qquad \frac{dy}{dx} = -2x^{-3}$$

Notice that the derivative is given by the same rule as (1); we get

$$\frac{d}{dx}\{x^r\} = rx^{r-1} \tag{2}$$

if we set $r = -2$. This suggests that the rule (2), proved above for integral values $r = 0, 1, 2, \ldots$, is actually valid for many other choices of the exponent r. In fact, this rule is valid for *every* real number r. We shall use this fact without going into its proof, which is more technical than the proof of (1).

Differentiation Rule for Powers $y = x^r$ If r is a real number, the function $f(x) = x^r$ has derivative

$$\frac{dy}{dx} = f'(x) = rx^{r-1}$$

That is

$$\frac{d}{dx}\{x^r\} = rx^{r-1} \tag{3}$$

Example 2 Find the derivatives of the functions

$$\text{(i) } f(x) = \frac{1}{x} \qquad \text{(ii) } g(x) = \sqrt{x} \qquad \text{(iii) } h(x) = x^{\sqrt{3}}$$

Solution   We may apply formula (3) once we express each function as a power of x. In (i) we have $y = 1/x = x^{-1}$; taking $r = -1$ in (3), we get

$$f'(x) = rx^{r-1} = (-1)x^{-2} = \frac{-1}{x^2}$$

In (ii), $g(x) = \sqrt{x} = x^{1/2}$. Taking $r = 1/2$ in (3), we get

$$g'(x) = \frac{1}{2}x^{1/2-1} = \frac{1}{2}x^{-1/2} = \frac{1}{2x^{1/2}} = \frac{1}{2\sqrt{x}}$$

In (iii), $r = \sqrt{3}$ and

$$h'(x) = \sqrt{3}x^{\sqrt{3}-1}$$

Four special functions turn up frequently in certain applications:

$$y = e^x \qquad \text{the exponential function}$$

$$y = \log x \qquad \text{the natural logarithm function}$$

which appear in growth and compound-interest problems, and

$$y = \sin x \qquad \text{the sine function}$$

$$y = \cos x \qquad \text{the cosine function}$$

which occur in trigonometry and in descriptions of all kinds of periodic phenomena. Instead of taking time to discuss these useful functions in detail we shall adopt a pragmatic viewpoint, regarding them as special functions whose values are found by referring to suitable tables or by using a pocket calculator. We shall handle their derivatives by referring to the differentiation rules listed without proof in Table 3.1. It is not necessary to know anything more about these functions to understand our occasional use of them in Chapters 3–6.*

* For readers who have encountered these functions before, we remark that e refers to the special real number $e = 2.71828\ldots$; $y = e^x$ is just e raised to the x power. Here $\log x$ is the so-called *natural logarithm*, taken with base $e = 2.718\ldots$. You may have encountered the *logarithm to base* 10, $y = \log_{10}(x)$, which is a different function. Its connection with $y = \log x$ is indicated in Chapter 6. In the trigonometric functions $y = \sin x$ and $y = \cos x$ the "angle" x is measured in *radians* rather than degrees. Angles θ given in degrees are converted to radians by taking $x = (2\pi/360)\cdot\theta$. Thus $360° = 2\pi$ radians, $90° = \pi/2$ radians, $30° = \pi/6$ radians, and so forth. Measuring x in radians makes the derivatives of $\sin x$ and $\cos x$ have the simple form given in Table 3.1.

$y = e^x$	$\dfrac{dy}{dx} = e^x$
$y = \log x$	$\dfrac{dy}{dx} = \dfrac{1}{x}$
$y = \sin x$	$\dfrac{dy}{dx} = \cos x$
$y = \cos x$	$\dfrac{dy}{dx} = -\sin x$

Table 3.1
Derivatives of the special functions e^x, $\log x$, $\sin x$, and $\cos x$.

Basic facts about $y = e^x$ and $y = \log x$ are presented in Chapter 6, and tables of values are given in Appendixes 3 and 4. We shall make very little use of the trigonometric functions $y = \sin x$ and $y = \cos x$ in this book, and so have not included tables for these functions.

We next show how to express the derivative of a combination of functions in terms of the derivatives of the functions we started with. If we multiply a function $f(x)$ by a constant k, we obtain a new function $g(x) = kf(x)$. The derivative of this new function is just the constant k multiplied by the derivative df/dx of the original function, $g'(x) = kf'(x)$. In other words

$$\frac{d}{dx}\{kf(x)\} = k \cdot \frac{df}{dx} \tag{4}$$

The proof is quite simple. If $\Delta x \neq 0$ then

$$\frac{\Delta g}{\Delta x} = \frac{g(x + \Delta x) - g(x)}{\Delta x} = \frac{kf(x + \Delta x) - kf(x)}{\Delta x} = k \cdot \frac{\Delta f}{\Delta x}$$

By definition, $\Delta f/\Delta x$ approaches $f'(x)$ as Δx approaches zero. Clearly $k(\Delta f/\Delta x)$ must approach $kf'(x)$, so that

$$g'(x) = \lim_{\Delta x \to 0} \frac{\Delta g}{\Delta x} = \lim_{\Delta x \to 0} \left\{ k \cdot \frac{\Delta f}{\Delta x} \right\} = kf'(x)$$

Example 3   Find the derivative dy/dx of $y = -7x^5$.

Solution   Let $f(x) = x^5$ and $g(x) = -7f(x) = -7x^5$. By formula (3), $df/dx = 5x^4$, and by (4) we get

$$g'(x) = \frac{d}{dx}\{-7x^5\} = -7\frac{d}{dx}\{x^5\} = -7(5x^4) = -35x^4$$

The sum $f + g$ of two functions $f(x)$ and $g(x)$ is a new function obtained by adding the values of f and g:

$$(f + g)(x) = f(x) + g(x) \qquad \text{for all } x \tag{5}$$

If $f(x)$ and $g(x)$ are differentiable functions, their sum $h(x) = f(x) + g(x)$ has derivative $h'(x) = f'(x) + g'(x)$. In other words

$$\frac{d}{dx}\{f(x) + g(x)\} = \frac{df}{dx} + \frac{dg}{dx} \tag{6}$$

To verify this, consider an increment $\Delta x \neq 0$ away from a point x. Then

$$\frac{\Delta h}{\Delta x} = \frac{f(x + \Delta x) - f(x)}{\Delta x} + \frac{g(x + \Delta x) - g(x)}{\Delta x} = \frac{\Delta f}{\Delta x} + \frac{\Delta g}{\Delta x}$$

By definition of the derivatives, $\Delta f/\Delta x$ approaches $f'(x)$ and $\Delta g/\Delta x$ approaches $g'(x)$ as Δx approaches zero. Clearly, their sum $\Delta h/\Delta x$ approaches $f'(x) + g'(x)$, which proves (6).

Example 4   Find the derivative dy/dx of the function $y = x^6 - 7x^5$.

Solution   By (3) and (4) we get

$$\frac{d}{dx}\{x^6\} = 6x^5 \quad \text{and} \quad \frac{d}{dx}\{-7x^5\} = -35x^4$$

Applying the rule for sums (6) we get our answer:

$$\frac{d}{dx}\{x^6 - 7x^5\} = \frac{d}{dx}\{x^6\} + \frac{d}{dx}\{-7x^5\}$$

$$= 6x^5 - 35x^4$$

Formulas (4) and (6) may be combined and restated as a single rule for differentiating linear combinations

$$a \cdot f(x) + b \cdot g(x) \qquad \text{(where } a \text{ and } b \text{ are constants)}$$

of the functions $f(x)$ and $g(x)$. Applying (6) and (4) in succession we get

$$\frac{d}{dx}\{a \cdot f(x) + b \cdot g(x)\} = \frac{d}{dx}\{a \cdot f(x)\} + \frac{d}{dx}\{b \cdot g(x)\}$$

$$= a\frac{df}{dx} + b\frac{dg}{dx}$$

Similarly, if we form a linear combination of several functions

$$a \cdot f(x) + b \cdot g(x) + c \cdot h(x) + \cdots \qquad (a, b, c \ldots \text{constants})$$

the derivative is

$$\frac{d}{dx}\{a \cdot f(x) + b \cdot g(x) + c \cdot h(x) + \cdots\} = a\frac{df}{dx} + b\frac{dg}{dx} + c\frac{dh}{dx} + \cdots \qquad (7)$$

A **polynomial** $P(x)$ is a linear combination of powers $x^0 = 1, x^1 = x, x^2, x^3, \ldots$

$$P(x) = a_0 + a_1 x + a_2 x^2 + \cdots + a_n x^n \qquad (a_0, \ldots, a_n \text{ constants})$$

We may differentiate $P(x)$ immediately by using (7), to get the differentiation formula for polynomials mentioned in Section 2.3.

$$P'(x) = a_0 \frac{d}{dx}\{1\} + a_1 \frac{d}{dx}\{x\} + a_2 \frac{d}{dx}\{x^2\} + \cdots + a_n \frac{d}{dx}\{x^n\}$$

$$= a_0 \cdot 0 + a_1 \cdot 1 + a_2 \cdot 2x + \cdots + a_n \cdot nx^{n-1}$$

$$= a_1 + 2a_2 x + 3a_3 x^2 + \cdots + na_n x^{n-1} \qquad (8)$$

Example 5   Find the slope of the curve $y = f(x) = x^3 - 3x^2 + 2x + 1$ at the point $(2, 1)$ on its graph.

Solution   The slope of the tangent line through (2, 1) is just the derivative $f'(x)$ at $x = 2$. Since $f(x)$ is a polynomial, its derivative is

$$f'(x) = \frac{d}{dx}\{x^3\} - 3\frac{d}{dx}\{x^2\} + 2\frac{d}{dx}\{x\} + \frac{d}{dx}\{1\}$$

$$= 3x^2 - 3(2x) + 2(1) + 0$$

$$= 3x^2 - 6x + 2$$

Hence, slope $= f'(2) = 3(2)^2 - 6(2) + 2 = 2$.

Exercises

● 1. Use the differentiation formula (3) to calculate the derivatives of the following functions:

    (*i*) $f(x) = x^3$ (*vi*) $f(x) = x^{-1/2}$

    (*ii*) $f(x) = 1/x^3$ (*vii*) $f(x) = x^{118}$

    (*iii*) $f(x) = \sqrt[3]{x}$ (*viii*) $f(x) = 1/x^{50}$

    (*iv*) $f(x) = 1/\sqrt[3]{x}$ (*ix*) $f(x) = x^{3.21}$

    (*v*) $f(x) = x^{5/3}$ (*x*) $f(x) = x^3 \cdot x^{-1/4}$

● 2. Find the following derivatives:

    (*i*) $f(x) = x^{10}$, $f'(1) = ?$

    (*ii*) $f(t) = t^{3/2}$, $f'(9) = ?$

    (*iii*) $f(t) = (\sqrt{t})^3$, $f'(1/4) = ?$

    (*iv*) $f(x) = 1/x^2$, $f'(-3) = ?$

    (*v*) $f(x) = x^3/\sqrt{x}$, $f'(8) = ?$

● 3. The surface area of a sphere of radius r is $A = 4\pi r^2$. Find the rate of change dA/dr.

● 4. Find the equation of the line tangent to the graph.

    (*i*) $y = \sqrt[3]{x}$ at the point (8, 2)

    (*ii*) $y = 1/x^3$ at the point (1, 1)

    (*iii*) $y = x^4 - x^{2/3}$ at the point (1, 0)

● 5. Suppose the demand function for a certain product is given by

$$p(q) = \frac{1000}{\sqrt{q}}$$

where q is the production level and p the unit price. Find the marginal demand dp/dq and the marginal revenue dR/dq when $q = 100$. HINT: Recall that $R = q \cdot p(q)$.

● 6. Calculate the derivatives of the following functions:

(i) $f(x) = 1 - x^6$ (vii) $P(q) = -4,000,000 + 87q - 0.000102q^2$

(ii) $V(r) = (4/3)\pi r^3$ (viii) $f(x) = \sqrt{x} + 1/\sqrt{x}$

(iii) $f(x) = 4x^5 - 8x^4 + x + 1024$ (ix) $f(t) = t^2 + 1 + 20 \cos t$

(iv) $s = 16t^2$ (x) $f(x) = x + e^x + \log x$

(v) $f(t) = 100\sqrt{2} + 7t^2 - t^3$ (xi) $f(x) = (1 - x^3)/x$

(vi) $C(q) = 4320 + 0.30q - 0.001q^2$ (xii) $f(x) = x^2(1 + \sqrt{x})$

7. The cost function of a manufacturer is

$$C = C(q) = 100 + 100q - q^2$$

and the demand function is

$$p = p(q) = 200 - 2q$$

where q is the level of production.

(i) Evaluate the marginal cost dC/dq.

(ii) Find the profit function $P(q) - q \cdot p(q) - C(q)$.

(iii) Evaluate the marginal profit function dP/dq.

● 8. The population N of a bacteria culture varies with time t according to the formula

$$N = 2000 + 300t + 18t^2 \qquad (t \text{ in minutes})$$

How fast is the population growing at $t = 10$ minutes?

9. A stone is thrown straight up from ground level. Its height h (in feet) after t seconds is given by $h(t) = 64t - 16t^2$.

(i) What is its velocity dh/dt at $t = 1$? at $t = 2$? at $t = 3$? Is the stone rising or falling at these times?

(ii) Find the maximum height.

(iii) Find the speed of the stone when it strikes the ground.

HINT: Ground level corresponds to $h = 0$.

●10. The radius of the Earth is $r = 3950$ miles. The average depth of its oceans is $1/2$ mile. Use the approximation principle (Section 2.5) to estimate the volume of an ocean layer $1/2$ mile deep covering the surface of the Earth. HINT: The volume of a sphere is $V = (4/3)\pi r^3$.

●11. A rectangular box with a square base, and height equal to twice the base length, has

$$\text{Volume} = V = 2s^3 \qquad \text{Area} = A = 10s^2$$

where $s = $ base length. Suppose the base length is measured to be 5 feet with a possible error of ± 0.01 foot. Use the approximation formula to estimate the uncertainty in V and A due to the uncertainty in measuring s. HINT: Take base value $s = 5.0$ and $\Delta s = \pm 0.01$. Then estimate the corresponding values of ΔV and ΔA.

●12. Give a formula estimating $\sqrt{1 + \Delta x}$ in terms of Δx for small increments. Give a formula estimating $(1 + \Delta x)^r$ in terms of Δx (r an arbitrary exponent). HINT: Consider the functions $y = \sqrt{x}$ and $y = x^r$ near the point $x = 1$. ANSWERS: $y \approx y(1) + y'(1) \cdot \Delta x = 1 + \frac{1}{2}\Delta x$; $y \approx 1 + r \cdot \Delta x$.

3.2   The Product Rule and the Quotient Rule

If $f(x)$ and $g(x)$ are functions their **product** $f \cdot g$ is the function

$$h(x) = (f \cdot g)(x) = f(x) \cdot g(x) \qquad \text{for all } x$$

obtained by multiplying their values for each x. Thus, if $f(x) = x$ and $g(x) = x^2 - x + 1$, the product is $h(x) = x(x^2 - x + 1) = x^3 - x^2 + x$ for all x. Or if $f(x) = 1 + x^2$ and $g(x) = e^x$, then $(f \cdot g)(x) = (1 + x^2)e^x = e^x + x^2 e^x$. The differentiation formula for products is more complicated than that for sums.

Product Rule for Derivatives   If $f(x)$ and $g(x)$ are differentiable, their product $h(x) = f(x) \cdot g(x)$ has derivative

$$h'(x) = f'(x) \cdot g(x) + f(x) \cdot g'(x)$$

That is

$$\frac{d}{dx}\{f(x) \cdot g(x)\} = \frac{df}{dx} \cdot g(x) + f(x) \cdot \frac{dg}{dx} \qquad (9)$$

We will not give a proof of (9); it is rather technical and our main concern here is the correct use of this rule.

Example 6   Use the product formula to find dy/dx if $y = x^4(\sqrt{x} + 1)$. Evaluate dy/dx at $x = 1$.

Solution   The factors $f(x) = x^4$ and $g(x) = \sqrt{x} + 1$ are easy to differentiate:

$$\frac{d}{dx}\{x^4\} = 4x^3$$

$$\frac{d}{dx}\{\sqrt{x} + 1\} = \frac{d}{dx}\{x^{1/2} + 1\} = \frac{d}{dx}\{x^{1/2}\} + \frac{d}{dx}\{1\}$$

$$= \frac{1}{2}x^{-1/2} + 0 = \frac{1}{2\sqrt{x}}$$

From the product formula (9) we get

$$\frac{dy}{dx} = \frac{d}{dx}\{x^4\} \cdot (\sqrt{x} + 1) + x^4 \cdot \frac{d}{dx}\{\sqrt{x} + 1\}$$

$$= 4x^3(\sqrt{x} + 1) + \frac{x^4}{2\sqrt{x}}$$

By writing everything in terms of fractional powers of x we can simplify this answer to get $dy/dx = (9/2)x^{7/2} + 4x^3$. At $x = 1$ we find that $dy/dx = 17/2 = 8.5$.

Example 7   Find dy/dx if $y = x^3 \sin x$.

Solution   In (9) let us set $f(x) = x^3$, $g(x) = \sin x$, and $h(x) = f(x) \cdot g(x) = x^3 \sin x$. Using the differentiation formula for $\sin x$ given in Table 3.1, we get

$$\frac{dy}{dx} = f'(x) \cdot g(x) + f(x) \cdot g'(x)$$

$$= (3x^2) \sin x + x^3(\cos x)$$

$$= x^2(3 \sin x + x \cos x)$$

The **quotient** of two functions $f(x)$ and $g(x)$

$$\left(\frac{f}{g}\right)(x) = \frac{f(x)}{g(x)}$$

is defined by taking the quotient of their values for each x. This process yields such functions as $1/x$, where $f(x) = 1$ and $g(x) - x$, and $y - x/(x^2 + 1)$, which is the quotient of x and $x^2 + 1$. As with products, we state the differentiation rule without proof and concentrate on its use in examples.

Quotient Rule for Derivatives   If $f(x)$ and $g(x)$ are differentiable, their quotient $h(x) - f(x)/g(x)$ has derivative

$$h'(x) = \frac{f'(x) \cdot g(x) - f(x) \cdot g'(x)}{[g(x)]^2}$$

In other words

$$\frac{d}{dx}\left\{\frac{f(x)}{g(x)}\right\} = \frac{\frac{df}{dx} \cdot g(x) - f(x) \cdot \frac{dg}{dx}}{[g(x)]^2} \tag{10}$$

The formula applies only to those values of x for which $g(x) \neq 0$, since $h(x)$ is not defined where $g(x)$ is zero.

Example 8 Find $\dfrac{d}{dx}\left\{\dfrac{1}{x^2}\right\}$ by using the quotient rule.

Solution Here $f(x) = 1$ and $g(x) = x^2$, so that $f'(x) = 0$ and $g'(x) = 2x$. Thus

$$\frac{d}{dx}\left\{\frac{1}{x^2}\right\} = \frac{f'(x) \cdot g(x) - f(x) \cdot g'(x)}{[g(x)]^2} = \frac{0 \cdot x^2 - 1 \cdot 2x}{(x^2)^2}$$

$$= \frac{-2x}{x^4} = \frac{-2}{x^3}$$

for all $x \neq 0$. (The function and its derivative are not defined at $x = 0$.)

Example 9 If $y = x/(x^2 + 1)$, find dy/dx.

Solution Taking $f(x) = x$ and $g(x) = x^2 + 1$ in formula (10), we obtain

$$\frac{dy}{dx} = \frac{\dfrac{d}{dx}\{x\} \cdot (x^2 + 1) - x \cdot \dfrac{d}{dx}\{x^2 + 1\}}{(x^2 + 1)^2}$$

$$= \frac{1 \cdot (x^2 + 1) - x(2x)}{(x^2 + 1)^2} = \frac{x^2 + 1 - 2x^2}{(x^2 + 1)^2}$$

$$= \frac{1 - x^2}{(x^2 + 1)^2}$$

Exercises

1. Find dy/dx for the expression $y = (x^2 + 1)(x^3 - 2)$ by each of the following methods, and reconcile the results.

   (*i*) Multiply out the product and differentiate the resulting polynomial.

   (*ii*) Apply the product rule directly.

●2. Differentiate the following functions by using the product rule.

   (*i*) $(x^2 + 1)(x^2 - 1)$ (*iii*) $x^{1/3}(x^4 + 3x^2 + 1)$

   (*ii*) $x^4(1 - x - x^3)$ (*iv*) $x^{-3}(x^2 - 1)$

(v) $(x^4 + x^2 + 1)(14x^3 - 3x + 2)$ (ix) $t^2 e^t$

(vi) $x^{-3}(x^2 + 1)(x^2 - 1)$ (x) $(\sin x)/x$

(vii) $\left(x + \dfrac{1}{x}\right)(\sqrt{x} + 1)$ (xi) $(1 + x + x^2)e^x$

(viii) $x(\log x)$ (xii) $(\sin x)(\cos x)$

●3. Calculate the following derivatives by using the quotient rule.

(i) $\dfrac{1}{x}$ (vii) $\dfrac{x^2 + 3x + 2}{x^2 - x + 1}$

(ii) $\dfrac{1}{1 + x}$ (viii) $\dfrac{1 - 2x}{x^2 + x}$

(iii) $\dfrac{1 + x}{1 - x}$ (ix) $\dfrac{1 + \sqrt{x}}{1 - \sqrt{x}}$

(iv) $\dfrac{-4}{x^2 + 1}$ (x) $\dfrac{\sin x}{\cos x}$

(v) $\dfrac{1}{100 - 45x}$ (xi) $\dfrac{x \cos x}{x^4 + 5x + 1}$

(vi) $\dfrac{x + 2}{1 - x} + \dfrac{1}{x}$ (xii) $\dfrac{x^2 + \cos x + 2}{e^x + 1}$

●4. Find the equation of the line tangent to the graph of $y = 2x/(x^2 + 1)$ at the point $(1, 1)$. Likewise at the point $(2, 4/5)$.

●5. The *average cost per unit* in a manufacturing operation is defined to be

$$A(q) = \frac{\text{total cost}}{\text{number of units}} = \frac{C(q)}{q} \qquad \text{for } q > 0$$

Assuming that the cost function $C(q)$ is differentiable, express the rate of change dA/dq in terms of q, $C(q)$, and the marginal cost dC/dq. Show that $dA/dq = 0$ when the average cost equals the marginal cost, $A = dC/dq$.

*●6. Here is a way to prove the formula $\dfrac{d}{dx}\{x^n\} = nx^{n-1}$ from the product rule.

(i) We already know that $\dfrac{d}{dx}\{x\} = 1$; write x^2 as $x \cdot x$ and apply the product rule to obtain

$$\frac{d}{dx}\{x^2\} = 2x$$

(ii) Write x^3 as $x^2 \cdot x$. Apply the product rule and (i) to obtain

$$\frac{d}{dx}\{x^3\} = 3x^2$$

(iii) Continuing in this manner, explain how you can show that

$$\frac{d}{dx}\{x^n\} = nx^{n-1} \qquad \text{for } n = 1, 2, 3, \ldots$$

3.3   The Chain Rule for Composite Functions

Suppose we inflate a balloon in such a way that its radius r increases with time, say $r = 3t$. The volume V depends on the radius in the usual way, $V = (4/3)\pi r^3$. Thus

$$V = \frac{4}{3}\pi r^3 \quad \text{while} \quad r = 3t$$

The volume may be expressed as a function of t by substituting $r = 3t$ into $V = (4/3)\pi r^3$

$$V = V(t) = \frac{4}{3}\pi(3t)^3 = 36\pi t^3$$

This process of replacing the independent variable in one function by a function of some new variable is an example of **composition** of functions. In the example above we composed $V = (4/3)\pi r^3$ with $r = 3t$ to obtain the **composite function** $V = 36\pi t^3$. In this section we shall give an important rule for differentiating composite functions.

Suppose the independent variable u in one function $y = f(u)$ depends on some other variable x according to some formula $u = g(x)$. Substituting $g(x)$ for u everywhere u appears in $f(u)$, we express y as a function of x

$$y = f(g(x)) \tag{11}$$

This substitution is often denoted by the symbol

$$y = \left[f(u) \Big|_{u=g(x)} \right] \tag{12}$$

Here the vertical bar indicates that $u = g(x)$ should be substituted. For example if

$$y = f(u) = u^2 + 1 \quad \text{and} \quad u = g(x) = 3x + 2$$

we get the following composite function of x by substituting $u = 3x + 2$ into $y = f(u)$:

$$y = f(g(x)) = \left[u^2 + 1 \Big|_{u=3x+2} \right]$$

$$= (3x + 2)^2 + 1 = (9x^2 + 12x + 4) + 1$$

$$= 9x^2 + 12x + 5 \tag{13}$$

For a given value of x, say $x = -3$, the corresponding value of u is $u = g(-3) = 3(-3) + 2 = -7$. The corresponding value of y is obtained by substituting $u = -7$ into $f(u)$

$$y = f(u) = f(-7) = (-7)^2 + 1 = 49 + 1 = 50$$

We can obtain the same result by substituting $x = -3$ directly into (13).

The **chain rule** for differentiating composite functions tells us how to compute dy/dx from the derivatives of the original functions $y = f(u)$ and $u = g(x)$.

Chain Rule   If $y = f(u)$ and $u = g(x)$ are differentiable functions, their composite $y = h(x) = f(g(x))$ has derivative

$$h'(x) = f'(g(x)) \cdot g'(x) \tag{14}$$

This may be expressed in the form

$$\frac{dy}{dx} = \frac{dy}{du} \cdot \frac{du}{dx} \tag{15}$$

but here dy/du is a function of u and we must substitute $u = g(x)$ so that all functions involved have the same variable x. More precisely, this formula can be rewritten as

$$\frac{dy}{dx} = \left[\frac{dy}{du} \bigg|_{u = g(x)} \right] \cdot \frac{du}{dx} \tag{16}$$

Notice that (14)–(16) say the same thing with slightly different notation. This rule can be proved from the approximation principle, as we indicate at the end of this section.

The chain rule is often used to differentiate a complicated function $y = h(x)$. To use it we search for simpler functions $y = f(u)$ and $u = g(x)$ such that $h(x)$ is a composite of these new functions

$$h(x) = f(g(x)) = \left[f(u) \bigg|_{u = g(x)} \right]$$

If we know dy/du and du/dx, then we can find dy/dx.

Example 10   Differentiate the function $y = h(x) = (x^2 + 1)^{20}$.

Solution   We could expand $(x^2 + 1)^{20}$ by tedious multiplication to obtain a polynomial with 21 terms, then differentiate this polynomial. However, the required differentiation is easily accomplished by using the chain rule, taking $f(u) = u^{20}$ and $u = g(x) = x^2 + 1$. Now

$$y = h(x) = f(g(x)) = \left[u^{20}\Big|_{u=x^2+1}\right] = (x^2 + 1)^{20}$$

Furthermore

$$f(u) = u^{20} \qquad \text{so} \qquad \frac{dy}{du} = f'(u) = 20u^{19}$$

$$g(x) = x^2 + 1 \quad \text{so} \quad \frac{du}{dx} = g'(x) = 2x$$

Thus

$$\frac{dy}{dx} = (20u^{19}) \cdot (2x) = 20(x^2 + 1)^{19} \cdot 2x = 40x(x^2 + 1)^{19}$$

Example 11   Find the derivative of the function $y = (1 - x + x^2)^{1/2} = \sqrt{1 - x + x^2}$.

Solution   If we lump together the terms $1 - x + x^2$, denoting them by u, then y is a composite function

$$y(x) = \left[u^{1/2}\Big|_{u=1-x+x^2}\right]$$

Applying formula (15), we get

$$\frac{dy}{dx} = \frac{dy}{du} \cdot \frac{du}{dx}$$

$$= \left[\frac{1}{2} u^{-1/2}\Big|_{u=1-x+x^2}\right] \cdot \frac{d}{dx}\{1 - x + x^2\}$$

$$= \frac{1}{2\sqrt{1 - x + x^2}} \cdot (-1 + 2x)$$

$$= \frac{2x - 1}{2\sqrt{1 - x + x^2}}$$

By using the same ideas we may prove a general rule, a helpful special case of the chain rule (see Exercise 7). If $f(x)$ is a differentiable function and r a real number, let

$$h(x) = (f(x))^r = \left[u^r \Big|_{u=f(x)} \right]$$

Then

$$\frac{d}{dx}\{(f(x))^r\} = r(f(x))^{r-1} \cdot \frac{df}{dx} \tag{17}$$

Example 12   Find ds/dt if $s = \dfrac{t}{\sqrt{t^2+1}}$.

Solution   Here the dependent variable is s and the independent variable t. Now s is given as the quotient of two functions, but it is slightly more convenient to express it as a product

$$s = t \cdot (t^2 + 1)^{-1/2}$$

Using the rule for differentiating a product (9), we get

$$\frac{ds}{dt} = \frac{d}{dt}\{t\} \cdot (t^2 + 1)^{-1/2} + t \cdot \frac{d}{dt}\{(t^2 + 1)^{-1/2}\}$$

Now we use formula (17), taking $f(t) = t^2 + 1$ and $r = -1/2$, to get

$$\frac{d}{dt}\{t\} = 1$$

$$\frac{d}{dt}\{(t^2 + 1)^{-1/2}\} = \left(-\frac{1}{2}\right)(t^2 + 1)^{-3/2} \cdot (2t)$$

$$= -t(t^2 + 1)^{-3/2}$$

The final answer is

$$\frac{ds}{dt} = (t^2 + 1)^{-1/2} - t^2(t^2 + 1)^{-3/2}$$

which may be simplified algebraically by writing $(t^2 + 1)^{-1/2} = (t^2 + 1)(t^2 + 1)^{-3/2}$:

$$\frac{ds}{dt} = (t^2 + 1)^{-1/2} - t^2(t^2 + 1)^{-3/2}$$

$$= (t^2 + 1)^{-3/2}[(t^2 + 1) - t^2]$$

$$= (t^2 + 1)^{-3/2}$$

$$= \frac{1}{(t^2 + 1)^{3/2}}$$

Example 13 Differentiate $y = e^{-x^2/2}$.

Solution This function is the composite of two simpler functions $y = f(u) = e^u$ and $u = g(x) = -x^2/2$:

$$h(x) = \left[e^u \Big|_{u = -x^2/2} \right] = e^{-x^2/2}$$

In Table 3.1 we find that

$$\frac{dy}{du} = e^u$$

Hence, applying the chain rule (15), we get

$$\frac{dy}{dx} = \frac{dy}{du} \cdot \frac{du}{dx} = e^u \cdot \frac{d}{dx} \left\{ -\frac{x^2}{2} \right\} = e^u \cdot \left(\frac{-2x}{2} \right) = -xe^u$$

Since $u = -x^2/2$, we finally obtain a function of x:

$$\frac{dy}{dx} = -xe^{-x^2/2}$$

We remark parenthetically that the function $h(x) = e^{-x^2/2}$ plays a central role in probability and statistics. With a constant multiplier, it gives the well-known normal, or "bell-shaped," distribution.

Sketch Proof of the Chain Rule   If we give x an increment $\Delta x \neq 0$, the corresponding increment Δu in $u = g(x)$ is $\Delta u = g(x + \Delta x) - g(x)$. The increment in u in turn gives an increment Δy in $y = f(u)$ at the point $u = g(x)$:

$$\Delta y = f(g(x + \Delta x)) - f(g(x)) = f(u + \Delta u) - f(u)$$

Using the approximation principle twice (at each $\approx$ symbol), we get

$$f(u + \Delta u) - f(u) \approx f'(u) \cdot \Delta u$$

$$= f'(u)[g(x + \Delta x) - g(x)]$$

$$\approx f'(u) \cdot [g'(x) \cdot \Delta x]$$

so that

$$\frac{\Delta y}{\Delta x} \approx f'(u) \cdot g'(x) \cdot \frac{\Delta x}{\Delta x} = f'(u) \cdot g'(x) \qquad (u = g(x))$$

The degree of approximation gets better and better as Δx approaches zero. In the limit we find that

$$\frac{dy}{dx} = \lim_{\Delta x \to 0} \frac{\Delta y}{\Delta x} = f'(u) \cdot g'(x) = f'(g(x)) \cdot g'(x)$$

as required.

Exercises

- 1. Compute the composite function $f(g(x)) = \left[f(u)|_{u = g(x)} \right]$ if
    - (i) $f(u) = u^3$, $g(x) = 1 - x$
    - (ii) $f(u) = 1/u$, $g(x) = x^2 + 1$
    - (iii) $f(u) = u^2 + 1$, $g(x) = 1/x$
    - (iv) $f(u) = \sqrt{u}$, $g(x) = (1 + x)/(1 - x)$
    - (v) $f(u) = (1 + u)/(1 - u)$, $g(x) = \sqrt{x}$
    - (vi) $f(u) = u^2 + u + 1$, $g(x) = \sqrt{x^2 + 1}$

- 2. Express the following functions as composites $y = f(g(x))$ of simpler functions $y = f(u)$ and $u = g(x)$.
    - (i) $(x^2 - x + 1)^{45}$
    - (ii) $(7 - x)^5$
    - (iii) $\sqrt{1 - x^2}$
    - (iv) $\sqrt[3]{x^2 - x + 2}$
    - (v) $\dfrac{1}{\sqrt{x^2 + x + 3}}$
    - (vi) $\sqrt{1 + \sqrt{x}}$
    - (vii) e^{-x}
    - (viii) $\log(1 - x^2)$

- 3. Use the chain rule to calculate the derivatives of the functions in Exercise 2.

4. Express as composites of simpler functions:

(i) $\sqrt{\dfrac{1-x^2}{1+x^2}}$

(vi) $1 + 4\sin(9 + 3\pi x)$

(ii) $(x + \sqrt{x})^{1/5}$

(vii) $2 - e^{x^2+x+1}$

(iii) $\dfrac{1}{1 - \sqrt{x}}$

(viii) $(\sin x)^3$

(iv) $\sqrt{x+2} + \dfrac{1}{\sqrt{x+2}} + 10$

(ix) $\sin(x^3)$

(v) e^{4+3x}

● 5. Differentiate the functions listed in Exercise 4.

● 6. Differentiate the following functions by any combination of methods.

(i) $\sqrt{1-x^2}$

(vi) e^{kx} (k a constant)

(ii) $x\sqrt{1-x^2}$

(vii) xe^{-x}

(iii) $\dfrac{2x}{\sqrt{1-x}}$

(viii) $\sqrt{\dfrac{1-x}{1+x}}$

(iv) $\dfrac{1-x^2}{\sqrt{x^2+x+1}}$

(ix) $\cos(3 + 4\pi x)$

(v) $\left(\dfrac{x}{x+1}\right)^{10}$

(x) $\dfrac{x\sqrt{1+x^2}}{(x+1)}$

● 7. If $f(x)$ is a differentiable function and r a real number, prove the differentiation formula (17)

$$\frac{d}{dx}\{(f(x))^r\} = r \cdot (f(x))^{r-1} \cdot \frac{df}{dx}$$

by using the chain rule.

● 8. A small hydrogen generator produces a volume of hydrogen

$$V = \frac{1000t^2}{1+t^2} \text{ cubic feet}$$

in t minutes of operation. If the generator is used to inflate a weather balloon, find the radius of the balloon r (in feet) t minutes after the generator is started. Find dr/dt one minute after start-up.

● 9. As an object is moved to greater and greater heights above the Earth's surface, the force of gravity gets weaker, and consequently the weight of the object decreases. The weight at height h (miles) is given by

$$W(h) = \frac{W_0}{\left(\dfrac{h}{3950}+1\right)^2} = W_0\left(\frac{h}{3950}+1\right)^{-2}$$

where W_0 is the weight at sea level. If an object weighs 100 pounds at sea level ($W_0 = 100$), calculate its weight at altitudes $h = 0$ and $h = 50$ miles. Calculate the rate of change dW/dh

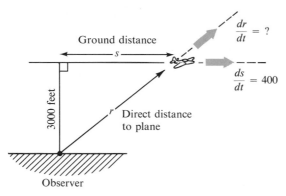

Figure 3.1
When $t = 10$ seconds, $s = 4000$ feet. (Why?) The triangle
shown is a right triangle.

as a function of h. Evaluate dW/dh when $h = 0$ (sea level). ANSWERS:

$$W'(h) = \frac{-1}{19.75}\left(\frac{h}{3950} + 1\right)^{-3}$$

$W(0) = 100$, $W(50) = 97.52$ pounds; $W'(0) = -0.05063$ pounds per mile.

●10. Use the result of Exercise 9 and the approximation principle to estimate the change in weight
of a 100-pound object if it is taken from San Francisco (sea level) to Denver (elevation 1 mile).
Estimate the change in weight if it is lifted from sea level to a height of 150 miles by rocket.
HINT: Use the answers to Exercise 9. There is no need to repeat those calculations.

●11. An airplane flies a straight course at constant speed $v = 400$ feet per second at a constant
altitude of 3000 feet, as shown in Figure 3.1. The triangle in this figure is a right triangle, so
by Pythagoras' Theorem its side lengths are related by the formula

$$r = \sqrt{(3000)^2 + s^2} \tag{18}$$

Compute s as a function of t (in seconds) if the plane is directly overhead at time $t = 0$.
Compute r as a function of t using (18). Compute dr/ds and dr/dt. How fast is the direct distance
r from the observer increasing 10 seconds after the plane passes overhead (find dr/dt at
$t = 10$)?

3.4   Maxima and Minima of a Function

Here are typical items that might be found in any newspaper.

   News item—"The rate of inflation last month reached an all-time peak."

   Advertisement—"The NRG Motor Company offers the lowest prices in town
on used cars."

Much of our everyday life is concerned with maximizing or minimizing certain variables. We have already presented some ways in which derivatives can be used to resolve such "optimization problems", in Section 2.6. We defer detailed solution of practical problems until Section 3.7. In this section we shall take up optimization problems for an arbitrary function $y = f(x)$, without attaching any special interpretation to the function. First we define some terms.

Definition   If a function $y = f(x)$ is defined at x_0, we say that x_0 is

    (*i*) a **relative maximum** if $f(x) \leqslant f(x_0)$ for all points x in the domain of definition that lie near x_0. That is, the value of f is at least as large at x_0 as it is at any *nearby* point where f is defined.

    (*ii*) an **absolute maximum** if $f(x) \leqslant f(x_0)$ for all points x in the domain of definition, whether they lie close to x_0 or not.

Relative (and absolute) minima are defined similarly; for minima, $f(x) \geqslant f(x_0)$ for all nearby points x (for all points x) in the domain of definition. If a point x_0 is either a maximum or a minimum, we sometimes combine these two possibilities by calling x_0 an **extremum** for f. Notice that we emphasize the place (value of x) where the largest or smallest value of f occurs, rather than the value $y = f(x)$. Once we know x the value of $y = f(x)$ is easy to calculate. Calculus methods will be used to locate the appropriate x. The nature of the graph of $y = f(x)$ near a relative maximum or minimum is shown in Figure 3.2. You might re-read the definition with these pictures in mind. In Figure 3.3 we show a fairly complicated graph. On it we have indicated all the relative extrema and absolute extrema.

We start our discussion of optimization with the following problem: locate the extrema of a function $y = f(x)$ that is *defined on a bounded interval $a \leqslant x \leqslant b$,* which we refer to as I. In many practical situations the feasible range of x is bounded from above and from below—hence our interest in this special problem. We shall assume that $f(x)$ is defined, but not necessarily differentiable, for all x in the interval I. A point x in the domain of definition of $y = f(x)$ is a **critical point** for f if either

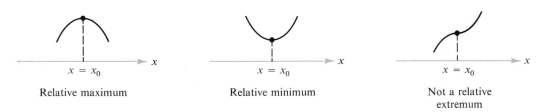

Relative maximum   Relative minimum   Not a relative
                                                                       extremum

Figure 3.2
We can decide whether $y = f(x)$ has a relative maximum or minimum at $x = x_0$ by comparing $y_0 = f(x_0)$ with the values $y = f(x)$ for points x close to x_0. Some of the possibilities are shown above.

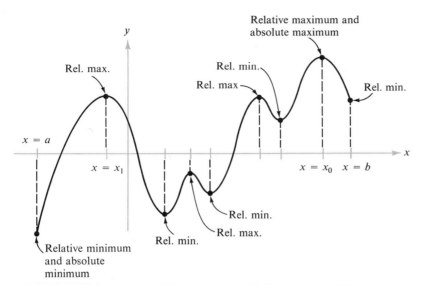

Figure 3.3

On the graph of $y = f(x)$, relative maxima correspond to high points (peaks) and relative minima to low points (valleys). If f is defined on the interval $a \leqslant x \leqslant b$, the largest value for y is achieved at $x = x_0$, which is the absolute maximum. A relative maximum occurs at $x = x_1$, but x_1 is not an absolute maximum since $f(x)$ has an even higher value at $x = x_0$, some distance away. The various absolute and relative extrema on the graph are labeled. Note carefully that a maximum or minimum may occur at either of the endpoints of the interval on which f is defined. Here the absolute minimum occurs at endpoint $x = a$. There is a relative minimum at the other endpoint $x - b$.

  (*i*) f fails to be differentiable at x; or

  (*ii*) f is differentiable at x with $f'(x) = 0$.

If $f(x)$ is differentiable at all points, finding the critical points amounts to solving the equation $f'(x) = 0$. The critical points of f are instrumental in locating the absolute extrema of f, as we indicate below.

Relative Extrema and Critical Points   If $y = f(x)$, defined for all x in an interval $a \leqslant x \leqslant b$, has a relative extremum at x_0, then x_0 must be either

  (*i*) a critical point within the interval $a < x < b$; or

  (*ii*) one of the endpoints $x = a$ or $x = b$.   (19)

In fact, if x_0 is not an endpoint and not a critical point, then f is defined at all points x to either side of x_0, f is differentiable at x_0, and $f'(x_0)$ is nonzero. Since by the approximation principle $\Delta f \approx f'(x_0) \cdot \Delta x$ for small increments away from x_0, we can increase $f(x)$ by moving in one direction and decrease $f(x)$ by moving in the opposite direction, starting from x_0. Thus a relative extremum cannot occur at x_0. By default, every relative extremum must occur at a critical point or an endpoint.

The important task in applications is to locate *absolute* maxima and minima. For example, if $P = P(q)$ is a profit function and q_0 is a relative maximum, we only know that profits at q_0 are higher than profits at *nearby* operating levels q. There may be other operating levels some distance from q_0 that yield even higher profit. Finding the critical points is the first step toward identifying the absolute extrema. Every absolute extremum is a relative extremum and so, according to (19), must appear among the critical points or endpoints. We need a procedure for actually picking out the absolute extrema. This can be troublesome if f has an unbounded domain of definition, say the whole number line. But if f is defined on a bounded interval $a \leqslant x \leqslant b$ there is a very simple procedure.

Locating Absolute Extrema in a Bounded Interval   Suppose that $y = f(x)$ is defined and continuous on an interval of the form $a \leqslant x \leqslant b$. Then

STEP 1   Locate all critical points $x_1, \ldots, x_k$ within the interval.

STEP 2   Calculate the values $y = f(x)$ at these critical points and at the endpoints $x = a$ and $x = b$.

STEP 3   Compare the values $f(a), f(x_1), \ldots, f(x_k), f(b)$. The largest of these is the absolute maximum for f on the interval $a \leqslant x \leqslant b$; the smallest is the absolute minimum.

To justify this procedure we invoke a result that is simple enough to state, but whose proof must be left to more advanced courses. *If $f(x)$ is continuous on a bounded interval $a \leqslant x \leqslant b$, then absolute maxima and absolute minima actually exist somewhere in the interval*. Simple examples (Exercise 5) show that absolute extrema need not exist at all if $f(x)$ is defined on an unbounded interval. Once the existence of absolute extrema is assured, we may argue as follows. An absolute maximum occurs somewhere, say at $x = p$. By (19), p must appear in our list of points $a, x_1, \ldots, x_k, b$ from Steps 1 and 2. Since p is an absolute maximum $f(p) \geqslant f(x)$ for all x, and in particular $f(p) \geqslant f(a), f(p) \geqslant f(x_1), \ldots, f(p) \geqslant f(x_k), f(p) \geqslant f(b)$. That is, p must be the point in our list at which f has the largest value, as stated in Step 3. The same reasoning applies to finding absolute minima.

Example 14   The following functions are defined and continuous on the interval $-1 \leqslant x \leqslant 1$:

(*i*) $f(x) = 3x - 2$

(*ii*) $g(x) = x^2 + 1$

(*iii*) $h(x) = x^3$

Find all critical points and absolute extrema for each function. What is the maximum value achieved by each function on this interval?

Solution

(*i*) This function is differentiable, with $dy/dx = 3$ (constant function). Since dy/dx is never zero, there are no critical points. Next we calculate the endpoint values

$$f(-1) = 3 \cdot (-1) - 2 = -5 \qquad f(+1) = 3 \cdot 1 - 2 = +1$$

to complete Step 2 of our procedure. Finally, the absolute maximum value is achieved at the right-hand endpoint $x = +1$, where $y = +1$. The absolute minimum occurs at $x = -1$.

(*ii*) For all x we get $g'(x) = 2x$. Therefore $g'(x) = 0$ at $x = 0$; $x = 0$ is the only critical point. The values $y = g(x)$ at this critical point and the endpoints $x = -1$ and $x = +1$ are

$$g(-1) = 2 \qquad g(0) = 1 \qquad g(+1) = 2$$

The absolute maximum value occurs at $x = -1$ and at $x = +1$, where $y = +2$. The absolute minimum occurs at $x = 0$.

(*iii*) Once again our function is everywhere differentiable, so we locate the critical points by solving the equation $h'(x) = 3x^2 = 0$. Obviously $x = 0$ is the only solution and the only critical point. Finally, list the values at $x = 0$ and the endpoints

$$h(-1) = -1 \qquad h(0) = 0 \qquad h(+1) = 1$$

The absolute maximum occurs at the right-hand endpoint $x = +1$, where $y = +1$. The absolute minimum occurs at the left-hand endpoint $x = -1$. Notice that the maximum and minimum here occur at the endpoints, rather than at a critical point. (By sketching the graph you can show that the critical point $x = 0$ isn't even a relative extremum.)

Example 15   Find the absolute maximum value of the function $y = f(x) = -x^4 + 4x^3 + 8x^2 + 3$ on the interval $-3 \leqslant x \leqslant +3$.

Solution   Since $f(x)$ is continuous on a bounded interval our procedure applies. To find the critical points we must solve the equation

$$f'(x) = -4x^3 + 12x^2 + 16x = 0$$

We do this by factoring the polynomial

$$-4x^3 + 12x^2 + 16x = -4x(x^2 - 3x - 4) = -4x(x - 4)(x + 1)$$

The only way this product can be zero is for one of the factors to be zero. Thus the only solutions of the equation $df/dx = 0$ are

$$x_1 = 0 \qquad x_2 = +4 \qquad x_3 = -1 \tag{20}$$

Since x_2 does not lie in the interval on which f is defined, we do not consider it any further; the remaining points $x_1 = 0$ and $x_3 = -1$ are the critical points for f on the interval $-3 \leqslant x \leqslant +3$.

Next we compute $y = f(x)$ at the critical points and at the endpoints $a = -3$ and $b = +3$.

$$f(a) = f(-3) = -114 \qquad f(x_3) = f(-1) = 6$$

$$f(x_1) = f(0) = 3 \qquad f(b) = f(+3) = 102$$

Clearly the largest of these values is $y = 102$; this is the absolute maximum value of f. It occurs at the endpoint $b = +3$.

We can vary this problem a bit by trying to maximize $f(x)$ on the interval $-3 \leqslant x \leqslant +5$. Now it turns out that all solutions (20) of the equation $df/dx = 0$ lie in the domain of definition of f, and so are critical points for f. In this case the absolute maximum value of f is $+131$; it occurs at the critical point $x_2 = +4$ (see Exercise 3 for details). Although we do not need the graph of f to answer these questions, you may find it interesting to refer to the graph (Figure 3.4) to see geometrically why the answers turn out as they do for the different intervals $-3 \leqslant x \leqslant +3$ and $-3 \leqslant x \leqslant +5$.

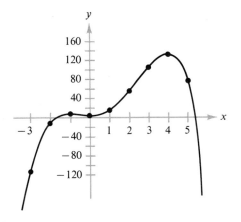

Figure 3.4
Graph of $y = -x^4 + 4x^3 + 8x^2 + 3$.

We must emphasize that this procedure applies only to functions defined on *bounded intervals*. In some applications to geometry, statistics, and the physical sciences, functions are used whose domains of definition are unbounded intervals, such as $0 < x < +\infty$ (all x such that $0 < x$) or the whole number line. Absolute maxima and minima might not exist for such functions (see Exercise 5), and even when they do exist a more detailed analysis of the function and its critical points is needed to identify them. These methods will be discussed in Section 3.6.

Exercises

●1. Find the critical points of the following functions:

(*i*) $y = -3x + 4$

(*ii*) $y = 4 + 7x - 3x^2$

(*iii*) $y = x^3 - 12x + 7$

(*iv*) $y = 3x^4 - 16x^3 + 18x^2 - 5$

(*v*) $y = x\sqrt{x^2 + 1}$

(*vi*) $y = x/(x^2 + 1)$

●2. Find the absolute maximum and minimum values of the following functions on the interval $-1 \leqslant x \leqslant 2$.

(*i*) $y = -3x + 4$ (*ii*) $y = 4 + 7x - 3x^2$ (*iii*) $y = x^3 - 12x + 7$

●3. Find the absolute maximum and absolute minimum values achieved by $y = -x^4 + 4x^3 + 8x^2 + 3$ on the bounded interval $-3 \leqslant x \leqslant +5$.

●4. Use the procedure given in this section to locate the absolute maxima and minima for the following functions on the bounded intervals indicated.

(*i*) $y = x + \dfrac{1}{x}$ on $\dfrac{1}{3} \leqslant x \leqslant 2$

(*ii*) $y = \dfrac{1}{3}x^3 + x^2 - 3x + 1$ on $-5 \leqslant x \leqslant 4$

(*iii*) $C = 4320 + 0.30q - 0.000005q^2$ on $0 \leqslant q \leqslant 40{,}000$

(*iv*) $s = \dfrac{4t}{t^2 + 1}$ on $0 \leqslant t \leqslant 10$

(*v*) $w = \dfrac{1 - r}{1 + r}$ on $0 \leqslant r \leqslant 100$

5. Sketch the graph of each of the following functions. In each case take the whole number line as the domain of definition.

(*i*) $y = x + 1$ (linear function)

(*ii*) $y = x^2$ (parabola)

(*iii*) $y = x^3$ (cubic curve)

By examining the graphs, decide whether there are any *absolute extrema*. Pay particular attention to what happens as x gets large positive or large negative.

6. Repeat Exercise 5, taking the bounded interval $-1 \leqslant x \leqslant +2$ as the domain of definition in each case.

•7. The profit function in Example 14, Section 1.6, was

$$P(q) = -5,000,000 + 61q - 0.000098q^2$$

for $0 \leqslant q \leqslant 1,000,000$. Find the absolute maximum and the corresponding value of q. Repeat the problem, assuming the feasible range of q to be $0 \leqslant q \leqslant 250,000$.

•8. At production level q, suppose that the cost function for a factory is

$$C(q) = 1000 + 100q - q^2$$

the demand function is

$$p(q) = 300 - 5q$$

and the feasible range of production levels is $0 \leqslant q \leqslant 100$.

    (*i*) Find the revenue function $R(q)$.

    (*ii*) Find the profit function $P(q)$.

    (*iii*) Find the value of q that maximizes profit.

3.5   Higher Derivatives

If a function $y = f(x)$ is differentiable, its derivative is another function $y' = f'(x)$. If $f'(x)$ is itself differentiable, we can apply the differentiation process to it. The resulting function, called the **second derivative**, is denoted by any one of the following interchangeable symbols:

$$\frac{d^2y}{dx^2} = \frac{d}{dx}\left(\frac{dy}{dx}\right) \qquad \frac{d^2f}{dx^2} \qquad y'' \qquad f'' \qquad f^{(2)}$$

Example 16   Find d^2y/dx^2 if $y = x^3 - 4x^2 + 2x - 3$.

Solution   Our rule for differentiating polynomials yields

$$\frac{dy}{dx} = 3x^2 - 8x + 2$$

We then differentiate the function dy/dx to obtain the second derivative

$$\frac{d^2y}{dx^2} = 6x - 8$$

There is no reason why this process cannot be continued, provided that we obtain differentiable functions at each step. Differentiating the second derivative function, we obtain a new function called the **third derivative** d^3y/dx^3; differentiating the third derivative yields the **fourth derivative** d^4y/dx^4, and so on.

Example 17   Find $\dfrac{d^n y}{dx^n}$ for all $n = 1, 2, \ldots$ if $y = x^3 - 4x^2 + 2x - 3$.

Solution   We have found the first derivative dy/dx and the second derivative d^2y/dx^2 in Example 16 above. Differentiating the function $d^2y/dx^2 = 6x - 8$, we obtain

$$\frac{d^3 y}{dx^3} = 6 \qquad \text{(a constant function)}$$

Differentiating again, we obtain

$$\frac{d^4 y}{dx^4} = 0$$

Now any further differentiation will yield the zero function, so that

$$\frac{d^n y}{dx^n} = 0 \qquad \text{for all } n \geq 4$$

Example 18   If $f(x) = (x^2 + 1)^{3/2}$, find $f''(x)$.

Solution   We first calculate $f'(x)$ using formula (17), with $r = 3/2$.

$$f'(x) = \frac{3}{2}(x^2 + 1)^{1/2} \cdot (2x) = 3x(x^2 + 1)^{1/2}$$

Differentiating once more, we get

$$f''(x) = \frac{d}{dx}\{3x\} \cdot (x^2 + 1)^{1/2} + 3x \cdot \frac{d}{dx}\{(x^2 + 1)^{1/2}\} \quad \text{(product rule)}$$

$$= 3(x^2 + 1)^{1/2} + 3x \cdot \left(\frac{1}{2}\right)(x^2 + 1)^{-1/2} \cdot (2x) \quad \text{(by (17); } r = \tfrac{1}{2})$$

$$= 3(x^2 + 1)^{1/2} + 3x^2(x^2 + 1)^{-1/2}$$

$$= 3(x^2 + 1)^{-1/2}[(x^2 + 1) + x^2]$$

$$= 3(x^2 + 1)^{-1/2}(2x^2 + 1)$$

$$= \frac{3(2x^2 + 1)}{\sqrt{x^2 + 1}}$$

The second derivative of a function f is useful both for what it tells us about the function, and also for applications. For example, what is it that causes the queasy feeling you sometimes get in a high-speed elevator? It does not occur when you travel at a constant velocity even though your velocity may be very great. You get this feeling when the elevator starts and stops; in other words, it is due to *change* in velocity. In both common parlance and physics, change in velocity is called acceleration. That is, the **acceleration** of a moving object is the instantaneous rate of change in its velocity $v(t)$ as a function of time. If the position of the object is given as a function of time by $s = f(t)$, the velocity of the object is (by definition) the first derivative

$$\text{velocity} = v(t) = \frac{ds}{dt} = f'(t)$$

Thus, the acceleration must be the second derivative

$$\text{acceleration} = \frac{d}{dt}\{v(t)\} = \frac{d}{dt}\left(\frac{ds}{dt}\right) = \frac{d^2s}{dt^2} = f''(t)$$

We shall illustrate the concept of acceleration in the next two examples, the first describing free fall and the second describing the motion of an elevator.

Example 19   A stone falls a distance $s = 16t^2$ feet in t seconds after it has been released. Find the acceleration as a function of time.

Solution   The velocity (measured in feet per second) is $ds/dt = 32t$ and the acceleration is $d^2s/dt^2 = 32$ (measured in units of *feet/second²* or *feet per second per second*). The acceleration is therefore *constant*, equal to 32 feet/second². This acceleration is a physical constant, characteristic of all dense objects falling freely under the influence of gravity on the Earth's surface. (On the surface of the moon a different constant would apply, roughly 5.33 feet/second², since $s = 2.66t^2$.)

Example 20   An elevator travels for 4 seconds between stops. Suppose that the distance travelled s (in feet) is given in terms of elapsed time t (in seconds) by the formula

$$s = \frac{32}{5}t - \frac{2}{25}(t-2)^5 - \frac{64}{25} \qquad \text{for } 0 \leqslant t \leqslant 4$$

Find the velocity and acceleration of the elevator.

Solution   The velocity v is given as a function of time by

$$v = \frac{ds}{dt} = \frac{32}{5} - \frac{2}{5}(t-2)^4$$

and the acceleration a is given by

$$a = \frac{dv}{dt} = \frac{d^2s}{dt^2} = -\frac{8}{5}(t-2)^3$$

Graphs of the functions are sketched in Figure 3.5. The acceleration has its largest magnitude at the start, when $t = 0$, and at the end, when $t = 4$. At these two instants the magnitude of a is 12.8 feet/second^2, about 40% as large as gravity (32 feet/second^2, as in Example 19 above). Large magnitudes of acceleration correspond to rapid changes in velocity. Our bodies are sensitive to such changes in velocity, but not to velocity itself, hence our discomfort at the beginning and end, but not the middle of the trip.

There is a useful geometric interpretation of the second derivative. Recall that a function is increasing if its derivative is positive, and decreasing if it is negative (Section 2.6). Now apply this remark to the function dy/dx and its derivative d^2y/dx^2 to conclude that

$$\frac{dy}{dx} \text{ is } \textit{increasing} \text{ if its derivative } \frac{d^2y}{dx^2} \text{ is } \textit{positive}$$

$$\frac{dy}{dx} \text{ is } \textit{decreasing} \text{ if its derivative } \frac{d^2y}{dx^2} \text{ is } \textit{negative}$$

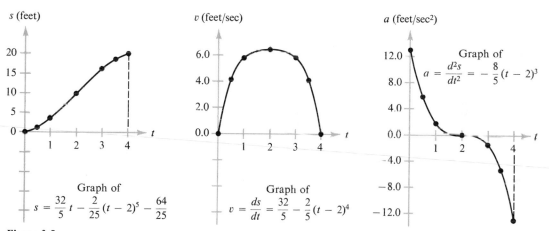

Figure 3.5
Graphs of the distance, velocity, and acceleration functions in Example 20. Between $t = 0$ and $t = 0.5$, velocity increases rapidly from $v = 0$ to $v = 4.4$ feet per second; this corresponds to the large (positive) acceleration near $t = 0$. Up to $t = 2$ the velocity continues to increase, but at a slower and slower rate, so that the acceleration, while still positive, decreases to zero. From $t = 2$ to $t = 4$ the velocity decreases, and consequently its rate of change (acceleration) is negative. This velocity decrease becomes more pronounced as we approach $t = 4$, so the acceleration becomes more negative.

But dy/dx is the slope of the graph of $y = f(x)$. If dy/dx increases as x increases, then the slope increases and the graph must "bend up" as in Figure 3.6(a). A curve with this shape is said to be **concave upwards**. Similarly, if the slope dy/dx decreases as x increases, then the graph "bends down" as in Figure 3.6(b), and is said to be **concave downwards**.

Example 21   The function in Example 20 gives distance as a function of time

$$s = \frac{32}{5}t - \frac{2}{25}(t-2)^5 - \frac{64}{25} \qquad \text{for } 0 \leqslant t \leqslant 4 \text{ seconds}$$

Where is the graph of this function concave upward? concave downward?

Solution   In Example 20 we calculated the second derivative

$$\frac{d^2s}{dt^2} = -\frac{8}{5}(t-2)^3$$

Clearly if $0 \leqslant t < 2$ then $(t-2) < 0$ and $(t-2)^3 < 0$, so that

$$\frac{d^2s}{dt^2} = -\frac{8}{5}(t-2)^3 > 0 \qquad \text{for } 0 \leqslant t < 2$$

The graph is concave upward over the interval $0 \leqslant t < 2$. Similarly, if $2 < t \leqslant 4$ then $d^2s/dt^2 < 0$; the graph is concave down for $2 < t \leqslant 4$, as shown in Figure 3.5. At $t = 2$ we have $d^2s/dt^2 = 0$. There the concavity changes from being upward (to the left of $t = 2$) to being downward (to the right of $t = 2$). Such a transition point is called an **inflection point** of the graph. The presence of an inflection point is usually marked by the occurrence of a zero value for the second derivative.

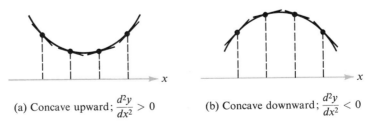

(a) Concave upward; $\dfrac{d^2y}{dx^2} > 0$ (b) Concave downward; $\dfrac{d^2y}{dx^2} < 0$

Figure 3.6
The concept of concavity and its relation to the second derivative d^2y/dx^2. In (a) the graph is concave upwards. The slope of the tangent line steadily increases as x moves to the right, so that $d^2y/dx^2 = $ *rate of change of slope* is positive. In (b) the graph is concave downwards; the slope steadily decreases (starting positive and finally becoming more and more negative), and $d^2y/dx^2 < 0$.

We conclude this section by briefly describing other uses of second derivatives. In economic theory the utility U of a commodity is a function $U = U(q)$ of the quantity consumed; it is a measure of the benefits derived by the consumer at various levels of consumption. As usual in economics, the rate of change dU/dq is called the *marginal utility* (recall Section 2.6). The *Weber-Fechner law* of decreasing marginal effect states that as q increases the marginal utility decreases. That is, in mathematical terms

$$\frac{d^2 U}{dq^2} < 0 \tag{21}$$

This means that the graph of the utility function $U = U(q)$ is concave downward. A typical graph with property (21) is shown in Figure 3.7. There are analogs of this "law of decreasing marginal effect" in many other fields, such as psychology. For example, the marginal effect of such stimuli as heat or pain tends to decrease as the total amount of stimulus increases.

Here is another case, a biological problem, in which the second derivative is important. One could chart the progress of an epidemic by plotting a graph that shows, as in Figure 3.8, the cumulative number $N(t)$ of reported cases as a function

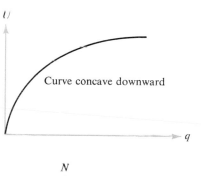

Curve concave downward

Figure 3.7
Graph of a typical function $U(q)$ with $d^2U/dq^2 < 0$.

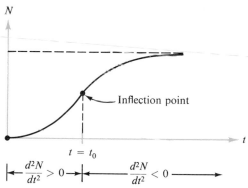

Figure 3.8
Cumulative number $N(t)$ of reported cases during an epidemic.

of time t (days from the start of the outbreak). The rate of change dN/dt gives the *infection rate*, the number of new cases per day. At first the infection rate increases, but finally it reaches its peak, and thereafter decreases toward zero. The transition point, shown as $t = t_0$ in Figure 3.8, is of great importance. It is directly related to the second derivative d^2N/dt^2. In fact, t_0 is the point at which the second derivative changes from

$$\frac{d^2N}{dt^2} > 0 \qquad \left(\text{infection rate } \frac{dN}{dt} \text{ *increasing*; graph concave *upward*}\right)$$

to

$$\frac{d^2N}{dt^2} < 0 \qquad \left(\text{infection rate } \frac{dN}{dt} \text{ *decreasing*; graph concave *downward*}\right)$$

At $t = t_0$ there is an inflection point, with $d^2N/dt^2 = 0$.

Exercises

●1. Calculate d^2y/dx^2 for the following functions:

   (i) $x^4 - 15x^2 - 1400$

   (ii) $\sqrt{x} - \dfrac{1}{\sqrt{x}}$

   (iii) $\dfrac{1}{x^2 - 1}$

   (iv) $\dfrac{x+1}{x-1}$

   (v) $1 + e^{4x-1}$

   (vi) $-3\sin(4x)$

●2. Find $f''(x)$ if

   (i) $f(x) = \sqrt{x}$
   (ii) $f(x) = \sqrt{1 - x^2}$
   (iii) $f(x) = x\sqrt{x^2 + 1}$

   ANSWERS: (i) $(-1/4)x^{-3/2}$; (ii) $-(1 - x^2)^{-3/2}$; (iii) $(2x^3 + 3x)/(x^2 + 1)^{3/2}$

●3. For the function $y = x^4 + 2x^3 - 12x^2$, find y''. Where is the graph of the function concave upward? concave downward? Find all inflection points.

●4. An object moving along a straight line has distance to the right of the origin

$$s = t^3 - 2t^2 + 1 \qquad \text{for } t \geqslant 0$$

   Find its speed and acceleration as functions of t. For which values of t is d^2s/dt^2 positive (acceleration to the right)? negative (acceleration to the left)?

●5. If the cumulative number of reported flu cases during a small-town epidemic is given by

$$N(t) = \frac{1500t^2}{1 + t^2} \qquad (t \text{ in weeks})$$

Calculate (*i*) the infection rate dN/dt; (*ii*) the second derivative d^2N/dt^2. When does the epidemic reach its peak ($d^2N/dt^2 = 0$)?

●6. Calculate d^3y/dx^3 if $y = x^{10} + 7x^6 - x^3 + 13x - \sqrt{5}$.

3.6   Derivatives and Curve Sketching

Up to now we have relied heavily on a table of values when graphing a function. This is a basic but rather primitive technique. Now we have at our disposal rules for calculating first and second derivatives; we also know how to interpret these derivatives geometrically, as properties of the graph of the function. It is time for us to return to the subject of graphing, bringing to bear our knowledge of derivatives. We shall also see how to locate absolute maxima and minima for functions with unbounded domains of definition, the case not covered by the discussion in Section 3.4.

Let us organize what we know about derivatives and graphs so we may apply this information in an orderly way. We begin with a differentiable function $y = f(x)$. The significance of its first derivative is indicated in Table 3.2. As shown in Section 2.6, wherever the derivative is nonzero its sign determines whether $f(x)$ is increasing (graph rising) or decreasing (graph falling) as x moves to the right.

Sign of $\dfrac{df}{dx}$	Information about the graph	Shape of the graph
$\dfrac{df}{dx} > 0$	$f(x)$ increases; graph rises	
$\dfrac{df}{dx} < 0$	$f(x)$ decreases; graph falls	

Table 3.2
The sign of df/dx determines whether the graph is rising or falling as x increases.

At the critical points, where $df/dx = 0$, there are various possibilities. The function might have a relative maximum or a relative minimum, or show some more complicated behavior (see Figure 3.9).

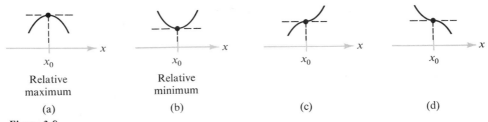

Figure 3.9
Types of behavior of $y = f(x)$ near a critical point x_0. In each case $f'(x_0) = 0$, so the tangent line is horizontal. Frequently there is a transition from rising to falling, or vice-versa, at a critical point, as in (a) and (b), but this is not always so, as can be seen in (c) and (d).

Table 3.3 recalls the significance of the second derivative. Where d^2f/dx^2 is nonzero its sign determines whether the graph is concave upward or downward. A point x_0 marking a transition from concave upward to concave downward, or vice versa, is called an **inflection point**. At such points $f'' = 0$, if the second derivative is defined there.

Sign of $\dfrac{d^2f}{dx^2}$	Information about the graph	Shape of the graph
$\dfrac{d^2f}{dx^2} > 0$	concave upward	(graph) or (graph)
$\dfrac{d^2f}{dx^2} < 0$	concave downward	(graph) or (graph)

Table 3.3
The sign of the second derivative d^2f/dx^2 determines whether the graph is concave upward or downward.

The graph of $y = f(x)$ may be sketched by carrying out the following steps.

Procedure for Curve Sketching

STEP 1   Calculate the first derivative $df/dx = f'(x)$. Determine where $f'(x)$ is positive, negative, or zero. This tells us where f is increasing, decreasing, or has a critical point.

STEP 2   Calculate the second derivative $d^2f/dx^2 = f''(x)$. Determine where $f''(x)$ is positive, negative, or zero. This tells us where the graph is concave upward or downward, or has a possible inflection point.

STEP 3   Plot the points on the graph corresponding to values of x such that $df/dx = 0$ (critical points) or $d^2f/dx^2 = 0$. These are important in making a sketch because the sign of df/dx or d^2f/dx^2 is likely to change at these points. If this is so, the nature of the graph also changes.

STEP 4   Use the information from the preceding steps to sketch the graph. Plot additional points as needed to make a reasonably accurate sketch.

In practice, the information provided by the first derivative is of primary importance; the second derivative is useful for fine details, but is less important.

Example 22   Sketch the graph of $y = x^3 - 2x^2 - 4x + 4$, defined for all x.

Solution   STEP 1   We observe that f has derivative $f'(x) = 3x^2 - 4x - 4 = (3x + 2)(x - 2)$. Thus

$$\frac{df}{dx} = 0 \qquad \text{at } x = +2 \text{ and at } x = -\frac{2}{3}$$

The sign of $f'(x) = (3x + 2)(x - 2)$ is determined from the signs of the individual factors $(3x + 2)$ and $(x - 2)$ by applying the rule of signs. The easiest way to keep track of the signs is to set up a diagram like Figure 3.10.

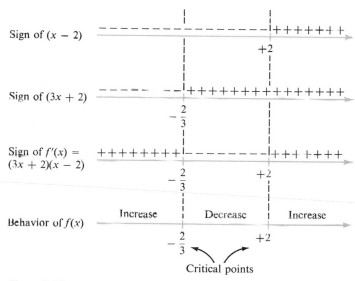

Figure 3.10
To determine the sign of $df/dx = (3x + 2)(x - 2)$ in various parts of the number line we first determine the signs of the factors $(3x + 2)$ and $(x - 2)$. For example, $x - 2 > 0$ when $x > 2$; similarly, $3x + 2 > 0$ when $x > -2/3$, as shown. Then we calculate the sign of their product df/dx by comparing signs (*Rule of Signs*, Section 1.1). The information in the last line follows immediately.

STEP 2   Since $f''(x) = 6x - 4 = 2(3x - 2)$, we see that $f''(x) = 0$ at $x = 2/3$. Furthermore

$$f''(x) > 0 \quad \text{for } x > \frac{2}{3} \qquad f''(x) < 0 \quad \text{for } x < \frac{2}{3}$$

This information is summarized in Figure 3.11.

STEP 3   Next we calculate the values $y = f(x)$ for the critical points $x = -2/3$ and $x = +2$, and for $x = +2/3$, where $y'' = 0$.

$$f\left(-\frac{2}{3}\right) = \frac{148}{27} = 5.48\ldots \qquad f\left(\frac{2}{3}\right) = \frac{20}{27} = 0.740\ldots \qquad f(2) = -4$$

These points are shown as dots in Figure 3.12. From the information displayed in Figure 3.10, it is apparent that the graph changes from increasing to decreasing at $x = -2/3$ since the sign of dy/dx changes, so that $x = -2/3$ is a relative maximum for f. Likewise, $x = +2$ is a relative minimum since f changes from decreasing to increasing as x passes $x = +2$. By examining Figure 3.11 we see that the sign of d^2f/dx^2 changes from $(-)$ to $(+)$ as x passes $+2/3$; thus the graph changes from being concave downward to concave upward (an inflection point).

STEP 4   With Figures 3.10 and 3.11 in mind, we sketch the graph so it is increasing/decreasing and concave upward/downward in the appropriate places. There is a relative maximum at $(-2/3, 148/27)$, a relative minimum at $(2, -4)$, and a change of concavity at $(2/3, 20/27)$. The final sketch is shown in Figure 3.12. To aid our rendering, we have plotted three additional points corresponding to $x = -2, x = 0$, and $x = 3$. Notice that this function has no absolute maximum or minimum.

Example 23   Draw the graph of $y = f(x) = 3x^4 + 4x^3 - 6x^2 - 12x$. Discuss the absolute maxima and minima of this function, using the graph.

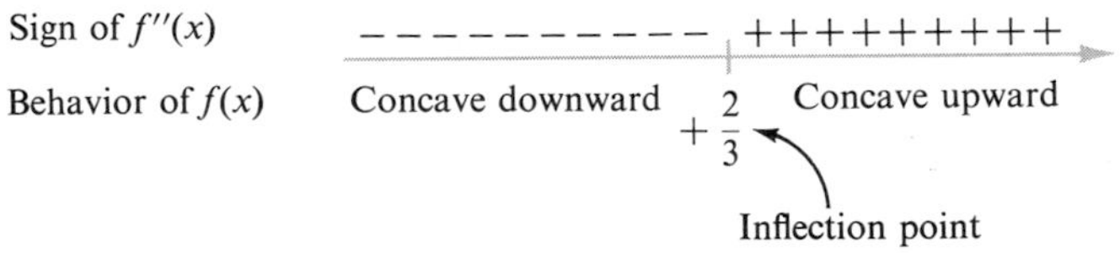

Sign of $f''(x)$	$-----------$	$+++++++++$
Behavior of $f(x)$	Concave downward	Concave upward

$$+\frac{2}{3}$$

Inflection point

Figure 3.11
The second derivative $f''(x) = 2(3x - 2)$ is zero at $x = +2/3$ (an inflection point), and has the signs shown to the right or left of $x = +2/3$. Notice that $3x - 2 > 0$ when $3x > 2$, or $x > 2/3$. The concavity of the graph changes from downward to upward as x increases past $x = +2/3$.

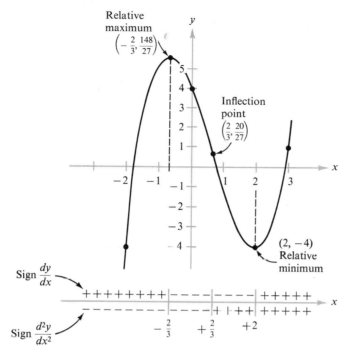

Sign $\dfrac{dy}{dx}$

Sign $\dfrac{d^2y}{dx^2}$

Figure 3.12
The graph of $y = x^3 - 2x^2 - 4x + 4$. The points corresponding to
the critical points are: a relative maximum $(-2/3, 148/27)$ and a
relative minimum $(2, -4)$. The point on the graph corresponding to
the inflection point $x = +2/3$ is $(2/3, 20/27)$. These are the points
mentioned in Step 3. We know that the graph rises until x reaches
$x = -2/3$, falls between $x = -2/3$ and $x = 2$, and rises again beyond
$x = 2$. Also, the graph is concave downward to the left of $x = +2/3$
and concave upward to the right.

Solution   We shall only outline the solution, leaving the details to the reader (Exercise
2). The first and second derivatives are easily factored:

$$f'(x) = 12x^3 + 12x^2 - 12x - 12 = 12(x + 1)^2(x - 1)$$

$$f''(x) = 36x^2 + 24x - 12 = 12(3x - 1)(x + 1)$$

The signs of $f'(x)$ and $f''(x)$ are shown in Figure 3.13, along with their geometric
meaning. The graph of f is shown in Figure 3.14. There are two critical points, at
$x = +1$ (relative minimum) and $x = -1$ (not a relative extremum). There are two
inflection points, at $x = -1$ and $x = 1/3$. The graph in Figure 3.14 has been
sketched taking these facts into account.

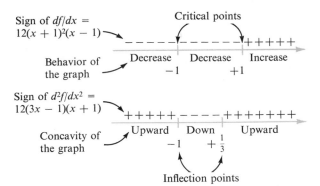

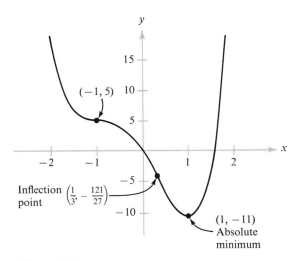

Figure 3.13
Signs of the derivatives of $y = 3x^4 + 4x^3 - 6x^2 - 12x$, and
their geometric meaning. The derivatives have been factored
and their signs determined from the signs of the factors (recall
Section 1.10). We leave the construction of detailed sign
diagrams, as in Example 22, to the reader.

Figure 3.14
The graph of $y = 3x^4 + 4x^3 - 6x^2 - 12x$. There is a
relative minimum at $(1, -11)$; points of inflection occur at
$(-1, 5)$ and $(1/3, -121/27)$. These points are indicated by
solid dots. The graph falls and is concave upward until it
reaches $x = -1$. At $x = -1$ the slope is zero (tangent line
momentarily horizontal). In the interval $-1 < x < +1/3$
the graph falls and is concave downward. For
$+1/3 < x < +1$ the curve is still falling, but is concave
upward. Finally, beyond $x = +1$ the graph rises and is
concave upward.

Now it is easy to discuss the absolute extrema. Since $f(x)$ decreases for all $x < 1$ and increases for $x > 1$, the relative minimum value at $x = 1$ is the smallest possible value for $f(x)$. This value $f(1) = -11$ is the absolute minimum value of f. There is no absolute maximum. As x moves toward infinity in either direction from $x = 1$, the values of $f(x)$ become larger, without any bound on their growth. There is no point p such that $f(p) \geqslant f(x)$ for all possible values of x.

If $y = f(x)$ is defined on a number of separate intervals rather than the whole number line, it may be helpful to study each interval separately when determining the signs of dy/dx and d^2y/dx^2 and sketching the graph.

Example 24   Sketch the graph of $y = \dfrac{1}{x} + 4x$, defined for $x \neq 0$.

Solution   The domain of definition is made up of two separate intervals $x < 0$ and $x > 0$. The derivatives

$$y' = -\frac{1}{x^2} + 4 \qquad\qquad y'' = \frac{2}{x^3}$$

are also defined for $x \neq 0$. The critical points, where $dy/dx = 0$, are located by solving the equation

$$y' = -\frac{1}{x^2} + 4 = 0 \quad \text{or} \quad 4x^2 = 1$$

The solutions are $x = +1/2$ and $x = -1/2$. As for the sign of dy/dx, let us write

$$\frac{dy}{dx} - -\frac{1}{x^2} + 4 = \frac{4x^2 - 1}{x^2} \qquad \text{for } x \neq 0$$

Here the denominator x^2 is *positive for all* $x \neq 0$; hence the sign of dy/dx is determined entirely by the sign of the numerator $4x^2$ 1. We have developed ways of determining the sign of such expressions in Section 1.10. First factor the expression $4x^2 - 1 = (2x + 1)(2x - 1)$; then determine the sign of each factor and set up a diagram like the one in Figure 3.15. (NOTE: dy/dx and its sign are undefined at $x = 0$, indicated by an open dot in the figure.) From this diagram we see that there is a relative minimum at $x = +1/2$ and a relative maximum at $x = -1/2$.

The sign of the second derivative $d^2y/dx^2 = 2/x^3$ is easy to determine. If $x > 0$ then $x^3 > 0$ and $y'' = 2/x^3 > 0$, so that

$$\frac{d^2y}{dx^2} > 0 \qquad \text{and the graph is concave upward}$$

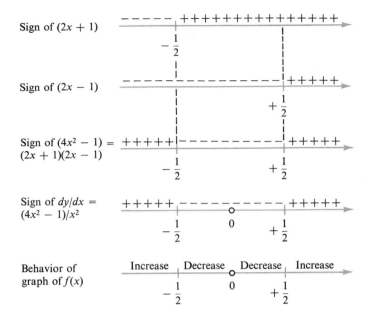

Figure 3.15
The sign of $dy/dx = (4x^2 - 1)/x^2$, defined for $x \neq 0$. The sign is entirely determined by the numerator $4x^2 - 1$, since the denominator is always positive. The quotient is not defined at $x = 0$.

Similarly, if $x < 0$ then $x^3 < 0$ and

$$\frac{d^2 y}{dx^2} < 0 \qquad \text{and the graph is concave downward}$$

The graph of a function is often badly behaved near any point where the formula used to define f has a zero in the denominator (here at $x = 0$), so we plot a few points on either side of $x = 0$ to get an accurate impression of the graph. We show the final graph in Figure 3.16.

There are no absolute extrema for this function. But suppose we restrict the domain of definition, say to $x > 0$. The restricted function does have an absolute minimum, at $x = 1/2$, but no absolute maximum, as you can see by inspecting the right half of the graph in Figure 3.16.

Exercises

●1. For each function below find dy/dx and d^2y/dx^2. Determine all critical points and the parts of the number line where the graph is increasing or decreasing. Determine where the graph is

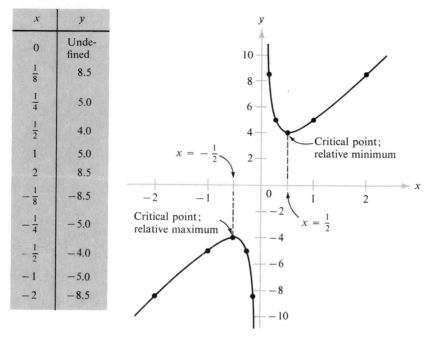

x	y
0	Unde-fined
$\frac{1}{8}$	8.5
$\frac{1}{4}$	5.0
$\frac{1}{2}$	4.0
1	5.0
2	8.5
$-\frac{1}{8}$	-8.5
$-\frac{1}{4}$	-5.0
$-\frac{1}{2}$	-4.0
-1	-5.0
-2	-8.5

Figure 3.16
The graph of $y = (1/x) + 4x$, defined for $x \neq 0$. Tabulated values are plotted as solid dots; $x = +1/2$ and $x = -1/2$ are critical points. The formula for $y = f(x)$ breaks down at $x = 0$, and the behavior of the graph is somewhat peculiar there, though entirely consistent with the information displayed in Figure 3.15. The values $y = f(x)$ become large negative as x approaches zero from the left, and become large positive as x approaches zero from the right (recall Example 9, Section 1.3).

concave upward or downward, and all inflection points. Then sketch the graph and locate the absolute extrema, if there are any

(i) $y = 7 - 4x + 2x^2$

(ii) $y = -2000 + 400x - 0.5x^2$

(iii) $y = x^3 - 3x^2 - 9x + 13$

(iv) $y = (1/27)(x^4 - 18x^2)$

(v) $y = 3x^4 - 4x^3 + 2$

2. Fill in the details of Example 23. In particular, work out the detailed sign diagrams that yield Figure 3.13.

●3. Apply the curve-sketching procedure to draw the graph of

$$y = \frac{1}{3}x^3 + x^2 - 3x + 1$$

Are there any absolute extrema? Label all relative maxima, relative minima, and inflection points.

●4. Sketch the graph of $y = -x^4 + 6x^3 - 9x^2 + 2$, labeling all relative maxima and minima. Are there any absolute maxima? absolute minima?

●5. Sketch the graph of $y = 1/(x^2 + 1)$. Find the absolute maximum value, if there is one. First use the differentiation rules and algebraic simplifications to show that

$$f'(x) = \frac{-2x}{(x^2 + 1)^2} \qquad\qquad f''(x) = \frac{6x^2 - 2}{(x^2 + 1)^3}$$

HINT: The expressions $(x^2 + 1)$, $(x^2 + 1)^2$, and $(x^2 + 1)^3$ are positive for all x, so the sign of f' or f'' is determined by the sign of the numerator. These derivatives are zero only when the numerators are zero. Factor $6x^2 - 2 = 2(\sqrt{3}x - 1)(\sqrt{3}x + 1)$.

●6. An object moves along a straight line with distance from an initial point given by

$$s = \frac{t}{t^2 + 1} \qquad \text{for } t \geqslant 0$$

Show that the derivatives can be written as

$$\frac{ds}{dt} = \frac{1 - t^2}{(t^2 + 1)^2} \qquad\qquad \frac{d^2s}{dt^2} = \frac{2t(t^2 - 3)}{(t^2 + 1)^3}$$

Sketch the graph of $s = s(t)$, defined for $t \geqslant 0$. Determine the maximum distance from the initial point. For which value of t is it achieved? HINT: In the derivatives the denominators are positive for all t.

●7. Sketch the graph of the function

$$y = x^2 + \frac{2}{x}$$

defined for $x > 0$. Explain why there is an absolute minimum. Give its location and the value of f there. ANSWER: Absolute minimum at $x = +1$, where $y = +3$; function decreases for $0 < x < 1$, then increases for $x > 1$.

●8. Repeat Exercise 7 taking the function to be defined for *all* $x \neq 0$ (both positive and negative). Is there still an absolute minimum? Is there an absolute maximum?

3.7   Applied Optimization Problems

We have now developed efficient mathematical methods of maximizing or minimizing a function. A major difficulty encountered in applied problems is translating this theory into practice. Usually a problem is described non-mathematically; we must translate this verbal description into a suitable mathematical one. Only common sense and reading comprehension are required—of course, with practice the task becomes easier. Here are some hints to help you accomplish this translation.

Procedure for Handling Verbal Problems

STEP 1   Read the problem carefully.

STEP 2   Label all the important variables in the problem; represent each variable by a different symbol.

STEP 3   Identify the variable that is to be maximized or minimized. This will be the dependent variable in the final differentiation problem.

STEP 4   Express the relationship between this dependent variable and the other variables in the problem by an equation.

STEP 5   Use the information given in the problem to eliminate all independent variables but one from the equation you have found. In this way the dependent variable is expressed as a function of *just one* independent variable. (If you cannot do this, either you have not extracted all the information from the original problem, or it is not possible to express the dependent variable in terms of only one independent variable. In the first case, go back and study the problem. In the latter case, the methods of this chapter do not apply. In Chapter 5 we shall develop techniques for optimizing functions of several variables.)

STEP 6   Determine the feasible range of the independent variable identified in Step 5. This gives the domain of definition of the function to be maximized.

STEP 7   Apply the techniques of Sections 3.4 and 3.6.

In most problems the last step can be carried out without going to the trouble of making a sketch of the graph. Often, absolute maxima can be found by examining just the first derivative; then it is not necessary to compute the second derivative, or to discuss concavity and inflection points. The explicit shape of the graph does not concern us if the absolute maximum and absolute minimum can be located with less effort. In solving a problem, you should use the simplest of the following techniques that will do the job:

1. If the domain of definition is bounded (of the form $a \leqslant x \leqslant b$), then the simple method of Section 3.4 suffices.

2. If the domain is unbounded, calculate the first derivative and use it to determine where the function is increasing or decreasing (the pattern of the signs of df/dx). With luck, this information suffices to locate the absolute extrema.

3. As a last resort, study the second derivative and make a detailed sketch of the graph of the function, as in Section 3.6. Sometimes we can use our intuititive

understanding of the problem at hand to make some shortcuts, as in Example 30 below.

Example 25   Find the rectangle of largest area whose perimeter (sum of lengths of four sides) is 12 inches.

Solution   First observe that this is an optimization problem; the word "largest" tells us at once that it is a maximization problem. What variable is to be maximized? Of course it is the area, which we denote by A. Upon what variables does A depend? Since the area of a rectangle is the product of the length and the width, let us call these variables l and w respectively. Then

$$A = lw \qquad (22)$$

We must next express A as a function of only one variable. To do this we use the condition that the perimeter is 12. Two sides of the rectangle have length l and the other two have length w, so that

$$2l + 2w = 12 \quad \text{or} \quad l + w = 6$$

thus

$$w = 6 - l \qquad (23)$$

Using equation (23) we eliminate w from equation (22) and express A as a function of the variable l alone:

$$A = lw = l(6 - l) \qquad (24)$$

Is there any restriction imposed by the problem on the independent variable l? In fact, the sides of the rectangle cannot have negative length, so that $l \geqslant 0$ and $w \geqslant 0$. The latter inequality, combined with (23), yields

$$w = 6 - l \geqslant 0$$

so that

$$l \leqslant 6$$

Thus l is restricted by two inequalities, $0 \leqslant l \leqslant 6$. We have now recast the original problem in mathematical form: Find the absolute maximum value of the function $A = A(l) = l(6 - l)$ defined on the interval $0 \leqslant l \leqslant 6$. We may apply our optimization techniques directly to this problem.

The methods of Section 3.4 suffice here. First locate the critical points of

$$A = A(l) = l(6 - l) = 6l - l^2$$

by setting dA/dl equal to zero

$$\frac{dA}{dl} = 6 - 2l = 0$$

There is just one critical point, namely $l = 3$. Then compare the values of $A(l)$ at the critical point $l = 3$ and at the endpoints $l = 0$ and $l = 6$:

$$\text{If } l = 0, A = A(0) = 0(6 - 0) = 0$$

$$\text{If } l = 3, A = A(3) = 3(6 - 3) = 9$$

$$\text{If } l = 6, A = A(6) = 6(6 - 6) = 0$$

The largest value, $A = 9$, is the absolute maximum value achieved by $A(l)$; it occurs at $l = 3$. Note that, from (23), $w = 6 - l = 3$ if $l = 3$, so that the rectangle is a *square*. The same analysis can be used to show that of all rectangles with a given perimeter, the one with largest area is always a square.

Example 26 The sum of two numbers is equal to 6. For which choice(s) of these numbers is their product a maximum?

Solution This example is almost identical to Example 25. We shall emphasize their mathematical similarity by using the same symbols. Let l and w be the two numbers and let $A = lw$ be their product. Then $l + w = 6$ and we may express A as a function of l alone:

$$A = A(l) = l(6 - l) = 6l - l^2$$

There is one important difference between this example and the preceding one: in this problem l is not restricted; it can take on any real value, positive or negative. Thus we seek the absolute maximum value of $A = A(l) = 6l - l^2$, with no restrictions on the independent variable l.

Since l is not restricted to a bounded interval, the method of Section 3.4 does not apply. Instead, we solve the problem by examining the first derivative dA/dl. The only critical point for $A(l)$ is $l = 3$, as before. Where is $A(l)$ increasing or decreasing? Since $dA/dl = 6 - 2l = 2(3 - l)$, we have

$$\frac{dA}{dl} = 2(3 - l) > 0 \qquad \text{for } l < 3$$

so A is increasing for $l < 3$. Similarly, A is decreasing for $l > 3$ as shown in Figure 3.17, since

$$\frac{dA}{dl} = 2(3 - l) < 0 \qquad \text{for } l > 3$$

Since $A(l)$ increases steadily until we reach $l = 3$ and decreases thereafter, the largest possible value of $A(l)$ occurs at $l = 3$. The two numbers we seek are therefore $l = 3$ and $w = 6 - l = 3$.

Example 27   In Example 14, Section 1.6, the profit function for a manufacturer of TV sets was

$$P(q) = -5,000,000 + 61q - 0.000098q^2$$

The feasible range of production levels was $0 \leqslant q \leqslant 1,000,000$. Find the (feasible) level of production that maximizes the profit.

Solution   Since $P(q)$ is defined on a bounded interval $0 \leqslant q \leqslant 1,000,000$, the procedure of Section 3.4 applies. To maximize P we first find all critical points.

$$P'(q) = 61 - 0.000196q$$

so there is just one critical point, obtained by solving the equation

$$0 = \frac{dP}{dq} = 61 - 0.000196q$$

Thus $q = 61/(0.000196) = 311,225$ (to the nearest integer). For this value of q, P is positive. At each of the endpoints $q = 0$ and $q = 1,000,000$ the dependent variable P is negative. Thus it is clear that the optimum feasible production level is $q = 311,225$. Compare the great simplicity and accuracy of this solution with the graphical technique employed in Section 1.6.

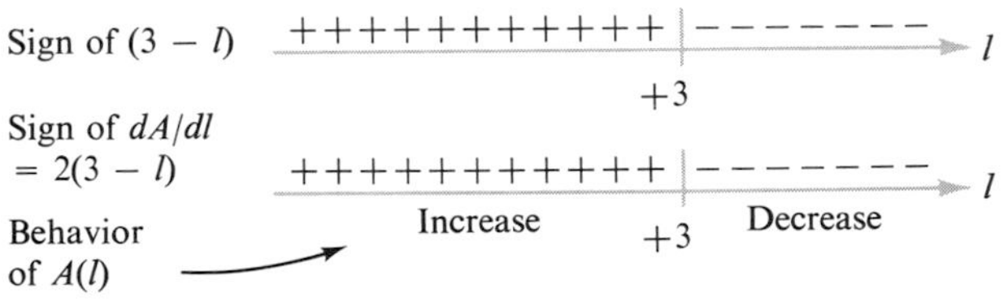

Sign of $(3 - l)$ $+ + + + + + + + + + +$ $| - - - - - - -$ $\longrightarrow l$
                                          $+3$

Sign of dA/dl
$= 2(3 - l)$ $+ + + + + + + + + + +$ $| - - - - - - -$ $\longrightarrow l$

Behavior   Increase $+3$ Decrease
of $A(l)$ $\longrightarrow$

Figure 3.17
Analysis of the sign of $dA/dl = 2(3 - l)$.

Example 28   In a manufacturing operation, suppose that the quantity sold q is related to the selling price (dollars per unit) p by the demand function $q = Q(p)$. As a measure of how q responds to changes in p, economists use the important concept of **elasticity of demand**, which is defined to be

$$E = -\frac{p}{q} \cdot \frac{dq}{dp} = -\frac{p}{q} Q'(p) \tag{25}$$

This quantity E may be interpreted as follows. For small increases in price Δp, the change in demand Δq is negative because demand decreases. Thus $-\Delta q$ is positive. The percentage changes are

$$100\, \frac{\Delta p}{p} = \text{(percent increase in price)} \qquad 100\, \frac{-\Delta q}{q} = \text{(percent decrease in demand)}$$

(both positive numbers due to our use of $-\Delta q$) and their ratio is

$$\left(\frac{-\Delta q}{q} \right) \bigg/ \left(\frac{\Delta p}{p} \right) = -\frac{p}{q} \cdot \frac{\Delta q}{\Delta p}$$

For small price increases Δp, this ratio is approximately equal to $(-p/q) \cdot dp/dq$. Thus elasticity E may be interpreted by noting that

$$\frac{\text{(percent decrease in demand)}}{\text{(percent increase in price)}} \approx E(p)$$

or

$$\text{(percent decrease in demand)} \approx E(p) \cdot \text{(percent increase in price)}$$

for small changes in p.

Economists use the following basic rule:

$$\text{Revenue is maximized when } E = 1. \tag{26}$$

Justify this rule mathematically.

Solution   In this example we seek to maximize the revenue R. As usual, revenue is the product of selling price p and the number q of units sold, $R = p \cdot q$. Substituting the demand function $q = Q(p)$ into this relation, we may express R as a function of p alone:

$$R = R(p) = p \cdot Q(p) \tag{27}$$

The price cannot be negative, so p must satisfy the condition $p \geqslant 0$. Also, there is a price $p = p_0$ so ridiculously high that there will be absolutely no demand for the product at that price; that is, $Q(p_0) = 0$. Thus we may restrict p to the bounded interval $0 \leqslant p \leqslant p_0$.

To find the absolute maximum of $R(p) = p \cdot Q(p)$ for p in the range $0 \leqslant p \leqslant p_0$, we may immediately exclude the endpoints $p = 0$ and $p = p_0$, because $R = 0$ there. Therefore the absolute maximum must occur at a critical point. However, at a critical point we have $dR/dp = 0$ (we assume our demand function is differentiable at all points). Applying the product rule for differentiation to (27), we get

$$\frac{dR}{dp} = p \cdot \frac{dQ}{dp} + \frac{dp}{dp} \cdot Q = p \cdot \frac{dQ}{dp} + Q = p \cdot \frac{dq}{dp} + q$$

Setting dR/dp equal to zero, we get

$$0 = \frac{dR}{dp} = p\frac{dq}{dp} + q \quad \text{or} \quad -p\frac{dq}{dp} = q$$

so that

$$-\frac{p}{q} \cdot \frac{dq}{dp} = 1$$

Thus, at the absolute maximum we must have $E = 1$.

Example 29   A publisher decides to print the pages of a book with one-inch margins at the top and bottom, and $\frac{1}{2}$-inch side margins. He is willing to vary the page dimensions, subject to the condition that the area of the page is 50 square inches (this is equivalent to specifying the paper cost per page). What dimensions will maximize the printed area of the page (thereby minimizing the paper cost for the book)?

Solution   For most of us, intuition fails to reveal the solution of this problem. Is a square page optimal? (How many books have you read with square pages?) Obviously, we should try to transform this into a mathematical optimization problem.

Let the height and width of the page be h and w respectively (see Figure 3.18). We want to maximize the printed area P. Now P is a rectangle with height $(h - 2)$ and width $(w - 1)$, so that

$$P = (h - 2)(w - 1) \tag{28}$$

We next express P as a function of only one independent variable. The total page area is 50, so that

$$hw = 50 \quad \text{or} \quad h = \frac{50}{w} \tag{29}$$

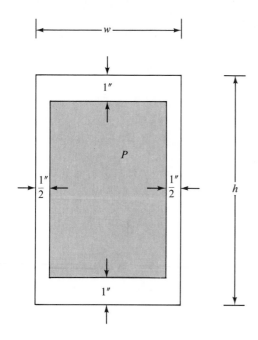

Figure 3.18
The printed page in Example 29. The printed area P is shaded; the rest of the page is taken up by margins. The total area of the page is $hw = 50$ square inches.

Substituting (29) into (28) we get

$$P = \left(\frac{50}{w} - 2\right)(w - 1) = 50 - 2w - \frac{50}{w} + 2$$

$$= 52 - 2w - 50w^{-1}$$

The page dimensions must be positive, so that the only restriction on the independent variable is $w > 0$ (unbounded domain). Now consider the first derivative

$$\frac{dP}{dw} = -2 + 50w^{-2} = -2 + 50\frac{1}{w^2} \qquad \text{for } w > 0$$

The critical points are determined by setting $dP/dw = 0$

$$0 = \frac{dP}{dw} = -2 + 50w^{-2}$$

Thus

$$2 = 50w^{-2}, \quad 2w^2 = 50, \quad \text{or} \quad w^2 = 25$$

The only solutions of the equation $w^2 = 25$ are $w = +5$ and $w = -5$. Since we consider only $w > 0$, we rule out $w = -5$; the only *feasible* critical point is $w = +5$.

It is a simple matter to determine the sign of

$$\frac{dP}{dw} = -2 + \frac{50}{w^2} = \frac{2(25 - w^2)}{w^2} = \frac{2}{w^2}(5 - w)(5 + w)$$

by determining the signs of the factors $(5 - w)$ and $(5 + w)$. (The term $2/w^2$ is positive for every choice of w, so it does not affect the sign of dP/dw.) For $w > 0$, we find that dP/dw is positive on the interval $0 < w < 5$ and negative for $w > 5$. Since P increases until $w = 5$, and decreases thereafter, $w = 5$ must give an absolute maximum for P. From (29), the corresponding value of h is $h = 50/w = 50/5 = 10$ inches. The optimal shape of the page is 10 inches high by 5 inches wide. You might want to compare the printed area of a page of this shape with that of a square page—the optimal page has roughly 4% more printed area.

There are some shortcuts that can save us the trouble of analyzing the signs of df/dx in detail. The maximum or minimum we seek must lie at one of the critical points, which we locate by solving the simple equation $df/dx = 0$. We may test the shape of the graph near each critical point by computing d^2f/dx^2 there. If $d^2f/dx^2 > 0$, the graph is concave upward and there is a relative minimum; if $d^2f/dx^2 < 0$, there is a relative maximum. Combining the results of this **second-derivative test** with our intuition about the problem we can often decide where the extremum lies without further effort. If not, we can always resort to the detailed analysis described in Section 3.6.

Example 30   The cost of constructing an apartment building x stories high is

$$C(x) = 1,800,000 + 200,000x + 2000x^2$$

The term $C(0) = \$1,800,000$ represents the cost of buying land and leasing equipment, incurred before construction begins. Each floor costs about \$200,000, but the higher the floor the greater the labor costs for that floor; hence the term $2000x^2$. Find the building height at which the average cost per floor $A(x) = C(x)/x$ is a minimum.

Solution   The function

$$A(x) = \frac{1,800,000}{x} + 200,000 + 2000x$$

is defined for $x > 0$. Intuitively, we know the problem has an answer; the minimum exists. This minimum must occur among the critical points. The derivative

$$\frac{dA}{dx} = \frac{-1,800,000}{x^2} + 2000$$

is zero when $2000 = 1,800,000/x^2$ or $x^2 = 900$, so that $x = +30$ or $x = -30$. The only *feasible* $(x > 0)$ critical point is $x = 30$. This critical point is the only possible candidate for a solution, so the minimum must occur when $x = 30$ stories. The (minimal) average cost per floor is $A(30) = \$320,000$.

To check our calculation, let us test the graph near $x = 30$. At $x = 30$

$$\frac{d^2 A}{dx^2} = \frac{3,600,000}{x^3} = \frac{3,600,000}{27,000}$$

is positive and the graph is concave upward, so we really do have a minimum there. Notice that we have relied heavily on intuition and our good fortune in having just one feasible critical point. Furthermore, we did not have to factor the numerator in

$$\frac{dA}{dx} = \frac{-1,800,000 + 2000x^2}{x^2}$$

(a messy job), or analyze the sign of dA/dx in detail.

Exercises

● 1. Among all rectangles whose area is 100 square inches, find the one with the minimum perimeter.

● 2. Find two numbers whose sum is 10, such that the sum of their squares is as small as possible.

● 3. If the price per ticket for a bus tour is set at x dollars, $1 \leqslant x \leqslant 5$, past experience indicates that $50 - 10x$ customers can be expected. Find the tour price x that maximizes the total revenue under these conditions.

● 4. Suppose that the cost of operating a truck is $(10 + \frac{1}{4}v)$ cents per mile when the truck runs at a steady speed of v miles per hour. Suppose the driver is paid $\$6.50$ per hour. Find the most economical speed for a 1000-mile trip. (Total cost = driver's wages + operating costs is to be minimized.) HINT: At speed v, how many hours does the trip take? ANSWER: $v = \sqrt{2600} \approx 51$ mph.

● 5. A piece of wire of length L inches is to be cut into two pieces. One piece will be formed into a square, and the other into a circle. How should the wire be cut so that the combined area of the square and circle is a maximum? ANSWER: Use all of L in the circle, none in square (endpoint maximum).

● 6. If $P(q)$, $R(q)$, and $C(q)$ are the profit, revenue, and cost functions for a manufacturer, show that the profit achieves a maximum value when the marginal revenue is equal to the marginal cost

$$\frac{dR}{dq} = \frac{dC}{dq}$$

● 7. Show that the average cost per unit $A(q) = C(q)/q$ for a manufacturer is minimized when the marginal cost is equal to the average cost.

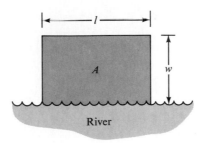

Figure 3.19
The farmer's field in Exercise 8.

- 8. A farmer with a field adjacent to a river wishes to fence off a rectangular area for grazing, as in Figure 3.19. No fence is required along the river, and he has available 1600 feet of fencing. What choice of dimensions encloses the maximum area? What is the value of the maximum area? What ratio l/w gives the maximum area? HINT: Feasible ranges are $l > 0$ and $w > 0$.

- 9. Repeat Example 29, taking the margins of the page to be 1 inch on one side and 2 inches on the other (to allow room for binding). The top and bottom margins are 1 inch, as before. If the page area is to be 50 square inches, find the optimal dimensions. HINT: Unbounded domain of definition $w > 0$. Can you use shortcuts?

- 10. A box with a square bottom and no top is to hold 5 cubic feet. Material for the sides costs 0.8¢ per square foot, but material for the bottom costs 1.0¢ per square foot. Find the dimensions that minimize the material costs.

- 11. Suppose a manufacturer's costs are

$$C(q) = 1600 + 20q + 0.01q^2$$

for $q \geqslant 0$. Then the average cost per unit is

$$A(q) = \frac{\text{total cost}}{\text{number of units}} = \frac{C(q)}{q} = \frac{1600}{q} + 20 + 0.01q$$

for $q > 0$. For which production level is the average cost per unit minimal?

- 12. An object moves along a straight line. Its distance to the right of the origin is

$$s = \frac{1}{t+1} \qquad \text{for } t \geqslant 0 \quad \text{(unbounded domain of definition)}$$

Determine the maximum distance from the origin. For which value of $t \geqslant 0$ is it achieved? HINT: Does ds/dt ever change sign for $t \geqslant 0$? ANSWER: $t = 0$, $s = 1$ (endpoint maximum).

- 13. A rectangular box with an open top and square bottom is to be formed from 36 square feet of cardboard. How should the height h and base length s be chosen so as to maximize the volume of the box?

- 14. Repeat Exercise 13, imposing an additional constraint on the dimensions of the box: the bottom must measure at least 4 feet by 4 feet. When this condition is imposed, what is the feasible range of the base length? ANSWERS: Feasible range is $4 \leqslant s \leqslant 6$; maximum volume when $s = 4$ (endpoint maximum); maximum volume $V = 20$ cubic feet.

- 15. The volume of a cylindrical can with height h and radius r is $V = \pi r^2 h$. The surface area (sides, top, and bottom) is $S = 2\pi r^2 + 2\pi rh$. Suppose we want to fabricate a can containing 16 cubic inches. If the cost of the can is proportional to the amount of sheet metal used (surface area), how should we choose the dimensions r and h so as to minimize the cost? What is the ratio height/diameter $= h/2r$ for the optimal dimensions of the can? ANSWERS: Height/diameter $= 1; r = 2/\sqrt[3]{\pi} \approx 1.37; h = 4/\sqrt[3]{\pi} \approx 2.73$.

*●16. Let $P = (30, 0)$ and $Q = (0, -20)$ be points in the coordinate plane. Starting at time $t = 0$, P moves *left* along the x-axis at a speed of 7 units per minute, while Q moves *up* along the y-axis with speed 5 units per minute.

(i) Calculate both coordinates of P, and of Q, after t minutes.

(ii) Do the moving points ever collide (occupy the same position) at any time?

(iii) Calculate the distance D between P and Q as a function of t. At what time $t \geqslant 0$ is D a minimum?

HINT: Make a drawing. Distance between two points (x,y) and (x',y') in the plane is obtained from their coordinates by the Pythagorean formula $D = \sqrt{(x' - x)^2 + (y' - y)^2} = \sqrt{(\Delta x)^2 + (\Delta y)^2}$. Use this to answer (iii). Minimize $D(t)$.

*3.8 Implicit Differentiation and Related Rate Problems

The method of **implicit differentiation** is an outgrowth of the chain rule. Often a function $y = f(x)$ is described as the solution of an equation involving x and y, such as

$$x^2y + y = 1 \tag{30}$$

or

$$e^{x^2y} = x - y \tag{31}$$

Sometimes we can solve the equation, rearranging it by algebraic manipulations to get y on one side and a formula involving x on the other. For example, it is easy to solve equation (30) above to get

$$y = \frac{1}{x^2 + 1}$$

Equation (31) is not so obliging; there is no simple formula that expresses y directly in terms of x. Nevertheless, equation (31) *implicitly* determines y as a function of x. If we take a definite value for x, there is precisely one value $y = f(x)$ that satisfies the equation (even though the value might be difficult to compute). Using the chain rule, we may discuss the derivatives of such functions without solving the equation that relates x and y. If we regard y as a function of x in (31), then the left side e^{x^2y} and the right side $x - y$ are functions of x and they are equal. Their derivatives (with respect to x) must also be equal. On the left-hand side we get

$$\frac{d}{dx}\{e^{x^2y}\} = e^{x^2y} \cdot \frac{d}{dx}\{x^2y\} \qquad \text{(chain rule)}$$

$$= e^{x^2y} \cdot \left(\frac{d}{dx}\{x^2\} \cdot y + x^2 \cdot \frac{dy}{dx}\right) \qquad \text{(product rule)}$$

$$= e^{x^2y}\left(2xy + x^2\frac{dy}{dx}\right)$$

and on the right-hand side

$$\frac{d}{dx}\{x - y\} = \frac{d}{dx}\{x\} - \frac{dy}{dx} = 1 - \frac{dy}{dx}$$

Since the left-hand side equals the right-hand side, we get

$$e^{x^2y}\left(2xy + x^2\frac{dy}{dx}\right) = 1 - \frac{dy}{dx}$$

Simplifying this we get

$$x^2e^{x^2y} \cdot \frac{dy}{dx} + \frac{dy}{dx} = 1 - 2xye^{x^2y}$$

so that

$$\frac{dy}{dx} = \frac{1 - 2xye^{x^2y}}{1 + x^2e^{x^2y}} \tag{32}$$

Though the derivative we have found is expressed in terms of both x and y, this is not much of a disadvantage. When x is specified, y is determined from (31) and dy/dx from (32). In particular, if $x = 0$ we find that $y = -1$ and $dy/dx = 1$.

Example 31   If $y^3 + xy = x^2 + 1$, (*i*) find dy/dx by implicit differentiation and (*ii*) find the equation of the tangent line to the graph (solution set) of $y^3 + xy = x^2 + 1$ at the point corresponding to $x = 0$.

Solution   In part (*i*), implicit differentiation yields

$$\frac{d}{dx}\{y^3 + xy\} = \frac{d}{dx}\{x^2 + 1\}$$

so that

$$\frac{d}{dx}\{y^3\} + \frac{d}{dx}\{xy\} = \frac{d}{dx}\{x^2\} + \frac{d}{dx}\{1\}$$

and

$$3y^2\frac{dy}{dx} + \frac{d}{dx}\{x\}\cdot y + x\frac{dy}{dx} = 2x$$

$$(3y^2 + x)\frac{dy}{dx} = 2x - y$$

$$\frac{dy}{dx} = \frac{2x - y}{3y^2 + x}$$

If $x = 0$, we get the corresponding value of y by noticing that

$$y^3 + 0\cdot y = 0^2 + 1$$

that is, $y^3 = 1$ and $y = +1$. We seek the tangent line passing through $P = (0, 1)$. The slope of this line is the derivative; taking $x = 0$ and $y = 1$, we get

$$\text{slope} = \frac{dy}{dx} = \frac{2\cdot 0 - 1}{3\cdot 1^2 + 0} = -\frac{1}{3}$$

The equation of the tangent line is

$$(y - 1) = \left(-\frac{1}{3}\right)(x - 0) = -\frac{1}{3}x$$

or

$$y = -\frac{1}{3}x + 1$$

If two (or more) interrelated variables turn up in a problem, the chain rule and implicit differentiation can be used to understand how a change in one of the variables affects the other variables.

Example 32   A pebble is dropped into a pond, causing a circular ripple to expand. The radius of the ripple is increasing at a rate of 2 inches per second when the radius is 7 inches. How fast is the area enclosed by the ripple increasing at that moment?

Solution   Let r be the radius of the ripple, and A the area of the enclosed circle. Then both A and r are functions of the elapsed time, which we denote by t. However A and r are also related to each other, since

$$A = \pi r^2 \tag{33}$$

Regard A and r as functions of t and differentiate each side of (33) with respect to t. We get

$$\frac{dA}{dt} = 2\pi r \frac{dr}{dt} \tag{34}$$

We have been told that r is increasing at the rate of 2 inches per second when $r = 7$, which means that $dr/dt = 2$ at that moment. We may evaluate dA/dt by using (34):

$$\frac{dA}{dt} = 2\pi r \frac{dr}{dt} = 2\pi(7)(2) = 28\pi \text{ square inches per second}$$

Example 33   Suppose that a car located at A in Figure 3.20 is 4 miles due south of an intersection C, travelling north at 40 miles per hour. At the same instant, suppose a car at B is 3 miles east of C, moving east at 50 miles per hour. Are the cars approaching one another at that instant, or moving apart? How fast?

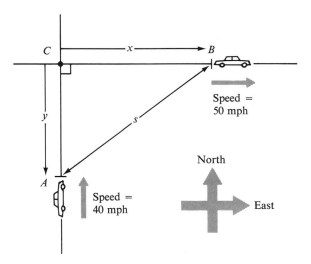

Figure 3.20
Two cars A and B in motion with respect to a highway intersection C. Distances x and y from the cars to the intersection (measured as shown) and the distance s between cars are each functions of time t.

Solution   Referring to Figure 3.20 let y be the distance of car A south of C, let x be the distance of car B east of C, and let s be the straight-line distance between A and B. Then x, y, and s vary with time, and are therefore functions of the time t. The three variables x, y, and s are also related to each other; by Pythagoras' theorem on right triangles

$$s^2 = x^2 + y^2 \tag{35}$$

Differentiating both sides of (35) with respect to t, we get

$$2s\frac{ds}{dt} = 2x\frac{dx}{dt} + 2y\frac{dy}{dt}$$

or

$$s\frac{ds}{dt} = x\frac{dx}{dt} + y\frac{dy}{dt} \tag{36}$$

Now at the instant of time mentioned in the problem, $x = 3$ and $y = 4$ (miles). Therefore, $s^2 = 3^2 + 4^2 = 25$ and $s = 5$. Furthermore, $dy/dt = -40$ (since y is decreasing) and $dx/dt = +50$ (since x is increasing). Substituting these values into (36), we get

$$5\frac{ds}{dt} = 3(50) + 4(-40) = 150 - 160 = -10$$

so that

$$\frac{ds}{dt} = -2$$

Hence s is decreasing and the two cars are approaching one another at the rate of 2 miles per hour.

Exercises

● 1. Find dy/dx by implicit differentiation.

     (i) $2x + 3y = 4$ (iii) $x^3 + y^3 = x + y$

     (ii) $x^2 + y^2 = 16$ (iv) $xy = x^3 + y^3$

● 2. Find the equation of the tangent line to $x^2 + xy - y^2 = 1$ at the point $(1, 1)$ on its graph.

● 3. Suppose the cost function $C = C(q)$ of a manufacturer satisfies the equation

$$q^3C + C^3 = 1$$

Find an expression for the marginal cost dC/dq. ANSWER: $dC/dq = -3q^2C/(q^3 + 3C^2)$.

● 4. Consider the point $P = (1, 1)$ on the graph of $x^2y + xy^2 = 2$, and a nearby point $Q = (x,y)$ lying on the graph. If $x = 0.95$, find the corresponding value of y approximately, using the approximation principle and regarding y as a function of x. ANSWER: $y \approx 1.05$.

*● 5. Find dy/dx and d^2y/dx^2 by implicit differentiation if $x^3 + xy + y^3 = 0$.

● 6. The volume V of a hot-air balloon is increasing at the rate of 10 cubic feet per minute. How fast is the radius r increasing when $r = 5$ feet? Assume the balloon is spherical in shape and recall that $V = (4/3)\pi r^3$ where r is the radius. ANSWER: $dr/dt = 1/10\pi = 0.0318$ feet per minute.

● 7. A particle moves along the curve $y = 1 + x^3$. At a certain instant it is observed that $x = -2$ and $dx/dt = 10$ units per second. Find dy/dt at that instant.

● 8. A low-flying jet aircraft covering a straight course is tracked by a radar station offset 6 miles to one side of the flight path, as in Figure 3.21. Here $x =$ distance from a reference marker on the course, and $s =$ direct distance from aircraft to radar unit. A radar unit can measure only the "range" s and the rate of change ds/dt. Suppose that the observed values are $s = 10$ miles and $ds/dt = 800$ miles per hour. Calculate the actual speed dx/dt of the aircraft. HINT: By Pythagoras' Theorem, the side lengths of the right triangle in Figure 3.21 are related by $s^2 = x^2 + 6^2 = x^2 + 36$.

● 9. In Figure 3.22, car A is 400 miles from an intersection C, moving toward it at 50 miles per hour. Car B is 300 miles from the intersection, moving toward C at 70 miles per hour. How fast are the cars approaching one another at this instant? (What is the value of ds/dt?) ANSWER: $ds/dt = -82$ miles per hour (minus sign since distance decreases, cars approach each other).

●10. In Exercise 9, calculate x, y, dx/dt, and dy/dt as functions of t. Use implicit differentiation to obtain a formula analogous to (36) for ds/dt. Determine the time when the cars are as close together as possible ($ds/dt = 0$). Will they collide?

●11. The population P of a certain parasite varies with the size H of the host population according

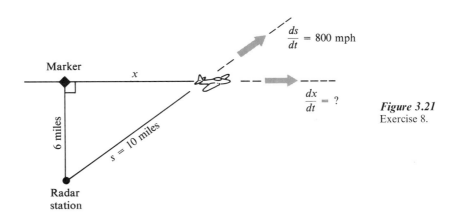

Figure 3.21
Exercise 8.

to the law

$$P = 3H + 0.0001H^2$$

Find the rate of increase in P if the host population is 3000, and is increasing at the rate of 200 per year.

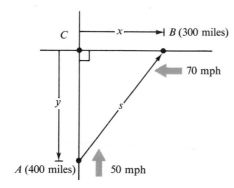

Figure 3.22
Exercise 9.

CHAPTER 4

Integration

4.1 Indefinite Integrals

In this chapter we shall examine an important new operation: *integration*. In a sense, integration is the inverse of differentiation, so we start by saying a few words about reversing the process of differentiation.

An **indefinite integral** of a function $f(x)$ is any function $F(x)$ whose derivative is the original function

$$\frac{dF}{dx} = f(x)$$

For example, what is an indefinite integral for $f(x) = x^2$? This is a new and unfamiliar problem; but we do know a lot about derivatives, so it is not hard to make an informed guess. Recall that the derivative of any power x^r is a constant times a power of one lower degree, namely rx^{r-1}. If we want a function $F(x)$ such that $dF/dx = x^2$, this suggests that we consider x^3. Now

$$\frac{d}{dx}\{x^3\} = 3x^2$$

so $F(x) = x^3$ is not quite the correct choice. But if we choose $F(x) = \frac{1}{3}x^3$, then

$$\frac{dF}{dx} = \frac{d}{dx}\left\{\frac{1}{3}x^3\right\} = \frac{1}{3} \cdot \frac{d}{dx}\{x^3\} = \frac{1}{3}(3x^2) = x^2$$

Thus $F(x) = \frac{1}{3}x^3$ is an indefinite integral of $f(x) = x^2$. Similarly, by reversing the differentiation formula

$$\frac{d}{dx}\{x^{r+1}\} = (r + 1)x^r \qquad (r \text{ any real number})$$

we see that the function $f(x) = x^r$ has an indefinite integral of the form

$$F(x) = \frac{x^{r+1}}{r + 1} \tag{1}$$

except when $r = -1$. (Then the denominator $r + 1$ is zero and the formula for $F(x)$ makes no sense; $f(x) = x^{-1} = 1/x$ has a different kind of indefinite integral, as we shall see below.) For example, an indefinite integral for $f(x) = x^{10}$ is given by $F(x) = \frac{1}{11}x^{11}$. Or taking $r = -1/2$, we find that

$$f(x) = x^{-1/2} = \frac{1}{\sqrt{x}} \qquad (\text{defined for } x > 0)$$

has an indefinite integral

$$F(x) = \frac{x^{(-1/2)+1}}{(-\frac{1}{2}) + 1} = \frac{x^{1/2}}{\frac{1}{2}} = 2\sqrt{x} \qquad (\text{for } x > 0)$$

Here are a few common indefinite integrals worth noting:

Function	Indefinite integral	
$f(x) = 0$ (constant)	$F(x) = 1$ (constant)	
$f(x) = 1$ (constant)	$F(x) = x$	(2)
$f(x) = x$	$F(x) = \frac{1}{2}x^2$	

Formula (1) gives an indefinite integral of any power x^r, except for $x^{-1} = 1/x$. The indefinite integral of the troublesome power $1/x$ can be found by examining the differentiation formula for the natural logarithm function $\log x$ (see Table 3.1):

$$\frac{d}{dx}\{\log x\} = \frac{1}{x}$$

Thus the indefinite integral of $f(x) = 1/x$ is *not* some other power of x, but rather $F(x) = \log x$.

A function $f(x)$ may have more than one indefinite integral. Indeed, if $F(x)$ is an indefinite integral and if c is a constant, we get another indefinite integral $G(x) = F(x) + c$ by adding a constant to $F(x)$ because

$$\frac{dG}{dx} = \frac{d}{dx}\{F(x) + c\} = \frac{dF}{dx} + \frac{d}{dx}\{c\} = \frac{dF}{dx} + 0 = f(x)$$

for all x. This leads us to ask: how can we find *all* indefinite integrals of a function $f(x)$? Given one indefinite integral $F(x)$ there are others of the form

$$F(x) + \text{constant} \tag{3}$$

Actually, there are no other indefinite integrals. In other words, if $f(x)$ has an indefinite integral at all this indefinite integral is "unique up to an added constant." For example, $f(x) = x^2$ has $F(x) = \frac{1}{3}x^3$ as an indefinite integral; all possible indefinite integrals are of the form

$$\frac{1}{3}x^3 + c \qquad (c \text{ any constant})$$

This can be summed up as follows:

Uniqueness of the Indefinite Integral   Suppose that $f(x)$ is defined on an interval $a < x < b$ and has an indefinite integral $F(x)$ on this interval. Then all other indefinite integrals of $f(x)$ have the form $F(x) + c$ where c is an arbitrary constant.

Sketch Proof   Suppose $G(x)$ is any other indefinite integral for $f(x)$. Then

$$\frac{dF}{dx} = f(x) \quad \text{and} \quad \frac{dG}{dx} = f(x)$$

for $a \leqslant x \leqslant b$. Their difference $H(x) = G(x) - F(x)$ has derivative zero, because

$$\frac{dH}{dx} = \frac{d}{dx}\{G(x) - F(x)\} = \frac{dG}{dx} - \frac{dF}{dx} = f(x) - f(x) = 0$$

That is, the rate of change of $H(x)$ is identically zero for all x. Intuitively it is obvious that this forces $H(x)$ to be a constant function, $H(x) = c$ for all x (c some constant). Since $G(x) - F(x) = H(x) = c$, we get $G(x) = F(x) + c$ for all x, as desired.

Indefinite integrals of $f(x)$ are indicated by the special symbol

$$\int f(x)\, dx \tag{4}$$

Thus

$$\int x^2\, dx$$

stands for an arbitrary indefinite integral of $f(x) = x^2$. By (1) we see that

$$\int x^2\, dx = \frac{1}{3} x^3 + \text{const}$$

where "const" indicates the arbitrary added constant associated with an indefinite integral. Similarly, we may rewrite formula (1) using this notation: if $r \neq -1$, the indefinite integral of x^r is

$$\int x^r\, dx = \frac{x^{r+1}}{r+1} + \text{const} \tag{5}$$

The case $r = -1$ is an exception:

$$\int \frac{1}{x}\, dx = \log x + \text{const} \tag{6}$$

With our previous comments about indefinite integrals in mind, we may compile a list of indefinite integrals for future reference (see Table 4.1).

Function	Indefinite Integral
x^r	$\int x^r\, dx = \dfrac{x^{r+1}}{(r+1)} + \text{const} \quad (r \neq -1)$
$\dfrac{1}{x}$	$\int \dfrac{1}{x}\, dx = \log x + \text{const}$
e^x	$\int e^x\, dx = e^x + \text{const}$
$\sin x$	$\int \sin x\, dx = -\cos x + \text{const}$
$\cos x$	$\int \cos x\, dx = \sin x + \text{const}$

Table 4.1
A basic list of indefinite integrals.

There is a useful generalization of the first formula in the table (see Exercise 2): If k is any constant, the indefinite integral of $f(x) = kx^r$ is

$$\int kx^r \, dx = k\frac{x^{r+1}}{r+1} + \text{const} \qquad (r \neq -1) \tag{7}$$

To avoid errors in using this notation, let us write out the special cases in (2). The constant function $f(x) = 0$ for all x has $F(x) = 0$ for an indefinite integral. Thus

$$\int 0 \, dx = \text{const}$$

A *nonzero* constant function $f(x) = k \, (k \neq 0)$ has a rather different indefinite integral, namely

$$\int k \, dx - kx + \text{const}$$

In particular, $\int 1 \, dx = x + \text{const}$.

Several differentiation rules can be reinterpreted as statements about indefinite integrals. The rule for differentiating a linear combination

$$\frac{d}{dx}\{k_1 f(x) + k_2 g(x)\} = k_1\frac{df}{dx} + k_2\frac{dg}{dx}$$

(k_1, k_2 constants) leads directly to the following rule for indefinite integrals, which will be useful in our calculations.

Indefinite Integral of a Linear Combination If $f(x)$ and $g(x)$ have indefinite integrals, then

$$\int (k_1 f(x) + k_2 g(x)) \, dx = k_1 \int f(x) \, dx + k_2 \int g(x) \, dx + \text{const} \tag{8}$$

To verify this, notice that $F(x) = \int f(x) \, dx$ and $G(x) = \int g(x) \, dx$ are just indefinite integrals of $f(x)$ and $g(x)$, so that

$$\frac{d}{dx}\{k_1 F(x) + k_2 G(x)\} = k_1\frac{dF}{dx} + k_2\frac{dG}{dx} = k_1 f(x) + k_2 g(x)$$

Thus on the right in (8), $k_1 F(x) + k_2 G(x)$ is an indefinite integral of $k_1 f(x) + k_2 g(x)$. By definition

$$\int (k_1 f(x) + k_2 g(x)) \, dx = \text{any indefinite integral of } k_1 f(x) + k_2 g(x)$$

so the left and right sides must agree up to an added constant, which we indicate by "const."

Example 1   Calculate the indefinite integral of $f(x) = x^3 + 6000x - \sqrt{2}$.

Solution   By formula (5)

$$\int x^3 \, dx = \frac{1}{4} x^4 + \text{const}$$

$$\int x \, dx = \frac{1}{2} x^2 + \text{const}$$

$$\int 1 \, dx = x + \text{const}$$

Now apply (8) and combine the undetermined constants.

$$\int (x^3 + 6000x - \sqrt{2}) \, dx = \int x^3 \, dx + 6000 \int x \, dx - \sqrt{2} \int 1 \, dx + \text{const}$$

$$= \frac{x^4}{4} + 3000x^2 - \sqrt{2}x + \text{const}$$

Do not be confused by the constants 6000 and $-\sqrt{2}$. They are brought outside of the integrals where they can be handled without difficulty.

Example 2   Calculate the indefinite integral of $f(t) = (3t^4 - 4)/t^2$.

Solution   First divide through by t^2, writing $f(t)$ as a sum of powers of the variable t

$$f(t) = 3t^2 - \frac{4}{t^2}$$

Taking $r = 2$ and $r = -2$ in formula (5), we get

$$\int t^2 \, dt = \frac{t^3}{3} + \text{const}$$

$$\int \frac{1}{t^2} \, dt = \int t^{-2} \, dt = \frac{t^{-2+1}}{(-2+1)} + \text{const} = \frac{t^{-1}}{-1} + \text{const}$$

$$= \frac{-1}{t} + \text{const}$$

Therefore

$$\int \frac{3t^4 - 4}{t^2}\, dt = \int \left(3t^2 - \frac{4}{t^2} \right) dt$$

$$= 3 \int t^2\, dt - 4 \int \frac{1}{t^2}\, dt = t^3 + \frac{4}{t} + \text{const}$$

We may calculate the indefinite integral of any polynomial or sum of powers x^r ($r \neq -1$) by these methods. Indefinite integrals involving $x^{-1} = 1/x$ are calculated by using formula (6).

Example 3   Calculate the indefinite integral $\int \left(1 - \frac{1}{x} \right) dx$.

Solution   The appropriate indefinite integrals are

$$\int 1\, dx = x + \text{const} \quad \text{and} \quad \int \frac{1}{x}\, dx = \log x + \text{const}$$

Thus

$$\int \left(1 - \frac{1}{x} \right) dx = \int 1\, dx - \int \frac{1}{x}\, dx = x - \log x + \text{const}$$

Example 4   Calculate the indefinite integral of $f(s) = \sqrt{s} + \frac{4}{\sqrt{s}} + 3e^s$.

Solution   Formula (5) is easier to apply if we rewrite $f(s)$ with fractional exponents:

$$f(s) = s^{1/2} + 4s^{-1/2} + 3e^s$$

Now

$$\int s^{1/2}\, ds = \frac{s^{(1/2)+1}}{(\frac{1}{2} + 1)} + \text{const} = \frac{s^{3/2}}{\frac{3}{2}} + \text{const} = \frac{2}{3} s^{3/2} + \text{const}$$

$$\int s^{-1/2}\, ds = \frac{s^{1-(1/2)}}{(1 - \frac{1}{2})} + \text{const} = \frac{s^{1/2}}{\frac{1}{2}} + \text{const} = 2s^{1/2} + \text{const}$$

$$\int e^s\, ds = e^s + \text{const}$$

so that

$$\int \left(\sqrt{s} + \frac{4}{\sqrt{s}} + 3e^s \right) ds = \int s^{1/2} \, ds + 4 \int s^{-1/2} \, ds + 3 \int e^s \, ds$$

$$= \frac{2}{3} s^{3/2} + 8s^{1/2} + 3e^s + \text{const}$$

We should mention that there are functions without indefinite integrals; our comments on the uniqueness of indefinite integrals only tell us what happens if an indefinite integral is known to exist. However, most standard functions do have indefinite integrals, as can be seen from Table 4.1. Later we shall find that any continuous function has an indefinite integral.

Exercises

● 1. Use Table 4.1 and formula (8) to find all indefinite integrals of the following functions:

(i) $f(x) = 2$ (constant function)   (vi) $f(s) = \dfrac{-5}{s^2}$

(ii) $f(x) = 0$ (constant function)   (vii) $f(t) = \dfrac{1}{2t}$

(iii) $f(x) = -4x^3$ (viii) $V(r) = \dfrac{4}{3} \pi r^3$

(iv) $f(x) = \dfrac{1}{\sqrt{x}}$ (ix) $f(x) = x + 1$

(v) $f(x) = x^{-4/5}$ (x) $f(x) = 4 - x^2$

Check your answers by differentiation.

2. If k is a fixed constant, prove that kx^r has indefinite integral

$$F(x) = k \frac{x^{r+1}}{(r+1)} + \text{const}$$

(provided that $r \neq -1$). Calculate indefinite integrals of the functions

(i) $-x$ (ii) $\dfrac{-7}{\sqrt{x}}$ (iii) $2.5x^4$

● 3. Calculate the indefinite integrals $\int f(x) \, dx$ for the following functions:

(i) $f(x) = 2x + 4$ (iv) $f(x) = 1 + \dfrac{1}{x^2}$

(ii) $f(x) = 3 - \dfrac{1}{2\sqrt{x}}$ (v) $3x^7 - 4x^5 + 2x^2 - 7$

(iii) $f(x) = 1 - 3x$ (vi) $5\sqrt{x} + \dfrac{1}{\sqrt{x}} + 10$

(vii) $-0.03x^2 - 10x + 4500$ (viii) $\dfrac{4}{x} + 2e^x$

● 4. Find the following indefinite integrals:

(i) $\displaystyle\int 3\,dx$ (vi) $\displaystyle\int (\sqrt{x} - 5\sqrt{2})\,dx$

(ii) $\displaystyle\int (5 - 2x)\,dx$ (vii) $\displaystyle\int (0.03x^2 - 100x + 1000)\,dx$

(iii) $\displaystyle\int (4x^3 + x^2 + 2x)\,dx$ (viii) $\displaystyle\int (x + e^x)\,dx$

(iv) $\displaystyle\int \dfrac{x^3 - 1}{x^2}\,dx$ (ix) $\displaystyle\int (\sin x - \cos x)\,dx$

(v) $\displaystyle\int (1 - x + x^5)\,dx$ (x) $\displaystyle\int \dfrac{3x - 2}{x}\,dx$

5. Find all indefinite integrals of $f(x) = x$. Choose any three indefinite integrals of f and sketch their graphs on the same piece of graph paper. Geometrically, how do these graphs relate to one another? Find the particular indefinite integral $F(x)$ whose graph passes through the point $(2, 0)$. How many indefinite integrals satisfy the condition $F(0) = -1$?

● 6. Verify the following useful formula for indefinite integrals ($k \neq 0$ a constant):

$$\int e^{kx}\,dx = \frac{1}{k}e^{kx} + \text{const}$$

by differentiating the function on the right (use the chain rule). Use this integration formula to calculate the indefinite integrals

(i) $\displaystyle\int e^{-x}\,dx$ (ii) $\displaystyle\int e^{(3/2)x}\,dx$

● 7. In more advanced texts are found more complicated integration formulas than the ones listed in Table 4.1. Some of these were discovered by guesswork, others by complicated deductive methods. Verify the following integration formulas by differentiation.

(i) $\displaystyle\int \dfrac{1}{x^2 - 1}\,dx = \dfrac{1}{2}\log\left(\dfrac{x - 1}{x + 1}\right) + \text{const}$

(ii) $\displaystyle\int \dfrac{1}{a^2 - x^2}\,dx = \dfrac{1}{2a}\log\left(\dfrac{a + x}{a - x}\right) + \text{const}$ ($a \neq 0$ fixed)

(iii) $\displaystyle\int xe^{-x}\,dx = -xe^{-x} - e^{-x} + \text{const}$

HINT: Use the chain rule.

● 8. A **differential equation** is an equation involving an unknown function $y = f(x)$ and also its derivatives. Use the remarks of this section to find functions f satisfying the following differential equations.

(i) $\dfrac{dy}{dx} = 1 + x^2$ (iii) $\dfrac{dy}{dx} - \dfrac{1}{x^2} = 0$

(ii) $\dfrac{dy}{dx} = \sqrt{x}$ (iv) $\dfrac{dy}{dx} = \dfrac{1}{x} + 1$

● 9. Find the equation of the curve $y = f(x)$ that passes through the point $(1, 2)$, if the slope at every point (x, y) on the curve is $2x$. (This amounts to solving the differential equation $dy/dx = 2x$, and finding the particular solution $y = f(x)$ for which $f(1) = 2$.) Solve the same problem if the slope is given by x^3 everywhere. ANSWERS: (*i*) $x^2 + 1$; (*ii*) $(1/4)x^4 + 7/4$.

*●10. If an object moves along a straight line under the influence of a force $F = F(t)$ (force may vary with time), its position $s = s(t)$ must satisfy **Newton's second law of motion**:

$$\text{force} = (\text{mass}) \times (\text{acceleration})$$

so that

$$F = m\frac{d^2 s}{dt^2} \quad \text{or} \quad \frac{d^2 s}{dt^2} = \frac{1}{m} F \tag{9}$$

Since the speed of the object at time t is $v = ds/dt$, Newton's law may be rewritten as

$$\frac{dv}{dt} = \frac{1}{m} F \tag{10}$$

Consider a force $F(t) = 5t$ acting on an object of mass $m = 2$. Assume that $s = 0$ and $v = 0$ when $t = 0$ (object starts at the origin with zero initial speed). Use your knowledge of indefinite integrals to

(*i*) find the speed $v(t)$ as a function of time, using (10).

(*ii*) find the position $s(t)$ as a function of time, using (*i*) and the fact that $ds/dt = v$.

ANSWER: $dv/dt = 5t/2$, so that $v = 5t^2/4$ and $s = 5t^3/12$.

*●11. Repeat Exercise 10 if the force is given by

$$F = 32m \qquad (\text{a constant} \times \text{the mass } m)$$

and the object has mass m (now the force does not vary with time).

4.2   Integrals and Areas

In this section we shall use indefinite integrals to calculate areas. Even in antiquity the problem of calculating areas was important, because of the need to survey land. Greek geometers regarded it as one of the central problems of plane geometry. Our method will go far beyond any geometric technique for determining areas. We start with certain simple facts:

(*i*) The area of a rectangle is given by the usual formula

$$A = lw \qquad (l = \text{length}, \ w = \text{width})$$

(*ii*) If a region R is broken up into several non-overlapping pieces $R_1, R_2, \ldots, R_n$ the areas of the pieces must add up to that of R

$$\text{Area}(R) = \text{Area}(R_1) + \text{Area}(R_2) + \cdots + \text{Area}(R_n)$$

(*iii*) If a region R is bracketed between regions R_1 and R_2, so that R_1 is entirely contained within R, which in turn lies entirely within R_2, then

$$\text{Area}(R_1) \leqslant \text{Area}(R) \leqslant \text{Area}(R_2)$$

We shall consider general regions such as the one shown in Figure 4.1(a). Such a region R is obtained by taking the part of the plane bounded by a continuous curve $y = f(x)$, the x-axis, and two vertical lines $x = a$ and $x = b$. How shall we calculate the area of R? The crucial idea is to study how the area *changes* as it is swept out from $x = a$ to $x = b$. For each x such that $a \leqslant x \leqslant b$ we let $R(x)$ be the region between the x-axis and the curve $y = f(x)$, lying over the interval $[a,x]$ (see Figure 4.1(b)). The function $A(x) = \text{Area}(R(x))$ is defined for $a \leqslant x \leqslant b$. When $x = a$, the interval $[a,a]$ reduces to a point, and $A(a)$ is the area of a line segment (length $= f(a)$, width $= 0$), so that

$$A(a) - 0 \tag{11}$$

When $x = b$, we get the area of the original region R

$$A(b) = \text{Area}(R) \tag{12}$$

Let us calculate the rate of change of area $A'(x) = dA/dx$ for a typical function $f(x)$, as in Figure 4.2. We first form the difference quotients

$$\frac{\Delta A}{\Delta x} = \frac{A(x + \Delta x) - A(x)}{\Delta x} \qquad \text{for small displacements } \Delta x \neq 0$$

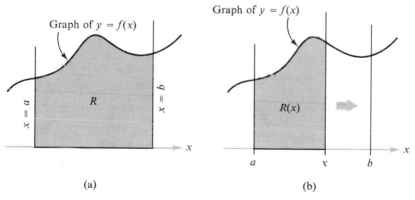

(a)   (b)

Figure 4.1
In (a) is shown a region R bounded by a curve $y = f(x)$, the x-axis, and two lines parallel to the y-axis. In (b) the shaded subregion $R(x)$ is the part of R lying above the segment $[a,x]$ in the horizontal axis. As x moves from a to b, the region $R(x)$ covers more of R. When $x = b$ we get $R(b) = R$.

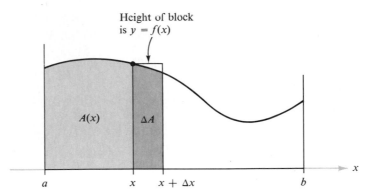

Height of block is $y = f(x)$

Figure 4.2
The area function $A(x)$ gives the area of the (lightly shaded) region above
the interval $[a,x]$. If x is increased slightly to $x + \Delta x$, then $A(x + \Delta x)$
measures the area lying above the larger interval $[a,x + \Delta x]$. Then
$\Delta A = A(x + \Delta x) - A(x)$ is the area of the region (heavy shading) above
the small interval $[x,x + \Delta x]$. Since f is continuous, ΔA is approximately
equal to $f(x) \cdot \Delta x$, the area of the rectangular block over $[x,x + \Delta x]$ with
height $y = f(x)$.

For simplicity, we take $\Delta x > 0$, as shown in Figure 4.2. Then ΔA represents the area
above the short line segment $[x,x + \Delta x]$ in the horizontal axis. Since f is continuous,
the values of f above the interval $[x,x + \Delta x]$ stay very close to the value $f(x)$ at the
left-hand endpoint of this interval. Thus the area ΔA, which corresponds to the
heavily shaded region in Figure 4.2, is very nearly equal to that of a rectangle with
base length Δx and height $f(x)$. That is, ΔA is approximately equal to $f(x) \cdot \Delta x$:

$$\Delta A \approx f(x) \cdot \Delta x \qquad \text{for small increments } \Delta x \tag{13}$$

Therefore, the difference quotient is

$$\frac{\Delta A}{\Delta x} \approx \frac{f(x) \cdot \Delta x}{\Delta x} = f(x)$$

This approximate formula becomes increasingly accurate as Δx is made smaller,
so that

$$A'(x) = \lim_{\Delta x \to 0} \frac{\Delta A}{\Delta x} = f(x) \tag{14}$$

Thus if we differentiate the area function $A(x)$ we get back the original function
$f(x)$ whose graph determines the region R. The function $A(x)$ is an indefinite integral
for $f(x)$. Using the uniqueness of indefinite integrals, we arrive at a truly remarkable
result that allows us to evaluate the areas of many regions.

Fundamental Theorem of Calculus   Let R be a region bounded by a continuous curve $y = f(x)$, the x-axis, and vertical lines $x = a$ and $x = b$, as in Figure 4.1. Suppose we know an indefinite integral $F(x)$ for f (say by applying the methods of Section 4.1). Then Area(R) is given by the difference in "endpoint values" of $F(x)$

$$\text{Area}(R) = F(b) - F(a) \tag{15}$$

Proof   We know an explicit indefinite integral $F(x)$ for $f(x)$. But the area function $A(x)$ is also an indefinite integral for $f(x)$. By the uniqueness of indefinite integrals, there is a constant c such that $F(x) = A(x) + c$ for all $a \leqslant x \leqslant b$. By definition of the area function, we have

$$\text{Area}(R) = A(b) = A(b) - A(a)$$

since $A(a) = 0$. But this means that

$$F(b) - F(a) = \big[A(b) + c\big] - \big[A(a) + c\big] = A(b) - A(a) = \text{Area}(R)$$

which completes the proof.

NOTE: If we take any other indefinite integral $G(x)$ in place of $F(x)$ in (15) then $G(x) = F(x) + c$ for some constant c, and this constant cancels. It simply does not matter which indefinite integral we use in this formula; once any indefinite integral is in hand, we may calculate areas with ease.

Example 5   Let $f(x) = 3$ for $1 \leqslant x \leqslant 5$. The region R bounded by the graph of f is a rectangle (see Figure 4.3). Verify that the Fundamental Theorem of Calculus gives the usual area for R.

Solution   Here $y = f(x) = 3$ and the vertical boundary lines are given by $a = 1$ and $b = 5$. Indefinite integrals of $f(x) = 3$ have the form

$$\int f(x)\, dx = \int 3\, dx = 3x + \text{const}$$

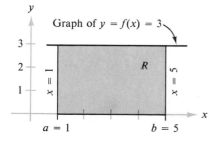

Figure 4.3
The region under the graph of $f(x) = 3$ over the interval $[1, 5]$.

It does not matter which indefinite integral we choose for formula (15), so let us take $F(x) = 3x$. Then

$$\text{Area}(R) = F(b) - F(a) = F(5) - F(1) = 3 \cdot 5 - 3 \cdot 1 = 12$$

This agrees with the usual area formula *Area = height × width*, since height = 3 and width = $5 - 1 = 4$.

We shall write the difference of endpoint values of a function $F(x)$ as

$$F(b) - F(a) = \left[F(x) \Big|_{x=a}^{x=b} \right] \tag{16}$$

In the last example, where $F(x) = 3x$, the area could be written

$$\text{Area} = \left[3x \Big|_{x=1}^{x=5} \right]$$

This notation is especially convenient if the formula for $F(x)$ is at all complicated. Notice that the value of $F(x)$ at the right-hand endpoint $x = b$ is taken first, and then the value at the left-hand endpoint $x = a$ is subtracted. Be sure you do not take the difference the wrong way around when you use this notation!

Here is a region whose area cannot be calculated by the usual methods of plane geometry. Finding the area would be very difficult without the Fundamental Theorem of Calculus.

Example 6 Calculate the area of the region R above the segment $-1 \leqslant x \leqslant 2$ in the x-axis and below the graph of $y = f(x) = x^2$ (see Figure 4.4).

Solution Here $y = f(x) = x^2$ and the vertical boundary lines are given by $x = a = -1$ and $x = b = 2$. We have already found indefinite integrals for $y = x^2$ in Section

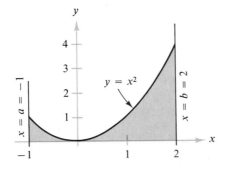

Figure 4.4
The region under the graph of $y = x^2$ over the interval $-1 \leqslant x \leqslant 2$.

4.1; we may use the particular indefinite integral

$$F(x) = \frac{1}{3}x^3$$

Applying formula (15), we find that

$$\text{Area}(R) = \left[\frac{1}{3}x^3 \Big|_{x=-1}^{x=2}\right]$$

$$= \frac{(2)^3}{3} - \frac{(-1)^3}{3} = \frac{8-(-1)}{3} = \frac{9}{3} = 3$$

So far we have avoided regions for which the graph of $f(x)$ is sometimes below the x-axis (that is, $f(x)$ is negative). Actually, the method described above works just as well whether the values of $f(x)$ are positive or negative, provided the areas calculated with the Fundamental Theorem of Calculus are interpreted as **signed areas**. If a region R lies partly above the x-axis and partly below, as in Figure 4.5(a), the signed area of R is obtained by counting the geometric area of the part above

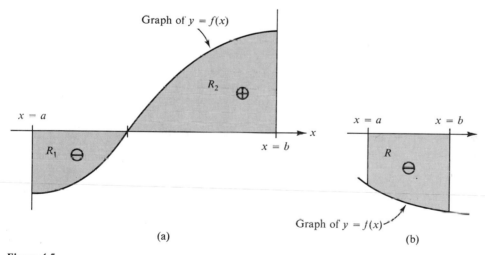

(a)   (b)

Figure 4.5
In (a) the full shaded region R lies between the x-axis and a curve $y = f(x)$ that crosses the x-axis. The signed area of R is given by $\text{Area}(R_2) - \text{Area}(R_1)$, where $\text{Area}(R_2)$ and $\text{Area}(R_1)$ are the geometric areas of the pieces above and below the x-axis. In effect, area above the x-axis is considered positive, while area below the x-axis is considered negative. For regions such as R, the Fundamental Theorem of Calculus gives the signed area rather than the geometric area. A region lying entirely below the axis, as in (b), has a negative signed area: Signed area$(R) = (-1)\,\text{Area}(R)$.

the axis with a (+) sign and the area of the part below the axis with a (−) sign. Thus in Figure 4.5(a)

$$\text{Signed area}(R) = \text{Area}(R_2) - \text{Area}(R_1)$$

In particular, if the region lies entirely below the axis, as in Figure 4.5(b), its signed area is the negative of its geometric area

$$\text{Signed area}(R) = (-1) \cdot \text{Area}(R)$$

If we adopt this definition, it is not hard to verify that the Fundamental Theorem of Calculus remains valid if we interpret it as saying*

$$\text{Signed area}(R) = F(b) - F(a) = \left[F(x) \, \Big|_{x=a}^{x=b} \right] \tag{17}$$

Here $F(x)$ is any indefinite integral of $f(x)$, and R is the region bounded by the curve $y = f(x)$, the x-axis, and vertical lines $x = a$ and $x = b$, as in Figure 4.5(a).

Example 7   Calculate the signed area of the region bounded by $y = x^3$, the x-axis, and the vertical lines $x = -1$ and $x = 0$.

Solution   This is the region R shown in Figure 4.6. Since x^3 is negative for $-1 \leqslant x \leqslant 0$, the region lies entirely below the x-axis. The Fundamental Theorem of Calculus therefore assigns a negative signed area to R. To compute its value, we first recall that indefinite integrals of $y = x^3$ have the form

$$\int x^3 \, dx = \frac{1}{4} x^4 + \text{const}$$

so we may take $F(x) = \frac{1}{4}x^4$ in formula (17). We get

$$\text{Signed area}(R) = \left[\frac{1}{4} x^4 \, \Big|_{x=-1}^{x=0} \right]$$

$$= \frac{(0)^4}{4} - \frac{(-1)^4}{4} = \frac{0 - (+1)}{4} = -\frac{1}{4}$$

Suppose that the curve $y = f(x)$ does cross the x-axis, as in Figure 4.5(a), and we wish to compute the geometric area of the shaded region R, counting the area

---

* The only change in the discussion of the Fundamental Theorem occurs when we examine the formula $\Delta A \approx f(x) \cdot \Delta x$. If the curve lies below the axis, the right side $f(x) \cdot \Delta x$ is negative because $f(x) < 0$ and Δx is positive. If we interpret "area" as meaning "signed area," the approximation formula still holds because ΔA is the area of a rectangular region lying *below* the axis, and is also negative.

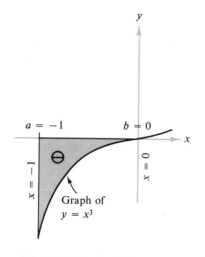

Figure 4.6
The region bounded by the graph of $y = x^3$, the x-axis, and the lines $x = -1$ and $x = 0$.

of each piece as positive. Direct application of the Fundamental Theorem would give the signed area, which is not what we want. Instead, we compute the signed area of *each* piece of R above and below the axis by using the Fundamental Theorem. Since each piece lies entirely above or below the x-axis, we get the geometric area of each piece by multiplying its signed area by $+1$ or -1. The geometric area of R itself is the sum of the geometric areas of the pieces. For the region in Figure 4.5(a)

$$\text{Area}(R_1) - (-1) \cdot \text{Signed area}(R_1)$$

$$\text{Area}(R_2) = \text{Signed area}(R_2)$$

so that

$$\text{Area}(R) = \text{Area}(R_2) + \text{Area}(R_1) - \text{Signed area}(R_2) - \text{Signed area}(R_1) \quad (18)$$

This idea applies just as well if the curve crosses the axis several times.

Example 8 Calculate the signed area and geometric area of the region bounded by $y = x^3$ and the x-axis, over the interval $-1 \leqslant x \leqslant +1$.

Solution The region R is shown in Figure 4.7. To calculate the signed area we apply the Fundamental Theorem of Calculus, taking the same indefinite integral $F(x) = (1/4)x^4$ as in Example 7. We get

$$\text{Signed area}(R) = \left[\frac{1}{4} x^4 \, \Big|_{x=-1}^{x=1} \right]$$

$$= \frac{(1)^4}{4} - \frac{(-1)^4}{4} = \frac{1 - (+1)}{4} = 0$$

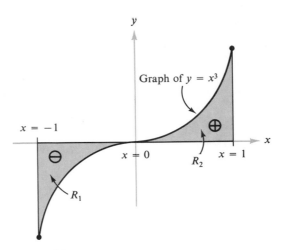

Figure 4.7
The region bounded by the graph of $y = x^3$, the x-axis,
and the lines $x = -1$ and $x = 1$.

This is to be expected because the signed areas of the pieces R_1 and R_2 are the same, but with opposite signs. Taking signs into account, the net area is zero. In Example 7 we calculated the signed area of the piece R_1 lying under the interval $-1 \leqslant x \leqslant 0$; clearly

$$\text{Area}(R_1) = (-1) \cdot \text{Signed area}(R_1) = (-1) \cdot (-\tfrac{1}{4}) = \tfrac{1}{4}$$

Similar reasoning shows that

$$\text{Area}(R_2) = \text{Signed area}(R_2) = \tfrac{1}{4}$$

so that formula (18) takes the form

$$\text{Area}(R) = \text{Area}(R_1) + \text{Area}(R_2) = \tfrac{1}{4} + \tfrac{1}{4} = \tfrac{1}{2}$$

If R is the region between a curve $y = f(x)$, the x-axis, and vertical lines $x = a$ and $x = b$ its signed area is traditionally referred to as the **definite integral** of $f(x)$ between $x = a$ and $x = b$. The definite integral is indicated by the symbol

$$\int_a^b f(x)\, dx$$

so that

$$\text{Signed area}(R) = \int_a^b f(x)\, dx$$

For example, the signed area between $y = x^3$ and the x-axis in Example 8 may be expressed as the definite integral

$$\int_{-1}^{+1} x^3 \, dx$$

Likewise, the definite integral $\int_{-1}^{2} x^2 \, dx$ stands for the area under the graph of $y = x^2$, between vertical lines $x = -1$ and $x = 2$, as in Figure 4.4. There is a connection between the definite integral $\int_{a}^{b} f(x) \, dx$ and indefinite integral $\int f(x) \, dx$ of a function $f(x)$. According to the Fundamental Theorem of Calculus, $\int_{a}^{b} f(x) \, dx =$ signed area is given by the difference of endpoint values for any indefinite integral $F(x) = \int f(x) \, dx$. Thus the Fundamental Theorem of Calculus may be rewritten as

$$\int_{a}^{b} f(x) \, dx = F(b) - F(a) = \left[\int f(x) \, dx \, \Big|_{x=a}^{x=b} \right] \tag{19}$$

using definite integrals.

Example 9   Interpret the definite integral $\int_{1}^{3} \dfrac{1}{x^2} \, dx$ as the area of a region bounded by the curve $y = 1/x^2$. Sketch the region. Calculate the definite integral by using the Fundamental Theorem of Calculus.

Solution   The graph of $y = 1/x^2$ is shown in Figure 4.8. The definite integral is the signed area of the shaded region R. Since R lies above the x-axis, the signed area is positive and equal to the geometric area. Using formula (5) of Section 4.1 we get an indefinite integral for $y = 1/x^2$

$$\int \frac{1}{x^2} \, dx = -\frac{1}{x} + \text{const}$$

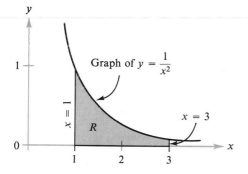

Graph of $y = \dfrac{1}{x^2}$

Figure 4.8
The region R corresponding to the definite integral $\int_{1}^{3} \dfrac{1}{x^2} \, dx$.

Taking $F(x) = -1/x$, we get

$$\int_1^3 \frac{1}{x^2}\, dx = \left[\int f(x)\, dx \Big|_{x=1}^{x=3}\right]$$

$$= \left[-\frac{1}{x}\Big|_{x=1}^{x=3}\right]$$

$$= \left(-\frac{1}{3}\right) - \left(-\frac{1}{1}\right) = 1 - \frac{1}{3} = \frac{2}{3}$$

Exercises

● 1. By using the Fundamental Theorem of Calculus, calculate the area of the region bounded by the curve $y = f(x)$, the x-axis, and the vertical lines indicated. Make a rough sketch of the region in each case.

   (i) $f(x) = x^2 + 1$ between $x = -1$ and $x = +1$

   (ii) $f(x) = \sqrt{x}$ between $x = 0$ and $x = +4$

   (iii) $f(x) = 8 - x^3$ between $x = 0$ and $x = 2$

   (iv) $f(x) = 1/x$ between $x = 1$ and $x = 5$

   (v) $f(x) = e^x$ between $x = 0$ and $x = 3$

   HINT: Use logarithm and exponential tables (Appendixes 3 and 4) to evaluate (iv) and (v).

● 2. Calculate the signed area and geometric area of the region bounded by $y = 2x - 1$ and the x-axis, over the interval $-1 \leqslant x \leqslant 3$. Check your answers by finding the areas of the (triangular) regions involved.

● 3. Consider the region bounded by the curve $y = (1/x^2) - 1$, the x-axis, and the vertical lines $x = 1/2$ and $x = 3$. Sketch the region and determine where the curve crosses the x-axis. Then calculate

   (i) the signed area of the region.

   (ii) the geometric area.

● 4. Sketch the graph of the function $y = 1 + x^2$ on graph paper. Draw a picture of the region under the graph whose area is given by the definite integral $\int_{-1}^{2} (1 + x^2)\, dx$.

5. Sketch pictures of the regions whose areas correspond to the following definite integrals:

   (i) $\int_{-1}^{1} (4 - x^2)\, dx$ (iii) $\int_0^4 \sqrt{x}\, dx$

   (ii) $\int_1^5 \frac{1}{x}\, dx$ (iv) $\int_{-5}^{-1} (t^2 + t + 1)\, dt$

   NOTE: In (iv) the variable is called t instead of x. The name we apply to the variable makes no difference.

● 6. Evaluate the following definite integrals. First find indefinite integrals.

(i) $\int_{-1}^{3} x \, dx$ (vi) $\int_{1}^{4} -5x \, dx$

(ii) $\int_{0}^{3} 2 \, dx$ (vii) $\int_{-1}^{+1} 6x^2 \, dx$

(iii) $\int_{-3}^{-1} x^2 \, dx$ (viii) $\int_{1}^{4} \dfrac{3}{\sqrt{x}} \, dx$

(iv) $\int_{0}^{8} x^{-1/3} \, dx$ (ix) $\int_{-1}^{5} (4 - 2x) \, dx$

(v) $\int_{1}^{10} \dfrac{1}{x^2} \, dx$ (x) $\int_{a}^{b} \dfrac{1}{x^3} \, dx$ $(0 < a < b)$

● 7. Evaluate the following definite integrals by using the Fundamental Theorem of Calculus.

(i) $\int_{-1}^{+3} 2 \, dx$ (vi) $\int_{1}^{4} (5 - \sqrt{x}) \, dx$

(ii) $\int_{-2}^{-1} (3x + 1) \, dx$ (vii) $\int_{-1}^{1} (x^2 - 4)^2 \, dx$

(iii) $\int_{0}^{2} (5 - t + t^2) \, dt$ (viii) $\int_{1}^{2} \dfrac{t + 1}{\sqrt{t}} \, dt$

(iv) $\int_{-2}^{0} (-x^3 + 10x + 9) \, dx$ (ix) $\int_{0}^{200} (0.03q^2 - 100q + 1000) \, dq$

(v) $\int_{-1}^{+1} (x^4 + x^3 - x + 5) \, dx$ (x) $\int_{1}^{3} \left(r - \dfrac{4}{r^2} \right) dr$

NOTE: In some cases we use a symbol other than x for the variable. The name applied to the variable makes no difference; just write out the indefinite integral with the same symbol for the variable.

◐ 8. Make a rough sketch of the region bounded by $y = f(x)$ and the x-axis, over the interval indicated. Determine where the curve crosses the axis (if it crosses at all). Calculate the signed area and the geometric area of the region.

(i) $y = x^2 - 2x$ over $I = [0, 3]$
(ii) $y = -2 + \sqrt{x}$ over $I = [1, 9]$
(iii) $y - 1 - x - x^2$ over $I = [1, 3]$

9. Consider $y = 1/x^2$ on the interval $-4 \leqslant x \leqslant -1$. Sketch the part of the graph over this interval. Sketch the region whose signed area is represented by

$$\int_{-4}^{-1} \dfrac{1}{x^2} \, dx$$

Evaluate this definite integral.

●10. Suppose that $f(x) = \dfrac{d}{dx} \{\sqrt{x^2 + x + 4}\}$. Calculate the definite integral $\int_{0}^{3} f(x) \, dx$. HINT: An indefinite integral of $f(x)$ is staring you in the face.

4.3   Definite Integrals

It is easy to find the area under the graph of a simple function $y = f(x)$ whose indefinite integral $F(x)$ can be found: just apply the Fundamental Theorem of Calculus. However, to apply this method we must be able to write out the indefinite integral quite explicitly, which can be difficult for a function as complicated as the one whose graph is shown in Figure 4.9. We need a new, more general method for computing such areas.

The graph in Figure 4.9 arises as follows. The rate at which a homeowner consumes electric power is measured in units called kilowatts, and the amount of energy consumed in units called kilowatt-hours. A 500-watt light bulb consumes power at the rate of 0.5 kilowatt; after, say, 3.5 hours of use the amount of energy it consumes is

(time) × (rate of power consumption)

= (3.5 hours) × (0.5 kilowatts) = 1.75 kilowatt-hours

and so on. The term *kilowatt-hours* (abbreviated kwh hereafter) should be familiar to

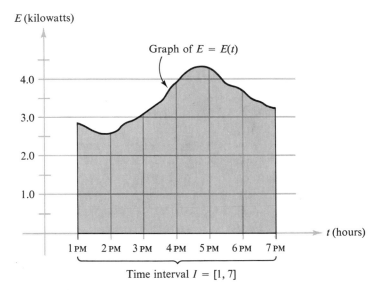

Figure 4.9
Rate of consumption of electric power (measured in kilowatts) as a function $E = E(t)$ of time t (measured in hours). The graph is plotted from measured data. The function $E = E(t)$ is not given by any simple algebraic formula. Total power consumed between 1 PM and 7 PM is numerically equal to the area of the shaded region under the graph.

anyone who has paid an electric bill, and was charged for the number of kwh used (at the rate of 10.94¢ per kwh in New York as of 1975). In Figure 4.9 we have recorded the rate E of power consumption as a function of elapsed time t during a typical afternoon. Consumption varies irregularly, depending on which appliances are in use.

Suppose we want to compute from this information the total number of kwh consumed, and thus the cost of electric service for this period. It turns out that the number of kwh is numerically equal to the area under the graph of $E = E(t)$ between $t = 1$ and $t = 7$.* The function $E(t)$ is not given by an algebraic formula, so it is not likely that we shall be able to apply the Fundamental Theorem of Calculus. Instead we shall estimate the area by setting up certain regions made up of rectangles that approximate the given region R. The sort of "approximating regions" we have in mind are the shaded regions R' and R'' shown in Figure 4.10. The areas of R' and R'' can be calculated, since they are made up of simple rectangular blocks. Further-more, the region R'' is larger than R, while R' is smaller, so we obtain an estimate for Area(R)

$$\text{Area}(R') \leqslant \text{Area}(R) \leqslant \text{Area}(R'') \qquad (20)$$

in terms of areas that we *can* calculate.

We set up typical approximating regions R' and R'' by dividing the base interval $I = [1, 7]$ on the t-axis into a number of subintervals $I_1, I_2, \ldots, I_n$, each of equal length $\Delta t = (7 - 1)/n = 6/n$. In Figure 4.10 we have divided I into $n = 6$ intervals,

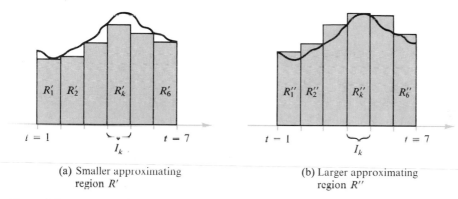

(a) Smaller approximating
region R'

(b) Larger approximating
region R''

Figure 4.10
The smaller and larger rectangular regions R' and R'', used to approximate the actual region R shown in Figure 4.9, are shaded in this diagram. Construction of the individual blocks R'_k and R''_k is described in the text.

---

* The reason for this equality is discussed in Section 4.4. For the moment we take this relation for granted and press on to the problem of evaluating this area.

each of length $\Delta t = 6/6 = 1.0$ hour. (The discussion would be similar if we considered a much finer subdivision of I consisting of, say, $n = 100$ intervals. There would be more numbers to keep track of, but the idea would be the same.) The smaller region R' is obtained by setting up rectangular blocks $R'_1, R'_2, \ldots, R'_n$ over each of the intervals $I_1, I_2, \ldots, I_n$. The block R'_k over the interval I_k is made as high as possible, keeping the entire block under the graph. The appropriate block heights can be read off of the graph without much trouble, and are tabulated in Table 4.2. Since Area(R'_k) = (height) $\times$ (width) we may also calculate the area of each block,

k	Interval I_k	Height of R'_k	Area (R'_k)
1	$1 \leqslant t \leqslant 2$	2.5	2.5
2	$2 \leqslant t \leqslant 3$	2.6	2.6
3	$3 \leqslant t \leqslant 4$	3.1	3.1
4	$4 \leqslant t \leqslant 5$	3.8	3.8
5	$5 \leqslant t \leqslant 6$	3.6	3.6
6	$6 \leqslant t \leqslant 7$	3.2	3.2

Table 4.2
Heights and areas of the rectangular blocks
$R'_1, \ldots, R'_6$ shown in Figure 4.10. Heights have
been read off of the graph in Figure 4.9.

and the total area of the region R' (full shaded region in Figure 4.10(a)),

$$\text{Area}(R') = \text{Area}(R'_1) + \cdots + \text{Area}(R'_n)$$

$$= 2.5 + 2.6 + \cdots + 3.2$$

$$= 18.8$$

Since the rectangular region R' lies inside the given region R we get an estimate Area$(R) \geqslant$ Area$(R') = 18.8$.

We construct the larger rectangular region R'' in much the same way. Over each interval I_k set up a rectangular block R''_k just large enough to cover the graph. These blocks fill the shaded region R'' shown in Figure 4.10(b). Again, the heights and areas of the blocks $R''_1, \ldots, R''_n$ may be determined by referring to the graph. The results are listed in Table 4.3. Clearly

$$\text{Area}(R'') = \text{Area}(R''_1) + \cdots + \text{Area}(R''_n) = 21.8$$

k	Interval I_k	Height of R_k''	Area(R_k'')
1	$1 \leqslant t \leqslant 2$	2.8	2.8
2	$2 \leqslant t \leqslant 3$	3.1	3.1
3	$3 \leqslant t \leqslant 4$	3.8	3.8
4	$4 \leqslant t \leqslant 5$	4.3	4.3
5	$5 \leqslant t \leqslant 6$	4.2	4.2
6	$6 \leqslant t \leqslant 7$	3.6	3.6

Table 4.3
Heights and areas of the rectangular blocks
$R_1'', \ldots, R_6''$ shown in Figure 4.10. Heights have
been read off of the graph in Figure 4.9.

Since R'' is larger than R we have Area(R) $\leqslant$ Area(R'') = 21.8, giving

$$18.8 = \text{Area}(R') \leqslant \text{Area}(R) \leqslant \text{Area}(R'') = 21.8$$

Thus we have estimated Area(R).

What if we divide $I = [1, 7]$ into many more pieces, of smaller length? The regions R' and R'' will then give a much better approximation to R, and the estimate

$$\text{Area}(R') \leqslant \text{Area}(R) \leqslant \text{Area}(R'')$$

will also be much better. Of course more calculation will be necessary; but if a computer is programmed to read the graph and do all the routine calculations, this will not be a serious difficulty. In fact, this is just what is done in practice. From this discussion we see that the exact area Area(R) is a limit of areas of rectangular approximating regions

$$\lim_{n \to \infty} \text{Area}(R') = \text{Area}(R) = \lim_{n \to \infty} \text{Area}(R'') \tag{21}$$

as the number n of equal-length subintervals gets larger and larger in the procedure described above.

The point of this discussion is that this procedure can be used to calculate the definite integral (signed area under the graph)

$$\int_a^b f(x)\, dx$$

of any reasonable function $y = f(x)$ over any interval $a \leqslant x \leqslant b$, or at least estimate it well enough for any practical purpose. The value of the definite integral is the limit of the signed areas of the rectangular approximating regions R' and R'' as we divide the base interval $I = [a,b]$ into smaller and smaller pieces

$$\int_a^b f(x)\,dx = \lim_{n\to\infty} \text{Area}(R') = \lim_{n\to\infty} \text{Area}(R'')$$

Example 10 Compare the exact value of $\int_0^1 (2 + x^2)\,dx$ (obtained by Fundamental Theorem of Calculus) with the approximate values Area(R') and Area(R'') computed by dividing $I = [0, 1]$ into $n = 10$ subintervals of equal length.

Solution The graph of $y = 2 + x^2$ is shown in Figure 4.11, along with the blocks $R_1'', \ldots, R_{10}''$ that make up R''. An indefinite integral for $y = 2 + x^2$ is

$$\int(2 + x^2)\,dx = 2\int 1\,dx + \int x^2\,dx = 2x + \frac{1}{3}x^3$$

so that Signed area(R) = Area(R) is given by

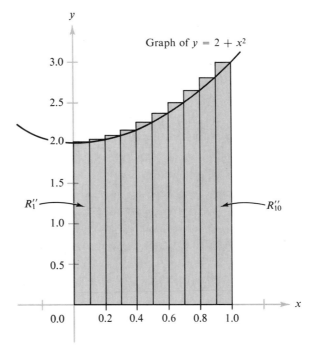

Figure 4.11
Graph of $y = 2 + x^2$ and the blocks $R_1'', \ldots, R_{10}''$ that make up the larger approximating region R''. Since the graph rises over the base interval $I = [0, 1]$, the height of each block R_k'' is just the value of $y = 2 + x^2$ at the right-hand endpoint of the interval I_k. Thus, over $I_1 = [0.0, 0.1]$ the block R_1'' has height $y = 2 + (0.1)^2 = 2.01$, as listed in Table 4.4.

$$\int_0^1 (2 + x^2)\, dx = \left[2x + \frac{1}{3} x^3 \ \Big|_{x=0}^{x=1} \right]$$

$$= \left(2 + \frac{1}{3} \right) - (0) = \frac{7}{3} = 2.333 \ldots$$

In Table 4.4 we list the heights and areas of the rectangular blocks R_k' and R_k''. These are easily computed from the formulas $y = 2 + x^2$ and $\text{Area}(R_k) = (\text{height}) \times (\Delta x) = (\text{height}) \times (0.1)$; there is no need to measure actual positions on the graph. Clearly $\text{Area}(R') = \text{Area}(R_1') + \cdots + \text{Area}(R_{10}') = 2.285$ and $\text{Area}(R'') = 2.385$. By

k	I_k	$Height(R_k')$	$Area(R_k')$	$Height(R_k'')$	$Area(R_k'')$
1	$0.0 \leqslant x \leqslant 0.1$	2.00	0.200	2.01	0.201
2	$0.1 \leqslant x \leqslant 0.2$	2.01	0.201	2.04	0.204
3	$0.2 \leqslant x \leqslant 0.3$	2.04	0.204	2.09	0.209
4	$0.3 \leqslant x \leqslant 0.4$	2.09	0.209	2.16	0.216
5	$0.4 \leqslant x \leqslant 0.5$	2.16	0.216	2.25	0.225
6	$0.5 \leqslant x \leqslant 0.6$	2.25	0.225	2.36	0.236
7	$0.6 \leqslant x \leqslant 0.7$	2.36	0.236	2.49	0.249
8	$0.7 \leqslant x \leqslant 0.8$	2.49	0.249	2.64	0.264
9	$0.8 \leqslant x \leqslant 0.9$	2.64	0.264	2.81	0.281
10	$0.9 \leqslant x \leqslant 1.0$	2.81	0.281	3.00	0.300

Table 4.4
Heights and areas of the rectangular blocks in Figure 4.11.

the basic estimate (20) we get

$$\text{Area}(R') \leqslant \text{Area}(R) = \int_0^1 (2 + x^2)\, dx \leqslant \text{Area}(R'')$$

The approximate values $\text{Area}(R')$ and $\text{Area}(R'')$ differ from the exact value 2.333 by -0.048 and $+0.052$, about 2.1% too low and 2.2% too high, respectively.

Exercises

●1. Consider the region R, shown in Figure 4.4, under the curve $y = x^2$ between $x = -1$ and $x = 2$. Divide $I = [-1, 2]$ into $n = 9$ equal subintervals. On graph paper make two sketches, one showing the smaller rectangular region R', and the other the larger rectangular region R'', for this partition of I.

2. For the following curves, sketch the smaller rectangular region R' obtained when the base interval $I = [a,b]$ is divided into n subintervals, taking $n = 2$, 4, and 6. Use graph paper.

    (*i*) $f(x) = 5 - 2x$, $I = [-1, 2]$

    (*ii*) $f(x) = 2x^2 - 1$, $I = [0, 2]$

    (*iii*) $f(x) = 1/x$, $I = [1, 5]$

Make similar sketches of the larger rectangular region R''.

●3. Consider the region R shown in Figure 4.4, bounded by $y = x^2$, the x-axis, and vertical lines $x = -1$ and $x = 2$. Divide $I = [-1, 2]$ into $n = 9$ subintervals of equal length. (*i*) Sketch the smaller and larger rectangular regions R' and R'' corresponding to this partition of I. (*ii*) Calculate Area(R') and Area(R''). Compare these with the exact area calculated in Example 6.

●4. Sketch the region R bounded by $y = f(x) = 4 - x^2$, the x-axis, and vertical lines $x = -2$ and $x = 2$. Sketch the smaller and larger rectangular regions approximating R when $I = [-2, 2]$ is divided into $n = 8$ subintervals. Calculate Area(R') and Area(R''). What is the exact area of R? (Use the Fundamental Theorem of Calculus.)

5. Sketch the region bounded by the curve $y = 1 + 3x$, the x-axis, and the lines $x = 1$ and $x = 3$. Calculate the numerical value of Area(R') and Area(R'') when $I = [1, 3]$ is divided into $n = 4$ pieces. Repeat, taking $n = 8$ and $n = 16$. NOTE: The exact area of R (a trapezoid) is 14.

●6. Estimate the area of the shaded region R shown in Figure 4.9 by dividing the base interval $I = [1, 7]$ into $n = 12$ subintervals and calculating Area(R') and Area(R''). Determine the heights of the rectangular blocks by inspecting the graph in Figure 4.9. Compare this estimate for Area(R) with that obtained in the text by using a coarser subdivision of I, into $n = 6$ pieces.

*●7. The value of the natural logarithm log s for any $s > 1$ is given by the definite integral

$$\log s = \int_1^s \frac{1}{x} \, dx$$

Thus, log s is numerically equal to the area under the curve $y = 1/x$, over the interval $I = [1, s]$. Consequently, if we divide $I = [1, s]$ into n subintervals of equal length, we have

$$\text{Area}(R') \leqslant \log s = \int_1^s \frac{1}{x} \, dx \leqslant \text{Area}(R'') \tag{22}$$

In other words, to compute log s we could divide I and calculate Area(R') and Area(R''), which give approximate values for log s. Formula (22) also gives an estimate for the error. A computer could easily be programmed to carry out this task, make sure that the error is at most 0.0001, and print out a table of logarithms like the one in Appendix 3.

    Estimate log 2 by hand: calculate Area(R') and Area(R'') for the integral $\int_1^2 \frac{1}{x} \, dx$ by dividing $I = [1, 2]$ into $n = 10$ pieces.

4.4   Further Applications of Integrals

The calculation of area is by no means the only use for definite integrals. They play a crucial role in physics, geometry, statistics, economics, and systems analysis. When a function $y = f(x)$ appears in a practical problem the definite integral $\int_a^b f(x)\, dx$ (signed area under its graph) takes on a meaning related to the significance of $f(x)$ in the problem at hand, and often plays an important role in solving the problem. We hinted at this in the power-consumption problem discussed in the last section. Here we discuss a few simple applications of definite integrals; a more sophisticated application will be given in Section 4.5.

Illustration: Areas of More Complicated Regions   Suppose a region R is bounded by vertical lines $x = a$ and $x = b$, and by *two* curves as in Figure 4.12(a). The upper boundary of R is given by $y = f(x)$, and the lower boundary by a different function $y = g(x)$. Over each x the height of the region is given by the function $h(x) = f(x) - g(x)$, for $a \leqslant x \leqslant b$. We shall show that Area(R) is given by the definite integral of this height function

$$\text{Area}(R) = \int_a^b h(x)\, dx = \int_a^b \left[f(x) - g(x) \right] dx \qquad (23)$$

Discussion   For simplicity we assume that the lower boundary curve stays above the x-axis for $a \leqslant x \leqslant b$. Then the region R lies completely above this axis. Write R_g for the region bounded by the curve $y = g(x)$, the x-axis, and vertical lines $x = a$ and $x = b$; and write R_f for the region bounded by $y = f(x)$ and the x-axis, between

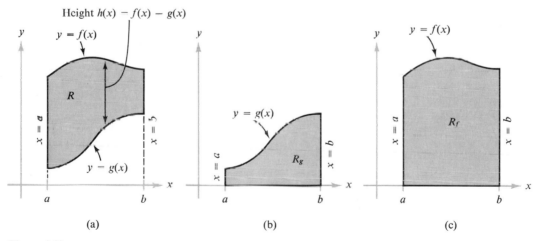

(a)	(b)	(c)

Figure 4.12
In (a) is shown a region R bounded by two curves, $y = f(x)$ and $y = g(x)$, and two vertical lines. The height of the region over x is $h(x) = f(x) - g(x)$. In (b) and (c) are shown the regions R_g and R_f underneath $y = g(x)$ and $y = f(x)$ respectively. It is clear that Area(R) + Area(R_g) = Area(R_f).

the lines $x = a$ and $x = b$ (see Figure 4.12(b) and (c)). Then R and R_g do not overlap, and together they fill up R_f. Hence Area(R) + Area(R_g) = Area(R_f) and

$$\text{Area}(R) = \text{Area}(R_f) - \text{Area}(R_g)$$

Since the areas of R_f and R_g are given by definite integrals of f and g we get

$$\text{Area}(R) = \int_a^b f(x)\, dx - \int_a^b g(x)\, dx$$

$$= \int_a^b [f(x) - g(x)]\, dx$$

$$= \int_a^b h(x)\, dx$$

A more careful analysis shows that the positions of the curves $y = f(x)$ and $y = g(x)$ relative to the x-axis do not matter. The formula (23) is valid as long as the curve $y = f(x)$ stays above $y = g(x)$ for a $\leqslant x \leqslant b$.

Example 11   Calculate the area of the region (Figure 4.13) bounded by the curves $y = f(x) = 4 - x^2$ and $y = g(x) = 4 - 2x$.

Solution   The curves cross at $x = 0$ and $x = 2$, so the shaded region R may be thought of as bounded by $y = f(x)$, $y = g(x)$, and vertical lines $x = 0$ and $x = 2$.

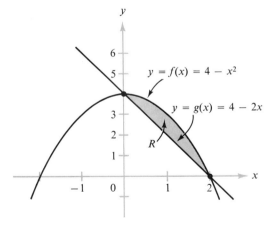

Figure 4.13
The shaded region R is bounded by the curves
$y = f(x) = 4 - x^2$ (upper curve) and $y = g(x) = 4 - 2x$
(lower curve). The crossover points for the curves are
shown as solid dots. They occur at $x = 0$ and $x = 2$.

Locating the crossover points is simple: they occur where $f(x) = g(x)$, so that

$$4 - x^2 = 4 - 2x \quad \text{or} \quad 0 = x^2 - 2x$$

Solving the equation $0 = x^2 - 2x = x(x - 2)$ we get $x = 0$ and $x = 2$.

The height function for this region is $h(x) = f(x) - g(x) = (4 - x^2) - (4 - 2x) = 2x - x^2$ for $0 \leqslant x \leqslant 2$. Thus

$$\text{Area}(R) = \int_0^2 h(x)\, dx = \int_0^2 (2x - x^2)\, dx$$

$$= 2 \int_0^2 x\, dx - \int_0^2 x^2\, dx$$

$$= 2 \left[\frac{x^2}{2} \Big|_0^2 \right] - \left[\frac{x^3}{3} \Big|_0^2 \right]$$

$$= 2 \left(\frac{4}{2} - \frac{0}{2} \right) - \left(\frac{8}{3} - \frac{0}{3} \right) = \frac{4}{3}$$

Sometimes integrals make their appearance in applications by way of the Fundamental Theorem of Calculus.

Illustration: Inertial Navigation   A submerged submarine starting from a certain location must keep track of its position, or net distance traveled. Surfacing to obtain a location fix is subject to the vagaries of weather, and may be unacceptable for other reasons. Modern navigation depends upon inertial guidance systems. Without relying upon external observations, these systems sense the accelerations of a boat and record its instantaneous velocity as a function of time. Unfortunately they cannot directly sense the position of the boat. How can we find the position from the data provided by the guidance system?

For simplicity let us assume that the submarine moves along a straight course with velocity $v(t)$, whose graph is shown as Figure 4.14(b). This velocity varies with time. It may be positive (forward motion) some of the time and negative (backward motion) at other times. We shall show that

$$\Delta s = \int_a^b v(t)\, dt \tag{24}$$

That is, Δs is determined from the data about $v(t)$ for $a \leqslant t \leqslant b$ by calculating the definite integral of $v(t)$. Although the integral gives the signed area under the graph, this area is numerically equal to the distance traveled, which is what we want to compute.

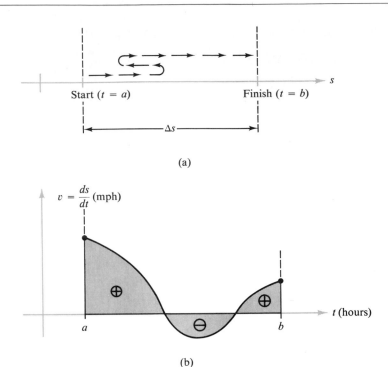

(a)

(b)

Figure 4.14
Motion of an object whose position varies with time is indicated
schematically in (a). The graph (b) shows the record of velocity $v(t) = ds/dt$
for $a \leqslant t \leqslant b$. The velocity is negative part of the time (the object moves
in the negative s-direction); but most of the time is spent in forward motion,
$v(t) > 0$, so the net distance moved Δs is positive. As explained in the text,
$\Delta s = \int_a^b v(t)\, dt$; that is, Δs is numerically equal to the signed area of the
region (shaded) between the curve $v = v(t)$ and the t-axis. The negative
area (which counts backward motion) must be subtracted from the positive
area (forward motion) to get the correct net motion Δs.

Discussion   To justify (24) we notice that, by definition, $v = ds/dt$; therefore, the
function $s(t)$ is an indefinite integral of $v(t)$. By the Fundamental Theorem of Calculus

$$\int_a^b v(t)\, dt = \left[s(t) \Big|_{t=a}^{t=b} \right] = s(b) - s(a)$$

$$= \text{(final distance)} - \text{(initial distance)} = \Delta s$$

as required.

   Exactly the same analysis applies to many different situations. Suppose we are
given the rate of change df/dx of *any* quantity with respect to some variable x. We want

to calculate from this the net change $\Delta f = f(b) - f(a)$ as x increases from $x = a$ to $x = b$. As above, the net change is given by a definite integral

$$\Delta f = \int_a^b \frac{df}{dx}\, dx = \int_a^b f'(x)\, dx \tag{25}$$

This is precisely why the area in Figure 4.9 was interpreted as the power consumed. If $Q(t)$ is the amount of power consumed after t hours (say, starting from 12 noon), then $dQ/dt = E(t)$ is the rate of power consumption. The total power consumed during the period $1 \leqslant t \leqslant 7$ is just $Q(7) - Q(1) = \Delta Q = \int_1^7 E(t)\, dt$, the area under the graph of $E(t)$.

Example 12   Suppose a recording speedometer in a race car indicates that the speed $v(t)$ during an acceleration test was given by

$$v(t) = 17.6(t - 0.003t^2) \text{ feet per second} \qquad (t \text{ in seconds})$$

Calculate the length of track (in miles) covered in time intervals $0 \leqslant t \leqslant 5$ and $0 \leqslant t \leqslant 10$ seconds (one mile $= 5280$ feet).

Solution   In each case, $\Delta s = \int_a^b v(t)\, dt$. Obviously $s(0) = 0$ (at starting position, no distance covered). Thus for $0 \leqslant t \leqslant 5$

$$\Delta s = s(5) - s(0) = \int_0^5 17.6(t - 0.003t^2)\, dt$$

$$= 17.6 \left[\frac{t^2}{2} - 0.001t^3 \Big|_{t=0}^{t=5} \right]$$

$$= 217.8 \text{ feet}$$

so that $\Delta s = 217.8/5280 = 0.0412$ miles. During the interval $0 \leqslant t \leqslant 10$

$$\Delta s = s(10) - s(0) = \int_0^{10} 17.6(t - 0.003t^2)\, dt$$

$$= 17.6 \left[\frac{t^2}{2} - 0.001t^3 \Big|_{t=0}^{t=10} \right]$$

$$= 862.4 \text{ feet}$$

or 0.1633 miles.

Exercises

●1. Sketch the region bounded by the curves $y = f(x) = x - x^2$, $y = g(x) = x^2 - 3x$, and vertical lines $x = 1$ and $x = 2$. Repeat, taking vertical lines $x = 0$ and $x = 2$.

●2. Calculate the area of the region bounded by the curves $y = f(x) = x^2$ and $y = g(x) = x^3$. HINT: First show that the curves cross at $x = 0$ and $x = 1$. Take these as the vertical lines determining R.

●3. Find the areas of the regions bounded by the following curves and vertical lines. If no vertical lines are specified, you must determine the crossover points for the curves, as in Example 11. Sketch the region in each case.

(i) $f(x) = \sqrt{x}$ and $g(x) = \frac{1}{2}x^2$ between $x = 0$ and $x = 1$

(ii) $f(x) = x + 2$ and $g(x) = x^2$

(iii) $f(x) = 4 + x - x^2$ and $g(x) = 0$ between $x = -1$ and $x = 1$

(iv) $f(x) = \sqrt{x}$ and $g(x) = \frac{1}{8}x^2$

(v) $f(x) = 4 - x^2$ and $g(x) = 3$

(vi) $f(x) = -x^2 + 3x - 3$ and $g(x) = x^2 - 2$

●4. During the first 16 weeks after birth, the weight $w(t)$ of a certain type of white mouse increases at a rate

$$\frac{dw}{dt} = \frac{2 + t}{100} \text{ ounces per week}$$

(i) Calculate the weight increase over the first 16 weeks.

(ii) If the weight at birth is 0.4 ounces, what is the net weight of the mouse after 16 weeks?

ANSWERS: $\Delta w = 1.6$ ounces; $w(16) = w(0) + \Delta w = 2.0$ ounces.

●5. A cost analysis has established the following formula for the marginal profit (profit per unit at various production levels) for producing a specialty item:

$$\frac{dP}{dq} = 10.50 - 0.01q + 0.0001q^2$$

When $q = 0$ we have $P = -300$ (equal to the fixed costs). Calculate the profit P at production levels $q = 50$ and $q = 100$. What is the profit $P(q)$ at an arbitrary production level q?

●6. If a rocket rises with a constant acceleration of 15 feet/sec², and starts with initial speed $v = 0$ when $t = 0$, find the velocity 10 seconds and 100 seconds after launch. HINT: By definition, acceleration $= dv/dt$.

*●7. A single-stage rocket is launched vertically from rest at ground level. Its engines burn for 90 seconds, producing an acceleration

$$a(t) = 300 - 2t \qquad \text{feet/sec}^2$$

for $0 \leqslant t \leqslant 90$. Find the velocity v at burnout (at $t = 90$ sec). Find the height h at burnout. HINT: By definition, $a = dv/dt$ and $v = dh/dt$, where $v(t)$ and $h(t)$ are functions of t. Find v as a function of t and set $t = 90$. Then find h as a function of t and set $t = 90$.

4.5   Describing Probability Distributions by Means of Integrals

Another important application of integrals deals with probability distributions. In this section we shall give an elementary, self-contained discussion that does not presume any familiarity with probability or statistical methods.

Suppose we wish to describe, as efficiently as possible, the distribution of heights among adult U.S. citizens in the year 1970. Let N stand for the number of adult citizens, $N \approx 140{,}000{,}000$. A very crude approach would be to label all individuals and list their heights. However, compiling such a list would be very expensive, and a list with 140,000,000 entries would be unwieldy, to say the least. How then are we to give a concise description of the distribution of heights? We must stop for a moment and see what kind of questions we may hope to answer by referring to statistical data. Here are a few:

A designer of a compact car that is comfortable only for individuals less than 6 feet tall might ask: "How many individuals have height $0 \leqslant h \leqslant 6$ feet?" or "What fraction of the total population has height $0 \leqslant h \leqslant 6$?" Clearly the answer to the second question is $1/N$ times the answer to the first.

A buyer of raincoats for a clothing chain would be interested in the fraction of the total population with height in the range $r_1 \leqslant h \leqslant r_2$ for various choices of $r_1 < r_2$, say $5.5 \leqslant h \leqslant 5.75$ or $5.75 \leqslant h \leqslant 6.0$. This way, the number of garments purchased in each size will match the demand for that size.

For a large population it is possible to summarize the statistical facts about height distribution by setting up a function $f(h)$, the **probability-density function** for heights, which allows us to determine the fraction of the population with height in any range $r_1 \leqslant h \leqslant r_2$ by calculating the definite integral $\int_{r_1}^{r_2} f(h)\, dh$.

Defining Property of the Density Function f(h)   Given any range of heights $r_1 \leqslant h \leqslant r_2$ with $r_1 < r_2$, the fraction of the population with height in this range is given by

$$\int_{r_1}^{r_2} f(h)\, dh$$

Numerically, the fraction of the population with height $r_1 \leqslant h \leqslant r_2$ is equal to the area under the graph of $y = f(h)$, above the interval $I = [r_1, r_2]$.

In Figure 4.15 we show the graph of $f(h)$; the heavily shaded strip corresponds to the fraction of the population with height $5.0 \leqslant h \leqslant 5.5$. Since few heights lie outside the range $3 \leqslant h \leqslant 8$, we may take $f(h)$ to be defined for $3 \leqslant h \leqslant 8$ without excluding any significant portion of our population.

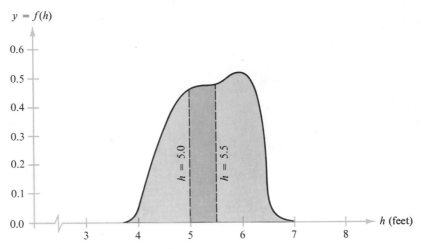

Figure 4.15
Probability density function $f(h)$ representing the distribution of heights among adult
U.S. citizens in 1970. For all h, $f(h) \geqslant 0$. On an interval $r_1 \leqslant h \leqslant r_2$, the integral
$\int_{r_1}^{r_2} f(h)\, dh$ gives the fraction of the population with height in this range. Since *all*
individuals have heights $3 \leqslant h \leqslant 8$, we must have $\int_3^8 f(h)\, dh = 1$; the total area under
the graph (shaded region) is equal to 1. The heavily shaded strip has area $\int_{5.0}^{5.5} f(h)\, dh$;
numerically this is just the fraction of the population with $5.0 \leqslant h \leqslant 5.5$. The two
bumps in the graph centered at slightly different heights correspond to the different
average heights for men and women.

Of course everything rests upon having the density function $f(h)$ in hand, so
a few words should be said about determining this function from raw statistical data.*
To set up an approximation to $f(h)$ we divide the interval $I = [3, 8]$ into subintervals
of equal length, say $n = 5$ intervals $I_1, \ldots, I_5$ each of length $\Delta h = (8 - 3)/5 = 1$ (see
Figure 4.16). For each interval I_k we refer to raw statistical data to find

$$F_k = \text{fraction of total population with height in the interval } I_k \qquad (26)$$

Then we plot a "step function," which has a constant value c_k over each interval I_k,
choosing the value c_k so that

$$F_k = \text{Area above } I_k = c_k \cdot \Delta h$$

Thus

$$c_k = \frac{F_k}{\Delta h} \qquad \text{for } k = 1, 2, \ldots \qquad (27)$$

---

* More detailed accounts can be found in any book on probability and statistics. In the rest of this
section we shall use predetermined density functions, and the reader will not be concerned with the way
they have been computed.

k	Interval I_k	N_k(millions)	F_k	$c_k = F_k/\Delta h$
1	$3 \leqslant h \leqslant 4$	0.15	0.001	0.001
2	$4 \leqslant h \leqslant 5$	39.73	0.284	0.284
3	$5 \leqslant h \leqslant 6$	68.17	0.487	0.487
4	$6 \leqslant h \leqslant 7$	31.81	0.227	0.227
5	$7 \leqslant h \leqslant 8$	0.15	0.001	0.001

Table 4.5
The interval $I = [3, 8]$ is divided into $n = 5$ pieces, each of
length $\Delta h = 1.0$. By examining raw statistical data we find N_k,
the total number of individuals with height in I_k (third column).
Then we calculate $F_k = N_k/N = N_k/140{,}000{,}000$, the fraction
of the population with height in I_k (fourth column). Finally, we
calculate the height $c_k = F_k/\Delta h$ of the vertical bar over I_k in
Figure 4.16.

Table 4.5 lists the values of F_k determined from statistical data and the calculated
values of the c_k for each of the subintervals I_k ($k = 1, 2, \ldots 5$). Figure 4.16 shows the
corresponding step function. The area of the bar over I_k is equal to F_k, and the total
area of the shaded bars is 1 since every individual height falls into one of the intervals
I_k. Such a step function is called a **histogram**. The rectangular areas that compose the

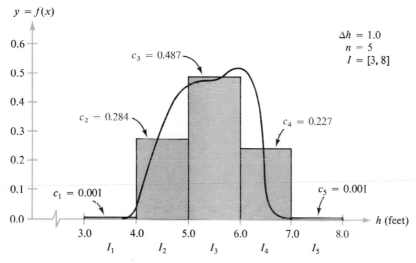

Figure 4.16
The histogram (step function) obtained by dividing $I = [3, 8]$ into $n = 5$ intervals,
each of length $\Delta h = 1.0$. The area of each rectangular bar gives the fraction F_k of the
total population with height in the interval I_k. The numerical values of F_k and the bar
heights $c_k = F_k/\Delta h$ are given in Table 4.5.

histogram in Figure 4.16 show at a glance the fraction of the population with height in each interval I_k, and so the histogram gives a rough picture of the actual density function. If we set up another histogram, dividing $I = [3, 8]$ into a larger number of subintervals, we get a much better idea of the density function. Figure 4.17 shows the histogram obtained by taking $n = 20$ subintervals (each of length $\Delta h = 0.25$). The numerical information used to plot the second histogram is tabulated in Table 4.6. Of course it requires more computation and closer scrutiny of the raw data to calculate the heights c_k of the 20 rectangles shown, but the resulting histogram presents much more information than the one in Figure 4.16.

As the number n of intervals increases (that is, as Δh gets small) these step functions closely approximate a smooth function $f(h)$; this is the desired density function. It is indicated by the solid curve in both figures.

This analysis of height distributions applies just as well to any variable x measured in a statistical survey of a large population of objects. For example, in a population of gas molecules x might stand for the velocities of individual molecules. A physicist might be interested in the distribution $f(x)$ of these velocities, say for $0 \leqslant x \leqslant 10{,}000$

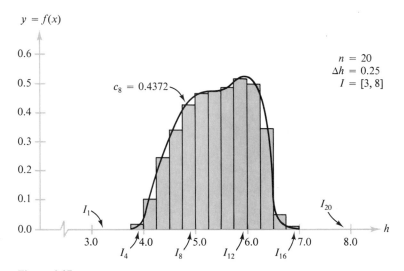

Figure 4.17
A closer approximation to the probability-density function for heights. This histogram was obtained by dividing $I = [3, 8]$ into $n = 20$ subintervals, each of length $\Delta h = 0.25$. The fraction of the population with height in the interval I_k is listed as F_k in Table 4.6; the value c_k gives the height of the rectangular bar above I_k. A few of the intervals $I_1, \ldots, I_{20}$ are labeled for easy reference to the data in Table 4.6. For example, over $I_8 = [4.75, 5.00]$ the height of the bar is $c_8 = 0.4372$, giving the bar an area $F_8 = c_8 \cdot \Delta h = 0.1093$. This is the fraction, about 11%, of the population with height $4.75 \leqslant h \leqslant 5.00$.

k	$N_k(millions)$	$F_k = N_k/N$	$c_k = F_k/\Delta h$
1	≈ 0	≈ 0	≈ 0
2	≈ 0	≈ 0	≈ 0
3	≈ 0	≈ 0	≈ 0
4	0.154	0.0011	0.0044
5	3.854	0.0275	0.1100
6	8.950	0.0632	0.2528
7	11.620	0.0830	0.3320
8	15.306	0.1093	0.4372
9	16.230	0.1159	0.4636
10	16.692	0.1209	0.4836
11	17.154	0.1225	0.4900
12	18.092	0.1289	0.5156
13	17.472	0.1248	0.4992
14	12.180	0.0870	0.3480
15	1.848	0.0132	0.0528
16	0.308	0.0022	0.0088
17	0.154	0.0011	0.0044
18–20	≈ 0	≈ 0	≈ 0

Table 4.6
Data for a histogram, dividing $I = [3, 8]$ into $n = 20$ pieces, each of length $\Delta h = 0.25$. From raw data we determine N_k = number of individuals with height in I_k, $F_k = N_k/N = N_k/140{,}000{,}000$ = fraction of population with height in I_k, and $c_k = F_k/\Delta h = 4F_k$. Then the vertical bar over I_k in Figure 4.17 has height c_k and an area equal to F_k.

feet per second. From this distribution he would be able to calculate almost all thermodynamic properties of the gas. Or we might consider the collection of all family units in the U.S. for the year 1974, and the variable x = gross family income. The density function $f(x)$ for this variable would be useful in formulating governmental economic and tax policy.

Suppose we have decided upon a variable x to be studied for a certain population of objects, and have chosen a range $a \leqslant x \leqslant b$ that includes essentially all values of x. Just as in the analysis of height distribution, there is a probability-density function

$f(x)$ that has the property

$$\int_{r_1}^{r_2} f(x)\,dx = \text{fraction of the total population for which} \\ x \text{ lies in the range } r_1 \leqslant x \leqslant r_2 \tag{28}$$

for every choice of $r_1 < r_2$. Some general properties of the density function follow directly from this definition:

(i) *The density function must be non-negative*; $f(x) \geqslant 0$ *everywhere*. For any range such as $r_1 \leqslant x \leqslant r_2$ the integral $\int_{r_1}^{r_2} f(x)\,dx$ is a positive fraction between 0 and 1. If $f(x)$ were negative its integral over certain ranges would also be negative, which is impossible.

(ii) *The total area $\int_a^b f(x)\,dx$ under the graph is* 1. This integral is precisely the fraction of the population for which $a \leqslant x \leqslant b$. But *all* values of x fall within this range.

By forming appropriate integrals we may answer many statistical questions involving x, such as the ones posed for height distributions. For example, if r is given

$$\int_a^r f(x)\,dx = \text{fraction of the population such that } a \leqslant x \leqslant r$$

Since all objects have $a \leqslant x$, this is just the fraction of the population with $x \leqslant r$. Similarly

$$\int_r^b f(x)\,dx = \text{fraction of the population such that } x \geqslant r$$

since $x \leqslant b$ for all objects. If we wish to find the total number of objects such that x lies in a certain range $r_1 \leqslant x \leqslant r_2$, we simply multiply the appropriate fraction by N, the total number of objects in the population under study; thus

$$N \int_{r_1}^{r_2} f(x)\,dx = \text{(total number of objects)} \times \text{(fraction with } r_1 \leqslant x \leqslant r_2) \\ = \text{total number of objects such that } r_1 \leqslant x \leqslant r_2$$

Example 13   The graph of the probability-density function

$$f(x) = (0.0012)(x^3 - 20x^2 + 100x) = 0.0012x^3 - 0.024x^2 + 0.12x$$

defined for $0 \leqslant x \leqslant 10$, is shown in Figure 4.18. Calculate the fraction of the popula-

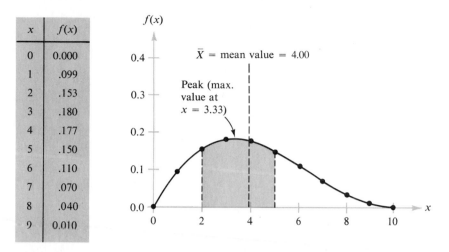

x	$f(x)$
0	0.000
1	.099
2	.153
3	.180
4	.177
5	.150
6	.110
7	.070
8	.040
9	0.010

Figure 4.18
The graph of the probability-density function $f(x) = 0.0012x^3 - 0.024x^2 + 0.12x$ studied
in Example 13. The shaded region corresponds to $\int_2^5 f(x)\, dx =$ fraction of population such
that $2 \leqslant x \leqslant 5$; this fraction is 0.507, slightly more than 50%. Simple differentiation
methods show that $f(x)$ has a maximum at $x = 3.333\ldots$ as indicated; the density is
greatest there.

tion such that the variable x lies in the range $2 \leqslant x \leqslant 5$ (corresponding to the shaded
region under the graph). Verify that the total area under the graph is equal to 1.

Solution   The fraction of the population such that $2 \leqslant x \leqslant 5$ is given by

$$\int_2^5 f(x)\, dx = (0.0012) \int_2^5 (x^3 - 20x^2 + 100x)\, dx$$

$$= (0.0012) \left[\frac{1}{4} x^4 - \frac{20}{3} x^3 + 50x^2 \Big|_{x=2}^{x=5} \right]$$

$$- (0.0012) \cdot (422.3) = 0.507$$

by definition of the probability-density function. An easy calculation shows that

$$\text{Total area} = \int_0^{10} f(x)\, dx = 1$$

In statistics certain numbers are helpful in describing density functions. The
most important of these is the **mean** or **mean value** of the distribution, and second in
importance is the **standard deviation**. These numbers are obtained from integrals
involving the density function $f(x)$.

The Mean Value $\bar{X}$ Intuitively, the mean value is the number about which the values x cluster. Suppose there are N objects and that the values of x have been compiled in a list $x_1, x_2, \ldots, x_N$. The **average value** or **mean value** of x for this population of objects is defined by giving equal weight $1/N$ to each of the values, and forming the average

$$\bar{X} = \frac{1}{N} \cdot (x_1 + x_2 + \cdots + x_N) \tag{29}$$

If N is very large this sum is difficult to calculate directly. For a large population with known density function $f(x)$ the mean value is given by the integral

$$\bar{X} = \int_a^b x \cdot f(x)\, dx \tag{30}$$

The Standard Deviation σ Once the mean value $\bar{X}$ has been calculated, the standard deviation is defined as

$$\sigma = \sqrt{\frac{(x_1 - \bar{X})^2 + (x_2 - \bar{X})^2 + \cdots + (x_N - \bar{X})^2}{N}} \tag{31}$$

The standard deviation σ is a positive number that measures the scatter of the values x_i away from the mean value $\bar{X}$. For large populations with known density function $f(x)$, the standard deviation is given by the integral

$$\sigma = \sqrt{\int_a^b (x - \bar{X})^2 \cdot f(x)\, dx} \tag{32}$$

The numbers $\bar{X}$ and σ tell us a lot about a population. The values of x cluster around the mean value $\bar{X}$. If σ is small they are concentrated close to $\bar{X}$, while if σ is large they are more spread out.

Example 14   Calculate the mean value $\bar{X}$ and standard deviation σ for the probability-density function given in Example 13.

Solution   We calculate the mean value according to the definition:

$$\bar{X} = \int_0^{10} x \cdot f(x)\, dx = (0.0012) \int_0^{10} (x^4 - 20x^3 + 100x^2)\, dx$$

$$= (0.0012)\left[\frac{1}{5}x^5 - 5x^4 + \frac{100}{3}x^3 \;\Big|_{x=0}^{x=10}\right]$$

$$= (0.0012)(2.00 - 5.00 + 3.33) \cdot 10,000$$

$$= 4.00$$

The location of $\bar{X}$ is shown in Figure 4.18.

In calculating the standard deviation σ, it helps to avoid entering the actual value $\bar{X} = 4.00$ until the very last step:

$$\sigma^2 = \int_0^{10} (x - \bar{X})^2 f(x)\, dx$$

$$= (0.0012) \int_0^{10} (x^2 - 2\bar{X}x + \bar{X}^2)(x^3 - 20x^2 + 100x)\, dx$$

$$= (0.0012) \int_0^{10} (x^5 - (20 + 2\bar{X})x^4 + (100 + 40\bar{X} + \bar{X}^2)x^3$$

$$- (200\bar{X} + 20\bar{X}^2)x^2 + (100\bar{X}^2)x)\, dx$$

$$= (0.0012)\left[\frac{x^6}{6} - \frac{20 + 2\bar{X}}{5}x^5 + \frac{100 + 40\bar{X} + \bar{X}^2}{4}x^4\right.$$

$$\left. - \frac{200\bar{X} + 20\bar{X}^2}{3}x^3 + \frac{100\bar{X}^2}{2}x^2 \;\Big|_{x=0}^{x=10}\right]$$

Upon setting $\bar{X} = 4.00$ we get $\sigma^2 = 4.0$, so that $\sigma = 2.0$.

Exercises

• 1. For a large population of objects a variable x is being studied. The values of x are found to lie between -1 and 1; the probability-density function for this variable has been determined to be

$$f(x) = \frac{3}{4}(1 - x^2) \qquad \text{for } -1 \leqslant x \leqslant 1$$

Calculate the fraction of objects for which x lies in the range $-0.25 \leqslant x \leqslant 0.25$. If there are 1,000,000 objects in all, how many have values of x in this range?

● 2. Consider the probability-density function $f(x)$ discussed in Example 13. For what fraction of the population of objects does the variable x lie in the range

   (i) $0 \leqslant x \leqslant 5$ (ii) $5 \leqslant x \leqslant 10$ (iii) $0 \leqslant x \leqslant 3$

● 3. The data in Table 4.7 are derived from the observed lifetimes t (measured in thousands of hours, $0 \leqslant t \leqslant 5$) for a lot of $N = 1000$ light bulbs. The range $I = [0, 5]$ of the variable t has been divided into $n = 10$ subintervals I_k, each of length $\Delta t = 0.5$ (thousand hours). Table 4.7 gives the total number N_k of bulbs whose lifetimes fall in the interval I_k.

   (i) Calculate $F_k = N_k/N$ for each interval.

   (ii) Calculate the heights $c_k = F_k/\Delta t$ of the vertical bars for an appropriate histogram showing the distribution of lifetime.

   Sketch the histogram on graph paper. On this picture superimpose the graph of the curve $y = e^{-t}$ (use exponential tables, Appendix 4, to find values). Does the smooth density function $f(t) = e^{-t}$ fit the data in the table reasonably well?

k	Time interval I_k (thousand hours)	Number of bulb failures N_k
1	0.0–0.5	389
2	0.5–1.0	230
3	1.0–1.5	150
4	1.5–2.0	93
5	2.0–2.5	61
6	2.5–3.0	36
7	3.0–3.5	21
8	3.5–4.0	13
9	4.0–4.5	4
10	4.5–5.0	3

Table 4.7
Results of testing a lot of $N = 1000$ lightbulbs, burned continuously until failure. The last column shows the number of failures during each consecutive period of 500 hours. These data can be used to plot a histogram for the expected lifetime t (measured in thousands of hours, $0 \leqslant t \leqslant 5$) of this type of bulb, as explained in Exercise 3. Note that time of failure = lifetime of the bulb, so the number of bulbs failing during time interval I_k is equal to the number of bulbs whose lifetimes fall within the interval I_k ($= N_k$ by definition).

● 4. Use the data in Table 4.7 to answer the following questions.

   (i) What fraction of the total sample of bulbs had a lifetime in the range $0 \leqslant t \leqslant 1$ (thousand hours)?

   (ii) What was the total number of bulbs in the sample with a lifetime greater than or equal to one thousand hours?

   (iii) What fraction of the bulbs had a lifetime of at least two thousand hours?

   ANSWERS: (i) 0.619; (ii) $0.381 \times 1000 = 381$; (iii) 0.138.

● 5. The function $y = e^{-x}$ occurs in a number of important density functions. Consider the density function $f(x) = 1.0067e^{-x}$ defined for $0 \leqslant x \leqslant 5$. Use the integration formula

$$\int xe^{-x}\, dx = -xe^{-x} - e^{-x} + \text{const}$$

to calculate the mean value $\bar{X}$ for this distribution. For what fraction of the population does x lie in the range $0 \leqslant x \leqslant 1$? NOTE: The formula may be verified by direct differentiation. Use the exponential tables (Appendix 4) to find any values of e^x or e^{-x} you need.

● 6. A precision bolt with diameter $D = 3.000$ inches is to be produced with a maximum allowable machining error of $\Delta D = \pm 0.005$ inches. From raw statistical data, the quality-control department has found that the variable

$$x = \text{error (or deviation) from design diameter}$$

(measured in 1/100ths of an inch) has the probability-density function

$$f(x) = \begin{cases} \dfrac{15}{16}(x^2 - 1)^2 & \text{for } -1 \leqslant x \leqslant 1 \\ 0 & \text{elsewhere} \end{cases}$$

shown in Figure 4.19.

(i) Show that $\int_{-1}^{1} f(x)\, dx = 1$, as required of a density function.

(ii) What fraction of the bolts produced will have machining errors within the acceptable range $-0.5 \leqslant x \leqslant +0.5$ (hundredths of an inch)?

ANSWER: (ii) $203/256 = 0.793$ (about 79%).

● 7. A variable x is restricted to the interval $1 \leqslant x \leqslant 3$. Over that interval, its probability distribution is described by a probability-density function of the form $f(x) = k \cdot x$, for a constant k. Find k. HINT: The density function must satisfy the condition $\int_{1}^{3} f(x)\, dx = 1$. ANSWER: $k = 1/4$.

● 8. The **uniform distribution** for a variable x restricted to the interval $0 \leqslant x \leqslant 1$ is described by the probability-density function

$$f(x) = 1 \quad \text{(constant)} \quad \text{for } 0 \leqslant x \leqslant 1.$$

Find the mean $\bar{X}$ and the standard deviation σ.

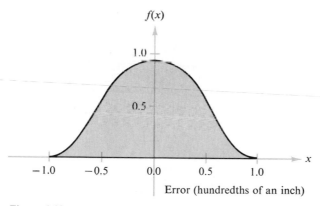

Figure 4.19
The probability-density function $f(x) = (15/16)(x^2 - 1)^2$ for $-1 \leqslant x \leqslant 1$ in Exercise 6. The function equals 0 for x outside the range $-1 \leqslant x \leqslant +1$.

● 9. A variable x associated with a large population of objects ranges through the interval $0 \leqslant x \leqslant 2$, and is described by a probability-density function of the form $f(x) = k \cdot x^3$, where k is a constant.

  (*i*) Find k (to insure that $\int_0^2 f(x)\, dx = 1.0$).

  (*ii*) Find the fraction of the population with $0 \leqslant x \leqslant 1$.

  (*iii*) Find the mean $\bar{X}$ for this population.

  (*iv*) Find the standard deviation σ.

  ANSWERS: (*i*) $k = 1/4$; (*ii*) $1/16 = 0.0625$; (*iii*) $\bar{X} = 1.6$; (*iv*) $\sigma = \sqrt{0.1066} = 0.327$.

●10. Consider a variable x ranging through the interval $0 \leqslant x \leqslant 1$, whose probability distribution function is $f(x) = 30(x^4 - x^5)$. (Graph shown in Figure 4.20.) Show that the total area under the graph is

$$\int_0^1 f(x)\, dx = 1.$$

Then find

  (*i*) the mean value $\bar{X}$.

  (*ii*) the value X_0 at which $f(x)$ is a maximum.

  (*iii*) the standard deviation σ.

Do $\bar{X}$ and X_0 coincide?

●11. The **median value** for a probability density $f(x)$ defined on an interval $I = [a,b]$ is the value $x = X_m$ such that half the population has values $x > X_m$ and the other half has values $x < X_m$.

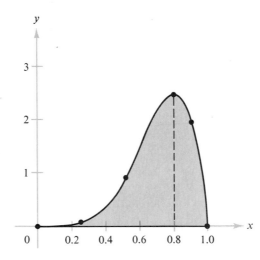

Figure 4.20
Graph of the probability-density function $f(x) = 30(x^4 - x^5)$. Tabulated values are plotted as solid dots. Maximum value occurs at $x = 0.80$.

x	y
0.00	0.000
.25	0.088
.50	0.936
.80	2.457
0.90	1.968
1.00	0.000

In other words, half the area under $y = f(x)$ lies to the left of $x = X_m$ and half to the right, so that

$$\int_a^{X_m} f(x)\, dx = \frac{1}{2} = \int_{X_m}^b f(x)\, dx$$

Find the median value for each of the density functions

(i) $f(x) = \frac{1}{2} x^{-1/2} = \frac{1}{2\sqrt{x}}$ on $1 \leqslant x \leqslant 4$

(ii) $f(x) = \frac{10}{9} \cdot \frac{1}{x^2}$ on $1 \leqslant x \leqslant 10$

HINT: Total area is 1, so it suffices to find X for which $\int_a^X f(x)\, dx = 1/2$.
ANSWERS: (i) $X_m = 9/4 = 2.25$; (ii) $X_m = 20/11 = 1.818$.

12. Calculate the mean values $\bar{X}$ for the probability-density functions in Exercise 11. Do they agree with the median values determined there?

4.6   Advanced Integration Techniques: Substitution

Almost every differentiation rule may be turned around and reinterpreted as a statement about indefinite integrals. This leads to new techniques for evaluating complicated integrals. We shall explain one of these, the **substitution method**, obtained by inverting the chain rule.

The chain rule tells us how to differentiate a composite function. Starting with a function $g(u)$ whose variable u depends upon a second variable x, so that $u = u(x)$, we substitute $u = u(x)$ in $g(u)$ to get a new function (composite function)

$$f(x) = g(u(x)) = \left[g(u) \Big|_{u = u(x)} \right]$$

with variable x. Its derivative df/dx is the product of derivatives dg/du and du/dx of the functions we combined to get $f(x)$ (see Section 3.3).

Consider the indefinite integral $\int f(x)\, dx$ of an arbitrary function $f(x)$. Suppose we can lump together a block of terms $u = u(x)$ so that the integrand $f(x)$ assumes the form

$$f(x) = g(u(x)) \cdot \frac{du}{dx}$$

for some function $g(u)$ in the new variable u. Then the problem of evaluating $\int f(x)\, dx$ reduces to the problem of evaluating a new integral, namely $\int g(u)\, du$ with variable u, which may be much easier to handle.

The Substitution Formula If $f(x)$ can be written as $g(u) \cdot \dfrac{du}{dx}$ for a suitable choice of $u = u(x)$, then

$$\int f(x)\, dx = \int g(u)\, du \Big|_{u=u(x)} \tag{33}$$

That is, we get $\int f(x)\, dx$ by evaluating $\int g(u)\, du$ as a function of u and then substituting $u = u(x)$ to get a function of the original variable x.

Example 15 Evaluate $\displaystyle\int_0^1 (x - 1)^{50}\, dx$.

Solution First we evaluate the indefinite integral. Although the integrand is a polynomial (of degree 50), it would be very tedious to multiply it out and integrate each term separately. Instead, we substitute $u = x - 1$; now $du/dx = 1$ and the integrand has the form

$$(x - 1)^{50} = u^{50} \cdot 1 = u^{50} \cdot \frac{du}{dx} = g(u)\frac{du}{dx}$$

where $u = x - 1$ and $g(u) = u^{50}$. Applying the substitution formula (33), we ma,
evaluate the integral with ease:

$$\int (x - 1)^{50}\, dx = \int u^{50}\, du \Big|_{u=x-1}$$

$$= \frac{u^{51}}{51}\Big|_{u=x-1} = \frac{(x - 1)^{51}}{51} + \text{const}$$

We can check this answer: differentiating $(x - 1)^{51}/51$ by means of the chain rule we get $(x - 1)^{50}$. The definite integral is just

$$\int_0^1 (x - 1)^{50}\, dx = \left[\frac{(x - 1)^{51}}{51}\Big|_{x=0}^{x=1} \right]$$

$$= \frac{0^{51}}{51} - \frac{(-1)^{51}}{51} = 0 + \frac{1}{51} = \frac{1}{51}$$

Example 16 Evaluate the indefinite integral $\displaystyle\int \frac{2x}{\sqrt{x^2 - 1}}\, dx$.

Solution   The integrand $f(x) = 2x/\sqrt{x^2 - 1} = 2x(x^2 - 1)^{-1/2}$ is not the derivative of a familiar function of x, so we have a problem. Life would be simpler if we could lump the expression $x^2 - 1$ into a new variable.

$$u = x^2 - 1 \qquad \left(\text{so that } \frac{du}{dx} = 2x \right)$$

Now $f(x)$ has the form

$$f(x) = \frac{2x}{\sqrt{x^2 - 1}} = \frac{1}{\sqrt{u}} \frac{du}{dx} = g(u) \cdot \frac{du}{dx} \qquad (\text{where } g(u) = u^{-1/2})$$

The new integral $\int g(u) \, du = \int u^{-1/2} \, du$ is quite familiar:

$$\int g(u) \, du = \frac{u^{(1 - (1/2))}}{(1 - \frac{1}{2})} = \frac{u^{1/2}}{\frac{1}{2}} = 2u^{1/2}$$

By the substitution formula (33) we get the desired integral

$$\int \frac{2x}{\sqrt{x^2 - 1}} \, dx = \int g(u) \, du \Big|_{u = x^2 - 1}$$

$$= 2\sqrt{u} \Big|_{u = x^2 - 1} = 2\sqrt{x^2 - 1} + \text{const}$$

The substitution formula (33) may be easier to use if we notice how $\int f(x) \, dx$ and $\int g(u) \, du$ are related for a correct choice of $g(u)$ and $u = u(x)$. The new integral $\int g(u) \, du$ should become the original integral $\int f(x) \, dx$ if we make the replacements

$$g(u) \to g(u(x)) \quad \text{and} \quad du \to \frac{du}{dx} \, dx$$

In Example 16, $u = x^2 - 1$ and $g(u) = 1/\sqrt{u}$, so

$$g(u) \to \frac{1}{\sqrt{x^2 - 1}} \quad \text{and} \quad du \to 2x \, dx$$

thus $\int u^{-1/2} \, du$ is converted into $\int \frac{2x}{\sqrt{x^2 - 1}} \, dx$, as expected.

Next we illustrate a common technique for preparing an integral so that the substitution method works. Essentially, we multiply and divide by a single constant, which does not change the integral.

Example 17   Evaluate $\int \dfrac{x}{(x^2 + 1)^2}\, dx$.

Solution   The derivative of $x^2 + 1$ is $2x$, so it seems reasonable to try $u = x^2 + 1$ and $g(u) = 1/u^2$. Then

$$g(u)\frac{du}{dx} = \frac{1}{u^2}\,2x = \frac{2x}{(x^2 + 1)^2}$$

This misses agreeing with the actual integrand $f(x) = x/(x^2 + 1)^2$ by only a multiplied constant 2. There is a standard trick for correcting this difficulty: before applying the substitution method we multiply and divide the integrand by the missing constant.

$$\int \frac{x}{(x^2 + 1)^2}\, dx = \int \frac{2}{2} \cdot \frac{x}{(x^2 + 1)^2}\, dx = \frac{1}{2}\int \frac{2x}{(x^2 + 1)^2}\, dx \tag{34}$$

We now apply the substitution method. This proceeds without difficulty if we take $u = x^2 + 1$ and $g(u) = 1/u^2$.

$$\int \frac{x}{(x^2 + 1)^2}\, dx = \frac{1}{2}\int \frac{2x}{(x^2 + 1)^2}\, dx = \frac{1}{2}\left[\int \frac{1}{u^2}\, du \,\Big|_{u = x^2 + 1}\right]$$

$$= \frac{1}{2}\left[-\frac{1}{u}\,\Big|_{u = x^2 + 1}\right]$$

$$= -\frac{1}{2(x^2 + 1)} + \text{const}$$

Example 18   Evaluate $\int_0^1 e^{-3x}\, dx$.

Solution   The main problem is to determine the indefinite integral $\int e^{-3x}\, dx$. We might try to reduce this to the known integral $\int e^u\, du = e^u + \text{const}$ (see Table 4.1) by setting

$$u(x) = -3x \qquad g(u) = e^u \tag{35}$$

Once again we are off by a multiplied constant (now -3): we have

$$f(x) = e^{-3x} \quad \text{while} \quad g(u)\frac{du}{dx} = -3e^{-3x}$$

But multiplying $f(x)$ by $1 = (-3)/(-3)$ gives

$$\int e^{-3x}\, dx = \int \left(\frac{-3}{-3}\right) e^{-3x}\, dx = \frac{-1}{3} \int -3e^{-3x}\, dx$$

Now the substitution (35) works, giving

$$\int -3e^{-3x}\, dx = \int e^u\, du \Big|_{u=-3x} = e^u \Big|_{u=-3x}$$

$$= e^{-3x} + \text{const}$$

Thus the integral we want is

$$\int e^{-3x}\, dx = \frac{-1}{3} \int -3e^{-3x}\, dx = \frac{-1}{3} e^{-3x} + \text{const}$$

and the definite integral is

$$\int_0^1 e^{-3x}\, dx = \left[\frac{-1}{3} e^{-3x} \Big|_{x=0}^{x=1} \right]$$

$$= \left(\frac{-1}{3} e^{-3} \right) - \left(\frac{-1}{3} e^{-0} \right) = \frac{1}{3}(1 - e^{-3}) = 0.31674$$

Remember: $e^{-x} = 1/e^x$ for any x, and $e^0 = 1$.

The same reasoning yields a useful integration formula for exponential functions. If $k \neq 0$ is any real number ($k = -3$ above), then

$$\int e^{kx}\, dx = \frac{1}{k} e^{kx} + \text{const} \tag{36}$$

Exercises

● 1. Show that $f(x) = 2x(4 + x^2)^5$ can be written as $g(u) \cdot (du/dx)$ if we take $g(u) = u^5$ and $u = 4 + x^2$. Apply the substitution rule to evaluate the indefinite integral $\int 2x(4 + x^2)^5\, dx$. Check your answer by differentiation.

●2. Calculate the following indefinite integrals by the method of substitution.

(i) $\int (x + 2)^3 \, dx$

(iv) $\int 3(3x + 2) \, dx$

(ii) $\int 2x\sqrt{x^2 + 4} \, dx$

(v) $\int \dfrac{1}{2x + 5} \, dx$

(iii) $\int \sqrt{x + 2} \, dx$

(vi) $\int e^{t+3} \, dt$

●3. Show that $f(x) = x^2/\sqrt{1 - x^3}$ can be written as $g(u) \cdot (du/dx)$, taking $g(u) = (-1/3)u^{-1/2}$ and $u = 1 - x^3$. Then apply the substitution method to evaluate

$$\int \frac{x^2}{\sqrt{1 - x^3}} \, dx$$

●4. Determine the following indefinite integrals:

(i) $\int (x^2 + 1)^{22} 2x \, dx$

(v) $\int \dfrac{t^3}{1 + t^4} \, dt$

(ii) $\int x\sqrt{x^2 + 4} \, dx$

(vi) $\int \dfrac{x}{(3 - x^2)^{17}} \, dx$

(iii) $\int x^2(1 - x^3)^{2/3} \, dx$

(vii) $\int \dfrac{\log x}{x} \, dx$

(iv) $\int \dfrac{1}{(2 - x)^3} \, dx$

(viii) $\int e^{-2x} \, dx$

●5. Calculate the following indefinite integrals:

(i) $\int \dfrac{x^2}{x^3 - 1} \, dx$

(v) $\int \dfrac{e^x}{2 + e^x} \, dx$

(ii) $\int (1 + x)^{4/3} \, dx$

(vi) $\int \dfrac{\sin x}{\cos x} \, dx$

(iii) $\int xe^{-x^2/2} \, dx$

(vii) $\int \left(1 + \dfrac{1}{x + 2}\right) dx$

(iv) $\int \sqrt{1 - x} \, dx$

(viii) $\int \sin(4\pi x + 7) \, dx$

●6. Calculate the following definite integrals by using the method of substitution.

(i) $\int_1^5 \sqrt{5 - x} \, dx$

(v) $\int_0^1 \dfrac{x}{(4 - 3x^2)} \, dx$

(ii) $\int_0^2 \dfrac{x}{\sqrt{x^2 + 1}} \, dx$

(vi) $\int_0^2 \dfrac{1}{2x + 5} \, dx$

(iii) $\int_{-2}^{-1} \dfrac{1}{(x + 3)^5} \, dx$

(vii) $\int_0^2 (2x + 1)(x^2 + x)^{3/2} \, dx$

(iv) $\int_0^5 e^{-x} \, dx$

(viii) $\int_{-a}^a xe^{-x^2/2} \, dx \qquad (a > 0 \text{ fixed})$

*4.7 Improper Integrals

Definite integrals $\int_a^b f(x)\,dx$ allow us to calculate the areas of many regions of finite extent. In some applications, and particularly when dealing with probability distributions, it is necessary to extend the notion of integral to regions of infinite extent. We do this by introducing **improper integrals**.

Consider the shaded regions R shown in Figure 4.21(a). These are bounded by the x-axis, the vertical line $x = 1$, and the curves $y = 1/x^2$ and $y = 1/\sqrt{x} = x^{-1/2}$ respectively. The shaded regions extend "out to infinity," so one might be tempted to suppose that their areas are infinite. On the other hand, the widths taper off rapidly to the right; if they taper off rapidly enough, it is conceivable that the total areas are finite. We can decide the issue by introducing a "cutoff" at some point $x = r$. Wherever we place the cutoff, we get truncated regions R_r of finite extent, as in Figure 4.21(b). The areas of the truncated regions are easily calculated in the usual way; in particular

$$\int_1^r f(x)\,dx = \int_1^r \frac{1}{x^2}\,dx = \left[-\frac{1}{x}\Big|_{x=1}^{x=r}\right] = 1 - \frac{1}{r} \tag{37}$$

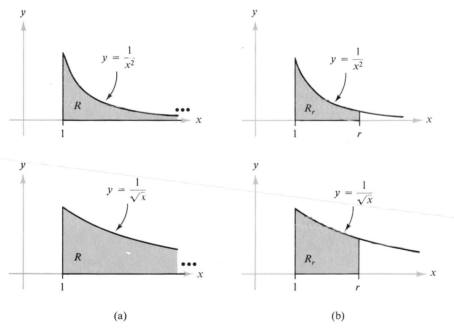

(a) (b)

Figure 4.21
(a) Regions of infinite extent. (b) Truncated regions, of finite extent.

for the curve $y = 1/x^2$, and

$$\int_1^r f(x)\, dx = \int_1^r \frac{1}{\sqrt{x}}\, dx = \left[2\sqrt{x} \;\Big|_{x=1}^{x=r} \right] = 2\sqrt{r} - 2 \qquad (38)$$

if $y = x^{-1/2}$. Now let the cutoff point $x = r$ move farther and farther to the right (indicated symbolically by writing "$r \to +\infty$"). There are two possibilities: either the area of the truncated region tends toward a finite limit value L, in which case we write

$$\lim_{r \to +\infty} \int_1^r f(x)\, dx = L$$

or else the area gets larger and larger without any bound, which we indicate by writing

$$\lim_{r \to +\infty} \int_1^r f(x)\, dx = +\infty$$

The limit value is called the **improper integral** of $f(x)$ from $x = a$ to $x = +\infty$.

Definition   Let $f(x)$ be positive and continuous for all x to the right of some point $x = a$. The **improper integral** of $f(x)$ from $x = a$ to $x = +\infty$, denoted by writing

$$\int_a^{+\infty} f(x)\, dx$$

is defined to be the limit value of the cutoff integrals $\int_a^r f(x)\, dx$ as r increases without limit:

$$\int_a^{+\infty} f(x)\, dx = \lim_{r \to +\infty} \int_a^r f(x)\, dx$$

If the limit does not exist, the improper integral is said to **diverge**, and we write

$$\int_a^{+\infty} f(x)\, dx = +\infty$$

In either case shown in Figure 4.21 we shall interpret the area of the full unbounded region R to be the limit value of the areas $\int_1^r f(x)\, dx$ of the truncated regions R_r,

$$\text{Area}(R) = \int_1^{+\infty} f(x)\, dx$$

In order to calculate improper integrals and the areas associated with them, we must examine the behavior of the integrals $\int_a^r f(x)\, dx$ as r gets larger and larger.

This is not difficult if we appeal to a few simple principles (recall Example 9, Section 1.3):

    (*i*) If r is a large positive (or negative) number, its reciprocal $1/r$ is a small positive (negative) number.

    (*ii*) If r is a large positive number, then any power r^a $(a > 0)$ is a large positive number.

(39)

The second rule insures that expressions such as $\sqrt{r}$, r^2, $r^{3/5}$, and so forth get larger and larger as r increases. Applying these ideas to the cutoff integrals in (37) and (38), we see that

$$\int_1^r \frac{1}{x^2}\, dx = \left(1 - \frac{1}{r}\right) \text{ approaches 1 as } r \text{ increases}$$

The constant 1 remains fixed, while $1/r$ gets very small as r increases. Thus, for $y = 1/x^2$

$$\text{Area}(R) = \int_1^{+\infty} \frac{1}{x^2}\, dx = \lim_{r \to +\infty} \int_1^r \frac{1}{x^2}\, dx = 1$$

On the other hand, for $y = x^{-1/2}$ the expression $\sqrt{r}$ gets very large as r increases, by (39*ii*), and so do $2\sqrt{r}$ and $2\sqrt{r} - 2$. Thus the integral diverges:

$$\text{Area}(R) = \int_1^{+\infty} \frac{1}{\sqrt{x}}\, dx = \lim_{r \to +\infty} \{2\sqrt{r} - 2\} = +\infty$$

In this case R contains subsets R_r with arbitrarily large area, so it is natural to say that Area(R) is infinite, written Area(R) $= +\infty$. Here are some additional examples.

Example 19   Calculate the improper integrals $\int_1^{+\infty} 1\, dx$ and $\int_2^{+\infty} \frac{1}{x^3}\, dx$. Interpret the answers as areas.

Solution   In the first integral, the cutoff integrals have values

$$\int_1^r 1\, dx = \left[x \Big|_{x=1}^{x=r} \right] = r - 1$$

Obviously, as r increases we have

$$\int_1^{+\infty} 1\, dx = \lim_{r \to +\infty} \int_1^r 1\, dx = \lim_{r \to +\infty} \{r - 1\} = +\infty$$

and the integral diverges. This is to be expected since the area of the strip in Figure 4.22(a) should be infinite. In the second integral

$$\int_2^r \frac{1}{x^3}\,dx = \left[\frac{x^{-2}}{-2}\Big|_{x=2}^{x=r}\right] = \frac{1}{2}\left(\frac{1}{2^2} - \frac{1}{r^2}\right) = \frac{1}{8} - \frac{1}{2r^2}$$

As r increases, r^2 takes on large positive values and $1/r^2$ very small positive values. Consequently, $-1/2r^2$ takes on small negative values tending toward zero, so that

$$\int_2^{+\infty} \frac{1}{x^3}\,dx = \lim_{r \to +\infty}\left(\frac{1}{8} - \frac{1}{2r^2}\right) = \frac{1}{8}$$

This is the area of the region shown in Figure 4.22(b).

If $f(x)$ is defined to the left of some point $x = a$, or on the entire number line, we can definite corresponding improper integrals

$$\int_{-\infty}^a f(x)\,dx \quad\text{and}\quad \int_{-\infty}^{+\infty} f(x)\,dx$$

just as we defined improper integrals of the form $\int_a^{+\infty} f(x)\,dx$ above. Thus, if $f(x)$ is positive and continuous for $x \leqslant a$, we take cutoffs to the left of $x = a$ and then move the cutoff point $x = r$ "toward $-\infty$," through larger and larger negative values, to define

$$\int_{-\infty}^a f(x)\,dx = \lim_{r \to -\infty}\int_r^a f(x)\,dx \tag{40}$$

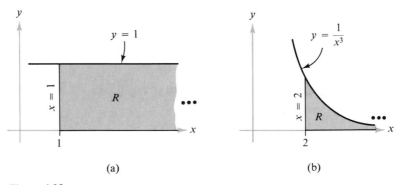

(a)   (b)

Figure 4.22
The regions whose areas correspond to the improper integrals $\int_1^{+\infty} 1\,dx$ and $\int_2^{+\infty} \frac{1}{x^3}\,dx.$

If $f(x)$ is positive and continuous for all x we take any convenient dividing point $x = a$, calculate the "one-sided" improper integrals $\int_{-\infty}^{a} f(x)\,dx$ and $\int_{a}^{+\infty} f(x)\,dx$ as above, and then define

$$\int_{-\infty}^{+\infty} f(x)\,dx = \int_{-\infty}^{a} f(x)\,dx + \int_{a}^{+\infty} f(x)\,dx \qquad (41)$$

This integral is considered to diverge if either of the one-sided improper integrals diverges, in which case we write $\int_{-\infty}^{+\infty} f(x)\,dx = +\infty$.

In Section 4.5 we indicated that statistical problems may be handled by means of integrals and probability densities. Without doubt the most important density function in statistics is the **normal density function**

$$f(x) = \frac{1}{\sqrt{2\pi}}\, e^{-x^2/2} \qquad \text{defined for all } x$$

whose graph is shown in Figure 4.23. One can show by means of advanced integration methods that

$$\int_{0}^{+\infty} \frac{1}{\sqrt{2\pi}}\, e^{-x^2/2}\,dx = \frac{1}{2} = \int_{-\infty}^{0} \frac{1}{\sqrt{2\pi}}\, e^{-x^2/2}\,dx$$

so that the total area under the graph equals 1:

$$\int_{-\infty}^{+\infty} \frac{1}{\sqrt{2\pi}}\, e^{-x^2/2}\,dx = 1$$

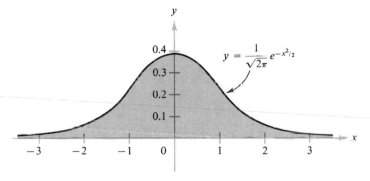

Figure 4.23
The normal density function $f(x) = (1/\sqrt{2\pi})e^{-x^2/2}$, commonly referred to as the "bell-shaped" density function because of the shape of its graph. It is symmetric about the y-axis ($f(-x) = f(x)$ for all x), has a maximum at $x = 0$, and has inflection points at $x = -1$ and $x = +1$. This density function plays a central role in statistics, where it is used to describe a wide variety of phenomena, such as the distribution of test scores, errors in precision tool manufacturing, and so on.

even though the region is unbounded. Thus $f(x)$ satisfies the principal condition required of any probability-density function. Since the variable x ranges over the entire number line, improper integrals must be used to carry out a number of statistical calculations involving the normal density function. Recall that $\int_a^b f(x)\,dx$ gives the fraction of the population for which the variable x lies in the range $a \leqslant x \leqslant b$. Suppose we want to know the fraction of the population for which $x \geqslant a$. Intuitively, we should compute

$$\int_a^r f(x)\,dx = \text{fraction of population such that } a \leqslant x \leqslant r$$

and let the upper limit r get larger and larger. Thus the fraction of the population for which $x \geqslant a$ is given by an improper integral

$$\lim_{r \to +\infty} \int_a^r f(x)\,dx = \int_a^{+\infty} f(x)\,dx$$

Here is an example involving a slightly different density function, in which the desired improper integral may be computed by means at our disposal. (Integrals involving the normal density function are very difficult to compute, and are usually evaluated by numerical methods.)

Example 20   In a study of the lifetime t (in hours of use) of a type of 60-watt light bulb, the probability-density function for lifetimes is found to be

$$f(t) = \frac{1}{1000}\, e^{-t/1000} \qquad \text{defined for } t \geqslant 0$$

(In probability theory this type of density is called *exponential*.) What fraction of the bulbs will have lifetimes exceeding 500 hours?

Solution   The fraction of bulbs for which $t \geqslant 500$ is given by $\int_{500}^{+\infty} f(t)\,dt$. The cutoff integrals $\int_{500}^r f(t)\,dt$ are readily evaluated by the substitution method (Section 4.6). Taking $u = -t/1000$ (so $du/dt = -1/1000$) we get

$$\int \frac{1}{1000}\, e^{-t/1000}\,dt = - \int e^u\,du \Big|_{u = -t/1000}$$

$$= \left[-e^u \Big|_{u = -t/1000} \right]$$

$$= -e^{-t/1000} + \text{const}$$

By the Fundamental Theorem of Calculus, this indefinite integral yields

$$\int_{500}^{r} f(t)\, dt = \left[-e^{-t/1000}\ \Big|_{t=500}^{t=r}\right] = e^{-1/2} - e^{-r/1000}$$

Thus

$$\int_{500}^{+\infty} f(t)\, dt = \lim_{r \to +\infty} \{e^{-1/2} - e^{-r/1000}\} = e^{-1/2} \approx 0.6065$$

Here we have used a simple fact about the exponential function e^x: as x gets larger and larger negative, e^x tends very rapidly toward zero. Thus the term $e^{-r/1000}$ gets very small as r increases, while the other term $e^{-1/2}$ remains constant. In all, about 61% of the bulbs will burn for 500 hours or more.

There are still other types of improper integrals, which we cannot discuss here. One of them appears in Exercise 8.

Exercises

●1. Evaluate the following improper integrals or show that they diverge.

(i) $\int_{1}^{+\infty} \dfrac{1}{\sqrt[3]{x}}\, dx$

(ii) $\int_{5}^{+\infty} \left(1 + \dfrac{1}{x^2}\right) dx$

(iii) $\int_{-\infty}^{-1} \dfrac{5}{x^4}\, dx$

(iv) $\int_{1}^{+\infty} x^{-3/2}\, dx$

(v) $\int_{0}^{+\infty} \dfrac{1}{(x+5)^2}\, dx$

(vi) $\int_{1}^{+\infty} \dfrac{1}{x}\, dx$

HINT: Use the ideas in (39). In (vi) use the fact that $\log x$ takes larger and larger positive values as x increases. In (v) use the substitution method.

●2. Suppose the unit lengths along the x-axis and y-axis are measured in feet. Find the volume of paint required to cover the following regions under the curve $y = 1/x^3$ and above the x-axis with a coat of paint 0.001 foot thick.

(i) The region above the interval $1 \leqslant x \leqslant 3$

(ii) The region above the interval $1 \leqslant x \leqslant 100$

(iii) The region above the interval $1 \leqslant x \leqslant 1000$

(iv) The full region bounded by $y = 1/x^3$, the line $x = 1$, and the x-axis.

ANSWERS: (cubic feet) (i) $4/9 \times 0.001 = 0.000444\ldots = 4.44 \times 10^{-4}$; (ii) 4.9995×10^{-4}; (iii) 4.999995×10^{-4}; (iv) 5×10^{-4}.

●3. Repeat Exercise 2 for the curve $y = 1/\sqrt{x}$. ANSWERS: (cubic feet) (i) 1.464×10^{-3}; (ii) 18×10^{-3}; (iii) 61.24×10^{-3}; (iv) $+\infty$.

●4. In Example 20, determine the fraction of light bulbs whose lifetime exceeds 2000 hours. What fraction have lifetimes in the range $0 \leqslant t \leqslant 2000$ hours? Of a lot of 10,000 bulbs, how many would you expect to last 2000 hours or more? ANSWERS: (*i*) 0.135 (13.5%); (*ii*) 0.865 (86.5%); (*iii*) 1353.

●5. Show that the areas under the graphs of the functions

(*i*) $f(x) = e^{-x}$

(*ii*) $f(x) = \dfrac{1}{2000} e^{-x/2000}$

defined for $x \geqslant 0$ satisfy the condition

$$\int_0^{+\infty} f(x)\, dx = 1$$

This shows that the functions are acceptable candidates for probability-density functions defined on the unbounded interval $x \geqslant 0$. HINT: Use methods similar to those of Example 20 to evaluate the improper integrals.

●6. Compute the mean value $\bar{X}$ for the normal density function

$$f(x) = \frac{1}{\sqrt{2\pi}} e^{-x^2/2}$$

defined for all x. This mean value is interpreted as the improper integral

$$\bar{X} = \int_{-\infty}^{+\infty} x f(x)\, dx$$

HINT: Use the substitution method, taking $u = -x^2/2$.

●7. Evaluate the following improper integrals or show that they diverge.

(*i*) $\displaystyle\int_1^{+\infty} \left(\frac{1}{x^2} + \frac{1}{\sqrt{x}} \right) dx$

(*iv*) $\displaystyle\int_0^{+\infty} \frac{x}{(1 + x^2)^2}\, dx$

(*ii*) $\displaystyle\int_1^{+\infty} \left(\frac{2}{x^2} - \frac{1}{x^3} \right) dx$

(*v*) $\displaystyle\int_{-\infty}^0 \frac{-x}{\sqrt{1 + x^2}}\, dx$

(*iii*) $\displaystyle\int_{-\infty}^{+\infty} x e^{-x^2/2}\, dx$

(*vi*) $\displaystyle\int_{-\infty}^{+\infty} e^{-x}\, dx$

HINT: Use the method of substitution in (*iii*)–(*vi*).

●8. Sometimes a function $y = f(x)$ is well-behaved within an interval $a < x < b$ but blows up at one endpoint, say $x = a$, as shown in Figure 4.24(a). In this case we may form a new kind of improper integral $\int_a^b f(x)\, dx$ by introducing cutoff points $x = r$ close to the "bad" endpoint $x = a$, as in 4.24(b). We then let r approach a, keeping $r > a$, and define the improper integral to be the limit value of the cutoff integrals

$$\int_a^b f(x)\, dx = \lim_{r \to a} \left\{ \int_r^b f(x)\, dx \right\}$$

Calculate the following improper integrals:

(*i*) $\displaystyle\int_0^1 \frac{1}{\sqrt{x}}\, dx = \lim_{r \to 0} \int_r^1 \frac{1}{\sqrt{x}}\, dx = 2$, where $f(x) = 1/\sqrt{x}$, $a = 0$, and $b = 1$.

(ii) $\int_0^3 \frac{1}{x^2}\,dx = \lim_{r\to 0}\int_r^3 \frac{1}{x^2}\,dx = +\infty$, where $f(x) = 1/x^2$, $a = 0$, and $b = 3$.

●9. Evaluate the following improper integrals or show divergence by using the methods of Exercise 8. In each case, which is the bad endpoint?

(i) $\int_0^1 x^{-1/3}\,dx$

(iv) $\int_1^2 \frac{1}{\sqrt{2-x}}\,dx$

(ii) $\int_{-1}^0 \frac{1}{x^4}\,dx$

(v) $\int_2^4 \frac{x}{\sqrt{16-x^2}}\,dx$

(iii) $\int_0^1 \frac{1}{x}\,dx$

HINT: In (iii) use the fact that $\log x$ tends toward $-\infty$ as x approaches 0 through positive values. ANSWERS: (i) 3/2 (endpoint $x = 0$); (ii) $+\infty$ ($x = 0$); (iii) $+\infty$ ($x = 0$); (iv) 2 ($x = 2$); (v) $\sqrt{12} = 2\sqrt{3} \approx 3.464$ ($x = 4$).

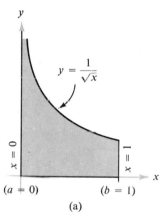 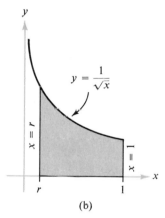

Figure 4.24
The function $y = f(x) = 1/\sqrt{x}$ is continuous for $0 < x \leqslant 1$, and takes on very large positive values as x approaches 0 from the right. If we take a cutoff point $x = r > 0$ and move it toward 0, the area under the graph over the interval $[r, 1]$, given by $\int_r^1 \frac{1}{\sqrt{x}}\,dx$. approaches the limit value 2.

We take this limit value to be the area under the graph over the full interval $[0, 1]$.

CHAPTER 5

Calculus of
Several Variables

5.1 Functions of Several Variables

If you have a carpenter build a rectangular box, you must independently specify several variables (namely length l, width w, and height h) in order to fully describe what you want. Then the other features may be described in terms of these variables. For example, the volume of the box is

$$V = V(l,w,h) = l \cdot w \cdot h$$

and the surface area (sum of areas of six rectangular sides) is

$$A = A(l,w,h) = 2lw + 2lh + 2wh$$

Previously we confined our attention to functions having a single independent variable. We did this to keep things simple while we introduced such notions as derivative, graph of a function, and so on. However, many problems in economics involve more than one independent variable; indeed, in a situation as complex as an "input-output" model of the U.S. economy we might have to distinguish hundreds or thousands of independent variables to obtain a realistic model. Thus we must come to grips with functions of several variables.

To begin, let us consider an economic problem with two variables. Suppose a pharmaceutical manufacturer produces just two antibiotics, neomycin and tetracycline. He must meet weekly fixed costs of $7400. Further, his plant produces capsules of neomycin at a unit cost of $159 per thousand and tetracycline capsules at $176 per thousand. How may we describe his weekly costs C?

There are two independent variables, the production levels

$$q_N = \text{thousands of neomycin capsules per week}$$

$$q_T = \text{thousands of tetracycline capsules per week}$$

That is, the operating state of the plant may be described by the pair of numbers (q_N, q_T). The weekly operating cost C is a function $C(q_N, q_T)$ of these variables. The variable cost is the sum of the costs for each product, $VC = 159q_N + 176q_T$. Thus

$$C(q_N, q_T) = FC + VC = 7400 + 159q_N + 176q_T \text{ dollars per week} \qquad (1)$$

for every choice of operating levels q_N and q_T. If the plant produces $q_N = 70$ (thousand capsules) and $q_T = 35$ (thousand capsules), weekly operating costs may be calculated by substituting these values into (1):

$$C(70, 35) = 7400 + 159(70) + 176(35) = 24,690 \text{ dollars per week}$$

If the plant is left idle (production levels $q_N = q_T = 0$) the cost reduces to the fixed cost

$$C(0, 0) = 7400 + 159(0) + 176(0) = 7400 \text{ dollars per week}$$

The operating states of the plant may be represented graphically by thinking of the pairs of numbers (q_N, q_T) as points in a plane whose coordinate axes are labeled q_N and q_T, as in Figure 5.1(a).

A manufacturer cannot set the production levels (q_N, q_T) arbitrarily. Certain **constraints** are imposed by plant capacity, for example. The production levels satisfying all production constraints, referred to as the **feasible** production levels, form the domain of definition for the cost function $C(q_N, q_T)$. If (q_N, q_T) lies outside the feasible set, the plant cannot operate at these production levels and it is not meaningful to speak of the operating costs C. As examples of constraints on the variables q_N and q_T, we always have $q_N \geq 0$ and $q_T \geq 0$; but there may be additional constraints. For example, limited plant capacity might impose constraints of the form $q_N \leq 100$ and $q_T \leq 120$; then the full system of constraints determining the feasible points would be given by

$$0 \leq q_N \leq 100 \quad \text{and} \quad 0 \leq q_T \leq 120 \qquad (2)$$

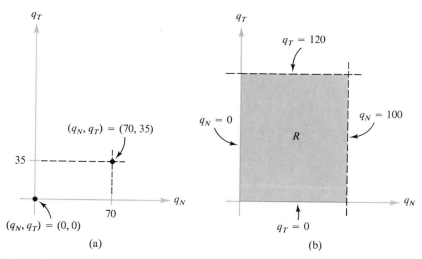

Figure 5.1

In (a) the possible operating states of a manufacturing plant are represented as points on a coordinate plane. The states $q_N = 70$, $q_T = 35$ and $q_N = 0$, $q_T = 0$ are shown as solid dots. The corresponding operating costs are calculated in the text. In (b) the shaded region R shows the feasible production levels determined by the constraints $0 \leqslant q_N \leqslant 100$ and $0 \leqslant q_T \leqslant 120$. The variables q_N and q_T are measured in thousands of capsules per week.

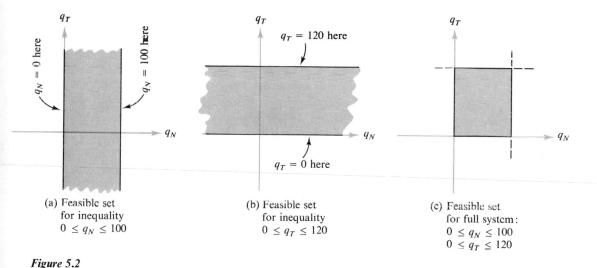

(a) Feasible set for inequality $0 \leq q_N \leq 100$

(b) Feasible set for inequality $0 \leq q_T \leq 120$

(c) Feasible set for full system:
$0 \leq q_N \leq 100$
$0 \leq q_T \leq 120$

Figure 5.2

In (a) the inequality $0 \leqslant q_N \leqslant 100$ restricts the first coordinate of a point $P = (q_N, q_T)$; thus P must lie between the vertical lines on which $q_N = 0$ or $q_N = 100$. Since the second coordinate is not restricted, all points in the shaded vertical strip satisfy the condition $0 \leqslant q_N \leqslant 100$. Similarly, the inequality $0 \leqslant q_T \leqslant 120$ is satisfied by points in the horizontal strip in (b), bounded by the horizontal lines on which $q_T = 0$ or $q_T = 120$. The points satisfying *both* inequalities at once are the points common to the sets shown in (a) and (b). These form the rectangle shown in (c).

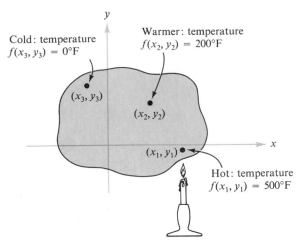

Figure 5.3
The domain of definition of a function $z = f(x,y)$ is a region
(shaded) in the xy-plane. The values $z = f(x,y)$ might be
thought of as a temperature distribution defined throughout
this region. The value of $f(x,y)$, the temperature at the point
$P = (x,y)$, varies as we examine different points $P_1 = (x_1,y_1)$,
$P_2 = (x_2,y_2)$, $P_3 = (x_3,y_3)$.

These inequalities determine the shaded rectangular region shown in Figure 5.1(b).
In the next section we shall explain how to sketch the feasible sets corresponding to
general systems of inequalities. The reasoning for the simple case (2) is explained in
Figure 5.2.

Any other function of two variables may be described in much the same way.
Suppose that $z = f(x,y)$ gives z in terms of independent variables x and y. We may
regard the pairs (x,y) as points in a coordinate plane. The function f may be defined
for some choices of (x,y) and not for others. Thus f has a domain of definition represented by some region in the plane, such as the one shown in Figure 5.3; f assigns
a real number $z = f(x,y)$ to each point in this region. The function might, pictur-
esquely, be thought of as describing a temperature distribution throughout the shaded
region, the value $z = f(x,y)$ being the temperature at the point (x,y).

Exercises

●1. Let $z = f(x,y) = 1 + 2x - y$ be defined for all x and y. Find the values $f(0, 0)$, $f(1, 2)$, $f(2, 1)$,
$f(-1, 2)$, and $f(-2, -1)$. Describe the set of points (x,y) for which $z = f(x,y) = 0$.

●2. Evaluate each of the following functions at the points $P = (2, 3)$ and $Q = (-1, 1)$.

   (*i*) $\sqrt{1 + x^2 + y^2}$ (*ii*) $1 - x + y$

(iii) $\dfrac{2xy}{x^2 + y^2}$

(vi) $30 - 2x^2 - 4y^3$

(iv) $\dfrac{x + y}{xy}$

(vii) $x^2y^2 - \sqrt{5x^2 - 8xy + 5y^2}$

(v) $5000 + 20x^2 + 100xy - 5y^2$

(viii) $e^{-(x^2+y^2)/2}$

●3. The height of a hyperbolic tent roof is described, relative to coordinates x and y laid out on the ground, by

$$h(x,y) = 30 + \frac{x^2}{250} - \frac{y^2}{100} \text{ feet}$$

The roof covers a rectangular area given by $-50 \leqslant x \leqslant 50$, $-20 \leqslant y \leqslant 20$ (coordinates measured in feet). Calculate the height above (i) the corners, (ii) the ends of the centerline (x-axis), and (iii) the center of the rectangle (where $x = 0$ and $y = 0$).

●4. A factory produces two lines of shoes, styles A and B. Overhead costs amount to $2000 per week and production costs (labor and materials) amount to $13 and $20 per pair of shoes. Shoes are sold to retail outlets at prices of $18 and $30 respectively. If q_A and q_B are the numbers of shoes produced per week, find (i) the weekly cost function $C = C(q_A,q_B)$, (ii) the weekly revenue $R(q_A,q_B)$ (assuming all shoes are sold), and (iii) the weekly profit $P(q_A,q_B)$.

●5. On graph paper sketch the regions in the coordinate plane determined by each set of inequalities.

(i) $y \geqslant 0$

(iv) $1 \leqslant y \leqslant 20$

(ii) $y \geqslant 1$

(v) $0 \leqslant x \leqslant 5$ and $-5 \leqslant y \leqslant 5$

(iii) $0 \leqslant x \leqslant 5$

(vi) $-1 \leqslant x \leqslant 1$ and $-1 \leqslant y \leqslant 1$

●6. Match the shaded sets in Figure 5.4 with the correct set of inequalities.

(i) $0 \leqslant x \leqslant 3$ and $0 \leqslant y \leqslant 2$

(ii) $-1 \leqslant x \leqslant 3$ and $-2 \leqslant y \leqslant 2$

(iii) $x \geqslant 0$

(iv) $-2 \leqslant y \leqslant 1$

Each set should consist of all points $P = (x,y)$ whose coordinates satisfy the inequalities. ANSWERS: (i) (d); (ii) (c); (iii) (a); (iv) (b).

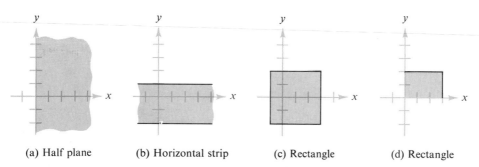

(a) Half plane   (b) Horizontal strip   (c) Rectangle   (d) Rectangle

Figure 5.4
The regions defined by the inequalities in Exercise 6.

●7. Consider the function of *three* variables defined by $f(x,y,z) = 3 - x - y + 2z$ for all x, y, and z. Find the values $f(0, 0, 0)$, $f(1, 2, 3)$, $f(-1, 1, 0)$, and $f(0, 1, 1)$. Show that

$$f(a,b,c) = f(b,a,c)$$

for all real numbers a, b, and c.

●8. Consider the function

$$z = f(x,y) = \sqrt{4 - x^2 - y^2}$$

Describe the domain of definition of f; that is, find all points $P = (x,y)$ in the plane for which f is well defined.

   (*i*) Find $f(0, 0)$, $f(-2, 0)$, $f(1, 1)$, $f(-\sqrt{2}, \sqrt{2})$.

   (*ii*) Find all points $P = (x,y)$ for which $f = 0$.

HINT: Geometrically, $x^2 + y^2 = r^2$ where r is the distance from $P = (x,y)$ to the origin $O = (0,0)$; f is defined when the expression under the square root is positive: $4 - x^2 - y^2 \geqslant 0$.

5.2 Describing the Domain of Definition: Linear Inequalities

For a function of one variable $y = f(x)$ the domain of definition is usually the whole number line or some interval described by inequalities, such as $0 \leqslant x \leqslant 100$ (interval with end points $x = 0$ and $x = 100$). Functions of two or more variables have, as a rule, more complicated domains of definition. In the pharmaceutical manufacturing problem described above, the feasible points formed a rectangle, shown in Figure 5.1(b). In practice we shall encounter production constraints more complicated than the inequalities in that problem. Frequently constraints are described by **linear inequalities**, in which the variables must satisfy an inequality of the form

$$Ax + By \leqslant C \quad \text{or} \quad Ax + By \geqslant C \quad \quad (A, B, \text{and } C \text{ constants}) \quad\quad\quad (3)$$

In the next example, where the variables are labeled q_N and q_T, we shall encounter an inequality of this form, namely

$$\frac{4}{3} q_N + 2q_T \leqslant 400$$

After dealing with it, we shall describe a general procedure for solving a linear inequality involving two variables.

Example 1 Suppose that the pharmaceutical manufacturer in Section 5.1 has removed a bottleneck, allowing unrestricted values $q_N \geqslant 0$ and $q_T \geqslant 0$. However, a new crimp in his operations has developed. He must use a scarce raw material to produce either drug. He can obtain up to 400 pounds per week of this substance, "ingredient X." Furthermore

> (*i*) each thousand capsules of neomycin require 4/3 pounds of ingredient X.
>
> (*ii*) each thousand capsules of tetracycline require 2 pounds of ingredient X.

(4)

Describe the corresponding constraint as a linear inequality relating q_N and q_T. Sketch the feasible set of production levels (q_N, q_T) under these new conditions.

Solution   If production levels q_N and q_T are specified, it follows from (4) that the week's operations will consume $(4/3)q_N + 2q_T$ pounds of ingredient X. Only 400 pounds are available; thus a feasible choice of production levels must satisfy

$$\frac{4}{3}q_N + 2q_T \leqslant 400 \tag{5}$$

Moreover, there are the obvious constraints

$$q_N \geqslant 0 \quad \text{and} \quad q_T \geqslant 0 \tag{6}$$

In all, three inequalities must be satisfied by any feasible choice of q_N and q_T. The simple inequalities (6), taken together, force $P = (q_N, q_T)$ to lie in the first quadrant of the coordinate plane (shaded region in Figure 5.5(a)); $q_N \geqslant 0$ forces P to lie to the right of the vertical axis (where $q_N - 0$), and $q_T \geqslant 0$ forces P to lie above the horizontal axis (where $q_T = 0$).

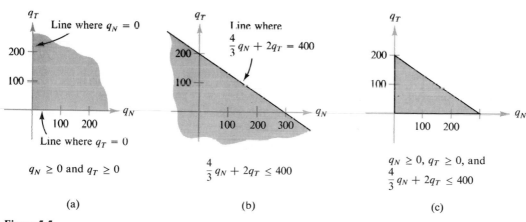

Figure 5.5
Solution sets for the various constraint inequalities discussed in Example 1. Note the position of the lines in (a) and (b) where the inequality reduces to an *equality*. These always form the boundary of the region where the desired inequality is valid.

As explained below, the solution set for the inequality $(4/3)q_N + 2q_T \leqslant 400$ is one of the half planes bounded by the line L where *equality*

$$\frac{4}{3} q_N + 2q_T = 400$$

holds. This line is shown in Figure 5.5(b); the correct half plane is the shaded one containing the origin. We can tell which is the correct half plane by testing the value of $(4/3)q_N + 2q_T$ at a point in each half plane to see whether it is less than 400.

Finally, we seek the points where all three inequalities are satisfied. These are precisely the points common to the shaded regions in (a) and (b). (The set of points common to two or more given sets is called the **intersection** of the sets.) This set of feasible points, the triangular region shown in Figure 5.5(c), is the domain of definition of the cost function under the new production conditions. As before, the cost function is given by the formula

$$C(q_N,q_T) = 7400 + 159q_N + 176q_T$$

for points $P = (q_N,q_T)$ in the new feasible set.

If x and y are independent variables, any condition of the form

$$Ax + By \leqslant C \quad \text{or} \quad Ax + By \geqslant C \qquad (A, B, \text{and } C \text{ fixed constants}) \qquad (7)$$

is called a **linear inequality** relating the variables. Its **solution set** consists of all points $P = (x,y)$ in the plane whose coordinates satisfy this inequality. Condition (5) is obviously a linear inequality relating q_N and q_T; so are each of the conditions in (6). Our task in Example 1 was to determine their solution sets, and then take their intersection. There is a simple procedure for solving any linear inequality. As we go through the steps you should refer to Figure 5.6 to see what they mean for the particular inequality $(4/3)x + 2y \leqslant 400$, in which $A = 4/3$, $B = 2$, $C = 400$.

Finding the Solution Set for a Linear Inequality $Ax + By \leqslant C$

STEP 1   Find the points $P = (x,y)$ for which *equality* holds. The equation $Ax + By = C$ determines a line L in the plane. This line divides the plane into two half planes, labeled H_1 and H_2 in Figure 5.6.

STEP 2   One of these half planes is the solution set for $Ax + By \leqslant C$. The other is the solution set for $Ax + By \geqslant C$, the reverse inequality.

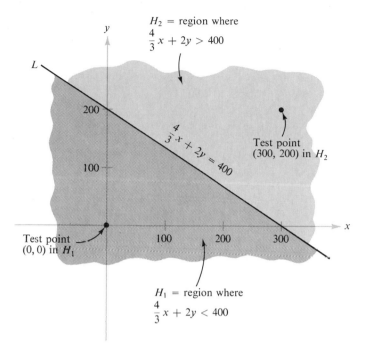

Figure 5.6
The solution set for the inequality $(4/3)x + 2y \leqslant 400$ is the heavily shaded half plane H_1. It includes the line L where equality holds: $(4/3)x + 2y = 400$. All linear inequalities can be solved by similar methods.

STEP 3   Decide which of the half planes gives the correct inequality $Ax + By \leqslant C$ by testing the value of $Ax + By$ at one point in each half plane (H_1 is the correct half plane in Figure 5.6).

The line L is part of the solution set. In Figure 5.6, L is the line $(4/3)x + 2y = 400$. Upon testing the value of $Ax + By = (4/3)x + 2y$ at points in H_1 and H_2 we get

$$\frac{4}{3}x + 2y = 0 \leqslant 400 \qquad \text{at } (x,y) = (0, 0) \text{ in } H_1$$

$$\frac{4}{3}x + 2y = 800 \geqslant 400 \qquad \text{at } (x,y) = (300, 200) \text{ in } H_2$$

Thus $(4/3)x + 2y \leqslant 400$ on H_1 and $(4/3)x + 2y \geqslant 400$ on H_2.

Example 2   Sketch the solution set for the inequality $x + y \leqslant 200$.

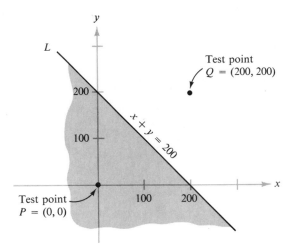

Figure 5.7
The solution set for the linear inequality $x + y \leqslant 200$ is
shaded.

Solution   First locate the line L where $x + y = 200$ by finding the points where L
crosses the x-axis or y-axis. Setting

$x = 0$, we find that $0 + y = 200$, so that $(0, 200)$ lies on L.

$y = 0$, we find that $x + 0 = 200$, so that $(200, 0)$ lies on L.

The inequality $x + y \leqslant 200$ holds on one of the half planes bounded by L, the reverse
inequality holding on the other half plane. Taking $P = (0, 0)$ and $Q = (200, 200)$
as test points, we get

$$x + y = 0 \leqslant 200 \text{ at } P \qquad x + y = 400 \geqslant 200 \text{ at } Q$$

so that the shaded half plane containing the origin is the solution set.

Example 3   A pottery shop decides to produce pitchers and bowls for a week. There
is a kiln that can fire up to 200 items per week. Craftsmen can prepare at most 100
pitchers and 150 bowls for firing in a week. Pitchers are sold for $9.50 each and bowls
for $12.50. Revenue from sales is offset by production costs of $5.00 for each pitcher
and $5.50 for each bowl. In addition, wages and other fixed costs amount to $1000
per week.
    Describe the feasible production levels, the cost function, the revenue function,
and the profit function for this shop.

Solution   Let

$$x = \text{number of pitchers} \qquad y = \text{number of bowls}$$

produced per week. Then weekly costs are

$$C(x,y) = 1000 + 5x + 5.5y \text{ dollars per week} \qquad (8)$$

Revenue is the sum of (sale price) × (quantity produced) for each item

$$R(x,y) = 9.5x + 12.5y \text{ dollars per week} \qquad (9)$$

and the profit is

$$P(x,y) = R(x,y) - C(x,y) = -1000 + 4.5x + 7.0y \text{ dollars per week} \qquad (10)$$

These functions are defined only for *feasible* choices of production levels. We must determine this domain of definition as well as the formulas (8), (9), and (10). Feasible choices (x,y) must satisfy the conditions

$$0 \leqslant x \leqslant 100 \quad \text{and} \quad 0 \leqslant y \leqslant 150 \text{ units per week} \qquad (11)$$

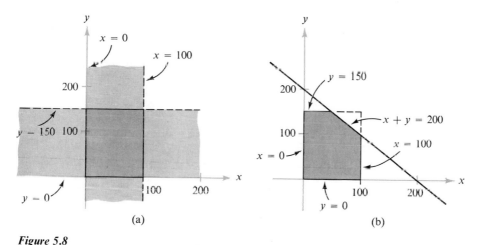

(a)   (b)

Figure 5.8
In (a) the solution set (heavily shaded rectangle) for the inequalities $0 \leqslant x \leqslant 100$ and $0 \leqslant y \leqslant 150$ is shown. The condition $x = \text{const}$ determines a vertical line, and $y = \text{const}$ a horizontal line. The solution set for $x + y \leqslant 200$ has been sketched in Figure 5.7. The set of points satisfying (11) and (12) is the intersection of these sets, the truncated rectangle in (b). Note that the boundary of this set is made up of line segments on which at least one of the constraint inequalities (11) and (12) reduces to an equality.

because only a limited number of items of each kind can be prepared for firing. Kiln capacity imposes the additional constraint

$$x + y \leqslant 200 \tag{12}$$

Now we sketch the solution sets for each of these linear inequalities; their intersection is the feasible set for this problem. The inequality $0 \leqslant x \leqslant 100$ does not restrict y in any way; it determines the vertical strip shown in Figure 5.8(a). Likewise $0 \leqslant y \leqslant 150$ determines a horizontal strip. The inequalities (11) taken together determine the heavily shaded rectangle in (a). On the other hand, we have determined the solution set for $x + y \leqslant 200$ in Example 2; it is the half plane shown in Figure 5.7. The actual set of feasible points, the intersection of the rectangle and this half plane, is shown in Figure 5.8(b). This rectangle with a corner sliced off is the domain of definition for each of the economic functions (8), (9), and (10).

Exercises

●1. Sketch the solution sets for the following elementary linear inequalities:

    (*i*) $x \geqslant 0$ (*v*) $x + 1 \geqslant 0$

    (*ii*) $y \geqslant 0$ (*vi*) $3x + 5 \geqslant 7$

    (*iii*) $y \leqslant 0$ (*vii*) $x + y \geqslant 2$

    (*iv*) $x \geqslant 2$ (*viii*) $x + y \leqslant 2$

●2. Which of the following points satisfy the linear inequality $y + 2x \leqslant 6$? (Test each point.)

    (*i*) $(0, 0)$ (*v*) $(0, 4)$

    (*ii*) $(-1, -2)$ (*vi*) $(2, 3)$

    (*iii*) $(-1, 9)$ (*vii*) $(1, 4)$

    (*iv*) $(2, 2)$ (*viii*) $(4, 1)$

Sketch the solution set of $y + 2x \leqslant 6$, showing the location of the points (*i*)–(*viii*).

●3. Sketch the solution sets for the following linear inequalities. Use graph paper; start by sketching the line where equality holds.

    (*i*) $x + y \geqslant 10$ (*iv*) $2y \geqslant 1 - x$

    (*ii*) $y - x \leqslant 1$ (*v*) $y + 2x \leqslant 4$

    (*iii*) $3y - 2x - 6 \geqslant 0$ (*vi*) $300 \leqslant 40x - 15y$

●4. Which of the following points satisfy the system of simultaneous inequalities: $x \geqslant 0$, $y \geqslant 0$, $y + x \leqslant 8$, $y - 2x \geqslant -4$. (Test all the points for each inequality.)

    (*i*) $(3, 1)$ (*iv*) $(3, 6)$

    (*ii*) $(3, 2)$ (*v*) $(4, 4)$

    (*iii*) $(3, 4)$ (*vi*) $(4, 5)$

      (*vii*) (1, 5)   (*viii*) (2, 7)

    Sketch the solution set for this system of inequalities.

○5. Sketch the solution set for each system of inequalities.

      (*i*) $x \geqslant 0$, $y \geqslant 0$, and $2x + 3y \leqslant 6$

      (*ii*) $0 \leqslant x \leqslant 10$ and $x + y \leqslant 20$

      (*iii*) $0 \leqslant x \leqslant 10$, $0 \leqslant y \leqslant 15$, and $x + y \leqslant 20$

      (*iv*) $x \geqslant 0$, $y \geqslant 0$, $3y + x \leqslant 30$, and $2y + 5x \leqslant 85$

      (*v*) $0 \leqslant x \leqslant 16$, $0 \leqslant y \leqslant 8$, $3y + x \leqslant 30$, and $2y + 5x \leqslant 85$

      (*vi*) $y \geqslant 0$, $2y + x \geqslant 4$, and $y - 2x \leqslant 5$

●6. A rancher must insure that his cattle eat at least 1000 pounds of protein and at least 200 pounds of fat per week. He mixes x pounds of fodder with y pounds of high-protein feed each week. The fodder contains 3% protein and 2% fat, and costs $150 per ton. The high-protein feed contains 10% protein and 1% fat, and costs $1000 per ton. Carefully describe the feasible set of choices of x and y in terms of linear inequalities. Sketch this set. Then describe the weekly cost function $C = C(x, y)$ for cattle feed.

●7. A power plant is designed to burn both coal and oil. Each ton of fuel burned produces the amount of pollutants (SO_2 = sulfur dioxide) indicated in Table 5.1. Pollution control regulations impose these allowable limits on pollutant emissions:

$$SO_2 \text{ at most 7.0 tons per hour}$$

$$\text{Dust at most 3.5 tons per hour}$$

If x = tons of oil burned per hour and y = tons of coal per hour, describe the pollutant limits as inequalities in x and y. On graph paper sketch the set of operating levels (x, y) that satisfy the pollution limits and the obvious additional constraints $x \geqslant 0$ and $y \geqslant 0$. HINT: Choose graph scales so 1 unit = 10 tons per hour.

●8. Two warehouses are to ship hundred-pound bags of fertilizer to two destinations, A and B. Due to varying distances, the shipping costs per bag differ, as indicated in Table 5.2. Suppose 40 bags are to be delivered to A and 30 bags to B. Warehouse 1 has on hand only 25 bags, while Warehouse 2 has only 60 on hand. Let x = number of bags delivered to A from Warehouse 1 and y = number of bags delivered to B from Warehouse 1. (Obviously the quantities delivered by Warehouse 2 must be $40 - x$ and $30 - y$, respectively.)

	Dust (tons)	SO_2 (tons)
Oil	0.002	0.035
Coal	0.055	0.093

Table 5.1
Pollutant emission per ton for fuels in Exercise 7.

	A	B
Warehouse 1	$2.54	$2.20
Warehouse 2	$3.70	$3.28

Table 5.2
Delivery costs per bag to destinations A and B in Exercise 8.

Write down all constraints on x and y as linear inequalities (include the trivial constraints $x \geqslant 0$, $y \geqslant 0$). Sketch the feasible set of (x,y). Then find the total delivery cost from *both* warehouses $C(x,y)$ as a function of x and y.

*5.3   Distances in the Plane

The distance between two points $P_1 = (x_1,y_1)$ and $P_2 = (x_2,y_2)$ in the plane may be expressed in terms of their coordinates. Writing $\Delta x = x_2 - x_1$ and $\Delta y = y_2 - y_1$ we get

$$\text{dist}(P_1,P_2) = \sqrt{(x_2 - x_1)^2 + (y_2 - y_1)^2} = \sqrt{(\Delta x)^2 + (\Delta y)^2} \qquad (13)$$

For example, the distance between $P_1 = (1, -2)$ and $P_2 = (4, 3)$ can be obtained without resorting to actual measurement:

$$\text{dist} = \sqrt{(4 - 1)^2 + (3 - (-2))^2} = \sqrt{3^2 + 5^2} = \sqrt{9 + 25} = \sqrt{34} \approx 5.83 \ldots$$

Formula (13) follows directly from Pythagoras' Theorem relating the side lengths of any right triangle, as explained in Figure 5.9. As a special case, the distance from any point $P = (x,y)$ to the origin $O = (0,0)$ is

$$\text{dist}(P,O) = \sqrt{x^2 + y^2} \qquad (14)$$

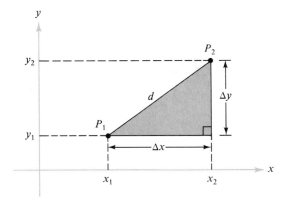

Figure 5.9
The distance $d = \text{dist}(P_1,P_2)$ between two points $P_1 = (x_1,y_1)$ and $P_2 = (x_2,y_2)$ is the length of the hypotenuse of the right triangle shown. Since the other sides of this triangle have length $\Delta x = x_2 - x_1$ and $\Delta y = y_2 - y_1$, by Pythagoras' Theorem $d^2 = (\Delta x)^2 + (\Delta y)^2 = (x_2 - x_1)^2 + (y_2 - y_1)^2$.

Some complicated functions $z = f(x,y)$ may be interpreted in a simple geometric way if we keep in mind the distance formula (13).

Example 4   If r is the distance from an arbitrary point $P = (x,y)$ to the fixed point $Q = (1, 0)$, express the functions $z = 1/(1 + r^2)$ and $z = 1/r$ as functions of x and y.

Solution   Since $r = \sqrt{(x - 1)^2 + (y - 0)^2} = \sqrt{x^2 - 2x + 1 + y^2}$, we get

$$\frac{1}{1 + r^2} = \frac{1}{1 + y^2 + x^2 - 2x + 1} = \frac{1}{y^2 + x^2 - 2x + 2}$$

$$\frac{1}{r} = \frac{1}{\sqrt{y^2 + x^2 - 2x + 1}}$$

for all x and y. If these functions had been presented without any geometric commentary, it would have been very difficult to comprehend their behavior. Using the distance formula, and the fact that $(x^2 - 2x + 1) = (x - 1)^2$, $y^2 = (y - 0)^2$, they have uncomplicated geometric meanings.

Sometimes the domain of definition of a function $z = f(x,y)$ is described by conditions involving the distance formulas (13) and (14). For example, consider the set of points $P = (x,y)$ determined by the constraints

$$(i)\ x \geq 0 \qquad (ii)\ y \geq 0 \qquad (iii)\ x^2 + y^2 \leq 4 \tag{15}$$

Inequalities (i) and (ii) are linear, and together force $P = (x,y)$ to lie in the first quadrant, the shaded region in Figure 5.10(b). The inequality $x^2 + y^2 \leq 4$ is not linear because it involves higher powers of the variables. But it does have a simple interpretation: $x^2 + y^2 \leq 4$ means that

$$[\text{dist}(P,O)]^2 \leq 4 \quad \text{or} \quad \text{dist}(P,O) \leq 2$$

where $P = (x,y)$ and $O = (0, 0)$ is the origin. Points such that $\text{dist}(P,O) = 2$ form a circle of radius $r = 2$ about the origin; those with $\text{dist}(P,O) \leq 2$ fill up the disc bounded by this circle. This solution set for $x^2 + y^2 \leq 4$ is shown in Figure 5.10(a). The solution set for the full system (15) of inequalities is the shaded region in Figure 5.10(c), the intersection of the regions in (a) and (b). Notice that, if $r > 0$ is fixed, the solution set for $x^2 + y^2 = r^2$ is the circle of radius r about the origin. The solution set for $x^2 + y^2 \leq r^2$ is the disc bounded by this circle, and the solution set for $x^2 + y^2 > r^2$ is the plane with this disc removed. For other examples, see exercises 3 and 4.

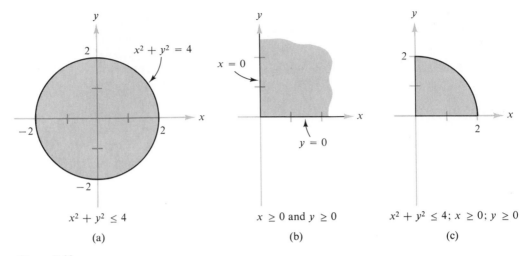

Figure 5.10
The solution sets for $x^2 + y^2 \leqslant 4$ and for $x \geqslant 0$, $y \geqslant 0$ are shown in (a) and (b). Their intersection, the shaded region in (c), consists of points satisfying all three inequalities.

Exercises

●1. Calculate the distances between the following pairs of points in the coordinate plane by using formula (13).

(*i*) $P_1 = (0, 0)$, $P_2 = (12, -5)$

(*ii*) $P_1 = (1, 1)$, $P_2 = (4, 5)$

(*iii*) $P_1 = (-1, 3)$, $P_2 = (-1, 4)$

(*iv*) $P_1 = (4, 5)$, $P_2 = (-2, -2)$

●2. Which of the following points satisfy the inequality $x^2 + y^2 \leqslant 9$?

(*i*) $(0, 0)$ (*iv*) $(3, 1)$

(*ii*) $(2, 2)$ (*v*) $(-2\sqrt{2}, -1)$

(*iii*) $(-2, 2)$ (*vi*) $(\sqrt{2}, 2)$

Sketch the solution set of the inequality $x^2 + y^2 \leqslant 9$. HINT: What does $x^2 + y^2$ represent geometrically?

●3. Sketch the solution sets for the following (sets of) inequalities by interpreting them as statements about the distance from $P = (x, y)$ to certain reference points in the plane.

(*i*) $(x - 1)^2 + (y - 2)^2 \leqslant 25$ (*iv*) $x^2 - 2x + 1 + y^2 \leqslant 3$

(*ii*) $x^2 + (y - 3)^2 \leqslant 7$ (*v*) $4 \leqslant x^2 + y^2 \leqslant 9$

(*iii*) $(x + 3)^2 + (y + 1)^2 \geqslant 4$ (*vi*) $x^2 + y^2 \geqslant 1$ and $x \geqslant 0$

4. Sketch the solution sets for the following systems of simultaneous inequalities:

   (i) $x \geqslant 0$, $y \geqslant 0$, $x + y \leqslant 7$, and $x^2 + y^2 \leqslant 25$

   (ii) $x \geqslant 0$, $y \geqslant 0$, $x + y \leqslant 7$, and $x^2 + y^2 \geqslant 25$

   (iii) $x \geqslant 0$, $y \geqslant 0$, $x + y \geqslant 7$, and $x^2 + y^2 \leqslant 25$

5.4   The Graph of a Function of Several Variables

One way to visualize a function $z = f(x,y)$ of two variables is to sketch the "graph" of the function, which is a surface in three-dimensional space instead of a curve in the plane. We shall define this concept below. We shall also introduce the notion of *level curve*, which reduces many questions about the function to exercises in map reading. There is, unfortunately, no easy way to visualize functions of more than two variables; they must be handled algebraically, without the aid of accurate pictures. However, our discussion of what happens with two variables does suggest what happens when f has many variables.

Before sketching the graph of a function $z = f(x,y)$ of two variables we must set up coordinates in three-dimensional space. We do this by marking an origin O and drawing three perpendicular coordinate axes through it. It is customary to identify the two horizontal axes with the independent variables x and y as shown in Figure 5.11(a), and the vertical axis with the dependent variable z. Each point P in space is described by three coordinates (a,b,c). Starting from the origin, we reach $P = (a,b,c)$ by moving a units in the x-direction, b units parallel to the y-direction, and then c units parallel to the z-axis, as in Figure 5.11(a). To put it another way, we may locate $P = (a,b,c)$ by setting up a rectangular box with side lengths a, b, and c in the x-, y-, and z-directions. Then $P = (a,b,c)$ is the corner point opposite the origin O (see Figure 5.11(a)). Figure 5.11(b) shows the locations of $(1, -2, 2)$, $(1, 2, -1)$, and $(-2, 2, 2)$. Obviously the origin O has coordinates $(0, 0, 0)$. The x-axis and the y-axis together determine a horizontal plane, which we call the **xy-plane**. It consists of all points $P = (x,y,z)$ such that $z = 0$; that is, it is the solution set of the simple equation $z = 0$. We do not move at all in the z-direction to reach points in this plane. Similarly, we define the **xz-plane** and the **yz-plane**, which are determined by the equations $y = 0$ and $x = 0$, respectively.

If $z = f(x,y)$ is a function of two variables, its **graph** is a surface S in three-dimensional space, determined as follows. First we sketch a copy of the domain of definition of f in the xy-plane, by identifying pairs (x,y) for which f is defined with points $(x,y,0)$ in the xy-plane (the shaded region in Figure 5.12). Over each point $Q = (x,y,0)$ in this region we find the point $P = (x,y,z)$ lying a distance $z = f(x,y)$ above Q. As Q varies within the domain of definition of f, the points $P = (x,y,z)$

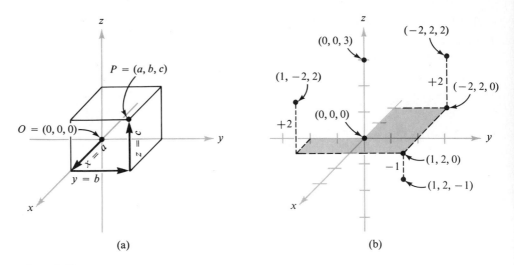

(a)   (b)

Figure 5.11
Cartesian coordinates in three-dimensional space. Unit lengths are marked off on each coordinate axis
in (b). In (a) we show how to locate a typical point $P = (a,b,c)$. In (b) we show the locations of a number
of specific points. Dashed lines are visual guidelines showing how far to move parallel to each axis.
Notice that all points (x,y,z) such that $z = 0$ lie in the horizontal plane determined by the x-axis and the
y-axis. This plane is often called the xy-plane; part of it has been shaded in (b).

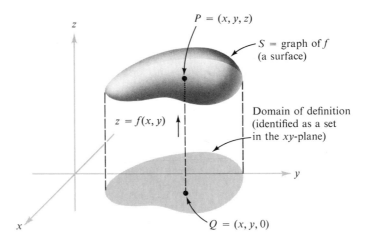

Figure 5.12
The graph of a typical function of two variables $z = f(x,y)$ is a surface
in three-dimensional space. Since all points on the graph S lie above the
xy-plane in this figure, $z = f(x,y)$ has positive values throughout its
domain of definition. The domain of definition is indicated by the shaded
region in the xy-plane.

with $z = f(x,y)$ trace out a surface. This surface is the graph of f. Conversely, if we are given the graph S of a function f, we may determine the value $z = f(x,y)$ geometrically. We simply locate the point $Q = (x,y,0)$ in the xy-plane and notice how far up or down we must move in order to reach the corresponding point $P = (x,y,z)$ on the surface. Then $z = f(x,y)$. Remember: We move *down* (move in the *negative* z-direction) to reach points (x,y,z) for which z is negative.

Linear functions

$$z = f(x,y) = Ax + By + C \qquad \text{(where } A, B, \text{ and } C \text{ are fixed constants)}$$

are the simplest functions of two variables. They have correspondingly simple graphs.

> The graph of any linear function $z - Ax + By + C$ is a plane in three-dimensional space.   (16)

This plane may be sketched by locating the three points where it crosses the coordinate axes. On any one of the axes, the other two variables are zero. Thus the point where the plane meets the x-axis may be found by setting $y = z = 0$ and solving $0 = Ax + C$ for x. The points on the other axes are located in the same way.

Example 5   Sketch the graph S of the linear function $z = 10 - x - 2y$.

Solution   To see where S meets the x-axis, we set $y = z = 0$. Then $0 = 10 - x$, or $x = 10$, so S meets the x-axis at $P_1 = (10, 0, 0)$. Similarly, setting

$$x = z = 0, \text{ we get } 10 - 2y = 0 \text{ or } y = 5$$

$$x = y = 0, \text{ we get } z = 10$$

Thus S meets the y-axis at $P_2 = (0, 5, 0)$ and the z-axis at $P_3 = (0, 0, 10)$. Figure 5.13 shows the part of the plane S determined by these points (shaded triangle). It is hard to visualize the whole plane S in a two-dimensional drawing. The orientation of S is more clearly revealed by drawing the shaded piece shown. However, the full solution set for $z = 10 - x - 2y$ is the full plane S. Actually, a plane is determined once we know *any* three points on it (as long as they are not collinear), not necessarily the particular points where it crosses the coordinate axes.

Example 6   Suppose that the linear function

$$f(x,y) = 8 - \frac{1}{2}x - \frac{1}{5}y$$

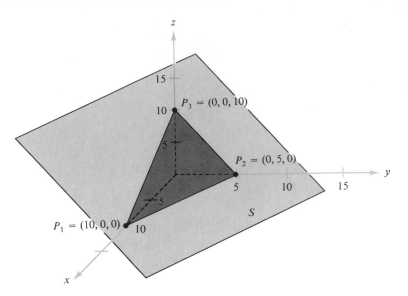

Figure 5.13
The plane S determined by the equation $z = 10 - x - 2y$ may be sketched by
locating the points P_1, P_2, and P_3 where it meets the x-axis, the y-axis, and the
z-axis.

is defined on the rectangle given by the constraints $0 \leqslant x \leqslant 4, 0 \leqslant y \leqslant 5$. Sketch
the graph of this function, showing the domain of definition.

Solution   This is a linear function of x and y, so its graph must be part of a plane in
three-dimensional space. The domain of definition is shown in Figure 5.14 as a
rectangular region in the xy-plane. The graph of f is the piece of surface lying over
this rectangle. The surface may be located by determining three or more points on it.
Figure 5.14 shows as solid dots the points on the plane lying over the corners of
the domain of definition; these corners have coordinates $Q_1 = (0, 0)$, $Q_2 = (4, 0)$,
$Q_3 = (4, 5)$, and $Q_4 = (0, 5)$. The corresponding z values of the points on the graph
are found by putting these values for x and y into the formula $z = f(x,y)$. Thus, over
$Q_3 = (4, 5)$ we get

$$z = 8 - \frac{1}{2}(4) - \frac{1}{5}(5) = 5$$

so the corresponding point on the graph has coordinates $(4, 5, 5)$, and so on. Once we
have plotted the points on the graph lying above the corners, the full graph is easily
filled in by drawing straight lines connecting these points, since we know that the
graph is part of a plane.

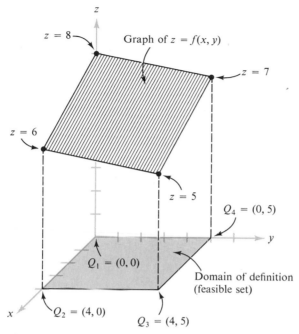

Figure 5.14
The graph of $z = f(x,y) = 8 - \frac{1}{2}x - \frac{1}{2}y$, defined for all (x,y)
such that $0 \leqslant x \leqslant 4$ and $0 \leqslant y \leqslant 5$. The domain of definition
is the shaded rectangle in the xy-plane. The graph of $z = f(x,y)$
(the striped surface) is the part of a certain plane in three-
dimensional space that lies over this rectangle. The corners of
the domain of definition $Q_1, \ldots, Q_4$ are labeled with their
coordinates. Solid dots on the graph are the points lying
directly above the corners of the domain of definition.

Exercises

1. Using graph paper, set up a system of coordinate axes as in Figure 5.11, and plot the locations
   of the following points:

   (*i*) $(0, 0, 1)$ (*v*) $(3, 4, 5)$

   (*ii*) $(0, 0, -1)$ (*vi*) $(-2, -1, 5)$

   (*iii*) $(1, -1, 1)$ (*vii*) $(4, 0, -3)$

   (*iv*) $(0, 0, 0)$ (*viii*) $(-3, -3, -3)$

2. Find all three coordinates of each point where the plane $2x + 3y + 4z = 12$ crosses the coordinate axes. Make a sketch of part of the plane, using Figure 5.13 as a model. ANSWERS: Crossover on x-axis $(6, 0, 0)$; y-axis $(0, 4, 0)$; z-axis $(0, 0, 3)$.

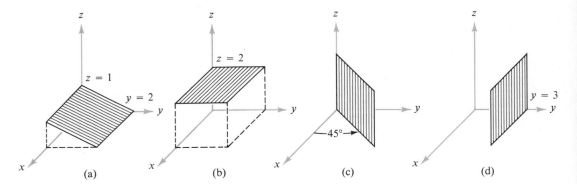

Figure 5.15
The planes in Exercise 3.

●3. The sketches in Figure 5.15 show parts of four planes. The planes are given by the equations

(*i*) $z = 2$ (*iii*) $6y - 18 = 0$

(*ii*) $x - y = 0$ (*iv*) $y + 2z - 2 = 0$

Match each plane with the correct equation. ANSWERS: (*i*) (b); (*ii*) (c); (*iii*) (d); (*iv*) (a).

●4. Sketch representative portions of the graphs of the following linear functions (defined for all x and y).

(*i*) $z = 10 - x - y$ (*iv*) $z = \frac{1}{2}x + \frac{1}{2}y$

(*ii*) $z = 10 - x$ (*v*) $z = 1 - x + \frac{1}{2}y$

(*iii*) $z = 10 - y$ (*vi*) $z = 3 + 2x + y$

Use Exercise 2 or Example 5 as models.

●5. Sketch graphs of the following linear functions, whose domains of definition are given by linear inequalities. In the xy-plane show the domain of definition, as in Figure 5.14.

(*i*) $z = f(x,y) = 3 - x - y$ $0 \leqslant x \leqslant 1, 0 \leqslant y \leqslant 1$

(*ii*) $z = f(x,y) = 3 + x;$ $0 \leqslant x \leqslant 2, 0 \leqslant y \leqslant 1$

(*iii*) $z = f(x,y) = 10 - 2x - 3y;$ $0 \leqslant x \leqslant 2, 0 \leqslant y \leqslant 1$

(*iv*) $z = f(x,y) = 14 - 2x - y;$ $1 \leqslant x \leqslant 3, 2 \leqslant y \leqslant 5$

*6. Show that the distance between two points $P_1 = (x_1,y_1,z_1)$ and $P_2 = (x_2,y_2,z_2)$ in three-dimensional space is given by

$$\text{dist}(P_1,P_2) = \sqrt{(x_1 - x_2)^2 + (y_1 - y_2)^2 + (z_1 - z_2)^2}$$

HINT: First find the distance between $Q_1 = (x_1,y_1,0)$ and $Q_2 = (x_2,y_2,0)$, the points obtained by projecting P_1 and P_2 perpendicularly into the xy-plane.

5.5 Visualizing Functions of Several Variables: Level Curves

The graph of an arbitrary function $z = f(x,y)$ may be rather difficult to sketch. Another way to portray the behavior of f is to sketch its **level curves**. These are the curves in the xy-plane consisting of all points such that $f(x,y) = $ constant $= c$. For each choice of the constant c there is a different level curve, the solution set of the equation $f(x,y) = c$. Information can be read out of the pattern of level curves for a function f much as you would read a contour map. Figure 5.16 shows the level curves $H(x,y) = c$ for a certain function $z = H(x,y)$, choosing values for c in steps of 500. The curves for $c = 9000$, $c = 10,000$, $c = 11,000$, $c = 12,000$, and $c = 13,000$ are labeled.

This diagram is, in fact, a contour map; $H(x,y)$ gives the altitude (in feet) for a certain part of the California Sierras. The curve $H(x,y) = c$ locates all points whose altitude is c. The coordinates x and y are measured in miles east and north of a geological reference marker located at the origin. Given only the pattern of level

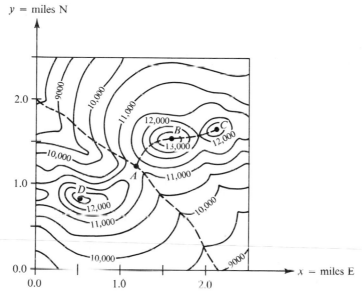

Figure 5.16
Altitude above sea level $H(x,y)$ as a function of position coordinates in a contour map. Solid curves are the level curves $H(x,y) = $ const, where the altitude is constant. A level curve may consist of several pieces; consider the contours $H = 11,000$ or $H = 12,000$. Contours are given every 500 feet, but only the thousand-foot contours are labeled. In a very accurate map the contours might be drawn for every 100-foot change in altitude.

curves, it is not hard to read out a great deal of information about the terrain. It is certainly not necessary to sketch the graph of $z = H(x,y)$ (that is, to make a per-spective drawing of the terrain) to see that the map depicts a mountain pass whose highest point A is about 11,250 feet above sea level. Points B, C, and D are mountain peaks. The dashed curve from bottom to top represents a trail from one side of the mountain range, across the pass, and down the other side. You might enjoy thinking over the following questions: (*i*) What happens if you follow the side trail ABC? (*ii*) Which of the peaks B, C, and D is the highest? (*iii*) What are the highest and lowest points on the map? (*iv*) In which part of the map is the terrain *steepest*?* The graph of a function $f(x,y)$, a surface above the xy-plane as in Figure 5.12, and the pattern of level curves $f(x,y) = $ const are different ways of presenting the same information. Surfaces are hard to draw and visualize in two dimensional sketches, so in this book we shall rely on patterns of level curves.

By examining the pattern of level curves we can determine where a function at-tains its maximum or minimum values. Let us apply this idea to an economic problem.

Example 7   Consider the profit function $P(x,y) = -1000 + 4.5x + 7.0y$ obtained in Example 3. This function is defined on the shaded feasible set shown in Figure 5.17. Sketch the level curves $P(x,y) = $ const and use them to decide where in the feasible set the profit is maximized.

Solution   The level curve consisting of all points (x,y) for which

$$-1000 + 4.5x + 7.0y = c \qquad (c \text{ a constant}) \qquad (17)$$

is a straight line in the xy-plane. For each of these lines, slope $= -4.5/7.0 = -0.64$; it does not depend at all on the choice of c. Thus the level lines are all parallel and slope downward as x increases. Figure 5.17 shows a few of these curves superimposed on the feasible set.† The curve $P = 0$ is particularly interesting since it shows where the operation "breaks even." Above this line the business would be making money.

If we let (x,y) move about within the feasible set, $P(x,y)$ stays constant if (x,y) moves parallel to the level curves, and increases as rapidly as possible if (x,y) moves perpendicular to them in the direction of increasing P (indicated by the shaded arrow). Starting from a particular point $A = (0,0)$ in the feasible set we could increase our profit by moving (x,y) along the dashed line up to the boundary at A'. Moving from A' to A'' leaves the profit unaltered, but the profit again increases as we move from A'' to $B = (50, 150)$. Now there is no way we can move *within the feasible set* to make

---

*ANSWERS: (*i*) You climb up to B, then down to and across a "saddle" (high pass), then up to peak C; (*ii*) B; (*iii*) Peak B is the highest point, lowest points are in the upper left corner, elevation about 8250 feet; (*iv*) Just north of D, where the contour lines bunch very closely together.

† We have drawn these lines by finding the points where they cross the x-axis and y-axis. This is done by substituting $x = 0$ or $y = 0$ into $-1000 + 4.5x + 7.0y = c$ and solving for the other variable.

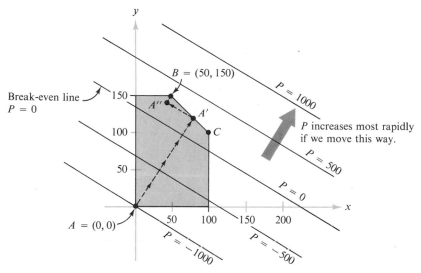

Figure 5.17
Level curves for $P(x,y) = -1000 + 4.5x + 7.0y$ are the parallel lines shown. We may
plot a typical line $-1000 + 4.5x + 7.0y = c$ by finding any two points on the line and
drawing a straight line through them. We show the lines taking steps $\Delta c = 500$, starting
with $c = -1000$. The shaded region is the feasible set, described in Example 3, where we
introduced this profit function $P(x,y)$. It should be clear that the profit is larger at B than
at C. As explained in the text, maximum feasible profit is attained when $(x,y) = B = (50, 150)$.

$P(x,y)$ larger. We have thus located the optimum choice of production levels in this
case.

We shall return to optimization problems of this kind in Section 5.14.

You will seldom have to determine the level curves of a function more complicated than a linear one like (17). This would require skills usually discussed only
in advanced courses. You are much more likely to encounter the (easier) converse
problem: given a detailed set of level curves, you must analyze the behavior of the
function, much as we did in figures 5.16 and 5.17. Economic data are often presented
in this way.

Exercises

●1. In Figure 5.18 we show level curves $f(x,y) = $ const for a certain function, superimposed on
a shaded triangular region R. By examining the figure, answer the following questions:

    (*i*) Where on R is the maximum value of f achieved?

    (*ii*) Where is the minimum value achieved?

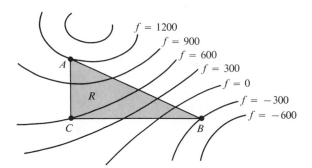

Figure 5.18
The level curves in Exercise 1.

(*iii*) What is the value of f at C?

(*iv*) How do the values of f vary if you move from B to A along the edge of R?

●2. Figure 5.19 shows the level curves for the profit function of an automobile assembly plant producing x Pintos and y Thunderbirds per month. Profit P is measured in thousands of dollars per month, and level curves are given in steps of $100,000 per month. The feasible set is the rectangle determined by $0 \leqslant x \leqslant 3000$, $0 \leqslant y \leqslant 1500$. By examining Figure 5.19, determine the choice of production levels that yields maximum profit. Is it possible to make a profit producing only Pintos? Thunderbirds? Estimate the fixed costs (profit when $x = 0$ and $y = 0$).

●3. Find the maximum value of $z = f(x,y) = 10 + x - y$ on the domain of definition determined by $0 \leqslant x \leqslant 8$ and $0 \leqslant y \leqslant 2$. HINT: First sketch the level curves $f(x,y) = $ const superimposed on a picture of the feasible set.

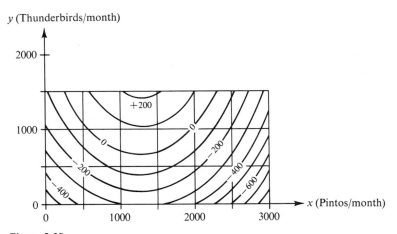

Figure 5.19
Profit function for an assembly plant (Exercise 2). Level curves $P = $ const are given in steps of $100,000 per month.

●4. In Exercise 6, Section 5.2, find the minimum feasible weekly cost for cattle feed. HINT: Sketch the level curves $C(x,y) = $ const in steps of \$500 per week, superimposed on an accurate sketch of the feasible set. Use graph paper, taking 4 units $= 10,000$ pounds of feed on both axes.

●5. In the xy-plane sketch the level curves $f(x,y) = c$ for the function $f(x,y) = 4 - x^2 - y^2$. Consider the cases $c > 4$, $c = 4$, $c < 4$ separately. Plot level curves in steps $\Delta c = 1$. By examining the pattern of curves, try to make a rough perspective sketch of the surface $z = f(x,y)$. HINT: $x^2 + y^2 = r^2$ where $r = $ distance from origin to $P = (x,y)$.

5.6   Partial Derivatives

If $z = f(x,y)$ is a function of two variables and $P = (x,y)$ is a fixed base point in the domain of definition of f, we may move in many directions to reach nearby points $Q = (x + \Delta x, y + \Delta y)$. For example, if Δx is arbitrary and $\Delta y = 0$, we move horizontally, parallel to the x-axis, to reach $Q' = (x + \Delta x, y)$; if Δy is arbitrary and $\Delta x = 0$, we move vertically from P to reach $Q'' = (x, y + \Delta y)$, as shown in Figure 5.20(a). However, the increments Δx and Δy are independent of one another, and we may reach any nearby point by choosing Δx and Δy appropriately. For example, if $P = (1, 1)$ as in Figure 5.20(b), and we wish to reach $Q = (4, -1)$, we should take $\Delta x = 3$ and $\Delta y = -2$, to get $(1 + \Delta x, 1 + \Delta y) = Q = (4, -1)$. As you can see, a "displacement" from one point $P = (x_1,y_1)$ to another point $Q = (x_2,y_2)$ is a quantity that has both a magnitude and a direction.

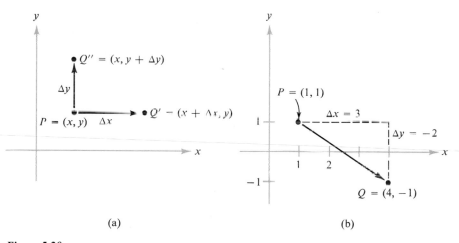

(a)   (b)

Figure 5.20
In (a) we show typical displacements from $P = (x,y)$. In (b) we set $P = (1, 1)$. To reach $Q = (4, -1) = (1 + \Delta x, 1 + \Delta y)$ we must must take $\Delta x = 3$, $\Delta y = -2$, as shown. By the Pythagorean Theorem the magnitude of this displacement, the distance between P and Q, is $\sqrt{(\Delta x)^2 + (\Delta y)^2} = \sqrt{13} = 3.605 \ldots$.

Now let $z = f(x,y)$ be any function defined at and near a point $P = (x,y)$. The value of the function there is just $f(P) = f(x,y)$. At a nearby point $Q = (x + \Delta x, y + \Delta y)$ its value is $f(Q) = f(x + \Delta x, y + \Delta y)$. Thus the change in the value of f is a real number

$$\Delta f = f(Q) - f(P) = f(x + \Delta x, y + \Delta y) - f(x,y)$$

while the change in the variable (the displacement from P to Q) is not a number. We cannot form averages

$$\frac{\Delta f}{\Delta P} = \frac{\text{change in value of } f}{\text{change in variable}}$$

as we did in Chapter 2, where we considered functions of one variable. A new idea is necessary to define rates of change and derivatives for functions of several variables. The idea is this: if a base point $P = (x,y)$ is given and we restrict attention to displacements from P in the x-direction only (Δx arbitrary, $\Delta y = 0$) then the average rate of change in the x-direction

$$\frac{\Delta f}{\Delta x} = \frac{f(x + \Delta x, y) - f(x,y)}{\Delta x} = \frac{f(Q) - f(P)}{\Delta x}$$

is defined for all small displacements $\Delta x \neq 0$. If these averages have a limit value as Δx approaches zero, we obtain the **rate of change of f with respect to x** (holding y fixed) at the point P. This rate of change, if it exists, is denoted by

$$\frac{\partial f}{\partial x}(x,y) = \frac{\partial f}{\partial x}(P) = \lim_{\Delta x \to 0} \left\{ \frac{f(x + \Delta x, y) - f(x,y)}{\Delta x} \right\} \tag{18}$$

It is called the **partial derivative of f with respect to x**. Similarly, we may define the **partial derivative of f with respect to y** as

$$\frac{\partial f}{\partial y}(P) = \lim_{\Delta y \to 0} \left\{ \frac{f(x,y + \Delta y) - f(x,y)}{\Delta y} \right\} \tag{19}$$

by considering displacements parallel to the y-axis. The number $\partial f/\partial y(P)$ gives the rate of change of f as we move away from the point P in the y-direction. Some books use other notations for these partial derivatives. Typical alternatives are

$$f_x \text{ and } f_y \qquad D_x f \text{ and } D_y f \qquad D_1 f \text{ and } D_2 f$$

We shall use the notation $\partial f/\partial x$ and $\partial f/\partial y$ throughout this book.

The partial derivatives $\partial f/\partial x$ and $\partial f/\partial y$ are usually defined whenever f itself is defined, so these partial derivatives are also functions of two variables. The functions $\partial f/\partial x$ and $\partial f/\partial y$ together play the role played by the ordinary derivative df/dx when we studied functions of one variable. They will be very useful when we search for maximum and minimum values of $f(x,y)$. Before we can use $\partial f/\partial x$ and $\partial f/\partial y$ we must be able to compute these partial derivatives. Fortunately, if you think of the limits (18) and (19) in the right way the problem of calculating $\partial f/\partial x$ and $\partial f/\partial y$ reduces to calculating ordinary derivatives of functions of one variable. Thus we can bring to bear all the techniques of Chapters 2 and 3.

To evaluate $\partial f/\partial x$ at a point $P = (x,y)$ we hold y fixed and see what happens as x varies; we defined $\partial f/\partial x$ this way. But if we hold y fixed then $f(x,y)$ becomes a function with only one variable, namely x. Let

$$F(x) = f(x,y), \text{ setting } y = \text{const wherever it appears}$$

By definition (18)

$$\frac{\partial f}{\partial x}(P) = \lim_{\Delta x \to 0} \left\{ \frac{f(x + \Delta x, y) - f(x,y)}{\Delta x} \right\}$$

$$= \lim_{\Delta x \to 0} \left\{ \frac{F(x + \Delta x) - F(x)}{\Delta x} \right\} = F'(x)$$

is just the ordinary derivative of F at x: $F' = dF/dx$. In other words:

Rule for Calculating Partial Derivatives   In order to calculate $\partial f/\partial x$, simply regard y as a constant wherever it appears in $f(x,y)$ and differentiate the resulting function of x in the ordinary way. The same rule of course applies to $\partial f/\partial y$: regard x as a constant wherever it appears.

Example 8   Let $f(x,y) = 400 + x^2 + y^2 + 3xy$. Calculate $\partial f/\partial x$ at $P = (1, 3)$. Calculate $\partial f/\partial x$ as a function of x and y: that is, calculate $\partial f/\partial x$ for an arbitrary point (x,y). Where is $\partial f/\partial x$ equal to zero?

Solution   First we shall calculate $\partial f/\partial x(P) = \partial f/\partial x(1, 3)$ by "brute force," according to the definition (18). Then we shall calculate $\partial f/\partial x$ by using the rule set forth above, to show how simply the rule works.

At $P = (1, 3)$ we have $f(P) = 400 + 1^2 + 3^2 + 3(1 \cdot 3) = 419$, and at $Q = (1 + \Delta x, 3)$ we have $f(Q) = 400 + (1 + \Delta x)^2 + 3^2 + 3(1 + \Delta x) \cdot 3$. Thus if $\Delta x \neq 0$

and $\Delta y = 0$, we get

$$\frac{\Delta f}{\Delta x} = \frac{f(1 + \Delta x, 3) - f(1, 3)}{\Delta x}$$

$$= \frac{400 + (1 + 2\,\Delta x + (\Delta x)^2) + 9 + 9(1 + \Delta x) - 419}{\Delta x}$$

$$= \frac{2\,\Delta x + (\Delta x)^2 + 9\,\Delta x}{\Delta x} = 11 + \Delta x$$

Clearly, as Δx approaches zero we get

$$\frac{\partial f}{\partial x}(1, 3) = \lim_{\Delta x \to 0} \left\{\frac{\Delta f}{\Delta x}\right\} = \lim_{\Delta x \to 0} \{11 + \Delta x\} = 11$$

To apply the rule above, we fix $y = $ const, leaving x as the variable. Regardless of what value we might assign to y, we carry out the calculation

$$\frac{\partial f}{\partial x}(x, y) = \frac{d}{dx}\{400 + x^2 + y^2 + 3xy\}$$

regarding y as a constant on the right side. Hence

$$\frac{\partial f}{\partial x}(x, y) = 2x + 3y$$

Naturally, if we set $x = 1$ and $y = 3$ we get $\partial f / \partial x (1, 3) = 11$, as above.

Finally, if $\partial f / \partial x = 0$ at a point (x, y), this means precisely that $0 = 2x + 3y$, or $y = (-2/3)x$. The solution set for the equation $\partial f / \partial x = 0$ consists of all points on a line determined by $y = (-2/3)x$. Notice that $\partial f / \partial x = 0$ at infinitely many points $P = (x, y)$.

Example 9   Calculate $\partial f / \partial x$ and $\partial f / \partial y$ for $f(x, y) = 1000 + x^2 + 3xy + 5y + 7y^2$. Find all points $P = (x, y)$ where both partial derivatives are simultaneously equal to zero.

Solution   Taking y as a constant everywhere it appears, we get

$$\frac{\partial f}{\partial x} = \frac{d}{dx}\{1000 + x^2 + 3xy + 5y + 7y^2\} = 2x + 3y$$

Similarly, treating x as a constant, we get

$$\frac{\partial f}{\partial y} = \frac{d}{dy} \{1000 + x^2 + 3xy + 5y + 7y^2\} = 3x + 5 + 14y$$

The solution set for $\partial f/\partial x = 0$ is the line given by $2x + 3y = 0$; $\partial f/\partial y = 0$ gives a different line, determined by $3x + 14y = -5$. The partial derivatives are both zero only if $P = (x,y)$ is a solution of the simultaneous equations

$$2x + 3y = 0$$

$$3x + 14y = -5$$

These are easy to solve. The first equation gives $y = (-2/3)x$; substituting this into the second equation, we get

$$-5 = 3x + 14\left(-\frac{2}{3}x\right) = -\frac{19}{3}x \quad \text{or} \quad x = \frac{15}{19}$$

Inserting $x = 15/19$ into either equation, we find the corresponding value for y:

$$3y + 2\left(\frac{15}{19}\right) = 0 \quad \text{or} \quad y = -\frac{10}{19}$$

Thus $P = (15/19, -10/19)$ is the only point where $\partial f/\partial x = 0$ and $\partial f/\partial y = 0$.

More complicated functions of x and y are differentiated in the same way.

Example 10   Calculate $\partial f/\partial x$ and $\partial f/\partial y$ for $f(x,y) = 1 + \sqrt{x^2 + xy + 3y^2}$.

Solution   It helps to write f with fractional exponents:

$$f(x,y) = 1 + (x^2 + xy + 3y^2)^{1/2}$$

Treating y as a constant everywhere it appears and applying the chain rule for ordinary derivatives (Section 3.3), we get

$$\frac{\partial f}{\partial x} = \frac{d}{dx} \{1 + (x^2 + xy + 3y^2)^{1/2}\}$$

$$= \frac{d}{dx} \{1\} + \frac{d}{dx} \{(x^2 + xy + 3y^2)^{1/2}\}$$

$$= 0 + \frac{1}{2}(x^2 + xy + 3y^2)^{-1/2} \cdot \frac{d}{dx} \{x^2 + xy + 3y^2\}$$

$$= \frac{2x + y}{2\sqrt{x^2 + xy + 3y^2}}$$

Similarly, regarding x as a constant, we get

$$\frac{\partial f}{\partial y} = \frac{d}{dy}\{1 + (x^2 + xy + 3y^2)^{1/2}\}$$

$$= \frac{1}{2}(x^2 + xy + 3y^2)^{-1/2} \cdot \frac{d}{dy}\{x^2 + xy + 3y^2\}$$

$$= \frac{x + 6y}{2\sqrt{x^2 + xy + 3y^2}}$$

Exercises

●1. Given the function $f(x,y) = x + x^3y^2$, calculate the values of $\partial f/\partial x$ and $\partial f/\partial y$ at $P = (2, 1)$ by direct examination of the limits

(i) $\displaystyle\lim_{\Delta x \to 0} \frac{f(2 + \Delta x, 1) - f(2, 1)}{\Delta x}$

(ii) $\displaystyle\lim_{\Delta y \to 0} \frac{f(2, 1 + \Delta y) - f(2, 1)}{\Delta y}$

●2. Given $f(x,y) = 2 + x + 3y - x^3y + 3xy^3$, find

(i) $\dfrac{\partial f}{\partial x}(0, 0)$ (iii) $\dfrac{\partial f}{\partial x}(-1, 1)$

(ii) $\dfrac{\partial f}{\partial y}(0, 0)$ (iv) $\dfrac{\partial f}{\partial y}(-1, 1)$

●3. Given $f(x,y) = 1 + 2x + 3y + x^2y - 3xy$, find the partial derivatives $\partial f/\partial x$ and $\partial f/\partial y$ as functions of x and y. Locate all points $P = (x,y)$ at which *both* partial derivatives are zero.

●4. Find $\partial f/\partial x$ and $\partial f/\partial y$ for each of the following elementary functions:

(i) $f(x,y) = 3$ (constant function)

(ii) $f(x,y) = x$

(iii) $f(x,y) = -y + 1$

(iv) $f(x,y) = x + y$

(v) $f(x,y) = xy + x^2 - y^2$

(vi) $f(x,y) = \dfrac{x}{y}$

●5. Find $\partial f/\partial x$ and $\partial f/\partial y$ for each of the following functions:

(i) $f(x,y) = x + \sqrt{x^2 + y^2}$ (iii) $f(x,y) = (x + y)^5$

(ii) $f(x,y) = 15x^{1/3}y^{4/5}$ (iv) $f(x,y) = \dfrac{1}{\sqrt{x^2 + 2x + 1 + y^2}}$

(v) $f(x,y) = -900,000 + (500x - 0.1x^2) + (700y - 0.2y^2) - 0.01xy$

(vi) $f(x,y) = \dfrac{1 + x^2}{1 + y^2}$

(viii) $f(x,y) = e^{-(x^2 + y^2)/2}$

(vii) $f(x,y) = \log(x - y)$

(ix) $f(x,y) = \dfrac{x + y}{xy} - x^3 + 2$

●6. The volume of a cone with radius r and altitude h is $V = \frac{1}{3}\pi r^2 h$. Calculate $\partial V/\partial r$ and $\partial V/\partial h$ as functions of r and h. Find their numerical values if $r = 2$ and $h = 10$. What do the partial derivatives $\partial V/\partial r(2, 10)$ and $\partial V/\partial h(2, 10)$ mean geometrically?

●7. Given a right triangle with side lengths x and y, the area A and length of hypotenuse l are given by the formulas

$$A = \frac{1}{2}xy \qquad l = \sqrt{x^2 + y^2}$$

Calculate the partial derivatives for $A(x,y)$ and $l(x,y)$. Calculate their numerical values at the point $P = (x,y) = (120, 160)$.

●8. An ideal gas in a container of variable volume satisfies Boyle's law:

$$PV = kT$$

where P = pressure, V = volume, and T = absolute temperature. Here k is a physical constant, measured experimentally. Express P as a function of V and T. Then calculate $\partial P/\partial V$ and $\partial P/\partial T$ as functions of V and T. NOTE: In physical terms, if V and T are set the gas will come to equilibrium with a definite pressure $P = P(V,T)$ given by the formula.

●9. Partial derivatives $\partial f/\partial x$, $\partial f/\partial y$, and $\partial f/\partial z$ for a function of three variables $f(x,y,z)$ are handled in almost the same way as those for functions of two variables. To compute $\partial f/\partial x$, treat the other variables, y and z, as constants and take the ordinary derivative with respect to x; the other partial derivatives are computed in the same way. Compute $\partial f/\partial x$, $\partial f/\partial y$, $\partial f/\partial z$ for the following functions of x, y, and z:

(i) $f(x,y,z) = x^2 + y^2 + z^2$

(iii) $f(x,y,z) = \dfrac{xy^2}{z + 1}$

(ii) $f(x,y,z) = 2xy + 2xz - y^2z^2$

(iv) $f(x,y,z) = x^2 + z^2 - xyz$

5.7 Applications of Partial Derivatives

Many applications of partial derivatives rest upon the interpretation of $\partial f/\partial x$ and $\partial f/\partial y$ as the rates of change of f in the x-direction and y-direction, as we move away from some base point. We shall illustrate this by re-examining the economic problem in Section 5.2 (Example 3).

Example 11 In Section 5.2 we determined the feasible set of production levels and the profit function $P(x,y) = -1000 + 4.5x + 7.0y$ for a ceramics shop. Suppose we start from the (feasible) operating point $Q = (50, 75)$ shown in Figure 5.21 and vary x. What is the rate of change in profit in the x-direction at this point? What does this suggest for economic strategy? Discuss the rate of change of profit in the y-direction at the same point.

Solution   First write down the partial derivatives of $z = P(x,y)$:

$$\frac{\partial P}{\partial x} = \frac{d}{dx} \{-1000 + 4.5x + 7.0y\} = 4.5$$

$$\frac{\partial P}{\partial y} = \frac{d}{dy} \{-1000 + 4.5x + 7.0y\} = 7.0$$

These partial derivatives have constant values throughout the plane. (This is true of any linear function $f(x,y) = Ax + By + C$, see Exercise 1. It is certainly *not* true of more complicated functions that involve powers or mixed products of the variables.) At the point $Q = (50, 75)$ we get

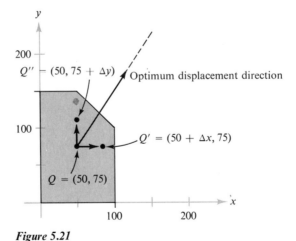

Figure 5.21
On the shaded feasible set, profit is $P(x,y) =$ $-1000 + 4.5x + 7.0y$. Since $\partial P/\partial x = 4.5$ and $\partial P/\partial y = 7.0$ at $Q = (50, 75)$, this means that $\Delta P \approx 4.5\Delta x$ for small displacements parallel to the x-axis, and $\Delta P \approx 7.0\Delta y$ for displacements parallel to the y-axis. Clearly P increases, but at different rates, if we take $\Delta x > 0$ or $\Delta y > 0$. This figure should be compared with Figure 5.17, which shows the level curves $P = $ const. There is an optimum direction of displacement from Q. Displacement in this direction produces the largest possible increase in profit. This direction, shown above, is perpendicular to the level curves in Figure 5.17.

$$\frac{\partial P}{\partial x}(50,\ 75) = 4.5 \qquad \frac{\partial P}{\partial y}(50,\ 75) = 7.0$$

But at any base point $Q = (a,b)$

$$\frac{\partial P}{\partial x}(a,b) = \text{rate of change of } P \text{ as } x \text{ increases past } x = a,$$
$$\text{holding } y \text{ fixed } (y = b)$$

$$\frac{\partial P}{\partial y}(a,b) = \text{rate of change of } P \text{ as } y \text{ increases past } y = b,$$
$$\text{holding } x \text{ fixed } (x = a)$$

This follows directly from the very definition of the partial derivatives. Thus if we move from $Q = (50, 75)$ a small distance in the x-direction to $Q' = (50 + \Delta x, 75)$, the change in profit is approximately $4.5\ \Delta x$.

$$\Delta P \approx \frac{\partial P}{\partial x}(50,\ 75) \cdot \Delta x = 4.5\ \Delta x \qquad \text{for all small increments } \Delta x \qquad (20)$$

Likewise, if we move in the y-direction from Q to $Q'' = (50, 75 + \Delta y)$, keeping $x = 50$, we get

$$\Delta P \approx \frac{\partial P}{\partial y}(50,\ 75) \cdot \Delta y - 7.0\ \Delta y \qquad \text{for all small increments } \Delta y \qquad (21)$$

We should recall the discussion of these approximation formulas in Section 2.6. They have immediate economic significance. In (20) ΔP is positive (profit increases) if $\Delta x > 0$, so it would pay to move our operating point horizontally to the right of point Q. Likewise, formula (21) shows that it would also be profitable to increase y, moving the operating point vertically up from $Q = (50, 75)$. It does not pay to move Q so as to *decrease* x or y. Notice that equal changes in the variables, say $\Delta x = 10$ and $\Delta y = 10$, do not produce equal changes in the profit:

$$\Delta P \approx 4.5\ \Delta x = 45 \quad \text{moving from} \quad Q = (50, 75) \quad \text{to} \quad Q' = (50 + \Delta x, 75) = (60, 75)$$

$$\Delta P \approx 7.0\ \Delta y = 70 \quad \text{moving from} \quad Q = (50, 75) \quad \text{to} \quad Q'' = (50, 75 + \Delta y) = (50, 85)$$

Moving 10 units in the positive y-direction produces \$25 per week more profit than moving 10 units in the x-direction.

We conclude by observing that the partial derivatives $\partial f/\partial x$ and $\partial f/\partial y$ allow us to approximate closely the behavior of $z = f(x,y)$ for points near a base point P by a linear combination of the partial derivatives and the increments Δx and Δy. If $Q = (x + \Delta x, y + \Delta y)$ is any point near $P = (x,y)$, then

$$\Delta f \approx \frac{\partial f}{\partial x}(P) \cdot \Delta x + \frac{\partial f}{\partial y}(P) \cdot \Delta y \qquad \text{for all small increments } \Delta x, \Delta y \qquad (22)$$

To put it another way, adding $f(P)$ to both sides of (22) we get

$$f(Q) = f(x + \Delta x, y + \Delta y) = f(P) + \Delta f \approx f(P) + \frac{\partial f}{\partial x}(P) \cdot \Delta x + \frac{\partial f}{\partial y}(P) \cdot \Delta y \qquad (23)$$

for all small increments. Since the point P is fixed, $f(P)$, $\partial f/\partial x(P)$, and $\partial f/\partial y(P)$ are constants in these formulas. Only the increments Δx and Δy vary. These increments may be chosen independently. Thus formulas (22) and (23) tell us approximately how f behaves as we move away from the base point in *any* direction, not just in directions parallel to the coordinate axes. If we set $\Delta x = 0$ or $\Delta y = 0$, we get the special cases

$$f(x + \Delta x, y) \approx f(P) + \frac{\partial f}{\partial x}(P) \cdot \Delta x \qquad \left(\text{that is, } \Delta f \approx \frac{\partial f}{\partial x}(P) \cdot \Delta x\right)$$

$$f(x,y + \Delta y) \approx f(P) + \frac{\partial f}{\partial y}(P) \cdot \Delta y \qquad \left(\text{that is, } \Delta f \approx \frac{\partial f}{\partial y}(P) \cdot \Delta y\right)$$

noted in Example 11.

Example 12   Consider the profit function $P(x,y) = -1000 + 4.5x + 7.0y$. Starting from point $Q = (50, 75)$, let us move a distance Δs along the line L shown in Figure 5.22. Estimate ΔP in terms of the distance Δs. Is displacement a unit distance ($\Delta s = 1$) in this direction more or less profitable than displacement one unit in the positive y-direction?

Solution   The line L is oriented $45°$ counterclockwise from the direction of the positive x-axis. If we move a distance Δs along L, the corresponding increments in x and y are

$$\Delta x = \frac{\Delta s}{\sqrt{2}} \qquad \Delta y = \frac{\Delta s}{\sqrt{2}}$$

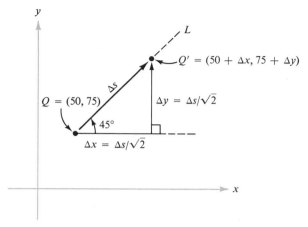

Figure 5.22
Moving Δs units along the line L (inclined $45°$ to the
positive x-axis) causes Δx to change by $\Delta x = \Delta s/\sqrt{2}$ units.
Similarly, $\Delta y = \Delta s/\sqrt{2}$. We consider the change $\Delta P =$
$P(50 + \Delta x, 75 + \Delta y) - P(50, 75)$, where $P(x,y) =$
$-1000 + 4.5x + 7.0y$.

(The triangle in the figure is a right triangle with legs of equal length.) We already
know that $\partial P/\partial x(50, 75) = 4.5$ and $\partial P/\partial y(50, 75) = 7.0$. Thus

$$\Delta P = P(50 + \Delta x, 75 + \Delta y) - P(50, 75)$$

$$\approx \frac{\partial P}{\partial x}(50, 75)\,\Delta x + \frac{\partial P}{\partial y}(50, 75)\,\Delta y$$

$$= 4.5\frac{\Delta s}{\sqrt{2}} + 7.0\frac{\Delta s}{\sqrt{2}} = \Delta s\left(\frac{11.50}{1.414}\right) = 8.13\,\Delta s$$

If $\Delta s = 1$, then $\Delta P \approx 8.13$. If we move one unit parallel to the positive y axis, then
$\Delta P = P(50, 75 + \Delta y) - P(50, 75) \approx \partial P/\partial y(50, 75)\,\Delta y = 7.0\,\Delta y$, so that $\Delta P \approx 7.00$.
Profits increase more rapidly if we displace our operating point along L.

Exercises

●1. Consider a general linear function $f(x,y) = Ax + By + C$ (where A, B, and C are fixed constants) defined for all x and y. Show that the partial derivatives are constant functions

$$\frac{\partial f}{\partial x} = A \qquad \frac{\partial f}{\partial y} = B$$

●2. A manufacturer of chain-link fencing produces two grades of fencing. Suppose his profit function is

$$P(x,y) = -700 + 0.5x + 0.3y - 0.00004xy$$

where x and y are the number of yards of heavy-duty and standard fencing produced (and sold) per week. Suppose his plant is operating at production levels $x = 400$ and $y = 4000$. Find the marginal profits $\partial P/\partial x$ and $\partial P/\partial y$ with respect to x and y. Is it profitable to produce (and sell) more standard fencing? Heavy-duty fencing? Should he tell his sales staff to push the standard or the heavy-duty fencing? HINT: In the last step, consider the effect of increasing output by $\Delta x = 1$ and $\Delta y = 1$. Which is more profitable?

●3. In Exercise 2, assume that

$$P(x,y) = -700 + 0.5x + 0.3y - 0.001xy$$

Starting from production levels $Q = (2000, 400)$, find the marginal profits $\partial P/\partial x$ and $\partial P/\partial y$ with respect to x and y. Will profit be increased by increasing x? By increasing y?

●4. The surface area of a solid cylinder with height h and diameter d (inches) is

$$A = \pi dh + \frac{\pi d^2}{2} \text{ square inches}$$

Find the area if $d = 10$ inches and $h = 12$ inches. How much does A change (approximately) if

(*i*) diameter is increased by 1 inch ($\Delta d = 1$), keeping h fixed?

(*ii*) height is increased by 1 inch ($\Delta h = 1$), keeping d fixed?

(*iii*) height is increased by 2 inches ($\Delta h = 2$) while diameter is decreased by 1 inch ($\Delta d = -1$)?

5. An ideal gas in a closed container satisfies Boyle's law:

$$PV = kT$$

where P = pressure, V = volume, and T = absolute temperature. Here k is a physical constant, measured experimentally. Express P as a function of V and T. Calculate $\partial P/\partial V$ and $\partial P/\partial T$ as functions of V and T. Suppose $V = V_0$ and $T = T_0$ are fixed (positive). Does the pressure increase or decrease as

(*i*) V increases to $V_0 + \Delta V$, keeping $T = T_0$ fixed?

(*ii*) T increases to $T_0 + \Delta T$, keeping $V = V_0$ fixed?

Does your answer agree with your intuition?

●6. Consider the function $f(x,y) = 3 + x - 2y$ and the point $P = (3, 2)$. Formula (23) tells us that

$$f(3 + \Delta x, 2 + \Delta y) \approx f(P) + \frac{\partial f}{\partial x}(P) \cdot \Delta x + \frac{\partial f}{\partial y}(P) \cdot \Delta y = 2 + \Delta x - 2\,\Delta y$$

for all small increments Δx and Δy. Show that this formula is more than approximate, that it is *exact* in this case and holds for all Δx and Δy, small or large. (The reason for this behavior is the linearity of the function f.)

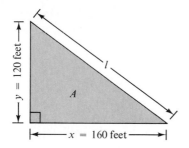

Figure 5.23
Triangle-shaped plot of ground in
Exercise 8.

●7. For the function $f(x,y) = 2 + x^2 - y^3$ and the point $P = (1, 1)$, compute $\partial f/\partial x(P)$ and $\partial f/\partial y(P)$ and show that formula (23) becomes

$$f(1 + \Delta x, 1 + \Delta y) \approx 2 + 2\,\Delta x - 3\,\Delta y$$

in this case. Calculate $f(0.9, 1.1)$ exactly; compare it with the approximation given by formula (23). Do the same for $f(1.2, 1.1)$.

●8. A plot of ground shaped like a right triangle (Figure 5.23) has legs of length $x = 160$ feet and $y = 120$ feet. Calculate

(i) $A = \text{area} = \dfrac{1}{2}xy$

(ii) $l = \text{hypotenuse length} = \sqrt{x^2 + y^2}$

Then use the approximation formula (22) to estimate the errors ΔA and Δl corresponding to errors $\Delta x = 0.5$ and $\Delta y = 0.5$ in measuring x and y.

5.8   Higher-order Partial Derivatives

If a function $z = f(x,y)$ has partial derivatives $\partial f/\partial x$ and $\partial f/\partial y$, we may be able to apply the operations $\partial/\partial x$ and $\partial/\partial y$ to each of these functions of two variables, thereby obtaining the **second partial derivatives** of f

$$\frac{\partial^2 f}{\partial x^2} = \frac{\partial}{\partial x}\left(\frac{\partial f}{\partial x}\right) \qquad \frac{\partial^2 f}{\partial y^2} = \frac{\partial}{\partial y}\left(\frac{\partial f}{\partial y}\right)$$

$$\frac{\partial^2 f}{\partial x\,\partial y} = \frac{\partial}{\partial x}\left(\frac{\partial f}{\partial y}\right) \qquad \frac{\partial^2 f}{\partial y\,\partial x} = \frac{\partial}{\partial y}\left(\frac{\partial f}{\partial x}\right)$$

For all the functions we shall meet, the "mixed" second partial derivatives agree:

$$\frac{\partial^2 f}{\partial x\,\partial y} = \frac{\partial^2 f}{\partial y\,\partial x}$$

This shortens the list of partial derivatives to keep track of. In many cases the operations $\partial/\partial x$ and $\partial/\partial y$ may be applied repeatedly to these second partial derivatives, yielding higher-order partial derivatives of f, such as

$$\frac{\partial^3 f}{\partial x^3} = \frac{\partial}{\partial x}\left(\frac{\partial^2 f}{\partial x^2}\right), \qquad \frac{\partial^3 f}{\partial y\,\partial x\,\partial y} = \frac{\partial}{\partial y}\left(\frac{\partial^2 f}{\partial x\,\partial y}\right), \qquad \text{and so on}$$

We shall not make much use of higher-order (or even second-order) partial derivatives. However, they are extremely important throughout the physical sciences, and in certain areas of economics.

Example 13   Calculate the first partial derivatives of $f(x,y) = 1/(x^2 + y^2 - 2y + 2)$, and locate all points $P = (x,y)$ such that $\partial f/\partial x(P) = 0$ and $\partial f/\partial y(P) = 0$. Then calculate the second-order partial derivatives

$$\frac{\partial^2 f}{\partial x^2} \qquad \frac{\partial^2 f}{\partial x\,\partial y} \qquad \frac{\partial^2 f}{\partial y^2}$$

Determine their values at the points where $\partial f/\partial x = \partial f/\partial y = 0$.

NOTE: Since $x^2 + y^2 - 2y + 2 = x^2 + (y-1)^2 + 1 = 1 + (\sqrt{(x-0)^2 + (y-1)^2})^2$, the function has the form $f(x,y) = 1/(1 + r^2)$ where r is the distance between the points $P = (x,y)$ and $Q = (0,1)$.

Solution   Taking x or y as a constant, and using the chain rule for ordinary derivatives, we get

$$\frac{\partial f}{\partial x} = \frac{d}{dx}\{(x^2 + y^2 - 2y + 2)^{-1}\}$$

$$= -(x^2 + y^2 - 2y + 2)^{-2}\,\frac{d}{dx}\{x^2 + y^2 - 2y + 2\}$$

$$= \frac{-2x}{(x^2 + y^2 - 2y + 2)^2}$$

$$\frac{\partial f}{\partial y} = \frac{-2y + 2}{(x^2 + y^2 - 2y + 2)^2}$$

These expressions are equal to zero when their numerators are zero. Thus $\partial f/\partial x = 0$ when $-2x = 0$; that is, when $x = 0$. Likewise $\partial f/\partial y$ is zero when $-2y + 2 = 0$, so that $y = 1$. Thus $P = (0, 1)$ is the only point where both first partial derivatives vanish simultaneously.

Next, treat y as a constant and calculate

$$\frac{\partial^2 f}{\partial x^2} = \frac{\partial}{\partial x}\left(\frac{\partial f}{\partial x}\right) = \frac{d}{dx}\{-2x(x^2 + y^2 - 2y + 2)^{-2}\}$$

$$= \frac{d}{dx}\{-2x\}\cdot(x^2 + y^2 - 2y + 2)^{-2} - 2x\cdot\frac{d}{dx}\{(x^2 + y^2 - 2y + 2)^{-2}\}$$

$$= -2(x^2 + y^2 - 2y + 2)^{-2} - 2x(-2)(x^2 + y^2 - 2y + 2)^{-3}(2x)$$

$$= \frac{-2}{(x^2 + y^2 - 2y + 2)^2} + \frac{8x^2}{(x^2 + y^2 - 2y + 2)^3}$$

$$= \frac{6x^2 - 2y^2 + 4y - 4}{(x^2 + y^2 - 2y + 2)^3}$$

Similarly

$$\frac{\partial^2 f}{\partial x\,\partial y} = \frac{\partial}{\partial x}\left(\frac{\partial f}{\partial y}\right) = \frac{d}{dx}\{(-2y + 2)(x^2 + y^2 - 2y + 2)^{-2}\}$$

$$= (-2y + 2)(-2)(x^2 + y^2 - 2y + 2)^{-3}(2x)$$

$$= \frac{8xy - 8x}{(x^2 + y^2 - 2y + 2)^3}$$

Treating x as a constant, we get

$$\frac{\partial^2 f}{\partial y^2} = \frac{\partial}{\partial y}\left(\frac{\partial f}{\partial y}\right) = \frac{d}{dy}\{(-2y + 2)(x^2 + y^2 - 2y + 2)^{-2}\}$$

$$= -2(x^2 + y^2 - 2y + 2)^{-2} + (-2y + 2)(-2)(x^2 + y^2 - 2y + 2)^{-3}(2y - 2)$$

$$= \frac{-2x^2 + 6y^2 - 12y + 4}{(x^2 + y^2 - 2y + 2)^3}$$

The values at $P = (0, 1)$ are obtained by substituting $x = 0$ and $y = 1$ into each formula:

$$\frac{\partial^2 f}{\partial x^2}(0, 1) = -2 \qquad \frac{\partial^2 f}{\partial x\,\partial y}(0, 1) = 0 \qquad \frac{\partial^2 f}{\partial y^2}(0, 1) = -2$$

These second derivatives may be used to locate maxima and minima of the function f, as we shall see in the following sections.

Exercises

●1. Calculate all first- and second-order partial derivatives of

$$f(x,y) = 4x^3 + 7xy^2 - x^2y^2 + \frac{1}{y} - 7$$

Give their numerical values at the point $P = (3, 1)$.

●2. Find all second partial derivatives of the functions

(i) $z = f(x,y) = 4x + 3y - 10xy$

(ii) $z = f(x,y) = 2xy + x^3 - y^3$

(iii) $z = f(x,y) = \log(x^2 + y^2)$

●3. For the function $f(x,y) = x^3 + x^2y - y$, locate all points $P = (x,y)$ for which $\partial f/\partial x(P) = 0$ and $\partial f/\partial y(P) = 0$. At these points calculate the second-order partial derivatives

$$\frac{\partial^2 f}{\partial x^2} \qquad \frac{\partial^2 f}{\partial y^2} \qquad \frac{\partial^2 f}{\partial x\, \partial y}$$

4. For each of the following functions calculate the "mixed" second partial derivatives

$$\frac{\partial^2 f}{\partial x\, \partial y} \quad \text{and} \quad \frac{\partial^2 f}{\partial y\, \partial x}$$

and check whether they agree.

(i) $z = 2x^4 - x^3y^2 + 3xy^3 - 24$

(ii) $z = \dfrac{1}{x + y^2}$

(iii) $z = xy \sin(x + 2y)$

(iv) $z = e^{x^2 - y^2}$

●5. Show that the partial derivatives of the functions $z = f(x,y)$

(i) $z = \log \sqrt{x^2 + y^2}$

(ii) $z = e^x \cos y$

satisfy the equation

$$\frac{\partial^2 f}{\partial x^2} + \frac{\partial^2 f}{\partial y^2} = 0 \qquad \text{(Laplace's equation)}$$

NOTE: This equation plays a central role in physics.

5.9 A Case Study in Optimization

Here is an economic model that will be used in several ways. Consider the profit function for an automobile-assembly plant that produces two types of cars, say Pintos and Mustangs. Suppose we let

$$x = \text{number of Pintos produced per month}$$

$$y = \text{number of Mustangs produced per month}$$

Suppose that the profit is given by the formula

$$P(x,y) = -900{,}000 + (500x - 0.1x^2) + (700y - 0.2y^2) - 0.01xy \qquad (24)$$

dollars per month for production levels $0 \leqslant x \leqslant 4000$ and $0 \leqslant y \leqslant 3000$. This is a reasonably complicated function; nevertheless, there is an intuitive interpretation of each group of terms in it. The constant $-900{,}000 = P(0, 0)$ gives the fixed costs, incurred even when there is no production at all. The term $(500x - 0.1x^2)$ gives the profit for producing x Pintos if no effort is made to produce Mustangs; to see this, set $y = 0$. In this term, $-0.1x^2$ reflects diseconomies of size in Pinto production; at low production levels there is roughly \$500 profit on each Pinto. Similarly, the term $(700y - 0.2y^2)$ reflects the profit for producing only Mustangs (set $x = 0$ in (24)). Finally, the term $-0.01xy$, which is nonzero only if production levels x and y are both positive, might arise because the same fabricating equipment must be used in certain production steps, whether for Pintos or for Mustangs. It measures diseconomy of size produced by, for example, congested facilities.

In Figure 5.24 are plotted the level curves $P(x,y) = \text{const}$ in steps of 100,000 dollars per month. This can be a tedious process; fortunately, it can be executed by a suitably programmed computer. All points (x,y) on the same curve represent equally profitable modes of operation. Notice that the plant loses money in many operating states, those outside the break-even curve, where $P = 0$. Our goal is to locate the optimum feasible choice of production levels. We could try to do this by searching through the pattern of level curves in Figure 5.24, but evidently we would need a much more detailed set of level curves $P = c$ in the range $200 \leqslant c \leqslant 300$ thousand. Instead, let us see what we can learn by methods of Calculus.

Suppose we select an operating level at random, say $Q = (1500, 2000)$. Can we displace Q so as to increase our profit? The answer is simple once we calculate the first partial derivatives. Regarding y as a constant, we get

$$\frac{\partial P}{\partial x} = \frac{d}{dx}\{-900{,}000 + (500x - 0.1x^2) + (700y - 0.2y^2) - 0.01xy\}$$

$$= 500 - 0.2x - 0.01y \qquad (25)$$

Similarly

$$\frac{\partial P}{\partial y} = 700 - 0.4y - 0.01x \qquad (26)$$

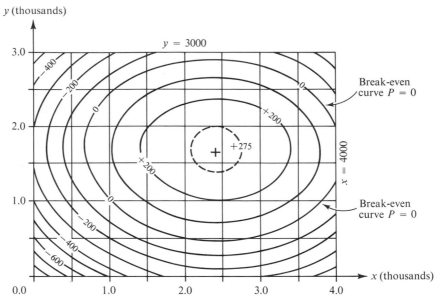

Figure 5.24
Level curves for the profit function $P(x,y) = -900{,}000 + (500x - 0.1x^2) + (700y - 0.2y^2) - 0.01xy$. Curves are given in steps $\Delta P = 100{,}000$ except for the dashed curve $P = 275{,}000$ near the point of maximum profit, which is marked by a cross. $P = 0$ is the break-even curve; inside it the assembly plant makes a profit. The feasible set is the rectangle determined by $0 \leqslant x \leqslant 4000$ and $0 \leqslant y \leqslant 3000$. Its boundary consists of four line segments determined by the respective conditions $x = 0$, $x = 4000$, $y = 0$, and $y = 3000$, as shown.

At the point $Q = (1500,\ 2000)$ we get

$$\frac{\partial P}{\partial x}(Q) = 500 - 0.2(1500) - 0.01(2000) = 180 \text{ dollars per Pinto}$$

$$\frac{\partial P}{\partial y}(Q) = 700 - 0.4(2000) - 0.01(1500) = -115 \text{ dollars per Mustang}$$

Formula (22) tells us that

$$\Delta P \approx \frac{\partial P}{\partial x}(Q) \cdot \Delta x = 180\,\Delta x \qquad \text{for small increments } \Delta x$$

if we move from $Q = (1500, 2000)$ to $Q' = (1500 + \Delta x, 2000)$. Obviously we may increase profits somewhat by increasing Pinto production (Δx positive), leaving Mustang production fixed. On the other hand, if we leave Pinto production fixed, it pays to *decrease* Mustang production (take $\Delta y < 0$). In fact, if we move to $Q' =$

$(1500, 2000 + \Delta y)$ we get

$$\Delta P \approx \frac{\partial P}{\partial y}(Q) \cdot \Delta y = -115\,\Delta y \qquad \text{for small increments } \Delta y$$

so that $\Delta P > 0$ if $\Delta y < 0$. Clearly, maximum feasible profit is not achieved at $Q = (1500, 2000)$. By moving Q in suitable directions we may increase the value of P while remaining within the feasible set.

The partial derivatives $\partial P/\partial x$ and $\partial P/\partial y$ of a profit function are often referred to as the **marginal profits** with respect to x and y (recall the terminology introduced in Section 2.6). They depend on the location of the point Q. For example, if we compare $Q = (1500, 2000)$ with another point $Q^* = (3000, 1000)$, we get different marginal profits with respect to x:

$$\frac{\partial P}{\partial x}(Q) = 180 \qquad \frac{\partial P}{\partial x}(Q^*) = -110$$

If we move away from Q^* while keeping Mustang production fixed, it pays to *decrease* Pinto production; starting from Q it pays to increase Pinto production, as we have seen.

The formula

$$\Delta P \approx \frac{\partial P}{\partial x}(Q) \cdot \Delta x + \frac{\partial P}{\partial y}(Q) \cdot \Delta y \qquad \text{for small increments } \Delta x \text{ and } \Delta y$$

applies to any base point Q. So long as *at least one* of the partial derivatives $\partial P/\partial x$ and $\partial P/\partial y$ is nonzero, we may displace Q in some directions to increase the value of P and in other directions to decrease the value of P. Thus, profits cannot achieve a maximum or minimum at Q. By default, the only points within the feasible set at which a maximum or minimum value can be achieved are those for which

$$\frac{\partial P}{\partial x} = 0 \quad \text{and} \quad \frac{\partial P}{\partial y} = 0 \quad \text{simultaneously} \tag{27}$$

These are called the **critical points** for the function $P(x,y)$.

There is one other possibility: a maximum or minimum value can be achieved on the boundary of the feasible domain. Maxima and minima located on the boundary do not necessarily signal their presence by the appearance of a critical point. There is a simple reason for this exception to the discussion in the preceding paragraph. At a boundary point $Q = (a,b)$ we are not permitted to move in *any* direction we wish; we are only allowed to move Q so that $Q' = (a + \Delta x, b + \Delta y)$ remains within the feasible set. Suppose we are looking for maxima. Even if the partial derivatives should be nonzero at a boundary point Q, we might not be allowed to displace Q in the directions suggested by formula (22) that would increase $P(x,y)$. Hence a boundary point can be a maximum without being a critical point. Maxima occurring *within* the feasible set, away from the boundary, must reveal their presence by satisfying the critical-point conditions (27).

We find the critical points for $P(x,y)$ by solving the simultaneous equations in x and y

$$\frac{\partial P}{\partial x} = 500 - 0.2x - 0.01y = 0$$

$$\frac{\partial P}{\partial y} = 700 - 0.4y - 0.01x = 0$$

Routine substitution of the second equation into the first gives

$$x = 2415 \text{ Pintos per month} \qquad y = 1689 \text{ Mustangs per month}$$

as the only critical point. Even if we defined $P(x,y)$ throughout the xy-plane by formula (24), this would be the only critical point. This point $Q^* = (2415, 1689)$, marked by a cross in Figure 5.24, lies within the feasible set. The value of P there is $P(2415, 1689) = 294$ thousand dollars per month. From the pattern of level curves it is clear that the profit decreases from this value no matter which way we move from Q^*. This point is the solution to our problem, unless a higher value of profit happens to occur on the boundary of the feasible set, where its presence might go undetected when we locate the critical points of $P(x,y)$. There are various ways to see that the values on the boundary of the rectangular feasible set in Figure 5.24 do not exceed the value at Q^*. We shall discuss systematic methods in Section 5.12. For now, we can examine the level curves. Clearly $P \leqslant 100,000$ on the boundary; in fact P is negative on most parts of the boundary, and $P > 0$ only on a small piece of the vertical boundary segment on the right-hand side of the rectangle.

Exercises

●1. Calculate the numerical values of the marginal profits $\partial P/\partial x$ and $\partial P/\partial y$ in (24) at production levels

$$Q_1 = (3000, 2500) \qquad Q_2 = (2000, 2500)$$

For each point calculate the (approximate) change ΔP in profit if

(*i*) Pinto production is increased by one car per month ($\Delta x = 1$), while Thunderbird production is kept constant.

(*ii*) Thunderbird production is increased by one car per month ($\Delta y = 1$), while Pinto production is kept constant.

●2. Suppose the profit $P(x,y)$ for an automobile-assembly plant is given by

$$P(x,y) = -900,000 + (500x - 0.1x^2) + (700y - 0.2y^2)$$

for production levels $0 \leqslant x \leqslant 4000$ and $0 \leqslant y \leqslant 3000$. (We have dropped the term involving xy in (24).) Find the marginal profits with respect to x and to y at point $Q = (1500, 2000)$. Find all critical points for the function $P(x,y)$.

●3. In the optimization case study of this section, suppose that a strike affecting a Pinto parts supplier limits Pinto production to at most 1500 month ($0 \leqslant x \leqslant 1500$), while Mustang production is unaffected. Use Figure 5.24 to estimate the point of maximum profit within the new feasible set: $0 \leqslant x \leqslant 1500, 0 \leqslant y \leqslant 3000$. Is this point a critical point for the function $P(x,y)$? Does it lie on the boundary of the feasible set? What is the maximum value achieved by P?

●4. Repeat Exercise 3, assuming now that Pinto production is unaffected, $0 \leqslant x \leqslant 4000$, but that Mustang production is limited to at most 1000 per month ($0 \leqslant y \leqslant 1000$). Estimate the point of maximum profit within the new feasible set: $0 \leqslant x \leqslant 4000, 0 \leqslant y \leqslant 1000$. Is this a critical point for $P(x,y)$?

●5. Examine the level curves in Figure 5.24 and verify that $P(x,y)$ never gets larger than $100,000 on the boundary of the feasible set. Find

(*i*) the lowest value achieved by P on the boundary. Where?

(*ii*) the highest value achieved by P on the boundary. Where?

5.10   Maxima and Minima for Arbitrary Functions

Our analysis of the profit function in the last section was based on the approximation formula (23)

$$f(x + \Delta x, \, y + \Delta y) \approx f(Q) + \frac{\partial f}{\partial x}(Q)\,\Delta x + \frac{\partial f}{\partial y}(Q)\,\Delta y$$

where $Q = (x,y)$, and Δx and Δy are small increments. This formula is valid for functions with well-behaved partial derivatives. We shall not make a precise technical definition of "well-behaved," an allusion to continuity of the partial derivatives.* It suffices to say that most functions arising in practice have this property, so we may apply the approximation principle (23) freely.

---

* We have not discussed continuity of functions of several variables. The definitions are rather technical; and since functions that arise in practice are almost invariably continuous, with continuous partial derivatives, this topic may safely be left for advanced courses. Intuitively, $z = f(x,y)$ is continuous if its graph could be modeled by deforming a flat sheet of elastic material without introducing any tears.

Definition   Given a function $z = f(x,y)$, we say that a point Q in its domain of definition is

    (*i*) a **relative maximum** if $f(Q) \geqslant f(Q')$ for all points Q' in the domain of definition which lie near Q. That is, the value of f is as large at Q as it is at any *nearby* point where f is defined.

    (*ii*) an **absolute maximum** if $f(Q) \geqslant f(Q')$ for all points Q' in the domain of definition, whether they lie close to Q or not.

Relative (absolute) minima are defined similarly: $f(Q) \leqslant f(Q')$ for all nearby points (all points) Q' in the domain of definition. If a point Q is either a maximum or a minimum, we shall sometimes combine these two possibilities by calling Q an **extremum** for f.

Near a relative maximum or minimum the graph of $z = f(x,y)$ has the shape shown in Figure 5.25. Clearly an absolute maximum is a relative maximum, though the reverse need not be true; likewise for minima. A function may achieve its extreme values on the boundary of the domain of definition (insofar as f is actually defined on this boundary) or at points interior to this domain. An **interior point** Q is one such that all points near Q lie within the domain of definition. Some possible locations of extrema are shown in Figure 5.26. There is an absolute minimum on the boundary of the domain of definition (point A); the absolute maximum is achieved at an interior point B. In addition, there are relative extrema that are not absolute extrema. For example, the value of f at the relative minimum C is lower than all nearby values, but higher than the value at the corner point A.

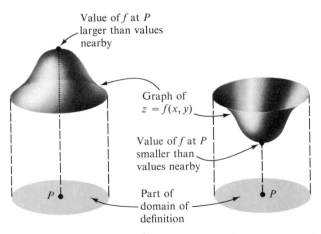

Relative maximum at P Relative minimum at P

Figure 5.25
Shape of the graph of f near a relative maximum or minimum.

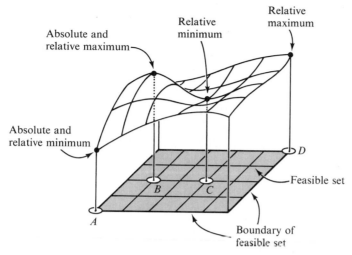

Figure 5.26
A surface exhibiting various kinds of maxima and minima. The shaded
rectangle (feasible set) lies in the xy-plane; its boundary consists of four
line segments. Here A is an absolute minimum occurring on the
boundary of the feasible set; B is an absolute maximum interior to the
feasible set; C is a relative minimum that is not an absolute minimum
(compare it with A); D, on the boundary, is a relative maximum that is
not an absolute maximum (compare it with B). The curved lines on the
surface lie over the straight lines $x =$ const and $y -$ const inscribed in
the feasible set.

The **critical points** of a function $z = f(x,y)$ are those points Q for which

$$\frac{\partial f}{\partial x}(Q) = 0 \quad \text{and} \quad \frac{\partial f}{\partial y}(Q) = 0 \quad \text{simultaneously}$$

The extrema lying interior to the domain of definition of f must appear among the
critical points of f. This observation is our basic tool for locating the extrema of f.

Extrema and Critical Points   If $f(x,y)$ has well-behaved partial derivatives, every
extremal point interior to the domain of definition is a critical point.

Proof   If Q is an interior point, all small displacements keep us within the domain
of definition of f. If Q is *not* a critical point, at least one of the partial derivatives
$\partial f/\partial x(Q)$ and $\partial f/\partial y(Q)$ is nonzero. By formula (23)

$$f(x + \Delta x, y + \Delta y) \approx f(Q) + \frac{\partial f}{\partial x}(Q) \cdot \Delta x + \frac{\partial f}{\partial y}(Q) \cdot \Delta y$$

there must be points Q' near Q where $f(Q') > f(Q)$, and other nearby points Q'' where $f(Q'') < f(Q)$. Therefore Q cannot be a relative maximum or minimum. By default, any extremum interior to the domain of definition must be a critical point.

The critical points may include points that are neither maxima nor minima. In searching for the extrema of f, we must locate the critical points, then sort out the honest extrema from the imposters. We have already encountered this problem for functions of one variable: consider $x = 0$ for $y = f(x) = x^3$. A typical example for two variables is the function

$$z = f(x,y) = 1 - \frac{1}{2}x^2 + \frac{1}{2}y^2$$

The surface $z = f(x,y)$ is "saddle shaped" above $Q = (0, 0)$, which is a critical point since $\partial f/\partial x = -x$ and $\partial f/\partial y = y$ are both zero there (see Figure 5.27). If we move away from Q along the y-axis, the value of f (height of the surface) increases; however, the value of f decreases if we move away from Q along the x-axis. Thus $Q = (0, 0)$ is not an extremum, although it is a critical point.

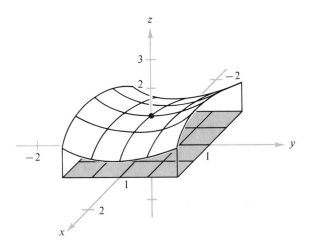

Figure 5.27
A critical point for $z = f(x,y) = 1 - \frac{1}{2}x^2 + \frac{1}{2}y^2$ that is neither a relative maximum nor a relative minimum. This is only part of the whole surface, which is defined for all x and y. The curves on the surface, which reveal its shape, lie above the lines $x = $ const (for $x = -1.0, -0.5, 0.0, 0.5, 1.0$) and $y = $ const (for $y = -1.0, -0.5, 0.0, 0.5, 1.0$) in the xy-plane. The critical point occurs at the origin $(0, 0)$, which is hidden from view by the surface. The solid dot on the surface lies over the origin.

How may we distinguish the critical points that are relative extrema from those that are not? The answer depends on what sort of computational tools are available. With a computer at our disposal, we might program it to calculate values $f(x + \Delta x, y + \Delta y)$ at 100 randomly selected points $Q' = (x + \Delta x, y + \Delta y)$ near $Q = (x,y)$, and compare these with the value at Q. The computer would report one of the following outcomes:

(i) $f(Q') \geqslant f(Q)$ for all nearby points.

(ii) $f(Q') \leqslant f(Q)$ for all nearby points.

(iii) Mixed outcome: say $f(Q') > f(Q)$ for 37 test points, $f(Q') = f(Q)$ for 4 points, and $f(Q') < f(Q)$ for 59 points.

We would be certain that Q was not an extremum in Case (iii), and reasonably certain that Q was a relative minimum in Case (i), a relative maximum in Case (ii). If our only aid is paper and pencil we must resort to studying the second partial derivatives of f and their geometric significance. Here are reasonably effective conditions for testing critical points with second partial derivatives:

Test for Extrema   Suppose that f has well-behaved partial derivatives of first and second order. Let $Q = (a,b)$ be a critical point for f, so that $\partial f/\partial x(Q) = 0$ and $\partial f/\partial y(Q) = 0$. To test Q for an extremum, we form the "discriminant"

$$D_Q = \frac{\partial^2 f}{\partial x^2}(Q) \frac{\partial^2 f}{\partial y^2}(Q) - \left(\frac{\partial^2 f}{\partial x \, \partial y}(Q)\right)^2 \tag{28}$$

out of the second partial derivatives.

(i) If $D_Q < 0$, then Q is not an extremum for f.

(ii) If $D_Q > 0$ and $\dfrac{\partial^2 f}{\partial x^2}(Q) > 0$, then Q is a relative minimum for f.

(iii) If $D_Q > 0$ and $\dfrac{\partial^2 f}{\partial x^2}(Q) < 0$, then Q is a relative maximum for f.

If $D_Q = 0$, the test gives no information about Q.

We shall not prove the test here, but we shall illustrate applications of it below. For a simple example, the profit function $P(x,y) = -900{,}000 + (500x - 0.1x^2) + (700y - 0.2y^2) - 0.01xy$ of Section 5.9 has

$$\frac{\partial P}{\partial x} = 500 - 0.2x - 0.01y \qquad \frac{\partial P}{\partial y} = 700 - 0.4y - 0.01x$$

$$\frac{\partial^2 P}{\partial x^2} = -0.2 \qquad \frac{\partial^2 P}{\partial x \, \partial y} = -0.01 \qquad \frac{\partial^2 P}{\partial y^2} = -0.4$$

(second derivatives are constant functions). At the one and only critical point $Q = (2415, 1689)$ we have

$$\frac{\partial^2 P}{\partial x^2}(Q) = -0.2 < 0 \quad \text{and} \quad D_Q = (-0.2)(-0.4) - (-0.01)^2 = 0.0799 > 0$$

Thus Q is a relative maximum for $P(x,y)$. Earlier, we determined this by examining the pattern of level curves $P(x,y) = $ const. But this is more or less the same as asking a computer to calculate nearby values—we used a computer to plot the level curves in the first place! By comparison, we need only do a little algebra to do the second-derivative test. The next example illustrates some algebraic techniques for locating the critical points; testing them is routine.

Example 14   Find all relative minima for $f(x,y) = x^3 - x + y^2 + xy$.

Solution   First we find the critical points, the choices of x and y that simultaneously satisfy the equations

$$0 = \frac{\partial f}{\partial x} = 3x^2 + y - 1$$

$$(29)$$

$$0 = \frac{\partial f}{\partial y} = x + 2y$$

Taking the simpler equation, we see that $x = -2y$ for any critical point. Substituting the condition $x = -2y$ (hence $x^2 = 4y^2$) into the first equation, we get

$$12y^2 + y - 1 = 0$$

Now solve for y by using the quadratic equation

$$y = \frac{-1 \pm \sqrt{1 + 48}}{24}$$

so that

$$y = -\frac{1}{3} \quad \text{or} \quad y = \frac{1}{4}$$

Thus if (x,y) is a critical point we must have $y = -1/3$ or $y = 1/4$. Substitute these y values into second equation (29) to get the corresponding x values $x = 2/3$ or $x = -1/2$;

there are just two critical points:

$$P = \left(\frac{2}{3}, -\frac{1}{3}\right) \qquad Q = \left(-\frac{1}{2}, \frac{1}{4}\right)$$

Next, calculate the second partial derivatives

$$\frac{\partial^2 f}{\partial x^2} = 6x \qquad \frac{\partial^2 f}{\partial y^2} = 2 \qquad \frac{\partial^2 f}{\partial x\, \partial y} = 1$$

and apply the second-derivative test. At $P = (2/3, -1/3)$ we get

$$D_P = 4(2) - 1^2 = 7 > 0 \quad \text{and} \quad \frac{\partial^2 f}{\partial x^2}(P) = 6\left(\frac{2}{3}\right) = 4 > 0$$

so P is a relative minimum. At $Q = (-1/2, 1/4)$ we get

$$D_Q = -3(2) - 1^2 = -7 < 0$$

so Q is not a relative extremum, and $P = (2/3, -1/3)$ is the only relative minimum for f. Neither point is a relative maximum; there are no relative maxima.

In certain applications *relative* extrema are precisely what we want to find. For example, if the coordinates x and y describe the state (position) of a mechanical system, and $f(x,y)$ the energy of the system, then the relative minima are of great interest because they are the states of the system that are **stable**. The system will return to such a state if perturbed slightly. This notion of stability also applies to chemical, ecological, and economic systems. In other cases we seek the *absolute* extrema of f, as when we want to find the most profitable production levels for a manufacturing plant. Although the absolute extrema must appear among the relative extrema, it can be very difficult to sort them out, or even to decide if there are any absolute extrema at all. The rest of the chapter is devoted to these problems.

Exercises

●1. Figure 5.27 shows the graph of $f(x,y) = 1 - \frac{1}{2}x^2 + \frac{1}{2}y^2$ if the domain of definition is taken to be the square $-1 \leqslant x \leqslant 1$, $-1 \leqslant y \leqslant 1$ (shaded). By examining the figure, classify the following points as absolute extrema, relative extrema, or nondescript. Which are boundary points?

    (*i*) $Q = (1, 0)$ (*ii*) $Q = (1, 1)$

(iii) $Q = (1, -1)$ *(v)* $Q = (\frac{1}{2}, \frac{1}{2})$

(iv) $Q = (0, 1)$ *(vi)* $Q = (0, 0)$

●2. Find all critical points for the function $f(x,y) = x^3 - x + y^2$. Use the second-derivative test to locate the relative maxima and minima. What are the values of f at these extrema?

●3. Find all critical points for $f(x,y) = 2x^3 + 3x^2 - 12x + y^2 - y + 2$. Test the critical points; make a list of all relative maxima and relative minima. Are there any critical points for which the second-derivative test fails to provide information? Are there any critical points that are not relative extrema?

●4. Find all critical points for the following functions $f(x,y)$:

(i) $x^2 + xy + y^2$ *(vi)* $4x + 3y + y^2$

(ii) $x^2 + 4xy + y^2 - x$ *(vii)* $\dfrac{1}{\sqrt{1 + x^2 + y^2}}$

(iii) $3xy - 2y^2 + y$ *(viii)* $x^2 + 2xy + y^2$

(iv) $\dfrac{1}{x} + \dfrac{1}{y} + xy$ *(ix)* $xe^{-(x^2+y^2)/2}$

(v) $470x + 550y - 0.10x^2 - 0.15y^2 - 0.04xy$

HINT: In *(viii)* there are infinitely many critical points. In *(ix)* use the fact that $e^a \neq 0$ for every real number a.

●5. Find all critical points and test for relative maxima and minima.

(i) $x^2 - 2y^2$ *(iv)* $y^2 + 3x^4 - 4x^3 - 12x^2 + 24$

(ii) $x^2 + y^2$ *(v)* $\dfrac{1 + x}{1 - y}$

(iii) $x^3 - xy - y^3$ *(vi)* $x^2y - xy^2 - x$

●6. The origin $P = (0, 0)$ is a critical point for the function $f(x,y) = x^3 - 2y^3$. Test the values of f at nearby points of the form $Q = (0 + \Delta x, 0 + \Delta y) = (\Delta x, \Delta y)$, taking $\Delta x = \pm 0.1$ and $\Delta y = \pm 0.1$. Is P a relative maximum? relative minimum?

5.11 Optimization Problems: No Boundary

The task of finding the absolute maximum or minimum of a function is commonly called an **optimization problem**. There are two parts to any optimization problem. First we must decide whether there are any absolute extrema at all; then we examine critical points in order to locate the extrema. Usually we do not give too much thought to the existence question. In applied problems, it is usually obvious from the start that the desired absolute maximum or minimum exists, unless there has been a serious mistake in posing the problem. For arbitrary functions $z = f(x,y)$ not connected with an intuitively meaningful application, there might not be any absolute extrema at all (see Example 17 below.) In general the existence question can be very difficult to resolve, requiring techniques that are beyond the scope of this book.

Once we are assured that absolute extrema actually exist, by appeal either to advanced methods or to intuition based on the problem at hand, there are straight-forward procedures for locating them. The extrema can appear either at points interior to the feasible set (among the critical points) or on the boundary. In practice the absolute extrema we seek frequently do lie on the boundary, giving us a **boundary extremum**. The profit function in Example 7 (Section 5.5) had an absolute maximum on the boundary of the feasible set. Indeed, in that problem there were *no* critical points interior to the feasible set, hence no interior extrema. Looking for extrema on the boundary can be a nasty, but important and unavoidable task. We reserve discussion of boundary extrema for the following three sections; we shall conclude this section with a few examples in which the boundary causes no trouble. By the nature of the problems the boundary points are not part of the feasible set, so that boundary extrema cannot occur.

Optimization Procedure: No Boundary   Suppose that $f(x,y)$ has well-behaved first partial derivatives, and that the feasible set consists entirely of interior points (no feasible boundary points). If an absolute maximum is known to exist, it may be found as follows:

STEP 1   Locate all critical points $Q_1, \ldots, Q_k$ in the feasible set and tabulate the values $f(Q_1), \ldots, f(Q_k)$ of f at these points.

STEP 2   Compare the values listed in Step 1; the largest value in the list is the absolute maximum value for f.

A similar procedure works for absolute minima, if they are known to exist.

The validity of the procedure is almost obvious; the main difficulty is in demon-strating that absolute extrema actually exist, so that we may legitimately use the procedure. If we are not sure of the existence of absolute extrema, we usually locate the critical points and apply the second-derivative test to each to learn what we can about absolute maxima and minima (see Example 17).

Example 15   By advanced methods one can show that the function

$$f(x,y) = 10 - (x-1)^2 - 20\left(y - \frac{1}{2}\right)^2 - xy$$

defined for all x and y actually achieves an absolute maximum. Given this informa-tion, locate the absolute maximum and determine the corresponding maximum value for f.

Solution   The domain of definition consists of the whole coordinate plane; there are no boundary points. It is convenient to multiply out the terms in f to get $f(x,y) = 4 - x^2 + 2x - 20y^2 + 20y - xy$. Then

$$\frac{\partial f}{\partial x} = -2x - y + 2 \qquad \frac{\partial f}{\partial y} = -x - 40y + 20$$

The simultaneous equations locating the critical points

$$0 = \frac{\partial f}{\partial x} = -2x - y + 2 \quad \text{and} \quad 0 = \frac{\partial f}{\partial y} = -x - 40y + 20$$

have just one solution, namely $Q = (-0.760, 0.481)$. There f has the value $f(-0.760, 0.481) = 6.888$. Since there are no other critical points, there is nothing to be done in Step 2. Hence, the absolute maximum must occur at Q.

There is no absolute minimum for this function. There aren't even any *relative* minima. If there were, they would appear among the critical points; but Q, a maximum, is the only critical point. How does the function avoid achieving a minimum? The answer is that $f(x,y)$ takes on larger and larger negative values as (x,y) moves away from the origin in any direction. Given any point $P = (x,y)$, there are always other points where f has lower (more negative) values, so no point can be an absolute minimum. This example shows why absolute extrema often fail to exist: $f(P)$ may take on larger and larger positive or negative values as $P = (x,y)$ moves around within the feasible set in a suitable way.

In the following example it is intuitively obvious that the absolute minimum we seek actually exists. Thus we may apply the optimization procedure described above.

Example 16   A closed rectangular box is to contain 15 cubic feet. Find the dimensions that yield the least possible surface area for the box. If the cost of fabricating a box of a given volume is proportional to its surface area, these dimensions give the most economical shape for the rectangular box.

Solution   Let l = length, w = width, and h = height, measured in feet. Since the volume is fixed

$$V = lwh = 15 \text{ cubic feet} \tag{30}$$

these three variables are not independent. We may use equation (30) to express one of them, say h, in terms of the others. If l and w are varied independently, we always get a box of the correct volume if we set $h = 15/lw$. For any choice of l and w the surface area of the corresponding box (six sides in all) is a function of l and w:

$$A(l,w) = 2lw + 2lh + 2hw = 2lw + 2l\left(\frac{15}{lw}\right) + 2\left(\frac{15}{lw}\right)w = 2lw + \frac{30}{w} + \frac{30}{l} \quad (31)$$

The feasible choices of l and w (domain of definition of A) are $l > 0$ and $w > 0$, indicated by the shaded region in Figure 5.28. This region is bounded by the lines on which $l = 0$ and $w = 0$ respectively. If either $l = 0$ or $w = 0$, we end up dividing by zero in (31), so the area function cannot be defined on the boundary. The reason for this is also clear geometrically: if one dimension is zero, giving us a "degenerate" box, no adjustment of the other dimensions can possibly give a volume of 15 cubic feet. Since $A(l,w)$ is not defined on the boundary, the absolute minimum must occur at an interior point.

Next we calculate the partial derivatives and find the critical points:

$$\frac{\partial A}{\partial l} = 2w - \frac{30}{l^2} \qquad \frac{\partial A}{\partial w} = 2l - \frac{30}{w^2} \qquad \text{for all } l > 0 \text{ and } w > 0$$

These are simultaneously zero when

$$2w - \frac{30}{l^2} = 0 \quad \text{and} \quad 2l - \frac{30}{w^2} = 0 \qquad (32)$$

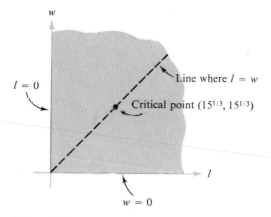

Figure 5.28
The feasible set for the area function $A(l,w)$ to be minimized in Example 16. The boundary consists of the two lines where $w = 0$ or $l = 0$. The function is not defined on these boundary lines, so the absolute minimum must be a critical point interior to the feasible set.

From the second equation we get $l = 15/w^2$. Substituting this into the first equation, we get

$$0 = 2w - \frac{30}{\left(\frac{15}{w^2}\right)^2} = 2w - \frac{2w^4}{15} \quad \text{or} \quad 2w\left(1 - \frac{w^3}{15}\right) = 0$$

This product can equal zero only if one of the factors is zero. One possibility is $w = 0$, which does not correspond to a feasible point. The other case

$$\left(1 - \frac{w^3}{15}\right) = 0 \quad \text{yields} \quad w^3 = 15$$

or $w = 15^{1/3} = \sqrt[3]{15} \approx 2.465$. Finally, substitute this value of w into either of the equations (32) to get the corresponding value of $l = 15/w^2$, namely $l = 15^{1/3}$. We have located the one and only critical point in the feasible set, namely

$$w = 15^{1/3} \qquad l = 15^{1/3} \tag{33}$$

This critical point must be the absolute minimum we seek, since it is intuitively obvious that there is a minimum somewhere, and the critical point is the only possible candidate, by our remarks about extrema and critical points on p. 279. For the critical values of l and w in (33), the corresponding value of h is

$$h = \frac{15}{15^{1/3} \cdot 15^{1/3}} = 15 \cdot 15^{-2/3} = 15^{1/3}$$

so the most economical dimensions are $l = 15^{1/3}$, $w = 15^{1/3}$, and $h = 15^{1/3}$ if $V = 15$ cubic feet. These dimensions are equal, so the optimal box is a *cube*. In fact, this is true regardless of the volume V of the box, as might be expected. In the following example intuition is not much help in deciding whether absolute extrema exist; we therefore appeal to the second-derivative test.

Example 17   Find all relative maxima and minima of

$$f(x,y) = 1 - \frac{1}{2} x^2 + \frac{1}{2} y^2$$

defined for all x and y. Are there any absolute maxima or minima?

Solution   Part of the graph of $z = f(x,y)$ has been shown in Figure 5.27. Now

$$\frac{\partial f}{\partial x} = -x \qquad \frac{\partial f}{\partial y} = y$$

so that $(x, y) = (0, 0)$ (the origin) is the only critical point. Since

$$\frac{\partial^2 f}{\partial x^2} = -1 \qquad \frac{\partial^2 f}{\partial y^2} = 1 \qquad \frac{\partial^2 f}{\partial x \, \partial y} = 0$$

(constant functions), the discriminant is negative everywhere $(D_{(x,y)} = (-1)(1) - 0^2 = -1)$, and there are no relative extrema *anywhere* for this function. Obviously, then, there cannot be any absolute extrema. In particular, $P = (0, 0)$ (the origin) is neither a maximum nor a minimum. This conclusion is entirely compatible with Figure 5.27. The values of f become large positive as we move toward infinity along the y-axis, and become large negative as we move toward infinity along the x-axis. There is no point in the plane where f is larger (or smaller) than it is at all other points.

Exercises

•1. The function $f(x,y) = 10 + 4x - x^4 + 4y^3 - y^4$, defined for all x and y, has an absolute maximum. Find it.

•2. The function $f(x,y) = x^2 + x - xy + y^2$ has an absolute minimum. Find it.

•3. Show that the function $f(x,y) = x^2 - 3xy + y^2$ has neither an absolute maximum nor an absolute minimum in the entire xy-plane. HINT: Every absolute extremum is a relative extremum. Show that $f(x,y)$ has no relative extremum.

•4. The function $f(x,y) = x/(1 + x^2 + y^2)$ has an absolute maximum and an absolute minimum. Find these extrema. Calculate the maximum and minimum values of f.

•5. Find all critical points for $f(x,y) = x^2 - 12y^2 - 4y^3 + 3y^4$. One can show that f actually has an absolute minimum. Where is it located, and what is the minimum value of f?

•6. A rectangular box without a top is to contain 108 cubic feet. Find the dimensions that yield the lowest possible surface area for the box. ANSWER: Base dimensions $l = 6$ and $w = 6$; height $h = 3$. (Minimize $A = 2lh + 2wh + lw$ for $l > 0, w > 0, h > 0$.)

•7. Find the minimum value of the function

$$f(x,y) = (x - 1)^2 + (y - 1)^2 + x^2 + y^2$$

defined for all x and y. NOTE: This function arises in a geometric problem: $f(x,y) = s^2$ where s is the distance in three-dimensional space from the point $Q = (1, 1, 0)$ to an arbitrary point (x,y,z) on the surface $z = \sqrt{x^2 + y^2}$. (This surface happens to be a cone with vertex at $(0, 0, 0)$ whose axis is the positive z-axis.) The minimum of f is the minimum distance from Q to the surface. It should be intuitively obvious that there is such a minimum distance.

•8. The distance between two points $P_1 = (x_1, y_1, z_1)$ and $P_2 = (x_2, y_2, z_2)$ in three-dimensional space is

$$s = \sqrt{(x_2 - x_1)^2 + (y_2 - y_1)^2 + (z_2 - z_1)^2} = \sqrt{(\Delta x)^2 + (\Delta y)^2 + (\Delta z)^2}$$

Consider a typical point on the surface determined by $z = f(x,y) = \sqrt{y^2 + x + 10}$. Write out a formula in terms of x and y for the distance from $Q = (1, 2, 0)$ to a typical point on the surface (the z-coordinate is determined once x and y are given). Find

(*i*) the minimum distance from Q to the surface.

(*ii*) all three coordinates of the point on the surface closest to Q.

ANSWERS: $s(x,y) = \sqrt{x^2 - x + 2y^2 - 4y + 15}$; (*i*) minimum distance $s = \sqrt{51/2} \approx 3.571$ at $x = 1/2$, $y = 1$; (*ii*) $(1/2, 1, \sqrt{23/2}) = (1/2, 1, 3.39)$.

● 9. Minimize the function of three variables $f(x,y,z) = x^2 - 2xy + x + z^2$ on the plane determined by the equation $x + y + z = 1$. Reduce this to a minimization problem in two variables x and y by substituting $z = 1 - x - y$ into f. The resulting function of two variables is defined for all x and y. It can be shown that the desired minimum exists; you may assume this.

5.12   Boundary Extrema: Eliminating a Variable

Many problems involve a function f defined on a **bounded set** (one that does not extend out to infinity) that includes all its boundary points. In this special case, a theorem from advanced calculus guarantees that both the absolute maximum and the absolute minimum *always exist*. To locate these extrema we must examine separately the behavior of f at interior points (easy) and on the boundary of the feasible set (more troublesome), by carrying out the following steps.

Optimization Procedure: Bounded Feasible Set   Suppose that f has well-behaved first partial derivatives, and is defined on the interior and the boundary of a bounded set in the plane. Then f has both an absolute maximum and an absolute minimum. The following procedure locates the maximum; the minimum is located in the same way.

STEP 1   Locate all critical points $Q_1, \ldots, Q_k$ in the interior of the feasible set and tabulate the values $f(Q_1), \ldots, f(Q_k)$ of f at these points. Note the largest of these values.

STEP 2   Examine f on the boundary of the feasible set and determine where on the boundary f achieves its maximum value. Note the value of f at this point.

STEP 3   Compare the results of steps 1 and 2. The larger of these is the absolute maximum value of f on the whole feasible set.

Once again, there is no need to test the critical points. However, in order to carry out Step 2 we must find ways of locating the absolute extrema that occur on the boundary. In this section we shall describe the method of **eliminating a variable**. Other methods of finding boundary extrema will be taken up in the next two sections.

Quite often the boundary of the feasible set breaks up into a finite number of pieces, on each of which x and y are related by some algebraic identity (one of the constraints determining the feasible set). In Example 19 below we shall encounter the feasible set shown in Figure 5.29(a). The boundary consists of the three curves $C_1, C_2,$ and C_3 shown in (b); the interior points form the rest of the shaded region. Each curve is determined by an algebraic equation:

$$\text{Points } (x,y) \text{ on } C_1 \text{ satisfy } x = 0$$

$$\text{Points } (x,y) \text{ on } C_2 \text{ satisfy } y = 0$$

$$\text{Points } (x,y) \text{ on } C_3 \text{ satisfy } x = 2 - 2y^2$$

Suppose that $z = f(x,y)$ is a function defined on this feasible set. On each piece of the boundary we may use the appropriate identity to eliminate one of the variables and express f as a function of the remaining variable. For example, consider $f(x,y) = x + 4y^2 + 4xy + 1$. The boundary curve C_3 may be described as all points (x,y) such that

$$x = 2 - 2y^2 \quad \text{and} \quad 0 \leqslant y \leqslant 1$$

By substituting this identity into $f(x,y)$, we can describe f as a function of *one variable*, namely y:

$$f(x,y) = (2 - 2y^2) + 4y^2 + 4(2 - 2y^2)y + 1$$

$$= -8y^3 + 2y^2 + 8y + 3$$

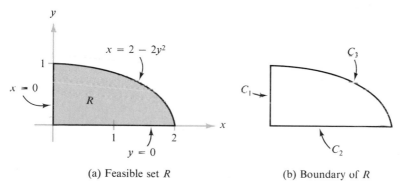

(a) Feasible set R (b) Boundary of R

Figure 5.29
In (a) is shown the feasible set R bounded by the curves $x = 0$, $y = 0$, and $x = 2 - 2y^2$. The curves $C_1, C_2,$ and C_3 form the boundary of R, as shown in (b).

for $0 \leqslant y \leqslant 1$. On C_1 and C_3 the substitutions are even simpler. For C_1, on which $x = 0$ and $0 \leqslant y \leqslant 1$, $f(x,y)$ becomes a function of y

$$f(x,y) = 0 + 4y^2 + 4(0)y + 1 = 4y^2 + 1 \qquad \text{for } 0 \leqslant y \leqslant 1$$

On C_2, $f(x,y)$ becomes a function of x

$$f(x,y) = x + 1 \qquad \text{for } 0 \leqslant x \leqslant 2$$

when we substitute $y = 0$.

As a result of this elimination process, on each piece of the boundary $f(x,y)$ becomes a function of *one variable* defined on some interval. If we wish to find the absolute maximum or minimum value of f on a piece of the boundary we may now apply the methods of Chapter 3 for functions of a single variable. We can then find the maximum (minimum) for the whole boundary by comparing the maximum (minimum) values on all the pieces.

Example 18   On the straight-line segment $2y + x = 5$, defined for $-3 \leqslant x \leqslant 2$, determine the absolute maximum and absolute minimum value of the function $f(x,y) = y^2 + x^2 + 4x + 4$.*

Solution   The feasible set for f is the line segment C shown in Figure 5.30. It has no interior points at all: the boundary is the segment itself. Thus Step 1 in the search procedure is irrelevant. On C we have $y = (5 - x)/2$ for $-3 \leqslant x \leqslant 2$. Substituting this into $f(x,y)$ we get a function of x

$$f(x) = \frac{1}{4}(5 - x)^2 + x^2 + 4x + 4 = \frac{5}{4}x^2 + \frac{3}{2}x + \frac{41}{4}$$

for $-3 \leqslant x \leqslant 2$. We can locate the absolute extrema by the methods of Section 3.4. First we calculate the derivative

$$\frac{df}{dx} = \frac{5}{2}x + \frac{3}{2}$$

This is zero when $5x + 3 = 0$ or $x = -3/5$. At this critical point f has the value $f(-3/5) = 49/5 = 9.8$. As in Section 3.4, we must also check the endpoint values;

---

* Here $f(x,y) = r^2$ where r is the distance from an arbitrary point $P = (x,y)$ to the point $Q = (-2, 0)$, since $r^2 = (x-(-2))^2 + (y - 0)^2 = y^2 + x^2 + 4x + 4$. We are, in effect, trying to determine the points *on the segment* closest to, or farthest from, the point $Q = (-2, 0)$ in Figure 5.30.

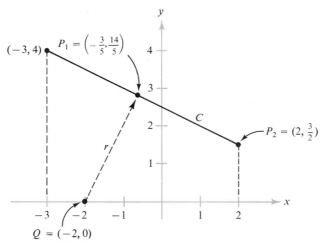

Figure 5.30
The function $f(x,y) = y^2 + x^2 + 4x + 4$, defined for all x and
y, gives r^2 where r is the distance from $Q = (-2, 0)$ to an
arbitrary point $P = (x,y)$ in the plane. If f is defined only for P
on the segment C determined by $2y + x = 5$, for $-3 \leqslant x \leqslant 2$,
then f gives the distance from Q to points on C. The absolute
minimum value of f on C is achieved at P_1 and the maximum at
P_2.

the values of f at the critical point and the endpoints $x = -3$ and $x = 2$ are

$$f(-3) = 17$$

$$f(-3/5) = \frac{49}{5} = 9.8$$

$$f(+2) = \frac{73}{4} = 18.25$$

The smallest value is 9.8, occurring at $x = -3/5$. This is the absolute minimum
on C. The absolute maximum occurs when $x = 2$. We locate the corresponding
points on C by substituting the values $x = -3/5$ and $x = 2$ into $y = (5 - x)/2$.
The minimum occurs at $P_1 = (-3/5, 14/5)$ and the maximum at the endpoint
$P_2 = (2, 3/2)$ as shown in Figure 5.30.

Example 19   Find the absolute maximum value of $f(x,y) = x + 4y^2 + 4xy + 1$
on the set shown in Figure 5.29(a) above.

Solution   First calculate the partial derivatives

$$\frac{\partial f}{\partial x} = 1 + 4y \qquad \frac{\partial f}{\partial y} = 8y + 4x$$

and locate the critical points interior to the set by solving the simultaneous equations

$$1 + 4y = 0 \qquad 8y + 4x = 0$$

Clearly $y = -1/4$, $x = 1/2$ is the only solution. It does not lie within the feasible set, and so may be discarded. This completes Step 1 of the search. In Step 2 we describe the pieces C_1, C_2, and C_3 of the boundary as follows:

$$C_1 \text{ is given by } x = 0, 0 \leqslant y \leqslant 1$$

$$C_2 \text{ is given by } y = 0, 0 \leqslant x \leqslant 2$$

$$C_3 \text{ is given by } x = 2 - 2y^2, 0 \leqslant y \leqslant 1$$

We must find the maximum value on each piece of the boundary (see Figure 5.31). On C_1, $f(x,y)$ reduces to a function of y

$$f(y) = f(0,y) = 0 + 4y^2 + 4(0)y + 1 = 4y^2 + 1 \qquad \text{for } 0 \leqslant y \leqslant 1$$

It is a routine exercise to show that the maximum value on $0 \leqslant y \leqslant 1$ is achieved when $y = 1$, at the point $Q_1 = (0, 1)$ on C_1, as shown in the figure. There the value of f is $f(Q_1) = f(0, 1) = 5$.

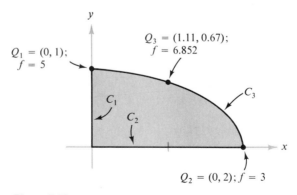

Figure 5.31
The boundary curves C_1, C_2, and C_3 in Example 19 and the location of the points Q_1, Q_2, and Q_3 where $f(x,y) = x + 4y^2 + 4xy + 1$ achieves its maximum value on each curve segment. The interior of the feasible set is shaded.

On C_2 we have $y = 0$, so that $f(x,y)$ is a function of x

$$f(x) = f(x,0) = x + 1 \qquad \text{for } 0 \leqslant x \leqslant 2$$

The maximum value of this linear function occurs at $x = 2$, corresponding to $Q_2 = (2, 0)$ on C_2, where the value of f is $f(Q_2) = f(2, 0) = 3$.

On C_3 we substitute $x = 2 - 2y^2$ to obtain a function of y, $f(y) = -8y^3 + 2y^2 + 8y + 3$, for $0 \leqslant y \leqslant 1$. Now

$$\frac{df}{dy} = -24y^2 + 4y + 8 = -4(3y - 2)(2y + 1)$$

Clearly $f'(y) = 0$ at $y = 2/3$ and $y = -1/2$; of these, $y = 2/3$ is the only feasible critical point (lying in the range $0 \leqslant y \leqslant 1$). Listing the values of f at this critical point and the endpoints $y = 0$ and $y = 1$, we get

$$f(0) = 3 \qquad f\left(\frac{2}{3}\right) = \frac{185}{27} = 6.852 \qquad f(1) = 5$$

Clearly the absolute maximum value on C_3 occurs when $y = 2/3$; then $x = 2 - 2y^2 = 10/9 = 1.11$ and the corresponding point on C_3 is $Q_3 = (1.11, 0.67)$, as shown in Figure 5.31. The value of f there is $f(Q_3) = 6.852$.

Comparing values of f at Q_1, Q_2, and Q_3, we see that the largest value of f on the whole boundary is achieved at Q_3, where $f = 6.852$. This completes Step 2. Since there were no critical points found inside the feasible set in Step 1, this is the absolute maximum value of f on the whole feasible set.

Finally, let us return to the case study of Section 5.9 and analyze it without resorting to a detailed plot of the level curves.

Example 20   Using calculus of several variables, find the absolute maximum value of the profit function $P(x,y) = -900,000 + (500x - 0.1x^2) + (700y - 0.2y^2) - 0.01xy$ on the feasible set $0 \leqslant x \leqslant 4000$, $0 \leqslant y \leqslant 3000$.

Solution   In Section 5.9 we located the only critical point for $P(x,y)$ lying within this rectangle. It occurs at $Q_0 = (2415, 1689)$, where $P(Q_0) = 294,000$. This finishes Step 1 of our search. The boundary segments shown in Figure 5.32 are described by the following conditions:

$$C_1 \text{ is given by } x = 0 \text{ and } 0 \leqslant y \leqslant 3000$$

$$C_2 \text{ is given by } y = 0 \text{ and } 0 \leqslant x \leqslant 4000$$

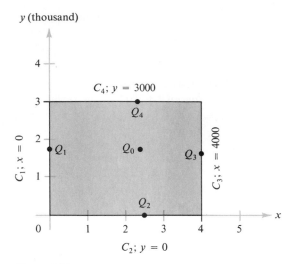

Figure 5.32
The boundary segments for the feasible set in Example 20.
The only interior critical point is Q_0. The maxima on the
individual boundary segments $C_1, \ldots, C_4$ are indicated
as $Q_1, \ldots, Q_4$.

$$C_3 \text{ is given by } x = 4000 \text{ and } 0 \leqslant y \leqslant 3000$$

$$C_4 \text{ is given by } y = 3000 \text{ and } 0 \leqslant x \leqslant 4000$$

On C_1, $P(x,y)$ becomes a function of y defined for $0 \leqslant y \leqslant 3000$; setting $x = 0$
we get

$$P(y) = P(0,y) = -900{,}000 + (700y - 0.2y^2)$$

with derivative

$$\frac{dP}{dy} = -0.4y + 700$$

Obviously $P'(y) = 0$ at $y = 1750$, where the value of P is $P = -287{,}500$. At the
endpoints $y = 0$ and $y = 3000$, the value of P is $P = -900{,}000$ and $P = -600{,}000$
respectively. The maximum thus occurs at $y = 1750$, which corresponds to the point
Q_1 on C_1, where $x = 0$ and $y = 1750$. There $P(Q_1) = P(0, 1750) = -287{,}500$.

Similarly, we may analyze $P(x,y)$ on the other boundary segments C_2, C_3, and
C_4. We shall only summarize the results of these calculations, which complete
Step 2 of our search:

$$\text{Maximum on } C_2 \text{ at } Q_2 = (2500, 0), \text{ where } P = -275{,}000$$

Maximum on C_3 at $Q_3 = (4000, 1650)$, where $P = 44,500$

Maximum on C_4 at $Q_4 = (2350, 3000)$, where $P = -47,750$

Now we carry out Step 3. Comparing the values $P(Q_0), \ldots, P(Q_4)$, we see that the largest value occurs at the interior point Q_0. The maximum profit occurs at Q_0, not at any boundary point. (This is precisely the conclusion we reached when we had a detailed set of level curves at our disposal.)

Exercises

● 1. Consider the line segment C determined by the conditions

$$y = \frac{5 - x}{2} \quad \text{for } -3 \leqslant x \leqslant 2$$

shown in Figure 5.30. Find the minimum distance from C to the point $P = (3, -1)$. Give both coordinates of the point Q on the segment lying closest to P.

● 2. Find the minimum distance from the line $2y + x = 5$ to the point $P = (3, -1)$. Give both coordinates of the point Q on the line lying closest to P.

● 3. Find the maximum and minimum values of the function $f(x,y) = xy$ on the line segment described by

$$x + 2y = 2 \quad \text{and} \quad 0 \leqslant x \leqslant 1.5$$

Sketch the segment, showing the locations of the extrema.

● 4. Find the maximum and minimum values of the function $f(x,y) = x^2 y^2$ on the half-ellipse (Figure 5.33) determined by

$$x^2 + 4y^2 = 4 \quad \text{and} \quad -1 \leqslant y \leqslant +1$$

Give both coordinates of the extrema.

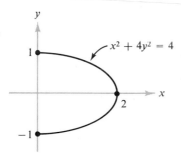

Figure 5.33
The half-ellipse described in Exercise 4.

● 5. Find the maximum value of $f(x,y) = x^2 + y^2$ on the triangular region bounded by the lines $x = 0$, $y = 0$, and $x + 2y = 2$. Make a rough sketch of the region and show the location of the maximum. NOTE: $x^2 + y^2 = r^2$ where r is the distance from the origin to a point $P = (x,y)$.

● 6. Find the minimum and maximum values of $f(x,y) = x^2 - 4x + y^2 - 4y + 8$ subject to the set of constraints $x \geqslant 0$, $y \geqslant 0$, $3x + 2y \leqslant 6$. Sketch the feasible set, showing the extrema.

● 7. Find the maximum value of $f(x,y) = x^2 + 2x + 1 + y^2$ on the square determined by $0 \leqslant x \leqslant 1$ and $0 \leqslant y \leqslant 1$. NOTE: Geometrically, f gives r^2 where r is the distance from $P = (x,y)$ to the fixed point $Q = (-1, 0)$.

● 8. Maximize the profit function $P(x,y) = -1000 + 45x - 0.1x^2 + 30y - 0.05y^2 - 0.1xy$ on the feasible set $0 \leqslant x \leqslant 200$, $0 \leqslant y \leqslant 200$.

● 9. Maximize the profit function $P(x,y) = -1000 + 45x + 30y - 0.3xy$ on the feasible set $0 \leqslant x \leqslant 100$, $0 \leqslant y \leqslant 50$.

●10. Postal regulations limit the size of a parcel-post package according to the following formula

$$h + g = \text{height} + \text{girth} \leqslant 100 \text{ inches}$$

where girth $=$ perimeter of the base (sum of 4 edges). Find the maximum possible volume of a rectangular parcel-post package with a square base. NOTE: h and g also satisfy the obvious constraints $h \geqslant 0$ and $g \geqslant 0$.

11. Repeat Exercise 10 to find the maximum volume of a cylindrical parcel-post package (circular base).

5.13   Lagrange Multipliers

Finding extrema of a function $f(x,y)$ on the boundary of a feasible set usually reduces to finding extrema when the variables x and y are obliged to satisfy some constraint equation

$$g(x,y) = 0 \tag{34}$$

that describes part of the boundary. Thus f is defined on a curve determined by the equation $g(x,y) = 0$, and we seek the extrema of f on this curve. One approach (Section 5.12) is to solve the constraint equation (34), expressing one variable in terms of the other. This allows us to eliminate one variable in $f(x,y)$ and yields an elementary one-variable extremum problem. Another approach, the method of **Lagrange multipliers**, involves introducing an extra independent variable λ. This procedure has several advantages, outlined below, but one disadvantage. If the curve on which $g(x,y) = 0$ is unbounded (extends out to infinity), the absolute extremum we seek might not exist. If it exists the method of Lagrange multipliers can locate it, but if it does not exist the method does not apply. Usually we rely on intuition to determine the existence of extrema.

Method of Lagrange Multipliers   Suppose $f(x,y)$ has well-behaved first partial derivatives, and we wish to find the absolute maximum of f on the set of points that satisfy a constraint equation $g(x,y) = 0$. If the absolute maximum we seek actually exists, its location may be found as follows (similar methods apply for minima):

STEP 1   Form a new function $F(x,y,\lambda)$ with three independent variables x, y, λ

$$F(x,y,\lambda) = f(x,y) - \lambda \cdot g(x,y)$$

This new function is defined for all values of x, y, λ; its variables are not subject to constraints.

STEP 2   Find the critical points of $F(x,y,\lambda)$. These are the points $P = (x,y,\lambda)$ for which

$$\frac{\partial F}{\partial x}(x,y,\lambda) = 0 \qquad \frac{\partial F}{\partial y}(x,y,\lambda) = 0 \qquad \frac{\partial F}{\partial \lambda}(x,y,\lambda) = 0$$

Tabulate the coordinates $P_1 = (x_1,y_1,\lambda_1), \ldots, P_k = (x_k,y_k,\lambda_k)$ of these critical points.

STEP 3   Tabulate the points in the xy-plane $Q_1 = (x_1,y_1), \ldots, Q_k = (x_k,y_k)$ given by the first two coordinates of the critical points $P_1, \ldots, P_k$. These automatically satisfy the constraint equation $g(x,y) = 0$.

STEP 4   Compare values $f(Q_1), \ldots, f(Q_k)$ of $f(x,y)$ at these points. The largest is the absolute maximum value of f on the curve $g(x,y) = 0$.

The partial derivatives of a function of three variables such as $F(x,y,\lambda)$ are computed in the usual way. To get $\partial F/\partial x$, treat all other variables as constants and differentiate with respect to x; similarly for the partials $\partial F/\partial y$ and $\partial F/\partial \lambda$.

The point of this procedure is to convert a two-variable extremum problem with a constraint $g(x,y) = 0$ to an extremum problem with one more variable but no constraint. In Step 2 we search for the critical points of $F(x,y,\lambda)$ without subjecting x, y, or λ to constraints. The method of Lagrange multipliers (adding a variable) and the method of elimination (removing a variable) both have the same goal. The Lagrange-multiplier method has the advantage that we need not solve the equation $g(x,y) = 0$ for one variable in terms of the other. This equation can be virtually unsolvable if $g(x,y)$ is even moderately complicated. Furthermore, the Lagrange-multiplier method can be generalized to handle functions (and constraints) involving more than two variables. On the other hand, endpoint conditions are a little troublesome with this method. The substitution method, when it works, handles these difficulties easily.

Example 21   By using Lagrange multipliers, find the minimum value of $f(x,y) = y^2 + x^2 + 4x + 4$ on the line described by the equation $2y + x = 5$. (In Example 18 we explained the geometric meaning of f; it is intuitively obvious that the minimum exists. In Example 18 we sought the extrema on a finite segment of the line; here we seek the minimum value on the whole line.)

Solution   Writing the constraint equation in the form $g(x,y) = 0$, we get

$$0 = g(x,y) = x + 2y - 5$$

The new function of the variables x, y, and λ is

$$F(x,y,\lambda) = f(x,y) - \lambda \cdot g(x,y) = y^2 + x^2 + 4x + 4 - \lambda(x + 2y - 5)$$

Its partial derivatives are

$$\frac{\partial F}{\partial x} = 2x + 4 - \lambda$$

$$\frac{\partial F}{\partial y} = 2y - 2\lambda$$

$$\frac{\partial F}{\partial \lambda} = -x - 2y + 5$$

We locate the critical points for $F(x,y,\lambda)$ by solving the equations

$$0 = \frac{\partial F}{\partial x} = \quad 2x \qquad\quad - \lambda + 4$$

$$0 = \frac{\partial F}{\partial y} = \qquad\qquad 2y - 2\lambda$$

$$0 = \frac{\partial F}{\partial \lambda} = -x - 2y \qquad\quad + 5$$

Combining these equations to eliminate x and y, we find that $\lambda = 14/5$. Entering $\lambda = 14/5$ in the second equation we get $y = \lambda = 14/5$. Setting $\lambda = 14/5$ in the first equation, we get $x = -3/5$. Thus $P_1 = (-3/5, 14/5, 14/5)$ is the only critical point for F, and Step 2 is completed.

   In the xy-plane P_1 corresponds to $Q_1 = (-3/5, 14/5)$, which lies on the line $x + 2y = 5$. Since this is the only critical point, and we intuitively know that there is an absolute minimum for the function f, the minimum must be achieved at Q_1. There the value of $f(x,y)$ is $f(Q_1) = f(-3/5, 14/5) = 9.80$. There are no endpoints to deal with because we take $f(x,y)$ to be defined on the entire unbounded line $x + 2y = 5$.

Example 22   Find the maximum and minimum values of $f(x,y) = 10xy$ subject to the three constraints

$$(i)\ x + y = 200 \qquad (ii)\ x \geqslant 0 \qquad (iii)\ y \geqslant 0$$

by using Lagrange multipliers.

Solution   Constraint (i) determines the line L in Figure 5.34; the others restrict us to the part of L on which $x \geqslant 0$ and $y \geqslant 0$, the solid segment shown. We first use Lagrange multipliers to locate extrema when $f(x,y)$ is subject to the constraint

$$0 = g(x,y) = x + y - 200$$

Then we shall see if these extrema fit the other constraints $x \geqslant 0$ and $y \geqslant 0$.
     Thus, we first set up $F(x,y,\lambda) = 10xy - \lambda(x + y - 200)$ and solve the following equations to locate its critical points:

$$0 = \frac{\partial F}{\partial x} = \quad 10y - \lambda$$

$$0 = \frac{\partial F}{\partial y} = 10x \quad - \lambda$$

$$0 = \frac{\partial F}{\partial \lambda} = -x - y \quad + 200$$

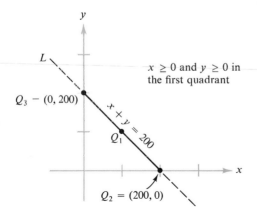

$x \geqslant 0$ and $y \geqslant 0$ in
the first quadrant

Figure 5.34
The heavy line segment is the feasible set for the constraints $x + y = 200$, $x \geqslant 0$, and $y \geqslant 0$. The function $f(x,y) = 10xy$ has its maximum value, $f = 100,000$, at $Q_1 = (100, 100)$ and its minimum value, $f = 0$, at both Q_2 and Q_3.

Combining all three equations to eliminate x and y, we get $\lambda = 1000$. Then from the first and second equations we see that $x = 100$ and $y = 100$. The only critical point is $P_1 = (x_1, y_1, \lambda_1) = (100, 100, 1000)$, which corresponds to $Q_1 = (x_1, y_1) = (100, 100)$ in the xy-plane. This is a feasible point, since $x \geqslant 0$ and $y \geqslant 0$; the value of f there is $f(Q_1) = f(100, 100) = 100{,}000$.

Our experience by now suggests that we also check the values of $f(x, y)$ at the endpoints of the feasible segment. At $Q_2 = (200, 0)$ and at $Q_3 = (0, 200)$ we get $f(Q_2) = f(Q_3) = 0$. Thus we may be reasonably certain that the maximum value occurs at Q_1, and that the minimum value $f = 0$ occurs at Q_2 and Q_3.

Exercises

●1. Maximize the function $f(x, y) = xy$ on the straight line $x + 2y - 2 = 0$ by using Lagrange multipliers.

●2. Find the real numbers x and y such that $x + y = 50$, and xy is a maximum.

●3. Find the maxima and minima of $P(x, y) = 3x + 4y$, subject to the constraint $x^2 + y^2 = 100$. (Thus, find the extrema of P on the circle of radius $r = 10$ about the origin.) HINT: Rewrite the constraint as $0 = g(x, y) = x^2 + y^2 - 100$.

●4. The surface $z = \frac{1}{4}x^2 + \frac{1}{9}y^2 + 10$ lies above the xy-plane in three-dimensional space. In the xy-plane consider the line L whose equation is $x + y = 1$. Find the point on L over which the surface has minimum height. What is the minimum height?

●5. Maximize the function $f(x, y) = xy$ on the curve $g(x, y) = x^2 + y^2 - 1 = 0$ by using Lagrange multipliers.

●6. Find the minimum distance from the line $3x + 4y - 25 = 0$ to the origin $O = (0, 0)$. HINT: The distance from a point $P = (x, y)$ to $O = (0, 0)$ is $r = \sqrt{x^2 + y^2}$. Minimizing the distance r is the same as minimizing the square of the distance $r^2 = x^2 + y^2$, which is easier to work with. Thus, minimize $f(x, y) = x^2 + y^2$ subject to the constraint $0 = g(x, y) = 3x + 4y - 25$.

7. Use the ideas in Exercise 6 to find the point on the line $x + 2y = 6$ closest to the point $P = (2, 4)$ in the plane. What is the value of the minimum distance?

*●8. To apply Lagrange multipliers to functions $f(x, y, z)$ and constraints $g(x, y, z) = 0$ involving *three* variables, just replace $f(x, y)$ and $g(x, y)$ by $f(x, y, z)$ and $g(x, y, z)$ in the discussion. Then $F = F(x, y, z, \lambda)$ and one more equation is added to the system in Step 2, yielding

$$\frac{\partial F}{\partial x} = 0 \qquad \frac{\partial F}{\partial y} = 0 \qquad \frac{\partial F}{\partial z} = 0 \qquad \frac{\partial F}{\partial \lambda} = 0$$

Use the modified procedure to find the point $P = (x, y, z)$ on the plane given by the equation

$$0 = g(x, y, z) = x + 2y - z + 12$$

at which the function $f(x, y, z) = x^2 + y^2 + z^2$ achieves a minimum. NOTE: Geometrically, you are finding the point on the plane closest to the origin, since the distance r between $P = (x,y,z)$ and $O = (0,0,0)$ satisfies $r^2 = x^2 + y^2 + z^2$. It is intuitively clear that the minimum distance exists.

5.14   Boundary Extrema: Linear Programming

If $f(x,y)$ is a linear function, that is, of the form

$$f(x,y) = Ax + By + C \qquad \text{where } A, B, \text{ and } C \text{ are fixed constants} \qquad (35)$$

and if f is defined on a bounded set determined by a finite number of linear in-equalities, then there is an elegant way to locate the absolute maximum and minimum values of f. We have already analyzed a typical problem of this kind in Example 7, but there we used the pattern of level curves $f = \text{const}$ to locate the production levels that yield maximum profit. Actually, there is a procedure for solving all such problems without the use of Calculus; it uses nothing more complicated than linear algebra. This procedure, called **linear programming**, is usually discussed in detail in texts on linear algebra. It can be generalized to handle any number of independent variables, but we shall confine our attention here to two-variable problems.

Suppose that $f(x,y) = Ax + By + C$ is defined on a bounded feasible set determined by a finite number of linear inequalities. For the sake of discussion, let us consider a specific feasible set, the one determined by the inequalities

$$(i) \ x \geqslant 0 \qquad (ii) \ y \geqslant 0 \qquad (iii) \ x + y \leqslant 200 \qquad (iv) \ 3x + y \leqslant 300$$

If f is a constant ($A = B = 0$) the optimization problem is trivial, so we assume f is not constant. The feasible set R, shown in Figure 5.35, is bounded by the lines $L_1, \ldots, L_4$ where these inequalities reduce to equalities. Since the feasible set is bounded, the absolute maximum and minimum must exist, as explained in Section 5.12. The partial derivatives of f are constant functions,

$$\frac{\partial f}{\partial x} = A \qquad \frac{\partial f}{\partial y} = B$$

at least one of which is nonzero, so there are no critical points (or extrema) within the feasible set. Therefore the absolute extrema must lie on the boundary. In fact, each extremum must occur at one of the vertices (corners) where two boundary lines meet, as we shall show in the next paragraph. Thus, to find the maximum and minimum of f all we have to do is find the coordinates of each vertex and compare the values of f at these points.

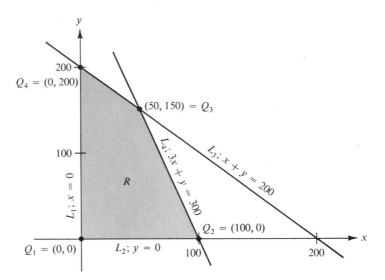

Figure 5.35
A typical bounded set determined by a finite number of linear inequalities
in the plane. If $f(x,y)$ is any linear function defined on such a set, the
maximum and minimum of f must occur at vertices (corners) of the set.

Locating Maxima and Minima by Linear Programming   Suppose $f(x,y)$ is a linear
function (35) defined on a bounded set that is determined by a finite number of
linear inequalities.

STEP 1   Sketch the feasible set by the methods described in Section 5.2.

STEP 2   Find the coordinates of each vertex $Q_1 = (x_1,y_1), \ldots, Q_k = (x_k,y_k)$ of
the feasible set. This can be done by noting which lines of equality
pass through the vertex in question, and solving the simultaneous pair
of equations in x and y.

STEP 3   Tabulate the values $f(Q_1), \ldots, f(Q_k)$ of f at the vertices.

STEP 4   The maximum (minimum) value of f on the feasible set occurs at the
vertex that gives the largest (smallest) value of f.

We can prove that the extrema occur at vertices by observing that the boundary is
made up of a finite number of line segments, as in Figure 5.35. The maximum (the
minimum is handled similarly) occurs on one of them, call it C. Now f is linear
on C, and a linear function on a segment either is constant or increases steadily
from one vertex to the other. In the first case the value of f at a vertex is as large
as it is anywhere else on C, so in a trivial way the maximum value is achieved at a
vertex. In the second case it is clear that the maximum occurs at one or the other

vertex because f steadily increases as (x,y) moves along C. In any event, the maximum on the boundary must occur at an endpoint of some segment (a vertex).

Example 23   Find the maximum and minimum values of $f(x,y) = 3x + 2y + 1$ on the set R shown in Figure 5.35.

Solution   Step 1 has been accomplished. The vertex Q_1 is determined by the lines where $x = 0$ and $y = 0$ respectively; thus $Q_1 = (0, 0)$. Vertex Q_2 is determined by the pair of equations

$$y = 0 \qquad 3x + y = 300$$

The only solution of this system is $x = 100$ and $y = 0$, so that $Q_2 = (100, 0)$. To locate Q_3 we must solve the system

$$3x + y = 300 \qquad x + y = 200$$

Substituting the equality $y = 200 - x$ into $3x + y = 300$, we find that $x = 50$. Thus $y = 150$ and $Q_3 = (50, 150)$. Finally, Q_4 is determined by the equations

$$x = 0 \qquad x + y = 200$$

so that $Q_4 = (0, 200)$. This completes Step 2. The values of f at these vertices can be calculated in a routine way:

$$f(Q_1) = f(0, 0) = 1 \qquad\qquad f(Q_3) = f(50, 150) = 451$$

$$f(Q_2) = f(100, 0) = 301 \qquad f(Q_4) = f(0, 200) = 401$$

The largest value is 451, achieved at Q_3; the smallest value is 1, achieved at Q_1. These are the maximum and minimum values of $f(x,y) = 3x + 2y + 1$ on R.

It might be interesting to re-examine Example 7 (Section 5.5), solving it by linear programming; we leave this as an exercise. Here is a practical problem solved by linear programming:

Example 24   An oil refinery produces two grades of gasoline, No-lead and Regular. Each is a blend of three products processed from crude oil in three separate plants. Table 5.3 gives the number of hours required by each plant to produce the ingredients for 1000 barrels of No-lead and of Regular gasoline. Let

$$x = \text{thousand barrels of No-lead}$$

$$y = \text{thousand barrels of Regular}$$

	Plant I	Plant II	Plant III
No-LEAD	2.0	1.2	2.6
REGULAR	2.1	2.8	0.8

Table 5.3
Hours required by plants I, II, and III to produce
the ingredients for 1000 barrels of each grade of
gasoline.

produced daily (24-hour operation). Suppose that at least 3000 barrels of No-LEAD must be produced daily to meet anticipated demand by recent-model cars equipped with pollution-control devices. Suppose that crude oil is available in essentially unlimited quantities (the crucial factor in this problem is the refinery capacity, the time required in each plant to produce the ingredients for amounts x and y of No-LEAD and REGULAR.) The profit on each product is

$2.60 per barrel of No-LEAD

$2.85 per barrel of REGULAR

Sketch the feasible set of production levels (x, y) and determine the most profitable choice of x and y.

Solution   First we list all the constraints implicit in the problem, beginning with the simple inequalities

$$x \geqslant 3 \quad y \geqslant 0 \tag{36}$$

We note that each processing plant can be run for at most 24 hours daily. The amount of time required by plant I is $2.0x + 2.1y$ hours, so we must have $2.0x + 2.1y \leqslant 24$. Treating the time requirements of plants II and III the same way, we get the full set of time constraints

$$2.0x + 2.1y \leqslant 24$$

$$1.2x + 2.8y \leqslant 24 \tag{37}$$

$$2.6x + 0.8y \leqslant 24$$

To determine the feasible set, we sketch the lines where each constraint in (36) and (37) reduces to an inequality. The equations $x = 3$ and $y = 0$ give simple vertical and horizontal lines (see Figure 5.36). The others (37) give slanting lines, as shown.

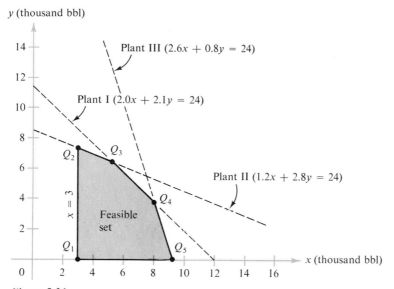

Figure 5.36
The feasible set for the oil-refinery problem. The vertical side corresponds to the constraint $x \geqslant 3$, the horizontal base line to $y \geqslant 0$. The slanted sides have the equations indicated; on each of these sides one of the inequalities (37) reduces to an equality.

Applying the methods of Section 5.2 to each constraint in (37) we find that the feasible set lies below and to the left of each of these lines. Combining all constraints we get the shaded polygonal region in Figure 5.36.

Next we calculate the coordinates of the vertices $Q_1, \ldots, Q_5$ by noting which boundary lines meet at each vertex. Obviously $Q_1 = (3.0, 0.0)$; Q_5 lies on the lines $y = 0$ and $2.6x + 0.8y = 24$, so that $x = 24/2.6 = 9.23$ and $Q_5 = (9.23, 0.0)$. Likewise, Q_2 lies on the lines $x = 3$ and $1.2x + 2.8y = 24$, so that $2.8y = 20.4$ or $y = 7.28$; thus, $Q_2 = (3.0, 7.28)$. Since Q_3 lies on the lines $1.2x + 2.8y = 24$ and $2.0x + 2.1y = 24$, its coordinates are located by solving the simultaneous equations

$$1.2x + 2.8y = 24 \quad \text{and} \quad 2.0x + 2.1y = 24$$

A little algebra yields $Q_3 = (5.45, 6.23)$. The coordinates of $Q_4 = (8.08, 3.73)$ are located similarly, by solving the equations

$$2.6x + 0.8y = 24 \quad \text{and} \quad 2.0x + 2.1y = 24$$

We calculate the profit P at each of these vertices by using the linear profit function of x and y

$$P = P(x,y) = 2.60(1000x) + 2.85(1000y) = 2600x + 2850y$$

Thus,

$$P(Q_1) = P(3.0, 0.0) = \$7800 \qquad P(Q_4) = P(8.08, 3.73) = \$31{,}639$$

$$P(Q_2) = P(3.0, 7.28) = \$28{,}548 \qquad P(Q_5) = P(9.23, 0.0) = \$23{,}998$$

$$P(Q_3) = P(5.45, 6.23) = \$31{,}926$$

The vertex with the largest value of P is Q_3, where $P = \$31{,}926$. The optimum choice of production levels is

$$x = 5.45 \text{ thousand barrels of No-lead per day}$$

$$y = 6.23 \text{ thousand barrels of Regular per day}$$

We conclude by reminding the reader that this method has severe limitations. If $f(x,y)$ is not linear, or if the feasible set is bounded by curves more complicated than line segments determined by linear inequalities, then one must turn to more advanced methods, using Calculus of several variables. Still, linear programming applies to many problems in economic analysis and is an important tool, whose usefulness can only be hinted at in this brief account.

Exercises

1. Find the maximum value of $f(x,y) = x - 2y + 10$ on the polygonal set whose vertices are $Q_1 = (0, 0)$, $Q_2 = (0, 1)$, $Q_3 = (3, 6)$, and $Q_4 = (5, 7)$. Sketch this polygonal set.

2. Find the minimum value of $f(x,y) = -2x + 3y + 100$ on the polygonal set with vertices $Q_1 = (-1, -2)$, $Q_2 = (5, 0)$, $Q_3 = (6, 1)$, $Q_4 = (4, 5)$, and $Q_5 = (0, 4)$. Sketch the set.

3. Find the maximum and minimum values of $f(x,y) = 2x - y + 5$ on the rectangle determined by $0 \leqslant x \leqslant 3$ and $2 \leqslant y \leqslant 5$.

4. Find the maximum and minimum values of $f(x,y) = 4x + 3y - 2$ on the feasible set determined by $x \geqslant 0$, $y \geqslant 0$, $x + y \geqslant 3$, and $9x + 6y \leqslant 54$. Sketch the feasible set.

5. In Example 1 (Section 5.2) a pharmaceutical manufacturer produces q_N thousand capsules of neomycin and q_T thousand capsules of tetracycline per week. The profit function is $P(q_N, q_T) = 28q_N + 23q_T$. Production is subject to certain constraints explained in the example. Find the maximum feasible profit. What choice of production levels (q_N, q_T) yields maximum profit?

6. Rework Example 7 (Section 5.5) as a linear-programming problem. (Now it is not necessary to examine level lines $P = $ const.)

7. An oil refinery produces gasoline and heating oil from petroleum crude. Three barrels of crude yield either one barrel of gasoline or two barrels of heating oil. The refinery can produce up to 1800 barrels of gasoline and 3600 barrels of heating oil each week. However,

the supply of crude is limited to at most 6000 barrels per week. If the profit on gasoline is $8 per barrel, and on heating oil $3 per barrel, find the maximum weekly profit. What choice of production levels yields the maximum profit?

● 8. Re-examine the warehouse problem in Exercise 8, Section 5.2. Sketch the feasible set. Determine the optimum number of bags of fertilizer each warehouse should send to destinations A and B in order to minimize shipping costs. What is the minimum shipping cost? ANSWERS: Warehouse 1 sends $x = 25$ bags to A, $y = 0$ bags to B; warehouse 2 sends $40 - x = 15$ bags to A, $30 - y = 30$ bags to B; minimum $= \$217.40$.

● 9. A factory produces two lines of shoes, the moderately priced J. C. Smith and the expensive Fleur models. A pair of J. C. Smith shoes requires 1.5 man-hours to produce and brings in a profit of $5, while a pair of Fleur shoes requires 2 man-hours and brings in $7 profit. Either pair of shoes requires one square foot of leather. Since leather is in scarce supply, at most 7000 square feet of leather can be supplied each month. Also, space limitations in the factory limit total monthly production to 12,000 man-hours. If all shoes can be sold without difficulty, how many pairs of each type should be produced monthly to maximize profits? What is the maximum feasible profit?

●10. Repeat Exercise 9, assuming now that each pair of J. C. Smith shoes yields $3.50 profit and each pair of Fleur shoes $4.50.

CHAPTER 6

Exponentials, Logarithms, and Growth Problems

6.1 Compound Interest

If you deposit $1200 in a bank account earning 6% annually, the interest after one year is 6% of $1200, or $(0.06) \times \$1200 = \$72$. Suppose the bank pays interest quarterly. This does not mean that at the end of each quarter you receive 6% of the amount invested; 6% is the *annual* rate of interest. Actually, at the end of one quarter you receive $\frac{1}{4}$ of the total interest, $\frac{1}{4} \times 6\% = 1.5\%$ of the invested amount, or $18. Interest paid monthly at a 6% *annual* rate is figured in the same way. After one month you receive $\frac{1}{12} \times 6\% = 0.5\%$ of the invested amount, or $6.

Suppose you deposit money in a savings account and that the interest payments periodically credited to your account are left in the account untouched. Soon you will be earning interest on the accumulated interest, a process called **compounding** of interest. Consider this example: You deposit $1200 on January 1 in an account paying 6% annual interest, compounded quarterly (paid in quarterly installments). How much will be in the account on the following January 1, or on January 1 several years later? As explained above, each quarter you are paid $\frac{1}{4} \times 6\% = 1.5\% = 0.015$ of the amount in the account, so that your investment grows as shown in Table 6.1.

We could extend the table, but there is a simple formula for the cumulative amount, valid for all interest rates and compounding schemes. To describe the

Payment number	Interest payment	Accumulated amount
Start	———	1200.00
1	18.00	1218.00
2	18.27	1236.27
3	18.54	1254.81
4	18.82	1273.63

Table 6.1
Interest on $1200 compounded quarterly at 6% annual interest.

compounding scheme we must know

(*i*) the initial investment P, called the **principal**.

(*ii*) the annual interest rate r (given in decimal form).

(*iii*) the number N of times that interest is paid per year. Thus, $N = 1, 2, 4$, and 12 for annual, semi-annual, quarterly, and monthly compounding, respectively. There are N payment periods in a year.

After k payment periods the accumulated amount A is given by

$$A = P\left(1 + \frac{r}{N}\right)^k \tag{1}$$

This is called the **compound-interest formula**. In particular, if the account is held for t full years there will be $k = Nt$ payment periods, and the balance will be

$$A = P\left(1 + \frac{r}{N}\right)^{Nt} \tag{2}$$

To justify (1) we can directly compute the balance at the end of successive payment periods $k = 1, 2, 3, \ldots$, simplify algebraically, and note the emerging pattern in Table 6.2.

Example 1   Find the amount accumulated after 7 years if $P = \$1200$ is compounded quarterly at 6% interest.

Payment number	Interest payment	Accumulated amount
(Start)	——	P
1	$P \cdot \dfrac{r}{N}$	$P + \dfrac{r}{N} \cdot P = P\left(1 + \dfrac{r}{N}\right)$
2	$\dfrac{r}{N} \cdot P\left(1 + \dfrac{r}{N}\right)$	$P\left(1 + \dfrac{r}{N}\right) + \dfrac{r}{N} \cdot P\left(1 + \dfrac{r}{N}\right) = P\left(1 + \dfrac{r}{N}\right)^2$
3	$\dfrac{r}{N} \cdot P\left(1 + \dfrac{r}{N}\right)^2$	$P\left(1 + \dfrac{r}{N}\right)^2 + \dfrac{r}{N} \cdot P\left(1 + \dfrac{r}{N}\right)^2 = P\left(1 + \dfrac{r}{N}\right)^3$
4	$\dfrac{r}{N} \cdot P\left(1 + \dfrac{r}{N}\right)^3$	$P\left(1 + \dfrac{r}{N}\right)^3 + \dfrac{r}{N} \cdot P\left(1 + \dfrac{r}{N}\right)^3 = P\left(1 + \dfrac{r}{N}\right)^4$
⋮	⋮	⋮
k	$\dfrac{r}{N} \cdot P\left(1 + \dfrac{r}{N}\right)^{k-1}$	$P\left(1 + \dfrac{r}{N}\right)^{k-1} + \dfrac{r}{N} \cdot P\left(1 + \dfrac{r}{N}\right)^{k-1} = P\left(1 + \dfrac{r}{N}\right)^k$
⋮	⋮	⋮

Table 6.2
Interest on P dollars, compounded N times a year, at an annual interest rate of r
(expressed in decimal form). At each step the interest paid is (r/N) times the previous
balance. After k steps the accumulated amount is clearly $P\left(1 + \dfrac{r}{N}\right)^k$ dollars.

Solution   Here $r = 0.06$, $N = 4$, and there are $Nt = 4 \cdot 7 = 28$ payment periods.
Substituting these values into (1) we get*

$$A = 1200\left(1 + \frac{0.06}{4}\right)^{28} = 1200(1.015)^{28} = 1200(1.517222) = 1820.67$$

Example 2   Find the amount accumulated after one year if a principal of \$1200
draws interest at an annual rate of 6% compounded monthly.

Solution   Here $P = 1200$, $r = 0.06$, $N = 12$, and there are $k = 12$ payment periods.
Using (1) we get

$$A = 1200\left(1 + \frac{0.06}{12}\right)^{12} = 1200(1.005)^{12} = 1200(1.061677) = 1274.01$$

* Multiplying 1.015 by itself 28 times is so tedious that a pocket calculator is very helpful in this and the
following examples. In Section 6.3 we shall see how to simplify these calculations by using logarithms.
The exercises for Section 6.1 have been designed to avoid unbearably long computations, and can be done
by hand.

Compare this with the amount 1273.63, which is accumulated if the same principal draws interest at 6% for the same time, but with quarterly compounding (Table 6.1). All other things being equal, more frequent compounding is advantageous to the depositor.

Example 3   Suppose you have two investment possibilities: you can lend $1000 to company A with repayment of $2000 in 10 years, or you can lend $1000 to company B for 10 years at an annual rate of 8% compounded annually. Assuming the companies are equally good risks, which investment should you choose?

Solution   If you choose to deal with company B in ten years your principal will grow to $1000(1 + 0.08)^{10} = 2158.92. This is greater than $2000, the amount company A will repay in 10 years; therefore you should lend to company B.

So far, our examples have involved realistic interest rates, at least for the U.S.A. Our next illustration may seem exaggerated, but considering recent rates of inflation in certain countries, it may not be far from the mark.

Illustration   In the country of Inflatia, things have reached a sorry state. Interest rates have climbed so rapidly that the government has declared a ceiling of 100% on the annual rate. The Inflatia National Bank desperately needs depositors. Realizing that competitors are offering a rate of 100% compounded quarterly, the Bank advertises a rate of 100% compounded monthly. Competing banks respond with the same rate compounded weekly. Inflatia National takes the challenge and immediately offers a 100% annual rate compounded daily. Where is all this leading?

Discussion   It is clear that more frequent compounding raises the "effective" rate of interest. To gauge this quantitatively, we can compare the final amount on a principal of $P = \$1$ for $t = 1$ year under different compounding schemes. With $r = 100\% = 1.00$ and $N = 4$, the final amount is $(1 + \frac{1}{4})^4 = 2.4414 \ldots$. (Banks refer to this as the **effective interest rate**: thus an annual rate of 100% compounded quarterly corresponds to a 244.14% effective annual rate.) In our illustration the annual rate is constant $r = 1.00$, while the number of payments N increases; the effective annual rate is therefore $(1 + (1/N))^N$. For $N = 12$ (monthly compounding), this rate is $(1 + \frac{1}{12})^{12} = 2.6130 \ldots$. For $N = 52$ (weekly compounding), it is $(1 + \frac{1}{52})^{52} = 2.6926 \ldots$. It appears that with more and more frequent compounding, the effective interest rate $(1 + (1/N))^N$ increases, approaching a definite limit value. That this is so is proved in more advanced texts; the limit value is universally denoted by the symbol

$$e = \lim_{N \to \infty} \left(1 + \frac{1}{N}\right)^N \tag{3}$$

Its decimal expansion is $e = 2.71828 \ldots$.

The banking situation is now clear. The mad rush to compound more frequently with the mandated 100% annual rate leads to effective interest rates that increase, approaching but never exceeding $e = 2.71828\ldots$. The limiting situation is called **continuous compounding**, for obvious reasons. We can get a pretty good idea of continuous compounding if we think of compounding interest every *microsecond* (1/1,000,000 second); this would be done $N = 31{,}536$ billion times per year. Then the effective interest rate $(1 + (1/N))^N$ agrees with $e = 2.71828\ldots$ to many decimal places.

If we take $r = 1.00$ in equation (2) and allow N to get larger and larger, then the amount accumulated after t years

$$A = P\left(1 + \frac{1}{N}\right)^{Nt} = P\left[\left(1 + \frac{1}{N}\right)^{N}\right]^{t}$$

is very nearly equal to Pe^t because $(1 + (1/N))^N$ approaches e. If the interest rate r is arbitrary (instead of $r = 1.00$ as above), similar calculations show that the amount A after a time t (in years) is given by the following **continuous-compounding formula**:

$$A = Pe^{rt} \qquad (r - \text{the annual interest rate expressed in decimal form}) \qquad (4)$$

A table of powers e^x and e^{-x} adequate for all computations in this book is given in Appendix 4. Most pocket calculators and slide rules are equipped to compute the powers of e needed to apply formula (4). Powers of e such as e^x make sense for all real numbers x, and the exponent laws discussed in Section 1.2 may be applied to simplify calculations. For example, $e^{-x} = 1/e^x$ and $e^{x+y} = e^x \cdot e^y$ for all real x and y.

Example 4   Find the amount accumulated after five years on a principal of $1000 if interest is continuously compounded at the annual rate of 8%. Compare this with the amount accumulated when the compounding is semi-annual (two payments per year).

Solution   In this example $P = 1000$, $r = 0.08$, and $t = 5$ years. If we substitute these values into (4) and use Appendix 4 to find values of e^x, we obtain after continuous compounding the amount

$$A = 1000e^{(0.08)5} = 1000e^{0.40} = 1491.80$$

If we compound semi-annually, then we apply (2) with $N = 2$ to obtain

$$A = 1000\left(1 + \frac{0.08}{2}\right)^{2 \cdot 5} = 1000(1.04)^{10} = 1000(1.48024) = 1480.24$$

Exercises

●1. Find the amount accumulated after two years if principal of $100 is invested at an annual rate of 7% compounded

   (*i*) annually

   (*ii*) semi-annually

   (*iii*) quarterly

   (*iv*) monthly

   (*v*) continuously

●2. A U.S. Treasury bond matures in one year, paying $10,000. Suppose the bond costs $9300. Is it better to buy the bond or to invest in a savings account paying 7% interest compounded quarterly? ANSWER: Buy the bond.

●3. If you borrow $600 through a credit card, you must pay back the original amount plus compound interest on the loan. Many credit cards charge you about 15% annually on unpaid loans. How much must you repay if you borrow $600 for

   (*i*) 3 months

   (*ii*) 6 months

   (*iii*) 1 year

   if interest is compounded quarterly?

●4. Compute the yield on $100 invested at 6% interest

   (*i*) for one year, compounded annually

   (*ii*) for one year, compounded continuously

   The yield on any other compounding scheme (with 6% annual interest) falls between these extremes. What is the annual yield on $1000 under each scheme? What is the effective annual interest rate in (*ii*); that is, what annual rate r, uncompounded, yields this amount on $100 after one year?

●5. What is the effective annual interest rate if interest is compounded continuously at the annual rate of 5%?

●6. How much money should you invest in an account paying 8% compounded annually if you wish to have $3000 in the account after 7 years?

●7. A certain municipal bond promises to pay its face value of $5000 when it matures 1.5 years hence. A bond salesman offers to sell you the bond now at a discount price of $4500. Alternatively, you could invest present funds at 8% interest, compounded quarterly. Should you buy the bond? (What will $4500 be worth when the bond matures?) At what price P does the bond become a bargain? ANSWERS: No ($4500 grows to $5067.73 after 1.5 years); $P \leqslant 5000/(1.02)^6 = \$4439.86$ is profitable to you.

●8. A manufacturer assumes, for tax-accounting purposes, that a certain piece of plant equipment **depreciates** in value by $r = 15\%$ each year. (That is, if the value at the beginning of the year is P, then its value at the beginning of the next year is $P - 0.15P = (1 - r)P$.) Assuming its value is $10,000 when new, compute its successive values $P(n)$ after n years, $n = 1, 2, \ldots$. If equipment is replaced once its value $P(n)$ falls below 1/3 of its original value, in which year should this equipment be replaced? ANSWERS: $P(1) = 8500$, $P(2) = 7225$, $P(3) = 6141$, $P(4) = 5220$, $P(5) = 4437$, $P(6) = 3771$, $P(7) = 3206$; replace after 7th year.

●9. A piece of manufacturing equipment becomes less valuable as time passes, due to wear and gradual obsolescence. This **depreciation** in value is often estimated by saying that the unit loses a certain percentage of its value each year. If it depreciates by r percent annually, and the value at the beginning of a year is P, then the value at the beginning of the next year is

$$P - rP = (1 - r)P \qquad (r \text{ in decimal form})$$

Prove that its value $P(N)$ after N years is related to its initial value P by the following **depreciation formula**

$$P(N) = P \cdot (1 - r)^N \qquad N = 0, 1, 2, \ldots$$

HINT: Refer to our discussion of the compound-interest formula (1).

6.2   The Exponential Function $y = e^x$

In Chapter 1 we reviewed the meaning of a^x for any $a > 0$ and summarized the laws of exponents (Section 1.2). Furthermore, we saw that functions of the form $f(x) = a^x$ describe growth phenomena (see Section 1.7, where we encountered $f(x) = 2^x$). For reasons that will become apparent, there is a particular choice of the base a in a^x that has overwhelming advantages, namely $a = e = 2.71828 \ldots$. The function defined by

$$f(x) = \exp(x) = e^x \qquad \text{for all real } x$$

is called the **exponential function**. Notice that the base e is constant, while the exponent x is the variable in this function. The domain of definition is the entire number line. A table of values of this important function is given in Appendix 4. Using values drawn from this table we may plot points and sketch the graph of $\exp(x)$ shown in Figure 6.1. The exponential laws of Section 1.2 force the exponential function $\exp(x)$ to have the following algebraic properties:

$$
\begin{aligned}
&(i)\ \ \exp(0) = e^0 = 1 \\
&(ii)\ \ \exp(1) = e^1 = e \\
&(iii)\ \ e^{x_1 + x_2} = e^{x_1} \cdot e^{x_2} \\
&(iv)\ \ e^{x_1 - x_2} = e^{x_1}/e^{x_2} \\
&(v)\ \ (e^{x_1})^{x_2} = e^{x_1 x_2} \\
&(vi)\ \ e^{-x} = 1/e^x
\end{aligned}
\qquad (5)
$$

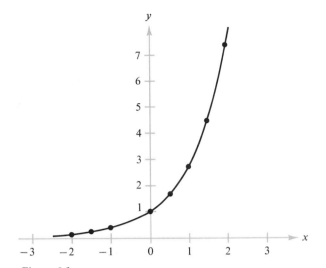

x	$y = e^x$
-3.0	0.0498
-2.0	.1353
-1.5	.2231
-1.0	0.3679
0.0	1.0000
0.5	1.6487
1.0	2.7183
1.5	4.4817
2.0	7.3891

Figure 6.1
Graph of the function $y = \exp(x) = e^x$. The tabulated values are plotted as solid dots. Because e^x is always positive, the graph lies above the x-axis. It rises very rapidly as x moves to the right, and approaches the x-axis as x moves to the left.

Here x, x_1, and x_2 are arbitrary numbers. For example $e^2 = (2.718\ldots)^2 = 7.3890\ldots$, so that $e^{-2} = 1/e^2 = 1/7.3890\ldots = 0.13533\ldots$.

Next we shall examine the derivative of the exponential function; only then shall we begin to understand the importance of this function.

Derivative of $y = e^x$ If $y = e^x$, then $dy/dx = e^x$. In other words

$$\frac{d}{dx}\{\exp(x)\} = \exp(x) \tag{6}$$

Thus the exponential function $y = e^x$ *is equal to its own derivative*. It is essentially the *only* function with this property, and it is this property that accounts for the appearance of exponential functions in growth problems, as we shall see in Section 6.4. Continuously compounded interest is an example of a growth phenomenon, the growth of invested capital with time; it can be described by the exponential function $A(t) = P \cdot e^{rt}$, as in (4). We shall not prove formula (6) here; the details may be found in any standard Calculus text.

The differentiation formula (6) is so simple because the base of the exponential function is e. Exponential functions $f(x) = a^x$ with different bases, such as 10^x or 2^x, have similar derivatives of the form

$$\frac{d}{dx}\{a^x\} = (\text{constant}) \cdot a^x \tag{7}$$

but a messy calculation is needed to evaluate the constant. For example

$$\frac{d}{dx}\{2^x\} = (0.6931) \cdot 2^x \qquad \frac{d}{dx}\{10^x\} = (2.3026) \cdot 10^x$$

for all x. Only if $a = e$ is this constant equal to 1. For this reason the particular exponential function e^x is universally employed in all advanced applications of mathematics.

Example 5   Find the derivatives

$$\frac{d^n}{dx^n}\{e^x\} \qquad \text{for } n = 1, 2, 3 \ldots .$$

What do they tell you about the graph of $y = e^x$?

Solution   From formula (6) we know that for $n = 1$ we have $\dfrac{d}{dx}\{e^x\} = e^x$. Applying the formula again we find that

$$\frac{d^2}{dx^2}\{e^x\} - \frac{d}{dx}\{e^x\} = e^x \tag{8}$$

and so on. In general

$$\frac{d^n}{dx^n}\{e^x\} - e^x \qquad \text{for } n = 1, 2, 3, \ldots$$

Recall that e^x is always positive. By (8) we know that

$$\frac{d}{dx}\{e^x\} = \frac{d^2}{dx^2}\{e^x\} = e^x > 0 \qquad \text{for all } x$$

Positivity of the first derivative tells us that the function $f(x) = e^x$ is increasing (graph rising), and positivity of the second derivative that the graph is concave upward. A glance at Figure 6.1 confirms these observations.

   If we now combine formula (6) with the chain rule, we obtain a very useful differentiation formula for more complicated functions. If $u(x)$ is a differentiable function, then

$$\frac{d}{dx}\{e^{u(x)}\} = e^{u(x)} \cdot \frac{du}{dx} \tag{9}$$

Example 6   Find dy/dx if $y = e^{-3x}$. What is the value of dy/dx at $x = 0$?

Solution   We use formula (9) with $u(x) = -3x$. Then

$$\frac{dy}{dx} = \frac{d}{dx}\{e^{-3x}\} = e^{-3x} \cdot \frac{d}{dx}\{-3x\} = -3e^{-3x}$$

In particular, if $x = 0$ we get $dy/dx = -3 \cdot e^0 = (-3) \cdot 1 = -3$.

If k is any constant, we may show by exactly the same method, taking $u(x) = kx$, that

$$\frac{d}{dx}\{e^{kx}\} = ke^{kx} \tag{10}$$

Example 7   Find dy/dx if $y = e^{2x+x^2}$.

Solution   The most efficient method is to employ (9), taking $u(x) = 2x + x^2$. Then

$$\frac{d}{dx}\{e^{2x+x^2}\} = e^{2x+x^2} \cdot \frac{d}{dx}\{2x + x^2\} = (2 + 2x)e^{2x+x^2}$$

Another method is to use (5*iii*), writing $y = e^{2x+x^2} = e^{2x} \cdot e^{x^2}$. Then use the product formula (Section 3.2) to obtain

$$\frac{dy}{dx} = \frac{d}{dx}\{e^{2x}\} \cdot e^{x^2} + e^{2x} \cdot \frac{d}{dx}\{e^{x^2}\}$$

$$= (2e^{2x}) \cdot e^{x^2} + e^{2x} \cdot (2xe^{x^2}) = (2 + 2x)e^{2x+x^2}$$

Finally let us consider integrals involving e^x. Recall that the indefinite integral $\int e^x \, dx$ is any function $F(x)$ for which $dF/dx = e^x$. But from formula (6) it is obvious that $F(x) = e^x$ meets this requirement, so that

$$\int e^x \, dx = e^x + \text{const} \tag{11}$$

Example 8   Find the area under the curve $y = e^x$ between $x = 0$ and $x = 1$.

Solution   The area is given by the definite integral $\int_0^1 e^x \, dx$. By the Fundamental Theorem of Calculus

$$\int_0^1 e^x \, dx = \left[e^x \Big|_{x=0}^{x=1} \right] = e^1 - e^0 = e - 1 = 1.71828\ldots$$

Example 9   Find the indefinite integral $\int xe^{-x^2}\,dx$.

Solution   We use the method of substitution (Section 4.6), letting $u = -x^2$ and $g(u) = e^u$. Then

$$\frac{du}{dx} = -2x \quad\text{and}\quad g(u)\cdot\frac{du}{dx} = e^u(-2x) = -2xe^{-x^2}$$

so evaluating $\int xe^{-x^2}\,dx$ reduces to evaluating $\int e^u\,du$, which is known:

$$\int xe^{-x^2}\,dx = -\frac{1}{2}\int -2xe^{-x^2}\,dx$$

$$= -\frac{1}{2}\left[\int e^u\,du\,\Big|_{u=-x^2}\right]$$

$$= -\frac{1}{2}\left[e^u\Big|_{u=-x^2}\right] = -\frac{1}{2}e^{-x^2} + \text{const}$$

SUGGESTION: Check the result by differentiating the answer.

Exercises

●1. Use the exponential tables, Appendix 4, to calculate the following exponentials:

(i) e^0 (v) $e^{2.14}$

(ii) $\sqrt{e} = e^{1/2}$ (vi) $e^{-3.19}$

(iii) $1/\sqrt{e} = e^{-1/2}$ (vii) $e^{-4/5}$

(iv) $e^{0.75}$ (viii) $1/e^2$

●2. Use the method of interpolation discussed in Appendix 1 to estimate the values of the following numbers:

(i) $e^{1/3}$ (iv) $e^{0.023}$

(ii) $e^{-1.742}$ (v) $e^{\sqrt{2}} \approx e^{1.414}$

(iii) $e^{1.827}$ (vi) $e^{1.0228}$

●3. For small values of Δx we may estimate the value of $e^{\Delta x}$ by using the approximation formula (Section 2.5), taking $f(x) = e^x$, $f'(x) = e^x$, and $p = 0$. Thus

$$e^{\Delta x} \approx e^0 + \Delta x \cdot e^0 = 1 + \Delta x$$

Using this method to estimate the values

(i) $e^{0.01}$ (ii) $e^{0.02}$

(*iii*) $e^{0.0001}$ (*iv*) $e^{0.0037}$

What are the exact values for (*i*) and (*ii*)?

4. Using the exponential tables, calculate the values of

$$f(x) = e^{-x^2}$$

for $x = 0.0, \pm 0.25, \pm 0.50, \pm 0.75, \pm 1.0, \pm 1.5,$ and ± 2.0. Use these to plot the graph of this function. NOTE: For a sketch of the graph see Figure 4.23.

●5. Use formula (4) to calculate the amount accumulated under the following *continuous-compounding* schemes:

   (*i*) $1000 at 6% for $4\frac{1}{2}$ years

   (*ii*) $10,000 at 6% for $4\frac{1}{2}$ years

   (*iii*) $1500 at 8% for 7 years

   (*iv*) $1 at 5% starting in 1875 and ending in 1975.

●6. For the function $f(x) = e^{-x^2/2}$, find $f'(x)$ and $f''(x)$.

●7. Find dy/dx if

   (*i*) $y = e^{3x}$ (*iv*) $y = 1/e^{2x}$

   (*ii*) $y = e^{x^2}$ (*v*) $y = (e^x + e^{3x})/e^{2x}$

   (*iii*) $y = e^{x^2 - 3x}$ (*vi*) $y = xe^x$

8. For the function $f(x) = e^{-x}$, find $f'(x)$ and $f''(x)$. Then sketch the graph of f. HINT: e^a is positive for *any* real number *a*.

●9. Evaluate:

   (*i*) $\int_0^1 e^{3x}\, dx$ (*iv*) $\int \dfrac{e^{2x} + 1}{e^x}\, dx$

   (*ii*) $\int e^{x-1}\, dx$ (*v*) $\int_0^2 u^2 e^{u^3}\, du$

   (*iii*) $\int \dfrac{1}{e^x}\, dx$ (*vi*) $\int (e^x + e^{-x})^2\, dx$

6.3   The Logarithm Function $y = \log(x)$

Generally, if an operation or function is useful in mathematics, so is its inverse. For example, subtraction is the inverse of the operation of addition; integration (via indefinite integrals) is the inverse of differentiation. Having defined the exponential function exp, we may introduce its inverse, the **logarithm function** $y = \log(x)$.

Logarithms arise when we ask such questions as:

For which value of *a* is $e^a = 2$?

Instead of starting with a number x and calculating e^x, we have reversed the roles of independent and dependent variables; given the value 2 we ask how the variable a should be chosen in order to get $e^a = 2$. The solution to this problem is the *logarithm of 2*, written log(2). Taking any other number x in place of 2, we may ask the same question:

$$\text{For which value of } a \text{ is } e^a = x?$$

The solution a (if there is one) is the *logarithm of* x, written $\log(x)$. Evidently

$$a = \log(x) \quad \text{means precisely that} \quad e^a = e^{\log(x)} = x \tag{12}$$

If we know how to compute values of e^x, say by using the tables in Appendix 4, it is not hard to evaluate logarithms such as log(2). The value e^a increases as a increases (see Figure 6.2); by searching through Appendix 4 for values of e^a close to 2.000, we find that

$$e^{0.69} = 1.9937, \text{ so that } a = 0.69 \text{ is too small}$$

$$e^{0.70} = 2.0137, \text{ so that } a = 0.70 \text{ is too large}$$

Thus log(2) lies between 0.69 and 0.70. The actual value $\log(2) = 0.693147 \ldots$ may be pinned down by trial and error, using a computer programmed to supply more accurate values of e^x. In this way, you could have a computer compile detailed tables for $\log(x)$, such as the one given in Appendix 3. Hereafter we shall refer to this table for values of $\log(x)$.

The equation $e^a = x$ has a solution $a = \log(x)$ only if $x > 0$, because e^a is positive for every real number a (see Figure 6.1). Thus $\log(x)$ is defined only for $x > 0$. Its graph, sketched in Figure 6.2 by plotting values of $\log(x)$ taken from Appendix 3, must therefore lie entirely to the right of the vertical axis.

Our logarithm function $y = \log(x)$ is sometimes called the **natural logarithm** or **logarithm to base e**. It is possible to define logarithm functions to an arbitrary base $a > 0$, $a = 10$ being the most common choice besides $a = e = 2.718 \ldots$. This is done by inverting the equation $a^y = x$ instead of the equation $e^y = x$ as above. We shall not do this. The same reasons that dictate the choice of e as the base of the exponential function apply as well to the choice of e as the base for the logarithm.

We have already noted that, by definition of log

$$e^{\log(x)} = x \qquad \text{for all } x > 0 \tag{13}$$

That is, if we successively apply the functions log and exp to a number $x > 0$, then exp undoes the action of log so that we end up with x. If we apply exp first and then

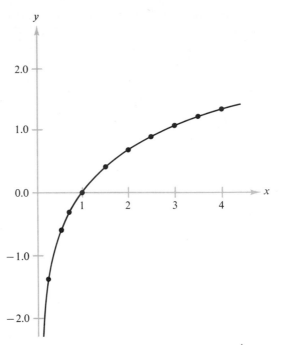

Figure 6.2
Graph of the natural logarithm function $y = \log(x)$. This function is defined only for $x > 0$. The values $y = \log(x)$ increase steadily as x increases. The value $\log(x)$ is large negative if x is small, and is large positive if x is large. Solid dots are points plotted by inspecting the table of values given in Appendix 3.

log, we again end up where we started

$$\log(e^x) = x \qquad \text{for all } x \tag{14}$$

This is why we say that log and exp are inverses of each other. The *inversion formulas* (13) and (14) are useful in algebraic manipulations of logarithms.

Example 10   Calculate $\log(1)$, $\log(e)$, and $\log(1/e^2)$.

Solution   Since $e^0 = 1$, we may apply (14) to get $\log(1) = \log(e^0) = 0$. Similarly $e = e^1$, so that $\log(e) = \log(e^1) = 1$; and $1/e^2 = e^{-2}$, so that $\log(1/e^2) = -2$.

Because exp and log are so closely related, the algebraic properties of exp summarized in (5) lead to corresponding algebraic properties of log that are extremely useful. If x, x_1, and x_2 are positive numbers, then

(i) $\log(1) = 0$

(ii) $\log(e) = 1$

(iii) $\log(x_1 x_2) = \log(x_1) + \log(x_2)$

(iv) $\log(x_1/x_2) = \log(x_1) - \log(x_2)$ (15)

(v) $\log(x^r) = r \cdot \log(x)$ (*r* any real number)

(vi) $\log(1/x) = -\log(x)$

These facts are easy to prove if we notice that different values of x give different values of e^x, since $y = e^x$ increases as x increases. Thus

$$a = b \quad \text{if and only if} \quad e^a = e^b \tag{16}$$

Consequently, an identity such as (15*iii*) is valid if and only if it remains valid after we apply exp to each side. But by (5*iii*) and the defining equation (13), we see that

$$e^{\log(x_1 x_2)} = x_1 x_2$$

$$e^{\log(x_1) + \log(x_2)} = e^{\log(x_1)} \cdot e^{\log(x_2)} = x_1 x_2$$

as required. Use of the algebraic rules (15) is illustrated in the following examples.

Example 11   Use logarithms to compute 8.24/2.37.

Solution   Let $x = 8.24/2.37$. Using the logarithms tabulated in Appendix 3 we get

$$\log x = \log\left(\frac{8.24}{2.37}\right) = \log(8.24) - \log(2.37) \qquad \text{by (15}iv)$$

$$= 2.1090 - 0.8629$$

$$= 1.2461 \ldots$$

Once we know $\log(x)$ we can find x by using formula (13) and the table of exponentials in Appendix 4:

$$x = e^{\log(x)} = e^{1.2461} = 3.4768 \ldots .$$

The table gives only $e^{1.24} = 3.4556$ and $e^{1.25} = 3.4903$, so $x = e^{1.2461}$ lies somewhere between these values, $3.4556 \leqslant x \leqslant 3.4903$. We may estimate x much more accurately by *linear interpolation* between the tabulated values of $e^{1.24}$ and $e^{1.25}$, as explained in Appendix 1. Since 1.2461 lies 61/100 of the way between 1.24 and 1.25, $e^{1.2461}$ lies roughly 61/100 of the way between the values $e^{1.24}$ and $e^{1.25}$ listed in Appendix 4:

$$e^{1.2461} \approx e^{1.24} + \frac{61}{100} \cdot (e^{1.25} - e^{1.24})$$

$$= 3.4556 + \frac{61}{100}(0.0347)$$

$$= 3.4556 + 0.0212 = 3.4768$$

which agrees to four decimal places with the exact answer 3.47679 ... .

Of course the last problem could have been done by long division, without use of logarithms. The following example cannot be worked so easily by arithmetical methods (try it to see how long it takes).

Example 12   Use logarithms to compute $1.5 \times (1.10)^{10}$.

Solution   Let $x = 1.5 \times (1.10)^{10}$. Taking logarithms we compute log x,

$$\log x = \log(1.5 \times (1.10)^{10})$$

$$= \log(1.50) + \log(1.10)^{10} \qquad \text{by } (15iii)$$

$$= \log(1.50) + 10 \cdot \log(1.10) \qquad \text{by } (15v)$$

$$= 0.4055 + 10(0.09531)$$

$$= 1.3586.$$

To recover x, we take exp of both sides. Using the tabulated values $e^{1.35} = 3.8574$ and $e^{1.36} = 3.8961$, we see that $x = e^{1.3586}$ lies about 86/100 of the way between $e^{1.35}$ and $e^{1.36}$. By making this linear interpolation, we may estimate x to four decimal places:

$$x = e^{1.3586} \approx e^{1.35} + \frac{86}{100} \cdot (3.8961 - 3.8574)$$

$$= 3.8574 + \frac{86}{100}(0.0387)$$

$$= 3.8907$$

The exact value is $x = e^{1.3586} = 3.89074$ ... .

The next example involves values of $\log(x)$ and e^x not listed explicitly in the tables (see also Exercise 2).

Example 13   Compute

$$(i)\ \log(0.0000471) \qquad (ii)\ \log(67{,}000{,}000) \qquad (iii)\ e^{20}$$

using the tables and the rules (5) and (15).

Solution   Write $0.0000471 = 4.71 \times 10^{-5}$. Using (15), we break things up into logarithms that are available in the tables:

$$\log(4.71 \times 10^{-5}) = \log(4.71) + \log(10^{-5})$$

$$= \log(4.71) + (-5)\log(10)$$

$$= 1.5497 + (-5)(2.3025) = -9.9628$$

Similarly, $67{,}000{,}000 = 6.70 \times 10^7$, so that

$$\log(67{,}000{,}000) = \log(6.70) + (7)\log(10)$$

$$= 1.9021 + 7(2.3025) - 18.0196$$

To find e^{20}, which is not in the table of exponentials, we use (5):

$$e^{20} = (e^5)^4 - (148.41)^4 \approx 4.851 \times 10^8$$

The following problems have a common theme. When we must find a certain number x, the algebra becomes much simpler if we first find $\log(x)$. Then we can find x itself by using the exponential tables and the formula $e^{\log x} = x$.

NOTE: Once $\log(x)$ has been found, many authors then determine x by referring to the logarithm tables, using them in reverse to locate the x that gives the proper value of $\log(x)$. This method eliminates the need for a table of exponentials, but it can be confusing. We use both exponential and logarithm tables to make hand calculations easier. Furthermore, our procedure (find $\log(x)$, then take $x = e^{\log(x)}$) is precisely the one to use when working with the aid of a modern calculator.

Example 14   Suppose an investment of \$1000 made 10 years ago in a mutual fund is now worth \$2000. At what interest rate, compounded quarterly, would you have had to invest the principal to achieve the same yield?

Solution Let r be the interest rate we seek. Substituting $P = 1000$, $N = 4$, $t = 10$, and $A = 2000$ into (2), we get

$$2000 = 1000\left(1 + \frac{r}{4}\right)^{40} \quad \text{or} \quad 2 = \left(1 + \frac{r}{4}\right)^{40}$$

Taking the logarithm on each side, we get

$$\log(2.00) = 0.6932 = \log\left[\left(1 + \frac{r}{4}\right)^{40}\right] = (40)\log\left(1 + \frac{r}{4}\right)$$

so that

$$\log\left(1 + \frac{r}{4}\right) = \frac{0.6932}{40} = 0.01733$$

From Appendix 4 we obtain, by linear interpolation between tabulated values $e^{0.01} = 1.0100$ and $e^{0.02} = 1.0202$,

$$1 + \frac{r}{4} = e^{0.01733} \approx 1.0175$$

$$\frac{r}{4} \approx 0.0175 \qquad r \approx 0.0700$$

or about 7%. (The exact answer is $r = 0.069924\ldots$.)

Example 15 How long will it take $1000 to grow to $1400 if it is invested at an 8% annual interest rate, compounded quarterly?

Solution Here $P = 1000$, $A = 1400$, $r = 0.08$, $N = 4$, and we want to find t in equation (2). Substituting these values into (2), we get

$$1400 = 1000(1.02)^{4t} \quad \text{or} \quad (1.02)^{4t} = 1.40$$

Taking logarithms of each side, we get

$$4t \cdot \log(1.02) = \log(1.40)$$

$$4t \cdot (0.0198) = 0.3365$$

$$t = 4.249 \approx 4\tfrac{1}{4} \text{ years}$$

After $4\frac{1}{4}$ years, or 17 interest periods, the account will have grown to slightly more than \$1400 (to \$1400.24 to be exact).

For some applications of Calculus, we must determine the derivative of the logarithm function $y = \log(x)$. Some technical details are needed to show that this function actually *is* differentiable; we shall not go into them here. Once dy/dx is known to exist it is easy to calculate it by implicit differentiation.

Derivative of $y = \log(x)$ The logarithm function $y = \log(x)$, defined for $x > 0$, has derivative

$$\frac{dy}{dx} = \frac{d}{dx}\{\log(x)\} = \frac{1}{x} \tag{17}$$

Proof   For all $x > 0$ we have $e^{\log(x)} = x$. Write $f(x) = e^{\log(x)}$ as a composite function

$$x = f(x) = \left[e^u \big|_{u = \log(x)} \right]$$

Now differentiate each side of this identity. On the left, $(d/dx)\{x\} = 1$. On the right, by the chain rule, we have

$$\frac{df}{dx} = \frac{d}{du}\{e^u\} \cdot \frac{du}{dx} = e^u \cdot \frac{d}{dx}\{\log(x)\}$$

$$= e^{\log(x)} \cdot \frac{d}{dx}\{\log(x)\}$$

$$= x \cdot \frac{d}{dx}\{\log(x)\}$$

Thus

$$1 = x \cdot \frac{d}{dx}\{\log(x)\} \quad \text{or} \quad \frac{1}{x} = \frac{d}{dx}\{\log(x)\}$$

If we combine formula (17) with the chain rule for differentiating composite functions, we get another useful formula. If $u(x)$ is differentiable and has positive values $u(x) > 0$, so that $\log(u(x))$ makes sense, then

$$\frac{d}{dx}\{\log(u(x))\} = \frac{1}{u(x)} \cdot \frac{du}{dx} \tag{18}$$

Example 16   Find dy/dx if $y = \log(1 + x^3)$.

Solution   Apply (18), taking $u = 1 + x^3$ to obtain

$$\frac{dy}{dx} = \frac{1}{u(x)} \cdot \frac{du}{dx} = \frac{1}{1 + x^3} \cdot (3x^2) = \frac{3x^2}{1 + x^3}$$

From the differentiation formula (17) we immediately obtain the following integration formula:

Indefinite Integral of $y = 1/x$ For $x > 0$, the indefinite integral of $f(x) = 1/x$ is given by

$$\int \frac{1}{x} dx = \log(x) + \text{const} \tag{19}$$

Example 17   Find the area under the graph of the curve $y = x/(1 + x^2)$ between the vertical lines $x = 0$ and $x = 1$.

Solution   We use the method of substitution (Section 4.6). Taking $u(x) = 1 + x^2$ and $g(u) = 1/u$, we find that

$$g(u) \cdot \frac{du}{dx} = \frac{1}{1 + x^2} \cdot 2x = \frac{2x}{1 + x^2}$$

Adjusting the integral by a constant multiplier, we get the indefinite integral

$$\int \frac{x}{1 + x^2} dx = \frac{1}{2} \int \frac{2x}{1 + x^2} dx = \frac{1}{2} \left[\int \frac{1}{u} du \Bigg|_{u = 1 + x^2} \right]$$

$$= \frac{1}{2} \left[\log(u) \Bigg|_{u = 1 + x^2} \right]$$

$$= \frac{1}{2} \log(1 + x^2) + \text{const}$$

Inserting the endpoint values $x = 0$ and $x = 1$, we get the definite integral

$$\text{Area} = \int_0^1 \frac{x}{1 + x^2} dx = \left[\frac{1}{2} \log(1 + x^2) \Bigg|_{x = 0}^{x = 1} \right]$$

$$= \frac{1}{2} \log(1 + 1) - \frac{1}{2} \log(1)$$

$$= \frac{1}{2} \log(2) - 0 = \frac{1}{2} (0.6932) = 0.3466$$

Exercises

● 1. Find the following logarithms by using the table in Appendix 3.

    (*i*) log(2)   (*v*) $\log(0.125) = \log(\frac{1}{8})$

    (*ii*) log(10)   (*vi*) log(100)

    (*iii*) log(2.72)   (*vii*) log(0.01)

    (*iv*) log(5.47)   (*viii*) $\log \sqrt{2}$

    HINT: Use the rules (15) if necessary.

● 2. Estimate the following logarithms to four significant figures using the method of interpolation described in Appendix 1.

    (*i*) log(1.027)   (*v*) log(0.1137)

    (*ii*) log(1.005)   (*vi*) log(0.9999)

    (*iii*) log(3.142)   (*vii*) log(0.003255)

    (*iv*) log(9.898)   (*viii*) log(101.7)

    HINT: See notes to Appendix 3 for log(*x*) if *x* falls outside the range $1 \leqslant x \leqslant 10.99$ given in the tables.

● 3. Use logarithms to compute

    (*i*) 3.42/1.27   (*iv*) $1.32 \times 7^{2/3}$

    (*ii*) 7.72 × 1.53 × 4.89   (*v*) $3^{1/3} \cdot 4^{1/4}$

    (*iii*) $\sqrt[3]{2} = 2^{1/3}$ (*vi*) $2 + \sqrt[3]{6.31}$

● 4. Evaluate the following to four significant figures by using any combination of methods.

    (*i*) $5^{7/13}$ (*vi*) $\sqrt[3]{108{,}000}$

    (*ii*) e^{10} (*vii*) $(0.00000389)^{3/4}$

    (*iii*) $e^{7.47}$ (*viii*) log(1000)

    (*iv*) $e^{-7.47}$ (*ix*) log(1490)

    (*v*) $(1.05)^{50}$ (*x*) log(0.0034)

    HINT: Use rules (5) and (15).

● 5. How much should you deposit in a savings account paying 6.25% annually, compounded quarterly, if you want the savings to amount to $10,000 after 5 years?

● 6. Find the interest rate that will double an investment in 8 years under continuous compounding. ANSWER: $r = \log(2)/8 \approx 8.66\%$.

● 7. After how many interest periods will a principal be tripled if invested at 9% compounded annually?

● 8. A large corporation offers to sell a bond issue to a broker. The bonds mature in 50 years to a face value of $1,000,000. How much are they worth now if investors have a choice between buying the bonds or investing money at 6% interest compounded annually? ANSWER: Their present value is $(1.06)^{-50} \cdot 1{,}000{,}000 \approx \$54{,}286$.

● 9. How much would \$1 be worth at the beginning of 1975, if it had been invested at the beginning of the year 1850 at

   (*i*) 5% interest compounded annually?

   (*ii*) 5% interest compounded quarterly?

   (*iii*) 5% interest compounded continuously?

   HINT: You will encounter exp(x) for numbers slightly larger than those tabulated in Appendix 4. But if you split off a power e^5 to get $e^x = e^5 \cdot e^{(x-5)}$, both factors can be found in the table.

●10. Legend has it that in 1626 Manhattan Island was sold to Peter Minuit by the Wappinger Indians for \$24. If the \$24 had been deposited immediately in a bank paying 3% compounded continuously, what would it be worth in 1976? ANSWER: $24e^{10.5} = 24e^5 e^5 e^{0.50} \approx \$871{,}500$.

●11. Find dy/dx if

   (*i*) $y = \log(2x)$ (*v*) $y = \log(4 + x^2)$

   (*ii*) $y = x \log(x)$ (*vi*) $y = x \log(x^3 + 1)$

   (*iii*) $y = e^x \log(x)$ (*vii*) $y = \log(\sqrt[3]{x^2 + 1})$

   (*iv*) $y = e^x + \log(x)$ (*viii*) $y = \log(x\sqrt{x^4 + 1})$

●12. Evaluate the following integrals:

   (*i*) $\displaystyle\int_1^7 \frac{1}{u}\, du$ (*iv*) $\displaystyle\int \frac{u^3}{1 + u^4}\, du$

   (*ii*) $\displaystyle\int_1^7 \frac{1}{x^2}\, dx$ (*v*) $\displaystyle\int \frac{2x^3 + x}{x^4 + x^2 + 1}\, dx$

   (*iii*) $\displaystyle\int \log(e^x)\, dx$ (*vi*) $\displaystyle\int \frac{e^x}{4 + e^x}\, dx$

 13. In Figure 1.19, Section 1.7, the size of a pheasant population was approximately described by the formula

$$N(t) = 8 \cdot 2^{1.6t} \qquad (t \geqslant 0 \text{ in years})$$

In order to plot the graph shown in that figure, it was necessary to calculate the values of $N(t)$ for $t = 0, 1, 2, 3, 4$, and 5. Use logarithms to calculate these values.

●14. In Section 1.7 we described the growth of a certain population by the formula

$$N(t) = 30{,}000{,}000 \cdot 2^{t/30} \qquad (t \geqslant 0 \text{ in years})$$

Use logarithms to compute the size of the population after (*i*) $t = 2$ years, (*ii*) $t = 10$ years, and (*iii*) $t = 45$ years. After how many years will the population triple in size from its initial value $N(0) = 30{,}000{,}000$?

●15. Use the formulas $2 = e^{\log(2)}$ and $10 = e^{\log(10)}$ and the algebraic rules (15) to show that the functions

$$(i)\ f(x) = 2^x \qquad (ii)\ f(x) = 10^x$$

can be written as $f(x) = e^{kx}$ for suitable choices of the constant k. Evaluate the constant in each case. ANSWERS: (*i*) $2^x = e^{kx}, k = \log(2) = 0.69315$; (*ii*) $10^x = e^{kx}, k = \log(10) = 2.3025$.

*●16. Show that the function $f(x) = a^x$ (with $a > 0$) can be expressed in terms of exponentials to base e in the form

$$a^x = e^{x \cdot \log(a)} \qquad \text{for all real } x$$

NOTE: In this way, calculations involving an arbitrary base a can be handled by the use of exponentials with base e. HINT: $a = e^{\log(a)}$.

6.4   Growth and Decay Phenomena

Growth and decay are opposites. In this section we shall show that both may be described by a single all-encompassing theory. Exponentials and logarithms are the key to this theory; as we shall see, the growth or decay of a quantity Q with time is often governed by an exponential equation

$$Q(t) = Ce^{kt} \qquad (C \text{ and } k \text{ suitably chosen constants})$$

Let us start with a particular problem, the decay of radioactive elements, before describing the general theory.

Since 1900 the concept of radioactivity has slowly become part of the public consciousness. No doubt you have heard about radioactive fallout from weapons tests, and its steady but excruciatingly slow decay into inert products. Or you may have heard about carbon dating of objects and archeological sites, which has revolutionized our understanding of past history. This dating method involves careful measurement of the decay of radioactive C^{14} (carbon-14), which is produced by the action of cosmic rays on (nonradioactive) atmospheric nitrogen (see Example 19 below).

In any object the amount of radioactive material steadily decreases as unstable radioactive atoms decay into stable inert products. To describe this decrease quantitatively, let Q be the weight of radioactive material. Then $Q = Q(t)$ is a function of time t that steadily decreases toward zero. The crucial fact is that the *rate of change* dQ/dt at any moment is proportional to the *amount of material* $Q(t)$ present at that moment. That is

$$\frac{dQ}{dt} = k \cdot Q(t) \qquad \text{for all } t \tag{20}$$

In a decay process material is lost, so Q decreases, dQ/dt is negative, and k is a negative number; in a growth process $k > 0$. This proportionality (20) can be justified by a "thought experiment." Suppose we take away part of the sample, leaving, say, 1/2 (or 1/3 or 15/27) of the original sample. Then the number dQ/dt of atoms decaying per second in the remaining sample is obviously 1/2 (or 1/3 or

15/27) the number in the full sample. That is, the decay rate dQ/dt, the number of atoms decaying per unit time, is proportional to the amount of radioactive material in the sample. The value of k determines the rate at which atoms decay. It depends on the material studied, and must be determined by physical experiment.

We have come to a crucial turning point in our discussion. Once we are assured that $dQ/dt = k \cdot Q$, the facts we have learned about Calculus completely determine the form of the function $Q(t)$. We have recently encountered functions whose derivatives are proportional to the original function; referring to equation (10) we see that $Q_1(t) = \exp(kt) = e^{kt}$ satisfies (20):

$$\frac{dQ_1}{dt} = \frac{d}{dt}\{e^{kt}\} = e^{kt} \cdot \frac{d}{dt}\{kt\} = k \cdot e^{kt} = k \cdot Q_1(t)$$

Are there other functions $Q(t)$ satisfying (20)? To find the answer, define $f(t) = Q(t)/Q_1(t) = Q(t)e^{-kt}$. Then

$$Q(t) = f(t) \cdot e^{kt} \tag{21}$$

Differentiating each side of this identity, we get

$$\frac{dQ}{dt} = f'(t)e^{kt} + f(t) \cdot ke^{kt}$$

Since $Q(t)$ is to satisfy (20) we must have $dQ/dt = k \cdot Q$, so that

$$f'(t)e^{kt} + f(t) \cdot ke^{kt} = \frac{dQ}{dt} = k \cdot Q(t) = k \cdot f(t)e^{kt}$$

Subtracting $f(t) \cdot ke^{kt}$ from each side we get

$$f'(t) \cdot e^{kt} = 0 \qquad \text{for all } t$$

which tells us that

$$f'(t) = 0 \qquad \text{for all } t$$

since e^x is *never* zero. The only functions with zero derivative are constant functions $f(t) = C$. Therefore, the most general solution $Q(t)$ of equation (20) is

$$Q(t) = Ce^{kt} \qquad \text{for all } t \tag{22}$$

where C is some constant. This constant C is always the *initial value* of Q, when $t = 0$; indeed, setting $t = 0$ in (22) we get $Q(0) = Ce^0 = C$.

Example 18   For the radioactive element radium, the constant k in (22) determined by experiment is $k = -4.27 \times 10^{-4}$ if t is measured in years. In how many years will an ounce of radium disintegrate so that only half the original amount remains? (In any decay process, the time it takes for half of the original material to disintegrate is characteristic of the material and is called its **half-life**.)

Solution   If $Q(t)$ is the weight remaining after t years we know that $dQ/dt = -4.27 \times 10^{-4} \cdot Q(t)$, so that in (22) we get

$$Q(t) = Ce^{(-4.27 \times 10^{-4}) \cdot t}$$

for a suitable choice of the constant C. Initially (when $t = 0$) there is one ounce or radium, so

$$1 = Q(0) = Ce^{(-4.27 \times 10^{-4}) \cdot 0} = Ce^0 = C$$

and $C = 1$. This completely determines the function $Q(t)$:

$$Q(t) = e^{(-4.27 \times 10^{-4})t} \qquad \text{for all } t \geq 0 \tag{23}$$

After a certain amount of time T (the half-life of radium) only $1/2$ ounce will remain:

$$\frac{1}{2} = Q(T) = e^{(-4.27 \times 10^{-4})T}$$

We solve for T by taking the logarithm on each side:

$$\log\left(\frac{1}{2}\right) = (-4.27 \times 10^{-4})T$$

Use Appendix 3 to find $\log(1/2) = \log(2^{-1}) = -\log(2.0) = -0.69315$. Then

$$T = \frac{-0.69315}{-4.27 \times 10^{-4}} = \frac{0.69315}{4.27} \times 10^4 = 1623 \text{ years}$$

Clearly, if we start with *any* initial amount of radium other than one ounce, half of that amount will remain after $T = 1623$ years; the half-life is independent of the amount we start with. There is no sense in talking about the "full" lifetime of radium: since $Q(t) = e^{(-4.27 \times 10^{-4})t}$ never reaches zero, there is always some radium left no matter how much time has passed.

Example 19   The half-life of C^{14}, the radioactive form of carbon, is 5720 years: half of any sample will decay in this period of time. Determine the constant k in formula (22) and write out the formula for the amount of C^{14} remaining after t years if initially there is 1 gram of pure material. Calculate the amount of C^{14} remaining after 1, 2, and 3 half-lives have elapsed. Calculate the amount remaining after 10,000 years.

Solution   In equation (22), $C = 1$, since initially there is 1 gram of material. From the definition of half-life we know that

$$Q(5720) = e^{5720k} = 0.5 \text{ grams}$$

Taking logarithms, we obtain k

$$5720k = \log(0.5) = -\log\left(\frac{1}{0.5}\right) = -\log(2.0) = -0.69315$$

$$k = \frac{-0.69315}{5720} = -1.212 \times 10^{-4} = -0.0001212$$

Thus the amount after t years is

$$Q(t) = e^{(-1.212 \times 10^{-4})t} \text{ grams} \tag{24}$$

If $t = 10,000 = 10^4$ we get

$$Q = e^{(-1.212 \times 10^{-4}) \times 10^4} = e^{-1.212} = 0.2976 \text{ grams}$$

or 29.8% of the original amount.
As successive half-lives elapse we have $t = 5720, 11,440, 17,160,$ and so on. We could substitute these values into (24) to get

$$Q = 0.500 = \tfrac{1}{2} \qquad \text{after 1 half-life}$$

$$Q = 0.250 = \tfrac{1}{4} \qquad \text{after 2 half-lives}$$

$$Q = 0.125 = \tfrac{1}{8} \qquad \text{after 3 half-lives}$$

and so on. However, at each step 1/2 of the previous amount remains, so it is actually obvious *without any computation at all* that we should get $Q = 1/2, 1/4, 1/8, 1/16, \ldots$ as successive half-lives elapse. For the reader's convenience we have sketched the graph of $Q(t)$ in Figure 6.3, plotting the points corresponding to successive half-lives $t = T, 2T, 3T,$ and so on.

Example 20   The carbon in the atmosphere is mostly the stable isotope C^{12}, with a small percentage of the radioactive isotope C^{14}. During the life of any plant or

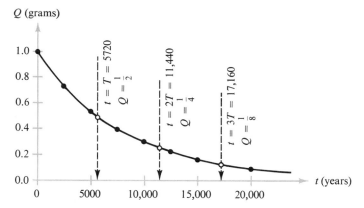

Figure 6.3
Graph of the exponential function $Q(t) = e^{kt}$, taking $k = -1.212 \times 10^{-4} = -0.0001212$. For any negative k the graph of $y = e^{kt}$ has the same general shape. Initially $y(0) = 1$; thereafter y values decrease steadily toward zero. This function gives the amount remaining after t years from a 1-gram initial sample of C^{14}. The half-life of C^{14} is $T = 5720$ years. Note the values of Q after successive half-lives have elapsed (open dots). Solid dots are values calculated by using Appendix 4.

animal the ratio of weights C^{14}/C^{12} in its body is almost identical to the corresponding ratio for carbon in the air; organic carbon is ultimately drawn from the air by plant photosynthesis, and biochemical processes cannot distinguish between C^{12} and C^{14}. After the death of the plant there is no further exchange of carbon between the air and the remains, so the radioactive C^{14} decomposes while the inert C^{12} remains unaltered. The ratio of C^{14} to C^{12} steadily decreases toward zero.

If bones discovered in an archeological dig contain 25% of their original C^{14} content, find their age t_0 by using the facts worked out in Example 19.

Solution   If C is the initial amount of C^{14}, then at any later time the amount remaining is given by formula (24)

$$Q(t) = Ce^{(-1.212 \times 10^{-4})t} \qquad (t - \text{years after death})$$

At present, t_0 years after death, the weight of C^{14} is only 25% of the original amount, so $Q(t_0) = 0.25C$ and

$$0.25C = Ce^{(-1.212 \times 10^{-4})t_0}$$

The (undetermined) constant C cancels out, leaving

$$0.25 = e^{(-1.212 \times 10^{-4})t_0}$$

$$(-1.212 \times 10^{-4})t_0 = \log(0.25) = \log(2.5) - \log(10) = -1.3862$$

so that the bones are

$$t_0 = \frac{-1.3862}{-1.212 \times 10^{-4}} = \frac{1.3862}{1.212} \times 10^4 = 11{,}437 \text{ years old}$$

In the exercises we shall examine other "decay processes" unrelated to radio-active decay. All can be described by equations (20) and (22). Growth phenomena obey the same equation

$$\frac{dQ}{dt} = k \cdot Q \tag{25}$$

except that the constant k is a positive number. The foregoing mathematical analysis applies, verbatim, to show that $Q(t)$ must have the form

$$Q(t) = Ce^{kt} \qquad (C \text{ a constant}) \tag{26}$$

Again C is the value of Q when $t = 0$; k determines the rate of growth. Exponential functions (26) have graphs of the form shown in Figure 6.4, according to whether $k > 0$ or $k < 0$.

Examples of **exponential growth** include continuous compounding of interest and certain types of population growth in both plants and animals. The most direct way to see this for continuously compounded interest is to notice that equations (26) and (4) are identical except for the names of the constants.

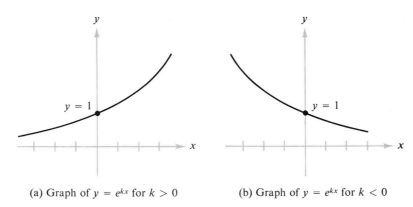

(a) Graph of $y = e^{kx}$ for $k > 0$ (b) Graph of $y = e^{kx}$ for $k < 0$

Figure 6.4
The graph of an exponential function $y = e^{kx}$ rises (a) or falls (b) according to whether the constant k is positive or negative. If $k = 0$ then $y = e^{kx} = e^0 = 1$ for all x (a constant function). The graphs are very steep if k is large positive or large negative. They pass through $(0, 1)$ no matter what the value of k.

As for population growth, an argument similar to that used for radioactive decay makes it plausible to assume that the rate of population growth is proportional to the size of the population at that instant, if family size, life expectancy, and so on remain stable.

Example 21   Country X, with a high birth rate, has a population that grows 3% annually. Estimate the size of the population in 50 years if the population now is 10 million.

Solution   The population after t years is given by an equation of the form

$$N(t) = Ce^{kt} \qquad (t \text{ in years})$$

Since $N(0) = 10{,}000{,}000$ we see that $C = C \cdot e^0 = 10{,}000{,}000$; our main task is to find k. To say that the population increases by 3% in one year means that

$$\frac{N(1) - N(0)}{N(0)} - 0.03 \qquad (= 3\% \text{ growth from initial value } N(0) \text{ in 1 year})$$

But $N(1) = Ce^{k \cdot 1} = N(0) \cdot e^k$; thus the value $N(0) = 10{,}000{,}000$ cancels out in the formula

$$0.03 = \frac{N(0) \cdot e^k - N(0)}{N(0)} = e^k - 1$$

Adding 1 to both sides, we get

$$1.03 = e^k \quad \text{or} \quad k = \log(1.03) = 0.02956$$

Consequently

$$N(t) = 10{,}000{,}000e^{(0.02956)t} \qquad (t \text{ in years}) \qquad (27)$$

In $t = 50$ years the population will be

$$N(50) = 10{,}000{,}000e^{(0.02956) \cdot 50}$$

$$= 10{,}000{,}000e^{1.478}$$

$$= 10{,}000{,}000(4.3842) \approx 43.8 \text{ million}$$

With formula (27) in hand we could go on to answer many other questions. For instance, how long does it take this population to double in size? (See Exercise 5.)

Exercises

- 1. A bacterial population, initially $N = 10,000$, increases to $N = 40,000$ after three hours in an incubated medium. The size of the population obeys a growth law of the form $N(t) = Ae^{kt}$ for suitably chosen constants A and k, as long as nutrients are plentiful. From the given values $N(0) = 10,000$ and $N(3) = 40,000$ determine the constants A and k and write down the explicit growth formula. After how many hours will the population double in size?

- 2. Carbon in the cloth wrapper of an Egyptian mummy has been found to contain 71% of its original C^{14} content. Presumably the wrappings and the mummy have nearly equal ages. What is the age of the entombed luminary? HINT: Refer to Example 20.

- 3. Country Y doubles in population every 37 years. Find the percentage increase in population during a ten-year period.

- 4. Country A has a population of 6,000,000 that doubles every 40 years. Country B's population is 4,000,000 and it doubles every 25 years. In how many years will the two countries have equal populations?

- 5. Countries W, X, Y, and Z have populations which grow by 1%, 2%, 3%, and 5% annually. Assuming that population growth is not suppressed by famine, disease, or a shift to smaller families, the population in each country will double in a certain amount of time. Calculate these "doubling times" by using ideas from Example 21. NOTE: Initial population is irrelevant.

- 6. Physical chemists have determined that uranium is radioactive, with the very long half-life of 4.5×10^9 years. Write out a formula for the amount $Q(t)$ left after t years if there is one kilogram of pure uranium when $t = 0$. How much remains after 1 billion years? 10 billion years? 100 billion years? ANSWERS: $Q(t) = e^{kt}$ kilograms, where $k = \log(\frac{1}{2})/(4.5 \times 10^9) = -0.154 \times 10^{-9}$; $Q(1 \times 10^9) = e^{-0.154} = 0.857$; $Q(10 \times 10^9) = e^{-1.54} = 0.214$; $Q(100 \times 10^9) = e^{-15.4} = e^{-5} \cdot e^{-5} \cdot e^{-5} \cdot e^{-0.4} = 2.05 \times 10^{-7}$.

- 7. Uranium decays into a form of lead that does not occur naturally. Thus chemical tests of a rock specimen can tell us what fraction of the uranium in the rock has decayed into lead since the rock solidified. Suppose the fraction of uranium *remaining* in three specimens of granite (from different locations) is

$$(i)\ 78\% \qquad (ii)\ 85\% \qquad (iii)\ 92\%$$

Determine the age of each rock. What conclusions can you draw about the age of the Earth? HINT: Refer to Exercise 6 and its answers.

- 8. Suppose that 0.157% of the original uranium in a sample of Canadian pitchblende (a rich uranium ore) has decayed to lead. Estimate the number of years since the ore mass was formed, using the facts discussed in Exercise 6. HINT: You must find $\log(1 - 0.00157) = \log(0.99843) = \log(9.9843) - \log(10)$; use interpolation to get $\log(9.9843)$.

- 9. The intensity I of sunlight reaching a depth of water x decreases exponentially with x according to the formula

$$I = I_0 e^{-0.5x} \qquad (x \text{ measured in feet})$$

where I_0 is the intensity at the water surface. At what depth is 50% of the sunlight absorbed? 70%? 90%?

●10. DDT absorbed in lake-bottom mud is slowly degraded by bacterial action into harmless products. Careful measurements show that 10% of the initial amount is eliminated in 5 years. As in all decay processes, the concentration of DDT is described by an equation of the form $C(t) = Ce^{kt}$, where C is the initial concentration. Determine k. What is the half-life of DDT in this environment (after how many years will half of the initial contaminant be degraded)? After how many years will 95% be degraded?

●11. Suppose that the growth of a variable $Q = Q(t)$ is governed by an exponential formula

$$Q(t) = Ae^{kt} \qquad (A \text{ and } k \text{ are positive constants})$$

Prove that there is a "doubling time" T such that Q doubles if we start at any time t and allow time T to elapse:

$$Q(t + T) = 2 \cdot Q(t) \qquad \text{for any starting time}$$

How is T related to k and A? ANSWERS: $Q(t + T)/Q(t) = e^{k(t+T)}/e^{kt} = e^{kT} = 2$ means $kT = \log(2)$ or $k = \log(2)/T$; T does not depend on A.

*6.5   Differential Equations with Separable Variables

In Section 6.4 we investigated the equation $dQ/dt = kQ$ (k a fixed constant). This is an example of a **differential equation**, an equation involving an unknown function *and its derivatives*. Such equations play an extremely important role in physics, engineering, biology, economics, and other subjects. A vast theory of differential equations exists; we shall barely scratch the surface.

Let us return to the convention of writing x for the independent variable and y for the dependent variable, and consider a special type of equation, a **differential equation with separable variables**. This is an equation that may be written in the form

$$\frac{dy}{dx} = \frac{f(x)}{g(y)} \tag{28}$$

where $f(x)$ and $g(y)$ are continuous functions of x and y respectively. For instance, the following equations may be rewritten this way after suitable algebraic manipulation:

$$\frac{dy}{dx} - 3y = 0 \qquad\qquad \frac{dy}{dx} = ky \qquad (k \text{ a fixed constant})$$

$$y\frac{dy}{dx} = x^2 + x \qquad\qquad \frac{dy}{dx} = yx^2 = \frac{x^2}{\left(\dfrac{1}{y}\right)}$$

In each case we seek a function $y = y(x)$ that reduces equation (28) to an identity if we set $y = y(x)$. Such functions are called the **solutions** of the differential equation.

Here is a formal procedure for finding all solutions of equation (28): A small change dx in the independent variable is related to the corresponding change dy in $y = y(x)$ by

$$g(y)\, dy = f(x)\, dx \tag{29}$$

Equation (29) cries out for some integral signs, which we now provide:

$$\int g(y)\, dy = \int f(x)\, dx \tag{30}$$

Performing the integrations in (30) amounts to finding the antiderivatives (indefinite integrals) of the given functions $f(x)$ and $g(y)$. This gives the desired solutions, if we remember to introduce an arbitrary added constant when we integrate. It would take us too far afield to verify that this formal procedure actually yields all solutions to the differential equation. Instead we shall illustrate the use of the procedure in a few examples.

Example 22   Solve the differential equation $dy/dx = ky$ where k is a fixed constant. What if $k = 1$?

Solution   We recognize that the variables are separable, with $f(x) = k$ (constant function) and $g(y) = 1/y$, so that

$$\frac{dy}{dx} = \frac{f(x)}{g(y)} = \frac{k}{(y^{-1})} = ky$$

Separating the variables, we get

$$\frac{1}{y}\, dy = k\, dx \quad \text{or} \quad \int \frac{1}{y}\, dy = \int k\, dx$$

so that

$$\log(y) = kx + c \qquad (c \text{ an arbitrary constant}) \tag{31}$$

is the most general solution. To obtain y as an explicit function of x, we take the exponential of each side in (31) to get

$$y = e^{kx+c} = e^c e^{kx} = Ce^{kx} \qquad (C \text{ an arbitrary constant})$$

If $k = 1$ we get $y = Ce^x$.

Example 23   Solve the differential equation $\dfrac{dy}{dx} = y - x$.

Solution   The variables are not separable in this case, so we cannot apply our procedure. In advanced courses methods are introduced for handling this sort of equation, but we shall not discuss them here. You might wish to verify that

$$y = 1 + x + Ce^x \qquad (C \text{ any constant})$$

is a solution, by direct differentiation and substitution into the differential equation.

Example 24   Find the solution of the differential equation $x\,\dfrac{dy}{dx} - 3y = 0$ for which $y = 1$ when $x = 1$ (that is, $y(1) = 1$).

Solution   The variables are separable, since the equation may be rewritten in the form

$$\frac{dy}{dx} = \frac{3y}{x} = \left(\frac{3}{x}\right)\Big/\left(\frac{1}{y}\right)$$

Separating the variables, we find that

$$\frac{1}{y}\,dy = 3\,\frac{1}{x}\,dx \quad \text{or} \quad \int \frac{1}{y}\,dy = 3 \int \frac{1}{x}\,dx$$

so that

$$\log(y) = 3 \log(x) + c = \log(x^3) + c \tag{32}$$

where c is an arbitrary constant. The particular solution we seek is the one for which $y(1) = 1$, so that

$$0 = \log(1) = 3 \log(1) + c = 3 \cdot 0 + c = c$$

Therefore $\log(y) = \log(x^3)$; taking the exponential on each side, we get

$$y = y(x) = x^3$$

It is easy to verify that this really is the desired solution.

Example 25   Simple models of population growth are based on the differential equation

$$\frac{dN}{dt} = kN$$

However, if deaths or external factors that limit population growth are to be taken into account, a more complicated equation must be used. One such modified growth equation has the form

$$\frac{dN}{dt} = kN(A - N) \tag{33}$$

Here k and A are constants that must be determined from observations. Roughly, equation (33) says that:

(*i*) When the population N is relatively small, so that $A - N \approx A$, the rate of population increase is approximately proportional to N, and thus grows more or less exponentially.

(*ii*) As N increases toward the "limiting value" A, both $A - N$ and $kN(A - N)$ get very small, which forces the growth rate dN/dt to slow down and approach zero.

Find all solutions of this modified growth equation.

Solution   By separating the variables N and t we obtain

$$\int \frac{1}{N(A - N)} \, dN = k \int dt$$

The antiderivative on the left can be evaluated by using the algebraic identity

$$\frac{1}{N(A - N)} = \frac{1}{A} \left[\frac{1}{N} + \frac{1}{A - N} \right]$$

Thus

$$\int \frac{1}{N(A - N)} \, dN = \frac{1}{A} \int \left(\frac{1}{N} + \frac{1}{A - N} \right) dN$$

$$= \frac{1}{A} \int \frac{1}{N} \, dN + \frac{1}{A} \int \frac{1}{A - N} \, dN = \frac{1}{A} \log N - \frac{1}{A} \log(A - N)$$

and

$$\frac{1}{A} \log \left(\frac{N}{A - N} \right) = kt + c \qquad (c \text{ an arbitrary constant})$$

Multiplying by A and taking exponentials on each side, we get

$$\frac{N}{A - N} = e^{Ac} e^{Akt} = C e^{Akt}$$

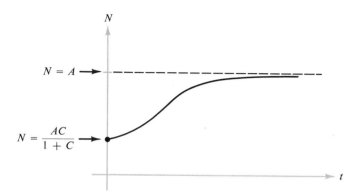

Figure 6.5
The graph of the growth function $N = ACe^{Akt}/(1 + Ce^{Akt})$ is S-shaped.
At first, for t near zero, $N(t)$ increases exponentially; but then the rate
of growth dN/dt gradually decreases toward zero as N approaches the
limiting value A. Since dN/dt is equal to the slope of the curve, the
graph levels off as shown.

where C is an arbitrary number. Solving explicitly for N, we have

$$N = (A - N)Ce^{Akt} = ACe^{Akt} - NCe^{Akt}$$

so that

$$N(1 + Ce^{Akt}) = ACe^{Akt}$$

and

$$N = \frac{ACe^{Akt}}{1 + Ce^{Akt}} \qquad (C \text{ an arbitrary constant}) \qquad (34)$$

The graph of such a function, shown in Figure 6.5, is called a sigmoid (literally,
S-shaped) curve, and arises quite often in realistic models of growth.

Exercises

●1. Solve the following differential equations:

(i) $y' = x$

(ii) $\dfrac{dy}{dx} = x^3 + 1$

(iii) $y' = y - 1$

(iv) $\dfrac{dy}{dx} - \dfrac{3x^2}{2y} = 0$

(v) $\dfrac{dy}{dx} = xe^y$ (vi) $\dfrac{dy}{dx} + x^2 y = x^2$

●2. Find the particular solution to the differential equation $dy/dx = y^2$ for which $y(2) = 1$. Check your answer by substituting it into the differential equation. Also verify that $y(2) = 1$.

●3. Solve $x \dfrac{dy}{dx} = y$, finding the solution for which $y = 2$ when $x = 1$.

●4. The population N of a certain bacteria culture is found to satisfy the differential equation

$$\frac{dN}{dt} = 0.1\sqrt{N}$$

If $N = 10{,}000$ when $t = 0$, find the population when $t = 100$.

●5. If an object is kept in surroundings of constant temperature, say 50°F, its temperature gradually tends toward that of its surroundings. **Newton's law of cooling** states that the rate of change dU/dt in the temperature U of the object is proportional to the difference in temperatures $U - 50$ between the object and the medium:

$$\frac{dU}{dt} = k(U - 50) \qquad \text{for some negative constant } k$$

Assume $k = -0.2$ and $U = 70°F$ when $t = 0$. Find U when $t = 3$. Find the formula for $U(t)$.

●6. In Exercise 5, how long does it take to cool an object to halfway between its initial temperature 70°F and its ultimate temperature 50°F?

Function Tables and Interpolation

When using tables to look up the value of a function f at a certain point x, you may often find that it falls between two values listed in the tables. By **interpolating** between these values of f, you can obtain an accurate estimate of the value of f at x. For example, the value of the square-root function $\sqrt{x}$ at $x = 2.14$ falls between the tabulated values (Appendix 2)

$$\sqrt{2.10} = 1.4491 \quad \text{and} \quad \sqrt{2.20} = 1.4832$$

Interpolation is based on the following simple idea: since $x = 2.14 = 2.10 + 0.04$ lies $4/10$ of the way from 2.10 to 2.20, the value of $\sqrt{2.14}$ should lie roughly $4/10$ of the way between the tabulated values $\sqrt{2.10}$ and $\sqrt{2.20}$. Since the difference between the tabulated values is $\Delta y = \sqrt{2.20} - \sqrt{2.10} = +0.0341$, this means that

$$\sqrt{2.14} \approx \sqrt{2.10} + \frac{4}{10} \cdot (\Delta y)$$

$$= 1.4491 + 0.4(0.0341)$$

$$= 1.4491 + 0.0136 = 1.4627$$

This estimate is pretty good. The exact value is $\sqrt{2.14} = 1.46287\ldots$. Here are some examples of interpolation using other tables.

Example Estimate log(2.1463) by interpolation.

Solution The nearest tabulated values of the logarithm (Appendix 3) are

$$\log(2.14) = 0.76081 \quad \text{and} \quad \log(2.15) = 0.76547$$

whose difference is $\Delta y = \log(2.15) - \log(2.14) = 0.00466$. Now $x = 2.1463$ lies $63/100$ of the way from 2.1400 to 2.1500. Thus $\log(2.1463)$ lies roughly $63/100$ of the way between $\log(2.14)$ and $\log(2.15)$:

$$\log(2.1463) \approx \log(2.14) + \frac{63}{100} \cdot (\Delta y)$$

$$= 0.76081 + 0.63(0.00466)$$

$$= 0.76081 + 0.00294 = 0.76375$$

The exact value is 0.763745 .... .

Example Estimate $e^{1.013}$ by interpolation.

Solution The nearest tabulated values of e^x (Appendix 4) are

$$e^{1.01} = 2.7456 \quad \text{and} \quad e^{1.02} = 2.7731$$

with difference $\Delta y = e^{1.02} - e^{1.01} = 0.0275$. Now $x = 1.013$ lies $3/10$ of the way from 1.010 to 1.020. Thus $e^{1.013}$ should lie roughly $3/10$ of the way between the values $e^{1.01}$ and $e^{1.02}$:

$$e^{1.013} = e^{1.01} + \frac{3}{10} \cdot (\Delta y) = 2.7456 + 0.3(0.0275)$$

$$= 2.7456 + 0.0083 = 2.7539$$

The exact value is 2.75385 .... .

Example Estimate $e^{-1.3172}$ by interpolation.

Solution The nearest tabulated values (Appendix 4) are for $x = 1.31$ and $x = 1.32$:

$$e^{-1.31} = 0.269820 \quad \text{and} \quad e^{-1.32} = 0.267135$$

As x increases from 1.31 to 1.32, the value of e^{-x} decreases:

$$\Delta y = e^{-1.32} - e^{-1.31} = -0.002685$$

Now $x = 1.3172$ lies $72/100$ of the way from 1.3100 to 1.3200, so $e^{-1.3172}$ lies roughly $72/100$ of the way between $e^{-1.31}$ and $e^{-1.32}$:

$$e^{-1.3172} \approx e^{-1.31} + \frac{72}{100} \cdot (\Delta y)$$

$$= 0.269820 + 0.72(-0.002685)$$

$$= 0.269820 - 0.001933 = 0.267887$$

The exact value is $e^{-1.3172} = 0.267884 \ldots$.

Example Estimate $\log(0.00714362)$.

Solution First notice that we may write (see Appendix 3)

$$\log(0.00714362) = \log(7.14362 \times 10^{-3})$$

$$= \log(7.14362) + \log(10^{-3}) = \log(7.14362) - 3 \cdot \log(10)$$

so we are really concerned with finding $\log(7.14362)$; $\log(10) = 2.3025$ is already in the table. Now $x = 7.14362$ lies $362/1000$ of the way between the nearest tabulated values, 7.14 and 7.15, for which

$$\log(7.14) = 1.9657 \quad \text{and} \quad \log(7.15) = 1.9671$$

The difference is $\Delta y = 0.0014$; thus $\log(7.14362)$ lies roughly $362/1000$ of the way between these tabulated values:

$$\log(7.14362) \approx \log(7.14) + \frac{362}{1000} \cdot (\Delta y)$$

$$= 1.9657 + 0.362(0.0014)$$

$$= 1.9657 + 0.0005 = 1.9662$$

Returning to our original problem, we find that

$$\log(0.00714362) = 1.9662 - 3(2.3025)$$

$$= 1.9662 - 6.9075 = -4.9413$$

Table of Square Roots

This table gives values of $\sqrt{x}$ to five significant figures, for x in the range $0 \leqslant x \leqslant 100$. To extend the range of the table, note that

$$\sqrt{100x} = \sqrt{100} \cdot \sqrt{x} = 10\sqrt{x}$$

$$\sqrt{1000x} = \sqrt{100} \cdot \sqrt{10x} = 10\sqrt{10x}$$

and so on. For example

$$\sqrt{440} = 10 \cdot \sqrt{4.40} = 10 \times 2.0976 = 20.976$$

$$\sqrt{0.0045} = \sqrt{45} \times \sqrt{0.0001} = 6.7082 \times 10^{-2} = 0.067082$$

When confronted with numbers presented as products or fractions, it may help to keep in mind the following rules (special cases of the laws of exponents):

$$\sqrt{a \cdot b} = \sqrt{a} \cdot \sqrt{b} \qquad \sqrt{\frac{a}{b}} = \frac{\sqrt{a}}{\sqrt{b}}$$

Square Roots of x and $10x$

x	$\sqrt{x}$	$\sqrt{10x}$	x	$\sqrt{x}$	$\sqrt{10x}$
0.0	.00000	0.0000	5.1	2.2583	7.1414
0.1	.31623	1.0000	5.2	2.2803	7.2111
0.2	.44721	1.4142	5.3	2.3021	7.2801
0.3	.54772	1.7320	5.4	2.3237	7.3484
0.4	.63246	2.0000	5.5	2.3452	7.4162
0.5	.70711	2.2360	5.6	2.3664	7.4833
0.6	.77460	2.4494	5.7	2.3874	7.5498
0.7	.83666	2.6457	5.8	2.4083	7.6157
0.8	.89443	2.8284	5.9	2.4289	7.6811
0.9	.94868	3.0000	6.0	2.4494	7.7459
1.0	1.0000	3.1622	6.1	2.4698	7.8102
1.1	1.0488	3.3166	6.2	2.4899	7.8740
1.2	1.0954	3.4641	6.3	2.5099	7.9372
1.3	1.1401	3.6055	6.4	2.5298	8.0000
1.4	1.1832	3.7416	6.5	2.5495	8.0622
1.5	1.2247	3.8729	6.6	2.5690	8.1240
1.6	1.2649	4.0000	6.7	2.5884	8.1853
1.7	1.3038	4.1231	6.8	2.6076	8.2462
1.8	1.3416	4.2426	6.9	2.6267	8.3066
1.9	1.3784	4.3589	7.0	2.6457	8.3666
2.0	1.4142	4.4721	7.1	2.6645	8.4261
2.1	1.4491	4.5825	7.2	2.6832	8.4852
2.2	1.4832	4.6904	7.3	2.7018	8.5440
2.3	1.5165	4.7958	7.4	2.7202	8.6023
2.4	1.5491	4.8989	7.5	2.7386	8.6602
2.5	1.5811	5.0000	7.6	2.7568	8.7178
2.6	1.6124	5.0990	7.7	2.7748	8.7749
2.7	1.6431	5.1961	7.8	2.7928	8.8317
2.8	1.6733	5.2915	7.9	2.8106	8.8881
2.9	1.7029	5.3851	8.0	2.8284	8.9442
3.0	1.7320	5.4772	8.1	2.8460	9.0000
3.1	1.7606	5.5677	8.2	2.8635	9.0553
3.2	1.7888	5.6568	8.3	2.8809	9.1104
3.3	1.8165	5.7445	8.4	2.8982	9.1651
3.4	1.8439	5.8309	8.5	2.9154	9.2195
3.5	1.8708	5.9160	8.6	2.9325	9.2736
3.6	1.8973	6.0000	8.7	2.9495	9.3273
3.7	1.9235	6.0827	8.8	2.9664	9.3808
3.8	1.9493	6.1644	8.9	2.9832	9.4339
3.9	1.9748	6.2450	9.0	3.0000	9.4868
4.0	2.0000	6.3245	9.1	3.0166	9.5393
4.1	2.0248	6.4031	9.2	3.0331	9.5916
4.2	2.0493	6.4807	9.3	3.0495	9.6436
4.3	2.0736	6.5574	9.4	3.0659	9.6953
4.4	2.0976	6.6332	9.5	3.0822	9.7467
4.5	2.1213	6.7082	9.6	3.0983	9.7979
4.6	2.1447	6.7823	9.7	3.1144	9.8488
4.7	2.1679	6.8556	9.8	3.1305	9.8994
4.8	2.1908	6.9282	9.9	3.1464	9.9498
4.9	2.2135	7.0000	10.0	3.1622	10.000
5.0	2.2360	7.0710			

Table of Natural Logarithms

This table gives values of $\log(x)$ for x in the range $1.00 \leqslant x \leqslant 10.99$, in steps of $\Delta x = 0.01$. To extend the range of the table, remember that any number x can be written as a power of 10 times a number between 1 and 10. Then use the rules

$$\log(a \cdot b) = \log(a) + \log(b)$$

$$\log(10^r) = r \cdot \log(10) = (2.3025) \times r$$

to evaluate $\log(x)$. For example

$$\log(450) = \log(4.5 \times 10^2) = \log(4.5) + 2 \cdot \log(10)$$

$$= 1.5041 + 2 \cdot (2.3025) = 6.1091$$

or

$$\log(0.0045) = \log(4.5 \times 10^{-3}) = \log(4.5) + (-3) \cdot \log(10)$$

$$= 1.5041 - 3 \cdot (2.3025) = -5.4034$$

When dealing with numbers presented as fractions it may help to recall the rules

$$\log\left(\frac{a}{b}\right) = \log(a) - \log(b) \qquad \log\left(\frac{1}{a}\right) = -\log(a)$$

Thus, without dividing out the fractions we may calculate

$$\log\left(\frac{4.58}{1.7}\right) = \log(4.58) - \log(1.7)$$

$$= 1.5217 - 0.5306 = 0.9911$$

or

$$\log\left(\frac{1}{2.13}\right) = -\log(2.13) = -0.75612$$

Natural Logarithms ($\log x$)

x	.00	.01	.02	.03	.04	.05	.06	.07	.08	.09
1.0	.00000	.00995	.01980	.02956	.03922	.04879	.05827	.06766	.07696	.08618
1.1	.09531	.10436	.11333	.12222	.13103	.13976	.14842	.15700	.16551	.17395
1.2	.18232	.19062	.19885	.20701	.21511	.22314	.23111	.23902	.24686	.25464
1.3	.26236	.27003	.27763	.28518	.29267	.30010	.30748	.31481	.32208	.32930
1.4	.33647	.34359	.35066	.35767	.36464	.37156	.37844	.38526	.39204	.39878
1.5	.40547	.41211	.41871	.42527	.43178	.43825	.44469	.45108	.45742	.46373
1.6	.47000	.47623	.48243	.48858	.49470	.50078	.50682	.51282	.51879	.52473
1.7	.53063	.53649	.54232	.54812	.55389	.55962	.56531	.57098	.57661	.58222
1.8	.58779	.59333	.59884	.60432	.60977	.61519	.62058	.62594	.63127	.63658
1.9	.64185	.64710	.65233	.65752	.66269	.66783	.67294	.67803	.68310	.68813
2.0	.69315	.69813	.70310	.70804	.71295	.71784	.72271	.72755	.73237	.73716
2.1	.74194	.74669	.75142	.75612	.76081	.76547	.77011	.77473	.77932	.78390
2.2	.78846	.79299	.79751	.80200	.80648	.81093	.81536	.81978	.82418	.82855
2.3	.83291	.83725	.84157	.84587	.85015	.85442	.85866	.86289	.86710	.87129
2.4	.87547	.87963	.88377	.88789	.89200	.89609	.90016	.90422	.90826	.91228
2.5	.91629	.92028	.92426	.92822	.93216	.93609	.94001	.94391	.94779	.95166
2.6	.95551	.95935	.96317	.96698	.97078	.97456	.97833	.98208	.98582	.98954
2.7	.99325	.99695	1.0006	1.0043	1.0080	1.0116	1.0152	1.0189	1.0225	1.0260
2.8	1.0296	1.0332	1.0367	1.0403	1.0438	1.0473	1.0508	1.0543	1.0578	1.0613
2.9	1.0647	1.0682	1.0716	1.0750	1.0784	1.0818	1.0852	1.0886	1.0919	1.0953
3.0	1.0986	1.1019	1.1053	1.1086	1.1119	1.1151	1.1184	1.1217	1.1249	1.1282
3.1	1.1314	1.1346	1.1378	1.1410	1.1442	1.1474	1.1506	1.1537	1.1569	1.1600
3.2	1.1632	1.1663	1.1694	1.1725	1.1756	1.1787	1.1817	1.1848	1.1878	1.1909
3.3	1.1939	1.1970	1.2000	1.2030	1.2060	1.2090	1.2119	1.2149	1.2179	1.2208
3.4	1.2238	1.2267	1.2296	1.2326	1.2355	1.2384	1.2413	1.2442	1.2470	1.2499
3.5	1.2528	1.2556	1.2585	1.2613	1.2641	1.2670	1.2698	1.2726	1.2754	1.2782
3.6	1.2809	1.2837	1.2865	1.2892	1.2920	1.2947	1.2975	1.3002	1.3029	1.3056
3.7	1.3083	1.3110	1.3137	1.3164	1.3191	1.3218	1.3244	1.3271	1.3297	1.3324
3.8	1.3350	1.3376	1.3403	1.3429	1.3455	1.3481	1.3507	1.3533	1.3558	1.3584
3.9	1.3610	1.3635	1.3661	1.3686	1.3712	1.3737	1.3762	1.3788	1.3813	1.3838

x	0	1	2	3	4	5	6	7	8	9
4.0	1.3863	1.3888	1.3913	1.3938	1.3962	1.3987	1.4012	1.4036	1.4061	1.4085
4.1	1.4110	1.4134	1.4159	1.4183	1.4207	1.4231	1.4255	1.4279	1.4303	1.4327
4.2	1.4351	1.4375	1.4398	1.4422	1.4446	1.4469	1.4493	1.4516	1.4540	1.4563
4.3	1.4585	1.4609	1.4633	1.4656	1.4679	1.4702	1.4725	1.4748	1.4771	1.4793
4.4	1.4816	1.4839	1.4861	1.4884	1.4907	1.4929	1.4952	1.4974	1.4996	1.5019
4.5	1.5041	1.5063	1.5085	1.5107	1.5129	1.5151	1.5173	1.5195	1.5217	1.5239
4.6	1.5261	1.5282	1.5304	1.5326	1.5347	1.5369	1.5390	1.5412	1.5433	1.5454
4.7	1.5476	1.5497	1.5518	1.5539	1.5560	1.5581	1.5603	1.5624	1.5644	1.5665
4.8	1.5686	1.5707	1.5728	1.5749	1.5769	1.5790	1.5810	1.5831	1.5852	1.5872
4.9	1.5892	1.5913	1.5933	1.5953	1.5974	1.5994	1.6014	1.6034	1.6054	1.6074
5.0	1.6094	1.6114	1.6134	1.6154	1.6174	1.6194	1.6214	1.6233	1.6253	1.6273
5.1	1.6292	1.6312	1.6332	1.6351	1.6371	1.6390	1.6409	1.6429	1.6448	1.6467
5.2	1.6487	1.6506	1.6525	1.6544	1.6563	1.6582	1.6601	1.6620	1.6639	1.6658
5.3	1.6677	1.6696	1.6715	1.6734	1.6752	1.6771	1.6790	1.6808	1.6827	1.6846
5.4	1.6864	1.6883	1.6901	1.6919	1.6938	1.6956	1.6975	1.6993	1.7011	1.7029
5.5	1.7047	1.7065	1.7083	1.7101	1.7119	1.7138	1.7156	1.7174	1.7191	1.7209
5.6	1.7227	1.7245	1.7263	1.7281	1.7298	1.7316	1.7334	1.7351	1.7369	1.7387
5.7	1.7404	1.7422	1.7439	1.7457	1.7474	1.7492	1.7509	1.7526	1.7544	1.7561
5.8	1.7578	1.7595	1.7613	1.7630	1.7647	1.7664	1.7681	1.7698	1.7715	1.7732
5.9	1.7749	1.7766	1.7783	1.7800	1.7817	1.7833	1.7850	1.7867	1.7884	1.7900
6.0	1.7917	1.7934	1.7950	1.7967	1.7984	1.8000	1.8017	1.8033	1.8050	1.8066
6.1	1.8082	1.8099	1.8115	1.8131	1.8148	1.8164	1.8180	1.8197	1.8213	1.8229
6.2	1.8245	1.8261	1.8277	1.8293	1.8309	1.8325	1.8341	1.8357	1.8373	1.8389
6.3	1.8405	1.8421	1.8437	1.8453	1.8468	1.8484	1.8500	1.8516	1.8531	1.8547
6.4	1.8563	1.8578	1.8594	1.8609	1.8625	1.8640	1.8656	1.8671	1.8687	1.8702
6.5	1.8713	1.8733	1.8748	1.8764	1.8779	1.8794	1.8809	1.8825	1.8840	1.8855
6.6	1.8870	1.8885	1.8901	1.8916	1.8931	1.8946	1.8961	1.8976	1.8991	1.9006
6.7	1.9021	1.9036	1.9050	1.9065	1.9080	1.9095	1.9110	1.9125	1.9139	1.9154
6.8	1.9169	1.9183	1.9198	1.9213	1.9227	1.9242	1.9257	1.9271	1.9286	1.9300
6.9	1.9315	1.9329	1.9344	1.9358	1.9373	1.9387	1.9401	1.9416	1.9430	1.9444

Natural Logarithms continued

x	.00	.01	.02	.03	.04	.05	.06	.07	.08	.09
7.0	1.9459	1.9473	1.9487	1.9501	1.9516	1.9530	1.9544	1.9558	1.9572	1.9586
7.1	1.9600	1.9615	1.9629	1.9643	1.9657	1.9671	1.9685	1.9699	1.9713	1.9726
7.2	1.9740	1.9754	1.9768	1.9782	1.9796	1.9810	1.9823	1.9837	1.9851	1.9865
7.3	1.9878	1.9892	1.9906	1.9919	1.9933	1.9947	1.9960	1.9974	1.9987	2.0001
7.4	2.0014	2.0028	2.0041	2.0055	2.0068	2.0082	2.0095	2.0108	2.0122	2.0135
7.5	2.0149	2.0162	2.0175	2.0189	2.0202	2.0215	2.0228	2.0241	2.0255	2.0268
7.6	2.0281	2.0294	2.0307	2.0320	2.0334	2.0347	2.0360	2.0373	2.0386	2.0399
7.7	2.0412	2.0425	2.0438	2.0451	2.0464	2.0476	2.0489	2.0502	2.0515	2.0528
7.8	2.0541	2.0554	2.0566	2.0579	2.0592	2.0605	2.0617	2.0630	2.0643	2.0656
7.9	2.0668	2.0681	2.0693	2.0706	2.0719	2.0731	2.0744	2.0756	2.0769	2.0781
8.0	2.0794	2.0806	2.0819	2.0831	2.0844	2.0856	2.0869	2.0881	2.0893	2.0906
8.1	2.0918	2.0931	2.0943	2.0955	2.0967	2.0980	2.0992	2.1004	2.1016	2.1029
8.2	2.1041	2.1053	2.1065	2.1077	2.1090	2.1102	2.1114	2.1126	2.1138	2.1150
8.3	2.1162	2.1174	2.1186	2.1198	2.1210	2.1222	2.1234	2.1246	2.1258	2.1270
8.4	2.1282	2.1294	2.1306	2.1318	2.1329	2.1341	2.1353	2.1365	2.1377	2.1388
8.5	2.1400	2.1412	2.1424	2.1435	2.1447	2.1459	2.1471	2.1482	2.1494	2.1506
8.6	2.1517	2.1529	2.1540	2.1552	2.1564	2.1575	2.1587	2.1598	2.1610	2.1621
8.7	2.1633	2.1644	2.1656	2.1667	2.1679	2.1690	2.1702	2.1713	2.1724	2.1736
8.8	2.1747	2.1758	2.1770	2.1781	2.1792	2.1804	2.1815	2.1826	2.1838	2.1849
8.9	2.1860	2.1871	2.1883	2.1894	2.1905	2.1916	2.1927	2.1938	2.1950	2.1961
9.0	2.1972	2.1983	2.1994	2.2005	2.2016	2.2027	2.2038	2.2049	2.2060	2.2071
9.1	2.2082	2.2093	2.2104	2.2115	2.2126	2.2137	2.2148	2.2159	2.2170	2.2181
9.2	2.2192	2.2202	2.2213	2.2224	2.2235	2.2246	2.2257	2.2267	2.2278	2.2289
9.3	2.2300	2.2310	2.2321	2.2332	2.2343	2.2353	2.2364	2.2375	2.2385	2.2396
9.4	2.2407	2.2417	2.2428	2.2439	2.2449	2.2460	2.2470	2.2481	2.2491	2.2502
9.5	2.2512	2.2523	2.2533	2.2544	2.2554	2.2565	2.2575	2.2586	2.2596	2.2607
9.6	2.2617	2.2628	2.2638	2.2648	2.2659	2.2669	2.2679	2.2690	2.2700	2.2710
9.7	2.2721	2.2731	2.2741	2.2752	2.2762	2.2772	2.2782	2.2793	2.2803	2.2813
9.8	2.2823	2.2834	2.2844	2.2854	2.2864	2.2874	2.2884	2.2895	2.2905	2.2915
9.9	2.2925	2.2935	2.2945	2.2955	2.2965	2.2975	2.2985	2.2995	2.3005	2.3015

	0	1	2	3	4	5	6	7	8	9
10.0	2.3025	2.3035	2.3045	2.3055	2.3065	2.3075	2.3085	2.3095	2.3105	2.3115
10.1	2.3125	2.3135	2.3145	2.3155	2.3164	2.3174	2.3184	2.3194	2.3204	2.3214
10.2	2.3223	2.3233	2.3243	2.3253	2.3263	2.3272	2.3282	2.3292	2.3302	2.3311
10.3	2.3321	2.3331	2.3340	2.3350	2.3360	2.3369	2.3379	2.3389	2.3398	2.3408
10.4	2.3418	2.3427	2.3437	2.3446	2.3456	2.3466	2.3475	2.3485	2.3494	2.3504
10.5	2.3513	2.3523	2.3532	2.3542	2.3551	2.3561	2.3570	2.3580	2.3589	2.3599
10.6	2.3608	2.3618	2.3627	2.3636	2.3646	2.3655	2.3665	2.3674	2.3683	2.3693
10.7	2.3702	2.3711	2.3721	2.3730	2.3739	2.3749	2.3758	2.3767	2.3776	2.3786
10.8	2.3795	2.3804	2.3814	2.3823	2.3832	2.3841	2.3850	2.3860	2.3869	2.3878
10.9	2.3887	2.3896	2.3906	2.3915	2.3924	2.3933	2.3942	2.3951	2.3960	2.3969

Tables of Exponential Functions e^x and e^{-x}

These tables give the values of e^x and $e^{-x} = 1/e^x$ for x in the range $0.00 \leqslant x \leqslant 6.09$, in steps of $\Delta x = 0.01$. To extend the range of the tables, we use the rule

$$e^{a+b} = e^a \cdot e^b$$

If x lies outside the range of the table, we may split off multiples of 5 until we get numbers that are listed. For example

$$e^{8.7} = e^{(5.00+3.70)} = e^{5.00} \times e^{3.70}$$

$$= 148.41 \times 40.447 \approx 6002.7$$

or

$$e^{-6.66} = e^{(-5.00-1.66)} = e^{-5.00} \times e^{-1.66}$$

$$= 0.006738 \times 0.19014 = 0.001281 = 1.281 \times 10^{-3}$$

For a more complicated example, consider the calculation

$$e^{12.02} = e^{5.00} \times e^{5.00} \times e^{2.02}$$

$$= (148.41)^2 \times 7.5383 = 166{,}035 \approx 1.660 \times 10^5$$

Actually, the table for e^{-x} is superfluous for anyone with access to a simple calculator, since e^{-x} is just the reciprocal $1/e^x$. Thus, using only the tables for $x \geqslant 0$, we find

$$e^{-3.17} = 1/e^{3.17} = 1/23.807 \approx 0.04200$$

Values of e^x

x	.00	.01	.02	.03	.04	.05	.06	.07	.08	.09
0.0	1.0000	1.0100	1.0202	1.0304	1.0408	1.0512	1.0618	1.0725	1.0832	1.0941
0.1	1.1051	1.1162	1.1275	1.1388	1.1502	1.1618	1.1735	1.1853	1.1972	1.2092
0.2	1.2214	1.2336	1.2460	1.2586	1.2712	1.2840	1.2969	1.3099	1.3231	1.3364
0.3	1.3498	1.3634	1.3771	1.3909	1.4049	1.4190	1.4333	1.4477	1.4622	1.4769
0.4	1.4918	1.5068	1.5219	1.5372	1.5527	1.5683	1.5840	1.5999	1.6160	1.6323
0.5	1.6487	1.6652	1.6820	1.6989	1.7160	1.7332	1.7506	1.7682	1.7860	1.8039
0.6	1.8221	1.8404	1.8589	1.8776	1.8964	1.9155	1.9347	1.9542	1.9738	1.9937
0.7	2.0137	2.0339	2.0544	2.0750	2.0959	2.1170	2.1382	2.1597	2.1814	2.2034
0.8	2.2255	2.2479	2.2705	2.2933	2.3163	2.3396	2.3631	2.3869	2.4109	2.4351
0.9	2.4596	2.4843	2.5092	2.5345	2.5599	2.5857	2.6117	2.6379	2.6644	2.6912
1.0	2.7182	2.7456	2.7731	2.8010	2.8292	2.8576	2.8863	2.9153	2.9446	2.9742
1.1	3.0041	3.0343	3.0648	3.0956	3.1267	3.1581	3.1899	3.2219	3.2543	3.2870
1.2	3.3201	3.3534	3.3871	3.4212	3.4556	3.4903	3.5254	3.5608	3.5966	3.6327
1.3	3.6693	3.7061	3.7434	3.7810	3.8190	3.8574	3.8961	3.9353	3.9749	4.0148
1.4	4.0552	4.0959	4.1371	4.1787	4.2207	4.2631	4.3059	4.3492	4.3929	4.4371
1.5	4.4816	4.5267	4.5722	4.6181	4.6645	4.7114	4.7588	4.8066	4.8549	4.9037
1.6	4.9530	5.0028	5.0530	5.1038	5.1551	5.2069	5.2593	5.3121	5.3655	5.4194
1.7	5.4739	5.5289	5.5845	5.6406	5.6973	5.7546	5.8124	5.8708	5.9298	5.9894
1.8	6.0496	6.1104	6.1718	6.2338	6.2965	6.3598	6.4237	6.4883	6.5535	6.6193
1.9	6.6858	6.7530	6.8209	6.8895	6.9587	7.0286	7.0993	7.1706	7.2427	7.3155
2.0	7.3890	7.4633	7.5383	7.6140	7.6906	7.7679	7.8459	7.9248	8.0044	8.0849
2.1	8.1661	8.2482	8.3311	8.4148	8.4994	8.5848	8.6711	8.7582	8.8463	8.9352
2.2	9.0250	9.1157	9.2073	9.2998	9.3933	9.4877	9.5830	9.6794	9.7766	9.8749
2.3	9.9741	10.074	10.175	10.277	10.381	10.485	10.590	10.697	10.804	10.913
2.4	11.023	11.133	11.245	11.358	11.473	11.588	11.704	11.822	11.941	12.061
2.5	12.182	12.304	12.428	12.553	12.679	12.807	12.935	13.065	13.197	13.329
2.6	13.463	13.599	13.735	13.873	14.013	14.154	14.296	14.439	14.585	14.731
2.7	14.879	15.029	15.180	15.332	15.486	15.642	15.799	15.958	16.119	16.281
2.8	16.444	16.609	16.776	16.945	17.115	17.287	17.461	17.637	17.814	17.993
2.9	18.174	18.356	18.541	18.727	18.915	19.105	19.297	19.491	19.687	19.885

x	.00	.01	.02	.03	.04	.05	.06	.07	.08	.09
3.0	20.085	20.287	20.491	20.697	20.905	21.115	21.327	21.541	21.758	21.977
3.1	22.197	22.421	22.646	22.873	23.103	23.336	23.570	23.807	24.046	24.288
3.2	24.532	24.779	25.028	25.279	25.533	25.790	26.049	26.311	26.575	26.842
3.3	27.112	27.385	27.660	27.938	28.219	28.502	28.789	29.078	29.370	29.665
3.4	29.964	30.265	30.569	30.876	31.186	31.500	31.816	32.136	32.459	32.785
3.5	33.115	33.448	33.784	34.123	34.466	34.813	35.163	35.516	35.873	36.234
3.6	36.598	36.966	37.337	37.712	38.091	38.474	38.861	39.251	39.646	40.044
3.7	40.447	40.853	41.264	41.679	42.097	42.521	42.948	43.380	43.816	44.256
3.8	44.701	45.150	45.604	46.062	46.525	46.993	47.465	47.942	48.424	48.910
3.9	49.402	49.898	50.400	50.906	51.418	51.935	52.457	52.984	53.517	54.054
4.0	54.598	55.146	55.701	56.260	56.826	57.397	57.974	58.556	59.145	59.739
4.1	60.340	60.946	61.559	62.177	62.802	63.434	64.071	64.715	65.365	66.022
4.2	66.686	67.356	68.033	68.717	69.407	70.105	70.809	71.521	72.240	72.966
4.3	73.699	74.440	75.188	75.944	76.707	77.478	78.257	79.043	79.838	80.640
4.4	81.450	82.269	83.096	83.931	84.774	85.626	86.487	87.356	88.234	89.121
4.5	90.017	90.921	91.835	92.758	93.690	94.632	95.583	96.544	97.514	98.494
4.6	99.484	100.48	101.49	102.51	103.54	104.58	105.63	106.69	107.77	108.85
4.7	109.94	111.05	112.16	113.29	114.43	115.58	116.74	117.91	119.10	120.30
4.8	121.51	122.73	123.96	125.21	126.46	127.74	129.02	130.32	131.63	132.95
4.9	134.28	135.63	137.00	138.37	139.77	141.17	142.59	144.02	145.47	146.93
5.0	148.41	149.90	151.41	152.93	154.47	156.02	157.59	159.17	160.77	162.38
5.1	164.02	165.67	167.33	169.01	170.71	172.43	174.16	175.91	177.68	179.46
5.2	181.27	183.09	184.93	186.79	188.67	190.56	192.48	194.41	196.36	198.34
5.3	200.33	202.35	204.38	206.43	208.51	210.60	212.72	214.86	217.02	219.20
5.4	221.40	223.63	225.87	228.14	230.44	232.75	235.09	237.46	239.84	242.25
5.5	244.69	247.15	249.63	252.14	254.67	257.23	259.82	262.43	265.07	267.73
5.6	270.42	273.14	275.88	278.66	281.46	284.29	287.14	290.03	292.94	295.89
5.7	298.86	301.87	304.90	307.96	311.06	314.19	317.34	320.53	323.75	327.01
5.8	330.29	333.61	336.97	340.35	343.77	347.23	350.72	354.24	357.80	361.40
5.9	365.03	368.70	372.41	376.15	379.93	383.75	387.61	391.50	395.44	399.41
6.0	403.42	407.48	411.57	415.71	419.89	424.11	428.37	432.68	437.02	441.42

Values of $e^{-x} = 1/e^x$

x	.00	.01	.02	.03	.04	.05	.06	.07	.08	.09
0.0	1.00000	.990050	.980199	.970446	.960789	.951229	.941765	.932394	.923116	.913931
0.1	.904837	.895834	.886920	.878095	.869358	.860708	.852144	.843665	.835270	.826959
0.2	.818731	.810584	.802519	.794534	.786628	.778801	.771052	.763379	.755784	.748264
0.3	.740818	.733447	.726149	.718924	.711770	.704688	.697676	.690734	.683861	.677057
0.4	.670320	.663650	.657047	.650509	.644036	.637628	.631284	.625002	.618783	.612626
0.5	.606531	.600496	.594521	.588605	.582748	.576950	.571209	.565525	.559898	.554327
0.6	.548812	.543351	.537944	.532592	.527292	.522046	.516851	.511709	.506617	.501576
0.7	.496585	.491644	.486752	.481909	.477114	.472367	.467666	.463013	.458406	.453845
0.8	.449329	.444858	.440432	.436049	.431711	.427415	.423162	.418952	.414783	.410656
0.9	.406570	.402524	.398519	.394554	.390628	.386741	.382893	.379083	.375311	.371577
1.0	.367879	.364219	.360595	.357007	.353455	.349938	.346456	.343009	.339596	.336216
1.1	.332871	.329559	.326280	.323033	.319819	.316637	.313486	.310367	.307279	.304221
1.2	.301194	.298197	.295230	.292293	.289384	.286505	.283654	.280832	.278037	.275271
1.3	.272532	.269820	.267135	.264477	.261846	.259240	.256661	.254107	.251579	.249075
1.4	.246597	.244143	.241714	.239309	.236928	.234570	.232236	.229925	.227638	.225373
1.5	.223130	.220910	.218712	.216536	.214381	.212248	.210136	.208045	.205975	.203926
1.6	.201897	.199888	.197899	.195930	.193980	.192050	.190139	.188247	.186374	.184520
1.7	.182684	.180866	.179066	.177284	.175520	.173774	.172045	.170333	.168638	.166960
1.8	.165299	.163654	.162026	.160414	.158817	.157237	.155673	.154124	.152590	.151072
1.9	.149569	.148080	.146607	.145148	.143704	.142274	.140858	.139457	.138069	.136695
2.0	.135335	.133989	.132655	.131336	.130029	.128735	.127454	.126186	.124930	.123687
2.1	.122456	.121238	.120032	.118837	.117655	.116484	.115325	.114178	.113042	.111917
2.2	.110803	.109701	.108609	.107528	.106459	.105399	.104350	.103312	.102284	.101266
2.3	.100259	.099261	.098274	.097296	.096328	.095369	.094420	.093481	.092551	.091630
2.4	.090718	.089815	.088922	.088037	.087161	.086294	.085435	.084585	.083743	.082910
2.5	.082085	.081268	.080460	.079659	.078866	.078082	.077305	.076536	.075774	.075020
2.6	.074274	.073535	.072803	.072078	.071361	.070651	.069948	.069252	.068563	.067881
2.7	.067206	.066537	.065875	.065219	.064570	.063928	.063292	.062662	.062039	.061421
2.8	.060810	.060205	.059606	.059013	.058426	.057844	.057269	.056699	.056135	.055576
2.9	.055023	.054476	.053934	.053397	.052866	.052340	.051819	.051303	.050793	.050287

x	.00	.01	.02	.03	.04	.05	.06	.07	.08	.09
3.0	.049787	.049292	.048801	.048316	.047835	.047359	.046888	.046421	.045959	.045502
3.1	.045049	.044601	.044157	.043718	.043283	.042852	.042426	.042004	.041586	.041172
3.2	.040762	.040357	.039955	.039557	.039164	.038774	.038388	.038006	.037628	.037254
3.3	.036883	.036516	.036153	.035793	.035437	.035084	.034735	.034390	.034047	.033709
3.4	.033373	.033041	.032712	.032387	.032065	.031746	.031430	.031117	.030807	.030501
3.5	.030197	.029897	.029599	.029305	.029013	.028725	.028439	.028156	.027876	.027598
3.6	.027324	.027052	.026783	.026516	.026252	.025991	.025733	.025476	.025223	.024972
3.7	.024724	.024478	.024234	.023993	.023754	.023518	.023284	.023052	.022823	.022596
3.8	.022371	.022143	.021928	.021710	.021494	.021280	.021068	.020858	.020651	.020445
3.9	.020242	.020041	.019841	.019644	.019448	.019255	.019063	.018873	.018686	.018500
4.0	.018316	.018133	.017953	.017774	.017597	.017422	.017249	.017077	.016907	.016739
4.1	.016573	.016408	.016245	.016083	.015923	.015764	.015608	.015452	.015299	.015146
4.2	.014996	.014846	.014699	.014552	.014408	.014264	.014122	.013982	.013843	.013705
4.3	.013569	.013434	.013300	.013168	.013037	.012907	.012778	.012651	.012525	.012401
4.4	.012277	.012155	.012034	.011914	.011796	.011679	.011562	.011447	.011333	.011221
4.5	.011109	.010998	.010889	.010781	.010673	.010567	.010462	.010358	.010255	.010153
4.6	.010052	.009952	.009853	.009755	.009658	.009562	.009466	.009372	.009279	.009187
4.7	.009095	.009035	.008915	.008826	.008739	.008652	.008566	.008480	.008396	.008312
4.8	.008230	.008148	.008067	.007937	.007907	.007828	.007750	.007673	.007597	.007521
4.9	.007447	.007372	.007299	.007227	.007155	.007083	.007013	.006943	.006874	.006806
5.0	.006738	.006671	.006605	.006539	.006474	.006409	.006346	.006282	.006220	.006158
5.1	.006097	.006036	.005976	.005917	.005858	.005799	.005742	.005685	.005628	.005572
5.2	.005517	.005462	.005407	.005354	.005300	.005248	.005195	.005144	.005092	.005042
5.3	.004992	.004942	.004893	.004844	.004796	.004748	.004701	.004654	.004608	.004562
5.4	.004517	.004472	.004427	.004383	.004339	.004296	.004254	.004211	.004169	.004128
5.5	.004037	.004046	.004006	.003966	.003927	.003887	.003849	.003810	.003773	.003735
5.6	.003638	.003661	.003625	.003589	.003553	.003518	.003483	.003448	.003414	.003380
5.7	.003346	.003313	.003280	.003247	.003215	.003183	.003151	.003120	.003089	.003058
5.8	.003028	.002997	.002968	.002938	.002909	.002880	.002851	.002823	.002795	.002767
5.9	.002739	.002712	.002685	.002658	.002632	.002606	.002580	.002554	.002529	.002504
6.0	.002479	.002454	.002430	.002405	.002382	.002358	.002334	.002311	.002288	.002265

Answers to Selected Exercises

Chapter 1

Section 1.1

1. See Figure A.1; (*i*) 0.333 ... ;
(*ii*) 2.14285714 ... ; (*iii*) −1.8333 ... ;
(*iv*) 2.500 .... **2.** $x > y$. **3.** (*i*) $x > y$;
(*ii*) $x > y$. **5.** 1.7475 ... largest,
0.8333 ... smallest. **6.** (*i*) −1.190; (*ii*) 3.474;
(*iii*) 0.173; (*iv*) 4.464; (*v*) −0.508. **7.** (*i*) T;
(*ii*) T; (*iii*) F; (*iv*) T; (*v*) F; (*vi*) F.
8. (*i*) $a < b$; (*ii*) $a < b$; (*iii*) $a > b$; (*iv*) $a > b$;
(*v*) $a < b$; (*vi*) $a = b$. **9.** See Figure A.2.
10. See Figure A.3.

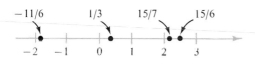

Figure A.1

Figure A.2

Section 1.2

1. Powers of $a = 0$ defined only for positive
exponents, other calculations routine except
for (*iii*) and (*viii*); (*iii*) $a = 1/3$, $a^4 = 0.01235$,
$a^1 = 0.3333$, $a^0 = 1$, $a^{-1} = 3$, $a^{-2} = 9$,
$a^{-3} = 27$, $a^{-4} = 81$; (*viii*) $a = \sqrt[3]{2} = 1.2599$:
$a^4 = 2.520$, $a^1 = 1.2599$, $a^0 = 1$,
$a^{-1} = 0.7937$, $a^{-2} = 0.6300$, $a^{-3} = 0.5000$,
$a^{-4} = 0.3969$. **2.** (*i*) 1; (*ii*) 2; (*iii*) 1/2;
(*iv*) 16; (*v*) 1/64; (*vi*) 4; (*vii*) 1/32;
(*viii*) $(1/8)^{1/3} = 8^{1/3} = 2$, $(8^2)^{1/3} - (8^{1/3})^2 = 8^{2/3} = 4$. **3.** (*i*) 1; (*ii*) 1; (*iii*) 0; (*iv*) 1; (*v*) 1/3;
(*vi*) 1/25; (*vii*) $32^{4/5} = 2^4 = 16$;
(*viii*) $16^{-2.50} = 16^{-5/2} = 4^{-5} = 1/1024$;
(*ix*) $(8/27)^{5/3} = (8^{1/3}/27^{1/3})^5 = (2/3)^5 = 32/243 = 0.1317$; (*x*) $(0.01)^{3/2} = (0.1)^3 = 0.001$.
4. If $t = 10$, $2^{10/30} = 2^{1/3} = 1.259$,
so $N = 37.77$ million; 47.55 million;

(i) at +3/2 ; *(ii)* at +3/2 ; *(iii)* at +3/2 ; *(iv)* between −5 and +2 ; *(v)* between −4.5 and −1.75 ; *(vi)* between −50 and 1000

Figure A.3

60 million; 75.54 million.   **5.** (*i*) $8^{-5/6} =$ $(2^3)^{-5/6} = 2^{-5/2} = 1/4\sqrt{2} = 0.1768$;
(*ii*) $27^{5/6} = (3^3)^{5/6} = 3^{5/2} = 9\sqrt{3} = 15.59$;
(*iii*) $125^{1/2} = (25 \cdot 5)^{1/2} = 5\sqrt{5} = 11.18$;
(*iv*) $125^{-1/2} = 1/125^{1/2} = 0.0894$; (*v*) $4^{-1.25} =$ $4^{-5/4} = (2^2)^{-5/4} = 2^{-5/2} = 1/4\sqrt{2} = 0.1768$;
(*vi*) $1000^{3/2} = (100^{1/2} \cdot 10^{1/2})^3 = (10\sqrt{10})^3 =$ $31,622.7 \ldots$; (*vii*) $(1/500)^{1/2} = 1/10\sqrt{5} =$ 0.0447; (*viii*) $(2/5)^{-3/2} = (5/2)^{3/2} = (\sqrt{5}/\sqrt{2})^3 =$ $(1.5811)^3 = 3.953$.   **6.** (*i*) 0.500; (*ii*) $1/32 =$ 0.03125; (*iii*) $(1/2)^{1.5} = (1/2)^{3/2} = 0.3535$;
(*iv*) $(1/2)^{7.5} = (1/2)^7 \cdot (1/2)^{1/2} = (1/2)^7 \cdot (1/\sqrt{2})$ $= 0.00552 \ldots$; only $r = 7.5$ will stop
all but 1% ($r = 5.0$ stops all but 3.1%);
none of these r will stop all but 0.1%.
7. (*i*) 6; (*ii*) 6; (*iii*) $1/32 = 0.03125$;
(*iv*) $32/243 = 0.1317$; (*v*) $2^{1/4} = (\sqrt{2})^{1/2} =$ $\sqrt{1.414} = 1.189$; (*vi*) 4; (*vii*) 3/4; (*viii*) 0.09.
9. (*i*) a^5; (*ii*) a^4; (*iii*) $b^{15}/a \cdot c^2$; (*iv*) a^6;
(*v*) $a^6 \cdot c^6$; (*vi*) b^4/a^4.   **11.** (*i*) 98×10^{-6};
(*ii*) 0.98×10^6; (*iii*) 1×10^1; (*iv*) 4.421×10^3;
(*v*) 9.842×10^9; (*vi*) 1×10^{-5}; (*vii*) 4.3×10^{-3}.
12. 96.04×10^{14}.   **13.** (*i*) 0.509×10^{-10};
(*ii*) 3.473×10^{-3}; (*iii*) 1.961×10^3;
(*iv*) $\sqrt{144} \times 10^3 = 12 \times 10^3$.
14. (*i*) $-320,000$; (*ii*) $1,200,000$; (*iii*) $2,320,000$.

Section 1.3
1. $-2, -5, 1, 22$; $f(x) = 4$ when $x = 2$.
2. (*i*) $30, 4, -2.5, -9, -61$; (*ii*) $15, 5, 5, 6, 50$;
(*iii*) $3620, 4000, 4099.6875, 4197.5, 4687.5$;
(*iv*) $\sqrt{84} = 9.165, 10, \sqrt{99} = 9.949$,
$\sqrt{96} = 9.798, 0$.   **3.** (*i*) $-20.55°C$;
(*ii*) $-17.77°C$; (*iii*) $0°C$; (*iv*) $21.1°C$;
(*v*) $32.2°C$; (*vi*) $37.0°C$; (*vii*) $100°C$.
4. (*i*) $h = 5'8'' = 5.67$ ft., $w = 163.8$ lbs;
(*ii*) $h = 6.0$, $w = 194.4$; (*iii*) wt. ratio $= 0.843$;

(*iv*) ht. ratio $= 0.945$.   **8.** (*i*) -5×10^6;
(*ii*) 1×10^6; (*iii*) $1,093,750$; (*iv*) $4,492,342$.
9. $A = \pi r^2$, so $r = \sqrt{A/\pi}$; valid for $A \geqslant 0$
(so the square root makes sense).
10. See Figure A.4.   **11.** See Figure A.5;
when $t = 1.25$, $s \approx 25$; $s = 70$ when $t = 2.1$.

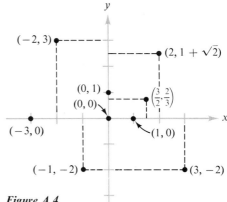

Figure A.4

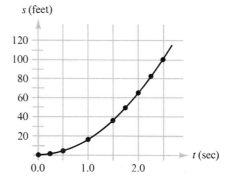

Figure A.5

12. See Figure A.6. **13.** See Figure A.7.
14. See Figure A.8 (p. 368). **16.** (*i*) The set
$1/x > 2$ shown in Figure A.9 (*i*); for $1/x < 1$
see A.9 (*ii*). **17.** (*i*) 1.24, 0.48; (*ii*) 1971;
(*iii*) 1968; (*iv*) 1938, 1934, 1929, 1915;
(*v*) $I = 1.64$ in 1974, $6098, $12,195.

18. See Figure A.10 for graph of $y = 2^x$.
19. See Figure A.11. **20.** See Figure A.12.

(*i*) $1/x > 2$

(*ii*) $1/x < 1$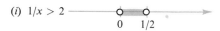

Figure A.9

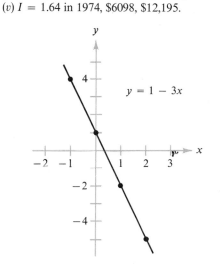

Figure A.6

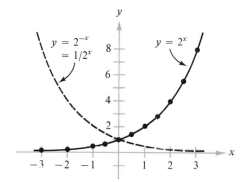

Figure A.10

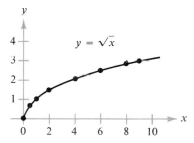

Figure A.11

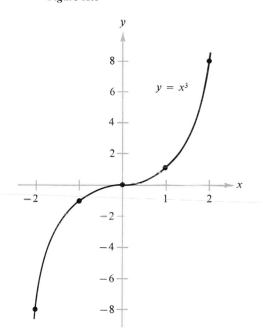

Figure A.7

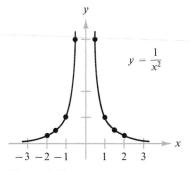

Figure A.12

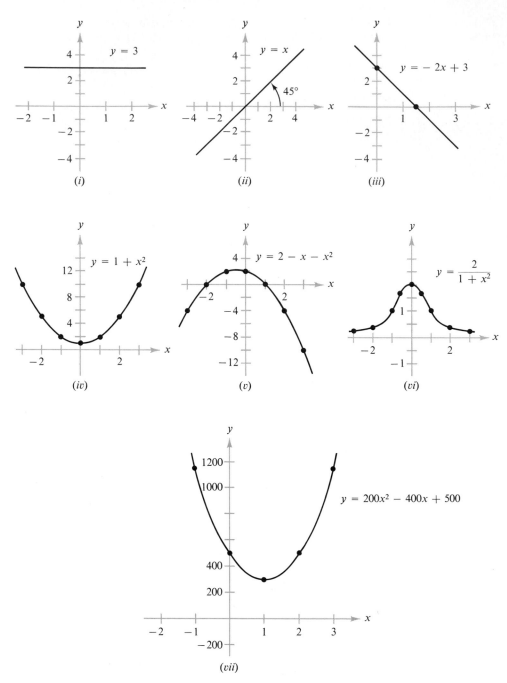

Figure A.8

Section 1.4

1. (*i*) 64 ft.; (*ii*) $s = 32$ when $t = \sqrt{s/16} = \sqrt{2} = 1.414$ sec. **2.** (*i*) 25 ft.; (*ii*) $s = 12.5$ ft. when $t = \sqrt{0.781} = \sqrt{78.1/10} = 0.884$ sec. **3.** 1.5 sec.; 1.18 sec.; falls the first $(36 - 20) = 16$ ft. in $t = 1.00$ sec. and falls the full 36 ft. in $t = 1.50$ sec., hence falls the *last* 20 ft. in $t = 1.50 - 1.00 = 0.50$ sec. **4.** $h(t) = 100t - 16t^2$; $h(t) = 0 = t(100 - 16t)$ when $t = 0$ (start) and $t = 6.25$ (hits ground); estd. max. ht. $= 156$ ft. as in Figure A.13. **5.** $h(t) = 48t - 16t^2$; (*i*) 32, 32; (*ii*) $h(t) = 0 = t(48 - 16t)$ when $t = 0$ (start) or $t = 3$ (impact); (*iii*) see Figure A.14; estd. max. ht. $= 36$ ft. **6.** $v_0 = 64$ ft./sec. and $h(t) = 64t - 16t^2$; estd. max. ht. $= 64$ ft.

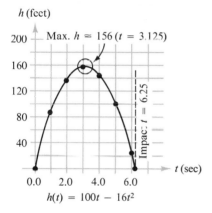

h (feet)

Max. $h \approx 156$ ($t = 3.125$)

Impact: $t = 6.25$

t (sec)

$h(t) = 100t - 16t^2$

Figure A.13

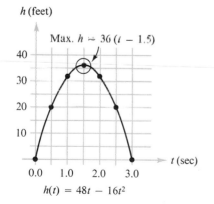

h (feet)

Max. $h \approx 36$ ($t = 1.5$)

t (sec)

$h(t) = 48t - 16t^2$

Figure A.14

Section 1.6

1. (*i*) $C = 1500 + 35q$; (*ii*) $R = q \cdot p(q) = 48q - 0.01q^2$; (*iii*) $P = R - C = -1500 + 13q - 0.01q^2$; (*iv*) $R(100) = 4700$, $P(100) = -300$, $R(300) = 13,500$, $P(300) = 1500$, $R(800) = 32,000$, $P(800) = 2500$, $R(1000) = 38,000$, $P(1000) = 1500$. **2.** $C = 1000 + 100q$; $R = q \cdot p(q) = 300q - 2q^2$; $P = R - C = -1000 + 200q - 2q^2$; graph in Figure A.15; for $0 \leqslant q \leqslant 40$, max. $P \approx \$3800$, when $q = 40$. **3.** $R = q \cdot p(q) = 0.80q - 0.00001q^2$; $P = R - C = -4320 + 0.50q - 0.00001q^2$; graph in Figure A.16; for $0 \leqslant q \leqslant 35,000$, max. $P \approx \$1930$, when $q = 25,000$ gal./month. **4.** $P = R - C = -4320 + 0.50q - 0.000005q^2$; for $0 \leqslant q \leqslant 30,000$, max. $P = \$6180$, when $q = 30,000$. **5.** (*i*) $P = 65x - 35(60 - x) = 100x - 2100$ for $0 \leqslant x \leqslant 60$; (*ii*) $R(x) = 200x$; (*iii*) $x = 21$ units; (*iv*) $C = R - P = 100x + 2100$; graph shown in Figure A.17. **6.** See Figure A.18. **7.** (*p*) decreases from 150 to 64; $q(p) = (150 - p)/0.000086 = 11,628(150 - p)$ for $64 \leqslant p \leqslant 150$. **8.** (*i*) 21,500, 9500, 5500, 3500; (*ii*) \$3.08; (*iii*) $p = \$1.48$. **9.** See Figure A.19. **10.** In millions, $P(0) = -5.00$, $P(100,000) = -0.12$, $P(200,000) = 2.32$, $P(250,000) = 2.63$, $P(300,000) = 2.32$, $P(500,000) = -5.00$, $P(600,000) = -12.32$; graph in Figure A.20; estd. max. $P = \$2.63$ million, when $q = 250,000$.

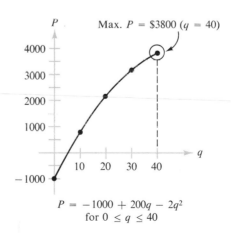

P

Max. $P = \$3800$ ($q = 40$)

q

$P = -1000 + 200q - 2q^2$
for $0 \leq q \leq 40$

Figure A.15

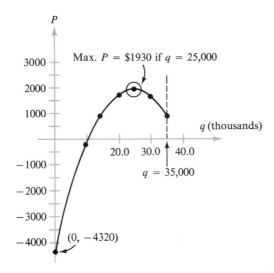

Figure A.16

Max. $P = \$1930$ if $q = 25,000$

$q = 35,000$

$(0, -4320)$

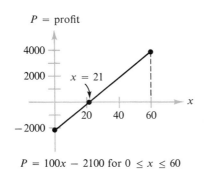

$P = \text{profit}$

$x = 21$

$P = 100x - 2100$ for $0 \leq x \leq 60$

Figure A.17

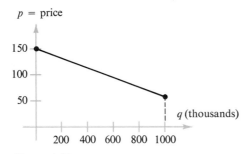

$p = \text{price}$

Figure A.18

11. $C(q) = 500 + 2.70q$, $A(q) = (500/q) + 2.70$; $C(10) = 527$, $C(50) = 635$, $C(100) = 770$, $C(200) = 1040$, $C(500) = 1850$, $C(1000) = 3200$;

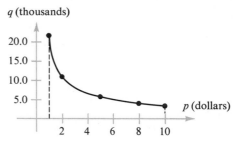

q (thousands)

p (dollars)

Figure A.19

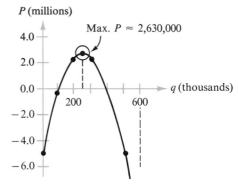

P (millions)

Max. $P \approx 2,630,000$

q (thousands)

Figure A.20

$A(10) = 52.70$, $A(50) = 12.70$, $A(100) = 7.70$, $A(200) = 5.20$, $A(500) = 3.70$, $A(1000) = 3.20$; as q gets large, $A(q)$ approaches \$2.70 per pound; breakeven at $q = 500$; graph in Figure A.21.   **12.** (*i*) $C = 4320 + 0.20q$ for $0 \leq q \leq 20,000$; (*ii*) $C = 5540 + 0.20(20,000) + 0.19(q - 20,000) = 5740 + 0.19q$ for $q > 20,000$; graph in Figure A.22, has a jump at $q = 20,000$; $C(15,000) = 7320$, $C(20,000) = 8320$, $C(25,000) = 10,490$.   **13.** $R(q) = 0.50q$, see Figure A.22; breakeven for $q = 14,400$ gal./wk.

Section 1.7
1. Recall Exercise 18, Section 1.3; graphs of $y = 2^x$, $y = 2^{-x}$ in Figure A.10; for $y = 8(2^x)$ multiply values by 8.   **2.** See Figure A.10.
4. $A = 50,000,000$ and $k = 1/50$, graph in Figure A.23; $P = 60$ million when $t = 13.2$, $P = 75$ million when $t = 29.3$.   **6.** (*i*) 100; (*ii*) see Figure A.24; (*iii*) $N = 500$ if $t \approx 3.2$, $N = 750$ if $t \approx 4.7$; (*iv*) N increases toward 1000 but never reaches it.   **7.** (*i*) 10,000;

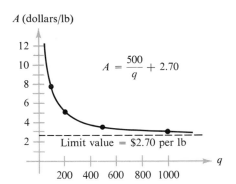

A (dollars/lb)

$$A = \frac{500}{q} + 2.70$$

Limit value = $2.70 per lb

q

Figure A.21

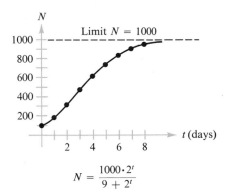

N

Limit $N = 1000$

t (days)

$$N = \frac{1000 \cdot 2^t}{9 + 2^t}$$

Figure A.24

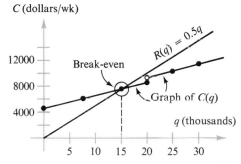

C (dollars/wk)

$R(q) = 0.5q$

Break-even

Graph of *C(q)*

q (thousands)

Figure A.22

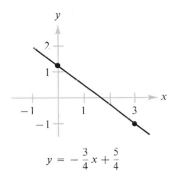

y

$$y = -\frac{3}{4}x + \frac{5}{4}$$

Figure A.25

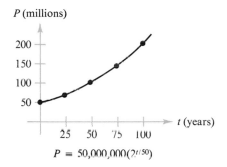

P (millions)

t (years)

$P = 50{,}000{,}000(2^{t/50})$

Figure A.23

(*ii*) $1/2 = 2^{-1} = 2^{-2t}$, so $2t = 1$, $t = 1/2$;
(*iii*) $1/2 = 2^{-2} = 2^{-2t}$, so $t = 1.0$.

Section 1.8

1. $\Delta x = 2$; $\Delta y = -4$; slope $= -2$.
2. (*i*) -3; (*ii*) 0; (*iii*) $1/3$; (*iv*) -3; (*v*) 3;
(*vi*) $1/3$.   **4.** slope $= -3/4$; equation is
$(y - 2)/(x + 1) =$ slope $= -3/4$ or
$y = (-3/4)x + (5/4)$; graph in Figure A.25.

5. $(y + 1)/(x - 2) = 1/3$ or $y = (1/3)x - (5/3)$;
graph is Figure A.26.   **8.** (*i*) $y - x = 1$;
(*ii*) $5y + 7x = -3$; (*iii*) $(y - 4)/(x - 1) = -1/2$
or $2y + x = 9$; (*iv*) $y + 5x = 5\pi + 1 + \sqrt{5} =$
$18.944 \ldots$; (*v*) $(y - 5)/(x - 0) = -1/3$ or
$3y + x = 15$; (*vi*) $y = (2/7)x$ or $7y - 2x = 0$.

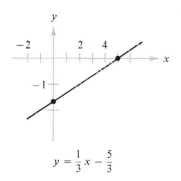

y

$$y = \frac{1}{3}x - \frac{5}{3}$$

Figure A.26

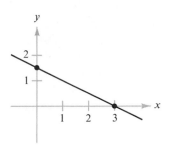

(*ii*) $x + 2y - 3 = 0$

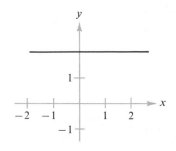

(*v*) $y - 2 = 0$

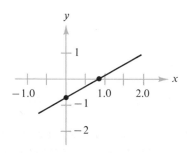

(*vii*) $0.67x - 0.80y = 0.59$

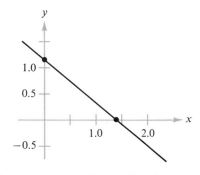

(*viii*) $350x + 420y - 500 = 0$

Figure A.27

9. See Figure A.27; slopes (*i*) $-4/3$; (*ii*) $-1/2$; (*iii*) 1; (*iv*) 4; (*v*) 0; (*vi*) 3/2; (*vii*) 0.67/0.8 = 0.8375; (*viii*) $-350/420 = -0.8333$.
10. slope $\Delta p/\Delta q = -10/600 = -1/60$, so $(p - 90) = (-1/60)(q - 1000)$ or $p = -q/60 + 106.67$; $p = 82.50$ when $q = 1450$; if $p = 87.00$, $q = 1180$.   **11.** Yes, line equation: $(q - 860)/(p - 80) = $ slope $= -18$ or $q = -18p + 2300$, for $80 \leqslant p \leqslant 100$.
12. (1, 2); (2, 10); slope = 8; equation $(y - 2)/(x - 1) = 8$ or $y = 8x - 6$.

Section 1.9

1. $q = 50$; $p = 1.33$; graph in Figure A.28.
2. (*i*) $x = -15/7$, $y = 10/7$; (*ii*) $x = 7/2$, $y = 3/2$; (*iii*) $x = 37.5$, $y = 212.5$.   **3.** $x = 8/5$, $y = 14/5$.   **4.** See Figure A.29; (*i*) cross at (5, 16) and $(-3, 0)$; (*ii*) cross at (3, 4) and $(-1, 0)$; (*iii*) cross at $(-2, -8)$ and (1, 1).
5. (*i*) $(3 + \sqrt{5})/2 \approx 2.62$, $(3 - \sqrt{5})/2 \approx 0.38$; (*ii*) none; (*iii*) $-2 + 2\sqrt{3} \approx +1.46$,

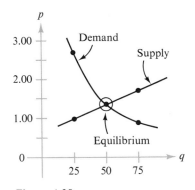

Figure A.28

$-2 - 2\sqrt{3} \approx -5.46$; (*iv*) $x = +1/20$, $x = -1/20$; (*v*) none; (*vi*) $10,000 + 5000\sqrt{2} \approx 17,071$ and $10,000 - 5000\sqrt{2} \approx 2929$; (*vii*) none.   **6.** $R = 110q$; $P = R - C = -50,000 + 10q + 0.1q^2$; $P(250) \approx -41,250$; breakeven at $q \approx 659$.   **7.** (*i*) $x = +1$, $x = -1$; (*ii*) $x = -2$, $x = +1$; (*iii*) none;

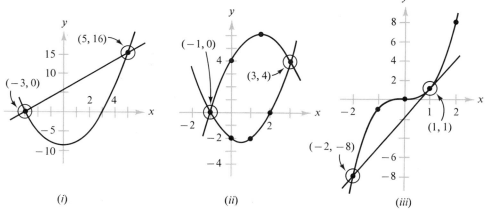

Figure A.29

(*iv*) $x = -1$, $x = +1$; (*v*) $x = (2 + \sqrt{116})/8 \approx$ 1.60, $x = (2 - \sqrt{116})/8 \approx -1.10$.
8. (*i*) $(x + 7)(x - 3)$; (*ii*) $(x - (1 + \sqrt{3})) \cdot (x - (1 - \sqrt{3}))$.

Section 1.10
1. See Figure A.30. **2.** Choose A if $x < 150$, H if $x > 150$. **3.** See Figure A.31; factor (*iii*) as $(x - 5)(x + 3)$; factor (*vi*) as $(x + 2)(x + 2)$; rewrite (*vii*) as $-8x + 2 \geqslant 0$; rewrite (*viii*) as $0 \leqslant x^2 + x - 6 = (x - 2)(x + 3)$.
5. See Figure A.32 for $p \geqslant 0$; $p(x) = 0$ if $x = 0$, 1, $+3$. **6.** See Figure A.33.
7. See Figure A.34. **8.** For $x > 0$, $1/x < 4$ when $1 < 4x$ or $x > 1/4$; if $x < 0$, $1/x < 4$ when $1 > 4x$ or $x < 1/4$ (but $x < 0$ already!);

thus you get $1/x < 4$ on the shaded set in Figure A.35. **9.** $10 \leqslant n \leqslant 100$.

Chapter 2
Section 2.1
1. (*i*) $4 = s_1$; (*ii*) $s_2 = 4 + 16(\Delta t) + 16(\Delta t)^2$; (*iii*) $\Delta s/\Delta t = 16 + 16(\Delta t)$ approaches 16 ft./sec.
2. Inst. speed 40 ft./sec. after $t = 1.25$ sec.
3. (*i*) 3.2 ft./sec. = 2.18 mph; (*ii*) 32 ft./sec. = 21.8 mph; (*iii*) 64 ft./sec. = 43.6 mph; (*iv*) 320 ft./sec. = 218.2 mph; (*mph*) = (*ft./sec.*) × (3600/5280) = (*ft./sec.*) × (0.6818).
4. $t = \sqrt{s/16} = 1.50$ sec.; speed = 48 ft./sec.
5. $t = \sqrt{s/16}$; (*i*) 0.25 sec.; (*ii*) $\sqrt{10}/4 = 0.791$ sec.; (*iii*) $10/4 = 2.5$ sec.; (*iv*) $10\sqrt{10}/4 = 7.91$ sec. **6.** First find impact time $t = \sqrt{s/16}$;

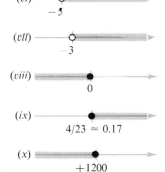

Figure A.30

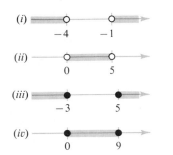

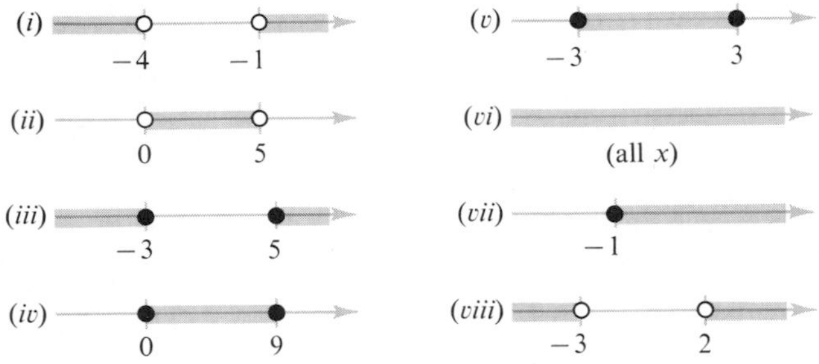

Figure A.31

Figure A.32

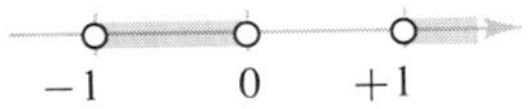

Figure A.33

Figure A.34

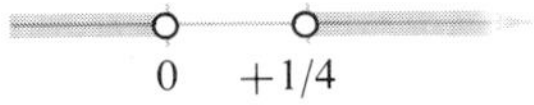

Figure A.35

(*i*) $t = 2.50$, (*ii*) $t = 10\sqrt{2}/4 = 3.54$; then speed $= 32t$ is (*i*) 80 ft./sec. $= 54.5$ mph, (*ii*) 113.28 ft./sec. $= 77.24$ mph; weight of object is irrelevant.

Section 2.2

1. (*i*) 0; (*ii*) 2; (*iii*) 2; (*iv*) $\Delta y = 3(\Delta x) + (\Delta x)^2$.
2. (*i*) 0; (*ii*) 2; (*iii*) -1; (*iv*) $3 + \Delta x$.
3. (*i*) $-1/6$; (*ii*) $-1/10$; (*iii*) $1/2$; (*iv*) $1/6$.
5. (*i*) 4; (*ii*) 2.   **6.** (*i*) $C(500) = 75,000$;
(*ii*) $C(600) = 74,000$; $\Delta C/\Delta q = -\$10$ per unit.

Section 2.3

3. $f'(x) = -2x$; $f'(2) = -4$; $f' = 4$ when $x = -2$; $f' = 0$ when $x = 0$.   **4.** (*i*) -3 (constant function); (*ii*) $2x - 1$; (*iii*) $1 - 3x^2$.
5. See Exercise 4.   **6.** (*i*) $f'(x) = 7x^6$;
(*ii*) $f'(1) = 7$; (*iii*) $f'(-2) = -2$; (*iv*) $f'(x) = 4x^3 - 2x + 2$; (*v*) $P'(q) = 3$ (constant function); (*vi*) $f'(x) = -4x^3$; (*vii*) $f'(r) = -4r^3$;

(*viii*) $f(x) = 1 + x + x^2 + x^3$, so $f'(x) = 1 + 2x + 3x^2$.   **7.** $dh/dt = 64 - 32t$ ft./sec.

Section 2.4

2. $P = (1, 2)$; $Q = (1 + \Delta x, 2 + 3(\Delta x) + (\Delta x)^2)$; $\Delta y/\Delta x$ approaches $3 =$ slope of tangent line.
3. (*i*) 4; (*ii*) 0; (*iii*) 3.   **4.** slope $= 2$; tangent line is $(y - 1) = 2(x - 1)$ or $y = 2x - 1$; see Figure A.36.   **5.** $dy/dx = 2x - 12$; slope $= dy/dx = 0$ when $x = 6$, $y = -36$.
6. (*i*) $y = 3x + 2$, slope $= 3$; (*ii*) $y = 0$, slope $= 0$; (*iii*) $y = 12x - 16$, slope $= 12$.
7. Slope $= -2$; tangent line $(y - 1) = -2(x - 1)$ or $y = -2x + 3$.

Section 2.5

2. Take $p = 49$, so $\Delta y \approx f'(49) \cdot \Delta x = (1/2\sqrt{49}) \cdot \Delta x = \Delta x/14$; then $\sqrt{48} \approx 7 + (-1)/14 = 6.929$, $\sqrt{53} \approx 7 + (4)/14 = 7.286$; exact values are $\sqrt{48} = 6.9282\ldots$, $\sqrt{53} = 7.2801\ldots$.   **3.** $\sqrt{49 + \Delta x} \approx 7 + \Delta x/14$.
4. $f' = -2/x^3$ so $f'(1) = -2$ and $f(1 + \Delta x) \approx f(1) + f'(1) \cdot \Delta x = 1 - 2 \cdot \Delta x$; thus $f(1.01795) \approx 1 - 2(.01795) = 0.96410$;

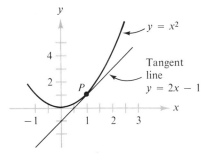

Figure A.36

exact value 0.96504. **5.** Exact $\Delta V = 3.951 \times 10^9$; approx. $\Delta V = 3.921 \times 10^9$.
6. Volume 1.96×10^9 cu. mi. **7.** Depth Δr gives Volume $= 4\pi(3950)^2(\Delta r) \approx 8.3 \times 10^6$, so that $\Delta r \approx 0.0423$ mi. $= 223.5$ ft.
8. $P'(q) = 40 - 0.04q$; if $q = 500$, $P'(500) = +20$ so $\Delta P \approx 20 \cdot \Delta q$; thus $P(520) - P(500) = \Delta P \approx 20(20) = \$400$; exact value $\Delta P = 5392 - 5000 = \$392$.
9. $A'(s) = 2s$, so if $s = 100$, uncertainty is $\Delta A \approx A'(100) \cdot \Delta s = 200 \cdot \Delta s$; taking $\Delta s = \pm 0.2$ ft., then $\Delta A = \pm 40$ sq. ft.
10. $v = 2$; uncertainty $\Delta v \approx 2kr \cdot \Delta r = \pm 0.4$ cm./sec.

Section 2.6

3. $dy/dx = 3x^2 - 3$; increasing, decreasing, decreasing, increasing. **4.** $dy/dx = 1 - 6x$; increasing if $x < 1/6$; decreasing if $x > 1/6$.
5. $dy/dx = 3x^2 - 3 = 3(x - 1)(x + 1)$; increasing/decreasing as in Figure A.37.

Behavior of $y = x^3 - 3x$

Figure A.37

6. See Figure A.38; (*i*) $dy/dx = -13$; (*ii*) $dy/dx = 1 + 2x$; (*iii*) $dy/dx = 6x^2 - 6x - 12$; (*iv*) $dy/dx = 3 + 6x + 3x^2$; (*v*) $dy/dr = 3r^2$; (*vi*) $dP/dq = 153 - 0.006q$.

Section 2.7

2. (*i*) 14; (*ii*) 0; (*iii*) -4; (*iv*) $\lim(h^2 - h)/h = \lim(h - 1) = -1$; (*v*) $\lim(t^2 - t - 2)/(t + 1) = \lim(t - 2) = -3$; (*vi*) $\lim x^3/x^2 = \lim x = 0$; (*vii*) 0; (*viii*) $\lim(x^2 - 4x + 4)/(x^2 - 4) = \lim(x - 2)^2/(x + 2)(x - 2) = \lim(x - 2)/(x + 2) = 0$. **3.** $1/x$ continuous if $x \neq 0$; $1/(1 - x^2)$ continuous if $x \neq -1$, $x \neq +1$. **4.** See Figure A.39;

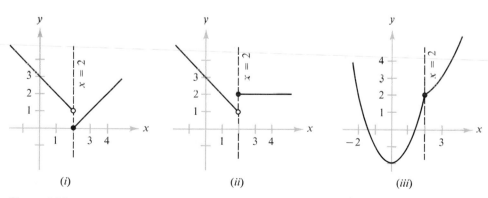

Figure A.38

Figure A.39

(*i*) discontinuous; (*ii*) discontinuous; (*iii*) continuous. **5.** $\lim(x - x^3)/(x - 1) =$ $\lim -x(x - 1)(x + 1)/(x - 1) =$ $\lim -x(x + 1) = -2$; take $f(1) = -2$ for continuity at $x = 1$. **6.** $a = f'(p)$.

Chapter 3

Section 3.1

1. (*i*) $3x^2$; (*ii*) $-3/x^4$; (*iii*) $(1/3)x^{-2/3}$; (*iv*) $(-1/3)x^{-4/3}$; (*v*) $(5/3)x^{2/3}$; (*vi*) $(-1/2)x^{-3/2}$; (*vii*) $118x^{117}$; (*viii*) $-50/x^{51}$; (*ix*) $(3.21)x^{2.21}$; (*x*) $y = x^{11/4}$, $dy/dx = (11/4)x^{7/4}$. **2.** (*i*) 10; (*ii*) 9/2; (*iii*) 3/4; (*iv*) 2/27; (*v*) $40\sqrt{2}$. **3.** $8\pi r$. **4.** (*i*) $y = (1/12)x + (4/3)$; (*ii*) $y = -3x + 4$; (*iii*) $y = (10/3)x - (10/3)$. **5.** $dp/dq = -500q^{-3/2}$; $p'(100) = -\$0.50$ per unit; $R = 1000\sqrt{q}$; $dR/dq = 500/\sqrt{q}$; $R'(100) = \$50$ per unit. **6.** (*i*) $-6x^5$; (*ii*) $4\pi r^2$; (*iii*) $20x^4 - 32x^3 + 1$; (*iv*) $32t$; (*v*) $14t - 3t^2$; (*vi*) $0.3 - 0.002q$; (*vii*) $87 - 0.000204q$; (*viii*) $\frac{1}{2}x^{-1/2} - \frac{1}{2}x^{-3/2}$; (*ix*) $2t - 20\sin t$; (*x*) $1 + e^x + 1/x$; (*xi*) $f = (1/x) - x^2$, $f' = (-1/x^2) - 2x$; (*xii*) $2x + (5/2)x^{3/2}$. **8.** $N'(10) =$ 660 bacteria/min. **10.** $\Delta V \approx 9.80 \times 10^7$ cu. mi. **11.** Max. error $\Delta V \approx V'(5) \cdot \Delta s = 150 \cdot \Delta s = \pm 1.5$ cu. ft.; max. error $\Delta A \approx A'(5) \cdot \Delta s = 100 \cdot \Delta s = \pm 1.0$ sq. ft.

Section 3.2

2. (*i*) $2x(x^2 - 1) + (x^2 + 1)2x = 4x^3$; (*ii*) $4x^3(1 - x - x^3) + x^4(-1 - 3x^2) = 4x^3 - 5x^4 - 7x^6$; (*iii*) $(1/3)x^{-2/3}(x^4 + 3x^2 + 1) + x^{1/3}(4x^3 + 6x) = (13x^4 + 21x^2 + 1)/3x^{2/3}$; (*iv*) $-x^{-2} + 3x^{-4} = (3 - x^2)/x^4$; (*v*) $(4x^3 + 2x)(14x^3 - 3x + 2) + (x^4 + x^2 + 1)(42x^2 - 3)$; (*vi*) $1 + 3x^{-4} = (x^4 + 3)/x^4$; (*vii*) $(1 - 1/x^2)(\sqrt{x} + 1) + (x + 1/x)(1/2\sqrt{x})$; (*viii*) $1 + \log(x)$; (*ix*) $e^t(t^2 + 2t)$; (*x*) $(-1/x^2)\sin x + (1/x)\cos x$; (*xi*) $(2 + 3x + x^2)e^x$; (*xii*) $(\cos x)^2 - (\sin x)^2$. **3.** (*i*) $-1/x^2$; (*ii*) $-1/(1 + x)^2$; (*iii*) $2/(1 - x)^2$; (*iv*) $8x/(x^2 + 1)^2$; (*v*) $45/(100 - 45x)^2$; (*vi*) $3/(1 - x)^2 - 1/x^2$; (*vii*) $(-4x^2 - 2x + 5)/(x^2 - x + 1)^2$; (*viii*) $(2x^2 - 2x + 1)/(x^2 + x)^2$; (*ix*) $1/\sqrt{x}(1 - \sqrt{x})^2$; (*x*) $[(\cos x)^2 + (\sin x)^2]/(\cos x)^2 = 1/(\cos x)^2$; (*xi*) $[(\cos x - x \cdot \sin x) \cdot (x^4 + 5x + 1) - (x \cdot \cos x)(4x^3 + 5)]/$

$(x^4 + 5x + 1)^2$; (*xii*) $[(2x - \sin x)(e^x + 1) - (x^2 + \cos x + 2)e^x]/(e^x + 1)^2$. **4.** $dy/dx = (2 - 2x^2)/(x^2 + 1)^2$; $(y - 1) = 0(x - 1)$ or $y = 1$ (horizontal); $y - (4/5) = (-6/25)(x - 2)$ or $25y + 6x = 32$. **5.** $dA/dq = C'(q)/q - C(q)/q^2$.

Section 3.3

1. (*i*) $(1 - x)^3$; (*ii*) $1/(x^2 + 1)$; (*iii*) $(1 + x^2)/x^2$; (*iv*) $\sqrt{1 + x}/\sqrt{1 - x}$; (*v*) $(1 + \sqrt{x})/(1 - \sqrt{x})$; (*vi*) $x^2 + 2 + \sqrt{x^2 + 1}$. **2.** (*i*) $y = u^{45}$, $u = x^2 - x + 1$; (*ii*) $y = u^5$, $u = 7 - x$; (*iii*) $y = \sqrt{u}$, $u = 1 - x^2$; (*iv*) $y = u^{1/3}$, $u = x^2 - x + 2$; (*v*) $y = 1/\sqrt{u} = u^{-1/2}$, $u = x^2 + x + 3$; (*vi*) $y = \sqrt{u}$, $u = 1 + \sqrt{x}$; (*vii*) $y = e^u$, $u = -x$; (*viii*) $y = \log u$, $u = 1 - x^2$. **3.** (*i*) $45(x^2 - x + 1)^{44}(2x - 1)$; (*ii*) $-5(7 - x)^4$; (*iii*) $-x/(1 - x^2)^{1/2}$; (*iv*) $(1/3)(x^2 - x + 2)^{-2/3}(2x - 1)$; (*v*) $(-1/2)(x^2 + x + 3)^{-3/2}(2x + 1)$; (*vi*) $(1/2)(1 + \sqrt{x})^{-1/2}(1/2)x^{-1/2}$; (*vii*) $-e^{-x}$; (*viii*) $-2x/(1 - x^2)$. **5.** (*i*) $-2x[(1 - x^2)/(1 + x^2)]^{-1/2}/(1 + x^2)^2 = -2x/(1 + x^2)^{3/2}(1 - x^2)^{1/2}$; (*ii*) $(1/5)(x + \sqrt{x})^{-4/5}(1 + 1/(2\sqrt{x}))$; (*iii*) $-(1 - \sqrt{x})^{-2}(-1/2\sqrt{x}) = 1/(2\sqrt{x}(1 - \sqrt{x})^2)$; (*iv*) $(1/2)(x + 2)^{-1/2} - (1/2)(x + 2)^{-3/2}$; (*v*) $3e^{(4 + 3x)}$; (*vi*) $12\pi \cos(9 + 3\pi x)$; (*vii*) $-(2x + 1)e^{(x^2 + x + 1)}$; (*viii*) $3(\sin x)^2(\cos x)$; (*ix*) $3x^2 \cdot \cos(x^3)$. **6.** (*i*) $-x/\sqrt{1 - x^2}$; (*ii*) $\sqrt{1 - x^2} - x^2/\sqrt{1 - x^2} = (1 - 2x^2)/\sqrt{1 - x^2}$; (*iii*) $(2 - x)/(1 - x)^{3/2}$; (*iv*) $(-2x^3 - 3x^2 - 6x - 1)/2(x^2 + x + 1)^{3/2}$; (*v*) $10x^9/(x + 1)^{11}$; (*vi*) ke^{kx}; (*vii*) $e^{-x} - xe^{-x}$; (*viii*) $-[(1 - x)/(1 + x)]^{-1/2}/(1 + x)^2$; (*ix*) $-4\pi \sin(3 + 4\pi x)$; (*x*) $(x^3 + 2x^2 + 1)/(x + 1)^2\sqrt{1 + x^2}$. **8.** $V = (4/3)\pi r^3$, so $r = \sqrt[3]{3V/4\pi}$; but $V = 1000t^2/(1 + t^2)$, so $r(t) = 10 \cdot [3t^2/4\pi(1 + t^2)]^{1/3}$; $dr/dt = (10/3) \cdot [3t^2/4\pi(1 + t^2)]^{-2/3} \cdot [3t/2\pi(1 + t^2)^2] = (10/3) \cdot \sqrt[3]{3/8\pi} \approx 1.64$ ft./min. at $t = 1$. **10.** $\Delta W \approx W'(0) \cdot \Delta h = -0.05063$ lb. if $\Delta h = 1$ mi.; $\Delta W \approx -7.59$ lb. if $\Delta h = 150$. **11.** Obviously $s = 400t$, $ds/dt = 400$, so $r = [(3000)^2 + (400)^2t^2]^{1/2}$; now $dr/ds = s/[(3000)^2 + s^2]^{1/2}$ and $dr/dt = dr/ds \cdot ds/dt = 400s/[(3000)^2 + s^2]^{1/2} = (400)^2t/[(3000)^2 + (400)^2t^2]^{1/2}$; at $t = 10$, $dr/dt = 320$ ft./sec.

Section 3.4

1. (*i*) none; (*ii*) 7/6; (*iii*) $-2, 2$;
(*iv*) $y' = 12x^3 - 48x^2 + 36x = 12x(x-3)(x-1) = 0$ if $x = 0, 1, 3$;
(*v*) none, numerator in $y' = (2x^2 + 1)/\sqrt{x^2 + 1}$ is never zero; (*vi*) $y' = (1 - x^2)/(x^2 + 1)^2 = 0$ when numerator $(1 - x^2) = (1 - x)(1 + x) = 0$, $x = -1$ or 1.   **2.** (*i*) Min. $y = -2$ at $x = 2$, max. $y = 7$ at $x = -1$; (*ii*) min. $y = -6$ at $x = -1$, max. $y = 97/12 \approx 8.08$ at $x = 7/6 \approx 1.17$; (*iii*) min. $y = -9$ at $x = 2$, max. $y = 18$ at $x = -1$.   **3.** min. $y = -114$ at $x = -3$; max. $y = 131$ at $x = 4$.
4. (*i*) Min. $y = 2$ at $x = 1$, max. $y = 10/3$ at $x = 1/3$; (*ii*) min. $y = -2/3$ at $x = 1$ and $x = -5$, max. $y = 26.333$ at $x = 4$;
(*iii*) min. $C = 4320$ at $q = 0$, max. $C = 8820$ at $q = 30,000$; (*iv*) min. $s = 0$ at $t = 0$, max. $s = 2$ at $t = 1$; (*v*) min. $w = -99/101 \approx -0.980$ at $r = 100$, max. $w = 1$ at $r = 0$.
7. On $0 \leqslant q \leqslant 1,000,000$ max. $P = \$4.49$ million at $q = 311,224$; on $0 \leqslant q \leqslant 250,000$ max. $P = \$4.13$ million at $q = 250,000$.
8. (*i*) $R - 300q - 5q^2$;
(*ii*) $P = -1000 + 200q - 4q^2$;
(*iii*) max. $P = \$1500$ at $q = 25$.

Section 3.5

1. (*i*) $12x^2 - 30$; (*ii*) $(-1/4)x^{-3/2} + (-3/4)x^{-5/2}$; (*iii*) $(6x^2 + 2)/(x^2 - 1)^3$;
(*iv*) $4/(x - 1)^3$; (*v*) $16e^{4x-1}$; (*vi*) $48 \sin(4x)$.
3. $y'' = 12x^2 + 12x - 24 = 12(x + 2)(x - 1)$; concave upward if $x < -2$ or $x > 1$; concave downward if $-2 < x < 1$; inflections at $(-2, -48)$ and $(1, -9)$.   **4.** Speed $ds/dt = 3t^2 - 4t$; acceleration $d^2s/dt^2 = 6t - 4$ is positive if $t > 2/3$, negative if $t < 2/3$.
5. (*i*) $dN/dt = 3000t/(1 + t^2)^2$; (*ii*) $d^2N/dt^2 = 3000(1 - 2t^2 - 3t^4)/(1 + t^2)^4 = 3000(1 - 3t^2)/(1 + t^2)^3$ is zero when $t = 1/\sqrt{3} \approx 0.577$ weeks $= 4.04$ days.
6. $y''' = 720x^7 + 840x^3 - 6$.

Section 3.6

1. See Figure A.40; (*i*) $y' = -4 + 4x$; $y'' = 4$; abs. min. $x = 1$; no abs. max.;
(*ii*) $y' = 400 - x$; $y'' = -1$; abs. max. $x = 400$; no abs. min.;
(*iii*) $y' = 3x^2 - 6x - 9 = 3(x - 3)(x + 1)$; crit. pts. $x = 3$ and -1; $y'' = 6x - 6$;

inflection at $x = 1$; no abs. extrema;
(*iv*) $y' = (4x^3 - 36x)/27$; crit. pts. $x = 0$, -3, and 3; $y'' = 4(x^2 - 3)/9$; inflections at $x = -\sqrt{3}, +\sqrt{3} \approx 1.732$; abs. min. at $x = -3$ and $+3$; no abs. max.; (*v*) $y' = 12x^2(x - 1)$; crit. pts. $x = 0$ and 1; $y'' = 12x(3x - 2)$; inflections at $x = 0$ and $x = 2/3$; abs. min. at $x = 1$; no abs. max.
3. See Figure A.41; $y' = x^2 + 2x - 3 = (x + 3)(x - 1)$; $y'' = 2x + 2$.   **4.** See Figure A.42; $y' = -4x^3 + 18x^2 - 18x = -2x(2x - 3)(x - 3)$; $y'' = -12x^2 + 36x - 18$.
5. See Figure A.43; abs. max. $y = 1$ at $x = 0$; no abs. min.   **6.** See Figure A.44; abs. max. $s = 0.5$ at $t = 1$.   **8.** See Figure A.45; no abs. extrema; rel. min. at $x = +1$.

Section 3.7

1. Min. $= 40$ in. ($l = w = 10$, a square).
2. Min. sum of squares $x^2 + y^2 = 50$ when $x = 5$ and $y = 5$.   **3.** $R = 50x - 10x^2$ for $1 \leqslant x \leqslant 5$; max. $R = \$62.50$ if $x = \$2.50$.
7. See Exercise 5, Section 3.2.   **8.** $w = 400$; $l = 800$; max. $A = 320,000$ sq. ft.; $l/w = 2$.
9. Since you know an optimum exists, just find where $dA/dw = 0$; $A(w) = 56 - 2w - (150/w)$; max. A at $w = \sqrt{75} \approx 8.66$ in.; $h = 50/w \approx 5.77$ in.   **10.** Let $s =$ length of edge of square, $h =$ height; then $V = s^2 h = 5$ and $C = s^2 + 16/s$; min. C when $s = 2$ ft. and $h = 1.25$ ft.   **11.** $q = 400$.
13. Area $= 36 = 4sh + s^2$, so $h = (36 - s^2)/s$ and volume $V = s^2 h = 36s - s^3$; feasible s when $0 \leqslant s \leqslant 6$; max. V when $s = 2\sqrt{3} \approx 3.464$ ft. and $h = \sqrt{3} \approx 1.732$ ft.
16. (*i*) P coordinates $(30 - 7t, 0)$, $Q = (0, 5t - 20)$; (*ii*) no collision, (*iii*) $D(t) = (74t^2 - 620t + 1300)^{1/2}$; min. when numerator in dD/dt is zero, that is, when $t = 620/148 \approx 4.19$ sec.; min. $D = D(4.19) \approx 1.16$ units.

Section 3.8

1. (*i*) $-2/3$; (*ii*) $-x/y$; (*iii*) $(1 - 3x^2)/(3y^2 - 1)$; (*iv*) $(3x^2 - y)/(x - 3y^2)$.   **2.** $y' = (2x + y)/(2y - x)$; when $x = 1$ and $y = 1$ we get $y' = 3$; tangent line $y = 3x - 2$.
5. $y' = -(3x^2 + y)/(x + 3y^2)$; $y'' = -(6x + 2y' + 6y(y')^2)/(x + 3y^2) = 2xy/(x + 3y^2)^3$.   **7.** $dy/dt = 120$ units/sec.

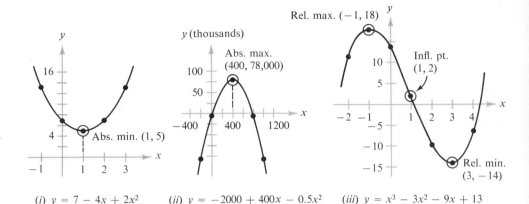

(i) $y = 7 - 4x + 2x^2$ (ii) $y = -2000 + 400x - 0.5x^2$ (iii) $y = x^3 - 3x^2 - 9x + 13$

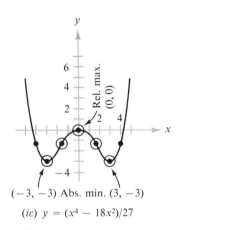

(iv) $y = (x^4 - 18x^2)/27$ (v) $y = 3x^4 - 4x^3 + 2$

Figure A.40

8. $2s \cdot ds/dt = 2x \cdot dx/dt = 2(s^2 - 36)^{1/2} \cdot dx/dt$, so $dx/dt = 1000$ mph. **10.** $x(t) = 300 - 70t$; $dx/dt = -70$; $y(t) = 400 - 50t$; $dy/dt = -50$; no collision; $ds/dt = 0$ when $x(dx/dt) + y(dy/dt) = -70 \cdot x(t) - 50 \cdot y(t) = 0$, so $t = 205/37 = 5.811$ hrs. **11.** $dP/dt = 720$ parasites per year.

Chapter 4

Section 4.1

1. (i) $2x + $ const; (ii) const; (iii) $-x^4 + $ const; (iv) $2\sqrt{x} + $ const; (v) $5x^{1/5} + $ const; (vi) $5/s + $ const; (vii) $\frac{1}{2}\log(t) + $ const; (viii) $\frac{1}{5}\pi r^4 + $ const; (ix) $\frac{1}{2}x^2 + x + $ const; (x) $4x - \frac{1}{3}x^3 + $ const.
3. (i) $x^2 + 4x + $ const; (ii) $3x - \sqrt{x} + $ const; (iii) $x - (3/2)x^2 + $ const; (iv) $x - (1/x) + $ const;

(v) $(3/8)x^8 - (2/3)x^6 + (2/3)x^3 - 7x + $ const; (vi) $(10/3)x^{3/2} + 2\sqrt{x} + 10x + $ const; (vii) $-0.01x^3 - 5x^2 + 4500x + $ const; (viii) $4\log x + 2e^x + $ const. **4.** (i) $3x + $ const; (ii) $5x - x^2 + $ const; (iii) $x^4 + x^3/3 + x^2 + $ const; (iv) $\frac{1}{2}x^2 + (1/x) + $ const; (v) $x - x^2/2 + x^6/6 + $ const; (vi) $(2/3)x^{3/2} - 5\sqrt{2x} + $ const; (vii) $0.01x^3 - 50x^2 + 1000x + $ const; (viii) $x^2/2 + e^x + $ const; (ix) $-\cos x - \sin x + $ const; (x) $3x - 2\log x + $ const. **6.** (i) $-e^{-x}$; (ii) $(2/3)e^{3x/2}$. **8.** (i) $x + x^3/3$; (ii) $(2/3)x^{3/2}$; (iii) $-1/x$; (iv) $x + \log x$. **11.** $v = 32t$; $s = 16t^2$.

Section 4.2

1. (i) $8/3$; (ii) $16/3$; (iii) 12; (iv) $\log(5) - \log(1) = 1.6094$; (v) $e^3 - e^0 = 19.086$. **2.** Geom.

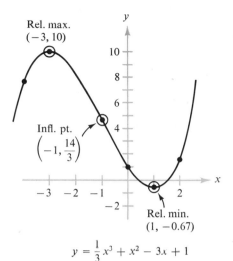

Rel. max.
$(-3, 10)$

Infl. pt.
$\left(-1, \dfrac{14}{3}\right)$

Rel. min.
$(1, -0.67)$

$$y = \frac{1}{3}x^3 + x^2 - 3x + 1$$

Figure A.41

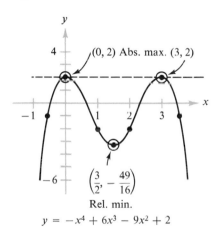

$(0, 2)$ Abs. max. $(3, 2)$

$\left(\dfrac{3}{2}, -\dfrac{49}{16}\right)$
Rel. min.

$$y = -x^4 + 6x^3 - 9x^2 + 2$$

Figure A.42

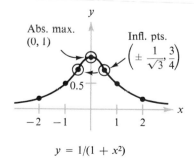

Abs. max.
$(0, 1)$

Infl. pts.
$\left(\pm \dfrac{1}{\sqrt{3}}, \dfrac{3}{4}\right)$

$$y = 1/(1 + x^2)$$

Figure A.43

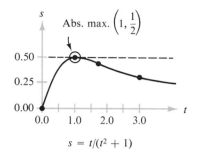

Abs. max. $\left(1, \dfrac{1}{2}\right)$

$$s = t/(t^2 + 1)$$

Figure A.44

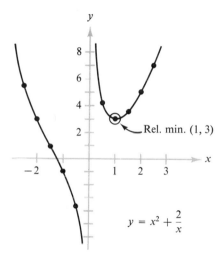

Rel. min. $(1, 3)$

$$y = x^2 + \frac{2}{x}$$

Figure A.45

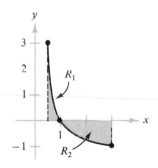

R_1

R_2

Figure A.46

area $= 17/2$; signed area $= 4$. **3.** See Figure A.46; crossover $x = 1$; Area $R_1 = +1/2$; Area $R_2 = +4/3$; geom. area $= 11/6$; signed area $= (1/2) - (4/3) = -5/6$. **4.** See Figure A.47. **6.** (*i*) 4; (*ii*) 6; (*iii*) 26/3; (*iv*) 6; (*v*) 9/10;

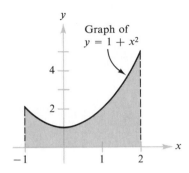

Figure A.47

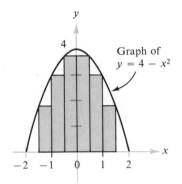

Figure A.49

(*vi*) $-75/2$; (*vii*) 4; (*viii*) 6; (*ix*) 0; (*x*) $(1/2a^2) -$ $(1/2b^2)$. **7.** (*i*) 8; (*ii*) $-7/2$; (*iii*) $32/3$; (*iv*) 2; (*v*) $52/5$; (*vi*) $31/3$; (*vii*) $406/15 = 27.07$; (*viii*) $(10\sqrt{2} - 8)/3 \approx 2.05$; (*ix*) $-1,720,000$; (*x*) $4/3$. **8.** (*i*) Cross at $x = 2$, signed area $= 0$, geom. area $= 8/3$; (*ii*) cross at $x = 4$, signed area $= 4/3$, geom. area $= 4$; (*iii*) no crossover, signed area $= -32/3$, geom. area $= 32/3$. **10.** $F(3) - F(0) = 2$.

Section 4.3
1. See Figure A.48. **3.** (*i*) See Figure A.48; (*ii*) Area $R' = 20/9 = 2.22$, Area $R'' = 35/9 = 3.88$, exact area $= 3$. **4.** Figure A.49 shows R'; R'' similar; Area $R' = 8.5$, Area $R'' = 12.5$, exact area $= 32/3 = 10.67$. **6.** Area $R' \approx 19.45$; Area $R'' \approx 21.05$. **7.** Area $R' = 0.6688$; Area $R'' = 0.7188$; exact area $= \log(2) = 0.6931$.

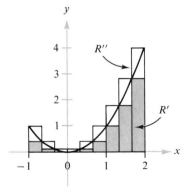

R' shaded; for R'' add
unshaded blocks

Figure A.48

Section 4.4
1. See Figure A.50. **2.** $y = x^2$ lies *above* $y = x^3$ if $0 \leqslant x \leqslant 1$, so geom. area $= \int_0^1 (x^2 - x^3)\, dx = 1/12$. **3.** (*i*) $1/2$; (*ii*) cross at $x = -1$, $x = 2$, area $= 9/2$; (*iii*) $22/3$; (*iv*) cross at $x = 0$, $x = 4$, area $= 8/3$; (*v*) cross at $x = -1$, $x = 1$, area $= 4/3$; (*vi*) cross at $x = 1/2$, $x = 1$, area $= 1/24$. **5.** (*i*) $P(50) - P(0) = \int_0^{50} (10.50 - 0.01q + 0.0001q^2)\, dq$, so $P(50) = P(0) + 516.66 = \$216.66$; (*ii*) $P(100) = \$733.33$; (*iii*) $P(q) = -300 + 10.50q - 0.005q^2 + 0.0001(q^3/3)$. **6.** $dv/dt = d^2s/dt^2 = 15$ and $v = 15t + \text{const}$, but $v(0) = 0$ so const $= 0$ and $v = 15t$; $v(10) = 150$ ft./sec.; $v(100) = 1500$ ft./sec. **7.** $v = 300t - t^2$; $v(90) = 18,900$ ft./sec.; $h(t) = 150t^2 - \tfrac{1}{3}t^3$; $h(90) = 972,000$ feet.

Section 4.5
1. (*i*) Fraction $= \int_{-.25}^{+.25} f(x)\, dx = 47/128 = 0.367$, total number $= .367 \times 10^6$.
2. (*i*) 0.688; (*ii*) 0.312; (*iii*) 0.348.
3. Read answers from Table 4.7 using conversions (*i*) $F_k = N_k/1000 = 0.001 \times N_k$ and (*ii*) $c_k = F_k/\Delta t = 0.001N_k/0.5 = 0.002N_k$; histogram in Figure A.51. **5.** Fraction with $0 \leqslant x \leqslant 1$ is $1.0067(1 - e^{-1}) = 0.6364$; $\bar{X} = 1.0067(1 - 6e^{-5}) = 0.9660$.
8. $\bar{X} = 0.5$; $\sigma^2 = \int_0^1 (x - 0.5)^2\, dx = 1/12$; $\sigma = 1/\sqrt{12} = 0.2887$. **10.** (*i*) $\bar{X} = 5/7 = 0.714$; (*ii*) $X_0 = 4/5 = 0.8$; (*iii*) $\sigma^2 = 5/196 = 0.02551$, so $\sigma = 0.1 \times \sqrt{2.551} = 0.1597$.

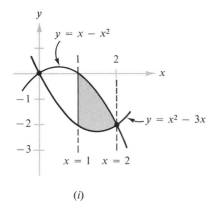

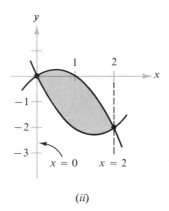

(i)   (ii)

Figure A.50

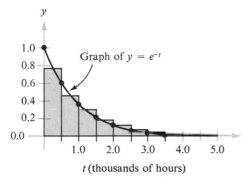

t (thousands of hours)

Figure A.51

Section 4.6
1. $(x^2 + 4)^6/6$. **2.** (i) $(x + 2)^4/4$;
(ii) $(2/3)(x^2 + 4)^{3/2}$; (iii) $(2/3)(x + 2)^{3/2}$;
(iv) $(3x + 2)^2/2$; (v) $\frac{1}{2}\log(2x + 5)$; (vi) e^{t+3}.
3. $(-2/3)(1 - x^3)^{1/2}$. **4.** (i) $(x^2 + 1)^{23}/23$;
(ii) $(1/3)(x^2 + 4)^{3/2}$; (iii) $(-1/5)(1 - x^3)^{5/3}$;
(iv) $1/2(2 - x)^2$; (v) $\frac{1}{4}\log(1 + t^4)$;
(vi) $1/32(3 - x^2)^{16}$; (vii) $\frac{1}{2}(\log x)^2$;
(viii) $-\frac{1}{2}e^{-2x}$. **5.** (i) $\frac{1}{3}\log(x^3 - 1)$;
(ii) $(3/7)(1 + x)^{7/3}$; (iii) $-e^{-x^2/2}$;
(iv) $(-2/3)(1 - x)^{3/2}$; (v) $\log(2 + e^x)$;
(vi) $-\log(\cos x)$; (vii) $x + \log(x + 2)$;
(viii) $(-1/4\pi) \cdot \cos(4\pi x + 7)$. **6.** (i) $16/3$;
(ii) $\sqrt{5} - 1 = 1.236$; (iii) $15/64$;
(iv) $1 - e^{-5} = 0.9933$; (v) $(\log(4) - \log(1))/6 = 0.2310$; (vi) $\frac{1}{2}(\log(9) - \log(5)) = 0.2940$;
(vii) $(2/5)6^{5/2} = 72\sqrt{6}/5 = 35.27$; (viii) 0.

Section 4.7
1. (i) diverge, (ii) diverge; (iii) 5/3; (iv) 1;
(v) 1/5; (vi) diverge. **6.** $\bar{X} = 0$.
7. (i) diverge; (ii) 3/2; (iii) 0; (iv) 1/2;
(v) diverge; (vi) diverge.

Chapter 5
Section 5.1
1. 1, 1, 4, -3, -2; $f(x,y) = 0$ on line given by
equation $y = 1 + 2x$. **2.** (i) $\sqrt{14}$, $\sqrt{3}$;
(ii) 2, 3; (iii) 12/13, -1; (iv) 5/6, 0;
(v) 5635, 4915; (vi) -86, 24;
(vii) $36 - \sqrt{17} \approx 31.87$, $1 - \sqrt{18} \approx -3.24$;
(viii) $e^{-6.5} = e^{-5} \cdot e^{-1.5} = 1.503 \times 10^{-3}$,
$e^{-1} = 0.3679$. **3.** (i) 36 ft.; (ii) 40 ft.;
(iii) 30 ft. **4.** (i) $C = 2000 + 13q_A + 20q_B$;
(ii) $R = 18q_A + 30q_B$; (iii) $P = -2000 + 5q_A + 10q_B$. **5.** See Figure A.52.
7. 3, 6, 3, 4. **8.** Defined when $(x^2 + y^2) \leqslant 4$,
so square root makes sense (disc of radius 2
about origin); (i) 2, 0, $\sqrt{2}$, 0; (ii) $f(x,y) = 0$
when $x^2 + y^2 = 4$ (circle of radius 2 about
origin).

Section 5.2
1. See Figure A.53. **2.** (i) Yes; (ii) yes;
(iii) no; (iv) yes; (v) yes; (vi) no; (vii) yes;
(viii) no; see Figure A.54. **3.** See Figure A.55.
4. (i) no; (ii) yes; (iii) yes; (iv) no; (v) yes;
(vi) no; (vii) yes; (viii) no. **5.** See Figure A.56.
6. $x \geqslant 0$; $y \geqslant 0$; $0.03x + 0.10y \geqslant 1000$;
$0.02x + 0.01y \geqslant 200$; $C = (150x + 1000y)/2000 = 0.075x + 0.5y$; see Figure A.57.

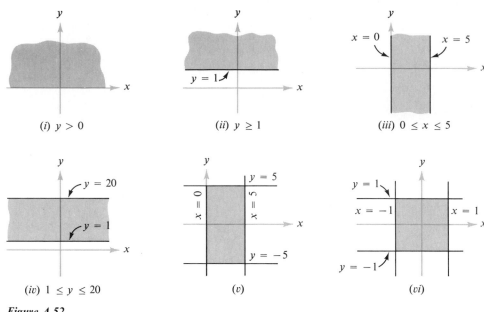

(i) $y > 0$ *(ii)* $y \geq 1$ *(iii)* $0 \leq x \leq 5$

(iv) $1 \leq y \leq 20$ *(v)*   *(vi)*

Figure A.52

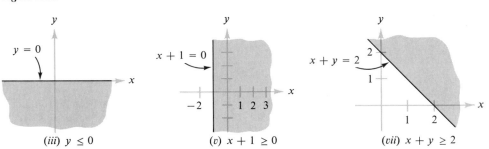

(iii) $y \leq 0$ *(v)* $x + 1 \geq 0$ *(vii)* $x + y \geq 2$

Figure A.53

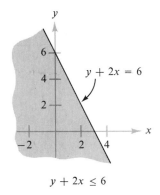

$y + 2x \leq 6$

Figure A.54

7. SO_2 constraint $0.035x + 0.093y \leq 7.0$; dust, $0.002x + 0.055y \leq 3.5$; see Figure A.58.
8. $x \geq 0$; $y \geq 0$; $x + y \leq 25$;
$(40 - x) + (30 - y) \leq 60$, or
$70 - x - y \leq 60$, or $10 \leq x + y$;
$C(x,y) = 2.54x + 2.20y + 3.70(40 - x) + 3.28(30 - y) = -1.16x - 1.08y + 246.40$;
see Figure A.59.

Section 5.3
1. *(i)* 13; *(ii)* 5; *(iii)* 1; *(iv)* $\sqrt{85} \approx 9.22$.
2. *(i)* Yes; *(ii)* yes; *(iii)* yes; *(iv)* no; *(v)* yes;
(vi) yes; solution set is disc of radius 3 about origin.   **3.** *(i)* Disc of radius 5 about (1, 2);

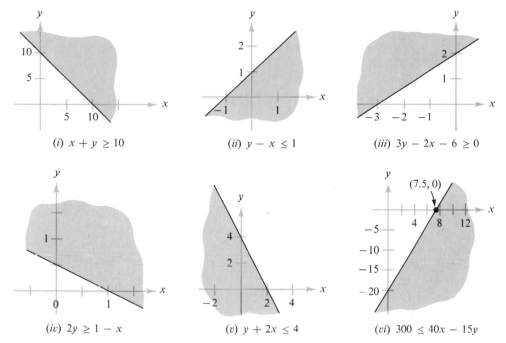

Figure A.55

(*ii*) disc of radius $\sqrt{7} \approx 2.65$ about $(0, 3)$;
(*iii*) distance from P to $(-3, -1)$ is ≥ 2, *exterior* of disc of radius 2 about $(-3, -1)$;
(*iv*) $x^2 + 2x + 1 + y^2 = (x - 1)^2 + y^2 \leq 3$, disc of radius $\sqrt{3} \approx 1.73$ about $(1, 0)$;
(*v*) ring-shaped set bounded by the circles about the origin of radius $r = 2$ and $r = 3$;
(*vi*) a notched half plane, half plane $x \geq 0$ with half-disc (radius 1 about origin) removed.

Section 5.4
4. See Figure A.60. **5.** See Figure A.61.

Section 5.5
1. (*i*) A; (*ii*) B; (*iii*) 600; (*iv*) increase from -600 to 1200. **2.** Max. $P \approx \$210{,}000$ when $x \approx 1350$ and $y = 1500$; P stays negative (no profit) when $x = 0$ (left edge) or $y = 0$ (bottom edge); fixed costs $= -P(0, 0) \approx \$600{,}000$. **3.** Max. $z = 18$ at $(x, y) = (8, 0)$. **4.** Min. $C = \$2500$ if $x = 33{,}333$ lbs. and $y = 0$ lbs. (vertex of feasible set lying on x-axis). **5.** See Figure A.62; no solution set if $c > 4$ since $x^2 + y^2$ cannot be negative;

$O = (0, 0)$ only solution if $c = 4$; circle of radius $r = \sqrt{4 - c}$ if $c < 4$, as shown; in (*i*) we show level curves $c = 4, 3, 2, \ldots$; in (*ii*) we show the graph of the function $z = 4 - (x^2 + y^2)$. Curves on this surface show where $z = c$ for $c = 4, 3, 2, 1, 0$.

Section 5.6
1. $\partial f/\partial x(P) = 13$; $\partial f/\partial y(P) = 16$. **2.** (*i*) 1; (*ii*) 3; (*iii*) 1; (*iv*) -5. **3.** $\partial f/\partial x = 2 + 2xy - 3y$; $\partial f/\partial y = 3 + x^2 - 3x$; $\partial f/\partial y$ is *never* zero (quadratic formula) so the partial derivatives are never zero simultaneously. **4.** (*i*) $\partial f/\partial x = 0$ and $\partial f/\partial y = 0$ (constant functions); (*ii*) 1, 0; (*iii*) 0, -1; (*iv*) 1, 1; (*v*) $y + 2x$, $x - 2y$; (*vi*) $1/y$, $-x/y^2$. **5.** (*i*) $\partial f/\partial x = 1 + \frac{1}{2}(x^2 + y^2)^{-1/2}(2x) = 1 + x/\sqrt{x^2 + y^2}$, $\partial f/\partial y = y/\sqrt{x^2 + y^2}$; (*ii*) $5x^{-2/3}y^{4/5}$, $12x^{1/3}y^{-1/5}$; (*iii*) $5(x + y)^4$, $5(x + y)^4$; (*iv*) $-(x^2 + 2x + 1 + y^2)^{-3/2}(x + 1)$, $-y(x^2 + 2x + 1 + y^2)^{-3/2}$; (*v*) $500 - 0.2x - 0.01y$, $700 - 0.4y - 0.01x$; (*vi*) $2x/(1 + y^2)$, $-2y(1 + x^2)/(1 + y^2)^2$;

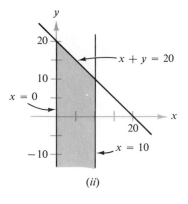

(ii)

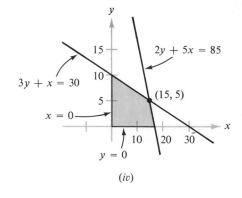

(iv)

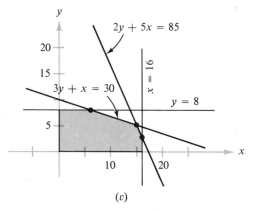

(v)

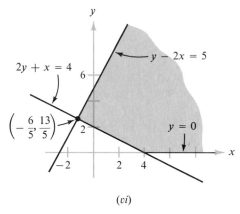

(vi)

Figure A.56

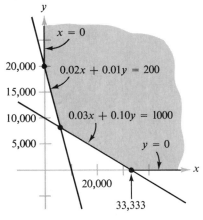

Figure A.57

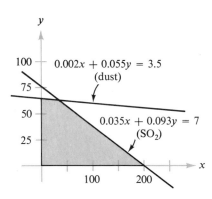

Figure A.58

(vii) $1/(x - y)$, $-1/(x - y)$; (viii) $-xe^{-(x^2+y^2)/2}$, $-ye^{-(x^2+y^2)/2}$; (ix) $-3x^2 - 1/x^2$, $-1/y^2$.

6. $\partial V/\partial r = 2\pi rh/3$; $\partial V/\partial h = \pi r^2/3$; at (2, 10), $\partial V/\partial r = 40\pi/3$ and $\partial V/\partial h = 4\pi/3$; these are rates of change in V as r or h increase, starting from base values $r_0 = 2$ and $h_0 = 10$.

7. $\partial A/\partial x = y/2$, $\partial A/\partial y = x/2$, $\partial l/\partial x = x/\sqrt{x^2 + y^2}$, $\partial l/\partial y = y/\sqrt{x^2 + y^2}$; values at $P = (120, 160)$ are 80, 60, 3/5, and 4/5.

8. $P = kT/V$; $\partial P/\partial V = -kT/V^2$; $\partial P/\partial T = $

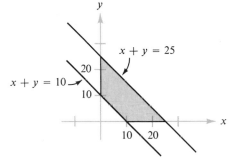

Figure A.59

k/V.   **9.** (i) $\partial f/\partial x = 2x$, $\partial f/\partial y = 2y$, $\partial f/\partial z = 2z$; (ii) $2y + 2z$, $2x - 2yz^2$, $2x - 2y^2z$; (iii) $y^2/(z + 1)$, $2xy/(z + 1)$, $-xy^2/(z + 1)^2$; (iv) $2x - yz$, $-xz$, $2z - xy$.

Section 5.7

2. If $Q = (400, 4000)$, $\partial P/\partial x = 0.34$ and $\partial P/\partial y = 0.284$; taking $\Delta x = 1$ and $\Delta y = 0$, $\Delta P \approx \$0.34$; taking $\Delta x = 0$ and $\Delta y = 1$, $\Delta P \approx \$0.284$; P increases if either x or y is increased, but increasing x is more profitable; push heavy-duty fencing.   **3.** If $Q = (2000, 400)$, $\partial P/\partial x = +0.10$ and $\partial P/\partial y = -1.70$; yes, no.   **4.** $\partial A/\partial h = \pi d$; $\partial A/\partial d = \pi h + \pi d$; at $Q = (10, 12)$, $A = 170\pi = 534.1$ sq. in. and $\Delta A \approx 10\pi(\Delta h) + 22\pi(\Delta d)$. Thus (i) $\Delta A \approx 22\pi = 69.1$ sq. in.; (ii) $\Delta A \approx 10\pi = 31.4$ sq. in.; (iii) $\Delta A \approx -2\pi = -6.28$ sq. in.   **7.** $f(0.9, 1.1) \approx 1.50$, exact $= 1.479$; $f(1.2, 1.1) \approx 2.10$, exact $= 2.109$.

8. (i) $A = 9600$; (ii) $l = 200$; $\Delta A \approx 60(\Delta x) + 80(\Delta y) = 70$ sq. ft.; $\Delta l \approx 0.8(\Delta x) + 0.6(\Delta y) = 0.7$ ft.

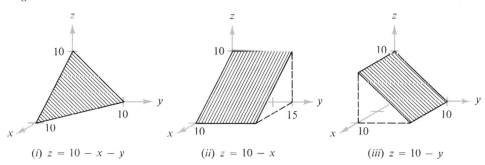

(i) $z = 10 - x - y$ (ii) $z = 10 - x$ (iii) $z = 10 - y$

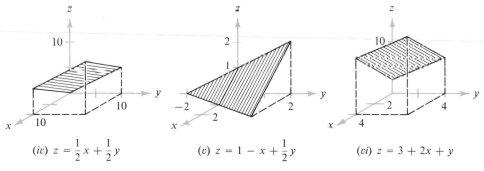

(iv) $z = \frac{1}{2}x + \frac{1}{2}y$ (v) $z = 1 - x + \frac{1}{2}y$ (vi) $z = 3 + 2x + y$

Figure A.60

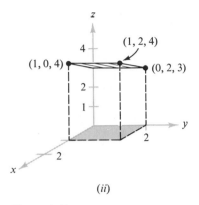 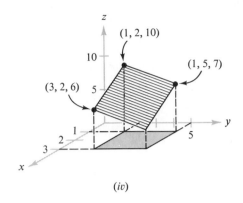

Figure A.61

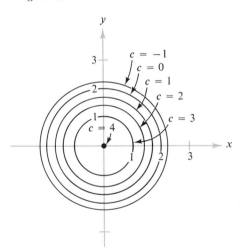 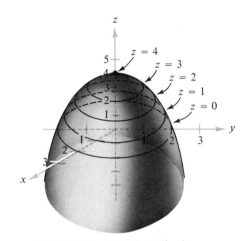

(*i*) Level curves
$4 - x^2 - y^2 = c$

(*ii*) Graph (surface) determined
by $z = f(x, y) = 4 - x^2 - y^2$

Figure A.62

Section 5.8

1. $\partial f/\partial x = 12x^2 + 7y^2 - 2xy^2$, $\partial f/\partial y = 14xy - 2x^2y - (1/y^2)$, $\partial^2 f/\partial x^2 = 24x - 2y^2$, $\partial^2 f/\partial x\,\partial y = \partial^2 f/\partial y\,\partial x = 14y - 4xy$, $\partial^2 f/\partial y^2 = 14x - 2x^2 + (2/y^3)$; values at $P = (3, 1)$ are 109, 23, 70, 2, and 26.

2. (i) $\partial^2 f/\partial x^2 = 0$; $\partial^2 f/\partial x\,\partial y = \partial^2 f/\partial y\,\partial x = -10$, $\partial^2 f/\partial y^2 = 0$; (ii) $\partial^2 f/\partial x^2 = 6x$, $\partial^2 f/\partial x\,\partial y = \partial^2 f/\partial y\,\partial x = 2$, $\partial^2 f/\partial y^2 = -6y$; (iii) $\partial^2 f/\partial x^2 = 2(y^2 - x^2)/(x^2 + y^2)^2$, $\partial^2 f/\partial x\,\partial y = \partial^2 f/\partial y\,\partial x = -4xy/(x^2 + y^2)^2$,

$\partial^2 f/\partial y^2 = 2(x^2 - y^2)/(x^2 + y^2)^2$. **3.** $\partial f/\partial x = 3x^2 + 2xy$ and $\partial f/\partial y = x^2 - 1$ simult. zero at $P = (1.0, -1.5)$ and $Q = (-1.0, 1.5)$, where values of second partials are 3, 2, 0 and $-3, -2, 0$ respectively.

Section 5.9

1. At Q_1, $\partial P/\partial x = -125$ and $\partial P/\partial y = -330$; at Q_2, $\partial P/\partial x = 75$ and $\partial P/\partial y = -320$; (*i*) $-\$125$ at Q_1, $\$75$ at Q_2; (*ii*) $-\$330$ at Q_1, $-\$320$ at Q_2. **2.** $\partial P/\partial x = 500 - 0.2x$ and $\partial P/\partial y = 700 - 0.4y$; values at Q are 200,

-100; only critical point is (2500, 1750).
3. Max. $P \approx \$210,000$ at boundary point
(1500, 1700); not a critical point for $P(x, y)$.
4. Max. $P \approx \$200,000$ at boundary point
(2400, 1000), not a critical point. **5.** (*i*) Lowest
boundary $P \approx -\$900,000$ at (0, 0); (*ii*) highest
boundary $P \approx \$30,000$ near (4000, 1600).

Section 5.10

1. (*i*) abs. min., boundary; (*ii*) not extremum,
boundary; (*iii*) not extremum, boundary;
(*iv*) abs. max., boundary; (*v*) not extremum,
interior; (*vi*) not extremum, interior.
2. Critical points $Q_1 = (1/\sqrt{3}, 0) \approx (0.577, 0)$
and $Q_2 = (-1/\sqrt{3}, 0) \approx (-0.577, 0)$; $D_{Q_1} =$
$4\sqrt{3} > 0$, $\partial^2 f/\partial x^2(Q_1) > 0$, Q_1 a rel. min.,
$f(Q_1) = -2/3\sqrt{3} \approx -0.384$; $D_{Q_2} =$
$-4\sqrt{3} < 0$, Q_2 not an extremum; no rel.
maxima. **3.** Critical points $Q_1 = (1, 1/2)$ and
$Q_2 = (-2, 1/2)$; $D_{Q_1} > 0$, $\partial^2 f/\partial x^2(Q_1) > 0$, Q_1
a rel. min.; $D_{Q_2} < 0$, not an extremum; test
works at each critical point. **4.** (*i*) (0, 0);
(*ii*) $(-1/6, 1/3)$; (*iii*) $(-1/3, 0)$; (*iv*) (1, 1);
(*v*) (2037.7, 1561.6); (*vi*) none; (*vii*) (0, 0);
(*viii*) all points on the line $x + y = 0$;
(*ix*) (1, 0) and $(-1, 0)$. **5.** (*i*) (0, 0) not
extremum; (*ii*) (0, 0) rel. min.; (*iii*) (0, 0) not
extremum, $(-1/3, 1/3)$ rel. max.; (*iv*) (0, 0) not
extremum, (2, 0) rel. min., $(-1, 0)$ rel. min.,
(*v*) no crit. points; (*vi*) $(2/\sqrt{3}, 1/\sqrt{3})$ and
$(-2/\sqrt{3}, -1/\sqrt{3})$, neither a rel. extremum.
6. Not a rel. extremum.

Section 5.11

1. (1, 3) where $f = 40$; at other critical point,
(0, 0), f has smaller value, $f = 13$.
2. $(-2/3, -1/3)$, the only critical point,
$f = -1/3$. **3.** $D_P < 0$ at only critical point
$P = (0, 0)$. **4.** Critical pts.: (1, 0) abs. max.,
$(-1, 0)$ abs. min., $f(1, 0) = 1/2$, $f(-1, 0) =$
$-1/2$. **5.** Abs. min. $f = -32$ at (0, 2); other
crit. pts. are $(0, -1)$ rel. min. and (0, 0) not rel.
extremum. **7.** Min. $f = 1$ at (1/2, 1/2), only
critical point. **9.** Min. $f = -1/8 = -0.125$
at $(1/4, 1, -1/4)$.

Section 5.12

1. Min. d when d^2 is minimum, d^2 is easier to
work with; min. $d = \sqrt{85}/2 \approx 4.61$ at $Q =$
(0, 5/2); endpoint minimum. **2.** Min. d when

d^2 is minimum, d^2 easier to work with; min.
$d = \sqrt{16/5} \approx 1.78$ at $Q = (19/5, 3/5) =$
(3.8, 0.6); all x feasible in this problem.
3. Max. $f = 1/2$ at (1, 1/2); min. $f = 0$ at
endpoint (0, 1). **4.** Max. $f = 1$ at $(\sqrt{2}, 1/\sqrt{2})$
and $(\sqrt{2}, -1/\sqrt{2})$; min. $f = 0$ at $(0, -1)$,
(2, 0), and (0, 1). **5.** Max. $f = 4$ at corner
(2, 0). **6.** Feasible set a triangle; max. $f = 8$
at corner (0, 0); min. $f = 16/13 = 1.23$ lies on
one of the edges, at (14/13, 18/13). **7.** Max.
$f = 5$ at (1, 1); problem can be solved by
geometry as well as Calculus. **8.** Max. $P =$
4625 at feasible critical point (150, 150); max.
on upper edge of boundary at (125, 200),
where $P = 4563$. **9.** Max. $f = 3500$; all
points on right-hand edge $x = 100$ give this
maximum value. **10.** $h = 33.3$ in.; $g =$
66.7 in.; base 16.7 in. each edge; max. $V =$
9259 cu. in.

Section 5.13

1. Max. $f = 1/2$ at (1, 1/2). **2.** Max. $xy = 625$
when $x = 25$ and $y = 25$. **3.** Max. $P = 50$
at (6, 8); min. $P = -50$ at $(-6, -8)$. **4.** Min.
ht. $= 131/13 = 10.08$ at (4/13, 9/13). **5.** Max.
$f = 1/2$ at $(1/\sqrt{2}, 1/\sqrt{2})$ and at
$(-1/\sqrt{2}, -1/\sqrt{2})$. **6.** Min. distance $=$
5 at (3, 4). **8.** Min. $f = 24$ at $(-2, -4, 2)$.

Section 5.14

1. Max. $= 10$ at (0, 0); min. $= 90$ at (5, 0).
3. Max. $= 9$ at (3, 2); min. $= 0$ at (0, 5).
4. See Figure A.63; max. $= 25$ at (0, 9);
min. $= 7$ at (0, 3). **5.** Max. $P = \$8400$ at

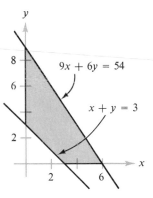

Figure A.63

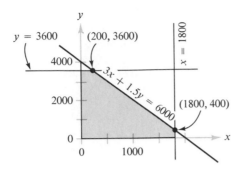

Figure A.64

$(q_N, q_T) = (300, 0)$.   **7.** Feasible set shown in Figure A.64; max. $P = \$15,600$ per week when $x =$ gasoline $= 1800$ and $y =$ htg. oil $= 400$; the nontrivial constraint is $3x + 1.5y \leqslant 6000$.   **9.** Max. $P = \$42,000$ when J. C. $= 0$ and $F = 6000$.   **10.** Max. $P = \$27,500$ when J. C. $= 4000$ and $F = 3000$.

Chapter 6

Section 6.1
1. (i) 114.49; (ii) 114.75; (iii) 114.89; (iv) 114.98; (v) 115.02.   **3.** (i) 622.50; (ii) 645.84; (iii) 695.19.   **4.** (i) 106; (ii) 106.18; 1060, 1061.80; 6.18%.   **5.** 5.12%.   **6.** 1750.47.

Section 6.2
1. (i) 1; (ii) 1.6487; (iii) 0.60653; (iv) 2.1170; (v) 8.4994; (vi) 0.04117; (vii) 0.44932; ($viii$) 0.13533.   **2.** (i) 1.3955; (ii) 0.17517; (iii) 6.2152; (iv) 1.0233; (v) 4.1124; (vi) 2.7809. **3.** (i) 1.01; (ii) 1.02; (iii) 1.0001; (iv) 1.0037. Exact: (i) 1.0100; (ii) 1.0202.   **5.** (i) 1309.90; (ii) 13,099; (iii) 2625.90; (iv) 148.41.   **6.** $f' = -xe^{-x^2/2}$; $f'' = -e^{-x^2/2} + x^2 e^{-x^2/2}$. **7.** ($i$) $3e^{3x}$; (ii) $2xe^{x^2}$; (iii) $(2x - 3)e^{x^2 - 3x}$; (iv) $-2e^{-2x}$; (v) $-e^{-x} + e^x$; (vi) $e^x + xe^x$. **9.** (i) $(e^3 - e^0)/3 = 6.3617$; (ii) $e^{x-1} + $ const; (iii) $-e^{-x} + $ const; (iv) $e^x - e^{-x} + $ const; (v) $(e^8 - e^0)/3 = 992.6$; (vi) $\frac{1}{2}e^{2x} + 2x - \frac{1}{2}e^{-2x} + $ const.

Section 6.3
1. (i) 0.69315; (ii) 2.3025; (iii) 1.0006; (iv) 1.6993; (v) $-\log 8 = -2.0794$;

(vi) $2 \log(10) = 4.6050$; (vii) $-2 \log(10) = -4.6050$; ($viii$) 0.34657.   **2.** (i) 0.02663; (ii) 0.00498; (iii) 1.1448; (iv) 2.2923; (v) $\log(1.137) - \log(10) = -2.1741$; ($vi$) $\log(9.999) - \log(10) = -0.0001$; ($vii$) $\log(3.255) - 3 \log(10) = -5.7273$; ($viii$) 4.6218.   **3.** ($i$) 2.693; ($ii$) 57.75; ($iii$) 1.2599; ($iv$) 4.8302; ($v$) 2.0396; ($vi$) 3.8478. **4.** ($i$) 2.3788; ($ii$) $e^5 \cdot e^5 = 22,025$; (iii) $e^5 \cdot e^{2.47} = 1754.5$; ($iv$) 0.0005699; ($v$) 11.467; ($vi$) $10 \cdot \sqrt[3]{108} = 47.619$; ($vii$) $389^{3/4} \times 10^{-6} = 87.58 \times 10^{-6}$; ($viii$) $3 \log(10) = 6.9075$; (ix) $\log(1.490) + 3 \log(10) = 7.3063$; ($x$) $\log(3.4) - 3 \log(10) = -5.6837$.   **5.** \$7335.   **7.** After 13 years. **9.** (i) 445.27; (ii) 495.82; (iii) 518.00. **11.** (i) $1/x$; (ii) $1 + \log x$; (iii) $e^x \log x + e^x/x$; (iv) $1/x + e^x$; (v) $2x/(4 + x^2)$; (vi) $\log(x^3 + 1) + 3x^3/(x^3 + 1)$; ($vii$) $2x/3(x^2 + 1)$; ($viii$) $(3x^4 + 1)/x(x^4 + 1)$.   **12.** (i) $\log(7) - \log(1) = 1.9459$; ($ii$) $6/7 = 0.8571$; (iii) $\int x \, dx = \frac{1}{2}x^2 + $ const; (iv) $\frac{1}{4} \log(1 + u^4) + $ const; (v) $\frac{1}{2} \log(x^4 + x^2 + 1) + $ const; (vi) $\log(4 + e^x) + $ const.   **14.** In millions, 31.4, 37.8, and 84.9; triple after 47.5 years.

Section 6.4
1. $N = 10,000e^{(0.4621)t}$; doubles in 1.50 hrs. **2.** 2826 years.   **3.** 20.6%.   **4.** 39 years. **5.** 69.7, 35.0, 23.4, 14.2 years.   **7.** $Q(t) = Q(0) \cdot e^{(-1.54 \times 10^{-10})t}$; in billions of years, 1.61, 1.05, and 0.54; age of Earth $\geqslant$ that of oldest rock.   **8.** $\log(0.99843) = -0.00157$; 10.2×10^6 years.   **9.** 1.39, 2.41, and 4.61 feet. **10.** $5k = \log(0.9)$, so $k = -0.02106$; half life $= 32.9$ years; after 142.2 years.

Section 6.5
1. Here $c = $ const: (i) $y = \frac{1}{2}x^2 + c$; (ii) $y = \frac{1}{4}x^4 + x + c$; ($iii$) $y = 1 + ce^x$; (iv) $y^2 = x^3 + c$ or $y = \pm\sqrt{x^3 + c}$; (v) $e^{-y} = -\frac{1}{2}x^2 + c$ or $y = -\log(c - \frac{1}{2}x^2)$; ($vi$) $y = 1 - ce^{-x^3/3}$.   **2.** $y = 1/(3 - x)$.   **3.** $y = 2x$. **4.** $N(t) = ((t/20) + 100)^2$; $N(100) = 11,025$. **5.** $U(t) = 50 + 20e^{-0.20t}$; $U(3) = 60.98°$F. **6.** $t = -\log(2)/-0.2 = 3.47$ hours.

Index